Company's Coming®

W9-BMZ-458

Italian with a Twist
Italian ❧ French ❧ Asian ❧ Canadian

Sonny Sung

CANADA COOKS

Italian with a Twist

First Printing November 2014

Library and Archives Canada Cataloguing in Publication

Sung, Sonny, author
Italian with a twist / Sonny Sung.
(Canada cooks)
Includes index.
ISBN 978-1-927126-40-0
1. Cooking, Italian. 2. Cookbooks. I. Title. II. Series:
Canada cooks series
TX723.S86 2014   641.5945   C2014-905157-3

Company's Coming Publishing Limited

87 Pender Street East
Vancouver, British Columbia, Canada V6A 1S9
www.companyscoming.com

Company's Coming is a registered trademark owned by Company's Coming Publishing Limited

We acknowledge the financial support of the Government of Canada through the Canada Book Fund (CFB) for our publishing activities.

Printed in China

PC: 27

Contents

DEDICATION
I dedicate this book to my family and friends, my loving wife and especially to my adorable and precious daughter.

ACKNOWLEDGEMENTS
I would like to express my sincere thanks to the Sorrentino's Restaurant Group, Bistecca, all my staff and customers, and to everyone who believed in me and supported me throughout my culinary career. *Grazie mille* to Carmelo Rago, Stella Rago, Frank Saccomanno and their families.

Special thanks to Gurvinder Bhatia for his amazing wine knowledge and expertise, his graceful commentary and his invaluable contribution to this book.

I would also like to thank the following people for their precious commentaries in regards to my cooking: Graham Hicks of the *Edmonton Sun,* Peter Graham, Bailli President of La Chaine des Rotisseurs de l'Alberta Nord, Vinod Varshney, manager of Culinary Team Alberta and Chairman of NAIT's School of Hospitality and Culinary Arts, and Nick Lees of the *Edmonton Journal.* Lastly, a heartfelt thanks to Company's Coming president Shane Kennedy, editor Wendy Pirk, editorial director Nancy Foulds and photographer Sandy Weatherall.

Foreword

There are many good chefs in the world. They have good technique, artistic plate presentations worthy of an art gallery showing, and their food is inoffensive, yet mediocre and uninspired. Truly great chefs champion the best quality ingredients, are blessed with an innate sense of combining flavours, and possess a passion and pleasure for sharing great quality food with others—a spirit that the Italians refer to as *La Convivialità.*

Over the past decade, it has been my distinct pleasure and good fortune to experience, share, participate in and be inspired by hundreds of meals prepared by Sorrentino's Executive Chef Sonny Sung. When it comes to food, Sonny embodies the Italian spirit of *La Convivialità.*

The beauty of Sonny's food is rooted in the fresh ingredients and simplicity of Italian cuisine. In the spirit of the Slow Food movement, he supports local products with real flavours grown and raised by caring people who share his same commitment to real food. But simple food doesn't have to mean unsophisticated food. Sonny's imagination and innovation enhance each of his creations without compromising quality or flavour. He understands simplicity, purity and subtlety and the pleasures than can result.

Sonny Sung is a friend, a fellow lover of real food and, quite simply, an immensely talented chef. This cookbook is a compilation of recipes that will allow you to discover the quality and simplicity of his cooking in your own home. When complimented on his food, Sonny's humble response is that he just "opened up a can." His desire is to show that by using great quality ingredients and proper technique, delicious food can be easy. Sonny's recipes will inspire you and instill in you the confidence to make great Italian food at home. Nothing would give him greater pleasure than knowing that this book could, in some small way, contribute to friends and family taking the time from their busy days to gather, laugh and share their lives over good food and good wine. "Opening a can" never tasted so good.

Gurvinder Bhatia
Quench Magazine wine editor
Edmonton Journal & Global TV Edmonton
wine columnist

Introduction

This book is about fusion—the fusion of Italian and French cuisine. The recipes in this book are the secrets behind my kitchens at Sorrentino's and Bistecca, where I am the Corporate Chef and, at the latter, partner. All the dishes in this book have been served in my restaurants, and many have become signature dishes. I have more than 14 years of experience as a chef preparing Italian cuisine and 10 years preparing French cuisine. I fell in love with Italian and French food when I was a young man travelling throughout Europe. I was impressed by the history, rich cultures, amazing people, delicious dishes and, especially, the romanticism of both Italy and France. It was during these travels that I decided I wanted to study and master the cuisines of both countries.

During my 24 years as a chef, I have realized that classical French cooking techniques and contemporary use of fresh, healthy, high quality ingredients blend seamlessly and harmoniously with the foundation of Italian cuisine. Italians put great emphasis in selecting the finest products and freshest fruits and vegetables. They love food and put the pride of their heritage into their cooking. A wonderful description of the Italian spirit of cooking is expressed by international wine judge and Italian wine specialist Gurvinder Bhatia. He writes, "truly great chefs champion the best quality ingredients, are blessed with an innate sense of combining flavours, and possess a passion and pleasure for sharing great quality food with others—a spirit that the Italians refer to as *la convivialità*." To recreate the Italian dining experience in Canada, we need to select the finest products and ingredients from our local farmers, growers and producers. In Canada, we are blessed with the finest quality beef and bison in the world. I use Sterling Silver premium beef and Alberta bison wherever possible in my restaurants and especially in Bistecca, which is the first Italian steakhouse in Alberta. When you use the finest quality ingredients, much of your work is done.

Italian cuisine is simple, flavourful, seasonal and healthy. My goal in this book is to share with you this philosophy of cooking and dining.

6

A Note on Ingredients

It isn't always easy to buy locally. Much of the produce grown in our country is shipped abroad, and many of the fruits and vegetables for sale here have been imported from distant lands. And then there is our short growing season. Gardens might grow year-round in some regions of France or Italy, but it is harder to buy locally year-round in most of Canada. So the philosophy of this cookbook is to shop locally and support regional farms rather than industrialized institutions as much as possible, but to also take advantage of the wealth of high-quality ingredients that are shipped to our stores from abroad. Truffles, European cheeses, wines and sausages—these items are well worth seeking out, and a little goes a long way to transform an ordinary dish into something amazing. Check ethnic grocery stores in your area for specialty items.

Italians care about their food and it shows. They go to the market daily if not twice a day to search for the freshest vegetables, finest fruits and best quality products. I will never forget the excitement I felt shopping at the food markets in Italy. In North America we are surrounded by supermarkets with flavourless, genetically modified, mass-produced products. As a result, additives are often used to "create" flavour. In Italy, flavourful dishes are based on using the best quality ingredients available. Additives are not necessary, and the dishes taste better and are better for our health.

Regional influences are important in Italy, as well. Minestrone soup in southern Italy, for example, looks much different than its equivalent in Milan. Every region has its own flavour profile and there is no firm recipe because it all depends on what vegetables are available in the season. The Italian philosophy of cooking is very similar to contemporary French cuisine. Food should be healthy, but tasty. Health should not be compromised for taste, but better still, it should be enhanced through the foods we consume. This book will guide you to what I called "the next level of cooking," which will not only preserve most of the nutrients and vitamins of the products, but also enhance the natural aromas, texture and taste.

Italian Cheeses

Italy has a long history of cheese-making. Historians believe the ancient Greeks introduced fresh, rindless cheeses to the Etruscans, who went on to create matured cheeses with rinds, which probably resembled the Parmesan and Pecorino cheeses we know today. In fact, Pecorino romano, a hard cheese made in the Lazio region from ewe's milk, may be the oldest Italian cheese, dating back to Roman times.

In Italy, cheese can be made from cow, ewe, goat or buffalo milk (or mixture thereof) and can be categorized into four types—hard, semi-soft, soft and fresh. Originally cheese makers probably used rennet from wild artichoke plants, and though some rural cheeses are still made in this way, most cheese today use animal rennet.

Many of Italy's finest cheese are now exported to Canada. You might find some hard varieties pre-packaged in supermarkets, but your better bet would be to buy a piece cut from a whole wheel. Similarly, I recommend using Parmigiano-Reggiano cheese where Parmesan is called for in these recipes.

Italians also love wine. A meal is not complete without a glass of wine. During my time as a chef, I have often been asked to suggest a wine that pairs well with a particular dish. I am honoured to have my good friend and colleague Gurvinder Bhatia share his insights about Italian wines and pairings for many of the recipes in this book. I hope that you will find his recommendations informative and inspiring.

After all, eating and cooking should be fun and exciting. Every moment we cook, we should cook with passion and creativity as it is a chance for us to celebrate our life. The recipes in this book place great emphasis on easy-to-find, high quality ingredients and products. The techniques are simple, and instructions are easy to follow. Most of the dishes can be prepared in 30 minutes or less. I sincerely hope my book will inspire you to take the time to cook for yourself, friends and family. We find time for what we value. Nothing is more precious than our health, and of course, nothing is more enjoyable than sharing a good meal with friends and family. I encourage you to try the recipes in this book using the best products from your local farmers and growers, to cook with your innate passion and creativity and, most importantly, with the Italian spirit of *la convivialità. Buon appetito!*

Wine Tips

by Gurvinder Bhatia

Wine in Italy is as integral to the country's cultural and social identity as is the food. Traditionally, Italians only served wine with food. Even today, wine is as important to a meal as are the individual ingredients that make up any dish.

For simplicity and practicality, I have not paired wines with each of Sonny's recipes. Instead, I have provided selections that can be served as aperitifs and with antipasti, and then I have a suggested a wine pairing with each entree.

Per Comminciare (To start)

Sparkling wine is the perfect way to begin any meal or gathering. Every country seems to have its own style of sparkling wine...Cava from Spain, Champagne from France and, of course, Prosecco from Italy.

Admittedly, I am an unapologetic Prosecco-file. There is something about the freshness, purity and simplicity of fine Prosecco that lifts my spirits along with my taste buds. It is traditionally light and refreshing, and there is no better way to bring a touch of conviviality to any occasion.

This classic Italian sparkling wine is from the alpine foothills of northeast Italy's Veneto region. The steep, well-drained slopes of this gorgeously scenic area combined with the cool breezes from the Alps and the warm influence from the Adriatic allow the grapes to develop a fresh acidity and a soft peachy character...the wine's hallmark features. Prosecco is a versatile food wine and will pair perfectly with antipasti, insalata and stuzzichini.

Recommended Prosecco Producers

Ruggeri, in my opinion, is the finest producer of Prosecco, bar none. The Bisol family has a long history in the region, but its modern era began in 1950 with the founding of Ruggeri by Giustino Bisol. Today, Paolo Bisol carries on the tradition of his father by working with a number of growers to produce a full range of Prosecco styles.

Other recommended Prosecco producers are Tenuta S. Anna, Masottina and Nino Franco.

Antipasti

When selecting wines to pair with antipasti, versatility and balance are the key. The wines should be fresh, with a purity of flavour and fine acidity. It is best to look for wines with soft tannins and a minimal (if any), well-integrated use of oak.

Recommended wines with antipasti (all wines listed are also great values and retail for less than $25):

Spumate
Ruggeri Rose di Pinot Brut, Veneto

Bianchi
Fabiano Soave Classico, Veneto
Fabiano Pinot Grigio, Veneto
Tenuta S. Anna Pinot Grigio, Friuli
S. Maria la Palma Vermentino
　　'Blu,' Sardegna
Marotti Campi Verdicchio dei Castelli
　　di Jesi 'Albiano,' Marche
Ceuso Scurati Bianco, Sicilia
DeAngelis Chardonnay
　　'Prato Grande,' Marche

Rosato
Tenuta S. Anna il Rosa Petillant, Veneto

Rossi
Fabiano Valpolicella, Veneto
Fabiano Valpolicella Classico
　　Superiore, Veneto
S. Maria la Palma Cannonau
　　'Le Bombarde,' Sardegna
DeAngelis Rosso Piceno, Marche
Solonio Montepulciano
　　'Fontanapiana,' Lazio
Gallo Mauro Barbera d'Asti, Piemonte
Ceuso Scurati Nero d'Avola, Sicilia
Capezzana Monna Nera, Toscana
Triacca Chianti Classico
　　'Bello Stento,' Toscana

GURVINDER BHATIA is an internationally known wine and food writer, consultant and educator. After leaving a career in law, Gurvinder was the wine columnist for CBC Radio Edmonton for more than 10 years. He is now the wine editor for Quench, *Canada's pre-eminent wine and food magazine; wine columnist for the* Edmonton Journal *and* Global TV Edmonton; *an international wine judge; creator of Vino-Aerobics; and the owner of Vinomania, named one of the 20 best wine stores in Canada. He also leads international wine tours and events, and speaks on wine and food-related topics around the world. This man knows his wine.*

Tomato and Gin Soup with Basil Oil

A grown-up version of tomato soup. For a professional appearance, use a squeeze bottle to drizzle the basil oil over top of the soup.

Soup

1/4 cup (60 mL) olive oil

1/2 cup (125 mL) diced onion

1/2 cup (125 mL) diced carrot

1/2 cup (125 mL) diced celery

2 Tbsp (30 mL) dried basil

2 Tbsp (30 mL) dried oregano

2 tsp (10 mL) minced garlic

1 cup (250 mL) coarsely chopped plum tomatoes

1/2 cup (125 mL) tomato paste

8 cups (2 L) vegetable broth

1 1/4 cups (300 mL) gin

sea salt and pepper, to taste

Basil Oil

1 cup (250 mL) fresh basil leaves

1 cup (250 mL) grape seed oil

1 tsp (5 mL) sea salt

Soup: Heat oil in a large pot on medium. Add onion, carrot, celery, basil, oregano and garlic. Cook for 5 minutes, stirring occasionally, until golden brown. Add tomatoes and tomato paste. Cook for 10 minutes, stirring occasionally. Add broth. Bring to a boil. Reduce heat to low. Simmer, covered, for 1 hour.

Add gin, salt and pepper. Stir. Simmer, covered, for about 20 minutes until vegetables are tender. Carefully process in blender until smooth, following manufacturer's instructions for processing hot liquids. Return to same pot. Bring to a boil. Divide soup among 6 individual bowls.

Basil Oil: Process all 3 ingredients in blender until smooth. Strain through sieve into small bowl. Drizzle over each bowl of soup. Serves 6.

Gin

Although the Dutch are credited with creating gin in the 16th century, Italian monks were making a juniper liquor as early as the 11th century.

Sterling Silver Premuim Beef Oxtail, Vegetable and Lentil Soup

This long-simmering soup is worth the wait.

1 Tbsp (15 mL) olive oil

2 lbs (1 kg) beef oxtail, cut into chunks

16 cups (4 L) beef broth or water

1 cup (250 mL) dried green lentils

1/2 cup (125 mL) diced carrot

1/2 cup (125 mL) diced celery

1/2 cup (125 mL) diced onion

1/2 cup (125 mL) diced leek

2 Tbsp (30 mL) minced garlic

***bouquet garni* of bay leaf, dried thyme, crushed peppercorns, parsley stems and crushed garlic cloves (see Tip)**

sea salt and pepper, to taste

Heat oil in a large saucepan on medium-high. Add beef. Cook for about 3 minutes until golden brown. Reduce heat to low. Add beef stock. Simmer for 2 hours. Skim and discard any fat from surface of liquid. Add lentils.

Combine carrot, celery, onion, leek and garlic in a frying pan on medium. Cook for about 20 minutes, stirring occasionally, until caramelized. Add vegetable mixture and *bouquet garni* to broth. Simmer, covered, for about 3 hours. Remove and discard *bouquet garni*. Add salt and pepper. Divide soup among 4 individual bowls. Serves 4.

Tip

A *bouquet garni* is a bundle of herbs that is removed from a dish before eating. Place *bouquet garni* ingredients on a piece of cheesecloth, then draw corners together and tie with butcher's string.

Fava Bean Soup

A creamy, rich soup that's topped with toasted lavender oil.

Soup

2 cups (500 mL) frozen fava beans, thawed

6 cups (1.5 L) chicken broth

1/4 cup (60 mL) olive oil

1 Tbsp (15 mL) minced garlic

1 tsp (5 mL) lemon juice

1/2 tsp (2 mL) ground coriander

1/2 tsp (2 mL) ground cumin

Lavender Oil

2 tsp (10 mL) lavender leaves

1/2 cup (125 mL) grape seed oil

1/2 tsp (2 mL) sea salt

Soup: Peel skins from fava beans. Place beans and chicken broth in a large saucepan on medium-high. Bring to a boil. Reduce heat to medium. Cook for 45 minutes until beans are softened.

Drain beans. Discard liquid. Carefully process in blender until smooth, following manufacturer's instructions for processing hot liquids. Return to pot. Bring to a boil. Add water if needed to thin slightly. Add olive oil, garlic, lemon juice, coriander and cumin. Stir. Bring to a boil. Simmer for 5 minutes. Divide among 6 individual bowls.

Lavender Oil: Heat a small saucepan on high. Add lavender leaves. Cook, stirring frequently, until golden brown. Add grape seed oil and salt, and bring heat up to 275°F (140°C). Remove from heat. Drizzle over each bowl of soup. Serves 6.

Fava Beans

Native to north Africa and southern Asia, fava beans are also grown throughout Italy. They are traditionally planted on November 2, All Souls Day, and are ready to harvest in early spring. These beans are especially popular in southern regions of the country and are eaten raw or cooked.

Minestrone Soup alla Calabrese

Topped with extra virgin olive oil and a bit of Parmesan cheese. Serve with a slice of bread.

1 Tbsp (15 mL) olive oil

1 cup (250 mL) diced carrot

1 cup (250 mL) diced celery

1 cup (250 mL) diced onion

1 cup (250 mL) diced prosciutto

2 Tbsp (30 mL) minced garlic

1 cup (250 mL) diced cabbage

8 cups (2 L) vegetable broth

1 cup (250 mL) diced tomato

1 cup (250 mL) elbow macaroni

2 Tbsp (30 mL) chopped fresh oregano

2 Tbsp (30 mL) chopped fresh basil

sea salt and pepper, to taste

grated Parmesan cheese, for garnish

extra virgin olive oil, for drizzling

Heat oil in a large pot on medium. Add carrot, celery, onion, prosciutto and garlic. Cook for 4 to 5 minutes, stirring occasionally, until golden brown.

Add cabbage. Cook for 1 minute. Add broth and tomato. Bring to a boil. Simmer for 45 minutes.

Cook pasta according to package directions. Drain. Add to stock. Add oregano, basil, salt and pepper. Stir. Divide among 8 individual warm bowls. Garnish with cheese and drizzle with oil. Serves 8.

Minestrone Soup

Minestrone soup is a dish with countless variations. It started out as a meal peasants would make with whatever vegetables and leftovers they had on hand. Meat was too expensive for the dinner table so the soup generally had beans as its base. When tomatoes where introduced into Italian cuisine in the mid-1600s, minestrone was transformed into the soup we are familiar with today.

Wild Mushroom Bisque with Truffle Crème Fraîche

Make the truffle crème fraîche at least 3 days before you make the soup.
The cultures in the buttermilk turn the cream into crème fraîche.
If desired, garnish each bowl with sliced black truffle.

Truffle Crème Fraîche

2 cups (500 mL) whipping cream

3 Tbsp (45 mL) buttermilk

1 Tbsp (15 mL) diced truffle

Soup

6 Tbsp (90 mL) olive oil

1 onion, finely diced

1/2 cup (125 mL) sliced oyster mushrooms

1/2 cup (125 mL) sliced shiitake mushrooms

1/2 cup (125 mL) sliced chanterelle mushrooms

1/2 cup (125 mL) sliced porcini mushrooms

6 Tbsp (90 mL) butter, softened

8 cups (2 L) chicken (or vegetable) broth

(see next page)

Truffle Crème Fraîche: In a small saucepan on low, warm cream slightly until just warm to the touch. Remove from heat. Stir in buttermilk. Transfer to a glass jar with a lid and let stand, covered, at room temperature for 24 hours. Stir every 6 to 8 hours. After 24 hours, stir well and put jar in refrigerator for 24 hours; liquid will continue to thicken. Add diced truffle and put jar back in refrigerator for 24 hours. Store in refrigerator for up to 7 to 10 days.

Soup: Heat oil in a medium pot on medium. Add onion. Cook for about 5 minutes, stirring often, until softened. Add all mushrooms and butter. Cook for about 8 minutes, stirring frequently, until onions are translucent but not browned. Stir in broth. Bring to a boil. Reduce heat to low. Simmer for about 1 hour. Remove from heat.

Carefully process in a blender or food processor until smooth, following manufacturer's instructions for processing hot liquids. Add cream, wine, thyme and oregano. Carefully process until smooth. Return to pot. Add salt and pepper. Bring to a boil. Add sherry and mix well. Divide among 6 individual bowls. Top with truffle crème fraîche. Serves 6.

Truffles

Truffles are one of the most expensive and coveted foods in the world. At least 25 truffle species grow in Italy, but only 8 or 9 are considered edible. The white truffle, which grows in the Piedmont region, is the most esteemed, but the black truffle is more widely available. Traditionally, female pigs were used to sniff out truffles, but many truffles fell victim to the sows' hearty appetites, so today in Italy, truffle seekers rely on specially trained dogs instead.

1 cup (250 mL) whipping cream

1/2 cup (125 mL) white wine

2 Tbsp (30 mL) dried thyme

1 tsp (5 mL) dried oregano

sea salt and pepper, to taste

1 cup (250 mL) sherry

Tuscan Vegetable and Bread Soup

Called *ribollita* in Italian, this Tuscan-inspired soup features crunchy bread cubes among diced tomatoes and other hearty vegetables.

2 Tbsp (30 mL) olive oil

1 large onion, finely chopped

2 Tbsp (30 mL) chopped fresh thyme

2 tsp (10 mL) minced garlic

1 cup (250 mL) diced tomato

1/2 cup (125 mL) diced carrot

1/2 cup (125 mL) diced celery

8 cups (2 L) vegetable broth

1/2 cup (125 mL) diced potatoes

2 Tbsp (30 mL) dried basil

sea salt and pepper, to taste

6 bread slices, cut into 3/4 inch (2 cm) cubes and toasted

1 cup (250 mL) grated Parmesan cheese

extra virgin olive oil, for drizzling

Heat oil in a large pot on medium. Add onion, thyme and garlic. Cook for 5 minutes, stirring often, until softened.

Add tomato, carrot and celery. Cook for 10 minutes. Add broth, potatoes and basil. Stir. Bring to a boil. Reduce heat to low. Simmer, covered, for 20 minutes.

Add salt and pepper. Simmer, covered, for about 10 minutes until vegetables are tender. Add bread cubes. Remove from heat. Let stand for 10 minutes. Add cheese. Stir. Divide among 6 individual bowls. Drizzle with oil and sprinkle with pepper. Serves 6.

Tuscan Bread

Bread in Tuscany is unlike any other you'll find throughout Italy. The bread does not contain salt so that its flavour will not compete with the foods it is typically served with. Baked fresh it is bland with a grainy texture and thick, chewy crust. Day-old bread is distinctly rock-like. Thrifty peasants created this soup to use up dried-out bread that would otherwise have gone to waste. Today, *ribollita* enjoys such popularity in Italy that it is even served in fine restaurants.

Caramelized Garlic and Onion Soup Infused with Cherry Liqueur

For this dish, you'll want to brown the onions very slowly. Just check them every once in a while. They will become very soft, golden brown and transparent. Garnish individual bowls with fresh herbs.

1/4 cup (60 mL) olive oil

2 cups (500 mL) sliced onions

1/2 cup (125 mL) minced garlic

6 cups (1.5 L) beef broth

sea salt and pepper, to taste

3/4 cup (175 mL) cherry liqueur

Heat oil in a large saucepan on medium. Add onions. Reduce heat to low. Cook for about 45 minutes, stirring occasionally. Add garlic. Cook for about 15 minutes, stirring occasionally.

Add broth. Bring to a boil on medium. Add salt and pepper. Simmer, uncovered, for 20 to 30 minutes. Divide among 6 individual bowls. Add 2 Tbsp (30 mL) cherry liqueur to each bowl. Serves 6.

Pea and Chicken Tortellini Soup

This soup was inspired by a similar soup I was served in a small, family-owned restaurant in Sienna. The simple ingredients are deceptive—they come together to create a dish with rich flavour that far exceeds the sum of its parts.

1/2 cup (125 mL) green split peas

1/4 cup (60 mL) olive oil

1/2 cup (125 mL) diced pancetta

1/2 cup (125 mL) diced carrot

1/2 cup (125 mL) diced celery

1/2 cup (125 mL) diced onion

1/2 tsp (2 mL) minced garlic

6 cups (1.5 L) chicken broth

bouquet garni of 2 bay leaves, 1/2 tsp (2 mL) dried thyme and 1/2 tsp (2 mL) crushed peppercorns (see Tip, page 13)

30 pieces of chicken tortellini

sea salt and pepper, to taste

Soak peas in water for 8 hours or overnight. Drain. Set aside.

Heat oil in a large saucepan on medium. Add pancetta. Cook slowly for about 10 minutes, allowing it to release fat. Add carrot, celery, onion and garlic. Cook for about 10 minutes, stirring often, until vegetables are softened but not browned.

Add broth, peas and *bouquet garni*. Bring to a boil. Reduce heat to low. Simmer, covered, for 20 to 30 minutes until peas are softened. Remove and discard *bouquet garni*.

Cook tortellini according to package directions. Drain. Add to broth mixture. Simmer, uncovered, for about 15 minutes. Add salt and pepper. Divide among 6 individual warm bowls. Garnish individual bowls with microgreens. Serves 6.

Tortellini

Tortellini originated in the Bologna region of Italy. Traditionally it was filled with a mixture of prosciutto, mortadella, Parmesan, egg and ox marrow and was served in broth, not cream or tomato sauce. To make the characteristic shape, egg pasta dough is cut into small squares, dabbed with filling and folded into a triangle, sealed and rolled around the end of a finger. It is said to resemble Venus' bellybutton.

Buffalo Mozzarella

Deep-fried buffalo mozzarella cheese with black garlic chutney and balsamic honey reduction sauce. Garnish with mixed greens and thinly sliced red peppers.

Black Garlic Chutney

1 tsp (5 mL) olive oil

1 cup (250 mL) finely chopped black garlic

1 Tbsp (15 mL) minced garlic

1/4 cup (60 mL) cold water

1 tsp (5 mL) sea salt

pinch of pepper

Balsamic Honey Reduction Sauce

2 cups (500 mL) balsamic vinegar

1 cup (250 mL) sugar

1/2 cup (125 mL) honey

1 Tbsp (15 mL) sea salt

Buffalo Mozzarella

1 cup (250 mL) flour, seasoned with sea salt and pepper

1 egg, fork-beaten

1 1/2 cups (375 mL) panko bread crumbs

12 × 3/4 inch (2 cm) slices buffalo mozzarella cheese

2 cups (500 mL) canola oil

Black Garlic Chutney: Heat oil, black garlic and garlic in a small saucepan on medium. Cook for about 1 minute. Add water. Bring to a boil. Add salt and pepper. Remove from heat and set aside.

Balsamic Honey Reduction Sauce: Combine all 4 ingredients in a medium saucepan. Cook on medium for 8 to 10 minutes until reduced to 1 cup (250 mL). Leftover sauce can be stored, covered, in the refrigerator for 7 to 10 days.

Buffalo Mozzarella: Place flour mixture, egg and panko in separate shallow dishes. Press both sides of cheese slices into flour mixture until coated. Dip into egg. Press both sides into panko, shaking off excess. Deep-fry in 350°F (175°C) oil in batches for 2 to 3 minutes per batch until golden brown. Discard excess flour mixture, egg and panko.

Heat black garlic chutney in microwave for about 1 minute. Arrange 3 slices of buffalo mozzarella in centre of each of 4 plates. Top with chutney and drizzle with 1 1/2 tsp (7 mL) reduction sauce. Serves 4.

Black Garlic

Black garlic is produced by fermenting regular garlic. It is available in the produce department of many grocery stores.

Bruschetta Trio

Bruschetta, from the Italian *bruscare* meaning "to roast over coals," is traditionally made by rubbing slices of toasted bread with garlic cloves, then drizzling the bread with extra virgin olive oil. The bread is salted and peppered, then heated and served warm. I've added toppings of cannellini beans, roasted spicy vegetables and roasted red pepper. Start the roasted red pepper mix the night before.

Roasted Red Pepper Mix

3 red peppers, quartered

1 Tbsp (15 mL) sea salt

1 Tbsp (15 mL) minced garlic

1 tsp (5 mL) fresh oregano

3 Tbsp (45 mL) olive oil

sea salt and pepper, to taste

Cannellini Bean Mix

19 oz (540 mL) can cannellini beans, rinsed and drained

1 Tbsp (15 mL) chopped garlic

1 Tbsp (15 mL) fresh oregano

1 tsp (5 mL) lemon juice

1/4 cup (60 mL) grape seed oil

sea salt and pepper, to taste

Spicy Vegetable Mix

2 × 3/4 inch (2 cm) slices zucchini

1 tomato, halved

(see next page)

Roasted Red Pepper Mix: Arrange peppers, skin side up, on ungreased baking sheet. Broil on top rack in oven for about 10 minutes until skins are blistered and blackened. Transfer to paper bag. Let stand for about 15 minutes. Remove and discard skins. Cut peppers into 3/4 inch (2 cm) pieces. Place in a sieve. Sprinkle with sea salt. Let stand overnight.

Transfer to a small bowl. Add garlic, oregano and oil. Toss. Add salt and pepper. Leftover red pepper mix will keep in refrigerator, covered, for 1 week.

Cannellini Bean Mix: Combine beans, garlic, oregano, lemon juice and oil. Toss. Add salt and pepper. Place in sealed container and chill. Serve cold. Leftover cannellini mix will keep in refrigerator, covered, for 1 week.

Spicy Vegetable Mix: Place zucchini, tomato, yellow pepper and eggplant on ungreased baking sheet. Bake in 350°F (175°C) oven for 10 to 15 minutes until tender-crisp. Let stand until cool enough to handle. Cut into small cubes. Transfer to small bowl. Set aside.

Toss chickpeas and oil in another bowl. Transfer to an ungreased baking sheet. Bake for 12 to 15 minutes until golden brown. Add chickpeas, garlic, basil, lemon juice and cayenne pepper to vegetable mixture. Add salt and pepper. Leftover spicy vegetable mix will keep in refrigerator, covered, for 1 week.

Bruschetta: Brush bread slices with oil and rub with garlic. Place on an ungreased baking sheet and toast bread in 350°F (175°C) oven for about 5 minutes until golden brown.

Arrange 3 slices of crostini on each of 4 individual plates. On each plate, spoon 2 Tbsp (30 mL) of red pepper mix on first crostini, 2 Tbsp (30 mL) cannellini bean mix on second and 2 Tbsp (30 mL) spicy vegetable mix on third. Garnish with Parmesan cheese and prosciutto as desired. Serves 4.

1/2 yellow pepper

2 × 3/4 inch (2 cm) slices eggplant

1 cup (250 mL) finely chopped canned chickpeas

1 Tbsp (15 mL) olive oil

1 tsp (5 mL) chopped fresh garlic

1 tsp (5 mL) chopped fresh basil

1 tsp (5 mL) lemon juice

pinch of cayenne pepper

sea salt and pepper, to taste

Bruschetta

12 crostini slices

1 Tbsp (15 mL) olive oil

3 garlic cloves, halved

shaved Parmesan cheese, for garnish

thinly sliced prosciutto, for garnish

Wild Mushroom and Olive Bruschetta

Wild mushrooms with Parmesan, and olives with toasted pine nuts, accompanied by toasted crostini.

Wild Mushroom Mix

3 Tbsp (45 mL) olive oil

3 Tbsp (45 mL) diced shallots

1 cup (250 mL) sliced chanterelle mushrooms

1 cup (250 mL) sliced cremini mushrooms

1 cup (250 mL) sliced shiitake mushrooms

1 cup (250 mL) sliced white mushrooms

2 Tbsp (30 mL) dried oregano

1 cup (250 mL) white wine

sea salt and pepper, to taste

1 Tbsp (15 mL) olive oil

Olive Mix

1 cup (250 mL) chopped sliced green olives

3 Tbsp (45 mL) chopped fresh oregano

3 Tbsp (45 mL) lemon juice

(see next page)

Wild Mushroom Mix: Heat oil in a medium pot on medium. Add shallots. Cook for 2 to 3 minutes, stirring often, until softened but not browned. Add all mushrooms. Cook for 10 minutes, stirring often.

Add oregano and wine. Cook for 10 to 15 minutes until liquid has evaporated. Add salt and pepper. Remove from heat. Let stand until cool. Add oil and toss.

Olive Mix: Combine olives, oregano, lemon juice, garlic and oil in a stainless steel bowl. Add salt and pepper.

Bruschetta: Place crostini slices on an ungreased baking sheet and toast in 350°F (175°C) oven for about 5 minutes until golden brown. Arrange 2 crostini slices on each of 6 individual plates. Spoon mushroom mixture on first crostini. Top with cheese. Spoon olive mixture on second crostini. Sprinkle with pine nuts. Serves 6.

Wild Mushrooms

Foraging for wild mushrooms is a popular pastime in Italy. Wild mushrooms abound in the Italian Alps and the Appenine. They are in season from April to November throughout much of the country, but in the south, the season can run into December. Porcini, pioppini, morels and chanterelles are some of the most sought-after types.

2 Tbsp (30 mL) minced garlic

2 Tbsp (30 mL) olive oil

sea salt and pepper, to taste

Bruschetta

12 crostini slices (or flatbread)

shaved Parmesan cheese, for garnish

1 Tbsp (15 mL) pine nuts, toasted (see Tip, page 37)

Panzanella Salad

Baby greens, red onion, cucumber and tomatoes with a lemon oregano vinaigrette. The vinaigrette will keep for about 1 month in a covered jar in the refrigerator. Use it in other salads, such as the Arugula Salad on page 36.

Lemon Oregano Vinaigrette

1/4 cup (60 mL) lemon juice

1 Tbsp (15 mL) chopped fresh oregano

1 Tbsp (15 mL) chopped shallots

1 cup (250 mL) grape seed oil

2 Tbsp (30 mL) honey

1 tsp (5 mL) Worcestershire sauce

1/2 tsp (2 mL) hot pepper sauce

sea salt and pepper, to taste

Salad

4 cups (1 L) mixed baby greens

4 red onion slices

24 cucumber slices

16 tomato wedges

sea salt and pepper, to taste

Lemon Oregano Vinaigrette: Combine lemon juice, oregano and shallots in a small bowl. Slowly whisk in oil. Whisk in honey. Add Worcestershire sauce, hot pepper sauce, salt and pepper.

Salad: Combine baby greens, red onion, cucumber and tomato in a medium bowl. Add salt, pepper and vinaigrette. Toss. Divide among individual 4 plates. Serves 4.

Insalata di Cesare

A classic Caesar salad topped with shaved crispy pancetta and Parmesan cheese.
Make the dressing 24 hours before serving.

Caesar Dressing

2 Tbsp (30 mL) minced garlic

1 tsp (5 mL) chopped capers

1/2 tsp (2 mL) black peppercorns, cracked

1 Tbsp (15 mL) chopped anchovies

1 Tbsp (15 mL) white wine vinegar

1 tsp (5 mL) Worcestershire sauce

1 Tbsp (15 mL) sea salt

2 egg yolks (large)

1 Tbsp (15 mL) Dijon mustard

1/2 cup (125 mL) olive oil

1 1/2 cups (375 mL) canola oil

2 Tbsp (30 mL) lemon juice

Salad

4 thin pancetta slices

2 cups (500 mL) cut or torn romaine lettuce

1/2 cup (125 mL) Caesar Dressing

1/4 cup (60 mL) grated Parmesan cheese, plus more for garnish

4 lemon wedges, for garnish

Caesar Dressing: Process garlic, capers, peppercorns, anchovies, vinegar, Worcestershire sauce and salt in a blender or food processor until well combined.

Whisk egg yolks and mustard in a stand mixer with whisk attachment until well mixed. With motor running, slowly add olive oil and canola oil. The mixture will thicken as you add the oil; slowly thin with lemon juice as needed. Add garlic mixture. Whisk. Transfer to a small resealable container. Chill, covered, for 24 hours. Leftover dressing will keep for 5 days, sealed, in the refrigerator.

Salad: Bake pancetta slices on an ungreased baking sheet in a 350°F (175°C) oven, until golden brown, about 5 minutes. Combine lettuce, Caesar dressing and cheese in a medium bowl. Divide among 4 individual plates. Garnish with pancetta, cheese and lemon wedges. Serves 4.

Caesar Salad

There is much debate about who created the Caesar salad, but one thing is certain—it wasn't Julius Caesar. In fact, this famous salad does not hail from Italy. Its origins have been traced back to Tijuana, Mexico, where restaurateur Caesare Cardini served it back in the 1920s. The original Caesar salad did not contain anchovies.

Arugula Salad

Arugula tossed with pine nuts, Sopressata sausage and shaved Santa Lucia goat cheese.
Look in an Italian grocery store for the sausage and goat cheese.

4 cups (1 L) arugula, lightly packed

1/4 cup (60 mL) pine nuts, toasted (see Tip)

20 thin slices Sopressata sausage

1/2 cup (125 mL) grated Santa Lucia goat cheese

1/2 cup (125 mL) Lemon Oregano Vinaigrette (see page 32)

1 cup (250 mL) mixed salad greens, lightly packed

Combine arugula, pine nuts, sausage slices and cheese. Toss with vinaigrette. Divide among 4 individual plates. Garnish with salad greens. Serves 4.

Tip

When toasting nuts, seeds or coconut, cooking times will vary for each type of nut—so never toast them together. For small amounts, place the ingredient in an ungreased shallow frying pan. Heat on medium for 3 to 5 minutes, stirring often, until golden. For larger amounts, spread the ingredient evenly in an ungreased shallow pan. Bake in a 350°F (175°C) oven for 5 to 10 minutes, stirring or shaking often, until golden.

Hot House Tomato and Stracchino Cheese

Sliced tomatoes piled high with Stracchino cheese, all drizzled
with white balsamic vinegar and truffle oil.

**4 medium tomatoes, cut
into 3/4 inch (2 cm) thick
slices**

sea salt and pepper, to taste

**2 Tbsp (30 mL) fresh
oregano**

**8 oz (225 g) Stracchino
cheese, cut into 3/4 inch
(2 cm) thick slices**

4 tsp (20 mL) truffle oil

**4 tsp (20 mL) white
balsamic vinegar**

microgreens, for garnish

Sprinkle tomatoes with salt, pepper and oregano. On each
of 4 individual plates, alternately stack tomato slices and
cheese slices. Drizzle with truffle oil and vinegar. Garnish
with microgreens. Serves 4.

Stracchino Cheese

Stracchino cheese, also called crescenza, is a soft, creamy, mild-flavoured cheese that originated in the Piedmont, Lombardy and Veneto regions of Italy. Traditionally it was made only in autumn and winter when the cows came in from mountain pastures, but it is now available year-round.

Tuscan Vegetable Insalata

Broiled eggplant, zucchini, asparagus, purple onion and tomatoes tossed with arugula, fresh goat cheese and roasted pine nuts. Make the chili oil at least 2 days in advance.

Chili Oil

1 cup (250 mL) olive oil

1 tsp (5 mL) dried crushed chilies

1/2 tsp (2 mL) cayenne pepper

1 tsp (5 mL) minced garlic

1 tsp (5 mL) hot paprika

Salad

8 × 3/4 inch (2 cm) thick eggplant slices

8 × 3/4 inch (2 cm) thick zucchini slices

8 asparagus spears

8 × 3/4 inch (2 cm) purple onion slices

8 tomato wedges

sea salt and pepper, to taste

1/4 cup (60 mL) pesto

1/2 cup (125 mL) arugula, lightly packed

1/2 cup (125 mL) goat cheese

4 tsp (20 mL) pine nuts, toasted (see page 37)

1/4 cup (60 mL) Chili Oil

Chili Oil: Heat oil in a small pot on low. Add chilies and cayenne pepper. Heat for 3 to 4 minutes. Add garlic and paprika. Stir. Transfer to a jar. Let stand, covered, at room temperature for about 2 days. Leftover chili oil will keep in a sealed container for a month in the refrigerator.

Salad: Blanch eggplant, zucchini and asparagus in boiling water in a medium pot for 1 to 2 minutes until asparagus is bright green. Place eggplant, zucchini, asparagus, onion and tomato on an ungreased baking sheet. Broil on centre rack in oven for 10 to 15 minutes, turning once, until vegetables are golden and tender. Add salt and pepper. Transfer to a bowl. Add pesto. Toss. Arrange vegetables, overlapping, on each of 4 individual plates.

Combine arugula and cheese in a small bowl. Place on top of grilled vegetables. Sprinkle with pine nuts. Drizzle with chili oil. Serves 4.

Variation

You can also grill the vegetables instead of broiling them. Grill
for 10 to 15 minutes, turning once, until vegetables are golden
and tender.

Tortino di Caprino

Lightly breaded goat cheese cakes served on a fig coulis with aged balsamic vinegar and microgreens. Use a deep frying thermometer to accurately test the temperature of your hot oil.

Fig Coulis

1 cup (250 mL) water

1/2 cup (125 mL) dried figs

1/2 cup (125 mL) port wine

Tortino di Caprino

8 oz (225 g) goat cheese

1 1/2 tsp (7 mL) sea salt

1/2 tsp (2 mL) white pepper

1 cup (250 mL) flour

2 eggs, beaten

1/2 cup (125 mL) homogenized milk

2 cups (500 mL) panko bread crumbs

2 cups (500 mL) olive oil

4 tsp (20 mL) 12-year-old balsamic vinegar

microgreens, for garnish

Fig Coulis: Heat water in a small saucepan on medium-high. Add figs. Bring to a boil. Simmer until figs are softened. Stir in wine. Carefully process fig mixture in a blender or food processor, following manufacturer's instructions for processing hot liquids, until smooth and thickened. Set aside.

Tortino di Caprino: Process cheese, salt and pepper in a blender or food processor until cheese is a paste-like consistency. Transfer to a small bowl. Chill, covered, in refrigerator for about 45 minutes. Use a melon baller or spoon to scoop out 2 oz (57 g) portions of cheese. Form each portion into a small ball. Flatten balls slightly into cakes. Place on an ungreased baking sheet. Freeze for about 1 hour until firm.

Place flour in a shallow bowl. Whisk together eggs and milk in a separate shallow bowl. Place panko in a third shallow bowl. Press both sides of cakes in flour until coated. Dip in egg mixture. Press in panko, shaking off excess. Discard any remaining flour, egg mixture and panko. Freeze on same baking sheet for 1 hour.

Heat oil in a small saucepan to 300°F (150°C). Shallow-fry cakes in hot oil for about 5 minutes until light golden brown. Remove to paper towels to drain.

Place fig coulis in centre of each of 4 individual plates. Place cakes on top. Drizzle vinegar around cakes. Garnish with microgreens. Serves 4.

Aged Balsamic Vinegar

Genuine balsamic vinegar comes from the Modena and Reggio Emilia provinces of Italy and has Protected Designation of Origin (PDO) status. To qualify as traditional balsamic vinegar, it must be made out of specific grapes and aged in an attic for at least 12 years in a series of barrels made of different types of wood. Aged balsamic has a syrup-like consistency and a sweet, full-bodied flavour. You most likely will not find it in your local supermarket, but it is available online.

Seafood Fritter Medley

Shrimp and other seafood are sold by the "count." For example, shrimp with a count of 21/25 means that there are 21 to 25 shrimp per pound.

Seafood Batter

1 cup (250 mL) rice
(or all-purpose) flour

1/2 cup (125 mL)
cornstarch

1 1/2 tsp (7 mL) baking
soda

pinch of kosher salt

1 egg yolk, large

1 cup (250 mL) ice-cold
sparkling water

Seafood

2 cups (500 mL) olive oil

8 shrimp (peeled and
deveined), size 21/25

8 prawns (peeled and
deveined), size 13/25

8 large sea scallops,
size 20/30

8 anchovies

8 sardines

1 mackerel fillets, cut into
8 pieces

8 squid pieces

sea salt and pepper, to taste

1 cup (250 mL) flour

4 lemon wedges (optional)

sliced red or yellow
peppers (optional)

microgreens (optional)

Seafood Batter: Combine flour, cornstarch, baking soda and salt in a medium bowl. Whisk egg yolk and sparkling water together in a separate bowl. Add egg mixture to flour mixture. Mix until a smooth batter forms.

Seafood: Heat olive oil to 325°F (160°C) in a heavy saucepan. Sprinkle all seafood with salt. Press all sides of seafood into flour. Dip into seafood batter. Deep-fry seafood, in batches, for 3 to 5 minutes until golden brown. Discard any remaining batter.

Arrange deep-fried seafood on 4 individual plates. If desired, garnish with a lemon wedge, red or yellow peppers and microgreens. Serves 4.

Venetian Seafood

This dish was inspired by a trip to Venice. Venice is known as much for its spectacular seafood as for its canals and gondolas. Lightly battered seafood that is then quickly deep fried to crispy perfection is a Venetian specialty.

Sautéed Jumbo Wild Prawns

Served with a flavourful vanilla coconut spicy curry reduction sauce.

Vanilla Coconut Spicy Curry Reduction Sauce

2 Tbsp (30 mL) olive oil

2 Tbsp (30 mL) diced shallots

8 oz (225 g) tub of Thai red curry paste

2 cups (500 mL) coconut milk

2 cups (500 mL) whipping cream

2 Tbsp (30 mL) vanilla paste

sea salt and pepper, to taste

Prawns

1/4 cup (60 mL) extra virgin olive oil

24 jumbo prawns (peeled and deveined)

2 Tbsp (30 mL) diced shallots

6 Tbsp (90 mL) white wine

3/4 cup (175 mL) Vanilla Coconut Spicy Curry Reduction Sauce

sea salt and pepper, to taste

dill or lemon thyme, for garnish

Vanilla Coconut Spicy Curry Reduction Sauce: Heat oil in a small saucepan on medium. Add shallots. Cook for about 5 minutes until slightly browned. Add curry paste. Stir. Slowly add coconut milk and cream. Bring to a boil. Cook for about 2 minutes, stirring often. Reduce heat to medium-low. Cook for about 10 minutes, stirring occasionally, until reduced to about 2 cups (500 mL). Add vanilla, salt and pepper. Remove from heat. Cover to keep warm. Leftover sauce will keep in refrigerator, covered, for 1 week.

Prawns: Heat oil in a separate small saucepan on medium. Add prawns and shallots. Cook for about 4 minutes, stirring occasionally, until prawns are pink. Add wine and reduction sauce. Simmer for 1 minute until heated through. Add salt and pepper.

Divide prawns among 4 individual plates. Top with sauce. Garnish with dill or lemon thyme. Serves 4.

Red Curry Paste

Red curry paste is a staple in Thai cuisine. Recipes vary, but the main ingredients include garlic, shallots, lemongrass, galangal (Asian ginger), peppercorns, cumin, coriander, dried chilies and shrimp paste. Vegetarian versions without the shrimp paste are also available commercially.

Grilled Shrimp Antipasti

Grilled shrimp on rosemary skewers served with tomatoes, chickpeas and bell peppers, sautéed with garlic oregano olive oil. Garnish with thinly shaved green onion.

16 shrimp (peeled and deveined), size 16/20 (see page 44)

4 × 6 inch (15 cm) sprigs of fresh rosemary, for skewers

3 Tbsp (45 mL) olive oil

1/4 cup (60 mL) canned chickpeas, rinsed and drained

1/4 cup (60 mL) diced tomato

1 Tbsp (15 mL) diced yellow pepper

1/2 tsp (2 mL) fresh oregano

1/2 tsp (2 mL) minced garlic

1/4 cup (60 mL) white wine

1/2 cup (125 mL) butter, softened

sea salt and pepper, to taste

thinly sliced green onion, for garnish

Preheat grill to medium. Thread 4 shrimp on each sprig of rosemary. Cook on greased grill for about 5 minutes, flipping once, until pink and cooked.

Heat oil in a frying pan on medium. Add chickpeas, tomato, yellow pepper, oregano and garlic. Cook for 2 to 3 minutes until softened. Add wine, butter, salt and pepper. Stir. Cook for about 2 minutes. Divide among 4 individual plates. Place skewered shrimp on top. Serves 4.

Antipasto

The Italian *antipasto* translates to "before the meal" and is the
first course of a formal meal, rather like an appetizer. In Italy,
it is usually a small portion and consists of olives, cold cuts,
anchovies, cheeses, crostini, bruschetta and the like. Antipasti
vary greatly depending on the region, with fish and seafood
playing more of a role in the south.

Wild Prawns and Coquilles St. Jacques

Prawns and scallops served with garlic mashed potatoes in a unique serving style—in scallop shells. Scallop shells can be found at a seafood shop. Garnish with green onion.

Garlic Mashed Potatoes

1 lb (454 g) Yukon gold potatoes, peeled and quartered lengthwise

1/2 cup (125 mL) whipping cream

2 Tbsp (30 mL) butter, softened

1 Tbsp (15 mL) minced garlic

pinch of nutmeg

sea salt and pepper, to taste

4 sea scallop shells

Cream Sauce

4 cups (1 L) whipping cream

1 cup (250 mL) chopped shallots

1 cup (250 mL) grated Parmesan cheese

sea salt and pepper, to taste

(see next page)

Garlic Mashed Potatoes: Pour water into a medium saucepan until about 1 inch (2.5 cm) deep. Add potato. Cover. Bring to a boil. Reduce heat to medium. Boil gently for 12 to 15 minutes until tender. Drain. Transfer to a medium bowl. Mash.

Heat cream, butter and garlic in a small pot on medium until butter is melted. Add to potatoes. Add nutmeg, salt and pepper. Stir. Scoop mashed potatoes into each scallop shell. Place potato-lined scallop shells on an ungreased baking sheet. Bake in 375°F (190°C) oven for about 5 minutes until golden brown.

Cream Sauce: Combine cream and shallots in a separate medium saucepan. Bring to a boil. Reduce heat to low. Simmer for about 10 minutes, stirring occasionally, until reduced by half. Add cheese, salt and pepper. Stir until smooth. Remove from heat. Cover to keep warm.

Butter Sauce: Combine wine, lemon juice, thyme and rosemary in a small saucepan on medium. Simmer for about 2 minutes until reduced by about 60%. Reduce heat to low. Remove thyme and rosemary. Slowly whisk in butter. Add salt and pepper.

Prawns and Scallops: Heat oil in a frying pan on medium. Cook prawns and scallops for 2 to 3 minutes per side until prawns are pink and scallops are opaque. Add shallots and wine. Add cream sauce, salt and pepper. Divide prawn mixture over scallop shells. Top with butter sauce. Serves 4.

Butter Sauce

1/2 cup (125 mL) white wine

1 Tbsp (15 mL) lemon juice

1 sprig of fresh thyme

1 sprig of fresh rosemary

1/2 cup (125 mL) cold butter

sea salt and pepper, to taste

Prawns and Scallops

1 Tbsp (15 mL) olive oil

12 prawns (peeled and deveined), size 16/20 (see page 44)

12 large sea scallops, size 10/20, patted dry

2 Tbsp (30 mL) chopped shallots

1/4 cup (60 mL) white wine

sea salt and pepper, to taste

Chilled Diver Scallops

With black truffle vinaigrette and mixed greens.

Black Truffle Vinaigrette

1 cup (250 mL) grape seed oil

1/2 cup (125 mL) champagne vinegar

1/2 cup (125 mL) truffle oil

2 Tbsp (30 mL) sea salt

1/2 tsp (2 mL) black pepper

1 Tbsp (15 mL) diced shallots

1/2 tsp (2 mL) hot pepper sauce

1/2 tsp (2 mL) Worcestershire sauce

Court Bouillon

4 cups (1 L) water

1 small carrot, thinly sliced

1 small onion, thinly sliced

1 celery rib, thinly sliced

8 bay leaves

2 sprigs of fresh rosemary

1 lemon, cut into wedges

1/2 tsp (2 mL) dried thyme

1/4 tsp (1 mL) sea salt

1 tsp (5 mL) black pepper

(see next page)

Black Truffle Vinaigrette: Whisk grape seed oil, vinegar, truffle oil, salt and pepper in a medium bowl until well combined. Add shallots, hot pepper sauce and Worcestershire sauce. Whisk until thickened. Set aside.

Court Bouillon: Combine all 10 ingredients in a large pot on medium-high. Bring to a boil. Boil for about 5 minutes. Remove bay leaves. Strain through sieve into a bowl. Discard solids.

Scallops: Place scallops in a round mesh strainer in a large saucepan or bowl. Pour court bouillon over scallops. Leave scallops in hot court bouillon for 1 to 1 1/2 minutes until medium-rare (or about 4 minutes until well done). Lift basket from court bouillon and transfer to ice water. Let scallops stand in ice for about 1 minute until cooled. Discard court bouillon.

Place scallops on serving plate. Garnish with mixed greens. Drizzle with black truffle vinaigrette. Top with oregano and black truffle. Serves 4.

Scallops

8 large sea scallops, size 10/20 (see page 44)

mixed greens, for garnish

1/2 tsp (2 mL) diced fresh oregano

2 Tbsp (30 mL) sliced black truffle

Escargots

Served with tomato concassé and black garlic butter. This presentation uses escargot dishes; alternatively, escargot shells from a seafood store can be used. Look for snails in cans, preferably a French variety.

Tomato Concassé

2 large tomatoes

1 Tbsp (15 mL) olive oil

1 Tbsp (15 mL) minced garlic

sea salt and pepper, to taste

Black Garlic Butter

1 1/4 cups (300 mL) butter, softened

6 Tbsp (90 mL) black garlic (see page 27)

1/4 cup (60 mL) Pernod liqueur

2 Tbsp (30 mL) chopped fresh parsley

2 Tbsp (30 mL) lemon juice

2 Tbsp (30 mL) minced garlic

2 tsp (10 mL) sea salt

1 1/2 tsp (7 mL) black pepper

Escargots

48 canned snails

Tomato Concassé: With a paring knife, cut an "X" on bottom of tomato just deep enough to penetrate skin. Blanch tomato in boiling water in small saucepan for about 30 seconds. Drain. Immediately plunge into ice water in small bowl. Let stand for about 10 minutes until cold. Drain well. Remove core. Peel tomato. Cut in half horizontally. Squeeze out and discard seeds and juice. Finely chop tomato.

Heat oil in a small pot on medium. Add tomato and garlic. Bring to a boil, stirring occasionally. Add salt and pepper. Remove from heat. Cover to keep warm.

Black Garlic Butter: Process all 8 ingredients in a food processor until smooth. Transfer to a small bowl. Chill, covered, until firm. Store leftover butter, covered, in the refrigerator.

Escargots: Place 2 snails in each compartment of 4 escargot dishes. Add 1/2 tsp (2 mL) concassé to each compartment and top with 1/2 tsp (2 mL) garlic butter. Bake in 350°F (175°C) oven for about 15 minutes. Serve hot. Serves 4.

Escargots

Although escargots are generally associated with French cuisine, there is a long history of snail consumption in Italy. Snail shells have been dug out of middens from around pre-Roman settlements, and snail farming (heliciculture) dates as far back as Roman times. The Roman scholar Pliny the Elder described the practice in his influential encyclopedia, *Naturalis Historia*, some of which was published posthumously after he died in the 79 AD eruption of Mount Vesuvius.

Mussels Siciliana

Mussels with crumbled Italian sausage in a white wine broth. Debeard mussels if necessary. Garnish with a lemon wedge and green onion if desired.

2 lbs (900 g) fresh mussels

2 Tbsp (30 mL) olive oil

1 cup (250 mL) crumbled Italian sausage

1 cup (250 mL) diced tomato

1/2 tsp (2 mL) chopped garlic

pinch of dried crushed chilies

sea salt and pepper, to taste

1/2 cup (125 mL) white wine

1/2 cup (125 mL) butter

parsley, for garnish

Put mussels into a medium bowl. Lightly tap to close any that are opened 1/4 inch (6 mm) or more. Discard any that do not close.

Heat oil in a frying pan on medium. Add sausage, tomato and garlic. Cook for about 7 minutes until sausage is browned. Add mussels, chilies, salt and pepper. Cook for 1 minute.

Add wine. Cook, covered, for 3 to 4 minutes until mussels have opened. Discard any unopened mussels. Stir in butter. Sprinkle with parsley. Divide among 4 pasta bowls. Serves 4.

Blue Mussels

Farmed blue mussels are big business in Canada. Prince
Edward Island is the top producer, but the other Atlantic
provinces, British Columbia and Quebec also play a significant
role. The mussels are grown on mussel socks suspended in
shallow bays or inlets along the coasts, a practice that is more
environmentally sustainable than dredging the ocean bottom.
Much of Canada's blue mussel yield is exported to the United
States.

Crispy Garlic Calamari

Garnish with thin strips of grated carrot.

1 1/2 lbs (680 g) small squid tubes and tentacles

1/4 cup (60 mL) minced garlic

sea salt and pepper, to taste

4 cups (1 L) olive oil

3/4 cup (175 mL) all-purpose flour

1 cup (250 mL) thinly sliced onion

Place squid tubes and tentacles in a bowl. Add garlic, salt and pepper. Let stand for 5 minutes.

Heat oil in a medium saucepan to 300°F (150°C). Place flour in a medium bowl. Toss squid and onion in flour until coated. Discard any remaining flour. Deep-fry squid and onion in hot oil, in batches, for about 1 minute until golden. Remove to paper towels to drain. Divide calamari and onion among 4 individual plates. Serves 4.

Calamari

Calamari is the plural version of *calamero,* the Italian word for squid. Squid plays a large role in Italian cuisine—it can be fried, grilled, stuffed, baked and even stewed in its own ink. In Canada when we think of calamari, we picture the lightly battered, deep-fried version that is a staple on appetizer menus across the land. This recipe uses the tentacles as well as the rings, much as you would see in Italy.

Crab Cakes

Panko-encrusted crab cakes with a spicy green curry reduction sauce, hearts of palm and pickled mango. Make the pickled mango 3 days in advance.

Pickled Mango

1 cup (250 mL) water

1 cup (250 mL) white wine vinegar

2 Tbsp (30 mL) brown sugar

2 Tbsp (30 mL) sea salt

5 whole cloves

2 bay leaves

1 green mango, cut into matchsticks (about 1/4 × 1/4 × 2 inches, 0.6 × 0.6 × 5 cm)

Spicy Green Curry Reduction Sauce

2 Tbsp (30 mL) olive oil

1 Tbsp (15 mL) chopped shallots

1 Tbsp (15 mL) Thai green curry paste

2 Tbsp (30 mL) white wine

1 cup (250 mL) homogenized milk

1 cup (250 mL) whipping cream

sea salt and pepper, to taste

(see next page)

Pickled Mango: Combine water, vinegar, brown sugar, salt, cloves and bay leaves in a small saucepan on medium-high. Bring to a boil. Remove from heat. Let stand until completely cooled. Place mango in a resealable jar. Pour vinegar mixture over to cover. Chill, covered, for 3 days. Remove bay leaves.

Spicy Green Curry Reduction Sauce: Heat oil in a separate small saucepan on medium. Add shallots and green curry paste. Cook for 1 minute. Add wine, milk and cream. Cook for about 6 minutes until reduced to 1 cup (250 mL). Add salt and pepper.

Crab Cakes: Heat oil in a frying pan on medium. Add bell peppers. Cook for about 4 minutes until tender.

Carefully pick through crabmeat, removing any pieces of shell but keeping lumps of crab as large as possible. Combine crabmeat, peppers, panko, cream, egg, shallots, parsley, mustard and garlic. Add salt and pepper. Drizzle a baking sheet with oil. Form crab mixture into 8 cakes. Place on baking sheet. Bake in 350°F (175°C) oven for 5 to 8 minutes until golden brown.

Divide hearts of palm and pickled mango among 8 individual plates. Top with crab cakes. Drizzle curry sauce around crab cakes. Garnish with mixed greens. Serves 8.

Crab Cakes

1 Tbsp (15 mL) olive oil

1 cup (250 mL) diced bell peppers (your choice of red, green and yellow)

2 cups (500 mL) fresh crabmeat

1/2 cup (125 mL) panko bread crumbs

1/2 cup (125 mL) whipping cream

1 large egg

1 Tbsp (15 mL) chopped shallots

1 Tbsp (15 mL) chopped Italian parsley

1 Tbsp (15 mL) Dijon mustard

1 tsp (5 mL) minced garlic

sea salt and pepper, to taste

1 Tbsp (15 mL) grape seed (or olive) oil

2 cups (500 mL) hearts of palm

mixed greens, for garnish

Sour Cherry Risotto Cakes with Braised Beef Short Ribs

An onion and garlic gremolata tops a tower of ribs and risotto cakes.

Ribs

1/2 cup (125 mL) olive oil

1 lb (454 g) beef short ribs, bone-in

1/2 cup (125 mL) chopped carrot

1/2 cup (125 mL) chopped celery

1/2 cup (125 mL) chopped onion

8 cups (2 L) beef broth

4 sprigs of fresh rosemary

4 bay leaves

2 cinnamon sticks (4 inches, 10 cm, each)

sea salt and pepper, to taste

Risotto Cakes

2 Tbsp (30 mL) olive oil

1/2 cup (125 mL) diced onion

2 cups (500 mL) arborio rice

8 cups (2 L) vegetable broth

1 1/2 cups (375 mL) grated Parmesan cheese

(see next page)

Ribs: Heat oil in a heavy ovenproof pot on high. Add ribs. Cook for 5 to 6 minutes until well browned. Transfer to a plate. Cover to keep warm.

Add carrot, celery and onion to same pot. Cook for about 5 minutes until onion is softened. Add ribs, broth, rosemary, bay leaves, cinnamon sticks, salt and pepper. Bake, covered, in 350°F (175°C) oven for about 3 1/2 hours.

Risotto Cakes: Heat oil in a medium pot on medium. Add onion and rice. Cook for 1 to 2 minutes, stirring often, until toasted.

Heat broth in a separate pot on medium until boiling gently. Add 1 cup (250 mL) of broth to rice, stirring constantly, until broth is absorbed. Repeat with remaining broth, 1 cup (250 mL) at a time, until broth is absorbed and rice is *al dente* (slightly firm but not crunchy). Entire process will take 15 to 20 minutes.

Add cheese, butter, cherries, salt and pepper. Stir. Use a 3-inch (7.5 cm) stainless steel ring mould to form risotto into 4 cakes.

Cipollini Onion and Garlic Gremolata: Wash and completely dry parsley. Pick off leaves from stems. Discard stems. Finely chop leaves. Combine parsley, pickled onion and zest in a small bowl. Add oil, salt and pepper.

Cut ribs into 2 oz (57 g) portions. Heat pan juices on medium-low until reduced to about 1/2 cup (125 mL). Discard rosemary, bay leaves and cinnamon sticks. Place 1 risotto cake on each of 4 individual plates. Top with short ribs and gremolata. Drizzle with reduction sauce and butter sauce. Garnish with microgreens. Serves 4.

1 cup (250 mL) butter, softened

1 cup (250 mL) finely chopped pitted sour cherries

sea salt and pepper, to taste

Cipollini Onion and Garlic Gremolata

1 bunch Italian parsley

1/2 cup (125 mL) chopped pickled cipollini onion

1/2 tsp (2 mL) lemon zest

1 Tbsp (15 mL) olive oil

1/2 tsp (2 mL) sea salt

pepper, to taste

1/4 cup (60 mL) Butter Sauce (see page 51)

microgreens, for garnish

Contorni

A side dish of sautéed wild mushrooms. You can substitute other types of mushrooms in place of wild mushrooms. Garnish with fresh herbs.

6 Tbsp (90 mL) olive oil

2 1/2 cups (625 mL) chopped wild mushrooms

1 Tbsp (15 mL) chopped shallots

3/4 cup (175 mL) vegetable broth

1/4 cup (60 mL) lemon juice

sea salt and pepper, to taste

6 Tbsp (90 mL) butter, softened

Heat oil in a medium saucepan on high. Add mushrooms and shallots. Cook for 1 to 2 minutes, stirring often, until golden.

Add broth, lemon juice, salt and pepper. Cook for 3 to 5 minutes until liquid is evaporated. Add butter and stir until melted. Serves 4.

Baked Asparagus Parmesan

A simple way to serve asparagus.

2 1/2 cups (625 mL) asparagus

1/2 cup (125 mL) butter, softened

1/2 cup (125 mL) grated Parmesan cheese

sea salt and pepper, to taste

1 Tbsp (15 mL) Butter Sauce (see page 51)

Blanch asparagus in boiling salted water in medium saucepan for 1 to 2 minutes until bright green. Drain. Immediately plunge into ice water in medium bowl. Let stand for about 10 minutes until cold. Drain well.

Place asparagus in a medium baking dish. Top with butter, cheese, salt and pepper. Bake in 350°F (175°C) oven for 6 to 8 minutes until butter is melted and asparagus is tender. Broil on centre rack for 3 to 5 minutes until golden. Top with butter sauce. Serves 4.

Parmigiano-Reggiano Cheese

Parmigiano-Reggiano cheese is a hard, dry, sharp-flavoured cheese that has PDO status in Italy. It must be produced in the Bologna, Parma, Reggio Emilia or Modena provinces and meet strict requirements to bear the Parmigiano-Reggiano name. Otherwise it is called Parmesan. High quality Parmesan cheeses are produced in many countries, but true Parmigiano-Reggiano outshines them all.

Caramelized Butternut Squash

A delicious side dish, and so simple.

**5 medium (or 3 large)
butternut squash**

**2/3 cup (150 mL) grated
Parmesan cheese**

pinch of nutmeg

sea salt and pepper, to taste

Bake butternut squash in 350°F (175°C) oven for 45 minutes to 1 hour until tender. Let stand until cool enough to handle.

Peel squash. Remove seeds. Chop. Process squash, cheese, nutmeg, salt and pepper in a food processor until smooth. Transfer to a medium baking dish. Bake for about 15 minutes until caramelized. Serves 4.

Squash

Squash features heavily in the cuisine of northern Italy. Zucchini may be the most common, but butternut squash is also a top contender. The tender flesh is incorporated into risotto, soup and pasta, among other dishes, and squash flowers are considered a great delicacy.

Sautéed Spinach

Works well as a simple side on its own, or can be incorporated into many main dishes in this book (such as Wild King Salmon, page 100, and Veal Vincenza, page 136).

1/4 cup (60 mL) olive oil

3 Tbsp (45 mL) chopped shallots

2 1/2 cups (625 mL) spinach

pinch of nutmeg

sea salt and pepper, to taste

3/4 cup (175 mL) vegetable broth

1/4 cup (60 mL) lemon juice

Heat oil in a medium saucepan on high. Add shallots. Cook about 3 minutes, stirring often, until golden brown.

Add spinach, nutmeg, salt and pepper, stirring often. Add broth and lemon juice. Cook for about 5 minutes, stirring often, until liquid is evaporated. Serves 4.

Conchiglietle

Shell pasta stuffed with spinach and ricotta, with a porcini mushroom
ragu cream jus and shaved Parmesan.

Stuffed Pasta

2 cups (500 mL) spinach

**2 cups (500 mL) ricotta
cheese**

**1/2 cup (125 mL) grated
Parmesan cheese**

**1/2 cup (125 mL) grated
pecorino cheese**

1/2 tsp (2 mL) nutmeg

sea salt and pepper, to taste

1/2 tsp (2 mL) salt

**1 lb (454 g) jumbo shell
pasta (about 16 shells)**

1 Tbsp (15 mL) olive oil

Porcini Mushroom Ragu

1 Tbsp (15 mL) olive oil

**1 cup (250 mL) sliced
porcini mushrooms**

1 tsp (5 mL) dried thyme

**1 tsp (5 mL) finely chopped
shallots**

3 Tbsp (45 mL) white wine

**1 cup (250 mL)
homogenized milk**

**1 cup (250 mL) whipping
cream**

(see next page)

Stuffed Pasta: Blanch spinach in boiling salted water in
medium saucepan for 1 to 2 minutes until bright green.
Drain. Immediately plunge into ice water in medium bowl.
Let stand for about 10 minutes until cold. Drain well. Mix
spinach, ricotta, Parmesan cheese, pecorino cheese and
nutmeg in a large bowl. Add salt and pepper. Set aside.

Heat water in a large pot on medium-high. Add salt. Bring
to a boil. Add pasta. Cook for about 13 minutes until
al dente. Drain well. Return to pot. Add oil. Toss to coat. Let
cool. Spoon about 2 Tbsp (30 mL) spinach mixture into each
shell. Squeeze shells gently to seal shut. Place shells in
baking dish. Set aside.

Porcini Mushroom Ragu: Heat oil in a frying pan on medium. Add mushrooms, thyme and shallots. Cook for 3 to 4 minutes, stirring often, until lightly browned. Add wine, milk and cream, stirring constantly. Cook on high until reduced by half.

Reduce heat to low. Add Parmesan cheese. Simmer for 5 to 6 minutes, stirring occasionally, until sauce thickens. Add salt and pepper. Pour sauce over stuffed shells. Cover with foil. Bake in 350°F (175°C) oven for 10 minutes. Garnish individual servings with Parmesan cheese and basil. Serves 4.

1/2 cup (125 mL) shaved Parmesan cheese, plus more for garnishing

sea salt and pepper, to taste

1/4 cup (60 mL) fresh basil, julienned

Baked Elbow Macaroni

With porcini mushrooms and truffles in a thick, rich cream.

1 Tbsp (15 mL) olive oil

2 Tbsp (30 mL) sliced porcini mushrooms

1 Tbsp (15 mL) shallots

6 Tbsp (90 mL) white wine

2 cups (500 mL) vegetable broth

2 cups (500 mL) whipping cream

1/2 cup (125 mL) grated Parmesan cheese

2 Tbsp (30 mL) butter

sea salt and pepper, to taste

1 lb (500 g) elbow macaroni

3 slices mozzarella cheese

2 Tbsp (30 mL) sliced truffles

Heat oil in a frying pan on medium. Add mushrooms and shallots. Cook for about 5 minutes, stirring occasionally, until lightly browned. Add wine, broth and cream, stirring constantly. Bring to a boil. Cook, stirring occasionally, until reduced to about 2 cups (500 mL). Add Parmesan cheese, butter, salt and pepper. Stir until butter is melted. Remove from heat and set aside.

Cook pasta in a pot of boiling salted water for about 8 minutes until *al dente*. Drain. Add to sauce. Toss. Transfer to a baking dish. Top with mozzarella. Bake in 350°F (175°C) oven for 6 to 8 minutes until cheese is melted and slightly browned. Garnish with truffles. Serves 4.

Macaroni

Macaroni, which in Canada generally refers to the
elbow-shaped noodle beloved by children across
the land, comes from the Italian *maccheroni*. In
Italy, *maccheroni* seems to have a bit of an identity
crisis—the word is used to describe any short,
tubular pasta, and yet flat, fresh noodles are often
called *maccheroni* as well.

Linguine Frutti di Mare

Shrimp, scallops, squid and clams in a marinara sauce. This recipe makes 4 very generous servings—it could easily also serve 6.

1/2 cup (125 mL) extra virgin olive oil

12 shrimp, size 16/20 (see page 44)

8 large sea scallops, size 10/20, patted dry

15 squid rings

8 oz (225 g) canned whole baby clams

2 cups (500 mL) tomato sauce

2/3 cup (150 mL) white wine

1/4 cup (60 mL) minced garlic

1/4 cup (60 mL) vegetable broth

pinch of basil

sea salt and pepper, to taste

36 oz (1 kg) linguine (about 4 cups)

1/2 cup (125 mL) butter, softened

fresh basil, julienned, for garnish

Heat oil in a large frying pan on medium. Add shrimp, scallops, squid and clams. Cook for about 1 minute. Add tomato sauce, wine, garlic, broth and basil. Cook, stirring occasionally, until reduced to 2 1/2 cups (625 mL). Add salt and pepper. Set aside.

Cook linguine in boiling salted water for about 12 minutes until *al dente*. Drain. Add to seafood mixture. Add butter. Toss. Transfer to individual pasta bowls. Garnish with basil. Serves 4.

Frutti di Mare

Frutti di mare translates to "fruits of the sea" and is a popular pasta dish in coastal regions of Italy. As with all Italian cuisine, each region has its own version, but common ingredients include mussels, clams, scallops, shrimp and squid.

Capellini al Salmone

Topped with thinly sliced smoked salmon and fresh basil.

1/2 cup (125 mL) extra virgin olive oil

2 tsp (10 mL) chopped garlic

1/2 cup (125 mL) white wine

3/4 cup (175 mL) butter, softened

2 Tbsp (30 mL) chopped Italian parsley

sea salt and pepper, to taste

1 lb (454 g) angel hair pasta

12 oz (340 g) thinly sliced smoked salmon

2 Tbsp (30 mL) julienned fresh basil

6 Tbsp (90 mL) thinly sliced green onion

1 Tbsp (15 mL) extra virgin olive oil

Heat oil in a large frying pan on medium. Add garlic. Cook for about 2 minutes. Add wine, butter, parsley, salt and pepper. Set aside.

Cook pasta in boiling salted water for about 5 minutes until *al dente.* Drain well. Add to butter sauce. Toss. Transfer to individual pasta bowls. Top with salmon, basil and green onion. Drizzle with oil. Serves 4.

Salmon

Salmon is native to the north Atlantic and Pacific oceans and is not a traditional Italian ingredient, but BC's smoked salmon is so renowned that it is in demand in Italy and has found its way onto restaurant menus in the country, particularly in Venice and Sicily.

Tagliolini al Nero di Seppia

Striking black squid ink noodles and cremini mushrooms in a mascarpone reduction.
Look for the noodles in an Italian shop.

1 Tbsp (15 mL) olive oil

1 cup (250 mL) sliced cremini mushrooms

1 cup (250 mL) white wine

1 cup (250 mL) homogenized milk

1 cup (250 mL) whipping cream

1 cup (250 mL) mascarpone cheese

1 cup (250 mL) grated Parmesan cheese

sea salt and pepper, to taste

1 lb (454 g) black tagliolini pasta

shaved Parmesan cheese, for garnish

chopped fresh basil, for garnish

Heat oil in a large saucepan on medium. Add mushrooms. Cook for about 2 minutes, stirring often, until lightly browned. Add wine, milk and cream. Cook for 3 to 4 minutes, stirring occasionally, until reduced to 2 cups (500 mL). Add mascarpone cheese, Parmesan cheese, salt and pepper. Stir until smooth. Remove from heat. Cover to keep warm.

Cook pasta in boiling salted water for about 3 minutes until *al dente.* Drain. Add to cheese sauce. Toss. Transfer to individual pasta bowls. Garnish with Parmesan cheese and basil. Serves 4.

Squid Ink Pasta

When squid ink is added to pasta, it does more than just colour the noodles, it also imparts a briny flavour that pairs well with seafood dishes. Squid ink pasta is available at Italian shops and can sometimes be found in large supermarkets.

Gluten-free Corn Fusilli

A tasty pasta with diced chicken, cherry tomatoes, garlic and pecorino cheese.

1/2 cup (125 mL) extra virgin olive oil

1/2 lb (225 g) diced chicken

1 cup (250 mL) halved cherry tomatoes

2 Tbsp (30 mL) minced garlic

1/2 cup (125 mL) white wine

1/4 cup (60 mL) butter, softened

sea salt and pepper, to taste

1 lb (454 g) corn fusilli pasta

1 Tbsp (15 mL) extra virgin olive oil

1/2 cup (125 mL) shaved pecorino cheese

chopped fresh basil, for garnish

Heat oil in a frying pan on medium. Add chicken, tomatoes and garlic. Cook for 5 to 8 minutes until chicken is golden brown and no longer pink inside. Add wine, butter, salt and pepper. Cook, stirring, until smooth. Remove from heat. Cover to keep warm.

Cook pasta in a pot of boiling salted water for about 11 minutes until *al dente.* Drain. Add to chicken mixture. Add oil and cheese. Toss. Transfer to individual pasta bowls. Garnish with basil. Serves 4.

Pasta

Traditional pasta in Italy is made from durum wheat, a hard wheat with a high gluten content that prevents the pasta from cracking as it dries, and helps it keep its shape as it cooks. At one time, wheat-free pastas were a mushy disappointment at best, but they've come a long way in the past few years. Now good quality pastas made of corn, quinoa or rice, to name a few, are readily available.

Chicken Penne Arrabbiata

Chicken with tomato sauce, fresh herbs and chili flakes.
I use Full Red plum tomatoes, available at Italian shops. The sauce can keep
in the refrigerator for 1 week or in the freezer for 6 months.

Tomato Sauce

6 Tbsp (90 mL) extra virgin olive oil

1/2 cup (125 mL) diced carrot

1/2 cup (125 mL) diced celery

1/2 cup (125 mL) diced onion

1/4 cup (60 mL) minced garlic

1 Tbsp (15 mL) dried basil

4 cups (1 L) chopped tomatoes

5 to 6 bay leaves

sea salt and pepper, to taste

Chicken Penne

6 Tbsp (90 mL) olive oil

12 oz (340 g) diced chicken

1 Tbsp (15 mL) chopped shallots

1 Tbsp (15 mL) minced garlic

2/3 cup (150 mL) butter, softened

1/4 cup (60 mL) white wine

(see next page)

Tomato Sauce: Heat oil in a heavy saucepan on medium. Add carrot, celery, onion, garlic and basil. Cook for about 5 minutes, stirring occasionally, until light golden brown. Add tomatoes. Bring to a boil, stirring often. Remove from heat. Carefully process in a blender or food processor until smooth, following manufacturers instructions for processing hot liquids. Transfer to same saucepan. Add bay leaves. Cook on low for about 10 minutes until sauce is thickened. Add salt and pepper. Remove bay leaves. Remove from heat. Cover to keep warm.

Chicken Penne: Heat oil in a large frying pan on medium. Add chicken, shallots and garlic. Cook for about 2 minutes. Add butter, wine, tomato sauce, chilies, rosemary, salt and pepper. Cook, stirring, until smooth. Remove from heat. Remove rosemary. Cover to keep warm.

Cook pasta in boiling salted water for about 8 minutes until *al dente.* Drain. Add to chicken mixture. Cook on high, stirring frequently, for 1 minute. Transfer to individual pasta bowls. Top with Parmesan cheese and basil. Serves 4.

Penne Arrabbiata

Penne arrabbiata translates to "angry penne" and is named for the fiery tomato sauce, which gets its heat from the chili flakes.

2 cups (500 mL) Tomato Sauce

1 tsp (5 mL) dried crushed chilies

4 sprigs of fresh rosemary

sea salt and pepper, to taste

1 1/2 lbs (680 g) penne pasta

1/4 cup (60 mL) shaved Parmesan cheese

chopped fresh basil, for garnish

Gnocchi with Braised Beef Short Ribs

Finished with horseradish gremolata.
You can serve the ribs with the carrot, celery and onion as well.

Braised Beef Short Ribs

1/3 cup (75 mL) olive oil

1 lb (454 g) beef short ribs, bone-in

1 cup (250 mL) flour, seasoned with sea salt and pepper

1/2 cup (125 mL) chopped carrot

1/2 cup (125 mL) chopped celery

1/2 cup (125 mL) chopped onion

2 cups (500 mL) red wine

12 cups (3 L) beef broth

3 cinnamon sticks (4 inches, 10 cm, each)

6 bay leaves

3 Tbsp (45 mL) whole black peppercorns

sea salt and pepper, to taste

(see next page)

Braised Beef Short Ribs: Heat oil in a large frying pan. Press both sides of ribs into seasoned flour in a small shallow dish until coated. Cook in frying pan for about 3 minutes per side until browned on all sides. Transfer to a plate. Cover to keep warm.

Add carrot, celery and onion to same frying pan. Cook for about 20 minutes until caramelized. Transfer to a large baking dish. Add ribs, wine, beef broth, cinnamon sticks, bay leaves, peppercorns, salt and pepper. Bake, covered, in 350°F (175°C) oven for about 3 hours until meat is tender. Discard cooking liquid.

Horseradish Gremolata: Combine parsley, horseradish, oil and lemon zest in a small bowl. Add salt and pepper. Set aside.

Potato Gnocchi: Place potatoes in a steamer or cover with water in a saucepan. Bring water to a boil. Simmer for about 45 minutes until potatoes are softened. Drain. Peel. Process slightly in a food mill.

Mix together potatoes, egg, salt and nutmeg in a medium bowl. Add flour. Mix lightly to form a medium-soft dough. Add more flour if necessary. Turn out onto lightly floured surface. Divide dough into 6 portions. Roll 1 portion at a time to 1/2 inch (12 mm) thickness. Let stand until cool. Cut into 3/4 inch (2 cm) squares. Roll squares gently along tines of a fork to create ridges and form a small shell shape. Cook gnocchi in boiling salted water for 3 to 5 minutes, stirring occasionally, until gnocchi float to the top. Cook for 1 minute before removing with slotted spoon to sieve. Drain. Cover to keep warm.

Heat oil in a frying pan on medium. Add garlic. Heat and stir for 1 to 2 minutes until fragrant. Add wine, butter and chilies. Cook, stirring, until smooth. Add parsley, salt and pepper.

Add gnocchi and cheese. Place gnocchi and ribs on 4 individual plates. Garnish with horseradish gremolata. Serves 4.

Horseradish Gremolata

1 cup (250 mL) finely chopped fresh flat-leaf parsley

1/2 cup (125 mL) prepared horseradish

1/4 cup (60 mL) extra virgin olive oil

1 Tbsp (15 mL) lemon zest

sea salt and pepper, to taste

Potato Gnocchi

2 lbs (900 g) russet potatoes

1 large egg

1 tsp (5 mL) sea salt

1/2 tsp (2 mL) nutmeg

2 cups (500 mL) all-purpose flour

1/4 cup (60 mL) olive oil

2 Tbsp (30 mL) chopped garlic

1/4 cup (60 mL) white wine

6 Tbsp (90 mL) butter, softened

1 tsp (5 mL) dried crushed chilies

2 Tbsp (30 mL) chopped fresh parsley

sea salt and pepper, to taste

1/2 cup (125 mL) grated Parmesan cheese

Bison Cannelloni

With a wild mushroom cream sauce. For a nice touch, bake in 4 individual baking dishes and serve straight from the oven—but be careful, the dishes will be very hot. This signature dish was an award winner in the Alberta Bison Commission's Best of Alberta Buffalo Culinary Competition.

Basic Pasta Dough

7 eggs

1 Tbsp (15 mL) olive oil

4 cups (1 L) all-purpose flour

Mushroom Cream Reduction Sauce

3 Tbsp (45 mL) olive oil

1 cup (250 mL) mixed mushrooms (such as porcini, portobello, cremini and shiitake)

2 Tbsp (30 mL) chopped shallots

2 Tbsp (30 mL) lemon juice

1 cup (250 mL) vegetable broth

1 cup (250 mL) white wine

2 1/2 cups (625 mL) whipping cream

3 Tbsp (45 mL) butter, softened

2 Tbsp (30 mL) sea salt

1/2 tsp (2 mL) white pepper

Cannelloni

1/4 cup (60 mL) olive oil

1/2 cup (125 mL) diced onion

(see next page)

Basic Pasta Dough: Whisk eggs and oil in a medium bowl. Place flour in a large bowl. Make a well in centre. Add egg mixture to well. Mix until dough begins to come together. Turn out onto lightly floured surface. Knead until ball forms. Wrap with plastic wrap. Let stand for 30 minutes. Using a pasta machine, roll out dough to thinnest setting. Cut pasta sheets crosswise into 5 inch (12.5 cm) lengths. Cook noodles, in batches, in boiling salted water for 1 to 2 minutes per batch until *al dente.* Transfer to a bowl of cold water. Spread noodles in a single layer on paper towels to drain.

Mushroom Cream Sauce: Heat oil in a small pot on medium. Add mushrooms. Cook for about 2 minutes, stirring often, until lightly browned. Add shallots and lemon juice. Cook for 2 minutes.

Add broth, white wine and cream. Bring to a boil. Reduce heat to low. Add butter, salt and pepper. Simmer for 5 to 6 minutes until reduced to 2 1/2 cups (625 mL).

Cannelloni: Heat oil in a large saucepan on medium. Add onion and garlic. Cook for about 5 minutes until golden brown. Add bison. Scramble-fry on high for about 10 minutes until no longer pink.

Add tomato, red wine, cream and oregano. Bring to a boil. Reduce heat to medium-low. Simmer for 1 to 1 1/2 hours until liquid is evaporated. Add Parmesan cheese, mozzarella cheese, salt and pepper. Stir. Remove from heat. Let stand until cooled.

Spoon 1/4 cup (60 mL) of bison mixture down centre of 1 noodle. Roll noodle to enclose filling. Transfer cannelloni, seam side down, to a well-greased baking dish. Repeat with remaining noodles and bison mixture, arranging in a single layer in baking dish. Pour cream sauce over top. Sprinkle with Parmesan cheese and mozzarella cheese. Bake in 350°F (175°C) oven for 10 minutes until bubbling. Broil 4 inches (10 cm) from heat in oven for about 2 minutes until cheese is golden. Garnish with oregano. Serves 4.

2 Tbsp (30 mL) minced garlic

2 lbs (900 g) ground bison

2 cups (500 mL) chopped plum tomatoes

1 cup (250 mL) red wine

1 cup (250 mL) whipping cream

2 Tbsp (30 mL) dried oregano

1 cup (250 mL) grated Parmesan cheese, plus extra for topping

1 cup (250 mL) grated mozzarella cheese, plus extra for topping

sea salt and pepper, to taste

chopped fresh oregano, for garnish

Orecchiette alla Potentina

Orecchiette, or "little ears" pasta, with veal meatballs, sweet cherry tomatoes and mozzarella cheese. The pasta is shaped like little ears, hence their name.

Veal Meatballs

1 lb (454 g) ground veal

1 cup (250 mL) fine dry bread crumbs

2 Tbsp (30 mL) finely chopped shallots

1 egg, fork-beaten

1/2 cup (125 mL) extra virgin olive oil

1/2 cup (125 mL) chopped Italian parsley

1/2 cup (125 mL) milk

3 Tbsp (45 mL) dried oregano

sea salt and pepper, to taste

1/2 cup (125 mL) extra virgin olive oil

1 Tbsp (15 mL) minced garlic

6 Tbsp (90 mL) white wine

6 Tbsp (90 mL) butter, softened

3 Tbsp (45 mL) chopped fresh parsley

1 Tbsp (15 mL) dried oregano

sea salt and pepper, to taste

(see next page)

Veal Meatballs: Combine veal, bread crumbs, shallots, egg, oil, parsley, milk, oregano, salt and pepper in a medium bowl. Roll into 20 small meatballs.

Heat oil in a frying pan on medium-high. Cook meatballs and garlic for 5 to 6 minutes, turning often, until fully cooked and no longer pink inside. Add wine, butter, parsley, oregano, salt and pepper. Remove from heat. Cover to keep warm.

Orecchiette: Cook pasta in boiling salted water for about 13 minutes until *al dente*. Drain. Add to meatball mixture. Add mozzarella. Toss. Transfer to individual pasta bowls. Top with tomatoes. Serves 4.

Orecchiette

Orecchiette is a type of pasta native to Apulia whose shape resembles a small ear. *Orecchiette* originates from *orecchio,* the Italian word for "ear."

Orecchiette

1 lb (454 g) orecchiette pasta

6 Tbsp (90 mL) grated mozzarella cheese

1 cup (250 mL) cherry tomatoes

Cacciucco

The truffle rouille isn't pictured, but it makes for a wonderful addition to this dish. You can buy truffles in jars at an Italian shop. If desired, season the cooked salmon with freshly ground black pepper.

Fennel Tomato Stock

3 Tbsp (45 mL) olive oil

2 Tbsp (30 mL) minced garlic

2 Tbsp (30 mL) finely chopped shallots

6 cups (1.5 L) fish (or vegetable) broth

1 fennel bulb (white part only), thinly sliced

2 cups (500 mL) diced tomatoes

1/4 cup (60 mL) Pernod

sea salt and pepper, to taste

Truffle Rouille

2 egg yolks

1 tsp (5 mL) Dijon mustard

1 cup (250 mL) grape seed oil

2 Tbsp (30 mL) truffle oil

(see next page)

Fennel Tomato Stock: Heat oil in a medium saucepan on medium. Add garlic and shallots. Heat and stir for 1 to 2 minutes until fragrant. Add broth, fennel and tomato. Bring to a boil. Reduce heat to low. Add Pernod, salt and pepper. Set aside.

Truffle Rouille: Process egg yolks and mustard in a food processor until combined. With motor running, add grape seed oil through feed chute until thickened. Add truffle oil, truffle, lemon juice, salt and pepper. Stir. Set aside.

Cacciucco: Put mussels into a medium bowl. Lightly tap to close any that are opened 1/4 inch (6 mm) or more. Discard any that do not close. Add salmon to tomato fennel stock. Bring to a boil. Add shrimp, scallops and mussels. Simmer for about 2 minutes until mussels open. Discard any unopened mussels. Arrange salmon, shrimp, scallops and mussels around 4 individual bowls. Divide stock among bowls. Add a dollop of truffle rouille in centre of each bowl. Serves 4.

S. Maria la Palma Cannonau 'Le Bombarde,' Sardegna

The perfect example of a red wine that is flavourful without being heavy, the Cannonau is extremely versatile and will pair with heavier dishes, but its brightness and fresh acidity also complements delicate dishes such as seafood without overpowering them.

Cacciucco

Cacciucco is a Tuscan seafood stew that originated in Livorno. It was a poor man's stew, made with the leftover catch that wouldn't sell at market. This stew was traditionally made with 5 types of fish, 1 for every "c" in its name (not 5 specific types, just 5 types at a time). Today many recipes call for more shellfish than fish, reflecting modern palates that prefer not to eat the bony fish.

1 tsp (5 mL) finely chopped truffle

2 tsp (10 mL) lemon juice

sea salt and pepper, to taste

Cacciucco

20 mussels

4 × 5 oz (140 g) salmon fillets

8 shrimp (peeled and deveined), size 21/25 (see page 44)

8 large sea scallops

Prawn Risotto

Risotto with spicy prawns *al pomodoro*, spring peas and grated Parmesan.

Risotto

2 Tbsp (30 mL) olive oil

1/2 cup (125 mL) diced onion

2 cups (500 mL) arborio rice

8 cups (2 L) vegetable broth

2 cups (500 mL) frozen tiny peas

1 cup (250 mL) butter, to taste

1 1/2 cups (375 mL) grated Parmesan cheese

sea salt and pepper, to taste

Prawns

1/4 cup (60 mL) olive oil

20 prawns (peeled and deveined), size 21/25 (see page 44)

2 Tbsp (30 mL) minced garlic

1/2 tsp (2 mL) dried crushed chilies

(see next page)

Risotto: Heat oil in a medium saucepan on medium. Add onion and rice. Cook for 1 to 2 minutes, stirring often, until toasted.

Heat broth in a separate pot on medium until boiling gently. Add 1 cup (250 mL) of broth to rice, stirring constantly until broth is absorbed. Repeat with remaining broth, 1 cup (250 mL) at a time, until broth is absorbed and rice is *al dente*. Entire process will take 15 to 20 minutes.

Add peas, butter, cheese, salt and pepper. Stir. Remove from heat. Cover to keep warm.

Prawns: Heat oil in a frying pan on medium. Add prawns, garlic, chilies, salt and pepper and cook for 1 to 2 minutes until garlic is fragrant. Add wine, tomato sauce and butter. Cook for about 2 minutes until prawns just start to turn pink.

Place risotto on one side of 4 individuals plates. Place prawns on other side. Spoon tomato sauce over prawns. Garnish with basil. Serves 4.

Fabiano Lugana 'Argillaia', Lombardia

Bright, fresh wine with a bit of minerality. The minerality works with the prawns, and the freshness of the acidity works to cleanse the palate of the fattier seafood.

Risotto

Risotto's creamy texture is in large part a result of the high starch content of the rice. In North America, arborio rice is most commonly used, but in Italy there are many more options including carnaroli, Calriso and vialone nano. Risotto can be served as a first course, main course or side dish and can be embellished with meat, seafood, cheese or vegetables.

sea salt and pepper, to taste

2 Tbsp (30 mL) white wine

1 cup (250 mL) tomato sauce

2 Tbsp (30 mL) butter

fresh basil, for garnish

Wild Halibut Piccata

With shrimp, caperberries, artichokes, tomatoes, lemon,
white wine, olive oil jus and sautéed spinach.

1 Tbsp (15 mL) olive oil

24 oz (680 g) halibut, cut into 4 portions

1 Tbsp (15 mL) olive oil

8 shrimp (peeled and deveined), size 21/25 (see Tip, page 44)

2 Tbsp (30 mL) minced garlic

2 tsp (10 mL) finely chopped fresh oregano

12 caperberries

30 artichoke bottoms, cut into 3/4 inch (2 cm) cubes

3/4 cup (175 mL) diced Roma tomatoes

1/2 cup (125 mL) white wine

4 tsp (20 mL) lemon juice

3/4 cup (175 mL) butter, softened

sea salt and pepper, to taste

2 1/2 cups (625 mL) Sautéed Spinach (see page 70)

Heat first amount of oil in a medium saucepan on medium. Add halibut. Cook for about 4 to 5 minutes per side until golden brown and flakes easily when tested with a fork. Remove from heat. Set aside.

Heat second amount of oil in a frying pan on high. Add shrimp, garlic, oregano, caperberries, artichoke bottoms and tomatoes. Cook for about 2 minutes, stirring often, until shrimp is just starting to turn pink. Add wine and lemon juice. Cook for 3 to 4 minutes until reduced by half. Add butter, salt and pepper. Stir until butter is melted.

Arrange spinach on 4 individual plates. Place halibut and shrimp on top. Spoon sauce over top. Serves 4.

Ceuso Scurati Bianco, Sicilia

Everything from the delicacy of the halibut to the flavours of the caperberries, tomato, artichoke and lemon are ideal with the soft, fresh, savoury quality of this Sicilian white.

Caperberries

Caperberries are the immature fruit of the caper shrub. They are usually sold still attached to the stalk and look rather like fat capers (which are the immature flower buds of the same plant) or small green grapes. They have a much milder flavour than capers and are often used in dishes that feature green olives.

Grilled Salmon Puttanesca

With a spicy mélange of tomatoes, capers, black olives, garlic and scallops.

Puttanesca Sauce

1 Tbsp (15 mL) olive oil

1 tsp (5 mL) finely chopped anchovies

1 tsp (5 mL) finely chopped capers

1 tsp (5 mL) minced garlic

2 cups (500 mL) tomato sauce

1/2 tsp (2 mL) dried oregano

sea salt and pepper, to taste

1 tsp (5 mL) chopped black olives

2 tsp (10 mL) extra virgin olive oil

Seafood

1 Tbsp (15 mL) olive oil

4 × 6 oz (170 g) salmon fillets

1 Tbsp (15 mL) olive oil

8 large sea scallops, size 10/20 (see page 44)

anchovies, for garnish (optional)

Puttanesca Sauce: Heat oil in a medium saucepan on medium. Add anchovies, capers and garlic. Heat and stir for 1 to 2 minutes until golden brown. Add tomato sauce, oregano, salt and pepper. Cook until heated through. Just before serving, add olives and oil.

Seafood: Heat first amount of oil in a large ovenproof saucepan on medium. Add salmon. Cook for about 5 minutes, without flipping, until golden. Bake in 350°F (175°C) oven for 7 to 8 minutes until fish flakes easily when tested with a fork.

Heat second amount of oil in a separate saucepan. Cook scallops for about 1 minute per side until golden brown on sides and opaque in centre. Place scallops in centre of 4 individual plates. Top with salmon. Drizzle puttanesca sauce over top. Top with anchovies if desired. Serves 4.

COS Ceresuolo di Vittoria, Sicilia

This versatile wine, with its bright cherry and licorice flavours, touch of spice and bright juicy finish, is a natural complement to salmon and the Mediterranean flavours with which it is accompanied.

Puttanesca Sauce

Puttanesca is a rich, spicy sauce with somewhat murky origins. We know it's from Naples, but no one is sure why it has such a racy name. *Puttanesca* is derived from the Italian *puttana* and translates to "in the style of the whore." Possible explanations for the name abound; one suggests that the sauce's spicy aroma was used to draw men off the streets and into the boudoir; another suggests that this dish was a favourite amongst prostitutes because it is quick to prepare and so the meal would be only a short interruption in a working lady's day.

Wild King Salmon

With saltimbocca sauce, prosciutto, sage, tomatoes, capers, lemon and white wine.

Saltimbocca Sauce

2 Tbsp (30 mL) olive oil

1/3 cup (75 mL) diced tomatoes

1 Tbsp (15 mL) minced garlic

2 tsp (10 mL) chopped capers

2 Tbsp (30 mL) white wine

2 Tbsp (30 mL) lemon juice

1/2 cup (125 mL) butter, softened

2 Tbsp (30 mL) chopped fresh sage

sea salt and pepper, to taste

Seafood

2 Tbsp (30 mL) olive oil

4 × 6 oz (170 g) wild salmon fillets

2 Tbsp (30 mL) olive oil

8 prawns (peeled and deveined), size 13/15 (see page 44)

sea salt and pepper, to taste

(see next page)

Saltimbocca Sauce: Heat oil in a saucepan on medium. Add tomatoes, garlic and capers. Cook for about 2 minutes until golden brown. Add wine and lemon juice. Reduce heat to low. Add butter. Cook, stirring constantly, until butter is melted. Add sage, salt and pepper. Remove from heat. Cover to keep warm.

Seafood: Heat first amount of oil in an ovenproof frying pan on medium. Add salmon. Cook for about 5 minutes, without flipping, until salmon is golden. Bake in 350°F (175°C) oven for about 5 minutes until fish flakes easily when tested with a fork.

Heat second amount of oil in a separate frying pan. Cook prawns for 5 to 6 minutes until pink. Add salt and pepper.

Place spinach in centre of 4 individual dishes. Place salmon and prawns on top. Top with sauce. Garnish with prosciutto, shallots and fresh herbs. Serves 4.

Borgo Magredo Pinot Nero, Friuli

Pinot Noir and salmon are a natural match. The salty, sweet and savoury preparation of the fish works well with the soft texture and bright, juicy finish of the wine.

Saltimbocca Sauce

Literally translated, *saltimbocca* means "jump in the mouth." It refers to a Roman specialty made of finely sliced veal sprinkled with sage, topped with a thin slice of prosciutto and sautéed in butter.

2 1/2 cups (625 mL) sautéed spinach (see page 70)

1/2 cup (125 mL) thinly sliced prosciutto

2 tsp (10 mL) chopped shallots

fresh herbs such as thyme or oregano, for garnish

Seared Sablefish

With a green pea and fava bean ragu and a tomato coulis.

Tomato Coulis

6 to 7 medium vine-ripened tomatoes

2 Tbsp (30 mL) olive oil

2 Tbsp (30 mL) finely chopped shallots

2 Tbsp (30 mL) minced garlic

2 tsp (10 mL) dried basil

sea salt and pepper, to taste

Garlic and Anchovy Extra Virgin Olive Oil

1 cup (250 mL) extra virgin olive oil

1/2 cup (125 mL) finely chopped anchovies

2 Tbsp (30 mL) chopped garlic

1/2 tsp (2 mL) dried crushed chilies

3 Tbsp (45 mL) lemon juice

Sablefish

1 Tbsp (15 mL) olive oil

4 × 6 oz (170 g) sablefish fillets

sea salt and pepper, to taste

(see next page)

Tomato Coulis: Drop tomatoes into boiling water for about 30 seconds. Remove from water. Peel. Squeeze out and discard seeds and juice. Chop coarsely.

Heat oil in a heavy saucepan on medium. Add shallots and garlic. Cook for 1 to 2 minutes until golden but not brown. Add tomato. Cook for 6 to 7 minutes until mixture is thickened. Remove from heat. Stir in basil, salt and pepper.

Garlic and Anchovy Extra Virgin Olive Oil: Whisk together all 5 ingredients in a small bowl until thickened. Leftover olive oil will keep in fridge, covered, for 3 to 4 days.

Sablefish: Heat oil in an ovenproof frying pan on medium. Sprinkle both sides of fillets with salt and pepper. Cook for 3 to 4 minutes on each side until golden. Bake in 350°F (175°C) oven for 4 to 5 minutes until fish flakes easily when tested with a fork.

Green Pea and Fava Bean Ragu: Heat oil in frying pan on medium. Add beans, peas, shallots, cream, salt and pepper. Cook for 4 to 5 minutes, stirring occasionally, until beans and peas are tender-crisp. Transfer to 4 individual dishes. Place fillets on top. Drizzle with tomato coulis and garlic and anchovy extra virgin olive oil. Garnish with thyme and microgreens. Serves 4.

DeAngelis Chardonnay 'Prato Grande,' Marche

The delicate sablefish is a lovely match with the delicate, almost tropical fruit-like flavours of this unoaked Chardonnay.

Sablefish

Sablefish is a sleek, black-scaled fish that is found in the deep, cold waters of the north Pacific. It has pearly white flesh that flakes into large chunks when prepared. With a rich and buttery flavor, sablefish is considered a delicacy by chefs across the country. Although it is often sold smoked, this fish is also available year-round both fresh and frozen. Sablefish has a high oil content which allows it to be cooked at high temperatures. It also makes this fish an ideal source of Omega-3 fatty acids, which many health experts suggest reduce the risk of heart disease.

Green Pea and Fava Bean Ragu

2 tsp (10 mL) olive oil

1 1/2 cup (375 mL) fava beans

1 1/2 cup (375 mL) fresh peas

2 Tbsp (30 mL) shallots

2 cups (500 mL) cream

salt and pepper, to taste

1/2 cup (125 mL) Garlic and Anchovy Extra Virgin Olive Oil

4 sprigs of fresh thyme, for garnish

microgreens, for garnish

Arctic Char

Serves 4

Pan-seared arctic char with a saffron, shrimp and clam sauce, accompanied by braised fennel and heart of palm. You can buy saffron cream at specialty stores.
Garnish with microgreens.

Arctic Char

1 Tbsp (15 mL) olive oil

1 lb (454 g) arctic char fillets, cut into 4 portions

1 Tbsp (15 mL) olive oil

20 clams

20 shrimp (peeled and deveined), size 21/25 (see page 44)

2 Tbsp (30 mL) chopped shallots

1 cup (250 mL) white wine

3 cups (750 mL) saffron cream

sea salt and pepper, to taste

Braised Fennel and Heart of Palm

1 Tbsp (15 mL) olive oil

1 1/2 cups (375 mL) chopped fennel bulb (white part only)

(see next page)

Arctic Char: Heat first amount of oil in an ovenproof frying pan on medium. Add fillets. Cook for about 2 minutes per side until golden. Bake in 350°F (175°C) oven for 4 to 5 minutes until fish flakes easily when tested with a fork.

Heat second amount of oil in a separate frying pan. Put clams into a medium bowl. Lightly tap to close any that are opened 1/4 inch (6 mm) or more. Discard any that do not close. Add clams, shrimp and shallots. Cook for 2 to 3 minutes until clams are opened. Discard any unopened clams. Remove to a bowl. Add wine to frying pan. Add saffron cream. Cook for 3 to 4 minutes until reduced by half. Return shrimp, clams and shallots to pan. Add salt and pepper.

Braised Fennel and Heart of Palm: Heat oil in a Dutch oven on medium. Add fennel and heart of palm. Cook for about 2 minutes. Add broth, salt and pepper. Bake in 350°F (175°C) oven for about 30 minutes until liquid is evaporated and vegetables are tender. Divide among 4 individual plates. Place fillets on top. Scatter shrimp and clams around fillets. Drizzle with sauce. Serves 4.

Poggiobello Ribolla Gialla, Friuli

This wine has a bite of ripe fruit that contrasts with the savoury saffron flavours, but a delicate soft acidity that marries well with the seafood. Texture plays a big part.

Arctic Char

Arctic char, a cold-water member of the salmon family, is native
to the Arctic Ocean and many rivers and lakes in the Canadian
far north. It is also farmed in Canada in land-based systems that
are considered some of the most environmentally responsible
fish farming designs in the world. Arctic char is considered
a "Best" choice by the Monterey Aquarium Watch Guide for
Healthy Oceans.

**1 1/2 cups (375 mL)
chopped heart of palm**

**2 cups (500 mL) vegetable
broth**

sea salt and pepper, to taste

Seared John Dory Beurre Meuniere

Served with grilled prawns, sautéed porcini mushrooms and truffle celery root purée.
Garnish with thin slices of red pepper and green onion.

Truffle Celery Root Purée

1 lb (454 g) celery root

6 Tbsp (90 mL) truffle oil

6 Tbsp (90 mL) butter

1/2 cup (125 mL) whipping cream

2 Tbsp (30 mL) minced garlic

sea salt and pepper, to taste

John Dory

1 Tbsp (15 mL) olive oil

4 × 8 oz (225 g) John Dory fillets

2 tsp (10 mL) olive oil

12 prawns (peeled and deveined), size 21/25 (see page 44)

sea salt and pepper, to taste

1 cup (250 mL) chopped porcini mushrooms

1 tsp (5 mL) minced garlic

Truffle Celery Root Purée: Steam celery root until slightly soft. Process in a food mill or food processor until smooth. Transfer to a medium bowl. Add truffle oil, butter, cream, garlic, salt and pepper. Stir until combined.

John Dory: Heat oil in a frying pan on medium. Add fillets. Cook for about 2 minutes per side until golden. Bake in 350°F (175°C) oven for about 3 minutes until fish flakes easily when tested with a fork.

Heat second amount of oil in a separate frying pan. Add prawns. Cook for about 1 minute until just pink. Add salt and pepper. Transfer to a bowl.

Add mushrooms and garlic to a frying pan. Season with salt and pepper, if desired. Cook for 1 to 2 minutes.

Divide celery root purée among 4 individual plates. Place fillets and prawns over top. Top with mushrooms. Serves 4.

COS Rami, Sicilia

This white wine has enough freshness, weight and texture, without oakiness, to complement all aspects of this dish including the earthiness of the mushrooms, truffle and celery root. The wine's freshness and minerality works well with the seafood.

John Dory

John dory is a white-fleshed, deep-sea fish with a flat body and
long spines on its dorsal fin. It is native to the western Pacific,
eastern Atlantic and Indian oceans, and though it is not well
known in North America, it is popular in Europe, Australia and
New Zealand. It has a mild, slightly sweet flavour.

Tuscan Roasted Chicken

Let the chicken marinate for 24 hours and the tomatoes soak
overnight before making this recipe.

Marinade

**1 cup (250 mL) dry white
wine**

1/2 cup (125 mL) olive oil

**2 Tbsp (30 mL) minced
garlic**

1 Tbsp (15 mL) fennel seed

2 tsp (10 mL) dried oregano

1 1/2 tsp (7 mL) paprika

2 tsp (10 mL) sea salt

1 tsp (5 mL) black pepper

**1 1/2 lbs (680 kg) chicken
breasts or thighs**

Spicy Sun-dried
Tomato Sauce

**1 cup (250 mL) sun-dried
tomatoes**

**1 1/2 cups (375 mL)
vegetable broth**

**1 tsp (5 mL) cayenne
pepper**

2 tsp (10 mL) sea salt

**freshly ground black
pepper, to taste**

1 cup (250 mL) olive oil

**1/2 cup (125 mL) grated
Parmesan cheese**

(see next page)

Marinade: Combine wine, oil, garlic, fennel, oregano, paprika, salt and pepper in a stainless steel bowl. Add chicken. Stir to coat. Chill, covered, for 24 hours. Drain and discard marinade.

Spicy Sun-dried Tomato Sauce: Soak tomatoes in water overnight. Dry thoroughly.

Cook tomatoes, broth, cayenne pepper, salt and pepper in a medium saucepan on medium for 10 to 12 minutes until liquid is evaporated. Remove from heat. Let stand to cool.

Process in food processor with oil and cheese until smooth. Store, covered, in the refrigerator for up to 1 week.

Rosemary Flatbread: Stir water and sugar in a large bowl until sugar is dissolved. Sprinkle yeast over top. Let stand for 10 minutes. Stir until yeast is dissolved. Add flour in 4 additions, stirring after each addition until just combined. Add first amount of salt. Turn out dough onto lightly floured surface. Knead until smooth. Place in greased extra-large bowl, turning once to grease top. Cover with greased waxed paper and tea towel. Let stand in oven with light on and door closed for about 45 minutes until doubled in bulk. Punch dough down. Divide into 4 portions. Flatten each on a greased baking sheet to 3/4 inch (2 cm) thickness.

Brush top of dough with oil. Let stand for about 15 minutes until doubled. Sprinkle with rosemary and second amount of salt. Bake in 400°F (200°C) oven for 7 to 9 minutes until lightly browned.

Col d'Orcia Rosso di Montalcino, Toscana

A bright, fresh style of red wine for chicken. It has more weight than a white to go with the bigger flavours of sun-dried tomato and oregano, rosemary and basil, which are herbs typically used to flavour meat in Tuscany.

Chicken: Heat oil in an ovenproof frying pan on medium. Cook marinated chicken for 4 to 5 minutes, stirring often, until browned on all sides. Bake in 375°F (190°C) oven for 6 to 7 minutes or until fully cooked and no longer pink inside. Slice chicken into small pieces.

Spread 6 Tbsp (90 mL) tomato sauce evenly on each piece of flatbread, leaving a 1/2 inch (12 mm) edge. Place chicken pieces and eggs over top. Sprinkle with cheese, salt, pepper and basil. Drizzle with oil. Serves 4.

Rosemary Flatbread

1 1/2 cups (375 mL) warm water

1 Tbsp (15 mL) sugar

1 Tbsp (15 mL) active dry yeast

2 cups (500 mL) all-purpose flour

1 1/2 tsp (7 mL) sea salt

2 tsp (10 mL) olive oil

1 tsp (5 mL) crushed rosemary

1/2 tsp (2 mL) sea salt

Chicken

1 Tbsp (15 mL) olive oil

1 1/2 cups (375 mL) Spicy Sun-dried Tomato Sauce

4 large hard-cooked eggs, sliced

Parmesan cheese, for sprinkling

sea salt and pepper, to taste

fresh basil, julienned, for sprinkling

olive oil, for drizzling

Free-range Chicken Breast

Chicken stuffed with goat cheese and topped with caramelized pear chutney, roasted garlic purée and beurre blanc. Traditionally shallots are strained out of the sauce before serving, but they can be left in if desired. Garnish with thin slices of red pepper and green onion.

Caramelized Pear Chutney

2 Tbsp (30 mL) butter, softened

1/2 cup (125 mL) sugar

1 tsp (5 mL) sea salt

2 cups (500 mL) diced peeled pear

1/4 cup (60 mL) lemon juice

Roasted Garlic Purée

1/2 cup (125 mL) minced garlic

2 Tbsp (30 mL) olive oil

1/2 tsp (2 mL) sea salt

2 Tbsp (30 mL) cold water

Beurre Blanc Sauce

1 tsp (5 mL) diced shallots

1 tsp (5 mL) chopped fresh thyme

1 tsp (5 mL) chopped fresh rosemary

1/4 cup (60 mL) white wine

(see next page)

Caramelized Pear Chutney: Heat butter in a Dutch oven on medium. Add sugar and salt. Heat and stir until browned. Add pears and lemon juice. Cook for 1 to 2 minutes, stirring constantly (do not let pears burn). Bake in 350°F (175°C) oven for about 5 minutes until pears are golden brown. Let stand until cool.

Roasted Garlic Purée: Place garlic, oil, salt and water on an 8 inch (20 cm) square piece of foil. Fold foil in on all four sides, like an envelope. Bake in 375°F (190°C) oven for 25 to 30 minutes until tender. Let stand until cool. Process in blender or food processor until smooth. Chill, covered.

Beurre Blanc Sauce: Heat shallots, thyme, rosemary and wine in a saucepan on medium-high. Bring to a boil. Reduce heat to low. Simmer for 3 to 4 minutes until reduced to about 2 Tbsp (30 mL).

Add 1 or 2 cubes of butter to saucepan at a time, whisking constantly, until all butter is added and melted. Remove from heat. Whisk. Sauce should be thick and smooth. Season with salt and pepper.

Chicken: Combine goat cheese, salt and pepper in a small bowl. Set aside.

Cut deep pocket in thickest part of each chicken breast half, almost but not quite through to other side. Spoon goat cheese stuffing into pocket. Do not overstuff.

Marotti Campi Verdicchio dei Castelli di Jesi 'Salmariano,' Marche

The wine is fresh, elegant and misleadingly structured, allowing it to complement the chicken, match the fresh herbaceousness of the creamy goat cheese and stand up to the richness of the sauce.

Heat oil in an ovenproof frying pan on medium. Cook chicken for about 10 minutes, turning occasionally, until golden brown on all sides. Bake in 375°F (190°C) oven for about 8 minutes until internal temperature of chicken (not stuffing) reaches 170°C (77°C). Internal temperature of stuffing should reach 165°F (74°C). Slice chicken. Divide among 4 individual plates. Top with pear chutney and roasted garlic purée. Spoon sauce around plates. Serves 4.

1 cup (250 mL) butter, cut into 1/2 inch (12 mm) cubes

1 tsp (5 mL) sea salt

1/2 tsp (2 mL) white pepper

Chicken

8 oz (225 g) goat (chèvre) cheese

sea salt and pepper, to taste

4 × 10 oz (285 g) boneless free-range chicken breast halves

2 Tbsp (30 mL) olive oil

Roasted Guinea Hen Portofino

Stuffed with shrimp, prosciutto and provolone cheese and served with a mustard seed vermouth cream reduction sauce. Garnish with your choice of fresh herbs.

Mustard Seed Vermouth Cream Reduction Sauce

1 tsp (5 mL) olive oil

1 Tbsp (15 mL) chopped shallots

1 cup (250 mL) homogenized milk

1 cup (250 mL) whipping cream

2 Tbsp (30 mL) mustard seed

1/2 cup (125 mL) vermouth

sea salt and pepper, to taste

Guinea Hen

4 × 8 oz (225 g) guinea hen breasts

sea salt and pepper, to taste

8 shrimp (peeled and deveined), size 16/20 (see page 44)

8 oz (225 g) provolone cheese, sliced in 4 portions

4 prosciutto slices

1/2 cup (125 mL) flour, for dredging

1/4 cup (60 mL) butter

Mustard Seed Vermouth Cream Reduction Sauce: Heat oil in a saucepan on medium. Add shallots. Cook for 1 to 2 minutes, stirring occasionally, until softened but not browned. Add milk, cream and mustard seed. Bring to a boil. Boil gently until reduced by half. Add vermouth, salt and pepper. Heat, stirring, for 1 to 2 minutes. Remove from heat.

Guinea Hen: Place guinea hen breasts between sheets of waxed paper and flatten with a meat mallet or rolling pin to 1/8 inch (3 mm) thick. Season with salt and pepper.

Wrap 2 shrimp with a slice of provolone and a slice of prosciutto. Place 2 wrapped shrimp on each guinea hen piece and roll up, securing open ends of rolls with toothpicks.

Place flour in shallow bowl. Dredge guinea hen pieces in flour, shaking off excess. Melt butter in heavy, large skillet on medium. Add guinea hen and sear for 2 to 3 minutes per side until golden. Slice each guinea hen into four 1/2 inch (12 mm) slices and place on plate. Drizzle sauce around guinea hens. Serve immediately. Serves 4.

Poggiobello Friulano, Friuli

The stuffing and cream reduction add richness and flavour, which lends well to the round texture of this fresh white. The wine's pleasant acidity also works to cut the richness of the cream sauce and melted cheese in the stuffing.

Cornish Hens

Marinated with red wine and finished with an aromatic lemon jus.
The creamy mushroom risotto is a nice complement.

Cornish Hens

1 1/2 cups (375 mL) red wine (Amarone or Barolo or your choice)

1 tsp (5 mL) dried oregano

1/2 cup (125 mL) olive oil

2 Tbsp (30 mL) diced garlic

2 Tbsp (30 mL) sea salt, plus extra for seasoning

1 tsp (5 mL) black pepper, plus extra for seasoning

4 × 1 lb (454 g) Cornish game hens

1 cup (250 mL) butter

sea salt and pepper, to taste

Lemon Jus

1/4 cup (60 mL) lemon juice

1/4 cup (60 mL) white wine

2 Tbsp (30 mL) chopped shallots

sea salt and pepper, to taste

6 Tbsp (90 mL) butter, softened

Creamy Mushroom Risotto

2 Tbsp (30 mL) olive oil

2 cups (500 mL) sliced mushrooms

(see next page)

Cornish Hens: Mix wine, oregano, oil, garlic, salt and pepper in a stainless steel bowl.

Place Cornish hens on breast. Using a rigid boning knife, cut alongside backbone from bird's tail to head. Lay Cornish hens flat in a large baking dish and pour red wine mixture over top. Marinate in refrigerator for 12 hours or overnight. Drain and discard marinade.

Lay birds flat on cutting board and remove backbone by cutting through ribs connecting to breast. Bend birds back, breaking breastbone free. Run a finger along bone to separate breast meat from it. Pull bone completely free. Be sure to remove flexible cartilage completely. Place meat in a baking dish. Brush with butter and season with salt and pepper. Bake in 400°F (200°C) oven for 35 to 45 minutes until juices run clear and internal temperature reaches 170°F (77°C).

Lemon Jus: Heat lemon juice, wine and shallots in a saucepan until reduced by half. Season with salt and pepper. Add butter 1 Tbsp (15 mL) at a time, stirring after each addition. Set aside.

Creamy Mushroom Risotto: Heat oil in a medium saucepan on medium. Add mushrooms and rice. Cook for 1 to 2 minutes, stirring often, until toasted.

DeAngelis Rosso Piceno Superiore, Marche

Rosso Piceno has fleshy plum flavours and a touch of earthiness to mirror the earthiness of mushrooms. The acidity of the lemon jus works well with the fresh juiciness of the wine. A red wine with a lot of versatility.

Heat broth in a separate saucepan on medium until boiling gently. Add 1 cup (250 mL) of broth to rice, stirring constantly, until broth is absorbed. Repeat with remaining broth, 1 cup (250 mL) at a time, until broth is absorbed and rice is *al dente* (slightly firm but not crunchy). Entire process will take 15 to 20 minutes.

Add butter, cheese, salt and pepper. Cut hen pieces in half and arrange on plate with risotto. Drizzle lemon jus around hen and serve immediately. Serves 4.

2 cups (500 mL) arborio rice

8 cups (2 L) vegetable broth

1/4 cup (60 mL) butter, softened

1 1/2 cups (375 mL) grated Parmesan cheese

sea salt and pepper, to taste

Parmesan Risotto Cakes with Shaved Smoked Duck

With morello cherry compote and peppercorn oil. Make the peppercorn oil 2 days before serving. Garnish with microgreens.

Peppercorn Oil

1 tsp (5 mL) whole black peppercorns

1 tsp (5 mL) whole green peppercorns

1 tsp (5 mL) whole red peppercorns

1 tsp (5 mL) whole white peppercorns

2 Tbsp (30 mL) Hungarian paprika

1 cup (250 mL) grape seed oil

Risotto Cakes

2 Tbsp (30 mL) olive oil

1/2 cup (125 mL) diced onion

2 cups (500 mL) arborio rice

8 cups (2 L) vegetable broth

1 1/2 cups (375 mL) grated Parmesan cheese

1 cup (250 mL) butter, softened

sea salt and pepper, to taste

(see next page)

Peppercorn Oil: Bake all peppercorns on a baking sheet in 350°F (175°C) oven for 10 to 15 minutes until toasted.

Transfer to a sauté pan on medium. Add paprika and oil. Whisk until combined. Remove from heat. Store in a covered container at room temperature for 48 hours before using. Any leftover peppercorn oil will keep in a sealed container in the fridge for 1 to 3 months.

Risotto Cakes: Heat oil in a medium pot on medium. Add onion and rice. Cook for 1 to 2 minutes, stirring often, until toasted.

Heat broth in a separate saucepan on medium until boiling gently. Add 1 cup (250 mL) of broth to rice, stirring constantly, until broth is absorbed. Repeat with remaining broth, 1 cup (250 mL) at a time, until broth is absorbed and rice is *al dente* (slightly firm but not crunchy). Entire process will take 15 to 20 minutes.

Add Parmesan cheese, butter, salt and pepper. Stir. Use a 3 inch (7.5 cm) stainless steel ring mould to form risotto into 4 cakes.

Morello Cherry Compote: Place cherries, lemon juice, sugar, salt and allspice in a saucepan and bring to a boil. Boil, uncovered, for 4 to 5 minutes.

Marotti Campi Lacrima di Morro d'Alba 'Orgiolo,' Marche

The slight bitter cherry and natural sweetness and richness of the duck are ideal with the fresh and aromatic Orgiolo with its nose of roses and fresh berries, smokiness and hint of black pepper. The wine also possesses great structure without overwhelming the dish.

Whisk together water and cornstarch. Add to cherry mixture. It should be thick enough to coat a spoon but not too thick. Adjust seasoning with salt and sugar if desired.

Duck: Heat risotto cakes in microwave for 90 seconds. Arrange on a plate and top with sliced smoked duck. Spoon compote and peppercorn oil around plate. Serve immediately. Serves 4.

Morello Cherry Compote

2 cups (500 mL) morello cherries or sour cherries

1 Tbsp (15 mL) lemon juice

1/2 cup (125 mL) sugar

1 tsp (5 mL) sea salt

pinch of ground allspice

1/2 cup (125 mL) cold water

2 tsp (10 mL) cornstarch

Duck

12 slices of smoked duck

1 cup (250 mL) Morello Cherry Compote

2 tsp (10 mL) Peppercorn Oil

Coniglio Bracciola

Rabbit braised in Tuscan Montalcino, pearl onions, mushrooms and pancetta. Serve with polenta, pasta or mashed potatoes, and garnish with microgreens.

1 Tbsp (15 mL) olive oil

2 lbs (900 g) rabbit legs or shoulder

1 cup (250 mL) pearl onions

1 cup (250 mL) wild mushrooms

1/2 cup (125 mL) diced pancetta

1 1/4 cups (300 mL) beef broth

3 cups (750 mL) Tuscan Montalcino wine

1 Tbsp (15 mL) minced garlic

2 sprigs of fresh rosemary

3 sprigs of fresh thyme

sea salt and pepper, to taste

Heat oil in a saucepan on medium. Add rabbit and sear until nicely golden brown. Transfer to a large baking dish.

In same saucepan, cook onions and mushrooms until golden brown. Cook pancetta in a separate pan until crispy, then crumble. Transfer onions, mushrooms and pancetta to baking dish with rabbit.

Add broth, wine, garlic, rosemary, thyme, salt and pepper. Bake in 375°F (190°C) oven for 2 to 3 hours until tender. Serves 4.

Bussola Valpolicella Classico, Veneto

The braised rabbit has a natural milder meat sweetness, which is complemented by the ripeness of the wine. The wine also possesses a rich, silky mouthfeel that complements the mouthfeel of the creamy polenta.

Rabbit

Rabbit, both wild and farmed, is often used in the place of veal, chicken or turkey in Italian cuisine. It is a lean meat that tastes a bit like chicken.

The Big Apple

Sterling Silver premium beef strip loin served with
sautéed yellow chanterelles and green peppercorn jus.

Green Peppercorn Jus

1 Tbsp (15 mL) olive oil

2 tsp (10 mL) minced shallots

2 tsp (10 mL) green peppercorns

2 tsp (10 mL) cognac

2 cups (500 mL) beef broth

1/2 cup (125 mL) whipping cream

2 tsp (10 mL) butter, softened

sea salt and pepper, to taste

Beef

1 Tbsp (15 mL) olive oil

4 × 12 oz (340 g) beef strip loin steaks

2 Tbsp (30 mL) olive oil

1 Tbsp (15 mL) shallots

1 1/4 cups (375 mL) yellow chanterelles

sea salt and pepper, to taste

sprigs of fresh rosemary, for garnish

Green Peppercorn Jus: Heat oil in a saucepan on medium. Add shallots and peppercorns. Cook, stirring, for 2 minutes. Slowly add cognac and broth, stirring constantly and scraping any brown bits from bottom of pan. Bring to a boil. Reduce heat to low. Simmer until liquid is reduced to 1 cup (250 mL). Add cream, butter, salt and pepper and stir until butter is melted.

Beef: Preheat grill to medium. Heat first amount of oil in a saucepan on medium. Sear steaks until both sides are golden brown. Transfer to grill (or broiler) and cook on hottest part of grill for 4 to 5 minutes until beef reaches an internal temperature of 120°F (50°C) for medium-rare or until desired doneness. Let stand for 5 minutes.

Heat second amount of oil in same saucepan on high. Add shallots. Cook for 2 to 3 minutes. Add chanterelles. Cook until golden brown. Season with salt and pepper. Place a steak and some chanterelles on each of 4 dishes, and pour green peppercorn jus over top. Garnish with rosemary. Serve immediately. Serves 4.

Capezzana Carmignano, Tuscany

The wine has structure, elegance and depth with a beautiful earthy quality that not only holds up to the full flavour of the dish, but also works with the mushrooms and spice. Flavours in both the wine and the dish mirror each other.

Trio of Sterling Silver Premium Beef

A trio of beef with a trio of sauces: prime beef tenderloin, beef strip loin and braised beef short ribs, served with recioto foie gras reduction sauce, green peppercorn jus and horseradish gremolata.

Braised Beef Short Ribs

1/2 cup (125 mL) olive oil

1 lb (454 g) beef short ribs, bone-in

1/2 cup (125 mL) chopped carrot

1/2 cup (125 mL) chopped celery

1/2 cup (125 mL) chopped onion

8 cups (2 L) beef broth

4 sprigs of fresh rosemary

4 bay leaves

2 sticks of cinnamon

sea salt and pepper, to taste

Recioto Foie Gras Reduction Sauce

2 Tbsp (30 mL) butter

2 Tbsp (30 mL) chopped shallots

1 cup (250 mL) recioto wine

4 oz (115 g) fresh foie gras, grade B or C

2 cups (500 mL) whipping cream

sea salt and pepper, to taste

(see next page)

Braised Beef Short Ribs: Heat oil in a heavy Dutch oven or ovenproof pot on high and brown ribs. Transfer to a plate and keep warm. Add carrot, celery and onion to pan. Cook for about 5 minutes, stirring, until onion is softened. Return ribs to pan and add broth, rosemary, bay leaves, cinnamon sticks, salt and pepper. Bake, covered, in 350°F (175°C) oven for about 3 1/2 hours. Remove ribs and cut into 2 oz (57 g) portions. Discard sauce. (Or, instead of discarding sauce, use it as a fourth sauce: heat on low until reduced to 1 cup (250 mL). Remove bay leaves and cinnamon sticks before using.)

Recioto Foie Gras Reduction Sauce: Heat butter in a pan on medium. Add shallots. Cook for 2 to 3 minutes until softened. Add wine and cook until liquid is evaporated. Add foie gras in chunks and cook until very soft. Whisk in cream a little bit at a time. Cook for 5 to 7 minutes until sauce coats the back of a spoon. Season with salt and pepper. Leftover sauce will keep in a sealed container in the fridge for 2 weeks.

Montevetrano di Silvia Imparato, Campania

A stunning wine with richness, elegance, an abundance of fruit, great structure and multi-layers works incredibly well with the multiple preparations of the beef. The wine has the ability to match the richness of the foie gras reduction on the tenderloin, stand up to the spice of the peppercorn jus on the succulent striploin and highlight the tender richness of the short ribs and intensity of the horseradish gremolata. The wine will change with each component of the dish, drawing out more flavours and complexities with each taste.

Beef: Heat oil in an ovenproof sauté pan on medium. Sear tenderloin and strip loin until golden brown on both sides. Season with salt and pepper. Transfer to 375°F (190°C) oven. Bake for 4 to 6 minutes until internal temperature reaches 145°F (63°C) for medium-rare or until desired doneness.

On a dinner plate, arrange tenderloin, strip loin and beef short ribs. Serve with recioto foie gras reduction sauce, green peppercorn jus and horseradish gremolata. Serves 4.

Beef

1 Tbsp (15 mL) olive oil

5 oz (140 g) beef tenderloin

4 oz (113 g) beef strip loin

sea salt and pepper, to taste

1/4 cup (60 mL) Recioto Foie Gras Reduction Sauce

1/4 cup (60 mL) Green Peppercorn Jus (see page 120)

2 Tbsp (30 mL) Horseradish Gremolata (see page 87)

Sterling Silver Premium Beef Tenderloin

With goat cheese quenelles and a recioto foie gras reduction sauce. Serve with your choice of vegetables and garnish with microgreens.

Goat Cheese Quenelles

1 cup (250 mL) goat cheese

sea salt and pepper, to taste

Tenderloin

2 Tbsp (30 mL) olive oil

4 × 6 oz (170 g) beef tenderloin steaks

sea salt and pepper, to taste

1 1/2 cups (375 mL) Recioto Foie Gras Reduction Sauce (see page 122)

Goat Cheese Quenelles: Process cheese, salt and pepper in a food processor. Dip two spoons in hot water, then scoop and shape a portion of cheese into a quenelle (an oval shape, like a football). Repeat. Chill until ready to serve.

Tenderloin: Heat oil in a large ovenproof pot on medium. Season both sides of beef with salt and pepper. Sear beef on both sides until browned. Transfer to 350°F (175°C) oven. Bake for 4 to 5 minutes until internal temperature of beef reaches 145°F (63°C) for medium-rare or until desired doneness. Remove from oven. Let stand for 5 minutes.

Heat foie gras sauce in a small pot. Top beef with goat cheese quenelles and foie gras sauce. Serves 4.

DeAngelis Anghelos, Marche

The foie gras reduction adds to the sweet richness of the dish, which works beautifully with the wine's structure, elegance and rich meaty and earthy flavours.

Quenelle

Traditionally a quenelle was a dumpling made of minced meat or fish, sometimes combined with vegetables, and bound with egg or flour, then shaped with two spoons into an oval and boiled in broth or water. Now the term can refer to any soft food that is shaped in that way. Chefs often use a quenelle to add a decorative flair to a dish's presentation.

45-Day Aged New York Steak

Bring your steaks to room temperature before cooking—cooking steaks when they're cold tends to toughen them up. Garnish the tomatoes with thin slices of black garlic.

Spicy Black Garlic Steak Sauce

2 cups (500 mL) ketchup

1 1/2 cups (375 mL) brown sugar

1 cup (250 mL) diced onion

1 cup (250 mL) soy sauce

1 cup (250 mL) vegetable broth

1/2 cup (125 mL) lemon juice

1/2 cup (125 mL) apple cider vinegar

1/2 cup (125 mL) Dijon mustard

2 Tbsp (30 mL) Hungarian paprika

2 Tbsp (30 mL) chili powder

2 Tbsp (30 mL) sea salt

1 Tbsp (15 mL) black pepper

1 Tbsp (15 mL) minced black garlic

(see next page)

Spicy Black Garlic Steak Sauce: Combine all 13 ingredients in a medium saucepan. Bring to a boil. Reduce heat to low. Simmer for 15 to 20 minutes until thickened. Carefully process in a food processor until mixture becomes paste-like. Sauce will keep in a sealed container in the fridge for up to 6 months.

Steaks: Preheat barbecue to medium-high. Place steaks on barbecue. Close lid. Cook for about 3 minutes per side, basting with butter occasionally, until internal temperature reaches 145°F (63°C) for medium-rare or until desired doneness. Season with salt and pepper.

Roasted Roma Tomatoes: Toss tomatoes with oil, garlic, basil, salt and pepper on a baking sheet with sides. Bake in 400°F (200°C) oven for about 10 minutes. Serve immediately with steak and spicy garlic steak sauce. Serves 4.

Col d'Orcia Brunello di Montalcino, Toscana

Full flavours, structured and elegant with just the right amount of acidity makes this wine a natural with the richness of the steak, spice and acidity of the tomatoes.

45-day Aged Beef

Most beef is aged anywhere between 15 and 21 days to give the meat good flavour and increase its tenderness. Beef that has been aged for 45 days is so tender it can be cut with a fork and it has a stronger, almost cheese-like flavour.

Steaks

4 × 10 oz (285 g) 45-day aged New York steak

melted butter, for basting

sea salt and pepper, to taste

Roasted Roma Tomatoes

8 Roma tomates, sliced

2 Tbsp (30 mL) olive oil

1 Tbsp (15 mL) minced garlic

1 Tbsp (15 mL) chopped fresh basil

sea salt and pepper, to taste

1 1/2 cups (375 mL) Spicy Black Garlic Steak Sauce

Marinated Flank and Flat Iron Steak Duo

This tender marinated beef would go nicely with mashed potatoes and asparagus. Garnish with thinly sliced red pepper.

Italian Herb Olive Oil

1 cup (250 mL) olive oil

2 Tbsp (30 mL) dried oregano

2 Tbsp (30 mL) minced garlic

2 Tbsp (30 mL) sea salt

1 1/2 tsp (7 mL) pepper

1 tsp (5 mL) paprika

1/2 tsp (2 mL) fennel seed

1/2 tsp (2 mL) ground coriander

Steak

4 × 6 oz (170 g) flank steak

4 × 6 oz (170 g) flat iron steak

2 Tbsp (30 mL) olive oil

sea salt and pepper, to taste

Italian Herb Olive Oil: Combine all 8 ingredients in a stainless steel bowl and whisk together until thickened. Set aside a small amount to brush on finished steak. Use the rest as marinade.

Steak: Place flank and flat iron steaks in a shallow dish. Cover with marinade. Chill for about 2 hours. Drain and discard marinade.

Heat oil in an ovenproof sauté pan on medium. Sear steaks until brown on both sides. Season with salt and pepper. Transfer to 375°F (190°C) oven. Bake for 4 to 5 minutes until internal temperature reaches 145°F (63°C) for medium-rare or until desired doneness. Thinly slice steak and brush with reserved Italian herb olive oil. Serve immediately. Serves 4.

Capezzana Barco Reale di Carmignano, Toscana

Full flavoured, yet fresh and elegant, the wine, which is composed mostly of Sangiovese, mirrors the savoury quality of the herbs while the Cabernet Sauvignon component gives additional structure to stand up to the beef. The wine's acidity helps to cleanse the palate, readying you for the next taste.

Flank Steak

Flank steak is cut from the belly muscles of the animal. Long and flat, flank steak is best when it is bright red. Because it comes from a strong, well-exercised part of the cow, it is best prepared when cut across the grain. Flat iron steak is cut from the shoulder. It usually has a significant amount of marbling.

Baked Veal Meatballs

Tender, tasty meatballs that could be served with grilled veggies or rice.

1 lb (454 g) ground veal

1 cup (250 mL) Italian seasoned bread crumbs

2 Tbsp (30 mL) minced shallots

1 egg

1/2 cup (125 mL) extra virgin olive oil

1/2 cup (125 mL) chopped Italian parsley

1/2 cup (125 mL) milk

3 Tbsp (45 mL) dried oregano

sea salt and pepper, to taste

2 cups (500 mL) tomato sauce

1 cup (250 mL) grated mozzarella cheese

pinch of basil

Combine veal, bread crumbs, shallots, egg, oil, parsley, milk, oregano, salt and pepper in a medium bowl. Roll into 20 meatballs. Arrange in a single layer on a parchment paper–lined baking sheet with sides. Bake in 325°F (160°C) oven for 6 to 8 minutes until browned.

Transfer meatballs to a baking dish. Pour tomato sauce and cheese over top. Sprinkle with basil. Bake for 5 to 8 minutes until meatballs are no longer pink inside and cheese is golden brown. Serve immediately. Serves 4.

DeAngelis Rosso Piceno, Marche

The wine's youthful freshness, bright fruit, smokiness and fresh meatiness highlight the natural meatiness of the dish. This unoaked wine is a natural match with tomato sauce.

Veal Chops

Serve with vegetables and garnish with fried onions.

4 × 14 oz (395 g) veal chops

2 tsp (10 mL) sea salt

1/2 tsp (2 mL) black pepper

6 Tbsp (90 mL) olive oil

1/4 cup (60 mL) minced garlic

extra virgin olive oil, for brushing

sea salt, for sprinkling

Preheat barbecue to medium-high. Season veal with salt and pepper. Combine first amount of olive oil and garlic in a shallow dish. Add veal. Turn until coated. Let stand for about 5 minutes.

Cook veal on greased grill for 3 minutes per side until golden brown. Place in baking dish. Bake in 375°F (190°C) oven for 4 to 5 minutes until internal temperature of veal reaches 145°F (63°C) for medium-rare or until desired doneness. Brush with second amount of oil. Sprinkle with salt. Serve immediately. Serves 4.

Ceretto Barbaresco 'Asij,' Piemonte

Soft, round manifestation of the Nebbiolo grape. The acidity and elegant tannins work incredibly well with the meatiness of this flavourful but simply prepared dish. A great example of quality and balance acting as a perfect pair.

Veal's Significance

Veal plays a significant role in the cuisine of both France and Italy, and in Italy it is the most popular meat throughout the country. Meat from calves up to 9 months old is called *vitello*, and thereafter up to 3 years is *vitellone*. The most sought-after veal is *vitello di latte*, or milk-fed veal, from the Piedmont and Lombardy regions.

Scaloppine di Vitello al Limone

Scaloppine refers to a thin cut of meat, often veal. Here small cuts of veal are served with wild mushrooms, tarragon and a lemon reduction sauce. Serve with pasta or grilled vegetables.

4 tomatoes, cut in half

1/4 cup (60 mL) olive oil

sea salt and pepper, to taste

2 Tbsp (30 mL) olive oil

2 cups (500 mL) flour seasoned with sea salt and pepper, for dredging

16 × 1 1/2 oz (43 g) pieces of veal scaloppine

1 1/2 cups (375 mL) wild mushrooms (shiitake, chanterelle, oyster)

1 tsp (5 mL) fresh tarragon

2 tsp (10 mL) white wine

2 tsp (10 mL) lemon juice

1/2 cup (125 mL) butter, softened

sea salt and pepper, to taste

2 1/2 cups (625 mL) sautéed spinach (see page 70)

Preheat grill to medium-high. Toss tomatoes in first amount of oil. Cook, cut side down first, on grill for about 4 minutes per side until soft and charred. Set aside.

Heat second amount of oil in a sauté pan on medium. Place flour in a shallow bowl. Press both sides of veal into flour until coated. Cook for 1 1/2 to 2 minutes per side until golden brown. Remove veal from pan. Set aside.

Add mushrooms and tarragon to same pan. Cook for 2 minutes. Slowly add wine and lemon juice, stirring constantly and scraping any brown bits from bottom of pan. Add veal and butter. Bring to a boil. Add salt and pepper.

Place spinach on 4 individual plates. Top with tomatoes, veal, mushrooms and sauce. Serve immediately. Serves 4.

Bricco dei Guazzi Barbera d'Asti, Piemonte

Both the wine and the dish possess bright acidity and a subtle earthiness. The wine has enough body for the veal and the freshness and no oak tannins to match the lemon reduction.

Veal Vincenza

Veal scaloppine with sun-dried tomato, caramelized onion,
Asiago cheese and roasted red pepper sauce.

Sun-dried Tomato Chutney

1 cup (250 mL) sun-dried tomatoes in oil, blotted dry

1 tsp (5 mL) diced garlic

1 tsp (5 mL) diced shallots

2 Tbsp (30 mL) olive oil

sea salt and pepper, to taste

Roasted Red Pepper Sauce

1 red pepper

1/2 cup (125 mL) olive oil

2 Tbsp (30 mL) lemon juice

1 Tbsp (15 mL) sea salt

pepper, to taste

Caramelized Onions

3 Tbsp (45 mL) olive oil

2 sweet onions, cut into thin strips

sea salt and pepper, to taste

(see next page)

Sun-dried Tomato Chutney: Grind tomatoes, garlic, shallots and oil to a smooth paste, adding a little water if needed. Season with salt and pepper. Chill in refrigerator until served.

Roasted Red Pepper Sauce: Preheat barbecue to medium-high. Cook pepper, skin side down, on greased grill (or broil skin side up in oven) for about 10 minutes until skin is blistered and blackened. Transfer to small bowl. Cover with plastic wrap. Let stand for 10 to 15 minutes. Remove and discard skin. Cut pepper in half. Core and remove seeds. Slice pepper into strips.

Process pepper and remaining 4 ingredients in a blender until smooth. Transfer to a sauté pan. Heat on medium for 2 to 3 minutes until warmed.

Caramelized Onions: Heat oil in a saucepan on medium. Cook onions for 15 minutes until softened and golden brown. Season with salt and pepper. Stir for 1 to 2 minutes. They are ready to serve when they begin to stick to bottom of pan and turn dark in colour.

Fabiano Valpolicella Classico Superiore, Veneto

A regional pairing of food and wine. Light cherry flavours, silky palate and pleasant acidity in the wine complement the light meat flavours with savoury sweetness.

Veal: Cut veal into 3/4 inch (2 cm) slices. Place veal slices between 2 sheets of plastic wrap. Pound with mallet or rolling pin to 3/4 inch (2 cm) thickness. Heat oil in a sauté pan on medium. Place flour in a shallow pan. Press both sides of veal pieces into flour until coated. Cook for about 2 minutes per side until golden brown.

Arrange spinach and sun-dried tomato chutney on 4 ovenproof plates. Add veal, caramelized onion and Asiago cheese. Broil just until cheese is melted. Top with roasted red pepper sauce and butter sauce. Serves 4.

Veal

1 lb (454 g) veal strip loin, silver skin removed

2 Tbsp (30 mL) olive oil

2 cups (500 mL) flour seasoned with salt and pepper, for dredging

2 1/2 cups (625 mL) sautéed spinach (see page 70)

2 oz (57 g) Asiago cheese

1/2 cup (125 mL) Roasted Red Pepper Sauce

1/4 cup (60 mL) Butter Sauce (see page 51)

sea salt and pepper, to taste

Veal Osso Bucco

Veal shanks braised in a rustic tomato sauce with chestnut gremolata and creamy orzo risotto. The 100 oz (3 L) can of 80+40 tomatoes (a type of tomato from California) can be purchased at an Italian grocery store.

Chestnut Gremolata

1 cup (250 mL) chopped chestnuts

1/2 cup (125 mL) chopped fresh parsley

1/2 cup (125 mL) olive oil

1 Tbsp (15 mL) grated lemon zest

1 tsp (5 mL) chopped garlic

sea salt and pepper, to taste

Creamy Orzo Risotto

2 cups (500 mL) orzo

2 cups (500 mL) chicken (or vegetable) broth

1 Tbsp (15 mL) chopped fresh thyme

zest of 1 orange

1/4 cup (60 mL) grated Parmesan cheese

3 Tbsp (45 mL) butter, softened

1 tsp (5 mL) sea salt

pepper, to taste

(see next page)

Chestnut Gremolata: Combine all 7 ingredients in a medium stainless steel bowl. Transfer to a sealable container, cover and chill.

Creamy Orzo Risotto: Bring a pot of salted water to a boil. Add orzo. Cook for 4 to 5 minutes until softened but still hard in centre. Remove from pot. Drain well.

In same pot, bring broth, thyme and zest to a simmer on medium. Add parboiled orzo and stir well. Simmer, stirring often, until liquid is absorbed. Stir in Parmesan cheese, butter, salt and pepper.

Veal: Place carrot, celery, leek and onion on a baking sheet with sides. Drizzle with oil. Bake in 350°F (175°C) oven for about 20 minutes until golden brown.

Heat second amount of oil in a very large cast-iron skillet on medium. Sear veal until golden brown on all sides. Remove to a plate. Slowly add wine, scraping any brown bits from bottom of pan. Cook on high for 15 to 20 minutes until sauce is a very thick syrup.

Triacca Sforzato 'San Domenico,' Lombardia

The richness of the wine, which is made with Nebbiolo grapes that have been dried, is the perfect match with the richness and deep flavours of the slow-braised osso bucco. The structure of the wine is almost masked by the rich, fruit-laden tannins, which pair with the rich meatiness of the dish while cleansing the palate in anticipation of the next taste.

Add veal, broth, tomatoes, garlic, bay leaves and roasted vegetables. Bake, covered, for about 3 hours, checking every 30 minutes, until veal is soft and tender.

Add water to cooking liquid. Heat, covered, on medium until sauce is slightly reduced and desired consistency. Remove bay leaves. Arrange veal on each of 4 plates. Top with sauce and chestnut gremolata. Serve with creamy risotto garnished with shaved Parmesan cheese. Serves 4.

Veal

1 cup (250 mL) diced carrot

1 cup (250 mL) diced celery

1 cup (250 mL) diced leek

1 cup (250 mL) diced onion

olive oil, for drizzling

2 Tbsp (30 mL) olive oil

2 lbs (900 g) veal shank, cut into 2 inch (5 cm) pieces

1/4 cup (60 mL) red wine

12 cups (3 L) beef broth

100 oz (3 L) can 80+40 tomatoes

10 garlic cloves

10 bay leaves

2 cups (500 mL) water

shaved Parmesan cheese (optional)

Bison Rib Eye Steak

A simple recipe and a simple presentation—bison rib eye *au poivre* finished with green peppercorn jus. Serve with a simple side of chopped and seasoned tomatoes. This signature dish also won an award in the Alberta Bison Commission's Best of Alberta Buffalo Culinary Competition.

1 Tbsp (15 mL) olive oil

4 × 10 oz (280 g) bison rib eye steak

1 Tbsp (15 mL) olive oil

1 Tbsp (15 mL) chopped shallots

1 cup (250 mL) chopped white mushrooms

sea salt and pepper, to taste

1 cup (250 mL) Green Peppercorn Jus (see page 120)

Heat first amount of oil in an ovenproof saucepan on high. Sear steak for 2 to 3 minutes per side until golden brown. Broil for 3 to 4 minutes per side until internal temperature reaches 145°F (63°C) for medium-rare or until desired doneness. Let rest for 5 minutes.

Heat second amount of oil in a sauté pan on high. Add shallots. Cook for about 3 minutes. Add mushrooms. Cook for about 5 minutes until browned. Season with salt and pepper.

Arrange steak, shallots and mushrooms on each of 4 plates. Top with green peppercorn jus and serve immediately. Serves 4.

Ceuso Fastaia, Sicilia

Great structure, but with lush tannins and ripe fruit, this wine possesses a fresh herbaceous quality to match the flavourful bison and green spiciness of the jus.

Bison Farming

Bison farming has really taken off in Canada, from 745 farms in 1996 to more than 1200 farms in 2014. Most of the farms are in Alberta and Saskatchewan, with a sprinkling in Manitoba and BC. Bison meat is in demand, and Canada exports much of the meat, primarily to the US, but also to Italy, Germany, France and Switzerland.

Medallions of Lamb

Lamb loin with apple mint chutney and crumbled goat cheese.

Apple Mint Chutney

1 Tbsp (15 mL) olive oil

3 Gala apples, diced

1 cup (250 mL) apple juice

1/4 cup (60 mL) sugar

3 Tbsp (45 mL) diced fresh mint

1 tsp (5 mL) sea salt

pepper, to taste

Fennel

1 cup (250 mL) whipping cream

2 fennel bulbs (white part only), thinly sliced

2 Tbsp (30 mL) chopped shallots

Roasted Red Peppers

13 oz (370 mL) jar of roasted red peppers, drained

2 Tbsp (30 mL) olive oil

1 tsp (5 mL) minced garlic

sea salt and pepper, to taste

(see next page)

Apple Mint Chutney: Heat oil in a sauté pan on medium. Add apples. Cook until golden. Add apple juice, sugar, mint, salt and pepper. Cook until liquid is evaporated. Carefully process in a blender or food processor until smooth.

Fennel: Combine cream, fennel and shallots in a small saucepan on medium. Cook, stirring occasionally, for about 10 minutes until shallots are softened.

Roasted Red Peppers: Sauté red peppers, oil, garlic, salt and pepper in a small sauté pan on medium for about 5 minutes until softened. Set aside.

Lamb: Cut lamb into 3/4 inch (2 cm) slices. Place slices between 2 sheets of plastic wrap. Pound with mallet or rolling pin to uniform 3/4 inch (2 cm) thickness. Heat oil in a sauté pan on medium. Pour flour into a shallow dish with sides. Press both sides of lamb into flour until coated. Cook for about 2 minutes per side until golden brown. Season with salt and pepper.

Divide fennel among 4 individual plates. Top with roasted red peppers, lamb, butter sauce, apple mint chutney and goat cheese. Garnish with parsley. Serve immediately. Serves 4.

Donatella Cinelli Colombini Cenerentola, Toscana

The wine has flavours of ripe red and blue fruit, the earthiness of tobacco, toasted nuts and just a hint of funkiness and fresh herbacious flavours to match the mint, goat cheese and the richness of the lamb.

Lamb Meat

Lamb meat does not enjoy the same popularity in North America as it does in Europe, but the production of ewe milk for cheese making is a growing market, particularly in Ontario and Quebec. In Italy, lamb is eaten most in the south, but roasted lamb is the traditional Easter meal throughout the country.

Lamb

1 lb (454 g) medallions of lamb loin, butterflied into large rounds, silver skin removed

2 Tbsp (30 mL) olive oil

2 cups (500 mL) flour seasoned with sea salt and pepper, for dredging

sea salt and pepper, to taste

2 Tbsp (30 mL) Butter Sauce (see page 51)

1/2 cup (125 mL) crumbled goat cheese

parsley, for garnish

Lamb Loin en Croute

Lamb loin, mushroom duxelles and foie gras finished with an apple chutney. The amarone jus is not pictured but perfectly complements the lamb.

Apple Chutney

2 cups (500 mL) peeled, sliced Granny Smith apples

1/2 cup (125 mL) brown sugar

1/3 cup (75 mL) apple cider vinegar

1/4 onion, finely chopped

2 Tbsp (30 mL) chopped fresh mint leaves

1/4 tsp (1 mL) sea salt

Amarone Jus

1 Tbsp (15 mL) butter

1/2 cup (125 mL) chopped onion

1 cup (250 mL) amarone wine

2 cups (500 mL) beef broth

1 Tbsp (15 mL) butter

sea salt and pepper, to taste

(see next page)

Apple Chutney: Combine all 6 ingredients in a medium saucepan. Bring to a boil on medium, stirring frequently. Reduce heat to low. Simmer for 4 to 5 minutes, stirring often, until apples are soft and begin to break apart and mixture thickens. Remove from heat. Let stand for 5 minutes, then pour into a jar with a lid. Cover tightly and store in the refrigerator. Leftover chutney will keep in sealed container in the refrigerator for up to 2 weeks.

Amarone Jus: Heat first amount of butter in a small pot on medium. Add onion. Cook, stirring occasionally, for 4 to 5 minutes until golden brown. Add amarone. Heat and stir for 2 minutes, scraping any brown bits from bottom of pan. Add beef stock. Heat for 6 to 8 minutes until reduced to about 1 cup (250 mL). Add second amount of butter. Stir until melted. Season with salt and pepper. Set aside.

Mushroom Duxelles: Heat butter in a small saucepan. Add shallots and garlic. Cook for 3 minutes until tender. Add mushrooms. Cook, stirring occasionally, until liquid is evaporated. Season with salt and pepper. Carefully process in food processor following manufacturer's instructions for processing hot liquids.

Lamb: Roll each puff pastry sheet out and cut in half to form four 7 x 8 inch (18 x 20 cm) rectangles. Place pastries on baking sheet. Spread a layer of mushroom duxelles on each pastry and arrange lamb loin on top. Spread foie gras on lamb. Wrap and seal packages. Brush packages lightly with egg yolk. Bake in 350°F (175°C) oven for 8 to 10 minutes until internal temperature of lamb reaches 145°F (63°C) for medium-rare or until desired doneness.

Fabiano Amarone della Valpolicella, Veneto

The richness of the dish is enhanced by the foie gras and amarone jus, requiring a wine with structure and richness to match. The amarone provides richness and deep flavours but also possesses velvety tannins and texture and a great structure. The apple chutney and the fresh finish of the wine prevent the dish from being overly rich.

Cut each package in half or into 5 slices and arrange on each plate with apple chutney. Spoon amarone jus over lamb and garnish with thyme. Serves 4.

Mushroom Duxelles

1 Tbsp (15 mL) butter

2 Tbsp (30 mL) minced shallots

1 tsp (5 mL) minced garlic

2 cups (500 mL) finely chopped mushrooms

sea salt and pepper, to taste

Lamb

2 sheets puff pastry, thawed

4 × 7 oz (200 g) lamb loin

2 oz (57 g) foie gras

1 egg yolk (large), fork-beaten

1/4 cup (60 mL) Apple Chutney

1/4 cup (60 mL) Amarone Jus

sprigs of fresh thyme, for garnish

Alberta Pork Mix

A savoury combination of marinated and grilled pork sausage, pork chop and pork tenderloin.
Serve with red cabbage and your choice of vegetables.

6 Tbsp (90 mL) minced garlic

2 Tbsp (30 mL) dry mustard

2 Tbsp (30 mL) fresh thyme

2 Tbsp (30 mL) paprika

1 Tbsp (15 mL) cayenne pepper

4 × 6 oz (170 g) pork chops

1 lb (454 g) pork tenderloin

4 x 3 oz (85 g) pork sausages

6 Tbsp (90 mL) olive oil

1 Tbsp (15 mL) sea salt

1 1/2 tsp (7 mL) black pepper

Combine garlic, mustard, thyme, paprika and cayenne pepper in a large bowl.

Add all pork. Stir until coated. Chill for 2 hours.

Preheat barbecue to medium. Cook tenderlion for about 10 minutes. Add chops and sausage and cook for 5 to 6 minutes per side until golden brown or until desired doneness. Brush with olive oil. Sprinkle with salt and pepper. Remove from barbecue. Let tenderloin stand for 5 minutes, and then slice. Arrange 1 pork chop, 1 portion of pork tenderloin and 1 pork sausage on each of 4 plates. Serve immediately. Serves 4.

Triacca Chianti Classico Riserva 'La Madonnina,' Toscana

A touch of barrel age on the wine softens the tannins just enough to play off the fattiness of the pork, while the ripe cherry flavours and touch of vanilla from the oak act to tame and complement some of the spiciness of the mustard, paprika and cayenne. The savoury earthiness of the thyme is mirrored by the underbrush flavours in the wine.

Pork Tenderloin

When it comes to healthy meat choices, pork tends to get a bad rap, but depending on the cut, it can be a good option. Sure, bacon and sausage are not paragons of healthy eating, but ounce for ounce, pork tenderloin has less fat than chicken breast.

Alberta Pork Tenderloin

Spicy rubbed pork tenderloin finished with apricot anisette chutney.
Serve with your choice of vegetables.

Spicy Rub

1 cup (250 mL) paprika

2 Tbsp (30 mL) cayenne pepper

2 Tbsp (30 mL) dried thyme

2 Tbsp (30 mL) dry mustard

2 Tbsp (30 mL) sea salt

1 Tbsp (15 mL) garlic powder

1 Tbsp (15 mL) ground cloves

1 Tbsp (15 mL) Chinese five-spice powder

Apricot Anisette Chutney

2 cups (500 mL) water

1 cup (250 mL) diced dried apricot

2 Tbsp (30 mL) anisette (anise-flavoured liqueur)

2 Tbsp (30 mL) coarsely chopped ginger root

4 garlic cloves, chopped

1/2 cup (125 mL) sugar

1 tsp (5 mL) sea salt

(see next page)

Spicy Rub: Place all 8 ingredients in a large bowl and mix together. Transfer to a container and store, covered, at room temperature.

Apricot Anisette Chutney: Combine all 7 ingredients in a medium pot. Bring to a boil. Simmer for 6 to 8 minutes until liquid is mostly evaporated. Remove from heat and let cool. Process in a food processor until smooth.

Pork: Rub spicy rub all over pork. Heat oil in an ovenproof sauté pan on medium. Sear pork on both sides until golden brown. Transfer to 350°F (175°C) oven and cook for about 5 to 8 minutes until internal temperature reaches 160°F (71°C) for medium or until desired doneness.

Slice meat. Arrange on 4 plates. Spoon butter sauce over each serving and garnish with apricot anisette chutney. Serve immediately. Serves 4.

Ceuso Scurati Nero d'Avola, Sicilia

Wild berry fruit with traditional Nero d'Avola flavours of spice and licorice mirror the anisette flavours in the dish. A bit of spiciness in the wine mirrors the spicy rub used on the pork.

Anisette

Anisette is a clear, anise-flavoured liqueur that is popular in Italy, Spain, Portugal and France. It tends to be sweeter than other anise-flavoured alcohols. Anisette generally isn't consumed straight because its alcohol content is so high. Instead, this liqueur is mixed with water, coffee, gin or bourbon, and in Italy it is used to make anisette cookies, a Christmas tradition.

Pork

1 lb (454 g) pork tenderloin, cut into 4 pieces

1 Tbsp (15 mL) olive oil

1 cup (250 mL) Butter Sauce (see page 51)

Ginger Honey Gelato with Panettone Pudding

You need an ice cream maker for this recipe.

Gelato

2 cups (500 mL) whipping cream

2 cups (500 mL) homogenized milk

2 Tbsp (30 mL) ground ginger

1 vanilla bean

8 egg yolks

1/2 cup (125 mL) honey

Panettone Pudding

3 cups (750 mL) panettone bread

4 cups (1 L) whipping cream

1 cup (250 mL) milk

2 large eggs

1 cup (250 mL) sugar

1/2 tsp (2 mL) ground cinnamon

1/2 tsp (2 mL) nutmeg

1 Tbsp (15 mL) vanilla bean paste

6 Tbsp (90 mL) butter, softened

1/4 cup (60 mL) dark rum

Gelato: Bring cream and milk to a boil in a small saucepan. Stir in ginger. Split vanilla bean in half lengthwise. Scrape seeds from pod into mixture. Add pod halves.

Whisk egg yolks and honey in a medium bowl. Add 2 Tbsp (30 mL) hot milk mixture. Stir. Slowly add egg yolk mixture to hot milk mixture, stirring constantly until boiling and thickened. Remove vanilla pod halves. Strain and chill, covered, for at least 30 minutes. Pour into ice cream maker. Freeze until firm.

Panettone Pudding: Tear panettone into chunks and place in a large bowl. Pour cream and milk over bread. Let stand until bread is softened.

Beat eggs and sugar until smooth and thick. Add cinnamon, nutmeg, vanilla bean paste, butter and rum. Gently toss egg mixture with bread to blend. Pour into 2 inch (5 cm) round ramekins. Bake in 350°F (175°C) oven for about 1 hour until browned and almost set. Serve warm with gelato. Serves 8.

Panettone

Panettone, meaning "big bread," is a yeast bread with a rather cake-like texture that usually contains sultanas, candied fruit and spices. It was originally a specialty of Milan but now is readily available throughout the country (and in Italian shops throughout Canada), around Christmas when it is given as a gift.

Crème Brûlée Trio

A trio of pistachio, pineapple and coffee. You'll need 12 small ramekins to serve this dish (and you could serve up to 12 and give 1 ramekin to each guest). Invest in a small propane torch for that perfect caramelized topping. If you don't have one, broil for 2 to 3 minutes until browned and caramelized. Pineapple paste can be found in the freezer section of your local grocery store.

20 egg yolks (large)

8 cups (2 L) whipping cream

2 cups (500 mL) sugar

2 Tbsp (30 mL) vanilla bean paste

1/4 cup (60 mL) pistachio paste

1/4 cup (60 mL) pineapple paste, or puréed pineapple

1/4 cup (60 mL) finely ground coffee beans

granulated sugar, for sprinkling

Place egg yolks in a large bowl.

Bring cream, sugar and vanilla to a boil in a medium saucepan. Slowly add to egg yolks, stirring constantly. Strain through a fine sieve into a separate large bowl.

Divide liquid into three parts, each about 4 cups (1 L). Add pistachio paste to 1 part, pineapple paste to another, and coffee beans to the other. Transfer to 3 1/2 inch (9 cm) ramekins. Set into a large baking dish or roasting pan.

Pour boiling water into baking dish until water comes three-quarters of the way up sides of ramekins. Bake in 300°F (150°C) oven for 45 minutes to 1 hour until a knife inserted in centre of custard comes out clean. Remove ramekins from water to wire rack to cool completely. Chill, covered, for about 15 minutes.

Sprinkle sugar on top of custard until completely covered. With a propane torch, heat sugar until golden brown but not dark, making sure all sugar melts and caramelizes. Let sugar cool slightly before serving. Serves 4.

Banana Saffron Panna Cotta with Raspberry Coulis

Gelatin sheets, also called gelatin leaves, are often used by professionals instead of powdered gelatin—it is said to give the dish a purer flavour. If you can't find gelatin sheets, try substituting 1 Tbsp (15 mL) powdered gelatin for the 4 gelatin sheets. You can garnish this dessert with mint or chocolate. Look for banana paste in the freezer section of your local grocery store.

Panna Cotta

2 cups (500 mL) whipping cream

1 cup (250 mL) milk

1/2 cup (125 mL) fresh banana purée or banana paste

1/2 cup (125 mL) sugar

2 tsp (30 mL) vanilla bean paste

pinch of saffron

4 gelatin sheets

Raspberry Coulis

1 cup (250 mL) frozen raspberries

1/2 cup (125 mL) sugar

2 Tbsp (30 mL) water

Panna Cotta: Combine cream, milk, banana and sugar in a medium saucepan. Add vanilla bean paste and saffron. Bring to a boil on medium. Cook for about 5 minutes, stirring occasionally.

Soak gelatin in cold water until soft. Remove gelatin from water. Pat away excess water with a towel. Add to cream mixture, whisking until gelatin is dissolved. Strain through a fine sieve. Divide panna cotta into 6 ramekins and refrigerate for about 4 hours until set.

Raspberry Coulis: Combine raspberries, sugar and water in a small pot and bring to a boil. Boil for 5 minutes. Remove from heat. Process with hand blender until smooth. Strain through a double layer of cheesecloth into a small bowl. Discard solids. Invert ramekins onto 6 individual plates. Top with raspberry coulis and serve. Serves 6.

Panna Cotta

Panna cotta is a light, silky, custard-like dessert made of sweetened cream that is set with gelatine. It originated in the Piedmont region of Italy but is now popular throughout the country as well as in North America, where it graces dessert menus of even the finest restaurants.

Fabiano Recioto della Valpolicella Sorbetto

A refreshing frozen dessert, flavoured with juice and wine. Serve garnished with grapes, berries or mint.

1/2 cup (125 mL) water

1 cup (250 mL) granulated sugar

1/2 tsp (2 mL) whole cloves

pinch of cinnamon

1 cup (250 mL) grape juice

1 cup (250 mL) apple juice

2 cups (500 mL) Fabiano Recioto wine

Bring water, sugar, cloves and cinnamon to a boil in a saucepan. Reduce heat to low. Simmer for about 5 minutes. Remove from heat. Let cool. Add grape juice, apple juice and wine. Pour into ice cube trays. Freeze. Process in a food processor until slushy. Serves 6.

Index

ADVOCACY
— for —
SOCIAL JUSTICE

ADVOCACY
— *for* —
SOCIAL JUSTICE

A Global Action and Reflection Guide

David Cohen
Rosa de la Vega
Gabrielle Watson

Kumarian
Press, Inc.

Advocacy for Social Justice: A Global Action and Reflection Guide
Published 2001 in the United States of America by Kumarian Press, Inc.
1294 Blue Hills Avenue, Bloomfield, CT 06002 USA.

Exclusive distributor for Europe and non-exclusive distributor for the rest of the world excluding the USA and Canada: Oxfam Publishing, Oxfam GB, 274 Banbury Road, Oxford OX2 7DZ, UK.

This project was developed by Oxfam America and The Advocacy Institute, and the views expressed in it are those of the two organizations, not necessarily those of Oxfam GB or Oxfam International.

Oxfam America and Oxfam GB are members of Oxfam International, a company limited by guarantee and registered in England No. 612172. Oxfam GB is a registered charity, No. 202918.

Production and design by ediType, Yorktown Heights, N.Y.

The text of this book is set in 10/13 Adobe Garamond.
Printed in Canada on acid-free paper by Transcontinental Printing and Graphics, Inc.
Text printed with vegetable oil–based ink.

∞ The paper used in this publication meets the minimum requirements of the American National Standard for Information Sciences–Permanence of Paper for Printed Library Materials, ANSI Z39.48–1984.

Library of Congress Cataloging-in-Publication Data

Advocacy for social justice : a global action and reflection guide / [edited by] David Cohen, Rosa de la Vega, Gabrielle Watson.
    p. cm.
   "Oxfam America, Advocacy Institute."
   Includes bibliographical references.
   ISBN 1-56549-131-9 (pbk. : alk paper)
   1. Social justice – Handbooks, manuals, etc. 2. Social advocacy – Handbooks, manuals, etc. I. Cohen, David, 1936- II. De la Vega, Rosa, 1973- III. Watson, Gabrielle, 1963- IV. Oxfam America. V. Advocacy Institute (Washington, D.C.)

HM671 .A38 2001
303.3′72 – dc21

2001023399

10 09 08 07   10 9 8 7 6 5 4   First Printing 2001

Contents

Part I: Reflections on Advocacy – David Cohen

Part II: Advocacy Skills – Rosa de la Vega

Part IV: Advocacy Resource Directory –
Gabrielle Watson with Angela Orlando, Jennifer Shea, and Karin Lockwood

Acknowledgments

The Advocacy Institute and Oxfam America, partners in the Advocacy Learning Initiative (ALI), are proud to present materials that reflect a community of voices and perspectives on advocacy. *Advocacy for Social Justice* is the result of a team effort. We are indebted to many for their ideas, stories, feedback, and support.

Advocacy for Social Justice is the product of the combined efforts of the core Advocacy Institute and Oxfam America staff and many others. The primary authors, David Cohen, Rosa de la Vega, and Gabrielle Watson, toiled for many hours to share our institutions' learnings with a wider community. The contributing authors shared stories that enrich our work and graciously allowed us to excerpt and edit their longer contributions. We are indebted to Saleemul Huq, Mahbubul Karim, and Mohammad Zakaria from Bangladesh; Srey Chanthy from Cambodia; Suneeta Dhar, Ulka Mahajan, Madhusudan Mistry, Vivek Pandit, and John Samuel from India; Codou Bop from Senegal; Warren Krafchik, Gladys Sonto Kudjoe, and Adèle Wildschut from South Africa; and Diana MTK Autin, Andrew Bauck, Tamara L. Jezic, Sofía Quintero, Karen Watson, and John Zippert from the United States.

The authors have special individual thanks we want to give. David wishes to thank Carla Cohen for understanding and encouragement. Rosa wishes to thank Diana MTK Autin, Jorge Du-Breuil, Valerie Miller, Timothy Saasta, Gordana Stojanovic, Paul Vleermuis, Phil Wilbur, and Ina Zoon for their help with examples; and Melanie Moses for patience and understanding. Gabrielle wishes to thank Patricia Watson for her support throughout this process.

In the course of developing the project, we turned to numerous colleagues, friends, and mentors to help us conceive and shape this book. We are grateful to, at the Advocacy Institute, Maureen Burke, Keiko Koizumi, Kathleen D. Sheekey, Wylie David Chen, Laura M. Chambers, and Ellen Mackenzie for their stalwart support throughout the initiative. At Oxfam America, our sincere thanks go to James Arena-DeRosa, Michael Bedford, Kelly Brooks, Carolina Castrillo, Lisa Collins, Peggy Connolly, Julio de Souza, Susan Holcombe, Danielle Klainberg, Veronica Lemus, Pamela Moore, Rama Niang, Lucy Nichols, Ray Offenheiser, Bernadette Orr, Michael Ounstead, Laura Roper, John Ruthrauff, Margaret Samuriwo, Martin Scurrah, Ibrahima Thiam, Elizabeth Umlas, Suzanne Wallen, and Emira Woods.

The ALI team is immensely grateful to our readers—Advocacy Institute and Oxfam America alumni, colleagues, partners, and staff whose perspectives range from activist to policy researcher, from grassroots to international, and from Bangladesh to Zimbabwe. They read through many drafts, gave thoughtful and provocative comments, and pushed us to go that extra step to make this a better resource for activists and advocates. Additionally, their comments have affirmed our belief that we are making a significant contribution to understandings of "advocacy." Our readers for Parts I, II, and III were Kamal Siddiqqui from Bangladesh; Gordana Stojanovic from Croatia; Mahesh Upadhyaya from India; Darmiyanti Muchtar and Anik Wusari from Indonesia; Prakash Singh Adhikari from Nepal; Peter van Tuijl from the Netherlands; Danilo Songco from the Philippines; Nancy Alexander, Diana MTK Autin, Joel Charny, John Brown Childs, Jonathan A. Fox, Sofía Quintero, Kay Treakle, and Nondas Hurst Voll from the United States; and Rudo Chitiga from Zimbabwe.

Part IV, the Advocacy Resource Directory, would not have been possible without the invaluable information, comments, access to their networks, and space offered by many colleagues, including Sladjana Dankovic of the Advocacy Institute; Leslie Fox and Roberto Mugnani from the School for International Training; Peter van Tuijl from NOVIB; and Jessica Greenberg and Lisa VeneKlassen from The Asia Foundation's Global Women in Politics program. During an Institute for Development Research workshop, Jane Covey and Valerie Miller created valuable space for discussion and strategizing about this initiative. Our thanks also go to our many colleagues within Oxfam America and Oxfam International, especially those in the regional offices. Our readers for Part IV were Carolina Castrillo, Rudo Chitiga, Rosa de la Vega, Justin Forsyth, Jonathan A. Fox, John Gershman, Kevin Healy, Andrew Hewitt, Moustafa Karim, Marieme Lo, Valerie Miller, Martin Scurrah, Julio de Souza, Jane Sparrow-Niang, Rajesh Tandon, Peter van Tuijl, Lisa VeneKlassen, and Rodrigo Villar.

Many people played key roles from behind the scenes, including dedicated staff, interns, and volunteers who put in long hours and generously pitched in to make the day-to-day work possible. We are grateful to Amanda C. Rawls, Farah Nazarali-Stranieri, Laura Scott, Mary Ellen Tsekos, Moco McCaulay, Nicole Gergens, Timothy Saasta, Naomi Lucks, Nancy Singer, Colin Moffett, Kelly Mack, and Malik Sakil. The resourceful and diligent directory production team included Karin Lockwood, Angela Orlando, and Jennifer Shea with Katherine Adams Ball, Eamon Aghdasi, Kathy Ausenhmer, Michael Berger, Laura Brezin, Marlene Roy, Ritirupa Samanta, and Kavita Shukla.

We want to thank Rob Cornford of Oxfam Great Britain Publishing for helping us find a US publisher for our book. Thanks also go to Jeff Wolfson of Goulston and Storrs for his able and always sensible behind-the-scenes support in this endeavor. We especially want to thank everyone at Kumarian Press for believing in this project and giving it wings. Despite the best efforts of all those who helped us, any errors and omissions are the responsibility of the authors.

This book would not have been possible to create without the generous support of the Ford Foundation and the John D. and Catherine T. MacArthur Foundation. We are especially grateful to the guidance and support of Srilatha Batliwala of the Ford Foundation and Melanie Oliviero of the MacArthur Foundation.

Finally, *Advocacy for Social Justice* would not exist without our alumni, partners, and colleagues. Their passion, commitment, mutual respect, belief that change is possible, and willingness to exchange stories, ideas, and lessons all sustain our work. This book is dedicated to these advocates and others working to create just, decent societies around the world.

Foreword

The 1990s offered unprecedented opportunities for civil society organizations to engage in building democratic institutions and practice and in shaping crucial policy dialogues at the local, national, and international levels. The end of the Cold War has been accompanied by an end to many of the most brutal and authoritarian regimes and ushered in a "democratic spring." Suddenly, building civil society and nurturing democracy became part of the mainstream development discourse.

Meanwhile, at the international level, multilateral institutions began to recognize the importance of engaging civil society organizations in the process of development. They began to actively seek out civil society leaders in order to assure better quality and more effective outcomes for their programs and as a way of leveraging better performance from state actors. At the same time, civil society organizations turned the spotlight around on multilaterals, questioning everything from the logical consistency of their programs to their political independence and their right to inflict punishing political, social, and economic conditionalities on the poor populations of highly indebted nations.

For many civil society organizations in the developing world, these opportunities to engage were novel. Many were born and had survived under authoritarian regimes for so long that the only forms of civil society actions they were familiar with were street demonstrations and mass rallies. They had never before had the possibility of governing or engaging with the state in a process that was respectful and congenial, yet also strategic and effective at fostering change. Civil society organizations were quick to see the opportunities afforded them by these new openings. Yet often, they believed they lacked the competencies among their staff to assume the new roles in policy advocacy, public education, issue campaigning, and media relations that these new circumstances called for.

Nonetheless, many forged ahead. They engaged their governments on a wide range of issues. They attended UN summits and all kinds of preparatory meetings. They launched new collaborations that focused explicitly on making links between grassroots development work and public-policy decision making. They boldly created their own advocacy experience. As it became clear that advocacy was going to become an even greater part of what civil society organizations needed to do during this new era, many began to seek out advocacy capacity building wherever they could find it.

This book, *Advocacy for Social Justice,* was born as a response to this growing interest on the part of civil society organizations from around the world for practical materials that would enrich and accelerate their organizational learning processes about advocacy. The project set out with the modest goal of producing a book that could help these organizations understand what the elements of advocacy are, how it can be practiced in diverse settings, and what the best practices might look like. The core premise of the project was that there were some very effective social justice campaigns underway that could provide excellent case material for those wishing to better understand the nature of advocacy.

The perceived need for this kind of work led to a unique collaboration between Oxfam America and the Advocacy Institute, two quite distinct institutions with a shared commitment to social justice and building the capacity of civil society organizations to influence public policy. The Advocacy Institute brought to the process the wisdom that comes with years of practice as advocates and working with activists to be reflective and confident practitioners. For its part, Oxfam America brought ground-based experience in communities, organizations, and social movements practicing advocacy at the local, national, and international level all around the world and an activist presence on major foreign and development policy issues in Washington, D.C. Together, both organizations brought a strong commitment to a process of learning that would draw lessons from the experience of practitioners working in diverse social, cultural, and economic contexts. At its heart, the project approached advocacy as an art that motivates and inspires people to fulfill their visions. It also requires craft—craft that might be practiced differently in different circumstances, but craft that could be guided by some basic and transferable skills.

The work that follows brings together materials for teachers, trainers, and practitioners in the field of advocacy and students of social movements and transnational advocacy. This book is meant to be absorbed and used in whatever order suits the practitioner-reader. It begins by setting forth a general conceptual foundation and then moves on to provide illustrations of tools and tactics that might be adapted to different circumstances. It offers a set of case studies of some specific campaigns that offer diverse lessons. Finally, it lists hundreds of leading advocacy support organizations that can help groups doing advocacy around the world. *Advocacy for Social Justice* has been written by and for practitioners. The authors hope it will serve as an inspiration to others who may want to set down their own experiences and add to this growing new literature on the messy world of social justice movements and non-linear social change processes.

For both Oxfam America and the Advocacy Institute, the process of producing this publication has been a transforming institutional experience. The iterative learning approach that was used to engage participants, test materials, and cultivate ideas touched a very wide circle of people in both institutions and challenged all of us in many important ways. This process has further reinforced the dedication of both organizations to be active learners, a welcomed but unanticipated by-product of the project for which we are most grateful. More important, however, the project involved broad participation and consultation, which are rare in producing materials of this sort. We are grateful to our funders for allowing us to engage in such a dynamic process with many of the kinds of institutional actors who we hope will be primary users of this work.

In every project, there must be leaders and heroes. This project was no exception. Our heroes are Gabri-elle Watson of Oxfam America and Rosa de la Vega of the Advocacy Institute, who deserve special recognition for nursing this writing project along from the beginning. In addition to taking on a significant share of the conceptualizing and writing, they successfully navigated many obstacles and forged a productive collaboration through persistence, stamina, and good cheer. A project of this scope and ambition could come to fruition only under the care and direction of the able shepherds that they are.

Gabrielle and Rosa worked through the cultural and institutional differences between Oxfam America and the Advocacy Institute to play a leading role in creating a clear, coherent, and compelling document. With empathy and understanding, they helped the practitioners and authors capture the many years of institutional learning and individual reflections—stories, histories, and institutional legacies—that had not been previously captured. In their own writing, they drew together lessons in insightful ways that will help bring our understanding to the next level. Each day they sustained our organizations' dedication to and focus on the project.

Finally, we would like to acknowledge the support of both the Ford Foundation and the MacArthur Foundation, whose generous support made this work possible. Many foundations speak the language of social justice, but few have the courage to support the advocates who make social change happen. We wish to salute the staff and leadership of these institutions for their support of a project we hope will inspire and guide individuals and organizations to raise their voices as advocates for human rights and social justice. We are grateful to these institutions for giving us the means to help others chart a path and perhaps find a vocation in this important work.

RAYMOND C. OFFENHEISER JR.   DAVID COHEN
President   Co-Director
Oxfam America   Advocacy Institute
Boston   Washington, D.C.

About the Authors and Contributors

Authors

DAVID COHEN, author of "Part I: Reflections on Advocacy," is Co-Director of the Advocacy Institute. He has spent his adult life working as an advocate, organizer, lobbyist, and strategist on major social justice and political reform issues in the United States. From 1975 to 1981, he served as President of Common Cause, the largest US voluntary membership organization working on issues of government accountability and abuse of power. After that, he formed a coalition of professionals—doctors, scientists, lawyers, social workers—to use their expertise and clout to address the threats stemming from nuclear arms. In 1985, he co-founded the Advocacy Institute, where, among other responsibilities, he pioneered the Institute's international capacity building program and counsels social justice leaders in the U.S. and abroad on strategies to advance their public agenda.

ROSA DE LA VEGA, author of "Part II: Advocacy Skills," was Coordinator of Capacity Building Programs at the Advocacy Institute. To write Part II, she drew from five years of learning from Advocacy Institute alumni and working closely with the Advocacy Institute's lead facilitators—Maureen Burke, David Cohen, Kathleen D. Sheekey, and Michael Pertschuk. Rosa has been instrumental in creating language and models to describe the Advocacy Institute's work and served as editor of *ChangeExchange,* an advocacy journal for Advocacy Institute alumni to exchange lessons and resources. Rosa de la Vega is currently Program Coordinator with YouthBuild New Mexico Coalition, Inc., which provides job training and education services for teenagers who have dropped out of high school.

GABRIELLE WATSON, author and editor of "Part III: Advocacy Case Studies" and coordinator of "Part IV: Advocacy Resource Directory," was a researcher in the Policy Department at Oxfam America. She conducted joint fieldwork with case study writers and coordinated the overall case study project. Prior to her work with Oxfam America, she worked for five years researching and writing about social movements and community participation in urban services throughout Latin America. Gabrielle Watson is currently Co-Director of the Centro de Derechos Económicos y Sociales in Quito, Ecuador.

Contributors

DIANA MTK AUTIN, 1998 Advocacy Institute Global Advocacy Leadership Team Fellow, is the Executive Director of the Statewide Parent Advocacy Network of New Jersey (SPAN). SPAN engages in public policy research and advocacy with the U.S. and New Jersey Departments of Education, Health, and Human Services and collaborates with school districts in implementing effective educational practices. Contact Ms. Autin at SPAN via e-mail at *span@spannj.org* and via fax at (973) 642-8080.

ANDREW BAUCK, case writer of the debt relief case study, is a graduate student at the Evans School of Public Affairs and Jackson School of International Studies at the University of Washington. His course work has focused on issues of international development and global economic justice. He has a particular regional interest in South Asia and has spent two years studying and working in India and Pakistan.

CODOU BOP, case writer of the Senegal gender violence case study, is a Senegalese researcher, evaluator, and trainer in gender, development, and communication. For over twenty years, she has participated in and served the women's movement in Senegal and throughout Africa as a consultant and as an activist. Ms. Bop trained at Rutgers University, Princeton University, the University of Paris, and the University of Dakar.

DR. SALEEMUL HUQ, 1996 Bangladesh Advocacy Fellow, is Executive Director of the Bangladesh Centre for Advanced Studies (BCAS). BCAS is a major nongovernmental research and policy institute working on environmental and development issues. Contact Mr. Huq via e-mail at *saleemul@citechco.net* and at BCAS via e-mail at *bcas@bdonline.com,* web at *http://www.bcas.net,* or via fax at (880-2) 811-344.

TAMARA L. JEZIC, case writer of the Ecuador campaign against Texaco case study, holds a J.D. from Harvard Law School and has worked since 1998 with a number of the key organizations involved in the Texaco case. She has worked as a lawyer with the Center for Economic and Social Rights (CESR) and as a legal adviser to the Independent Shuar Federation of Ecuador (FIPSE) and to the Secoya Indigenous Organization of Ecuador (OISE).

MAHBUBUL KARIM, 1994 Bangladesh Advocacy Fellow, is Senior Vice President of Proshika and former Head of the Institute for Development Policy Analysis and Advocacy (IDPAA) at Proshika. Proshika conducts an extensive and intensive participatory sustainable development process through empowerment of the poor. IDPAA provides systematic advocacy interventions for the creation of a macro-policy environment committed to the alleviation of poverty in Bangladesh. Contact Mr. Karim at Proshika via e-mail, *mkarim@proshika.bdonline.com* or via fax at (880-2) 805-811.

WARREN A. KRAFCHIK is Manager of the Budget Information Service (BIS) at the Institute for Democracy in South Africa (Idasa). Idasa is committed to promoting a sustainable democracy in South Africa by building democratic institutions, educating citizens, and advocating social justice. Contact Mr. Krafchik at Idasa via e-mail, *warren@idasact.org.za* or via web at *http://www.idasa.org.za* or via fax at (27-21) 462-0162.

GLADYS SONTO KUDJOE, 1996 South Africa Advocacy Fellow, is currently a Director in the Department of Foreign Affairs in South Africa. Previously, Ms. Kudjoe was a Research Consultant and Deputy CEO for the National Institute for Public Interest Law and Research (NIPILAR). NIPILAR was established in 1986 as a Black-led, anti-apartheid organization that provides legal assistance to individuals and community organizations adversely affected by apartheid laws, policies, and practices. More recently, NIPILAR has focused on customary law and juvenile justice in rural areas. Contact Ms. Kudjoe via e-mail at *nipilar@wn.apc.org* and via fax at (27-12) 328-5831.

ULKA MAHAJAN, 1996 India Advocacy Fellow, worked for five years with Samarthan, an advocacy group working in Maharashtra, India. Contact Samarthan via e-mail at *vsansad@bom3.vsnl.net.in* or via fax at (91-22) 343-7291.

MADHUSUDAN MISTRY, 1989 India Advocacy Fellow, is Director of Patheya, a center for budget analysis started by Developing Initiatives for Social and Human Action (DISHA). Contact Mr. Mistry, DISHA, and Patheya via e-mail at *disha@adl.vsnl.net* and via fax at (91-79) 755-6782.

VIVEK PANDIT, 1990 India Advocacy Fellow, is co-founder of Vidhayak Sansad and Shramajeevi Sanghatana, Director of Samarthan, and Secretary of the National Centre for Advocacy Studies. A human rights activist since his student days, Vivek has been instrumental in the release of bonded laborers, organizing the rural poor, and setting up organizations with a strong orientation toward strengthening human rights movements. Contact Mr. Pandit and Vidhayak Sansad via e-mail at *vsansad@bom3.vsnl.net.in* and via fax at (91-22) 343-7291.

SOFÍA QUINTERO, 1994 US Leadership Fellow and Advocacy Institute Board Member, is Director of Community Training and Support at the National Center for Schools and Communities. As a community organizer and activist, Sofía also works with Sista II Sista, a collective working toward the holistic development of young women of color between ages thirteen and eighteen; the multicultural Organizing Support Center in New York City; the Brecht Forum; and the North Star Fund. Contact Ms. Quintero via e-mail at *poderlatina@hotmail.com* and via fax at (212) 636-6033.

JOHN SAMUEL, 1995 India Advocacy Fellow, is the Executive Director of the National Centre for Advocacy Studies (NCAS). NCAS is a social change resource center working with social action groups, public interest professionals, and citizens all over South Asia. He is also Honorable Coordinator of INASIA, a social change networking initiative of activists, writers, and journalists in fifteen Asian countries. Contact Mr. Samuel at NCAS via e-mail at *ncas@wmi.co.in* and via fax at (91-212) 346-460.

SREY CHANTHY, case writer of the Cambodian land-law case study, is a Cambodian consultant with expertise in agronomy, agricultural policy, and rural development in Cambodia. He has prepared reports for numerous Cambodian and international development agencies, including the Asia Development Bank, UNDP, and Cambodian ministries.

KAREN WATSON, 1993 US Leadership Fellow and Advocacy Institute Board Member, is the Executive Director of the Positive Action Committee (PAC). Formed in 1988, PAC focuses on reforming the treatment of African American and low-income students in the public school system. Contact Ms. Watson and PAC via fax at (912) 564-0097.

ADÈLE WILDSCHUT, 1995 South Africa Advocacy Fellow, is the former Director of the Centre for Rural Legal Studies and now provides management consultancy services to the voluntary sector. The Centre addresses the need for legal intervention and policy formulation on labor and land rights in rural areas by researching the experiences of disadvantaged people, formulating possible solutions, and facilitat-

ing dialogue between major actors in the agricultural sector. Contact Ms. Wildschut via e-mail at *dushi@iafrica.com* or via fax at (27-21) 696-4348 and the Centre for Rural Legal Studies via e-mail at *rulegstu@iafrica.com* or via fax at (27-21) 886-5076.

MOHAMMAD ZAKARIA, 1994 Bangladesh Advocacy Fellow, is Executive Director of Gana Gabeshana o Unnayan Foundation (GoUF—the Participatory Research and Development Foundation). GoUF works in southwestern Bangladesh to alleviate poverty and promote grassroots democracy. Contact Mr. Zakaria via e-mail at *zakaria@citecho.net* and via fax at (880-2) 815-962.

JOHN ZIPPERT, case writer of the US Black-farmer case study, is Director of Programs with the Federation of Southern Cooperatives and was an active participant in many of the events described in his case study. He has participated as an expert witness in numerous government investigative commissions on the impact of racism on Black farmers. Mr. Zippert is the editor of the *Green County Democrat,* one of the few independent weekly newspapers in Alabama.

Introduction

In today's increasingly interconnected and "globalized" world, the struggle to create just societies has taken on new dimensions. Communities around the world are affected by decisions made in distant places by often unknown and powerful actors. More and more, grassroots groups and development organizations are going beyond direct development and service work and engaging in advocacy to confront underlying inequities in their communities, in their countries, and on a global level.

Today more than ever, advocacy resonates around the world. But questions abound: What is advocacy? What is distinct about *social justice* advocacy? How is it connected to civil society? Do advocates in the global South have a distinct perspective? Are common understandings shared by Southern and Northern activists? What insights, wisdom, experiences, and lessons learned can be shared across borders and contexts?

Advocacy for Social Justice: A Global Action and Reflection Guide poses these questions. In response, we offer a range of perspectives and experiences from around the world to better understand the dynamic processes of social justice advocacy.

Advocacy Learning Initiative

Advocacy for Social Justice is the result of the Advocacy Learning Initiative, a three-year collaboration between the Advocacy Institute and Oxfam America, respectively, a not-for-profit advocacy-capacity-building organization and a not-for-profit development agency. The partnership builds on our shared commitments:

- We share core values and a vision of a just, equitable world that is committed to peace, democracy, justice, and respect for human rights and dignity.

- We are part of extended networks of justice and equality advocates working for change at the grassroots, national, and international levels. The Advocacy Institute works with advocates, leaders, and social change agents in Bangladesh, India, Namibia, Nepal, South Africa, the United States, and other emerging or fragile democracies in Africa, Asia, and Europe. Oxfam America works with grassroots and development nongovernmental organizations in thirty countries in Asia, Africa, Latin America and the Caribbean, and the United States.

- We are "learning organizations" committed to ongoing reflection and learning about our own work and that of our partners and colleagues.

Our partners and colleagues work in rapidly changing contexts. Many countries have recently overcome repressive, antidemocratic governments or are emerging from conflict. Too many must continue to battle against hostile environments.

Regardless of differences in their specific political, economic, social, and historical contexts, our colleagues share many things in common:

- They work with the poor and other marginalized peoples to improve daily lives, to preserve dignity, and to facilitate empowerment, self-reliance, and civic participation.

- They work with limited financial resources and, despite the related constraints and tensions, invariably make a little go a long way.

- They challenge existing power dynamics and the laws, policies, and behaviors that hold them in place. The differences that oppress—race, gender, class, caste, and others—are under ongoing attack.

- In challenging power relationships, they often face risks to their lives and livelihoods. Yet these risks do not dampen their voices, determination, courage, hope, energy, and resilience.

- Increasingly, their lives are affected by forces and decisions that are made outside their local, regional, and national contexts, requiring them to work simultaneously on multiple levels.

- Some work within societies that follow democratic processes and some do not. Yet all struggle to foster accountability within government and civil society and to raise issues that fundamentally affect people's lives.

- The actions they take fill a spectrum from coordinated efforts and expected outcomes at one end, to chance opportunities and surprises at the other. In all cases, they are guided by a vision of a better society.

We believe that much can be learned from reflecting on the efforts of these social justice advocates. We know that one book will never capture all, or even most, of the lessons. Learning and reflection always continue. But it is important to share what we have learned so advocates can become more effective in setting or carrying out a public agenda that reflects justice.

To foster ongoing learning about social justice advocacy, *Advocacy for Social Justice* seeks to

- Celebrate the experiences of our partners and colleagues, by reflecting on what works, what doesn't, and why.

- Share insights from advocates around the world to broaden and deepen understandings of advocacy.

- Strengthen the capacity of grassroots and development organizations to advocate for constructive change.

- Build regional and international linkages, momentum, and energy to strengthen and carry movements forward.

Overview

Advocacy for Social Justice includes:

- *Part I: Reflections on Advocacy.* David Cohen, Advocacy Institute co-founder and Co-Director, reflects on the institute's capacity-building work and synthesizes understandings about advocacy. His reflections are enriched by seven brief cases by Advocacy Institute alumni and colleagues from Bangladesh, India, South Africa, and the United States.

- *Part II: Advocacy Skills.* Rosa de la Vega, Advocacy Institute Coordinator of Capacity-Building Programs, draws from the institute's capacity-building curriculum to present one model for strategy development and to discuss common advocacy skills: collaboration, using information and research, message development, and message delivery, including working with the mass media and lobbying. Her writing is enriched by five brief cases by Advocacy Institute alumni from Bangladesh, India, South Africa, and the United States, as well as other examples.

- *Part III: Advocacy Case Studies.* Gabrielle Watson, Oxfam America Advocacy Research Project Manager, together with research collaborators and Oxfam partner organizations, provides in-depth documentation and analysis of six advocacy experiences. The cases tell how people have organized to combat violence against women in Senegal, to fight racism in the United States, to defend human rights in Guatemala, to reform the land law in Cambodia, to stop oil companies from polluting the Ecuadorian Amazon, and to fight for debt relief for the poorest developing countries, principally in Washington, D.C. The conclusion synthesizes lessons running across the six cases and presents a framework for evaluating social justice advocacy work.

- *Part IV: Advocacy Resource Directory.* Gabrielle Watson, with Angela Orlando, Jennifer Shea, and Karin Lockwood, presents concise descriptions and contact information for 272 advocacy support organizations from Africa, Asia, Europe, Latin America, the Middle East, and North America. The directory is a global "clearinghouse" for grassroots groups to find advocacy support that meets their strategy development, funding, networking, and policy analysis needs.

- *Companion Advocacy for Social Justice Web Page.* The directory and other materials from the book also appear on the ALI (Advocacy Learning Initiative) web page launched in 2001. The web version of the directory is significantly expanded from the print version and offers a searchable database that includes full organizational descriptions as reported by the organizations themselves as well as annotated listing of over 350 printed and electronic resources. The *Advocacy for Social Justice* web page can be reached from the Advocacy Institute and Oxfam America websites, at *www.advocacy.org* and *www.oxfamamerica.org*.

Part I

Reflections on Advocacy

David Cohen

Introduction to Part I

What is advocacy? How can it serve the needs of social justice advocates—needs that are often unrecognized by others in society?

In Part I of *Advocacy for Social Justice,* I address these questions by reflecting on my own experiences as an advocate and facilitator and by drawing on the experiences of my colleagues. My reflections are interspersed with seven brief cases contributed by Advocacy Institute alumni and colleagues.

A Personal Perspective

From workshops and seminars in which I have participated, I have learned that people expect to hear about a speaker's core beliefs and experiences. What does the speaker bring to the discussion? In India and Bangladesh, people might ask, "What is your perspective?" In South Africa, "What is your ideology?" In the United States, "Who are you and what are you fighting for?" Whatever the orientation, it is only fair to learn what perspectives and ideology I bring to this writing.

I am not value-neutral. I have spent my adult life working as an advocate, organizer, lobbyist, and strategist on major social justice and political reform issues in the United States. Starting in the early 1960s, these issues have included civil rights, anti-poverty, ending congressional support for the Vietnam War, and reforming political processes by ending abuses of power and the corrupting influence of money on American politics. From 1975 to 1981, I served as President of Common Cause, the largest US voluntary membership organization working on issues of government accountability and abuse of power. After that, I formed a coalition of professionals—doctors, scientists, lawyers, and social workers—to use their expertise and clout to address the threats stemming from nuclear arms. I have also carved out a role as a pro bono counselor to many public interest groups.

In 1985, I co-founded the Advocacy Institute. Since its doors opened, the Advocacy Institute has been dedicated to strengthening the capacity of justice advocates

and movements to influence and change public policy. Until now, our main model for strengthening advocacy capacity has been the Fellows Program, a two- to four-week advanced leadership program for seasoned advocates and community-based leaders. The Fellows Program can be differentiated from a typical "training" program in two ways. First, we recognize there is no single right definition or approach to advocacy, and our methodology respects and affirms the rich diversity of advocacy experiences and perspectives. Second, we sustain ongoing relationship building between the alumni and the institute, and among the alumni.

In my role as facilitator, I counsel social justice leaders on their efforts to gain support for their public agendas. Our program emphasizes understanding the elements of advocacy and the place of people-centered organizing, civil society, and engaging policy-making systems in gaining their objectives.

Through the Fellows Program and other advocacy-capacity-strengthening work, my colleagues and I have been privileged to work with social justice leaders from Asia (Bangladesh, India, Indonesia, Nepal, the Philippines), Africa (Angola, Botswana, Ghana, Kenya, Malawi, Mozambique, Namibia, Senegal, South Africa, Uganda, Zimbabwe), the Middle East (Egypt, Israel, Palestine), central and eastern Europe (Bosnia-Herzegovina, Bulgaria, Croatia, Hungary, Macedonia, Romania, Russia, Serbia, Slovakia, Ukraine), and the Americas (Cuba, the United States).

I have drawn on these experiences, as well as extensive reading from many countries, to write this first part of *Advocacy for Social Justice.* As with all of the institute's work, this part also draws on firsthand stories, insights, and innovations. Seven brief cases—contributed by Advocacy Institute alumni and colleagues from Bangladesh, India, South Africa, and the United States—are interspersed throughout this part.

These reflections are only a beginning. They will take on new dimensions as you and others engage with, challenge, and use the ideas alongside your own experiences and understanding.

3

What We Have Learned: Value in Getting Started

In the Advocacy Institute's work with groups around the world, we have learned that people are ready to take action, to jump right in and use the tools of advocacy to bring about change. This is particularly true when they have the opportunity to participate and engage with their public institutions through organized actions that they believe will make a difference in their lives. Their practical actions are supported by ennobling visions. Even if not fully articulated, their visions of a future with justice—tempered by the need to overcome real obstacles—inspire action.

There is value in getting started. Nothing teaches more than experience, whether it is new skills being learned or confidence built to overcome the risks inherent in social change. When getting started, people must avoid becoming paralyzed by the need for comprehensive, systemic change. One rarely goes from "what is" to "what should be" in a single leap. Except in those rare times when revolution occurs (with its risk of violence and death), changes are rarely sweeping and comprehensive. Rather, they are realized through a long-term, incremental process that keeps sight of a larger vision.

Small changes and ongoing activities are vital. They can lead people to take action, to organize themselves, to shape ideas and policy demands, and to engage with public institutions. Such actions may relate to development that goes beyond alleviating poverty or affecting social structures, including the family. Protest can lead to facing issues that otherwise might be ignored. Examples abound of people finding ways to intervene at micro-levels in the places where they live and work. They neither wait for comprehensive, sweeping change nor are deterred by large institutions that are unresponsive and seemingly impenetrable.

Organized actions have value. Even if policy change is not fully understood or achieved, organized actions that engage decision-making bodies are a critical part of advocacy and influencing outcomes.

The following are illustrations of factors that our colleagues have seen change people's lives:

- Microcredit for women has changed relationships within families. Working in a group, negotiating a loan, and participating in repayment plans have resulted in improvements in women's standing in the community. The process creates a respect that may not have previously been present in the eyes of children. It can lead to husbands recognizing their wives as authority figures.

- Interventions that enable people to test their drinking water or treat diarrhea have given them a sense of their own power to improve their lives. They go on to meet with public officials to demand an end to unsafe drinking water.

- Resistance in one part of the world has inspired people in other parts. The anti-apartheid boycott led US educational, religious, and philanthropic institutions to divest themselves of stock holdings in South African companies. In turn, local and state government pension funds divested. The practical, effective idea has taken new forms: activists have pressured cities not to invest public funds with arms dealers and human rights abusers.

By themselves, such short-term steps do not create long-term change. They must be linked together, within countries and across borders. Doing so requires discipline, focus, and strategy.

Overview of Part I

To help advocates develop the necessary discipline, focus, and strategy, Part I aims to:

- Build understanding of advocacy within one's own political, economic, and social contexts.

- Strengthen leadership and people-centered movements.

- Develop the attitudes, knowledge, and skills needed to create long-term change.

- Build understanding of points of intervention for social justice advocacy.

Part I is written in three chapters:

- *Chapter 1—Advocacy: Its Many Faces and a Common Understanding.* Drawing from the Advocacy Institute's work with social justice advocates in South Asia, southern Africa, central and eastern Europe, the United States, and elsewhere, a working definition and characteristics of advocacy are shared.

- *Chapter 2—Lessons from Social Movement Advocacy.* Lessons about the nature of change, public problem-solving processes, and sustaining individuals, organizations, and movements are drawn from the Advocacy Institute's work.

- *Chapter 3—Advocacy in the Twenty-First Century.* Two factors affecting the modern context for advocacy—political liberalization and democratization, and economic liberalization and globalization—are discussed, along with common points of intervention drawn from our colleagues' experiences.

How to Use Part I

These writings present a synthesis of my learning as an advocate, organizer, lobbyist, strategist, and Advocacy Institute facilitator. Much is drawn from the specific experiences of our Advocacy and Leadership Fellows in Bangladesh, India, Namibia, South Africa, and the United States.

To help you reflect on your own experiences and to draw lessons that can be applied to your particular context, ask yourself the following questions as you read:

- Does this resonate with my own experiences and contexts? Do some parts resonate more than others? Which parts?

- Why or why not?

- Would I define some words and concepts differently? How?

- What new lessons or insights have I gained?

- What can I apply to my own social change work? How?

Chapter 1

Advocacy: Its Many Faces and a Common Understanding

What is advocacy? What makes social justice and social movement advocacy distinctive?

Part I discusses a working definition of advocacy, drawn from the experiences of the Advocacy Institute's colleagues around the world.

Social Justice Advocacy: Creating a Value-Based Definition

Experience shows that advocacy is not limited to the voices of virtue or social justice. Ideologues of all persuasions advocate. The changes they seek can bring good or harm to people's lives. Social justice advocates, then, have a special challenge—to differentiate the advocacy that they do in a way that resonates with their experiences and values.

To understand social justice advocacy requires stripping it bare. Here is one definition of *value-neutral advocacy:*

> *Advocacy is the pursuit of influencing outcomes— including public-policy and resource-allocation decisions within political, economic, and social systems and institutions—that directly affect people's lives.*

Even if technically true, this definition has serious limitations for social justice advocates. In theory, the list of those who advocate has no bounds. A society should hear from a plurality of interests—economic, ethnic, occupational, geographic, ideological, and so on. In reality, when decisions are made, many voices are left out and their issues are never considered.

Modern history offers many examples of the consequences faced by ordinary people:

• *Contemporary colonialism*, in which international financial institutions, like the World Bank and International Monetary Fund (IMF), and multinational corporations make decisions that over-

shadow the decisions made at the national level, thereby weakening national sovereignty and the ability of governments to meet the needs of their people.

• *The breakdown of society*—during periods of religious or ethnic violence, when the state uses non-state agents to infiltrate and spy on groups, when the state is so strong that it goes unchecked, when the state is too weak to protect people from harm or help improve their lives, when any sense of mutual responsibility fails. The breakdown of society can have many sources:

– *Laws* such as apartheid, which excommunicated Black South Africans from humankind.

– *Abusive behavior by institutions*, such as the government crackdown on peaceful protesters in Tiananmen Square in 1989.

– *Harassment and threats* to advocates' lives and safety by the state's apparatus—the military, police—or by holders of social power whose behavior is emboldened by government inaction.

– *Second-class citizenship*, patterns of exclusion, and discrimination that deny citizens their full political, economic, and social rights and try to keep people submissive.

– *Disrespect for a person's humanity* by corporations that treat workers like animals, exploiting them for low wages and creating unsafe working conditions with the permission, and even approval, of the state.

– *Disrespect for a person's or community's identity* or expression of their culture—such as birth language, race, rituals, celebrations, heroes, literature, symbols. Whether it is ridicule through

7

negative stereotypes or other actions, it makes people feel invisible, ignored, and devalued.

Whatever the source of society's breakdown, the result often brings about violence and loss of dignity.

From this reality of "what is," social justice advocates around the world have created different visions of "what should be" in a just, decent society. It is a society that:

- *Respects and protects human rights.* (A broad human rights framework is presented in Part III.)

- *Respects and preserves the dignity of all people*, regardless of differences.

- *Eradicates cruelty by protecting people* from abuse, violence, and humiliation caused by communities and institutions—including the government, international financial institutions, and multinational corporations.

- *Provides public space for people to challenge* unjust behaviors.

- *Engages people in decision-making* processes that affect their lives. People's participation should include:

  - Ratifying decisions, either formally or without protest, provided that opportunities for protest exist.

  - Visioning and planning solutions to issues that affect their lives in basic ways, such as building a road, cleaning a waterway, where to locate a large waste facility, repairing a school building, or modernizing a hospital for birth deliveries.

  - Assessing and providing feedback on programs that are initiated, indicating which ones work and should be continued and replicated and which ones do not and should be altered.

- *Protects people from risk and harassment* when they participate and exercise their rights.

- *Fixes responsibility on society's powerful institutions*, both within and outside of government, to protect people from harm and help improve their lives.

To make a just and decent society a reality, social justice advocates must meet the ongoing challenge of how to be heard so that those who hold power listen and respond. Otherwise, ideas and issues will not be addressed, necessary changes will not be created, and society will not be transformed.

A definition of *social justice advocacy*, then, must embrace power relationships, people's participation, and a vision of a just, decent society. Here is one working definition:

> *Advocacy is the pursuit of influencing outcomes— including public-policy and resource-allocation decisions within political, economic, and social systems and institutions—that directly affect people's lives.*
>
> *Advocacy consists of organized efforts and actions based on the reality of "what is." These organized actions seek to highlight critical issues that have been ignored and submerged, to influence public attitudes, and to enact and implement laws and public policies so that visions of "what should be" in a just, decent society become a reality. Human rights—political, economic, and social—is an overarching framework for these visions. Advocacy organizations draw their strength from and are accountable to people—their members, constituents, and/or members of affected groups.*
>
> *Advocacy has purposeful results: to enable social justice advocates to gain access and voice in the decision making of relevant institutions; to change the power relationships between these institutions and the people affected by their decisions, thereby changing the institutions themselves; and to result in a clear improvement in people's lives.*

Advocacy in Action

The specific strategies, points of intervention, and actions taken will vary based on each social justice advocate's political, economic, and social context. They may be different depending on:

- What the political space allows.

- Whether the setting is local, national, regional, or international.

- Whether the issue is micro or macro.

- Whether the issue is one of obvious human rights or rights not yet recognized by all.

In the Advocacy Institute's experience, when advocates from different contexts discuss and reflect on their experiences, they find commonalities that in no way diminish the distinctiveness of their local cultures. Across cultures, our colleagues:

- Resist and challenge the status quo, often using protest to find ways to engage governance institutions (when opportunities for protest exist).

- Raise critical issues—such as inequality—that otherwise would be avoided by those in power. In doing so, they begin to set a public agenda that reflects their goals and priorities.

- Place issue and policy demands on political and policy-making systems—whether they are strong or decaying—because those systems are not responding to people's needs.

- Ask others—individuals, groups, and institutions—to act and do something that can help create positive change.

- Initiate action and innovate policy solutions.

- Create space for public argument and advocacy.

- Actively engage members, supporters, and affected constituencies in advocacy efforts, thereby continually developing their skills and understanding and strengthening future efforts.

When asked to describe their efforts as a whole, our colleagues describe advocacy that takes one or more forms:

- *Ideological advocacy.* Groups push to make their set of beliefs and values dominant, battling others in the streets, in the halls of decision-making bodies, and in electoral campaigns. Those who have engaged in struggle—the war for freedom in Bangladesh, ending totalitarianism in the USSR and the countries it dominated, ending colonialism in Africa, Asia, the Middle East, and Latin America, poor people's struggles everywhere—recognize that total commitment and possible risk to security and life are required.

  Critics of ideological advocacy argue that it can become narrow in perspective and can exclude people, focusing on "enemies" rather than building support among "unlikely allies." Also, broad beliefs and values may not be translated into specific issue or policy battles.

- *Mass advocacy.* Public actions—petitions, protests, demonstrations, sit-ins, nonviolent civil disobedience—by large groups of people are used to air major grievances, to confront power holders, and to find ways to engage different decision-making systems. Mass participation and mobilization are essential elements.

  Critics of mass advocacy argue that such actions may influence specific situations but usually do not create comprehensive or systemic change. Also, some mass movements can be dominated by a single charismatic leader who may not encourage others to assume leadership roles. The result is a movement that is unable to sustain itself over the long term.

- *Interest-group advocacy.* Groups organize around a specific set of issues and place demands on the system, through lobbying or other persuasion efforts.

  Critics of interest-group advocacy argue that decision makers only listen to those who are organized and skilled at presenting arguments and working within the system. Such organization and skill often take money, meaning that people who are poor, near-poor, or historically underrepresented—women, children, racial and ethnic minorities—are often left out.

- *Bureaucratic advocacy.* Researchers, economists, and consultants from "think tanks" and universities try to influence bureaucrats and decision makers within the system. They are allowed access to present their findings and conclusions because they may be considered "experts." Official decisions are vetted through slow, deliberative processes and, when they are reached, are accepted as legitimate by many sectors of society.

  Critics of bureaucratic advocacy argue that it puts little value on public participation or the voices of grassroots and community-based nongovernmental organizations (NGOs), who are not considered experts despite their direct experience with the issues being addressed. Also, bureaucratic advocacy rarely responds quickly to crises or opportunities.

Taken alone, each form has both strengths and limitations. *Social justice advocacy*, in order to draw on the strengths—and avoid the limitations—of each, must:

- *Be people- and community-centered,* drawing on their experiences to shape objectives and finding ways to amplify their knowledge and expertise so they are heard by decision makers.

- *Build relationships* with officials, experts, and other parts of civil society to foster support for its goals.

- *Use organized mass action to find ways to engage decision-making systems,* but not limit itself to mass action.

- *Translate protest into policy demands for specific institutional change,* or move "from protest to politics," in the words of Bayard Rustin, a leading strategist of the US civil rights movement in the 1950s and 1960s.

The following section shares lessons about how to make operational a value-based definition of social movement advocacy toward a just, decent society.

Chapter 2

Lessons from Social Movement Advocacy

The Advocacy Institute finds advocates from all parts of the world who want to discuss and understand social movements from other countries. This is more than politeness. These advocates have a deep interest in history and making connections between others' struggles and their own.

All over the world, powerful social movements have pushed for change in the last half of the twentieth century and at the beginning of the twenty-first century. Whether we examine the US civil rights movement from the 1950s and 1960s, the fall of apartheid in South Africa in the mid-1990s, or the women's movement today, many core lessons can be drawn from social movements:

1. Drawing from one's own sources of power creates change.

2. People must be prepared to face immediate threats and risks that come from social change.

3. People-centered advocacy has a powerful result.

4. Advocates must understand the cycles of change to find points of intervention.

5. To build public support, advocates must engage in public argument.

6. Free spaces are critical for engaging in public argument and building public judgment.

7. Advocates must engage policy-making systems.

8. Stories provide a tremendous source of power—to both the narrator and those listening.

9. Innovation is born in innovative, learning organizations.

10. Effective leadership is a critical part of strengthening movements for the long term.

11. Effective social movements are built by well-rounded teams of storytellers, organizers, and "experts" alike.

12. It is easier to destroy a movement than to build one.

These lessons—about the nature of change, public problem-solving processes, and sustaining individuals, organizations, and movements—reflect the multiple dimensions of the Advocacy Institute's capacity-building work. Each lesson is discussed in the following sections.

Lesson 1:
Drawing from One's Own Sources of Power Creates Change

Social justice advocates, with good cause, rarely believe that they have a dominant hand in power relationships. Whether the change sought is transformative and systemic or incremental, one of public policy or public attitudes, nearly every issue is affected by unequal power relationships between advocates and decision makers.

Yet there are many accounts in which those with seemingly less power have overcome tremendous odds to thwart those with greater power—greater resources, experience, and access. Whether the leaders are historic (like Gandhi-ji or Reverend Martin Luther King Jr.) or anonymous at the start (like Rosa Parks), they knew that understanding power dynamics mattered.

Power can be defined as the "ability to create whatever effect is desired (change or status quo), especially in the face of opposition." Power takes different forms:

- *Political.* The ability to control, exercise authority over, or influence the institutions through which laws are made and implemented. For political power to be lasting, it must shape public judgment so it supports the laws. (Public judgment is discussed in Lesson 5.) Gandhi-ji, King, and Parks all understood that oppressive power ultimately loses its legitimacy when it can no longer claim to have the consent of the governed.

- *Economic.* The ability to control the means and place of production, including work conditions and wages.

- *Social.* The ability to control or influence people, especially in hierarchical relationships in family and other social contexts.

In an advocacy context, three characteristics of power are critical to understand:

- Power is a matter of degree. It can be absolute, or shared and limited. Social justice advocacy seeks to share the power to make decisions that will affect people's lives.

- Power changes. It is dynamic, always shifting—not static. Just because someone has power over you today, it does not mean they will have power over you tomorrow. Social justice advocates know from experience that power is rarely given or yielded. It must be won through resistance and struggle.

- Not all power relies on threats, coercion, command, or greater amounts of money. Social justice advocates draw tremendous strength from:

  - Strategic action that engages public problem-solving processes, defines and frames issues, fixes responsibility, and creates solutions.

  - Innovation, invention, and initiation.

  - Vision, commitment, and intensity.

  - Above all, people—their knowledge, experiences, and stories.

  - These sources of power can all rend asunder traditional measures of power.

Lesson 2:
People Must Be Prepared to Face Immediate Threats and Risks That Come from Social Change

In too many Southern and Northern societies, social change advocates face constant risk to their lives, families, and communities. People who do not want to lose their positions of power have fought change violently. Too many state authorities have neither the will nor strength to protect advocates' lives or choose to take part in intimidation and abuse. Even in countries with well-established democratic practices, including the United States, marginalized groups often face threats to essential liberties, including the right to be left alone. Whatever form risks take, the effect is the same: to silence people's voices.

When advocating for social change, some level of risk is inevitable. Yet history—from the US civil rights movement to the anti-apartheid movement in South Africa—tells us that people who prepare for risks are far less intimidated by threats and even violence. Their willingness to stand up and not be silenced is a tremendous source of power.

Any organization that wants to create change must directly tackle the issue of risk but not be paralyzed by it. Organizations must:

- Assess potential harm that may come from action.

- Help people prepare if they choose to take calculated risks.

- Protect them as best as possible when they do.

(Part II poses questions to help advocates do such assessment.)

Lesson 3:
People-Centered Advocacy Has a Powerful Result

So often when decisions are made, many voices are left out. Ordinary people must overcome isolation and bridge the gap between their authentic voices and the world of "experts" and officials. People-centered advocacy is fundamental to this process. Two principles are essential:

- *Ordinary people know what they need and want.* As Brazilian popular educator Paulo Freire taught us, ordinary people are often the best sources of knowledge about how a problem influences their lives and how possible solutions might work. Their experiences and knowledge need to be heard and respected by decision makers.

- *Learning about and participating in public life builds confidence* and facilitates the empowerment of people who don't believe change is possible. In many ways, these changes can be the most profound and lasting.

Social justice advocates can play a role in helping amplify other people's voices, as well as organizing people so they become their own confident advocates. In practice, this means creating opportunities for ordinary people to:

- *Define their own issues, objectives, and strategies based on their needs and wants.* Starting points may be creating a vision of "what should be," assessing the current reality of "what is," and identifying potential issues for action. The issues and objectives that emerge often combine the personal and the political. This may mean challenging the government and the political process, the effects of globalization and rapid changes on daily lives, and many other aspects of society—existing power dynamics within families, dominant ideology, personal social attitudes, and lifestyle and workplace issues.

- *Identify commonalities within groups and communities that may be divided by gender, race, class, and other differences.* Time and safe space are needed for people to understand—and even empathize with—perspectives different from their own and to evaluate alternative solutions that may affect different groups differently.

- *Work toward their goals by participating in many parts of an advocacy effort.* These may include leadership, strategy development, building relationships with experts and allies, meeting with officials and others in the community, and participating in protests and demonstrations.

- *Build their confidence to ask something of others—* individuals, groups, institutions, and decision makers.

- *Learn by doing, from both successes and mistakes.* Over time, people will develop the necessary skills, discipline, and deep understanding of the complex, often mysterious ways in which the political process works.

Even if a social justice advocacy organization is not membership-based, it must work to stay connected with and accountable to the people whose interests are being served. To make sure that an organization maintains significant relationships with its members, constituents, or those in affected groups, it needs to continuously ask itself three questions:

- Does it give voice to people whose voices are not fully heard?

- Does it enable and motivate people to become actively involved in the advocacy process?

- Does it take time to learn from the experiences of its members, constituents, or those in affected groups?

In creating significant relationships between advocacy organizations and ordinary people, people-centered advocacy not only helps amplify the voices that are seldom heard but also begins to transform existing power dynamics that determine who can be an "advocate" in the first place.

People-Centered Advocacy in India, John Samuel

Contributed by John Samuel, 1995 India Advocacy Fellow and Executive Director of the National Centre for Advocacy Studies (NCAS), Pune, India. Excerpted from his essay "Public Advocacy in the Indian Context," Straight-Talk *(July 1999).*

Although "advocacy" is used widely in social change and development discourse, it is difficult to clarify the term because it is often used to describe a wide range of activities, such as lobbying, public interest litigation, civil disobedience, public relations, and market research. Advocacy usually includes one or more of these, and thinking that one element constitutes all of public advocacy is to miss the forest for the trees.

Here, the attempt to define advocacy is based primarily on the perspective of many politically oriented social action groups and social change agents in India.

Among other things, public advocacy is a value-driven, people-centered political process. In a liberal democratic framework, public policies play a very important role in determining the directions of social justice, political and civil liberties, and the long-term interests of the environment and people at large. However, public-policy formulation usually falls to the dominant group. To effectively influence public policies, we have to question and shift existing unequal power relations in favor of the poor, the voiceless, and others who have historically been left out.

To be effective and efficient, people-centered advocacy needs to:

- *Empower those who have less conventional economic, social, or political power,* using grassroots organizing and mobilization as a means of awareness and assertion of the rights and social responsibilities of citizens.

- *Resist unequal power relations* (like patriarchy) at every level: from personal to public, and from family to governance. The challenge for public advocacy groups is to accomplish this using our meager financial, institutional, and human resources. To effectively influence government or corporate power structures, public advocacy can draw on five major sources that cost nothing:

  – The power of people or citizens.

  – The power of direct grassroots experience or linkages.

  – The power of information and knowledge.

  – The power of constitutional guarantees.

  – The power of moral convictions.

- *Bridge micro-level activism and macro-level policy initiatives.* Public advocacy initiatives that are practiced only at the macro-level run the risk that a set of urban elites, equipped with information and skills, will take over the voice of the marginalized. Public advocacy groups must make sure they are continually sensitive to the grassroots situation and organically bridge the gap between citizens and policy change.

  Moreover, grassroots organizing and mobilization lend credibility, legitimacy, and crucial bargaining power to public advocacy. In the Indian context, grassroots support and constituency are the most important factors that determine the credibility of the lobbyist—not his or her professional background or expertise. Activists with an adequate level of expertise and mass support have proven to be better lobbyists than professional experts. Grassroots mobilization and advocacy must work together if we are to achieve real progress at the macro-level.

Lesson 4:
Advocates Must Understand the Cycles of Change to Find Points of Intervention

Three cycles of change affect all advocacy efforts:

- Problem-solving cycle.

- Issue life cycle.

- Organizational life cycle.

By understanding each one and how they interact, advocates can better assess what actions to take at a given moment.

Problem-Solving Cycle

Whatever the problem, big or small, public or private, people go through stages trying to find a solution. These stages can be described generically:

- People experience a problem and decide something needs to change.

- Alternative solutions are considered, and one is chosen for identified reasons.

- The solution is implemented, and the necessary change happens.

This model is too simple. Advocates know that so much happens between "people experience a problem" and they "decide something needs to change." For one thing, the people who experience the problem are often not the ones with the power and authority to change it. For another, key decision makers and parts of the general public may actively resist change. To move the issue forward, then, advocates must engage in public argument and build support.

Issue Life Cycle

The challenge is to move an issue forward from discussion to action. To develop a strategic action plan, it is helpful to think about the stages that an issue goes through. While the transition from one stage to another is not always clear, even as an approximation, the issue life cycle has helped advocates learn how to assess their issue, judge organizational capacities that are needed but missing, and move the issue forward to some level of completion.

The following are the stages of an issue life cycle:

- *Birth.* A new demand, issue, idea, or proposal takes form. It is not yet recognized by others. Its proponents need to build support to advance the idea.

- *Childhood.* The issue or idea requires nurturing. Who else will support it? Do they consider it a priority? Will they help formulate policy solutions that won't be dismissed as impractical or too expensive?

- *Adolescence.* The issue or idea advances through the early stages of decision making. It gains champions within influential institutions and among some key decision makers. Others begin to contribute ideas about different paths to the desired result. This generates more interest and strengthens the idea's importance and legitimacy. Conclusive recommendations are not required. In time, differences will be sorted out. Discussion needs to be focused in ways that aren't divisive, but rather advance the issue so a decision will be made.

- *Adulthood.* The issue reaches a resolute decision. It either moves forward, with sufficient detail to make it workable, or it does not.

- *Maturity.* The idea is implemented and monitored and evaluated for effectiveness. What has worked well? What needs improvement?

- *Renewal.* Implementation is evaluated further. Should the program continue? If so, should anything be changed? Can the idea be applied to other issues?

At each stage, an advocacy effort will need different skills, take different actions, and create different roles and responsibilities for an organization's members and constituents. For example:

- *At an issue's birth,* the skill is in defining the issue and its impact on people and communities. Groups may raise the issue through protest or other ways to exert pressure.

- *At childhood,* groups move "from protest to politics," engaging in public argument and generating possible solutions. They may build alliances, work with the media, and analyze policy alternatives.

- *At adolescence,* groups may work inside the corridors of power, negotiating compromises with decision

makers, while exerting steady pressure from outside to maintain political will to take action.

- *At adulthood,* groups may analyze the budget to make sure the final solution has the commitment and resources needed to be effective.

- *At maturity,* groups work closely with their constituents to monitor the solution's impact. They may generate their own data and give feedback to decision makers.

- *At renewal,* groups need to review their progress and determine their next action steps.

Example of an Issue Life Cycle

To see how a policy may move through the issue life cycle, consider the following example:

- *Birth.* An idea takes shape: waive the law school fees for students who commit to becoming public interest practitioners when they graduate. The result would be more experienced lawyers to represent people with limited finances and to help amplify their voices. The idea could be given birth by a judge of a high court, by an experienced lawyer at a national meeting, or by an organization working to strengthen a culture of rights. A successful birth means that the issue is connected to people in other institutions that can help it move forward.

- *Childhood.* To advance the idea, a consortium of law schools and legal clinics conduct a study to show what public interest practice has meant to the professionals and the people they serve.

- *Adolescence.* Questions are teased out: Is the program just a convenient way to get a free law school education, or does it attract people to the law who otherwise could not afford such education? How great is the need for public interest practitioners? Does it help address serious societal problems? If adopted, does it have a chance of giving voice to those who are unheard?

- *Adulthood.* The idea is fleshed out with sufficient operational detail, and the program is adopted.

- *Maturity.* The program is implemented and the results are studied. What has happened to the people who have entered the program? Did the graduates fulfill their promise to serve as public interest practitioners? How has the program influenced their careers? How have people been served?

- *Renewal.* The program has been successful. Can it be adapted to help future teachers, nurses, and doctors who are prepared to spend their time in underserved communities?

Organizational Life Cycle

Should all advocacy groups engage equally in all stages of an issue? Is it the most effective use of a group's limited resources? Does the group have a particular strength?

Many skills and types of action will be needed. Rarely can one group do it all. Identifying which stage an organization is in can help its leaders assess what actions it can take on. The stages of an organization are similar to the stages of an issue life cycle:

- *Birth.* An organization is created and establishes its presence. Founding leaders must recognize that being present at an organization's birth does not mean one owns it permanently. They must help develop the leadership skills of others within the organization.

- *Childhood.* An organization begins to learn new skills and to build a solid, supportive organizational infrastructure. An organization in its childhood—especially one with a base of many motivated people—has great potential that needs to be nurtured by more experienced leaders, organizations, and funders.

- *Adolescence.* An organization becomes willing to experiment, take on more difficult challenges, and take responsibility for its action or inaction. It also needs to be willing to learn from and be mentored by those with more experience.

- *Adulthood.* An organization assumes a greater level of responsibility, taking the lead on an issue even if it forgoes significant credit, taking appropriate risks even if defeat is possible, and nurturing and mentoring organizations in their childhood and adolescence.

- *Maturity.* An organization turns over responsibility to others, shares its wisdom and experiences, and sets an example for personal and organizational renewal.

- *Renewal.* To stay vital, an organization needs to resist the urge to stay comfortable. It may develop a new strategic focus or new organizational leadership.

At each stage, an organization will grow in a number of ways:

- *Leadership.* Is the organization run by a single, charismatic founder? Or is second- and third-generation leadership being developed? Are staff members encouraged to take on greater levels of responsibility? The word "leadership" is used purposefully instead of "leaders." Within an organization and a larger social movement, many roles and talents are needed, all of which cannot and should not be drawn from one person.

- *Organizational infrastructure.* Does the organization have the people resources—staff and/or volunteers—to do the work? Does it have a sound financial base?

- *Skills and capacities.* What are the organization's strengths? What areas could be developed? For example, an organization may be strong in grassroots mobilization and raising awareness about an issue, but may need to improve at strategy development and seizing opportunities.

- *Relationships.* Does the organization have a constituency base? Does it work with other organizations, or compete against them for resources and recognition? Does it have productive relationships with other civil society organizations (CSOs), decision makers, the media, and funders?

- *Experience and confidence.* Is the organization willing to try new things and learn from its mistakes?

These questions can help a group identify its current strengths and—by matching these to the issue's current stage—which roles the group can best play and which skills and capacities it needs to develop.

Lesson 5:
To Build Public Support, Advocates Must Engage in Public Argument

Social justice advocacy goals almost always require public support to move forward. Therefore, public argument must be an essential part of any advocacy effort.

Public argument is about addition: finding ways to bring the unconvinced to your point of view. The phrase "public argument" is used deliberately. Argument organizes the discussion to try to persuade others. In contrast, "debate" polarizes and may intensify opposition from others. "Discussion" leaves many loose ends and lacks the closure needed to advance.

Over time, public argument leads to public judgment (a phrase coined by leading public opinion analyst Daniel Yankelovich). If public judgment is reached, when the time comes for a decision—regardless of which one is made—the public will accept or at least acquiesce to the proposed change, enabling decision makers to act with public permission. Without favorable public judgment, it will be far more difficult to implement changes that may be won and to protect them in the future.

Advocates who sustain relationships with those outside of their immediate communities have a better chance of learning how to influence others and to build public judgment. They need to build relationships with many groups:

- *The community and general public* who share an organization's interests but are not represented by the organization.

- *Like-minded organizations and coalitions* working in the same issue sector, such as education or health.

- *Civil society,* the panoply of organizations and individuals engaged in public life (see "Defining 'Civil Society' from a Social Justice Perspective" for definition).

- *Governance institutions*—local and regional, national and international—that affect people's lives. The multi-level focus is particularly important in the context of economic liberalization and other effects of globalization (discussed in Part III) that, operationally, mean that decision making is no longer confined to a country's borders.

Defining "Civil Society" from a Social Justice Perspective

What is the role of civil society? Who is part of it? Who is not? The answers will vary between countries and even among advocates from the same country. Understanding the idea of civil society and the form it takes in one's own context can help advocates to identify potential allies.

Here is one aspirational, working definition of *civil society:*

Civil society is a panoply of organizations and individuals that engage in public life. Those acting from a social justice perspective engage in public life to help people, groups, and governing institutions meet their mutual responsibilities to the society; to check and balance the power of the state and market; and to work toward making real a vision of a just, decent society.

Civil society includes, among others, nongovernmental organizations (NGOs), community-based organizations (CBOs), professional associations, philanthropic and religious organizations, and both ordinary and elite individuals. Taken as a whole, civil society represents a diversity of identities, issues, and perspectives. It can draw strength from its pluralism and diversity, even though it cannot represent or speak for the interests of all people all of the time, or even some of the time.

Overall, civil society excludes members of the state apparatus—the military, police, bureaucracy, elected officials—political parties, corporations, and donor agencies, such as the World Bank and International Monetary Fund (IMF). However, there is space for individuals from these institutions to engage in public roles that are separate from their work affiliations.

Civil society creates and uses public, free spaces to gather, think, exchange and refine views, organize, and take action. As part of this process, all participants accept debate and disagreement, compromise and negotiation. Participation in free spaces is open and/or representative.

Civil society's strength depends in large part on its genuine autonomy from the state. Civil society organizations (CSOs) and their leadership must be independent of government authorities even as they work to develop professional and public relationships with public officials at all levels of government. People and organizations that participate in civil society should be free from threats and harassment by both public officials and nongovernment "vigilantes" who operate outside the law.

To further understand the diversity within civil society, Larry Diamond in *Developing Democracy* identifies a number of perspectives commonly represented by civil society organizations (CSOs):

- *Civic.* Strengthening the political system's accountability by insisting on transparency and participation and by modeling it within organizations and civil society.

- *Human rights.* Monitoring government agencies at all levels and pushing for the protection and advancement of human rights.

- *Cultural.* Expressing and defending values and beliefs, including those of ethnic, racial, and religious minorities.

- *Social movement.* Giving voice to critical yet un-met public needs, often those affecting women, poor people, indigenous peoples, ethnic minori-ties, people with disabilities, workers, and the environment.

- *Developmental.* Strengthening participation and organization to improve institutions, infrastructure, and quality of life in the community.

- *Informational.* Producing and disseminating public knowledge, ideas, news, and information.

- *Educational.* Learning as an ongoing experience, from early childhood through mature adulthood.

- *Economic.* Producing and marketing, often by small-scale farmers and small-business owners, including street hawkers, vendors, and others in the informal economy.

The working definition presented here is an aspiration. When Advocacy Institute colleagues are asked to describe their civil society—who is included, who is not, who participates, who doesn't but should—they often paint a different picture. For example, a group of 1995 Namibia Advocacy Fellows drew the following diagram that clearly showed NGOs and

CBOs as distant from engaging with the Namibian government:

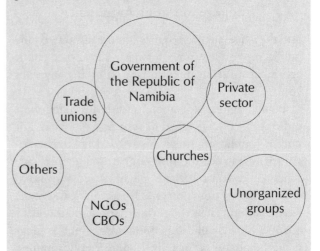

The key is for groups to use an aspirational, working definition of civil society to identify unorganized groups that should be active in civil society, which groups have less power than others, and ways to strengthen participation in public life.

Lesson 6:
Free Spaces Are Critical for Engaging in Public Argument and Building Public Judgment

Relationship building that leads toward public judg-ment benefits from the creation and use of free spaces, so eloquently described by Sara Evans and Harry Boyte.

Across different political contexts, *free spaces* are "public places in the community, between private lives and large-scale institutions," where people come together. In free spaces, people:

- *Organize,* share experiences, and raise issues that would otherwise be avoided.

- *Engage with people who are different* in some ways—constituency, generation, civil society role, and so on—but who share similar interests and may be-come "unlikely allies." This works best when the space is open and diverse and includes ordinary people and elites.

- *Learn to collaborate,* listen attentively, give and take, compromise, negotiate, problem solve, and act in solidarity—rather than succumb to controversy and conflict.

- *Sort through policy priorities and innovate ideas,* strategies, action plans, policies, and programs that will advance a vision of "what should be."

- *Generate demands on the political and policy systems* to challenge existing power relationships.

Free spaces can also be a safe space for decision makers and those affected by impending decisions to candidly discuss policy priorities, differences, and potential areas for agreement. In the United States, many "think tanks" make an effort to provide such space, but important parts of the community are often left out, particularly those that have been historically under-represented. In contrast, the Institute for Development Policy and Analysis (IDPAA) at Proshika has been successful in bringing together different parts of the Bangladesh NGO community to discuss the national budget and poverty alleviation. This method has been used successfully with other issues in many parts of the world.

The use of free spaces helps build many key characteristics of a strong democracy, including:

- A culture of listening.

- A sense of community responsibility.

- A culture of people's legitimate participation in public argument and problem solving.

Free spaces are not limited to organizations, buildings, or formal settings, but can be thought of more broadly as places where people gather to discuss experiences, ideas, and pressing issues. For example:

- Rivers and streams in rural Asia, Africa, and Latin America where women wash clothes have long been places for organizing and creating demands.

- In the US South before the civil rights revolution, beauty shops, barbershops, and pool halls in African American communities were places for studying the US Constitution—a prerequisite for registering to vote.

- In the United States, church basements, public libraries, bookstores, and performance halls are commonly used for community meetings convened by religious, ethnic, civic, neighborhood, women's, worker, and immigrant groups.

Free space can also be virtual, using the mass media or communication technology to span geographic distances. For example:

- The story is often told of villagers gathered around a television to watch a documentary. After the program, they discuss the program's meaning and application to their lives.

- In Indonesia where urban radio shows cannot reach remote areas, e-mail is used to feed news to rural radio stations.

- In many parts of the world, e-mail discussion lists are increasingly being used for networking, information sharing, problem solving, and strategizing.

Whether it is television, radio, or the Internet, communication technology can help ideas reach a wider audience and broaden participation in public argument. In creating virtual free spaces, however, advocates must be sure technology is used in ways that equalize access to information, rather than creating new groups of "haves" and "have nots."

Whatever form they take, free spaces, free speech, and freedom of assembly must be respected by the state's apparatus—the police, the army, and government officials—and protected from harassment, by either officials or nongovernment vigilantes. In cases where they are not, abuses often become a rallying point for advocacy efforts. The fight for press freedom and to protect journalists in many countries offer two examples.

Lesson 7:
Advocates Must Engage
Policy-Making Systems

Time and again, history has shown that real change only happens when mass mobilization and other forms of outside pressure are exerted on the institutions that need to change. But mobilization alone is not enough.

When the time comes to consider solutions to the problem, advocacy groups need to be involved in policy analysis and influence. Why? When issues move forward and alternative solutions are considered, many choices need to be made. It can be certain that experts—people from universities and think tanks—and public leaders will be involved. However, they are often distant from ordinary people's reality and have interests that are quite different. Without direct participation from social justice advocates, the solutions chosen will rarely serve people's needs. For example, think of structural adjustment programs (SAPs) imposed by the International Monetary Fund (IMF) and World Bank, with the support of the United States and other industrialized countries. These policies have thwarted relief and development efforts by NGOs in Asia, Africa, and Latin America in the past twenty years.

To engage with decision-making systems and create policy proposals and demands that decision makers cannot ignore, advocates need to pose critical questions: Will the solution reached reflect people's needs? Whose voices will be heard? Whose interests will be served? They need to be able to analyze, critique, and formulate policies; understand the political realities; identify the "art of the possible"; and stretch it to include the voices that are so often ignored.

In particular, advocates need to learn the stages of *policy analysis and influence:*

- *Define the problem.* Assemble evidence to make clear the extent and nature of the problem. Avoid stating the solution when defining the problem. Premature surfacing of a single solution will prevent a more comprehensive, systematic effort to test each alternative for strengths and weaknesses.

- *Construct alternatives to existing policy.* Alternatives are just that. They provide options and interventions to be considered and debated. Focus public argument by winnowing out the solutions that do not advance the organization's policy objective. To do this, it is helpful to learn from how similar problems were addressed and which policy solutions worked, which didn't, and why.

- *Select criteria to judge outcomes for each alternative.* First, focus public argument on values such as equality, equity, fairness, and justice. These values can be a powerful tool, especially when the

time comes for trade-offs and compromises. Second, temper these value-based criteria with what is practical. Is the policy alternative workable? Is it politically practical?

For example, in raising the minimum wage, a value-based criterion would be that people who work full-time should not stay steeped in poverty. This argument will run against the argument that employers cannot afford to increase workers' wages. Past experiences—such as phased-in increases—can be valuable in demonstrating an alternative's practicality.

- *Project outcomes for each alternative.* This is difficult because it means forecasting the future, which is always uncertain. The tendency is to be too optimistic, which often leads to unmet expectations and disappointment. In projecting outcomes, acknowledge that a particular policy may not be perfect, but it can be an improvement. Advocates should also warn about the harmful side effects of policies they oppose.

- *Face the trade-offs.* This is the hardest step. It means acknowledging that an ideal policy may not be politically viable, at least in the short term, and requires making choices. Trade-offs must be anticipated so an organization can decide what should and should not be traded. The organization must prepare its members and constituents for why the trade-offs are necessary and how they are chosen. One key is emphasizing that changing policy is a long-term, step-by-step process.

- *Decide and tell them what you want.* It is essential to tell decision makers and others—the media, lower-level bureaucrats responsible for implementing policy, affected constituencies, and the public—which policies you want. This can make your policy solution the center of public argument.

For example, after years of intensive mass mobilization, a reluctant President Kennedy finally addressed civil rights. Two groundbreaking laws—the Civil Rights Act of 1964 and Voting Rights Act of 1965—were enacted because the US civil rights movement had prepared its policy agenda and made it a critical part of public argument.

The Evolution of Civil Society and Advocacy in Bangladesh, Saleemul Huq

Contributed by Saleemul Huq, 1996 Bangladesh Advocacy Fellow and Executive Director of the Bangladesh Centre for Advanced Studies (BCAS), Dhaka, Bangladesh.

Nongovernmental organizations (NGOs) were set up in Bangladesh immediately following its independence in 1971. During the late 1970s and early 1980s, Bangladesh went from civilian rule to military rule and back again. The NGO community stayed out of politics and worked in humanitarian aid and development. The government, in turn, allowed NGOs to carry out their functions with some level of regulation, mainly with respect to obtaining foreign funding. In the main, however, the government regarded NGOs as outside its own development efforts, which concentrated more on the infrastructure to promote agriculture.

By the late 1980s and early 1990s, civil society in general began to change. Intellectuals, teachers, and the media began to take on a more policy-oriented advocacy role, and NGOs were no exception. Particular effort went into the environment in response to the devastating floods of 1987 and 1988. Thousands of people lost their lives and vast areas of the country were inundated with water. In response to the floods, the government of Bangladesh developed the so-called Flood Action Plan (FAP), along with donors such as the World Bank. The FAP aimed to tackle the problem of floods by building more embankments on the banks of main rivers, a strategy that was already questioned in many countries, including Germany and the United States.

Environmental groups in Bangladesh, though small, mounted a concerted and rather successful campaign to question the wisdom of the FAP on both environmental and social grounds. In time, they drew support from development NGOs, intellectuals, professional groups, the media, and international environmental groups in countries that gave aid to Bangladesh, particularly those supporting the FAP. This led to a major, sometimes acrimonious debate between proponents of the FAP (mainly the government and their donors) and opponents of the FAP (mainly environmental and other NGOs). Finally, in the mid-1990s, both the government and financial donors accepted that the solution to the problem of floods did not lay in constructing more embankments. Instead, they focused on developing a more environmentally sound strategy of year-round water management. They also recognized the importance of including public participation in the planning process.

In the early 1990s, another environmental action took place: the government's development of the National Environment Management Action Plan (NEMAP) in cooperation with NGOs and other sectors of civil society. The nation was invited to participate, demonstrating that the government and NGOs could work together and that it was possible to find ways to incorporate public concerns into development planning.

Today, the shape of political and civil discourse in Bangladesh has changed considerably. No longer are NGOs and other sectors of civil society outside the political and policy-making process. They are now recognized as a major force and are consulted on all major issues concerning the national agenda. Greater cooperation between the government and NGOs is underway in most fields of development, including the environment, women, children, education, health, family planning, and agriculture. Such cooperation is likely to grow and strengthen in the years to come, allowing the policy-development process to become much more people-centered. NGOs in Bangladesh will need to further develop analytical skills to draw lessons from their experiences so they can give coherent guidance toward national policy making.

Should all advocacy groups engage in policy analysis? Is it the most effective use of a group's limited resources? What if policy analysis isn't the group's strength? Not all organizations will have the time, expertise, or resources to analyze alternatives or the social or economic impact of a particular policy. Organizations can, however, play other important roles:

- *Gathering information based on people's experiences,* observations, and analysis, and developing powerful stories. Among other things, this helps an issue stay visible throughout the decision-making process.

- *Building relationships with and disseminating critical information to decision makers* to help them understand and see the issue differently. Advocates must continuously remind themselves that, if policy makers' hostile and stubborn *attitudes* do not change, then formal *policy* changes will create a new set of conflicts between advocates and the officials responsible for implementation. For example, remember the South African freedom government that inherited a long line of civil servants who did not accept the people's decision to elect Mandela and the African National Congress (ANC).

- *Building relationships with research institutions to stay informed* about the policy alternatives being considered and to offer critical insights from on-the-ground experiences. Similarly, organizations that don't have a grassroots membership need to build relationships with those that do, thereby maintaining a two-way channel of communication.

- *Testing programs on a small scale* to offer feedback on how policy alternatives, if implemented, would affect people's lives.

- *Monitoring the impact of programs that are implemented* and offering feedback when an issue enters its renewal.

For example, my former organization, the National Institute for Public Interest Law and Research (NIPILAR), was involved in monitoring Section 29 of the Amended Correctional Service Act of 1996. We sought the government's permission to visit prisons where children in conflict with the law were kept. Visiting the prisons was an eye-opener. It was an opportunity for the team to see the conditions under which the children were kept and to talk to the children. Armed with the information the team gathered from the visits, a submission was made to Parliament that led to review of the legislation.

Interacting and working closely with government departments provides opportunities for lobbying, getting information, and understanding how the government operates. In South Africa, this has enabled NGOs, CBOs, and individuals to formulate policies (white papers) that have led to the tabling (consideration) of bills before Parliament.

As a result, people feel that they are actually part of the process and have a say on issues that affect them. This is a success story for the community, and the people are now more willing to work with advocates to improve their way of life.

Disseminating Critical Information to Decision Makers, Gladys Sonto Kudjoe

Contributed by Gladys Sonto Kudjoe, 1996 South Africa Advocacy Fellow and a Director of the Department of Foreign Affairs in South Africa, Pretoria, South Africa.

The institutions of government play a vital role in creating, administering, and changing development policies. The government does not have the capacity to research and monitor implementation of its legislation. Nongovernmental organizations (NGOs) and community-based organizations (CBOs), though, are grassroots-based and have firsthand information on issues affecting the public. By conveying the difficulties and frustrations they and their constituents face, advocates can inform the government about the results of their decisions.

Monitoring Implementation

The selection of a solution and its implementation does not necessarily mean the problem is solved. Outcomes matter. Does the solution work? Do the changes improve people's lives? Advocates may ask: Do people have enough to eat? Do they have adequate shelter, safe drinking water, and basic sanitation? Do they earn enough money to keep clothes on their backs, food on the table? Do children stay in school and learn? Are people protected from harm?

Whatever the question, advocates need to develop benchmarks of success. They can be used to set goals for ongoing improvement at the local, national, or international level.

For example, many believe that the gross domestic product (GDP)—a measure of the total flow of goods and services produced by the national economy— ignores measures of natural and human capital and masks the social costs of economic growth and the widening gap between rich and poor. To focus public argument on critical social justice issues, advocates are using alternative measures of a nation's economic growth. Here are the most common examples:

- *Human Development Index (HDI).* Measures life expectancy, educational attainment (adult literacy and mean years of schooling), and income per capita.

- *Gender-related Development Index (GDI).* Adjusts the HDI to account for gender inequality and imbalances in basic health, education, and income.

- *Gender Empowerment Measure (GEM).* Measures whether women and men are able to actively participate in economic and political life and decision making.

- *Genuine Progress Indicator (GPI).* Measures the economy's performance in terms of social and environmental costs, such as crime, natural resource depletion, and limited leisure time. Also adds crucial aspects of the economy that are excluded from monetary transactions, such as housework and volunteering.

Southern nongovernmental organizations (NGOs) and their Northern allies use such indicators to ask: What is the real effect of debt payments, privatization, deregulation, and structural adjustment? Do they affect women and men differently? What is the impact on food supply and the social safety net? Are poor countries improving, staying the same, or getting worse over time?

These "effects" tests are an important tool for organizing public argument and showing how World Bank, International Monetary Fund (IMF), and other policies affect ordinary people's lives.

Lesson 8:
Stories Provide a Tremendous Source of Power—to Both the Narrator and Those Listening

Advocates love stories, and everyone has one to tell—colleagues, allies, family, friends, and even those with whom you may disagree. Stories can:

- Help people make connections between their day-to-day lives and other communities, issues, or strug-

gles. This is particularly important for building public argument and public judgment.

- Help people begin to understand and learn to navigate complicated issues and decision-making systems.

- Inspire realistic hope that unyielding forces can be overcome.

- Create a culture of participation, active listening, and learning.

- Enable advocates to reflect on their experiences, recognize their contributions, claim ownership of outcomes, reach closure on a particular effort, and translate lessons—about both successes and mistakes—into future action.

(See the texts that follow for examples of stories that have been told by Advocacy Institute colleagues.)

Organizations and movements need to find ways to encourage people to share—and learn from—their stories. A "diarist" can help, capturing stories in writing, pictures, songs, on audio or video cassette, or in other forms.

Placing Demands

Dalits are people in India and Nepal who have been deemed "untouchable" and relegated to the lower social strata. Dalits scavenge, picking up waste on the roads and in the sewers. Their labor is forced and pre-ordained by custom. They play the drums at others' weddings, but their own wedding processions may not enter the village.

Despite how inhumanely they are treated, Dalits have dignity that can give the confidence needed to confront injustice and challenge power. For example, one day a group of women scavengers said they would only continue to do the job if they had handles for their brooms—a simple means to dignify their work and allow them to sweep without continually stooping over. They were denied handles, so they organized themselves and refused to work until they received them. They did.

This story shows how advocacy—expressing power, placing demands—can be applied to realistic situations.

Creating the World That Should Be

In India, tribals are people who have traditionally lived off the land. Encroachment by modernization and urban expansion has led to their exploitation and loss of land, resources, and livelihood. Violations of their rights have been reinforced by authorities who fail to protect them from personal and social atrocities.

In 1998, a group of tribals in Mumbai (Bombay) asked to meet with police officials. The tribals wanted to discuss their land rights—they wanted their rights respected, and they knew the police had a responsibility under the law to enforce these rights. At the time, there were no serious disputes between the tribals and the police, and the police officials were working to improve the quality of law enforcement.

Over one hundred tribals—half men, half women—filled the police station. During the meeting, the senior police official had the bearer bring in tea for the group. The crowded room was electrified! To many, the tribals are outcasts. But by serving the tea—in the same glasses he would have offered to a group of professionals or businesspeople—the police official treated the tribals with the same respect he would give his peers. It was a riveting moment, and the tribals understood the symbolism.

This story offers an example of how a vision of "what should be" can be attained piece by piece, in ways that bring real difference to people's immediate lives.

Overcoming Racial Inequalities in the US South, Karen Watson

Based on an interview between Karen Watson— 1993 US Leadership Fellow, Advocacy Institute Board Member, and Executive Director of the Positive Action Committee (PAC), Sylvania, Georgia, USA—and Moco McCaulay and Rosa de la Vega of the Advocacy Institute, Washington, D.C., USA.

Screven County, Georgia, is a very small rural county in the US South. The population is about thirteen thousand, almost half of which are Black. What we in the progressive movement would recognize immediately as blatant injustices—things that are clearly wrong and very often illegal—are so often seen as normal procedure here. Doing justice-based work is difficult because both sides of the community—the power structure and the minority community— appear to have some comfort level around the injustices.

Since the Positive Action Committee (PAC) started organizing, we now have lots of allies, particularly in the African American community both inside and outside Screven County. As far as the power structure goes, we are at a point where we can actually have a conversation that is filled with a little less tension than it used to be.

For example, at a recent board of education meeting, the issue came up of whether to allow students to participate in the graduation ceremony if they had not passed the high school graduation test mandated by the State of Georgia. Most of the children who don't pass the test are African American. This is because of racially biased practices that have kept these children from getting the education that they need to pass the test.

The board passed the policy, saying that if the children hadn't passed the high school graduation test, they couldn't march in the ceremony. We don't necessarily disagree with the policy. But there was a time when that would have been the end of the discussion. The board would have passed the policy, and we would have had to really fight to get the issue on the table. We would have met some very stony faces of silence, sometimes open hostility, and we probably wouldn't have accomplished much.

At this meeting, we sat quietly to see how far down this road they were going. All the things that we were concerned about, they brought up themselves. We didn't have to say a word. The superintendent admitted that they have to take responsibility for the fact that these children can't pass the test and do something about it. A white man brought up the issues that PAC had been pushing all along: How do we let these children know that they're in trouble? How do we let their parents know? What is a better way for us to do this? How many chances were they given to pass the test? Another board member asked if we could prove that the things on the test had actually been taught to these children. There was a real discussion around how we close the gap, a conversation that was initiated by the board. Even though we participated in it, we did not have to initiate it.

We do understand that there will be other battles with this board. We've learned not to assume that because we have accomplished something in one arena, that when another issue hits the table, it will not be business as usual. But the fact that there has been that little bit of progress gives us great joy.

Analyzing Gender Dynamics in Advocacy Groups, Sofia Quintero

Contributed by Sofia Quintero, 1994 US Leadership Fellow, Advocacy Institute Board Member, and Director of Community Training and Support at the National Center for Schools and Communities, Fordham University, New York City, USA.

As a writer and advocate, I deeply appreciate the power of storytelling. I began to reflect on my experiences and sift through them for lessons on how gender dynamics affect advocacy groups. To my continuing surprise, I found that gender—whether we are aware of it or not—can alter relationships among advocates who seemingly have the same objective. Gender dynamics are often so deep that they are invisible. As these "tales from the front" show, marginalization of female advocates can occur unconsciously, even in the most admirable movements against marginalization.

First Lesson: Assume Gender Is a Dynamic
The Story
A group of young activists fighting police brutality organizes a know-your-rights forum. They discuss possible speakers, with an eye toward building a diverse panel. A female member of the group suggests they invite someone who can speak about the impact of police brutality on women.

Several men in the group openly resist the idea. Since police brutality largely falls on Black and Latino men, they argue that it makes little sense to approach the issue from a female perspective.

The woman points out a fact the men overlooked: many of the leaders in the fight against police

brutality are the mothers and wives of its victims. She describes the physical and psychological abuse they experience—sometimes in their own homes in front of their children—when they attempt to protect or advocate for their male loved ones, the initial targets of police harassment.

Eventually, the men give in, and the woman finds a Latina to speak at the forum. The forum is a success. One female member of the collective admits afterward, "I wasn't sure how police brutality affected women. But, as a woman, I couldn't sit there and let the men dismiss the possibility. If I hadn't spoken up, that speaker might not have been invited and I wouldn't have learned so many new things."

What Happened?
Revisiting this experience as a lesson in advocacy, I am struck by three points:

- Social problems that seem to affect only men actually concern the entire community. Even women who are not physically beaten by police can still be victims of brutality.

- Female activists must constantly remind our male colleagues that the gender differential exists and demystify its relation to the social ill we seek to remedy. If we don't do it, no one else will.

- Even women at the front of advocacy efforts can be invisible to their own colleagues. This was my most startling observation. When I think of the fight against police brutality and racial violence in New York City, Iris Báez and Altagracía Mayí immediately come to mind. These are women who have lost men they loved. I can also name the men who organized the marches and rallies at which they spoke. I know that if for some reason these men could no longer play this role, these women will continue the fight—and not only because they have been personally affected by these unpunished crimes. Yet I did *not* remember these women when we considered how police brutality affects women.

This last point is worth pursuing. We believe that when a man speaks out against injustice—even if that injustice has affected him personally—he crusades for us all. Yet we perceive a woman who does the same merely as a victim seeking justice to ease her personal pain. In doing so, we fail to draw larger lessons from women's experiences.

If that woman in our group had not seen a gender differential and insisted on pursuing it, our ignorance might have seriously undermined our campaign. Informed by a gender perspective, our efforts can only be improved. We can engage a broader constituency, pursue more data to support our claims, and shape more effective public policy to eliminate the problems of police brutality and racial violence.

Second Lesson: Never Underestimate the Intersection of Racism and Sexism

The Story

Two Black men and two white women are the ad hoc leadership of a network of activists for and about people of color. They coordinate the group's meetings and plan the agenda. Meetings occur regularly and run smoothly. People attend consistently and follow through on tasks. For quite a while, the organization functions well under the guidance of these four.

One day, the men, who founded the organization, decide that the two women are a threat to the network because they are white. They move to push the women out of the organization. This breaks the group into factions and completely halts its work. There are passionate ideological discussions about whether an organization of color should allow white people into its ranks. In the end, the white women leave the organization.

Their ouster severely cripples the organization in two ways:

- The ugliness surrounding their departure alienates not only members but also supporters. Many individuals and organizations withdraw their support.

- These women handled a great deal of the behind-the-scenes work that enabled the group to function. Their preparation and skill in facilitating each meeting are missed terribly when they leave.

It is primarily the women in the organization who struggle to restore the harmony disrupted by the incident. Through their efforts, they are able to keep enough members engaged in a major event they were planning. The event proves successful and interests many attendees in joining the organization. They

now have a base for rebuilding the organization if they decide they should.

What Happened?

To this day, I am amazed at how gender never entered our discussions. We all, myself included, were too wrapped up in debating the strategic advantages and cost of allowing whites in our organization. I firmly believe now that the group unconsciously used those women's race to disempower them when they stepped out of their gender roles. No one questioned their presence as long as they did "women's work"— organized the meetings, did outreach to boost attendance, took notes at meetings, and so on. The male founders did not move against them until the women began to put issues of gender and sexual orientation on the table and to assert their right as members to influence the organizational agenda.

The virtual dissolution of the organization over this incident was a costly lesson in how race and gender are intricately linked. Would bringing gender into our discussions have made a difference in keeping the group together?

Conclusion

These cautionary tales highlight the dangers and blessings that await us when we choose to address or ignore the influence of gender dynamics. Even as I document these experiences, I marvel at how they did not first come to me as lessons in gender. Only when I rummaged through my mental files with my gender glasses on did I realize that many of the experiences I have had were influenced by gender as much as by race or some other dynamic. We must always ask what lesson we are missing just because we are not looking for it.

Lesson 9: Innovation Is Born in Innovative, Learning Organizations

If they are to be transformative, social movements cannot mimic the behaviors that they oppose from government, corporations, or other institutions. In contrast, they must create environments where people feel safe to experiment, learn from mistakes, ask hard questions, and not be paralyzed by perfection.

Two organizational elements contribute to creating innovative, learning organizations:

- Values.

- Characteristics.

Understanding each can help leaders identify ways to strengthen their organizations, so that they will have the capacity to engage in advocacy on a sustained basis.

Organizational Values

In her work at the Advocacy Institute, Maureen Burke has identified a set of core values that we believe create an innovative, learning organization. The acronym THE RAMP symbolically means reaching greater heights:

- *Transparency* in decision making and communication. Those responsible for decisions have no hidden agendas, and encourage an open flow of communication among everyone involved in the effort, members and leaders alike.

- *Hope* that people's advocacy efforts will create change. When realistic hope is nurtured, it can motivate advocates, giving them something to look forward to as they engage in a long-term campaign.

- *Exchange* among peers and colleagues within an organization. Everyone has something to offer. Forums need to be created for people to learn from each other, and everyone should be modest enough to know they always have more to learn.

- *Respect* for members and leaders alike, given in one-on-one relationships and in group settings.

- *Affirmation* of people doing the work. This means not only the leaders but also those who provide administrative and logistical support and those who are relatively inexperienced.

- *Modeling,* setting a good example, or putting words and ideas into action. In other words, "walking the talk."

- *Pragmatism.* Actions are based on long-term and short-term objectives that are realistic, achievable, and practical. Actions just for the sake of doing something must be avoided.

When taken as a whole, THE RAMP creates a standard to which organizations aspire and hold themselves and demonstrates an organization's willingness to be a *learning* organization. Organizations that make THE RAMP operational provide opportunities for members and less experienced organizations to practice the skills and art of advocacy, gain confidence and self-respect, deepen their commitment, and broaden their experiences. These are key elements for sustaining social change movements.

Organizational Characteristics

In addition to values, five essential qualities have been outlined by Malcolm S. Knowles, a student of innovative organizations:

- *Structure:* flexible. Roles are defined broadly, and functional collaboration creates multiple links within the organization.

- *Atmosphere:* people-centered, caring, trusting, and informal.

- *Management philosophy and attitudes:* experimental. Willing to act despite ambiguity, to take risks, and to learn from mistakes, rather than place blame. Resources are mobilized effectively and members' potential is developed to the extent practical.

- *Decision making and policy making:* high value is placed on accessible decision making and participation by members in strategy development, problem solving, and policy formulation and implementation.

- *Communication:* open and multi-directional: top-down, bottom-up, and horizontal.

Lesson 10:
Effective Leadership Is a Critical Part of Strengthening Movements for the Long Term

Just as organizations cannot mimic the behaviors they oppose in society's institutions, neither can advocacy leadership. Three leadership elements must be understood:

- Style.

- Roles.

- Responsibilities.

Understanding each can help leadership identify ways to become more effective agents of social change and to strengthen organizations and movements for the long term.

Leadership Styles

To understand the leadership characteristics that best support innovative, learning organizations, it is helpful to compare *traditional* patterns of leadership with *emerging* patterns of leadership:

Traditional	Emerging
Authoritative	Participatory
Hierarchical	Empowering
Elitist	Democratic
Possessive of information, power	Sharing
Results-oriented	People-centered
One-person show	Cooperative effort
Vertical	Horizontal
Manipulative	Transparent
Leaders born	Leaders made

Traditional leadership uses "power over" organizations and members, creating an environment of command and control. In contrast, emerging leadership uses "power to," which enables organizations and their members to participate and contribute to the best of their abilities. This creates an environment of cooperation and learning.

In addition, emerging leadership recognizes that renewal, reflection, and sustenance are absolutely necessary to build emotional and intellectual reserves for the long-term nature of advocacy. The importance of renewal extends beyond the prevention of burnout. It is necessary for leadership to be creative, innovative, and supportive, to take initiative, and to create environments that sustain other advocates.

Leadership Roles

Throughout an advocacy effort, many roles and talents will be needed at different stages of the problem-solving cycle, issue life cycle, and organizational life cycle. (Section 6, "Collaboration," in chapter 6, presents a leadership taxonomy that describes such roles.) One individual may fill multiple roles, but no one person can do it all. Effective leadership, therefore, must rely on a *group* of leaders that share responsibility.

To build effective leadership, advocates and organizations need to:

- Assess themselves and their coalitions to identify who fills which roles and which roles are missing but needed.

- Identify which stages of the problem-solving cycle and issue life cycle best match their leadership strengths and stage of the organizational life cycle.

- Understand the limitations of their leadership abilities and create alliances to overcome their individual and institutional weaknesses.

- Develop abilities in more than one area of leadership.

In addition, to maintain an environment of innovation and sustenance, leaders of organizations and advocacy efforts need to make it an ongoing priority to:

- Cultivate second and third generations of leadership to ensure succession and sustain the effort when veteran leaders step aside.

- Encourage talent so new people regularly assume leadership roles.

- Develop systems to identify and draw in talented individuals with the potential to blossom.

- Build teams of individual leaders that complement each other's strengths.

Leadership Responsibilities

Movements, even when they are clear and coherent on a policy solution, do not march in lockstep. Leadership's challenge is to help buttress and bolster the various parts of the movement, keep the movement on its essential course, and make decisions about when to shift direction. This requires judgment that cannot be made in isolation.

Regardless of the specific leadership roles played, effective leadership must also be able to:

- *Translate* and decipher the workings of the political and policy processes and the symbols, metaphors, and subtexts used by their opponents. Leaders need to be able to explain what has happened and what will happen next in ways that clarify the choices in complex situations.

- *Glue* together and attach different parts within the movement and persuade the factions to unite. This will create an internal cohesion that buffers advocates and organizations against efforts that will try to tear them apart.

- *Connect* and solidify relationships with those outside the movement. US civic leader John Gardner describes the "networks of responsibility" that are needed:

    If our pluralistic system is to regain any measure of cohesion, leaders from various segments are going to have to come together in what I call "networks of responsibility" to appraise and seek to resolve the larger problems of their community, region, nation, or world.

    The mayor cannot turn a city into a community through sheer personal leadership skills. The fabric of community must be woven by many groups—municipal agencies, civic organizations, businesses, unions, schools, churches, neighborhood organizations, the community foundation, community colleges, and so on. Leaders from all segments, at all economic levels, must have formed networks that permit continuous collaboration, identify issues, and move towards consensus.

Lesson 11:
Effective Social Movements Are Built by Well-Rounded Teams of Storytellers, Organizers, and "Experts" Alike

Just as no one person has all the talents needed to *lead* an advocacy effort, no one person—or organization—can have all of the attitudes, skills, and knowledge needed to *carry out* the effort. Teams, organizations, and alliances need to be built to complement each other's strengths, ultimately forming a well-rounded, effective social movement.

The following is an illustrative—but not exhaustive—list of necessary attitudes, skills, and knowledge identified by frontline advocates across many cultures. Understanding what is required can help leaders identify ways to strengthen their organizations and what to look for in potential partners.

Attitudes

Necessary ones include:

- Hope and belief that change is possible despite obstacles and overwhelming odds. Belief that these can serve as opportunities for education and motivation.

- Willingness and the confidence to challenge entrenched, institutionalized power and the powerful, despite possible risks or threats. Understanding the risks that people take.

- Enough self-confidence not to be deterred by criticism from decision makers or by the fear of not being liked.

- Belief in and practice of non-discrimination, equality, and inclusion, regardless of one's race, class, caste, gender, sexual orientation, religion, ethnicity, ability/disability, credentials, or other differences.

- Belief in democratic values and processes. Respect for others' experiences and points of view. Belief in people's capacity to make their own decisions and, at times, mistakes.

- Recognition that there are different roles for different people at different times.

- Willingness to be transparent—honest and open—with colleagues, including not avoiding difficult matters, sharing critical feedback in a supportive and safe environment, and providing perspective on gains that are made.

- Commitment, patience, and stamina to engage in a long struggle to achieve and maintain significant change.

- Celebration of both substantive victories, like winning a new law, and "process" victories, like an organization's members meeting with elected officials or journalists.

Skills

Advocates need to be able to:

- Work with people who are different from them.

- Listen to one's members and constituents, allies, and opponents.

- Learn from experience and exchange with others, in formal and informal ways.

- Maintain a vision of what one wants—"what should be"—while staying grounded in the reality of "what is" and an assessment of how to get there.

- Analyze who has a stake in an issue (friends, foes, and the undecided), what motivates them, the positions they take, and possible common ground or ways to defuse opposition.

- Analyze opportunities to act and when to negotiate, drive a hard bargain, compromise, or hold firm.

- Adapt to new situations. Seize the moment and try something new, despite inevitable tensions or uncertainty.

- Admit uncertainty, mistakes, and what one wishes had been done differently. Create safe space to reflect on and move past errors in judgment.

- Provide constructive criticism without personalizing judgment.

- Express love and warmth, anger and disappointment, humor and playfulness in ways that will strengthen a team effort.

- Organize a campaign in ways that are appropriate for one's context and the risks that people face. Help people prepare to face potential risks.

- Build relationships—with obvious and unlikely allies, in coalitions and other collaborative relationships, within and outside of decision-making systems at all levels—that can survive disagreement and allow working with former adversaries. Mediate differences.

- Generate pressure through grassroots mobilizing and organizing. Influence international decision-making systems by generating domestic pressures.

- Tell stories that inspire and motivate others.

- Create, gather, analyze, synthesize, and disseminate complex and diverse information, including data, statistics, and anecdotes.

- Communicate effectively. Make public argument and messages understandable and persuasive. Write and edit quickly to take advantage of sudden opportunities.

- Build a team. Share responsibilities, obligations, and accountability within a community of advocates. Balance modesty and being in the background with confidence and being assertive.

- Raise money and build a solid financial base for an organization.

Knowledge

Advocates need to know:

- The political and policy systems. Where decisions are made, who makes them, and how they are made—formally and informally, at the local, national, regional, and international levels.

- Power relationships within a system and what influences decision makers and their decision-making processes. This includes understanding the effects of economic liberalization and globalization and the relationships among:

  - Civil society.

  - The media—local, national, and international.

  - The state.

  - The market—local and multinational corporations.

  - International financial institutions—the World Bank, International Monetary Fund (IMF), regional development banks.

  - The United Nations.

- Who the stakeholders are and on which issues they agree or conflict.

- Entry points to decision-making systems, how to intervene in the policy and budget processes, and how to counter corruption.

Any reflective practitioner of advocacy will agree that no one person has all the necessary attitudes and that new skills and knowledge constantly have to be learned (using computers and understanding globalization are prime examples). Reflective advocates will constantly test their open-mindedness and learning spirit.

Lesson 12:
It Is Easier to Destroy a Movement
Than to Build One

Advocacy requires many qualities: innovation, hope, stamina, drive, grit, determination, resolve, commitment. When an effort is clearly winning, it is easy to sustain these, as individuals and organizations. But when an issue suffers a setback or fades from public view, an organization's leadership faces its greatest challenges.

Leaders need to create strong organizations that motivate, energize, and support people engaged in the effort. Strong organizations must also buffer members against both external and internal tensions.

In the early 1980s, Byron Kennard, an organizer and leader in the US environmental movement, wrote of "ten ways to kill a movement." Advocacy Institute Co-Director Michael Pertschuk created a contemporary list based on his experiences with public health and tobacco control advocates. Pertschuk calls his list "eight ways to lead a movement to oblivion":

- Fight! Fight! Fight! or Talk! Talk! Talk!, but *never* balance struggle efforts with negotiation.

- Use your grass roots; then lose them.

- Lose track of your goals.

- Get drunk on your successes.

- Let a tender, bruised ego destroy your strategic judgment.

- Undermine all efforts at open and honest debate.

- Find a scapegoat and move on unenlightened.

- Keep doing what you are doing no matter how much the world changes.

Any one of these behaviors can be damaging to advocates and movements. When looked at in the reverse, they stand as a powerful reminder of the care that must be given to sustain advocates. Sustenance is particularly important when an effort does not successfully reach a short-term objective and frustrated advocates are tempted to find faults and lay blame on each other. The negative behaviors are noted here so advocates can avoid them.

In any advocacy effort, positive models of behavior deserve to be followed. Kennard's "ten ways to *kill* a movement" are reframed here as ten positive, proactive steps that an organization, coalition, or movement and its leadership can take to *build* a movement.

- Remember where you come from, that you are part of something larger. Celebrate your origins and roots.

- Listen to the insights and experiences of people who are affected by the issues and participate in the efforts. They are the real experts—amplify their voices. Keep professional experts "on tap, not on top."

- Keep balance in your work and personal life. Work hard, yes. Meet responsibilities, yes. Make an extra effort, yes. But also add humor and rest. Avoid pessimism and martyrdom.

- Recognize human frailty and accept it. Set the example by not holding yourself—or others—to rigid or impossible standards that drain the organization's energy.

- Motivate others by sharing responsibility, paying attention to others, and encouraging those who make the extra effort. Give praise when it is merited.

- Model behavior, or set a good example, by fostering cooperation, sharing information with others, and encouraging others' leadership. Don't dominate. Leave space for others to share their knowledge and skills.

- Insist on a calm approach to solving problems. Set real deadlines. Avoid a crisis mentality.

- Share credit generously within the organization, within the sector, and among allies.

- Be equally civil to those who share your views or tactics and those who do not. Agree to disagree and do so without personalizing disagreements.

- Recognize that there are incremental steps in the advocacy journey. Celebrate how far a group has come and what it means to the lives of people. New experiences—like meeting with a bureaucrat, politician, or editor—are as much a success as winning a favorable policy. They build confidence and empowerment that, in many ways, are the most profound and lasting changes. Savor them.

I have tried these behavior models out on experienced practitioners. They invariably respond enthusiastically.

Chapter 3

Advocacy in the Twenty-First Century

Great changes have occurred in the last quarter of the twentieth century and the beginning of the twenty-first century. Since the 1970s, fifty-four countries around the world have shed authoritarian governments or dictatorships and—for the first time in their histories—held multi-party elections. In Latin America, most of these occurred in the 1980s. In Africa and Asia, the overwhelming majority occurred in the 1990s. These elections—the first step in political liberalization and democratization—have changed the power dynamics between governments and their citizens.

At the same time, a neoliberal consensus has emerged among governing elites. Actors outside the nation-state are driving policy decisions that control and dominate developing and poor countries. This economic liberalization has weakened the ability of fragile and emerging democracies to govern effectively and to meet the needs of their people.

As advocates seek change in the twenty-first century, they need to understand political liberalization and democratization as well as economic liberalization and globalization. Chapter 3 discusses these and offers common points of intervention for social justice advocacy, drawn from the Advocacy Institute's exchanges with frontline advocates in different countries.

Political Liberalization and Democratization

In the last three decades, on every continent, many dictators have fallen, and authoritarian systems have ended. The people of South Africa have triumphed over apartheid.

A pattern emerges: authoritarian heads of government do not yield power willingly but do surrender political power when faced with the pressures of mass movements and mobilizations. (This was the case in the Philippines in 1987, Bangladesh in 1991 and 1996, and Indonesia in 1998.)

As a result, processes are often established for "free and fair" elections. On election day, people wait patiently in long lines to cast their votes. The atmosphere is celebratory, and some first-time voters wear special outfits to mark the occasion. When the results of the vote are announced, people accept them. The winners take office.

In examining elections as the first step in political liberalization and democratization, several qualities are often present:

- Movements, political parties, and even interest groups mobilize large numbers of people to vote.

- Many people participate by voting—at least in the hundreds of millions, perhaps even more.

- The sectors of people who vote expand to include indigenous people, women, young people, and people who are illiterate. Gender, age, class, caste, nationality, tribe, language, religion, ideology—none presents a bar to participation. No one is formally excluded.

- The process is egalitarian. Each vote is equal and counted individually.

- Voters trust the integrity of the process and choose freely whether to cast their vote or not to participate.

The common act of voting is an essential part of democratization, but does not equal democratization. Getting elected and governing are vastly different enterprises. When the winners take office, will they be fairer than previous leaders and accountable to the people? Will they respect a free press, freedom of association, and other basic freedoms? How will the state's institutions manage controversy and political differences that challenge the ruling elites' power? Will political and public space be created for civil society organizations (CSOs) to participate actively in democracy's work—forming arguments, shaping public opinion, providing feedback to decision makers, and making demands on the political system?

Economic Liberalization and Globalization

The story of political liberalization and democratization is not complete until the story of economic liberalization and globalization is told.

People demand democracy. The one-party state, dictatorship, and authoritarian government are overthrown. The government and legislative body, fairly elected, respond by adopting policies to clean up the excesses of the authoritarian government. But the hopes generated by the changes are short-lived, and disillusionment sets in. The realities of unemployment, poverty, and national debt are difficult to overcome, especially as people's lives are increasingly affected by external economic forces and policy decisions made outside of their nation-state.

The disillusionment cannot be overemphasized. The election campaign and movement work created expectations. People expect their lives to improve. Their hopes are voiced in glowing democratic terms. Yet, as Padraig O'Malley writes in *Southern Africa: The People's Voices,* "rather than standards of living increasing, people find they often decrease. The poor remain poor; the homeless homeless; the unemployed unemployed."

The shift in decision making and the effects on people's lives are just part of the many social, economic, and cultural transformations resulting from rapid modernization. Joshua Karliner in *The Corporate Planet* describes the issue crisply:

> The "globalization" we are witnessing in the 1990s is an acceleration of historical dynamics, hastened by the advent of increasingly sophisticated and rapid communication and transportation technologies, the decline of the nation-state, the absence or ineffectiveness of democratic systems of global governance, and the rise of neoliberal economic ideology.
>
> Its primary beneficiaries are both the transnational corporations and the privileged consumer classes in the North and, to a growing degree, in the industrializing nations of the South.

In contrast, globalization adversely affects a majority of people living in the South and many more in the North than political leaders acknowledge. Many have little or no say over the changes being forced on their lives. Public anxiety skyrockets as people are unable to cope with (let alone adapt to) the rapid changes, and each country's leadership—government, civil society, and corporations—faces greater stress in dealing with value conflicts.

Neoliberal economic ideology, which undergirds globalization, centers on these harmful principles:

- Economic growth is most important. Organized economic interests—corporations and their agents—need to be free to pursue what gives them economic advantage. The choices made will help not only them but also the wider community. Internal and global markets, then, must be free to operate with little government constraint or regulation.

- Free trade is good for all nations. A country will produce goods and provide services that give it a comparative advantage.

- Government spending contributes to inefficiency and waste—not all of it, but enough of it to suggest that public expenditures should be cut.

- In the distribution of economic goods, individual responsibility and social Darwinism replace the concepts of public good and community.

Neoliberal economic ideology provides the foundation for the economic liberalization policies created by international financial institutions—the World Bank, the International Monetary Fund (IMF), the World Trade Organization (WTO), and other institutions supported by Northern governments in North America, western Europe, and Japan. Their policies press governments to balance their budgets and fight inflation through lower public spending, deregulation, and privatization that will, in theory, enable open capital markets to promote economic development.

While there is a growing middle class in some Southern countries, overall, economic liberalization, for those who have not attained middle-class economic status, has failed to improve people's daily lives and, for many, brings harm instead. So far, political and policy responses have been inadequate in meeting the challenge.

David Korten, Peter Ewang in his essay "How

Africa Was Brought Low," and others contribute macro-data that tell a devastating story:

- A total of over 227 billion US dollars of international debt is owed by forty-two countries. Many countries in southern Africa now owe more money in international debt than they did at the start of the 1990s. For some, more than at the start of the 1980s.

  One cause is structural adjustment programs (SAPs) pressed on countries as a prerequisite to receiving development loans from international financial institutions. Critics contend that the SAPs are designed to benefit the developed countries traded with, rather than realistically helping the borrowing countries to attain sustainable development. As Kay Treakle observes in her essay in *The Struggle for Accountability*, SAPs undermine "social services, food producers, worker rights, the natural environment, and the viability of fragile democracies."

- To pay the debt, heavily indebted countries must use most of their export earnings and follow a short-term strategy of leasing or selling off valuable resources and land.

- People who are poor, near-poor, and marginalized are the ones who suffer:

  - With no substantial commitment to the public good and a safety net in tatters, the nation-state can neither protect people from the consequences of rapid modernization nor help them meet their basic needs—food, shelter, health, education. Nor are effective mechanisms in place to counter environmental health and safety threats caused by the markets and corporations.

  - With macroeconomic policy focused on deregulation and privatization, distributional questions—who gets what, who benefits, how lives are improved—are not open to public argument.

  - Even in specific cases where the *percentage* of the population living in poverty has decreased, the rise in *total* population numbers means a growing number of poor people in absolute terms. Oil-exporting and heavily indebted countries continue their decline in per capita income.

Since 1980, southern Africa has produced less food and has more hungry people.

  - Studies have shown that women bear a disproportionate share of the burden and face increasing incidents of domestic violence.

- In the absence of strong accountability measures, the politics of economic liberalization—privatization, deregulation, and incentives for accumulating private capital—exacerbate and encourage corruption at the national and local levels. Corruption spreads like cancer to the core of communities, harms people in their daily lives, and deeply damages the public's trust in and the legitimacy of those in authority.

- With poverty amidst plenty, and public squalor accompanied by private opulence, the society fails to live up to values that are critical for a just, decent society—including economic equity, gender fairness, sustainable development, and environmental responsibility.

By pressing economic liberalization policies on Southern countries, the power of international financial institutions overshadows national systems of decision making and weakens democracy. People-centered advocates in civil society organizations (CSOs), and nongovernmental organizations (NGOs) as one subset of CSOs, must push for transparency and accountability not only to deal within the governments under which they live but also to work within powerful institutions outside their countries.

Points of Intervention

For social justice advocates, the challenges in this picture may evoke the myth of Sisyphus—forever rolling the boulder uphill, only to have it tumble down again. Yet experience shows that advocates are not taking any of this passively. They are springing into action to make a difference in people's lives.

The Advocacy Institute's colleagues are finding imaginative ways to use the spaces created by political liberalization and democratization to intervene, raise public attention for neglected issues, force public argument, and present alternatives. They are focusing on two broad issues that link the micro- and macro-levels:

- *Accountability.* Advocacy efforts expose state officials' failures to meet their responsibilities and duties in relation to the citizens they serve, and how these failures weaken democratic decision making. They focus on the gap between noble words—constitutions and rights-oriented laws—and their implementation or restrictive laws that contradict them entirely.

- *Social, economic, and environmental policies.* Advocacy efforts challenge weak economic analysis and gaps in planning and highlight the real but ignored costs and benefits to ordinary people's lives.

In focusing on these broad issues, advocates recognize they need to locate who *really* makes the decisions that affect their country's people and where these decisions are made, whether at the national, regional, and international levels. Increasingly, they are targeting national-level officials in international financial institutions as well as pressuring their own national government officials who bear responsibility for implementing policies driven by harmful neoliberal ideology.

In addressing these two broad issues, our colleagues' experience suggests there are at least six points of intervention commonly being used by advocates:

- Strengthening the electoral process.

- Raising issues that link the personal and the political.

- Embracing a broad human rights framework.

- Countering corruption and creating a culture of transparency.

- Analyzing public budgets.

- Using UN conferences and their related declarations.

The following sections discuss each point of intervention along with recommendations drawn from practitioners in the field.

Strengthening the Electoral Process

While the act of voting does not equal democracy per se, the process offers critical opportunities for people to articulate their common demands and press for a response from their country's leaders. Participation,

then, must reach beyond simply casting a vote. It should include engaging in public argument before election day and taking steps to ensure that, when the votes are cast, the process has integrity.

To strengthen the electoral process and democratization, the following are some action steps that can be taken by advocates, civil society organizations (CSOs), and ordinary people:

- *Raise a political but nonpartisan voice,* beyond get-out-the-vote campaigns or party endorsements.

   Social justice advocates and other CSOs need to raise critical issues, based on their beliefs and values, to make sure they become part of public argument. Three steps can be taken:

   – *Ask questions of every candidate,* whether in writing or orally, formally or informally. Make demands on party platforms and manifestos. This is a way to secure a party's promise to which it can be held politically when it shifts away from keeping that promise.

   – *Get answers from political parties and candidates.* Answers should be received formally. This starts the necessary public relationship with political parties and candidates and lays the base for continuing discussions and relationships with the winners after the election.

      At first, candidates may be reluctant. Asking questions is not the kind of behavior they expect from voters. They expect to speak, not to be spoken to. Groups should be prepared to embarrass those who are silent or non-responsive.

   – *Give answers* to the public, political parties, and candidates. This carries the advocates' ideas to a broader audience and uses the election campaign to identify issues that will need to be resolved once the election is over.

      To understand this role's powerful influence, think about those candidates who run for office but do not win. Nonetheless, their ideas and proposals often become part of public argument and decision making. Civil society can make similar contributions to public argument. In the United States, third parties and strong nonpartisan movements—civil rights, labor, Christian fundamentalists—have all had major effects on mainstream politics. In India, Hindu fundamentalists—through the RSS—have dominated the political ideology of the BJP political party. They have turned the BJP from a minor party to a major party, enabling Hindu fundamentalists to acquire a political legitimacy they did not previously have.

When asking questions, getting answers, and giving answers, advocates have a special responsibility to ensure that those who are politically marginalized—whether by class, ethnicity, gender, race, or economic status—have their voices heard. This work must be ongoing, and not limited to the election cycle.

- *Follow the money.* Increasingly, money plays a major role in elections. In most countries, campaign contributions are secret, undisclosed, and unanalyzed. Even when laws prohibit bribery by companies and individuals, there are no restrictions on the uses of political money by political parties or candidates. Standards should be set to regulate and monitor the flow of money in electoral campaigns. (Suggested standards and actions are discussed later in the section on corruption and transparency.)

- *Engage the media* in the election effort beyond reporting what the candidates say and do. The media should also listen to what voters say, their priority issues, and how the candidates' promises will be kept.

- *Monitor the media's responsibility* to give equal and fair coverage to all candidates and parties. For example, efforts have begun in Bosnia-Herzegovina to counter the media's role in fanning hatred and spreading misinformation.

- *Create a team of domestic election monitors.* Their presence at the voting polls demonstrates that a group of people, regardless of their individual political preferences, stands for upholding the integrity of the election results.

- *Press the government to accept international election monitors for the whole process,* including what happens before the election days. They may ask: Are political differences respected? Is public argument robust? Do all candidates have a chance to present their views? Do people vote in privacy and without interference? Such monitoring helps validate the legitimacy of free and fair elections and improves the chance of an orderly transfer of power, enabling the elected officeholders to form their government so decisions can be made.

- *Establish an independent, statutory election commission.* Together with domestic and international monitors, it must conduct post-election monitoring to protect the integrity of the process. The experiences of Bangladesh, India, Malawi, and South Africa show this further strengthens the chance of successive, routinely free and fair elections—a necessary step to firmly setting a country on the path to democratization.

Raising Issues That Link the Personal and the Political

The issues raised by advocates, whether during election campaigns or at another time, are often those closest to their lives. By raising issues that link the personal and the political, people can learn from firsthand experience how to amplify their voices, participate in public life, and engage in politics and public argument to push for solutions. This was the case in Ecuador, where indigenous peoples' groups have organized around the impact of International Monetary Fund–imposed SAPs on rising consumer gas prices.

The work to end domestic violence offers another powerful example. Around the world, groups are organizing, often led by women who are survivors of domestic violence. These leaders have shed the sense of powerlessness that so often results from abuse and, despite the risks that may come, have found great power within themselves to act. In doing so, they discover the power of being part of a group and the creative energy that is released.

These advocates draw from their own experiences as well as relevant research to understand the power dynamics involved and to identify points of intervention. For example, David Levinson's pioneering work, *Family Violence in Cross-Cultural Perspective,* helps identify common factors related to high rates of domestic violence:

- Male control of family wealth and income.

- Male-dominant domestic authority.

- Severe divorce restrictions for women, whether by law or in implementation.

- A societal pattern of resolving conflicts violently.

Levinson also found that societies with little incidence of domestic violence have several common factors:

- Wives have some form of shared control over family wealth and income.

- Husbands and wives share in domestic decision making.

- Divorce is infrequent and equally easy or hard for men and women to obtain.

- Monogamy is expected from both men and women. Cultural norms expect neither men nor women to engage in pre-marital sex. Husbands and wives sleep together.

- Men resolve disputes with other men peacefully.

- The society's norm is to intervene immediately in wife-beating incidents.

The causes of domestic violence clearly make it a personal issue *and* a political issue, a family issue and a public issue. Recognizing this, advocates are creating holistic action plans. They are generating standards of unacceptable behavior that focus on:

- *Individual and community responsibility to change social attitudes.* Advocates are working with CSOs, such as churches and schools, to create a norm and expectation that violence is unacceptable and people have the responsibility to intervene.

  For example, Agisanang Domestic Abuse and Prevention Training (ADAPT) in South Africa works with men to organize support groups, to learn to control emotional and verbal violence, and to become active allies in preventing domestic violence. Other groups work on related issues, such as challenging hierarchical relationships within families and protecting women in their rights under inheritance laws.

  In Washington, D.C., teenage males who have engaged in violent behavior are being organized into peer groups by a group of men who have served in jail. The peer group models behavior that rejects violence, is socially responsible, and accepts the consequences of individual actions.

Another example is the work of Sisterhood Is Global (SIGI) with women in Muslim societies. SIGI facilitates empowerment by providing a safe environment for sharing experiences and building a common understanding of the problem. Participants identify the sources of violence in the family, community, state, and society and focus on those who bear the responsibility for ending it: police, doctors, judges, and government officials. In doing so, they connect international human rights treaties and other documents with ways to combat and end violence in the local setting.

- *Government responsibility to protect all of its citizens from violence, regardless of the source.* Advocates recognize that official actions and policies matter and are pressing the government to not stand idly by when violence and abuse occurs.

  Policy solutions focus on:

  - Sufficiently clear definitions to protect people against assault, battery, and marital rape.

  - Institutional protections, such as shelters for women who leave their abusive homes, and restraining orders and police protection to bar abusers from inflicting further harm.

  - Supportive child services that allow mothers to leave abusive relationships without losing child custody.

  - Social and health services for survivors of domestic abuse, including job training for women who cannot survive economically or support their families with their current skills.

  - Sensitivity training for police officers and judges who intervene in domestic abuse situations.

  - New institutional approaches, such as efforts by San Diego County in California to create a separate court to handle domestic violence cases. The court's approach focuses on the "total person," using criminal punishment as well as counseling for the abuser to prevent future domestic violence.

These illustrative actions in strengthening individual, community, and government responsibility make differences in people's lives while changing both culture and policy. Both types of changes are needed to tackle critical issues, such as gender segregation, physical and verbal assault, spousal abuse, rape, female genital mutilation, trafficking, and prostitution.

Embracing a Broad Human Rights Framework

To stop with the right to vote leaves out a wide range of other rights—including economic, social, and cultural rights—that also need to be protected and exercised. (See "Broad Human Rights Framework," below.)

Recognizing this, advocates around the world are helping people to bring their rights alive and to learn:

- What their legal rights are.

- How to reconcile a broad human rights framework with potentially conflicting cultural values and teachings.

- How to exercise their rights individually and as a community.

- How to assist others to exercise such rights.

- How to push for those rights that they do not yet legally have. This may include pressuring their governments to:

  - Ratify international human rights treaties and laws.

  - Change domestic law so that it conforms to international law.

  - Enforce the domestic laws that already exist.

Advocates are also using the human rights framework to organize allies and to expose, shame, and create political pressures on corporations and governments that (by their actions and inaction, respectively) do not protect people's enjoyment of their rights. For example:

- Using a US law that grants non-US citizens access to US courts in cases involving international law, thirty thousand Ecuadorian citizens filed a class-action lawsuit in New York against the Texaco oil corporation for pollution and contamination in the Ecuadorian Amazon. Drawing on the Rio Declaration and other international accords, the lawsuit claimed that actions like Texaco's 16.8 million gallon oil spill are a violation of their fundamental right to a clean and healthy environment.

- In Louisiana—a US state dominated by petrochemical, oil, and industrial facilities—organized groups of African American citizens have brought a case in front of the UN Commission on Human Rights. They claim that the location of these polluting facilities in or near poor minority communities is "environmental racism" and a violation of the Convention for the Elimination of All Forms of Racial Discrimination (CERD).

Broad Human Rights Framework

The Universal Declaration of Human Rights, created by the United Nations in 1948, first presented a normative framework of human rights focused on a person's dignity and relationship to their society.

Here is a basic overview, with illustrative examples:

- *Civil and political rights,* or claims to liberty, include:

  - Right to:

    - Life.

    - Liberty and security.

    - Privacy.

    - Protection as a child.

    - Opportunity to vote and run for elected office in periodic free and fair elections.

    - Equal treatment, protection, and recognition before the law, including presumption of innocence, a fair trial, and right to appeal.

  - Freedom of:

    - Movement and choice of residence.

    - Thought, conscience, and religion.

    - Opinion and expression.

    - Peaceful assembly.

    - Association.

  - Freedom from:

    - Torture or cruel, inhuman, or degrading treatment or punishment.

    - Slavery or forced labor.

~ Arbitrary arrest.

~ National, racial, or religious hatred that incites discrimination, hostility, or violence.

• Economic, social, and cultural rights, or claims against poverty, include the right to:

– Work.

– Fair pay and conditions.

– Social security.

– An adequate standard of living, including adequate food, clothing, and housing.

– The highest attainable standard of physical and mental health.

– Education.

– Practice of one's own culture, religion, and language with other members of one's group.

Economic, social, and cultural rights are often called "second-generation rights" because they are frequently neglected during political liberalization and democratization. Neglect—often accompanied by discrimination—causes chronic suffering and conditions that often escalate into armed conflict, humanitarian emergencies, and abuse of civil and political rights.

Taken as a whole, the human rights framework sets standards against which to measure a state's laws, policies, and behavior, as well as the policies and behaviors of corporations and international financial institutions, like the World Bank and IMF.

While no single law-making body, court, or police force currently exists to enforce human rights, the aspirations captured in the international treaties, conventions, and covenants provide a powerful advocacy tool.

Countering Corruption and Creating a Culture of Transparency

The right to vote and freely elect one's leaders is meaningless if electoral officials take bribes, thereby tainting public decisions that are made, or if officials look the other way and refuse to punish corrupt or repressive behavior, whether by actors within government or outside it.

Corruption takes many forms, as described by The Asia Foundation and others:

• *Bribery,* favor giving, or "greasing the palm" to gain access to decision makers and to receive favorable decisions, such as in tax policy or the awarding of government contracts.

Even when laws prohibit bribery, many countries practice a form of institutionalized bribery and gift giving through electoral campaign contributions. For example, money has so debased US politics that a system that worked reasonably well in the 1976–1984 presidential elections has now been decimated. Powerful special interests and wealthy individuals gain access to decision makers by contributing huge sums of money (often over $100,000) to finance both Democratic and Republican presidential campaigns. Such legal bribery adds to the cynicism of US voters and voter turnout plummets further.

Another form of legal bribery is the expectation that action on official decisions is designed to enrich officeholders. Indonesia, Nigeria, and Russia competed for the distinction of having the most virulent corruption in the 1990s.

• *Extortion,* using intimidation to demand "pay offs" or economic tribute from people. In the cities of South Asia, South Africa, and elsewhere, "muscle men" are a constant threat to street vendors working in the informal economy.

• *Embezzlement or distortion,* making government spending decisions in ways that siphon funds to the decision maker's pocket or political apparatus, rather than to programs that benefit the public welfare.

• *Patronage,* granting political appointments and other favors to supporters within the government.

• *Cronyism,* granting economic advantages, such as government contracts, to political supporters and personal friends, rather than following formal institutional laws and procedures. Cronyism can also mean allowing organized criminal elements to operate because of state inaction.

Indonesia offers a dramatic example of systemic corruption that remained uncorrected after

Suharto's overthrow. Rice distributors, in league with government regulators, habitually paid farmers too little, while they charged consumers too much for a basic dietary staple. These middle men gained at the expense of both—many of whom are poor to begin with.

In Colombia, Mexico, Russia, Taiwan, Thailand, and elsewhere, corruption and crime are inextricably linked. Organized criminal elements have power in society that translates into lasting immunity from prosecution and other favored treatment. The result is corruption of the political and judicial systems.

Whatever the form, corruption ultimately harms the powerless. It makes people cynical, believing there is little or nothing they can do. Such cynicism drains energy and threatens to extinguish the idealism and intensity needed to create change.

The purveyors of corruption expect people to surrender to its practice. Yet people do not. As pervasive as corruption is, every society has voices that continually challenge it. They are determined to uproot its systemic base.

Advocates have found that the most effective antidotes are transparency and accountability of public officials. Or in the words of US Supreme Court Justice Louis Brandeis, "Sunlight is the best disinfectant." When required by law and practiced, transparency and accountability prevent deeply embedded, institutional corruption.

Peter van Tuijl, in his article "NGOs and Human Rights: Sources of Justice and Democracy," and others describe a range of actions that can be taken to show that people are watching and have expectations of their public officials:

- Create sustained public pressure and outrage to change the habits of entrenched government officials or their counterparts in international financial institutions and multinational corporations.

- Set standards of "what should be" for officials to follow.

- Monitor the work of official agencies to determine whether declared policies and procedures are being followed.

- Monitor budget allocations to determine whether public programs have the money they need to function successfully.

- Follow implementation of programs on the ground to learn how the policies work. Is there an improvement in the lives of the poor? Is it substantial or marginal, long-lasting or transitory, thorough or casual?

In tackling systemic corruption and lack of transparency, standards of "what should be" need to be systemic as well, making it difficult and illegal for individuals to continue corrupt behavior.

The wide-ranging changes that are needed can seem daunting at first. However, as experiences in Chile, India, South Africa, and the United States show, there are a number of starting points to address systemic issues:

- An independent, statutory election commission should be established. Together with domestic and international monitors, it must conduct post-election monitoring to protect the integrity of the process. This further enhances the chance of successive free and fair elections that happen routinely.

- The flow of money should be transparent. Political parties and candidates should be expected to make full and timely disclosures of all contributions received, regardless of the timing in the election cycle. Disclosure should include contribution amounts; contributors' names, countries, and global corporate links; and dates of contribution. Strict penalties, including forfeiture of an election seat, should be applied to those who violate the law grossly or repeatedly. Just as an independent election commission is needed, so too is an independent enforcement agency for campaign contributions.

- Public officials (including judges) and their immediate family members should disclose their personal finances, including income, assets, loans, and gifts. Public disclosure should be made annually. Falsification, or omission of information, should lead to criminal charges.

- Government contracts and procurement should be performed according to standards of ethics and integrity. Conflicts of interest should be avoided by matching an official's financial disclosure with their official duties or voting on an issue. Ill-gotten gains should be forfeited with heavy fines and jail sentences. An independent enforcement body should make the decision as to whether a conflict exists.

- Companies, including multinational corporations, that violate the law should be barred from doing business with the government. Enforcement against wrong-doing must be certain and not haphazard.

- A public meeting log should be kept that says with whom an official met, where, when, and what public business was discussed.

- The rationale for all government decisions should be shared. A freedom of information act should make relevant data, memoranda, and background information for public programs—whether funded by government or by international financial institutions—available to the public in a timely manner. According to Lori Udall in her essay in *The Struggle for Accountability,* critical elements include "project objectives, expected or probable components, costs and financing, environmental issues, the status of procurement and consulting services, studies to be undertaken, implementing agencies, and relevant contact points." Such project information should neither hide nor distort what is known and the issues to be considered.

  Transparency and availability of such information will enable advocates and people directly affected by decisions to understand the basis of those decisions and to be able to argue for or against them in an informed manner.

- Organized groups of citizens should be able to attend open meetings when important public-policy decisions are developed and considered. This makes it harder for a few "insiders" to control how these decisions are made. Experiences in South Africa and the United States show that the ability to attend open meetings strengthens the citizen's power as a watchdog.

To strengthen the effectiveness of these steps, three broad principles must be embraced:

- Autonomous audit agencies as independent arms of government are necessary for controlling corruption, and governments must develop the capacity to create them.

- Advocates need to help create a culture of familiarity with one's rights.

- Independent civic bodies are needed to monitor decision-making systems at the local, national, and international levels.

There is no single recipe for countering corruption and creating a culture of transparency and accountability. These starting points should be adapted to fit a particular country's context and needs, based on a strategic assessment of power dynamics, how the decision-making systems operate, and how strong support can be built among civil society as well as businesses and corporations.

While there is much to do, there are certainly reasons to be encouraged:

- Many countries that hold competitive elections have been helped by independent election commissions. This strengthens the country's rule of law and leads to a legitimate government.

- People want to do something about corruption in their country. Surveys show that overwhelming majorities make the connection between corruption, criminal elements, lawlessness, and threats to democracy. This holds true throughout Latin America, South Asia, Russia, and Ukraine. The problems are not limited to a single country or region, but, on every continent, efforts are underway to attain transparency and accountability to tackle systemic corruption.

Analyzing Public Budgets

Public budgets ultimately determine policy outcomes. They show who benefits from public spending and who is bypassed, where the money is allocated and where it is not. Budget analysis can be a pivot to focus on local, national, and international issues.

Historically, public budgets have been formulated in secrecy by an elite corps of government bureaucrats, who mostly guide elected government officials, who in turn regularly respond to organized interests. In parliamentary systems, the finance minister is the major power. In the United States, it is the director of the Office of Management and Budget and, sometimes, the secretary of the treasury as well.

Macroeconomic policy that directs the budget's formulation is also barely debated and rarely challenged. Arguments do occur but only over slices of specific items. For all practical purposes, the public, even those who are most active, is left out of budget-policy deliberations.

To create space for public argument, organized advocates around the world have begun to analyze their national and local budgets. Their work includes summarizing official information that is readily available and sharing it with other advocates to be used in their efforts.

In the United States, major changes have taken place in fewer than twenty years. A small number of highly skilled budget analysts have emerged to work on the national and state levels. Premier among the national organizations is the Center for Budget and Policy Priorities. Born out of crisis during the Reagan administration's severe cutbacks to social programs, the center has played a significant role in showing how the US budget affects low-income families, the poor, and the near-poor—including millions of people who work for a living and yet remain poor. The Institute for Democracy in South Africa (Idasa), Developing Initiatives for Social and Human Action (DISHA) and Vidhayak Sansad in India, Proshika and the Institute for Development Policy Analysis and Advocacy (IDPAA) in Bangladesh, and many organizations in Latin America have started similar efforts, independently and in collaboration with the center. For example, in Bangalore, India, the Public Affairs Centre has launched a "report card" that enables users of urban public services to rate levels of performance and their satisfaction. The idea is catching on in other cities, thereby widening the numbers of people familiar with the budget and primed for action.

In these ways, social justice advocates are using budget analysis to:

• Amplify the voices of people who are not heard.

• Raise issues that would otherwise be neglected and draw the attention of the media and others in civil society.

• Confront unequal power dynamics that affect the distribution of public resources.

• Pressure governance institutions to treat marginalized people with dignity.

• Create new public spaces for people's participation.

• Connect micro-level experiences to macro-level economic and social policies.

• Learn how their decision-making system works and how to make interventions earlier in the policy-making process.

• Gain the skills needed to effectively participate in public argument.

A public document once created in secrecy by a small governing elite is no longer perfunctory. It is under public scrutiny and, increasingly, public pressure to be responsive to people's needs.

In many countries, national governments have devolved or are devolving power to local governments, as seen with neighborhood associations in Latin America, the Panchyat Raj in India, and the union *parishads* and other locally elected bodies in Bangladesh. Within this context, budget analysis has become an entry point for building relationships with local officials to address the problems closest to people's lives. These same local officials place pressure on national officials to change budget allocations so the coffers for poverty elimination, education, and other programs that help people are not left empty.

Budget analysis is also an entry point for tackling economic liberalization and globalization on an international level. For example, an international coalition—including faith-based organizations, development agencies, NGOs in the South and North, and others—has organized to critique SAPs and to push for cancellation of the vast majority of the debt created by these harmful programs. They see debt cancellation as a critical step in changing the direction of economic policies away from neoliberal ideology.

Through budget analysis, these advocates have been able to:

• Target the G7 countries of western Europe, North America, and Japan as the key decision makers in the IMF, World Bank, and other international financial institutions.

- Translate an international declarative policy (reduce absolute poverty by 50 percent by 2015) into a practical policy demand (forgive all or most of the debt based on a country's ability to repay).

- Use "jugular information" to frame the argument clearly and to make counterarguments ineffective. For example, in a short period of time, the stock market wealth in the richest countries has grown to fifty times more than the combined debt of the forty-two poorest countries. As wealth grows, the case for forgiving the debt becomes even more compelling.

- Show what each country has lost in paying off the debts rather than supporting public programs to meet people's basic needs: food, shelter, health, education. Such information may include the number of deaths that were preventable through basic health services, or the number of children—especially girl children—that go uneducated. For example, in Tanzania, the debt payments are nine times greater than what it spends on primary health care, four times what it spends on primary education. (See the two following texts for examples of these types of initiatives.)

The South African Women's Budget Initiative, Warren A. Krafchik

Contributed by Warren Krafchik, Manager of the Budget Information Service (BIS) at the Institute for Democracy in South Africa (Idasa), Cape Town, South Africa.

The South African Women's Budget Initiative was developed in 1995 to track and advance the interests of women during the political and economic transition after apartheid and to provide a comprehensive, critical set of analyses that can be integrated into the activities of both civil society and Parliament.

The initiative is a joint project of two civil society think tanks—the Institute for Democracy in South Africa (Idasa) and the Community Agency for Social Inquiry (CASE)—and the National Parliamentary Committee on the Status and Quality of Life of Women. The civil society–legislature partnership is critical to the initiative's success:

- Civil society contributes research capacity that is lacking in Parliament, while Parliament is able to guarantee direct access to the executive branch. The result is rigorous research that can take advantage of formal and informal channels of intervention.

- In other countries, women's budget research generally faces a trade-off between criticality and data access. In Australia, the women's budget is produced inside the government. The result is a detailed but largely uncritical report. In Canada, where a women's budget is produced entirely outside of government, the report is critical but stunted by lack of access to detailed data. We have not had to face this trade-off in South Africa. The partnership approach has enabled the initiative to be a "critical ally"—our critical analysis does not compromise our access to data.

- The partnership represents a broad alliance that covers a fairly wide political spectrum. It is therefore able to attract and include a wide range of organizations that are able to incorporate the research in their own work.

Methodology

Poverty is widespread in South Africa, but this is not simply the result of inadequate spending. In fact, in each of the major socioeconomic sectors—health, education, and welfare—South Africa spends as much as any other developing country at a similar stage of development. Therefore, rather than focusing on the budget as a whole, reallocations between departments, or increases to total department spending, the Women's Budget Initiative focuses on budgets in specific government departments and ways to redirect spending *within* departments.

The lack of availability of statistics, which is the case in most developing countries, means that it is not possible to conduct an accurate line-by-line audit of public spending to assess the budget's impact on women. Instead, to isolate the policy issues while being sensitive to the data limitations, each paper—written by trained budget analysts and researchers—considers four issues:

- The major gender issues facing the sector under discussion.

- How the state is involved in correcting these issues.

- Whether budget commitments are adequate to meet policy commitments.

- Alternative approaches to correct budget shortfalls.

Information Dissemination and Timing

The drafting process is a secretive, in-house government exercise, as is the case in most countries where it is the government's responsibility to develop the budget. Successful civil society interventions in the early drafting stage are more likely to be highly analytical, targeting the distribution of the budget between departments or levels of government.

The legislative stage is traditionally more open, but it occurs late in the process when only marginal changes are possible. Interventions at this stage may focus on re-prioritization within a department and offer practical, limited alternatives that maintain the overall budget amount for that department.

There is no one magical moment. Budget advocacy has to occur throughout the year with appropriate strategies for each stage of the process.

For example, the dissemination cycle for the Third Women's Budget (1998) began with training workshops in November 1997. By the end of February, draft research papers were completed. This left enough editing time to distribute unpublished papers as soon as the budget was tabled (considered) in March. The South African national budget takes eighteen months to produce, so budget processes overlap. The initiative's submissions, then, served two purposes: they provided a critique of last year's and the new year's budget; and they fed into the next year's budget formulation.

The submission was presented directly to the appropriate parliamentary committee, released to national newspapers, and posted on the Internet. Because it is difficult to compete against the private sector for media coverage on budget day, the initiative focused greater attention on radio coverage, especially community radio stations that attract listeners from community-interest groups. In addition, the initiative prepared a considered, analytical response that would appear as in-depth op-ed pieces in the national print media a week later.

Our efforts to publicize the work of the Women's Budget Initiative are not limited to the budget process. Throughout the year, researchers are involved in writing articles and submissions on current issues, delivering workshops, and assisting government departments and committees with digesting the implications of the recommendations.

Achievements of the Women's Budget Initiative

The Women's Budget Initiative has recorded several important and visible achievements:

- It directly provides budgetary skills to approximately twenty researchers. Many of these researchers have initiated budget work within their own organizations and continue to be involved in the initiative's reference team.

- It produces in-depth research on approximately thirty government departments.

- It provides crucial baseline research that regularly feeds into parliamentary submissions and sector policy research by several organizations. Partly as a result of the initiative, in 1997, the government committed itself to systematically monitoring the quality of life of women. Since this announcement, members of the initiative have been working with the Department of Finance and Central Statistical Services to implement this commitment.

Perhaps the most significant achievement of the initiative is not the most visible: there is a growing number of individuals and organizations that comprise the loose coalition of the initiative. This group is continually deepening its understanding of gender and strengthening its preparedness to respond flexibly to a growing set of issues confronting women, backed by solid budget analysis.

Budget Analysis: A Powerful Tool for Social Activists, Madhusudan Mistry

Contributed by Madhusudan Mistry, 1989 India Advocacy Fellow and Director of Patheya, a center for budget analysis started by Developing Initiatives for Social and Human Action (DISHA), Ahmedabad, India.

DISHA began to see the need for budget analysis when we lobbied the government to raise the wages for one million Tendu leaf-plucker tribal women and on other issues relating to the general welfare of communities living in the tribal areas of Gujarat state in western India. With each struggle, a realization grew: unless we had information on the money spent by the national and state governments, it would be difficult to fairly represent the issues of tribal development. Eventually, this realization forced us to learn how to analyze the state budget.

The word "budget" is enough to turn off most social activists. Our group was no exception. Reaction, debate, and studies on the national and state budgets are traditionally the domain of academics and researchers. This has always been alien territory for social activists. We discovered, however, that budget analysis can be a powerful tool for grassroots groups to use in negotiation or confrontation with the government.

Our Experience with Budget Analysis

In Gujarat, according to the budget manual, the budget process takes over six months. Until the budget is presented in assembly, there is no provision for the general public to participate directly in the budget-making process. They can only "take part" in the budget discussion through the press reports of their elected members' speeches in the assembly. The business community regularly invites finance ministers to listen to their proposals on the budget. The poor, on the other hand, have no influential connections with the finance minister, and their organizations know little about the budget. Our budget analysis aimed to change this.

Our first task was to get a copy of the budget document. We did not know where to look, but eventually found the easiest way was to get it from the elected representatives when it is tabled (considered) in the state assembly. This is what we did.

Budget numbers express an enormous volume of information about the expressed intention of the government, its policies, its allocation of financial resources, and its hidden priorities. However, when we first saw the budget documents, we were puzzled and overwhelmed. First, we had to classify the data. Next, we had to understand the government's accounting system. It took some time to build our self-confidence and create a foolproof system.

Finally, we published our analysis, *Injustices to the Tribals*. Because ours was the first attempt by any public group to disseminate such an analysis, we decided to emphasize how poor people are left out of the budget policies, and how these policies adversely affect the poor. We also used the budget figures extensively, showing that we had discovered 172 mathematical errors in the twenty-two budget documents.

We wanted our notes to stand out from the piles of paper that elected members get during the budget session. We decided to prepare notes that were short—six pages long at the most. We sent our notes to government ministers and bureaucrats and to the press, academic institutions, and voluntary agencies, and waited for a response.

Reactions to Our Budget Analysis

Injustices to the Tribals created a great deal of interest. The ruling party and the bureaucrats were caught unawares; they realized that somebody else was taking keen interest in the budget documents. The opposition parties took full advantage of our notes to press their own cause.

Before each day's budget discussion, we prepared more notes and handed them out to assembly members. Many of them became addicted to our notes. They were eager to receive them as early as possible to help them formulate their own arguments to create pressure on the government.

Every member in the state assembly found our notes useful in a number of ways:

- Our notes—prepared in the local language and with the elected members' educational backgrounds in mind—shaped the budget discussions in the assembly.

- Government officials became more alert to questions raised in the assembly. For the first time, the issues of the poor were discussed, questions were answered, and the debate became precise.

- Budget discussion became sharper and more factual, forcing the ministers to reply to the facts and making the government officials work.

- Our organization's name became familiar in the "corridors of power." Our access to officials, ministers, elected representatives, and the press became easier. Our notes also created strong positive impressions about us: we were not merely a struggle-oriented and slogan-shouting organization. We had the intellectual abilities to put our case across solidly in the government's own sacred terminology.

- Our notes became so popular that a number of Members of the Legislative Assembly (MLAs) asked us to conduct budget analysis training programs for them.

Lessons Learned

Budget analysis has taught us several important lessons:

- Our analysis shifted the balance of power. In general, NGOs and voluntary agencies have rarely addressed the whole field of "governance." Until recently, their role had been limited to receiving either "finance" or "information" from the government. By doing a budget analysis, the group acts as a partner in formulating the budget and pushes the state to collect information and provide it to the people.

- The budget is prepared by a very small group of people in the bureaucracy. In order to maintain their monopoly, they don't want others to know its intricacies. Knowing the process of making the budget documents breaks this monopoly. NGOs must know the process. The more one knows about the finances of the state, the more one becomes confident and powerful.

- Using factual information to discuss the issues of tribal development sharpened our arguments. The budget analysis also widened our vision and gave us ways to pick up certain issues and focus on them.

Budget analysis does have its limitations. We can't find the answers to all the actions of the state by analyzing its budget. Nonetheless, this process can certainly help us understand most of the issues that people are facing.

Using UN Conferences and Their Related Declarations

United Nations (UN) conferences, and other regional and international meetings, create international free spaces that can complement the work being done on the local and national levels.

During the 1990s, seven UN conferences strengthened international movement-building on core issues. These conferences are commonly referred to by the cities where they took place:

- *Rio de Janeiro* (1992). UN Conference on Environment and Development.

- *Vienna* (1993). World Conference on Human Rights.

- *Cairo* (1994). International Conference on Population and Development, including women's reproductive rights.

- *Copenhagen* (1995). World Summit for Social Development, including social policies and rights.

- *Beijing* (1995). Fourth World Conference on Women.

- *Istanbul,* a.k.a. Habitat II (1996). UN Conference on Human Settlements, including affordable, livable communities and housing.

- *Hamburg* (1997). UN Conference on Adult Education.

In 2000, follow-up to Beijing and Copenhagen occurred. Critics of UN conferences—and similar meetings at the regional and international levels—are often disillusioned that necessary policy changes do not follow smoothly from the declarations generated at these conferences.

However, many important outcomes are encouraging:

- *Building local and national civil society.* To prepare for UN conferences, many NGOs and advocates have organized from the bottom up—first locally, then nationally. For example, for the Beijing conference, NGOs created free spaces for women to come together and voice their concerns, demands, and priorities. This process strengthened both the legitimacy and accountability of the delegations that eventually represented their countries in Beijing and Hauirou (at the NGO forum).

- *Exchange.* At the conferences, NGOs and advocates share models of "good practices," patterns of intervention, and lessons from previous efforts, and test ideas for future work. In particular, models from the South and developing countries have made important challenges to the prevailing style and conventional wisdom of Western, industrialized democracies. Participatory, interactive processes often continue after the conferences. For example, Civicus, an international network of CSOs, has initiated discussions to evaluate the strength and autonomy of each country's civil society.

- *Networking.* After the conferences, ongoing working groups and the use of low-cost technology, like e-mail, can keep learning, exchange, and inspiration alive. Such momentum can help to connect issues from one conference to another and to create new campaigns and movements that cross borders. For example, follow-up to the Beijing conference includes extensive cross-border discussions on women's equity, political power, and health, and how to organize around such issues.

- *Legitimacy.* By convening under the auspices of the UN, the conferences make it clear that the issues raised by civil society are priorities to be addressed.

- *Framing public argument.* For example, the UN Conference on Environment and Development (UNCED) in Rio took the phrase "sustainable development" out of the mouths of ecologists and introduced it into the mainstream environmental movement, eventually making it a crucial declarative requirement of all new development projects.

- *Recommendations and declarative policy.* These reflect agreement on issues and priorities that has been negotiated across barriers of language, culture, and differences in political perspectives. Governments sign declarations to indicate their intent to pursue compatible national policies. Declarations, then, become a benchmark against which national policies can be measured and to which civil societies can hold their governments accountable. Even when a particular government does not ratify a declaration, the declaration still embodies aspirations around which advocates organize to pressure

their government. Reminding countries of commitments made at UN conferences is one way to create public argument about a government's non-performance, to inject new demands into the political and policy systems, or to bring life to old demands that have been ignored.

- *New civil society capacities.* Natural partnerships have formed between small and large CSOs working at all levels, leading to new capacities to monitor and evaluate the policy outcomes of the conferences. For example, the US-based international advocacy group Women's Economic Development Organization (WEDO) gathers information from local and national NGOs to highlight gaps between promises and action and to keep pressure on governments. Their annual reports help focus advocates' attention on successes to be built on and issues for future action.

- *New national government policies.* For example, the Uganda government has drawn up a strategic national plan focusing on four areas of concern addressed in the Beijing Platform. It has also reserved 30 percent of seats in local government for women. Although simply increasing the number of seats does not by itself increase the capacity of women to effectively develop and push through favorable policies, it is a critical starting point on which government and advocates can build.

- *New international institutional capacity.* Policy change (like the criminalization of human rights violations) is rarely effective if not coupled with institutional changes (such as the uncontested establishment of the rule of law and the designation of a court to hear human rights claims). Recognizing this, the United Nations has made key institutional changes, such as creating the post of high commissioner for human rights, further integrating human rights throughout all UN activities and increasing human rights field operations from one to twenty.

- *Sustaining public argument.* Five-year follow-up conferences—commonly known by the original location "plus five"—provide a forum for systematic evaluation of the progress made. In the case of the Rio follow-up, the backsliding of environmental issues since 1992 led organizers to call it

"Rio minus five." Whether they are "plus five" or "minus five," the follow-up conferences:

– Provide a valuable performance check.

– Sustain public argument within countries and in international institutions, including donor agencies.

– Serve as pressure points to aggregate common demands.

All this is the essence of advocacy.

These important outcomes are the building blocks for changing attitudes, policies, and institutions toward long-term transformative change.

Conclusion to Part I

Over the years, the Advocacy Institute has had the privilege of working with and learning from Southern and Northern frontline activists, grassroots organizers, lobbyists, strategists, researchers, and policy analysts—social justice advocates all. Our experience tells us that more and more advocates in Southern and Northern countries demonstrate confidence in demystifying, defining for themselves, and practicing advocacy. Particularly in the last ten years, people—ordinary and elite—are becoming agents of change through engaging in people-centered advocacy.

The results are twofold: these efforts are creating a changing power dynamic in people's immediate environments, whether in their community, state, or nation. Moreover, the opportunity to learn from experience and to participate in organizations and advocacy efforts is facilitating the empowerment of people who don't believe change is possible. In many ways, these changes can be the most profound and lasting, and are cause for celebration.

But this is not the end of the story. At the same time, advocates—particularly Southern advocates—are grappling with a rapidly changing world that presents new threats and forces outside their control. Each day, people face real risks to their lives and security.

To counter these threats, to build on the many positive small changes toward long-term sustainable change, and to transform societies, advocates around the world must continue to:

- Focus on participation, accountability, and transparency as core themes in pushing decision-making systems to be responsive to people's voices and needs.

- Enact these core themes within their own organizations and efforts.

- Organize civil society as a powerful force in public life by creating free spaces for people to exchange ideas and innovate actions.

- Engage with public argument and public decision-making systems to move "from protest to politics," from primarily opposition to initiating actions and policies.

- Learn how to navigate decision-making systems at all levels—local, national, and international.

- Hone strategy development skills to identify micro-level points of intervention that tackle macro-level problems, to build on advocates' sources of power, and to make judgments about what kinds of risks are worth taking.

Finally, to meet ongoing and emerging challenges, advocates—and their supporters—must recognize the necessity of time and space for reflection, storytelling, exchange, learning, networking, mentoring, and skill building. When combined, these elements will create an effective advocacy leadership that renews itself and builds depth in second and third generations of leadership, and those yet to come.

51

Part II

Advocacy Skills

Rosa de la Vega

Introduction to Part II

How is advocacy done? What skills are needed? How can social, economic, and political justice advocates become more effective?

Part II of *Advocacy for Social Justice* addresses these questions by drawing on the collective experiences of the Advocacy Institute staff and our colleagues around the world. Six brief cases contributed by Advocacy Institute alumni, as well as other examples, are interspersed throughout this part.

Learning by Doing

Since 1985, the Advocacy Institute has worked to demystify the concept of "advocacy" and to strengthen people's confidence and ability to create change through advocacy. We work as trainers, facilitators, and advisers. In doing so, many of us draw from our own frontline experience.

Our colleagues are grassroots activists, community leaders, and paid professionals working for social justice around the world. Through the Fellows Program—our intensive leadership development program—and other work, we have been privileged to work with hundreds of social justice leaders from Asia (Bangladesh, India, Nepal, Indonesia, the Philippines), Africa (Angola, Botswana, Ghana, Kenya, Malawi, Mozambique, Namibia, Senegal, South Africa, Uganda, Zimbabwe), the Middle East (Egypt, Israel, Palestine), central and eastern Europe (Bosnia-Herzegovina, Bulgaria, Croatia, Hungary, Macedonia, Romania, Russia, Serbia, Slovakia, Ukraine), and the Americas (Cuba, the United States).

Over the years, many have asked us for a recipe for "how to do advocacy." Our response is always the same: a single recipe doesn't exist. Every situation is different and everyone discovers for themselves what will work best.

We have, however, gained three insights about how advocacy is done:

- *Advocacy is an art.* The best advocates envision what they want to create, then piece by piece, layer by layer make it real. And, like many true masterpieces, advocacy toward long-term change takes more than one effort, each improving on the one before.

- *Reflection enhances effectiveness.* Those who pause to reflect on what they do instinctively often become more effective strategists, leaders, mentors, and teachers.

- *Around the world, advocates ask the same core questions* as they create their advocacy strategies and action plans.

Overview of Part II

To help advocates reflect on their own experiences, Part II draws on the Advocacy Institute's learning from our colleagues and aims to name what advocates often do instinctively.

Part II is written in three chapters:

- *Chapter 4—Social Justice Advocacy: Key Concepts.* Key concepts of social justice advocacy that are used throughout Part II are presented in this chapter.

- *Chapter 5—Strategy Development.* One model for strategy development is presented and discussed in this chapter.

- *Chapter 6—Skill Building.* Other generic skills that are needed in any advocacy effort—collaboration, use of information, message development and delivery, working with the mass media, and lobbying—are discussed in this chapter.

Part II combines lessons learned by the Advocacy Institute in our capacity-building work, assessment questions to help your group reflect on your own learning, and brief cases contributed by Advocacy Institute alumni and other examples from our colleagues. Together, we hope they will help you apply new lessons and insights to your future advocacy efforts.

The models presented here are only a beginning. They will take on new dimensions as you and others engage with, challenge, and use the ideas alongside your own experiences and understanding.

How to Use Part II

These writings present a synthesis of the Advocacy Institute's collective experience. Much is drawn from the specific experiences of our Advocacy and Leadership Fellows in Bangladesh, India, Namibia, South Africa, and the United States.

To help you reflect on your own experiences and to draw lessons that can be applied to your particular context, ask yourself the following questions as you read:

- Does this resonate with my own experiences and contexts? Do some parts resonate more than others? Which parts?

- Why or why not?

- Would I define some words and concepts differently? How?

- What new lessons or insights have I gained?

- What can I apply to my own social change work? How?

Chapter 4

Social Justice Advocacy: Key Concepts

As David Cohen writes in Part I of *Advocacy for Social Justice,* it is important to share what perspective informs one's writing. With this in mind, this chapter summarizes key concepts that are drawn upon in the following chapters and sections. Keep these in mind as you read Part II and reflect on the information presented alongside your own experiences.

The Advocacy Institute's understanding of "social justice advocacy" includes the following key concepts:

- When public decisions are made, many voices are left out of public argument. Too often, these voices belong to poor people and others who are marginalized or oppressed.

  Social justice advocacy seeks to change this by trying to:

  - Influence political, economic, and social *outcomes* that directly affect people's lives.

  - Change the *processes* by which decisions are made, including creating openings for those affected by decisions to be involved in making them.

- In the process, social justice advocacy focuses on four core themes: participation, representation, accountability, and transparency. Minimally, participation means having one's voice heard when public-policy solutions are formulated, considered, chosen, and implemented.

  While advocacy groups vary greatly—from community-based membership organizations to national-level policy-research organizations and cross-border coalitions—the core themes also relate to how these groups are connected to their constituents, members, or those who are affected by the issue. A group's answers to questions like "Who are we?" "What is our voice?" and "Who do we speak for?" will significantly affect the strategy developed and actions taken.

- The process of change is incremental. In most cases, the changes desired are large and complex, meaning they will be reached by stringing together a series of smaller steps and victories. To link one step to the next, planning, reflection, and vision are essential.

- Three cycles of change affect all advocacy efforts. Since Part I discusses these in greater depth, here is a brief description of each:

  - *Problem-solving cycle.*

    - People experience a problem and decide something needs to change.

    - Alternative solutions are considered, and one is chosen for identified reasons.

    - The solution is implemented, and the necessary change happens.

  - *Issue life cycle.* At each stage, different skills, actions, roles, and responsibilities are needed.

    - *Birth.* A new demand, issue, idea, or proposal takes form.

    - *Childhood.* The issue is nurtured, and support is built.

    - *Adolescence.* The issue advances through the early stages of decision making.

    - *Adulthood.* The issue reaches a resolute decision.

    - *Maturity.* The idea is implemented, monitored, and evaluated in the short term.

    - *Renewal.* Implementation is evaluated to determine if it should continue in the long term.

  - *Organizational life cycle.* Organizations have different skills, capacities, and resources as they grow. An organization needs to match its stage in the organizational life cycle to the issue-life-cycle stage to identify what it can do best and in what ways it needs to collaborate with others.

- ~ *Birth.* An organization is created.

- ~ *Childhood.* An organization learns new skills and builds infrastructure.

- ~ *Adolescence.* An organization becomes willing to experiment.

- ~ *Adulthood.* An organization takes the lead and mentors others.

- ~ *Maturity.* An organization shares its wisdom and experiences.

- ~ *Renewal.* An organization develops a new strategic focus or leadership.

- Change is multi-dimensional. The process of organizing demands and placing them on those with the power to make change affects individuals, organizations, families, communities, and civil society as well as society as a whole and its governing institutions. At the same time, change may occur on the local, national, or international levels.

- Even the best advocacy efforts will rarely know exactly which action, tactic, or tool moves a key audience to act in the desired way. Therefore, it is important to focus on several key audiences at once and to combine "inside" tools (such as lobbying a decision maker) with "outside" tools (such as mobilizing the grassroots, mass media, and other pressure makers).

  The combination of inside and outside tools serves another purpose: it helps organizations and advocacy efforts stay connected and accountable to the grassroots and those who are directly affected by the issue.

Throughout Part II, "advocacy" refers to these understandings of social justice advocacy and the nature of change.

Chapter 5

Strategy Development

Strategy development is at the core of effective advocacy efforts. The process will help your group to:

- *Assess your particular situation,* including the current reality, your sources of power and current capacity, and possible starting points for creating change.

- *Select achievable objectives* for getting started.

- *Create an action plan,* including how to use your resources, what capacities to build, and which actions, tactics, and tools to use.

- *Navigate the little victories,* setbacks, compromises, unexpected opportunities, and uncertainties that line the road to the long-term change you want to achieve.

One Model for Strategy Development

Many models have been created to help groups develop strategy. In our experience, one receives consistent praise from Advocacy Institute alumni: "the nine questions," developed by our colleague Jim Shultz from the Democracy Center. This model is effective because it simply names the questions that many advocates ask instinctively.

Like any masterpiece, what appears simple is actually the result of careful, disciplined work based on research, observation, and practice. To aid advocates in their own research and observation, a modified version is presented here. It includes five key elements:

- *Objectives.* What do we want?
- *Audiences.* Who has the power to make it happen?
- *Diagnosis.* What is possible?
- *Action plan.* How do we get started?
- *Evaluation.* How do we know our plan is working?

Each of the five key elements can be broken into further questions to help advocates understand their context as well as possible:

- *Objectives.* What do we want?
  - Who are we?
  - What is the problem?
  - What is our vision of change?
  - What objectives—or piece of our vision—will we focus on?

- *Audiences.* Who has the power to make it happen?
  - What is at stake?
  - How are changes made?
  - Who are the *key* audiences?

- *Diagnosis.* What is possible?
  - What is our capacity to engage in advocacy? Where is our group at the moment?
  - What is the external environment like?
  - When you put it all together, what is possible?

- *Action plan.* How do we get started?
  - How do we move each audience to make—or not block—change?
  - How will we protect our group members from risk?
  - What is our work plan?
  - Do we have what we need to get started?
  - What is our backup plan?

- *Evaluation.* How do we know our plan is working?
  - What has changed in the short term?
  - What has changed in the long term?

These questions are drawn from our colleagues' outstanding work, including the ACT ON model created by Phil Wilbur, our former media advocacy director;

the stakeholder analysis used by Zane Dangor and Owen Stuurman from the Development Resources Centre in South Africa; and the evaluation framework developed by Valerie Miller at the Institute for Development Research in Boston.

Sections 1 to 5 discuss the five key elements, and provide "Assessment Questions" and "Worksheets" that we have found helpful.

How to Use This Model

When using this model, keep in mind a few things:

- To be useful, the strategy development process requires:

    - Systematic and disciplined effort.

    - Ongoing action, reflection, and refinement.

    - Research and planning to tailor your strategy to your context and capacity.

    - Time—informally throughout the effort, or formally in sessions lasting one or more days.

    - Flexibility and the ability to work in a non-linear order.

    - The ability to give a diagnosis—to understand the current reality, what is possible, and how to get started—despite uncertainty or incomplete information.

    - Willingness to experiment and to learn by doing.

- Models are created to simplify otherwise complex processes. When you compare them to your own experience, some parts will work, some won't. For example, with strategy-development models in particular, one challenge is putting the questions in order. While the following sections and chapter present questions in one order, you may find you naturally ask the questions in a different order—or ask different questions entirely! We encourage you to try this model, pull it apart, and adapt it to fit your own style and experience.

- You may not be able to answer all of the questions at first and may need to gather more information along the way. You may return to one or more stages

throughout the advocacy effort. You may not have answers to all of the questions. Don't be discouraged! Over time, you will learn which questions to ask and how to find the answers you need.

- Strategy development often works best as a participatory process that draws upon multiple perspectives. We suggest working in a group—with members of your organization or within a coalition—to develop and refine your strategy.

- Some groups will need more time to address the questions. This may be true if the group is newly formed; does not yet believe that change is possible; or focuses on critical consciousness, social-analysis skills, group problem solving, and facilitating members' empowerment to advocate on their own behalf. Remember, learning by doing is a core principle of advocacy—we encourage you to take the time you need.

Section 1
Objectives: What Do We Want?

As we discussed in chapter 4, change is multi-dimensional, with small changes occurring simultaneously. When taken together, these incremental changes can build toward long-term, transformative change.

Your objectives, therefore, need to be multi-dimensional as well. They may:

- *Be long-term and short-term.*

    Many advocacy efforts start with broad, long-term objectives. To help draw people into the effort and create a belief that change is possible, long-term objectives need to be broken into smaller pieces—specific, short-term objectives that may be achieved in six months to two years.

    Some advocacy efforts focus only on short-term objectives, with no eye to the future. While their objectives may be achievable, they rarely build on short-term victories, momentum, and excitement toward a long-term objective.

    Both long-term and short-term objectives are critical. While your action plan will focus on the short-term, your long-term objectives will help you evaluate your progress and re-strategize as necessary.

- *Look outward and inward.*

    Many advocacy objectives look outward to *people and institutions*—such as government and corporations—that have the power and authority to make the desired changes, through law, policy, or behavior. Advocacy objectives may also look outward by focusing on the *processes* by which changes or decisions are made.

    It is important to also look inward. After all, winning a short-term policy victory can ultimately weaken an organization if it does not continue to involve those affected in any meaningful way. Without a strong grassroots group to monitor implementation of the policy and to hold the government accountable over time, policy victories can be hollow.

    There is another reason to look inward. Your group may lose a specific battle, but you may succeed in a number of other ways. You may stage a first-ever mass protest on your issue, gain increased press coverage, or develop new relationships, skills, expertise, knowledge, and, above all, confidence! Such successes are incredibly valuable, both building toward future efforts and making an immediate impact on the lives of those engaged in the struggle from day to day.

- *Focus on multiple levels.*

    Looking outward, your objectives may focus on the local, national, and/or international level.

    Looking inward, your objectives may seek to have a positive effect on individuals, organizations, communities, and/or civil society as a whole.

The selection of objectives is often based on careful analysis of the problem and who has the power to make change happen. At this stage, think of your objectives as first drafts.

Many questions will be presented in this section and the following sections to help you determine if your objectives are both appropriate and possible. You will revisit and refine your objectives in section 3, "Diagnosis."

Your refined objectives will guide the actions, tactics, and tools you choose to use in section 4, "Action Planning." Your objectives will also provide the framework for reflecting on your efforts and planning next steps in section 5, "Evaluation."

Assessment Questions

To help a group develop draft objectives, we have found the following questions helpful:

- Who are we?

- What is the problem?

- What is our vision of change?

- What objectives—or piece of our vision—will we focus on?

Who Are We?

Your group's identity will guide the objectives you ultimately choose. You may return to these kinds of questions throughout your strategy development. Think about:

- Who are we? What perspectives and identities do we bring to our work?

- Do we represent someone beside ourselves? If so, what is our accountability to these people?

- What are our sources of power?

- What are our sources of legitimacy and credibility? From the perspective of those we represent? From the decision makers' perspective?

- What risks do we face? What are we afraid of? What might happen if we take action?

- What are our values? Why are we engaged in advocacy? How do we want to work together as a group?

What Is the Problem?

To better understand the problem, create as full a picture as possible. (For more on this process see "Defining the Problem.") Share stories, experiences, and information with others. You might ask yourselves:

- Who does the problem affect? How? Be as concrete as possible. For example, how large is the affected group relative to the total population? How intensely does the problem affect people's lives? Does the problem affect different groups differently?

- What causes the problem?

- Who is responsible for addressing the problem?

- What are possible solutions?

- What will the impact of these different solutions be on the entire affected group? Subgroups?

Defining the Problem, Identifying Solutions: Relationships with Local Government Officials, Mohammad Zakaria

Contributed by Mohammad Zakaria, 1994 Bangladesh Advocacy Fellow, former Executive Director of Gana Gabeshana o Unnayan Foundation (GoUF), and current Regional Manager for ActionAid Bangladesh (Jessore, Bangladesh). Some observations emerged from the Capacity Building Initiative for NGOs (CABIN), jointly operated by CAPRe and GoUF and supported by the Swiss Development Corporation (SDC).

Gana Gabeshana o Unnayan Foundation (GoUF), the Participatory Research and Development Foundation, is a local nongovernmental organization (NGO) active in southwestern Bangladesh. As part of a long-term strategy to alleviate poverty, we have been working to promote grassroots democracy and to help local-level government officials serve the citizens more effectively.

GoUF has identified a number of problems that prevent such effectiveness:

- *Citizens are alienated from the government.* In the past, heroes, kings, and military dictators told the people what to do. As a result, the people have learned to feel helpless and the government has become paternalistic: "The people are helpless, they need to be helped. The people are without ideas, they need to be given ideas. The people are without resources, they need to be given resources as mercy."

- *The people do not know what resources are available.* Despite huge investment in the local infrastructure, the people do not have enough information about who is doing what and where to find help.

- *The people have poor relationships with government workers:*

  – Government officials are frequently transferred, and the people have to build rapport all over again with a new officer.

  – The job requires many more hours than the people actually work. This is discouraging for workers who are sincere and devoted to their jobs.

  – Non-local supervisors are sometimes threatened by the local power structure and make compromises in order to survive and keep their jobs.

  – NGOs say government officials lack the skills to handle flexible, field-oriented development activities and need to be better trained.

- *There is a lack of village-level democracy.* Even though the union *parishad* members—the people's locally elected representatives—could be the best advocates for the voters' rights, they spend much of their time and energy with Members of Parliament (MPs) and other party leaders and ignore the people they are supposed to serve.

How GoUF Addresses the Problem

The poor are not incapable of helping themselves; they are just out of practice. GoUF believes that changing this mindset is the basis of a new beginning. GoUF advocates a knowledge-intensive development approach that starts at the bottom, with the poor themselves:

- *Gathering information.* GoUF involves people in collecting and collating data about poverty. This new collective knowledge will provide clues to how they might work together to overcome poverty. This type of participatory research naturally evolves to the planning stage.

- *Education program.* GoUF runs an education program for semi-specialization in areas that target the needs of the village and the poor. After graduation, Village Experts teach other group members what they have learned in weekly group meetings and formal trainings.

- *Planning.* Village participatory planning is done collectively by the villagers. They approach different local-level government officers or employees and ask for help in implementing their ideas through training, technical assistance, and advice.

- *Training.* GoUF provides small loans and micro-credit to aid some group members, mostly women, in starting new ventures. GoUF then invites local-level government officers to provide training to the loanees. Trainee group members come with their own information from their respective villages and present their needs. This strategy inspires many government officials to offer ideas and builds rapport between them and the group.

- *Communication.* Most government officials begin with negative ideas. Through conversation, however, they tend to move toward the positive. We must have more than one conversation. We can return with follow-up questions and concrete action plans. The most important thing is to keep talking. The more we talk, the more clearly we will be able to understand each other.

What Is Our Vision of Change?

Your vision is important and can serve many purposes.

Your vision can help you "see" what you want to create, and, if you can see it, it will likely feel possible to achieve! When you get started on your advocacy effort, your vision will be your guiding light—inspiring, motivating, and helping you to focus when you reach a turning point or experience a setback.

The process of creating a vision can also be an effective way for a diverse group or coalition to identify common ground and build cohesion or to motivate people who do not yet believe change is possible.

To create such a vision, you might ask yourselves:

- If the changes we want happen, what would be different? Whose lives would be improved? How?

A vision based on your group values can also help your group to evaluate alternative solutions, as well as to identify practices and behaviors you can enact now. To create this kind of vision, you might ask yourselves:

- If we created a world based on our values of just, decent society, what would be different?

- Will the solutions we want help to create this world? How?

- What can we do *now* to begin to create this world on a smaller scale—in our personal relationships, families, communities, organizations, and/or civil society?

For some advocates, it is helpful to imagine a future world that is different for their children and grandchildren. They recognize that their vision may not be realized in their lifetimes but there is much they can do to build toward it. For many, such a sense of purpose is a significant sustaining force. To create this kind of vision, you might ask yourselves:

- Imagine that we resolve all the problems we described. Imagine a morning ten, twenty, fifty, one hundred years from now. When people awaken, how do we want the world to be?

Some advocacy efforts do not begin with a vision. It *is* possible to create a strategy and engage in advocacy without one. However, in the Advocacy Institute's experience, creating a vision—whether at the beginning of an effort or at mid-course—can be a significant sustaining force for those working for long-term, transformative change.

Sample Visions

Contributed by Gordana Stojanovic, 1997 International Policy Advocacy (IPA) alumna and President of the Association for Peace and Human Rights in Croatia; and Diana Autin, 1994 US Leadership Fellow and Executive Director of the Statewide Parent Advocacy Network (SPAN) in New Jersey, USA.

One minority Croat group in Serbia envisions a society with the right to go to school, normal electricity, and the right to speak openly about problems.

In the United States, the Statewide Parent Advocacy Network (SPAN) uses their vision to identify the benefits of potential solutions, including those that may "solve" one problem only by creating another. For example, one "solution" to low-quality public schools in urban communities is to give students vouchers to use at religious or private schools. Without a vision based on the importance of a strong *public* education system, this solution could be very attractive.

What Objectives—or Piece of Our Vision—Will We Focus On?

You may be able to see what you want to create, but your vision may seem so big, so complex—how could you possibly do it all? The key is to focus on one piece of your vision—one set of objectives.

To choose a set of objectives, think about which piece of your vision is:

- Important enough.

  - Will it build the support and/or active involvement of those affected by the issue? Of potential allies? (For example, is it a priority issue for them? If not, will they at least support your efforts?)

  - Will it engage the general public?

  - Will it build toward your vision?

- Small enough to achieve in the short term (six months to two years).

    Many steps—and people's sustained involvement—will be needed to reach your long-term objectives. A small, achievable step that leads to visible, concrete results will give your group a sense of progress and momentum while you build confidence, skills, and support.

- An opportunity to build skills and facilitate grassroots empowerment.

    Inward objectives are incredibly valuable. By drawing people in and creating opportunities for people to "learn by doing," an advocacy effort can build its long-term capacity and strengthen and sustain itself in the long run. By investing in "hands-on training" for those directly affected by the issue, advocacy efforts can also begin to shift the power of who can be an "advocate" and who can participate in public argument and problem solving.

    Inward objectives also link to outward objectives. By drawing people into the effort, especially those affected by the problem, an advocacy effort broadens its grassroots base and increases its credibility and legitimacy—both to the affected groups and to the key decision makers.

This series of questions has helped you identify potential objectives—short-term and long-term, outward and inward, and multi-level. The next sections will help you gather more information about your

specific context. In section 3, "Diagnosis," you will synthesize the information you gather and determine whether your objectives are SMART—specific, manageable, achievable, realistic, and timely.

Choosing a Piece of the Vision

Drawn from stories told by Kathleen D. Sheekey and David Cohen, Advocacy Institute Co-Directors and lead lobbyists in the campaign to stop the MX missile.

In 1982, the American public's growing fear of a nuclear holocaust was the catalyst for a large peace demonstration in Central Park, New York City. Clearly, it was an issue that engaged the general public.

However, although the rally organizers' vision—a nuclear-free world—was inspiring, it was not practical for an advocacy campaign. A broad arms control coalition narrowed the vision to one manageable piece: stop funding for the MX missile system. The MX was the perfect choice because there were so many doubts about its design and necessity, and a challenge to it was likely to build support among many unlikely allies.

Important enough and small enough to be more likely to achieve, the objective had another dimension. Until then, there were no public discussions about the MX. Focusing on the MX became an opportunity to organize grassroots pressure on decision makers to *share* decision-making power with citizens and, therefore, to transform the decision-making process. (*The story continues. See section 3, "Diagnosis."*)

Section 2
Audiences: Who Has the Power to Make It Happen?

Advocacy efforts mix actions that pressure, persuade, educate, and mobilize people and institutions that can make change happen. These people and institutions can be thought of as "audiences." Your effort will likely focus on multiple audiences simultaneously, especially since you will likely never know which combination of actions, tactics, and tools will lead to the change you want.

Your advocacy efforts will focus on two types of audiences:

- *Decision makers.* Those that have the power of authority—formal and/or informal—to make or to block change.

- *Pressure makers.* Those that have the power to influence or pressure decision makers or other pressure makers and to raise public opinion of an issue.

In some cases, pressure makers may be so influential that they become de facto or informal decision makers, overshadowing de jure or formal decision makers. For example, on paper, the New Jersey State Board of Education makes education policy. In practice, the board rarely disagrees with the commissioner of education. Therefore, the commissioner is an informal decision maker.

To choose which decision makers and pressure makers to focus on, you will need to carefully analyze the power dynamics involved, the processes—formal and informal—through which change happens, and who has a stake or interest in how the problem is resolved.

The questions in this section will help you to identify, categorize, and research various audiences and to determine if you are focusing on the right ones. They will also help you to assess potential risks and to begin gathering and analyzing information about each audience. You will use this information in section 3, "Diagnosis," to determine what may be possible to achieve and in section 4, "Action Planning," to create an action plan for getting started.

Assessment Questions

To help a group identify the right audiences, we have found the following questions helpful:

- What is at stake?

- How are changes made?

- Who are the *key* audiences?

What Is at Stake?

The push for social change is often met by resistance, especially by those who are threatened by the change or do not want to share the power to make decisions that affect people's lives.

In addition to helping you identify potential audiences for your demands, these questions will help you anticipate and prepare for resistance. Think about:

- Who is harmed by the status quo? What is their social status? What barriers do they face (for example, limited or no social mobility, a history of non-engagement)?

- Who wants to maintain the status quo? Who benefits?

- Who will benefit from change?

- Who will be threatened by change and become a potential antagonist?

How Are Changes Made?

To identify decision makers and pressure makers, think about both the formal and informal ways in which changes are made or blocked. These questions will also help you identify opportunities to participate in or exert pressure on the decision-making system.

Think about:

- *Decision makers.*

  - Who has the power and authority to make or block change? Who decides whether a problem is addressed or ignored?

  - What are their duties? For what can they be held accountable?

  - What are their limitations?

- *Pressure makers.*

  - Who has influence with or connection to these decision makers?

    ~ Think about those in civil society, the private sector, and the government. (See "Defining Civil Society" for one definition.)

    ~ Think about all levels (local, state, national, regional, international).

  - Who influences public opinion on an issue?

  - Why are they influential? What are their sources of power?

  - Are any of them so influential that they are informal decision makers?

- *Formal and informal structures.*

  – What are the decision-making bodies? Think about branches of government, ministries or departments, agencies, committees, councils, boards of directors, stockholders, and so on.

  – How are they organized? What is the relationship among different bodies? Between different levels?

- *Decision-making processes.*

  – How does an issue become part of the problem-solving agenda?

  – How is a solution considered, chosen, and implemented? What is the process? How much time can each stage take?

  – Are there openings for public participation? Do decision makers consult with civil society when deciding among alternative solutions? If so, at what stages of the process? Through what mechanisms?

  – Who has access to these mechanisms? Whose voices are sought out? Represented? Listened to? Considered important?

Defining "Civil Society" from a Social Justice Perspective

Here is one aspirational, working definition of "civil society":

Civil society is a panoply of organizations and individuals that engage in public life. Those acting from a social justice perspective engage in public life to help people, groups, and governing institutions meet their mutual responsibilities to the society; to check and balance the power of the state and market; and to work toward making real a vision of a just, decent society. Civil society includes, among others, nongovernmental organizations (NGOs), community-based organizations (CBOs), professional associations, philanthropic and religious organizations, and both ordinary and elite individuals.

(See Part I, lesson 5, "Public Argument," for further discussion.)

Understanding How Changes Are Made, Ulka Mahajan

Contributed by Ulka Mahajan, 1996 India Advocacy Fellow and former staff person at Samarthan, Mumbai, India.

The status of the common citizen needs to change from a beggar at the gate to a bargainer who sits at the table with the government. It is a journey from protest to politics. To bargain and apply pressure successfully, it is essential to understand government procedures. Here is an example from my practical experience.

Campaigning to Increase the Minimum Wage

In Maharashtra state, India, the government had not increased wages for five years. To protest government apathy, the agricultural laborers' unions mobilized people from all over the state for a huge rally. The delegation went to the minister's office with their demands. The minister, busy in the state legislative session, refused to meet with them. The next day, the delegation found that legislators from the opposition had raised the issue in the assembly but in a way that sidetracked it. This was an eye-opener for us. Most of our preparations had gone to waste, and we did not achieve any tangible results—clearly a consequence of not knowing how the system works.

After this experience, we made an effort to understand the state's legislative procedures and methods. We used two legislative tools:

- *Calling an "attention motion"* about an issue of urgent public importance. We created this urgency by initiating several simultaneous events—picketing, a hunger strike, demonstrations—at the local and state level. The media covered the events and the issue was taken up in the legislature. We learned how to draft the motion ourselves to make sure the core of the issue would be addressed.

- *Question hour,* during which six or seven questions are discussed on the floor. In one session, a legislative question on the agricultural laborers' issue was number twenty-four on the agenda and had no chance of being raised. We discovered, though, that the members can ask the speaker to take a question during the last ten minutes if it is a major issue.

Before the question hour, we spoke with the leader of the opposition and different party leaders. We convinced them of the issue's importance, and it was discussed in the last ten minutes during that session.

Within the next two years, we managed to get the issue discussed thoroughly and consistently on the legislative floor. We also managed to make it a sizable issue for the opposition, which had neglected it for years.

As a result of our consistent efforts, wages for agricultural laborers were increased in 1994. However, the wage increase was inadequate. This gave us another opportunity to intervene. We investigated and found out that we could challenge the inadequate wage increase by submitting petitions to the Minimum Wage Advisory Board. Seventeen unions of laborers submitted their objections in well-drafted, informed memoranda. For the first time in the state, the agricultural laborers recorded their say with the advisory board and, moreover, were well received. The wages were increased again in 1997, this time as a major cabinet decision.

Lessons Learned

Studying the rules, procedures, nature, and intricacies of the system can take you a long way in the process of resolving an issue. The following areas are particularly important to understand:

- *Mechanisms that support or apply pressure to particular decision-making processes,* such as committees and advisory boards.

- *The cycle of accountability and its dynamics in a given system.* For example, the executive machinery is accountable to the legislature and judiciary.

- *Key areas and trends of current politics.* For example, the present state government in Maharashtra has an urban face. They want to project their rural concerns to the public and the media, so the issue of agricultural laborers was a key issue for them.

Who Are the *Key* Audiences?

In answering many of the previous questions, you have started a list of possible audiences. If the list is long, how can you possibly focus on everyone? The key is to begin to narrow the list by identifying the *most important* audiences—those who can help or hurt your issue the most. They will be the focus of your action plan.

In addition to identifying key audiences, the following questions will help you gather information about each one. You will use this information to create your action plan.

To identify key audiences, ask yourself the following questions. Be as specific as you can. Take time to discuss each audience and to gather as much relevant information as possible.

- *Who holds a stake or an interest in the issue and whether or how it is resolved?* (See Worksheets 5.1–5.2.)

  - Start by listing those you identified in answering "What is the problem?" "What is at stake?" and "How are changes made?" Divide your list into decision makers (formal and informal) and pressure makers.

  - Add anyone else whose support you need or whose opposition you need to neutralize.

  - Did you forget anyone? Take another look. Think about all sectors of society at all levels (local, state, national, regional, international).

- *For each audience, how important are they to the issue? Why?* (See Worksheet 5.3.) "Important" may mean that an audience will be directly affected by the change, has the power and opportunity to make or block change, or is very influential with decision makers, pressure makers, or in raising public opinion. Think about three broad categories:

  - Very important.

  - Somewhat important.

  - Not important.

The audiences you identify as "very important" will be your *key* audiences and the focus of your action plan. You will also need to monitor the other audiences in case their level of importance changes.

Worksheet 5.1: Listing Your Audiences

First, list audiences that you identified in answering "What is the problem?" "What is at stake?" and "How are changes made?" Then add anyone else whose support you need or whose opposition you need to neutralize.

Audiences	Notes

Worksheet 5.2: Dividing Your Audiences

Divide your list from Worksheet 5.1 into decision makers (formal and informal) and pressure makers.

Formal Decision Makers	Informal Decision Makers	Pressure Makers

Worksheet 5.3: Ranking Your Audiences' Level of Importance

For each audience, how important are they to the issue? For each column, divide the list into three broad categories: very important, somewhat important, and not important. The audiences you identify as "very important" will be your *key* audiences and the focus of your action plan.

"Important" may mean that an audience will be directly affected by the change, has the power and opportunity to make or block change, or is very influential with decision makers, pressure makers, or in raising public opinion.

	Formal Decision Makers	Informal Decision Makers	Pressure Makers
Very Important			
Somewhat Important			
Not Important			

Worksheet 5.4: Evaluating Your Audiences

For each key audience, do they support the change? Or oppose it? Divide your list again into five categories: strong supporters, moderate supporters, fence-sitters (those who are uncommitted, undecided, or easily swayed), moderate opponents, and strong opponents. You will develop your action plan based on an audience's level of support or opposition.

	Very Important Formal Decision Makers	Very Important Informal Decision Makers	Very Important Pressure Makers
Strong Supporters			
Moderate Supporters			
Fence-Sitters			
Moderate Opponents			
Strong Opponents			

Worksheet 5.5: Matching Pressure Makers with Decision Makers

The more specific you can be about who influences whom, the more effective your action plan will be.
To match key pressure makers with key decision makers, first, write a decision maker's name into Circle 1.
Then, look at your list of other very important decision makers and pressure makers (see Worksheet 5.3). Which
ones are influential to the decision maker in Circle 1? Add their names to Circles 2–5. Use as few or as many
circles as you need. Repeat this for each key decision maker.

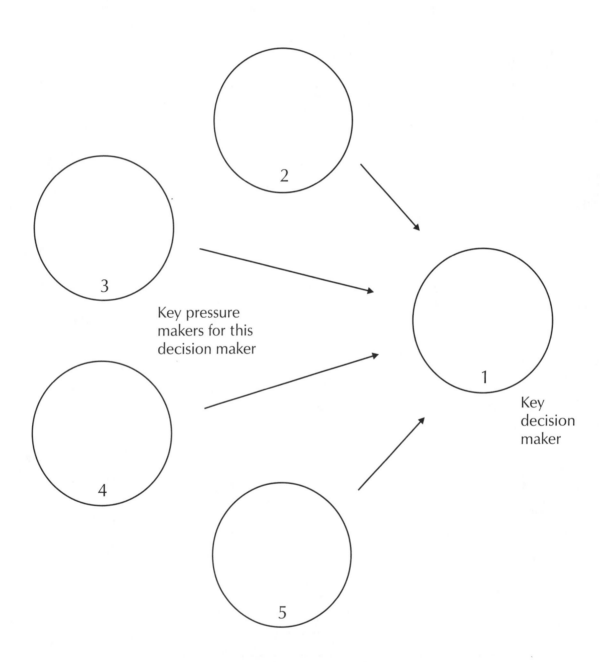

- *For each key audience, do they support the change? Or oppose it?* (See Worksheet 5.4.) Divide your list again into five categories:

  - Strong supporters.

  - Moderate supporters.

  - Fence sitters (those who are uncommitted, undecided, or easily swayed).

  - Moderate opponents.

  - Strong opponents.

  During section 4, "Action Planning," you will develop your action plan based on an audience's level of support or opposition.

- *Can you match key decision makers (formal or informal) with key pressure makers?* (See Worksheet 5.5.) The more specific you can be about who influences whom, the more effective your action plan will be.

- *What do you know about each key audience?* These questions will help you gather and analyze information about each audience. You will use this information to create an action plan in section 4, "Action Planning":

  - Is the audience a decision maker? Or a pressure maker? Why?

  - What is the audience's stated position, if any? How do we know? Give examples, such as an official's public statements, a legislator's voting record, or the type of coverage a particular newspaper gives to an issue.

  - Why does the audience support or oppose the issue? Who or what motivates the audience? Think about the audience's value base, personal background, and so on.

  - What prevents the audience from being involved?

  - Are there any splits or differences of opinion among key decision makers? If so, how can you take advantage of them?

This series of questions has helped you to identify, categorize, and research your key audiences. In

section 3, "Diagnosis," you will refine your draft objectives based on this information as well as additional information about your group's advocacy capacity and your external environment.

Identifying the Key Audiences

Excerpted from "Legislative Change through Public Advocacy: Czech Citizenship Law," written by Ina Zoon from the Tolerance Foundation for the 1997 Symposium on Public Interest Law in Eastern Europe and Russia.

In 1992, the Czech Parliament passed a citizenship law that limited the Roma's access to Czech citizenship and, in the long term, made it possible to exclude them from the Czech territory. One official stated the racial intent of the Czech law was an "open secret." Thousands of Roma—an already marginalized and vulnerable group—lost their right to vote, work, and receive social benefits. Most did not have identification documents and were at risk of expulsion at any moment.

The Tolerance Foundation's Equal Rights Project ruled out the use of litigation in either the Constitutional Court or the European Court of Human Rights. Instead, the project focused on legislative advocacy to amend the citizenship law.

The project then had to decide which audience to target on the national level: the Parliament or the government. The decision to target the government was based on a study of the Czech Parliament in 1993: out of sixty-three bills submitted by the government to Parliament, 100 percent were adopted. Of the twenty-four bills submitted by Members of Parliament (MPs), only 67 percent were adopted. Also, any bill initiated by Members of Parliament (MP) against the government's agreement did not pass. Consequently, the best way to ensure the success of a bill was to have it initiated by the government.

But how to convince the Ministry of Interior—which drafted the law—to amend it? How to erode its hard-line position? The ministry's decision to submit a restrictive draft to the Parliament had been a political decision based on the certainty that the Czech majority would agree with any measure aimed to exclude the Roma from the Czech lands. Therefore,

to address the executive directly would have been a waste of energy and resources. The ministry also did not have a history of accepting dialogue with human rights groups. So the project attempted to convince international organizations—the Council of Europe, UNHCR, OSCE, and the US Helsinki Commission—to urge the Czech government to amend the law.
(*The story continues. See section 3, "Diagnosis."*)

Section 3
Diagnosis: What Is Possible?

The art of advocacy lies in thinking strategically to leverage your sources of power against seemingly more powerful forces. History has shown this *is* possible. One key is—before taking action—to reflect on whether your draft objectives are possible, SMART (specific, manageable, achievable, realistic, and timely), and focused on the right audiences.

The questions in this section will help you gather more information and refine your objectives and audiences before creating an action plan.

Assessment Questions

To help a group revisit its objective based on what is possible and SMART, we have found the following questions helpful:

- What is our capacity to engage in advocacy? Where is our group at the moment?

- What is the external environment like?

- When we put it all together, what is possible?

What Is Our Capacity to Engage in Advocacy? Where Is Our Group at the Moment?

One part of action planning will be determining whether some steps need to happen before others. For example, you may decide that before taking action to pressure and persuade key decision makers, you need to build your group's capacity—people, skills, confidence, willingness to take calculated risks, money, organizational infrastructure, and so on.

The following questions represent the "A" and "C" in ACT ON, one model for doing an environmental assessment (see the text titled "ACT ON," below).

They will help you identify your group's current capacity, sources of power, and unique niche or ways to complement—rather than compete with—the work of other groups. They will also help you identify potential collaborators.

Look inward. Think first about your group or organization, then your allies, collaborators, and others who may share a common objective or desire for change.

- *What are your advantages, especially in relation to other groups?* What do you have that you can build on? Resources? Strengths? Gifts? Can you protect your members when they assume calculated risks? How?

- *What are your challenges?* What's missing? What do you need to develop or improve? People? Skills? Resources? Other gaps or barriers?

- *Where is your group in the organizational life cycle?*

What Is the External Environment Like?

The following questions represent the "T" and "O" in ACT ON. They will help you further identify potential risks as well as windows of opportunity.

Look outward. Think about timing, public opinion, and political, social, and economic trends in general.

- *What are the threats?* What are the external obstacles or barriers? Review your responses to the questions, "Who are we?" in section 1 and "What is at stake?" in section 2. Are there other risks or repercussions you would face if you take certain types of action?

- *What are the opportunities?* What can you build on? Who are potential allies?

- *Where are you in the issue life cycle and/or problem-solving cycle?*

ACT ON:
One Model for Doing
an Environmental Assessment

The Advocacy Institute frequently uses one strategy development tool, ACT ON, to help groups assess their advocacy capacity and external environment. ACT ON has its genesis in SWOT, a model familiar to many Southern development workers.

ACT ON	SWOT
Advantages	Strengths
Challenges	Weaknesses
Threats	Opportunities
Opportunities	Threats
Next Steps	

On the surface, there are no major differences between ACT ON and SWOT. In practice, they are significantly different.

In ACT ON, "Advantages" emphasizes assessing your group to find your niche. It also focuses on your allies' advantages, so you can best combine advantages—and offset challenges—in a collaborative relationship.

"Challenges" has a different psychology than weaknesses. Weaknesses have a sinking feeling to them and are rarely discussed openly. In contrast, challenges can be tackled and overcome. They encourage creativity and action.

In assessing the external environment, SWOT begins with opportunities and ends with threats. Again, psychologically, this approach ends the process on a low—threats. Advocacy requires a sense of possibilities, a sense that can be lost by stopping on threats. In contrast, ACT ON focuses on opportunities *after* threats.

When workshop participants in both Southern and Northern settings are asked to free associate about "advocacy," the words they use are action verbs—challenge, pressure, influence, persuade, mobilize, organize, participate. They understand the need for action. The ACT ON method—which adds an "N" for next steps—resonates because it leads analysis and planning into action.

When We Put It All Together, What Is Possible?

Take another look at the information and analysis you have generated so far. Pull together all of the components:

- Your draft objectives.
- Key decision makers.
- Key pressure makers.
- How changes happen.
- Potential risks.

- Your group's capacity, including willingness to take calculated risks and to protect its members.
- The external environment.

Do the pieces fit together? Think about:

- Are your objectives specific?
  - Can you state each in one sentence?
  - Can you say why each objective is important?
  - Can you identify the key decision makers and relevant pressure makers?
- Are your objectives realistic and achievable?
  - Are you targeting the right decision makers? Do they have the power and authority to make change happen?
  - Are you targeting the right pressure makers? Are they the most influential with the key decision makers?
  - Are they important enough to generate the support you need?
  - Are there sufficient openings in the decision-making process to get started? Or must you first advocate for those openings?
  - Do they include a short-term (six months to two years) objective?
- Are your objectives manageable?
  - What risks are you willing and able to take? Can you protect your group members against risk?
  - Do your organizational strengths match your objectives? Would your group be taking on too much?
  - Do you have what you need to get started? Or must you first build your capacity and resources?
- Are your objectives timely?
  - Can you seize an opportunity to catapult your issue into the forefront?

Based on your answers, refine your objectives—long-term and short-term, outward and inward, multi-level—and key audiences as needed. When you think you have identified the right ones, you are ready to create an action plan.

First Step:
Opening the Decision-Making System,
Diana MTK Autin

Contributed by Diana MTK Autin, 1994 US Leadership Fellow and Executive Director of the Statewide Parent Advocacy Network (SPAN) in New Jersey, USA.

When the New Jersey State Board of Education was revisiting one of its education codes, it planned to have only one opportunity for public input: a public hearing at 3 P.M. in Trenton. This was the worst time of day for concerned parents to testify and was far away from where most families live. For the Statewide Parent Advocacy Network (SPAN)—which wanted to revise the board's regulations—the first step was to get the state board to hold regional hearings at times and places accessible to families.

In addition to mobilizing our parent leaders, we were able to elicit the support and pressure of organizations and individuals who might not have agreed with us on the content of the regulations but who agreed that the decision should not be made with so little public input. Thousands of letters were written to the board pushing for the input process to be opened up.

As a result, we got regional hearings, and thousands of parents submitted testimony—the most ever. We were also successful in getting board members to stand up to the state commissioner of education and to revise some of the most onerous proposals. But gaining access to the public forums—where board members had to sit through actual testimony from parents around the state—was the first step.

Choosing Realistic Objectives

Excerpted from "Legislative Change through Public Advocacy: Czech Citizenship Law," written by Ina Zoon from the Tolerance Foundation for the 1997 Symposium on Public Interest Law in Eastern Europe and Russia.

From the beginning, the Tolerance Foundation's Equal Rights Project wanted to eliminate part of the citizenship law: the clean-criminal-record requirement. This was the ideal solution to the

problem. But was it reasonable? Certainly not. The citizenship law was already in force in September 1993 when the project started. The principle had already been generally accepted and tens of thousands of applications had been processed. It was late, very late, to re-discuss it.

The project had to accept that the main goal might not be reached and, from the start, to formulate a reasonable one with some chance of success: try to *alleviate the hardship* of the clean-criminal-record requirement.

It also made sense to target at the beginning a specific number of points to lose. Several additional objectives were added: liberalization of the residence requirements, reduction of administrative fees, improvement of regulations concerning children, etc. (*The story continues. See section 5, "Evaluation."*)

Refining Draft Objectives

Adapted from chapters 7–8 of "Giant Killers," an oral history of the MX missile campaign, written by Michael Pertschuk, Advocacy Institute Co-Director.

In May 1983, the House of Representatives voted 239 to 186 to release funds for the construction and deployment of MX missiles. The broad arms control coalition was convinced that stopping the MX's funding was winnable but—with a fifty-three-vote losing margin—understood the campaign to build opposition to the MX would have to be won in increments.

The coalition's objective—stop the MX—became a shorter-term one: *narrow the margin of defeat* with each new vote to fund the MX. While the coalition continued to lose the vote—in July 1983, they lost by twenty-seven votes; in November, by nine; on May 16, 1984, by six—its short-term objective helped maintain intensity and optimism throughout the campaign.

On May 31, 1984, the House voted 198 to 197 *against* the MX. While there were later votes, this was the turning point. It was the first time that the US Congress had voted to halt production of a major nuclear weapons system. It was also the first time that citizens working through their elected representatives had challenged the defense experts' wisdom and control over nuclear decision making.

Section 4
Action Planning: How Do We Get Started?

Organized, strategic action is at the core of advocacy and social change and can be a great source of power.

The questions in this section will help you create an action plan—for both your group and your key audiences.

Assessment Questions

To help a group develop an action plan, we have found the following questions helpful:

- How do we move each audience to make—or not block—change?

- How will we protect our group members from risk?

- What is our work plan?

- Do we have what we need to get started?

- What is our backup plan?

How Do We Move Each Audience to Make—or Not Block—Change?

In general, advocacy efforts mix actions that pressure, persuade, educate, monitor, and mobilize people and institutions that can make—or block—change. Specific actions—organizing public demonstrations, lobbying decision makers, working with the mass media, filing a public interest lawsuit, and so on—should be considered based on a strategic assessment of what could help you meet your objectives. (See Worksheet 5.6.)

Think about your objectives and where you are in the problem-solving or issue life cycle:

- What do you want each audience to do? How can their action (or inaction) help make or block change? Think about:

  - Decision makers and their ability to make the desired change.

  - Pressure makers—including your group's members, constituents, or those who are affected by the problem—and the influence they have with key decision makers or other pressure makers.

  - Each audience's current level of support or opposition.

  - Current windows of opportunity.

In general, you may want your supporters to demonstrate their support publicly, help influence other key audiences, or work more closely with your organization. You may want your opponents to question their position on the issue, be quiet on the issue, or be drowned out by your supporters' voices.

- What do we need to do to move the key audiences to act in these ways?

  - How can we consolidate support and build intensity?

  - How can we sway fence-sitters to become supporters or, at least, to not become active opponents?

  - How can we neutralize our opponents and their influence on decision makers or other key audiences? What pressures do they respond to?

  - How do we monitor other audiences that are currently not very important?

  - What message does each audience need to hear? (Section 8, "Message Development," discusses this question.)

  - How do we deliver these messages? What are the right media? Who are the right messengers? (Section 9, "Message Delivery," discusses this question.)

  - What other actions do we need to take to pressure, persuade, educate, monitor, and mobilize our key audiences and to meet our objectives?

How Will We Protect Our Group Members from Risk?

Your group will have asked itself this question throughout the strategy development process. It is particularly critical to ask it now *before* your group engages in actions or activities that could endanger your members. You will need to determine what calculated risks you are willing and able to take, why, and how you will prepare. Think about:

- Who opposes or will be threatened by change? What are their sources of power? What might they do to stop or intimidate us?

Worksheet 5.6: *Motivating Key Audiences*

The specific actions you take should be considered based on a strategic assessment of what could help you meet your objectives.

Think about your objectives and where you are in the problem-solving or issue life cycle. First, ask yourself, What do we want each audience to do? How can their action (or inaction) help make or block change? Next, ask yourself, what do we need to do to move the key audiences to act in these ways? Be as specific as possible.

Key Audiences	Level of Support or Opposition	Desired Action	Why Do We Want This?	Action *We* Will Take to Motivate the Audience's Actions
Decision Makers				
Pressure Makers				

- What risks will we face if we take action? Think about:

  - Physical risks.

  - Emotional and psychological risks.

  - Economic risks. For example, could we lose our jobs?

  - Political or organizational risks. For example, could a smear campaign weaken our group's credibility? Could we lose important allies or financial support?

- If we take certain risks, will it be worth it? Why?

- Given this, are there specific actions we *won't* take? Can any of our allies take these actions instead?

- If we go ahead and take certain risks, what preparation will we need? For example, role plays of the situation? Civil disobedience training? A fund to support workers on strike, to bail protesters out of jail, or to pay for hospital bills (just in case)?

Be sure to allow reflection and discussion time for group members to decide for themselves and to prepare emotionally and psychologically.

Assessing Risks and Taking Action, Vivek Pandit

Contributed by Vivek Pandit, 1990 India Advocacy Fellow, co-founder of Vidhayak Sansad and Shramajeevi Sanghatana, and Director of Samarthan, Mumbai, India.

Since 1979, my wife, Vidyullata, and I have worked alongside tribals, dalits, bonded laborers, and the rural poor in Maharashtra state, India. We have organized around the philosophy of nonviolence and avoided unnecessary risks. Yet we have seen violence as a group and as individuals. These physical attacks strengthened our organization. We not only survived, we grew.

Sometimes, we have carefully planned to get beaten as a strategy to further our cause. In each of these cases, our Satyagraha—nonviolent peaceful protest—drew its power from our willingness to die for the cause and from the enormity, sensitivity, and power of the issue itself.

In one such instance, a criminal Member of the Legislative Assembly (MLA) was nominated to serve on the Committee for Tribal Welfare. The MLA had instilled terror in the tribals' hearts; he had murdered them and grabbed their land. We appealed his nomination to the Chief Minister. When our appeals fell on deaf ears, we decided to demonstrate in the cordoned-off area in front of the Mantralaya, the seat of state governance. No more than five people are allowed to assemble there, so we knew we would have a confrontation with the police.

We planned a peaceful demonstration in front of the building. To try to understand what might happen, we selected strong, committed activists and role-played the entire demonstration twice. One group acted as police, and the other group as demonstrators. It soon became clear that the demonstration would result in the police beating back the crowd with their police sticks. Such beatings can cause injury or death. Knowing the risk, we decided to go ahead anyway.

On the day of the demonstration, sixty-five activists of Shramajeevi Sanghatana—nearly half of them women—sat outside the Mantralaya. They linked their hands and feet in a human chain and shouted slogans. Although the activists resisted arrest peacefully, they were beaten for forty-five minutes. Finally, they were thrown into police vans and arrested.

Our demonstration was a success. The next day, the MLA was removed from the committee.

That same day, we also discovered that one of our activists was pregnant. This young woman had known she was endangering two lives, yet she joined her husband in the demonstration. When we asked her what made her take that kind of risk, she replied she could not remain at home when there was action—come what may. There are many like her in the Sanghatana who are willing to put their lives at stake. They are angry at injustice and take pride in raising their voices when others keep quiet. They are the strength of the Sanghatana.

Lessons Learned

Fighting violence with nonviolence has not been easy. It takes a tremendous amount of thought and careful strategic planning. We have risked our lives, but they have been calculated risks. After every hard-earned victory, we have celebrated like there was no tomorrow.

We have learned many lessons from our work:

- Effective activism—taking the side of the poor and marginalized, demanding social justice laws and their implementation, challenging existing power structures—implies taking risks. We should not be surprised by violent reactions. We should expect them. The organizer must always be aware that danger is possible, even during the most spontaneous and nonviolent actions.

- Facing the moment of risk requires anger against injustice, courage, presence of mind, resilience, and optimism. The leader-organizer must have these qualities, and should be able to communicate them to the group.

- Every time people take a risk, they should be congratulated and celebrated, even if there is no victory. When activists come out of jail, they should be given a hero's welcome.

- Historically, the powerful always win and the poor always lose. Nobody has ever listened to the poor, and they are afraid of speaking out. It is not surprising that they are not ready to take a risk. The leader-organizer needs to ignite the spark of anger against injustice and instill confidence that even if "they" have always won in the past, "we" can win now.

- In spite of our readiness to put our lives on the line, we must avoid unnecessary risks. We do not want to die. We do not want to commit suicide. We want to win, and we want to live to celebrate the victory and tell the story.

What Is Our Work Plan?

In the long term, *organized* efforts are the most effective. One key is to develop a work plan, including activities, specific tasks, resources needed, assignments, and deadlines. (See Worksheet 5.7.)

To create a work plan, think about:

- What are our activities?

- Do some steps or activities need to happen before others? Think about:

  – Where are we in the organizational life cycle? Do we need to build our capacity before taking on certain types of work?

  – How are changes currently made? Are there existing openings for people's participation in the decision-making process? Or must we first advocate for such openings before advocating for a specific change in policy?

  – Where are we in the issue life cycle? Do we need to build public argument before we propose specific solutions?

- For each activity, think about:

  – What tasks are involved?

  – What resources are needed?

  – Who can do the work?

  – Are any of the tasks time-sensitive? If so, what is the deadline?

  – When will we evaluate our progress so far?

Do We Have What We Need to Get Started?

Your ability to carry out your action plan rests on your group's—or coalition's—capacity. Think about:

- Do we have what we need to get started? What's missing?

- How can we get what we need?

- Who do we need to work with? Who has advantages that offset our group's challenges? (Section 6, "Collaboration," discusses this question.)

- Do we need more information to identify entry points, to develop effective messages, or to support our position on the issue? (Section 7, "Information and Research," discusses this question.)

What Is Our Backup Plan?

Things are always changing—a key audience's position on the issue, political pressures on decision makers and advocates, resources within an organization, and so on. While you are now ready to create an action plan, it is important to recognize that it will only be as good as the assessments you did in sections 1 to 4.

Worksheet 5.7: Developing a Work Plan

To create a work plan, list the actions you will take and other activities, the tasks involved, the resources needed, who can do the work, and deadlines. Also, ask yourself, do some steps or activities need to happen before others?

Actions We Will Take and Other Activities	Why Will We Do This?	Tasks	Resources Needed	Assignments	Deadlines

You will need to periodically evaluate your action plan and your progress to see if your objectives, key audiences, and activities are still the right ones.

You will evaluate your action plan in more depth in section 5, "Evaluation." For now, think about:

- What could change? How would it affect our action plan?

- What could go wrong? What would be the worst-case scenario?

- If something does go wrong, do we have another plan?

This series of questions has helped you create an action plan based on a realistic assessment of possible risks and what you need to get started. In section 5, "Evaluation," you will periodically assess your action plan as you carry it out.

Chapter 6 will help you build generic skills that are needed in any advocacy effort.

Creating an Action Plan

Developed by a group of India Advocacy Fellows who were asked to create an action plan for a hypothetical advocacy effort to increase a state's minimum wage for agricultural workers.

- *Gather information.*

  - Information to demonstrate the need.

    - Current laws on minimum wage and related issues.

    - Current government programs, such as "food for work."

    - Current minimum wage.

    - Cost of living index.

    - Comparisons with other states, and between women and men.

  - Sources of information.

    - Labor department.

    - Agriculture department.

    - Legal department.

    - Nongovernmental organizations (NGOs); interviews with laborers, employers, and landlords.

    - Expert opinions from nutritionists and economists.

- *Formulate demands.*

  - Short-term objectives.

    - A specific increase now followed by regular, periodic increases.

    - Equal pay to women and men for equal work.

  - Long-term objectives.

    - Create a comprehensive agricultural labor policy.

    - Create state-level labor unions.

- *Activities.*

  - Disseminate information to laborers, local officials, and the public through seminars, studies, posters, pamphlets, wall writing, and street plays.

  - Form coalitions with laborers, media, government, political parties, and women's groups.

  - Draft a bill.

  - Demonstrate popular support for the bill through a signature campaign, rallies, marches, and asking for sympathetic statements from respected community leaders and the media.

  - Generate political will through a laborers' strike.

  - Create a strike fund to provide financial support to striking workers.

Getting Started:
Building Organizational Capacity
to Create Change,
Adèle Wildschut

Contributed by Adèle Wildschut, 1995 South Africa Advocacy Fellow and former Director of the Centre for Rural Legal Studies, Stellenbosch, South Africa.

In the mid-1980s, the South African farm worker's situation was almost the same as a hundred years before, when slavery was abolished in the Western Cape. Farm workers and their families lived and worked on the employer's property. Common law and paternalist practices governed their relationship, and any influence from the state (even the apartheid state) and civil society stopped at the farm gate.

As a result, farm workers were at the farmers' mercy and enjoyed privileges, not rights. Wages were low and working conditions highly exploitative. Farm workers could be dismissed or evicted at any time. The slightest misdemeanors were often punished with extreme violence, leading to severe injury or death.

Dependent on the employer for their most basic needs, generations of farm workers survived by being subservient and complying with the most dire conditions. Living with insecurity for generations, many farm workers considered challenging such a powerful employer foolhardy indeed. Each generation's chance to escape was limited by isolation, poverty, and what minimal education their parents could afford with their meager wages.

Creating Institutions to Address the Need

The 1980s in South Africa were a period of great political and social upheaval and massive state repression. During this period, activists from many walks of life—student leaders, academics, lawyers, community leaders—worked tirelessly to challenge the denial and violation of human rights of the poor and marginalized. They established advice centers all over the country. Stellenbosch, a sleepy university town and bastion of an Afrikaner academic elite, did not escape. A small, vibrant group proceeded to assist the poor of the town and the surrounding farms in their daily struggle with the powerful police, powerful local authorities, powerful employers, powerful farmers, and powerful commercial interests. There

were many small victories as they found spaces in the labyrinth of apartheid law to begin challenging various forms of injustice.

There were also many defeats. The biggest problem was the almost complete absence of space to challenge injustice when it came to assisting farm workers.

In 1990, a group of progressive organizations in Stellenbosch decided to investigate this situation. The report compiled found that "there is less access to the legal system in rural areas and a lack of legal protection for those who live and work on the farms." The report recommended that an institution be established to systematically "focus on two main issues: farm workers and their access to the legal system in rural areas." This report became the founding document of the Centre for Rural Legal Studies.

To help extend labor rights to farm workers, the centre needed to:

- More deeply understand what it meant to be a farm worker.

- Understand the legitimate concerns of farmers.

- Make very strong proposals on how labor legislation should include farm workers.

Next Steps: Protecting Social Justice Gains

By early 1994, farm workers were included in the most important labor acts. The new constitution and Bill of Rights also conferred new rights of citizenship—including the right to vote—to a class of South Africans that had been extremely marginalized.

The Centre for Rural Legal Studies realized that both these changes—labor rights and political rights—would be meaningless if farm workers did not know their rights, if employers did not respect these rights, and if workers could not access the courts to enforce their rights. We identified three ongoing needs and strategies:

- *Knowledge.* The centre produces accessible written materials on farm workers' rights and enforcement and disseminates them to a primarily farm worker audience. Training is also provided to farm worker leadership and community-based service providers in rural areas.

- *Assistance.* Armed with knowledge, many farm workers are keen to enforce their rights when they are infringed upon. They seek assistance from their nearest advice center, trade union, service organizations, or the centre directly. The centre regularly monitors and analyzes "test" cases.

- *Effective institutions.* Relevant state institutions are regularly monitored to ensure that farm workers are able to access them to enforce their rights. Relationships are maintained with relevant individuals within these institutions in order to maintain good communication channels to air problems. Regular roundtable discussions are convened between relevant players, users, and state service providers to improve enforcement and access.

Section 5
Evaluation: How Do We Know
Our Plan Is Working?

Strategy is based on the research and assessment done at a specific time. As you carry out your action plan, however, one or more parts of the situation will change. Therefore, you will need to periodically re-assess your strategy and evaluate the effectiveness of your efforts.

Evaluation serves other purposes as well. It is part of the critical learning that any innovative organization must do. It also helps you identify successes that should be celebrated. Remember that in any advocacy effort, "success" must mean more than simply changing a law or stopping something harmful. After all, your group may lose on a specific battle, but you may succeed in a number of other ways. You may stage a first-ever mass protest on your issue, gain increased press coverage, or develop new relationships, skills, expertise, knowledge, and—above all—confidence! Such successes are incredibly valuable—fueling the stamina, patience, and optimism needed for long-term efforts; building toward future efforts; and making an immediate impact on the lives of those engaged in the struggle from day to day. Whatever the success, be sure to take time to celebrate!

The questions in this section will help you evaluate progress toward your objectives in the short term and long term, and your successes along the way.

Assessment Questions

To help a group evaluate its progress, we have found the following questions helpful:

- What has changed in the short term?

- What has changed in the long term?

What Has Changed in the Short Term?

How often you ask this question will be determined by the pace of your campaign or efforts. For example, if your group is working on an intense lobbying campaign before a critical vote, you may ask yourself this question hourly, daily, and weekly. If you are working with the mass media to increase coverage of the issue, you may ask this weekly or monthly. If you are working to mobilize and organize members of the affected group, you may ask this every three to six months.

Regardless of when you ask the question, think about:

- Has anything changed in our initial ACT ON assessment? (See "ACT ON" in section 3, "Diagnosis.")

- Are our objectives still possible?

- Have our key audiences changed? Has anyone's position shifted in level of support or opposition? Has a new audience emerged that is very important to the issue?

- Has our group developed new capacities? Have we overcome an internal challenge that previously limited us? Are we able to take on new work as a result? Should we?

- Have we lost any of our capacities? For example, has a critical staff member left? Do we still have our members' active support? Do we have adequate finances?

- Has the external environment changed? Are there new opportunities we can seize? Have old ones disappeared? Are there any unexpected surprises?

- Was our risk assessment accurate? Did we overlook something?

- Did our calculated risks help us achieve our objective? Was it a bearable amount of risk? Was it worth it?

- Have any of our actions been effective? How? Why or why not?

- What can we celebrate?

- What are next steps?

  - What should we continue to do?

  - Do we need to move on to another step?

  - What (if anything) should we do differently?

Responding to a Surprise

Drawn from a conversation with Jorge Du-Breuil and Christine Leonard from the Cuban Committee for Democracy (CCD).

In January 1996, a few Cuban American groups developed a strategy for raising a unified progressive voice in the debate on US-Cuba policy. They planned to hold a lobby day in Washington, D.C., to build opposition to the Helms-Burton Bill, and began to organize their constituents at the state level.

One week before the lobby day, something unexpected happened: the Cuban government shot down a civilian plane, and congressional support for the Helms-Burton Bill intensified.

At first, the planning group disagreed on whether to hold the lobby day as planned. Eventually, they decided to go ahead since their constituents had already committed to participating. Even though the bill was passed, the response to the lobby day was very positive. Their press conference had a large turnout because of the crisis, and their allies—who could say they had the support of Cuban American groups—still voted against the bill.

After the lobby day, the planning group decided to take a break for a month and a half to analyze the impact of Cuba's actions and the passage of the bill, and to reassess their individual organization's strategies.

What Has Changed in the Long Term?

You may ask this question when your group comes to a significant turning point, is struggling with how to move forward, or wants to reach closure on past efforts.

Think about:

- Have we achieved our objectives? If so, which ones? Think about:

  - Long-term and short-term.

  - Outward and inward.

  - Multiple levels.

- Have we achieved something that we didn't expect?

- Which of our actions were effective? How? Why or why not?

- Are we stronger as individual advocates? Do we have greater confidence, new skills, new knowledge, and so on?

- Are we stronger as a group or organization? Have we built new relationships? Have we recruited more people to our effort? Have we supported emerging leaders?

- Are we stronger as a civil society or issue sector?

- Have we helped raise public awareness and support for the issue?

- Have we helped open the decision-making process to people's participation? Have we helped increase the legitimacy of people's participation in these processes?

- What have we learned?

- What can we celebrate?

- What are next steps?

  - What should we continue to do?

  - Do we need to move on to another step?

  - What (if anything) should we do differently?

Reaching Closure:
Assessing Lessons Learned

Excerpted from "Legislative Change through Public Advocacy: Czech Citizenship Law," written by Ina Zoon from the Tolerance Foundation for the 1997 Symposium on Public Interest Law in Eastern Europe and Russia.

As a result of the Tolerance Foundation's Equal Rights Project's efforts, the Czech citizenship law was amended three times in two years. Many problems created by the citizenship law were alleviated, though they did not disappear entirely.

In analyzing the campaign, the project recognized that one mistake was paying insufficient attention to a key player: President Vaclav Havel. Though not a decision maker, President Havel is considered the highest moral authority in his country.

The president, despite decrying individual acts of violence perpetrated against Romanies, failed to recognize the existence of any systematic state-sponsored racist policies. Further, there was no indication that he was prepared to publicly address the issue. It was, therefore, a very unpleasant surprise when, during a November 1994 radio interview, he advocated the government stance on the citizenship law. While recognizing it had a certain degree of negative impact on some groups, he only blamed the manner in which the law was implemented. He went no further in accepting that administrative measures might be useful in improving the situation. His statement was used many times by the executive as the best argument supporting their refusal to modify the law. It then became more difficult for the human rights community to allege that the law is discriminatory when the human rights champion President Havel said publicly that it is not.

We should have known better and tried harder to convince the president—if he was not prepared to support the legislative change—at least to not address the issue at all. Many of the people supporting the campaign were former members of Charter 77 and Havel's personal friends. Maybe all together we could have tried to avoid his damaging intervention. The fact that the president had no decision-making power is no justification for not trying to prevent a statement that obviously damaged the campaign.

Putting It All Together:
Influencing Policy to Assist
the Urban Poor,
Mahbubul Karim

Contributed by Mahbubul Karim, 1994 Bangladesh Advocacy Fellow, Senior Vice President of Proshika, and former Head of the Institute for Development Policy Analysis and Advocacy (IDPAA) at Proshika, Dhaka, Bangladesh.

Bangladesh has an alarmingly high rate of urban poverty and much to be desired in its approach to urban development. When the government considers it "necessary" to clear the slums, they evict people. These people are left on the street with no help finding housing and no solution to their economic problems. The slum-dwellers and squatters of Bangladesh live in constant fear of being evicted by the government.

Proshika realized that no sustainable solution is possible without a broad policy on resettlement of the urban poor. In 1995–1996, IDPAA at Proshika began two studies:

- *Urban Livelihoods Study* to create a substantial knowledge-base.

- *Resettlement of the Urban Poor in Dhaka* to explore policy options and to suggest models for viable housing for the poor.

With these two studies and the experience of Proshika's Urban Poor Development Program, we launched an advocacy campaign through an alliance of four groups: Coalition of the Urban Poor; Ain O Salish Kendra, a legal advocacy center; Bangladesh Environment Lawyers Association; and IDPAA at Proshika. We also mobilized the organized urban poor.

To convince policy makers of the need to resettle the slum-dwellers and to stop slum eviction without resettlement, we used street demonstrations, press briefings, and legal suits. The NGO community made a statement of our intentions to the prime minister. We also strongly and successfully pursued the issue with the Asian Development Bank, the major donor in the field of urban development in Bangladesh.

In February 1997, the Public Works Department—with the help of five hundred riot police and several hundred hoodlums—evicted ten thousand slum-dwellers in the Bhasantek area in Dhaka. This was a turning point for our campaign. The prime minister, approached by the NGO alliance, immediately intervened. She instructed the authorities concerned to resettle the evicted people in the same slum within twenty-four hours. She herself visited the area the next day and told a gathering of the evicted people that from now on, no slum-dweller would be evicted without a place to go. Moreover, the minister who ordered the eviction was forced to resign.

The Prime Minister then asked the State Minister for Land to take up a pilot project with the Association of Development Agencies in Bangladesh (ADAB) to rehabilitate sixteen thousand slum households by constructing multi-story buildings in Dhaka.

The Ministry of Land formed a steering committee that consisted of government officials, ADAB representatives, and members of the NGO alliance. With assistance from IDPAA at Proshika, the steering committee developed a proposal and gave it to the Executive Committee of the National Economic Council (ECNEC)—the government's highest project-approving authority. The proposal:

- Emphasized undertaking measures to eradicate urban poverty.

- Recommended constructing low-cost multi-story buildings for the urban poor.

- Pressed for a policy of resettling the slum-dwellers after eviction.

It took a long time for the project to receive pre-ECNEC approval. There was stiff opposition from a section of the bureaucracy and constant lobbying by vested-interest groups. However, with the support of the prime minister, the state minister for land stood firm. This made it possible for the project to get both pre-ECNEC and ECNEC approval, with some changes to the implementation plan.

Lessons Learned

A number of major factors contributed to the success of our campaign:

- The evolving democratic process.

- The existence of a vibrant civil society.

- A well-organized NGO sector.

- A strong network of people's organizations at the grassroots and national levels.

Our experience reveals at least three major problems:

- Most planners and decision makers come from the upper echelons of society and are generally not sympathetic to the causes of the poor. The national budget makers are also reluctant to give more money to social sectors, such as education and health, that directly contribute to poverty eradication.

- The government tends to hold the same old view: poverty will wither away if we achieve a high rate of growth. We know from experience that growth alone does not eliminate poverty and even widens the gap between the rich and the poor. Equity alongside growth is the way to address the problem of poverty.

- The political government is inexperienced and still largely depends on the bureaucracy for decision making. The bureaucracy is an elite, very powerful vested-interest group known for its anti-reform character. It can jeopardize any effort for policy change. Even when a change in the policy is initiated, it can delay implementation indefinitely.

The questions in this section have helped you to identify lessons learned, reasons to celebrate, and possible next steps. You are ready to begin the reflect-plan-act cycle again!

Chapter 6

Skill Building

To effectively carry out your action plan, a variety of skills, attitudes, and knowledge will be needed. In the Advocacy Institute's experience, the following generic skills are needed in any advocacy effort:

- Collaboration.

- Use of information and research.

- Message development.

- Message delivery, including working with the mass media and lobbying.

Chapter 6 presents theories about and frameworks for each skill to help groups reflect on their experiences and deepen their understanding. At the end of each section, a "Summary" recaps key points.

The information presented in these sections draws on the outstanding work of our colleagues, including Michael Pertschuk's leadership "taxonomy"; Valerie Miller's "What Is Success?"; the Advocacy Institute Tobacco Control Project's *Blowing Away the Smoke* series of media advocacy advisories; the Certain Trumpet Program's *Trumpet Notes;* the media advocacy expertise of Phil Wilbur, Larry Wallack, Makani N. Themba-Nixon, Susan Bales, and their colleagues at the Berkeley Media Studies Group, the Marin Institute, and the Benton Foundation, respectively; Amanda C. Rawls's "Media-Advocacy Relationships: The View from the Other Side"; and Kathleen D. Sheekey's "Six Tips: Practical Tips on How to Lobby Your Legislator or Elected Official."

Section 6
Collaboration:
Who Will We Work With? How?

In the Advocacy Institute's experience, advocates know instinctively that they need to work together—create strength in numbers—to create lasting change. How-ever, many are wary of the inevitable challenges that come with working in coalitions and other forms of collaboration.

To help a group assess its work within coalitions and other forms of collaboration, this section is divided into four parts:

- Frequently asked questions.

- How to decide whether to enter a coalition.

- Managing coalitions.

- Summary of key points.

Frequently Asked Questions

What Is "Collaboration"?

Collaboration is working with individuals and groups who share a common focus or interest. The purpose may range from sharing information to taking joint action.

Collaboration has many forms (ranging from informal to formal, temporary to permanent) that have many names—network, coalition, alliance, campaign, federation, and so on. The meaning and use of each name vary from country to country.

While the distinctions are fluid and change over time, it can be helpful to consider "networks" at one end of the spectrum and "coalitions" at the other:

Figure 6.1. Collaboration Spectrum

Networks	Coalitions
Information sharing	Joint action
Temporary	Possibly permanent
Informal	Formal
Limited structure	Structure needed
Full autonomy	Shared decision making and resources
	Coordinated activities

89

- *Networks* exist for sharing information, ideas, and support. A common interest may be the only membership requirement, allowing space for other differences to exist peacefully. A network's structure is often informal—members invest little and are free to benefit, contribute, or quit whenever they wish.

- *Coalitions* exist for joint action. To reach a specific goal, members invest significant resources, share decision-making power, and coordinate their strategies, messages, and action plans. In addition to a common interest, coalition members must share a high level of trust. A coalition's structure tends to be more formal, and skilled leadership is needed to guide members through their differences so the coalition can function. When a coalition's goal is achieved (or thwarted), the members must decide whether to disband or to continue working together toward another goal.

What Are the Benefits of Collaboration?

The benefits of joining a network include:

- Accessing information that can be hard to find.

- Accessing decision makers and power holders through other network members.

- Learning from others' experiences of what works well and what doesn't.

- Building relationships that can be activated for future action.

- Connecting to a larger like-minded community and combating isolation.

The benefits of working in a coalition include:

- *Strength in numbers.* Working together can create pressure on decision makers and legitimacy for the issue and can increase the ability of individuals to take calculated risks with the group.

- *Strength in diversity.* A wide variety of perspectives and constituents creates a broader, holistic picture of the issue; enhances problem solving; strengthens outreach and impact; and increases credibility.

- *Shared workload and resources.* A diversity of talents, work styles, and resources is needed to carry out a multi-faceted action plan and to reduce the burden on any one organization.

- *Cohesion and solidarity.* Shared values, goals, and experiences help advocates overcome isolation, build confidence, and renew faith that change is possible.

- *Creating a micro-model of a just, decent society.* Coalitions provide the opportunity to practice on a smaller level the skills and attitudes needed for a strong democracy—such as respect, transparency, accountability, equality, and commitment to working with diverse groups of people.

How to Decide Whether to Enter a Coalition

The benefits of coalitions are clear. Yet many advocates are wary of entering them because they demand high levels of coordination and interdependence among members. Such intensity triggers a number of common fears:

- Differences among members could paralyze the coalition, preventing it from making progress toward its goal and discouraging members from working in future coalitions.

- Working in a coalition may take time and energy away from working closely with constituents and members.

- The investment of resources could outweigh the benefits received, especially if other members don't do their share of the work.

- Shared decision-making power could mean members surrender control over the agenda, tactics, resource allocation, and other strategic decisions.

- An organization's identity could be masked by the coalition identity, making it difficult to act autonomously.

- The coalition may become too large or "bureaucratic" to function.

- Rather than cooperating with each other, members may end up competing with coalition partners for resources, funding, and public recognition.

With such potential pitfalls, how do you decide if it's worth your investment to join a coalition? There are a number of questions you may ask yourself:

- Is the issue a priority for our organization? Will joining a coalition help further our organization's agenda?

- Do we have the organizational capacity to commit resources to the coalition? Or will joining a coalition drain our organization's leadership or other resources?

- How will joining a coalition affect our relationship with our constituents and members? How do we stay accountable to them?

- Can we achieve our goal if we don't work with others? Do we have the resources and support we need? If we don't join a coalition, is there another way to achieve our goals?

- Who else will be involved? Do we have—or want to have—a relationship with any of the potential coalition members? Do we share similar ideologies and values? If not, are we willing and able to work through our differences so the coalition can function? Do other members demonstrate the same commitment to "agree to disagree"?

- What trade-offs will we be making if we join the coalition? If we don't join?

If you are wary of working in a coalition and don't have a compelling reason to do so, then it probably isn't worth the investment of time, energy, and other resources at this time. However, you do have alternatives:

- Continue building and maintaining new relationships, on both the individual and organizational level.

- Continue sharing information through networks.

- If no one else is ready to work on the issue, get started anyway and keep others informed about your work.

- Collaborate with each other in less intense ways. For example, work together on a single event or short-term campaign. Or develop parallel organizations that work separately toward the same goals. This may be an effective way to bridge large differences between organizations, such as the power differential between smaller and larger organizations or organizations from the global South and global North.

Such alternatives can help organizations develop trusting and respectful relationships and the potential for future action together.

Managing Coalitions

An organization that does enter a coalition will face tensions, conflicts, and "growing pains" that are unique to its history and mix of members. For example, one coalition may be born out of crisis, leaving little time to devote to trust building, creating coalition structures, and other group processes. Another may struggle to manage a diverse membership, large power differentials among members, or individual behaviors and work styles that clash. To manage such tensions, a coalition's leadership will need to create its own recipe of solutions.

Above all, the key ingredient to managing a coalition is willingness to experiment and to learn from mistakes. Through practice, time, and flexibility, a coalition's leadership and members will develop the comfort and confidence needed to minimize conflicts and work together effectively.

Based on the experiences of the Advocacy Institute's facilitators and alumni, a number of other ingredients are also critical:

- Skilled and diverse leadership.

- Diverse membership and broad outreach.

- Basic coalition structures.

- Trusting relationships among members.

- Effective communication and conflict management.

These ingredients are discussed below.

Skilled and Diverse Leadership

Within a coalition, leadership's goal is to balance action, strategy, and group process. Many roles, strengths, and talents will be needed, at different stages of the problem-solving cycle, issue life cycle, and organizational life cycle, and often at multiple levels—local, state, national, regional, and international. One individual may fill multiple roles, but no one person can do it all. Effective leadership, therefore, must rely on a *group* of leaders that share responsibility.

To help assess your coalition—who fills which roles, which roles are missing but needed—one helpful model is the leadership "taxonomy" developed by Advocacy Institute Co-Director Michael Pertschuk and US tobacco control leaders Karla Sneegas and Sally Malek. Here is a modified version:

- *Movement builders* are convenors and facilitators who:

  – Bring people together comfortably and foster respect and trust among coalition members.

  – Reach out to diverse individuals and groups, draw them in, and make them feel welcome, valued, listened to, and heeded.

  – Bridge differences, egos, and turf wars.

- *Problem solvers* cut through tensions, differences, and resistance to get the work done. They:

  – Mediate, invite feedback, listen well, and communicate openly.

  – Help members to "agree to disagree" and to stay focused on common ground and the coalition's goal.

  – Draw from a "great tangle of motives those that serve the purposes of group action in pursuit of shared goals," in the words of US civic leader John Gardner.

  – Create organizational structure and processes to manage group tensions.

- *Role models and mentors* demonstrate behaviors that help strengthen organizations and coalitions and help others develop their own leadership skills.

- *Visionaries* think long-term and lift our horizons beyond the readily attainable to the barely imaginable. They may use participatory exercises to draw their vision from their constituents' or members' indigenous knowledge and experience.

- *Strategists* choose parts of the vision that are readily attainable and develop a strategy to get there. They know how to plan and choose tactics strategically, plan for contingencies, seize new and uncharted opportunities, and—led by courage and wisdom— know when to resist premature compromise and when the time for compromise has come.

- *Historians* are keepers of the movement's memory, bringing to bear the learning of past experience.

- *Resource mobilizers* know how to cut through institutional inertia to harness the resources needed to act.

- *Statespersons* are "larger than life" public figures who are widely known outside the movement. They embody authority, credibility, and respect.

- *Communicators* are the public teachers. Speaking with experience and authority—moral, scientific, legal—they compress complex data into accurate, powerful messages and metaphors that can be instantly grasped by the broad public.

- *"Outside" sparkplugs* are aggressive and angry agitators who demonstrate in the streets, refuse to be reasonable or polite, and demand much more than negotiation is likely to produce.

- *"Inside" negotiators* are skilled and tough, know the system, are welcome in the seats of power, and are at the table to make demands. They know how to open doors, test out arguments that resonate with decision makers, and press them in ways that cannot be dismissed.

- *Generalists* bring multilayered skills to the effort, often cultivated through many years of experience.

Whatever the roles, coalition leadership must earn the members' trust. Three characteristics are key:

- *Chosen, not predetermined.* Members play an active role in choosing the coalition's leadership. Space is needed for newly recruited members to join the coalition leadership. Individuals who served as catalysts by convening the coalition may be asked to step aside.

- *Representative.* Leadership must reflect the diversity of coalition members. This is also an opportunity to shift traditional power dynamics of who leads, who decides, and whose voice is heard. In this way, coalitions have the potential to be a micro-model of the just, decent society that the group is working to create.

- *Accountable.* Processes are needed to determine which decisions require input from coalition members, how those decisions are made, and how an open flow of communication between members and leadership is maintained.

Diverse Leadership Styles

Adapted from The People Rising: The Campaign against the Bork Nomination, *written by Michael Pertschuk, Advocacy Institute Co-Director, and Wendy Schaetzel.*

On July 1, 1987, US president Ronald Reagan announced his nomination of Robert H. Bork for the upcoming vacancy on the Supreme Court. On July 2, representatives of eighty organizations met to form a coalition to block the Senate's confirmation of Bork's nomination. Just four months later, on October 23, the Senate voted fifty-eight to forty-two to reject the Bork nomination—the largest negative margin in history.

The coalition represented civil rights, organized labor, women's, ethnic minorities', disabled people's, senior citizens', education, and religious groups, and others. The diversity of interests had the potential to distract them from their common goal: defeat the Bork nomination. The coalition's ability to coalesce quickly, stay focused, and accomplish so much was due in part to its skilled leadership: Ralph Neas from the Leadership Conference on Civil Rights and Nan Aron from the Alliance for Justice.

Neas's eight years of experience on Capitol Hill enabled him to master the rhythms of the legislative process and to develop relationships with Congress members and staff. This experience served him well as the executive director of the Leadership Conference, a coalition established by the leaders of the oldest and largest civil rights organization—the National Association for the Advancement of Colored People (NAACP). Judging by his appearance alone—white, Catholic, male, Republican—Neas seemed an unlikely leader of a civil rights coalition. However, a magnificent organizer and lobbyist, Neas took a giant, unmanageable coalition—the Leadership Conference—and managed it.

While Neas was skillful at *managing* coalitions, Nan Aron was skilled at *building them from the ground up.* Coming from a social activism background, Aron had convinced twenty diverse public interest organizations to form the Alliance for Justice. Aron was known as a champion out-reacher, a bridger of diversities, a tempter and persuader of the reluctant ally. Aron was both a talent scout and recruiter of the right talent for the right job.

Both Neas and Aron presided over the coalition's formal and informal leadership structure. Their diverse backgrounds, experiences, and leadership strengths enhanced the capacity of the coalition to mobilize support both "inside" and "outside" the corridors of power and, ultimately, to succeed.

Diverse Membership and Broad Outreach

Diversity is a critical part of a coalition's strength and its ability to build public judgment. However, as many advocates know from experience, diversity can be difficult to build. Here are a few lessons drawn from the Advocacy Institute's work:

- *Think creatively, non-traditionally, "outside the box."* Reach beyond people who are just like you—that is, those who already share the same perspective on the issue, similar expertise, experience, personal backgrounds, or represent similar types of groups or communities. In doing so, you may identify "unlikely allies"—those whom you would not think of immediately but who indeed share a common interest.

- *Make time to build new relationships.* Seek understanding about different perspectives. Ask questions. Listen. Ask for recommendations for whom else to recruit.

- *Build diversity before the first formal meeting.* The more diverse the perspectives are around the table, the better your strategy development, analysis, and action planning will be.

- *Leave space for a shared agenda to be created or revised once others join the coalition,* rather than expecting others to simply sign on to your agenda. This is critical for building group cohesion and ownership in the coalition. If there *are* "no compromise" areas that are not open to revision, be open about them when recruiting coalition members.

- *Remember that "diversity" means difference.* Don't expect people who are different from you to think the same way and make the same decisions you do. Leave time to discuss and understand each other's perspectives and to form compromises.

Thinking "Outside the Box"

Diversity comes in many types, including:

- *Issue sector.* From those immediately connected to the issue or serving the same constituents to those focused on broader issues. For example, groups working on primary education may also work on affordable health care for children. A wide range of groups will likely be interested in broad issues that affect everyone, like campaign finance and corruption.

- *Civil society sector:*

  - From groups affected by the issue or historically marginalized to groups sympathetic to the issue.

  - From organizations—nongovernmental organizations (NGOs), community-based organizations (CBOs), people's organizations (POs), trade unions, professional groups, academics, students, churches, clubs—to individuals who work in the business or government sectors but who engage in public roles that are separate from their work affiliation.

- *Personal background.* Including race, ethnicity, class, caste, gender, religion, ability/disability, profession, residence (rural or urban), education, age, life experiences, and so on.

- *Geographic region and scope.* From village, town, and state to national, regional (global South or North), and international.

- *Organization size.* From small organizations working on a limited scale to large organizations.

- *Resources,* including:

  - *Legitimacy and credibility* in the eyes of key decision makers and your constituents alike.

  - *People power:*

    - Talented coalition members.

    - Grassroots base and other volunteers.

    - Paid staff dedicated exclusively to the coalition's work.

  - *Knowledge:*

    - Experience and perspective on the issue.

    - Information and data.

  - *Expertise:*

    - Community organizing and mobilizing.

    - Lobbying.

    - Communications (developing messages, working with the media, graphic design).

    - Research and analysis.

    - Facilitation.

  - *Relationships:*

    - Grassroots base and constituency.

    - Decision makers.

    - Journalists.

    - Donors.

    - Other networks.

  - *Money.*

  - *Facilities:*

    - Meeting space.

    - Office space, computer, copier, phone, fax, e-mail, and so on.

The types of diversity you need will be determined by your strategy, especially the key audiences you identify. Think about:

- For each key audience—especially the decision makers—what or who influences them? Who, therefore, needs to be involved in the effort to give it credibility and legitimacy?

- Whose expertise or information is needed to create an effective strategy?

- Who has the resources needed to carry out an action plan?

Identifying Unlikely Allies

Adapted from the Advocacy Institute's Stone Soup: Recipe for Successful Coalition Building.

An environmental coalition in Indiana, a midwestern US state, fought bitterly with a group of local farmers over the coalition's attempts to build a wildlife reserve. Later, though, when plans were made to build a bypass through their rural area, the coalition and farmers' group found themselves on the same side of an issue. The farmers did not want the city encroaching on their farmland, and the environmentalists did not want a bypass tearing through the wildlife in the area. One of the coalition's leaders took advantage of the similar interests and developed an unlikely alliance.

Basic Coalition Structures

Basic coalition structures help a coalition function and manage tensions or differences. The key is to keep it simple, creating structure, processes, and rules only when needed.

While each coalition will create its own structure to manage its unique tensions, the following areas are usually critical:

- *Membership:* Who can join the coalition? What criteria must be met?

  When new members join, a sense of common ground needs to be maintained. Coalitions often create a statement of principles and/or a set of membership criteria.

- *Participation:* How are members expected to participate?

  Effective coalitions leave space for members to participate and contribute to the best of their ability.

  – What is the minimum level of participation?

  – Who represents organizational members, attends meetings, and participates in discussions? Do they need to have decision-making authority within their home organization?

  – How are resource needs shared by members? Do larger organizations contribute more? Can smaller organizations contribute resources other than money?

  – How do members participate in decision making?

  – How are roles defined and assignments made? What are the consequences if assignments aren't completed?

- *Leadership:* How are the leaders chosen? How are they held accountable to the members?

- *Making decisions:* How are decisions for the coalition made?

  Basic, simple processes are needed to identify which decisions need group discussion, to create space for discussion, and to mediate conflicts over decisions.

  – Are decisions made by leadership after group discussion or by the full group?

  – By consensus or voting? If voting, is it proportional, meaning larger organizations have more votes? Or does each organization get one vote, allowing smaller groups to have an equal voice?

  – If a member doesn't have decision-making authority within their home organization, can more time be given before voting?

  – Are there different processes for strategic decisions, day-to-day decisions, and emergency decisions?

- *Coalition identity and members' autonomy:*

  – When do members act as a group?

  – Through what process is this decided? How long does that process take? Is there a shorter process during emergencies?

  – When and how can members act alone? What are the consequences for violating these agreements?

- *Communication:*

  – Are notes taken at each meeting? Are they distributed to members? How?

  – What information needs to be shared between meetings? How is it shared? Through phone? Fax? E-mail? Mail? A web page? Some combination?

  – How do members stay in touch when there is an emergency?

– What language(s) should be used? What impact does this have on time needed during meetings? On resources for interpreters, translating materials, and so on?

- *Logistics:*

    – How often does the coalition meet? How often do subgroups or task forces meet?

    – Where does the coalition meet? Is the location rotated or fixed?

    – Who facilitates each meeting? Is facilitation shared and/or rotated?

    – How is the meeting agenda created? At the beginning of the meeting? Through consultation with members before the meeting? Who prioritizes the agenda items?

Decision-Making Structures for Coalitions

Excerpted from "NGO and Grassroots Policy Influence: What Is Success?" by Valerie Miller, Senior Associate at the Institute for Development Research (IDR) in Boston, Massachusetts, USA. Miller's article is drawn from collaborative research sponsored by CODE-NGO (Caucus of Development NGO Networks) and Green Forum in the Philippines and IDR.

As examples from the Philippines show, decision-making structures affect a group's ability to influence policy and represent its members' interests and concerns. Speedy, agile, and clear decision-making processes allow groups to respond in a timely fashion to the fast-paced, multi-level nature of policy-influence work. Formal democratic structures of coalition decision making and accountability help establish common purpose, responsibility, and ownership and hold together ideologically diverse groups.

- When a decision was needed quickly, the Urban Land Reform Task Force secretariat would convene a meeting and whatever members were present made the decision by voting. This ad hoc process allowed for prompt responses but did not offer a system to ensure full representation, and there seemed to be no mechanism for providing accountability to the coalition as a whole. The secretariat's impartiality and commitment to keeping members involved may have ameliorated the structural problem of accountability. However, important groups were not always involved in crucial decisions.

A number of major factors contributed to the success of our campaign:

- The National Council of Leaders—the governing board of the Nation-wide Coalition of Fisherfolk for Aquatic Reform (NACFAR)—included officers from member fisherfolk federations and was responsible for major coalition decision making. In addition, these same officers formed NACFAR's advocacy and lobbying team along with four staff members from the secretariat. Working within the coalition's general guidelines, this combined team made and implemented decisions on advocacy strategies and, therefore, was able to quickly respond to the ever-changing political dynamics of the campaign and the different policy players. By incorporating structures of overall accountability, NACFAR seemed to be able to ensure effective participation and a high degree of member ownership and commitment.

- The Congress for People's Agrarian Reform had a much slower, more formalized decision-making process based on a strict adherence to consensus building. To make important decisions, each federation underwent a consultation process with its organizations and then had to reach consensus with all other federations. This inhibited the coalition's ability to be flexible or timely in its responses but was crucial for holding its ideologically diverse members together and maintaining a high level of accountability.

Creating Coalition Ground Rules

As a coalition discovers its unique tensions, it may create new ground rules to help manage them. The following are sample ground rules, identified by Advocacy Institute alumni when reflecting on their own experiences working in coalitions. While this is *not* a recipe, you may find some ingredients can be adapted to your own context:

- Respect others' opinions, confidentiality, organizational work styles, needs, and limitations. Don't question others' motives or commitment to the coalition.

- Criticize ideas, not people. No "zaps"—personal criticisms, insults, or digs. Don't criticize each other in public.

- Give credit where credit is due.

- Be transparent. Share information. Don't have hidden agendas.

- Be accountable. Divide the work and report back to the full group.

- Participate equally—everyone shares decision making, contributing resources, and doing the work. One member, one vote. Rotate facilitators and meeting location.

- Strategize collectively before making joint resolutions, interventions, and compromises.

- Contribute to the best of your ability. Play to your strength.

- Stay focused during meetings. Follow the agenda's discussion topics and time limits.

- Don't interrupt when someone is speaking. Take turns. If you are talking more than others, hold back so others can participate.

- Discuss the "undiscussables." (This is discussed further in "Effective Communication and Conflict Management" later in this section.)

- Agree to disagree.

- Check your ego at the door.

- Use humor appropriately.

Trusting Relationships among Members

A coalition's success relies on whether members trust and can rely on each other. Basic coalition structures and accountability processes lay the groundwork. Trust and confidence also come with time, working together on concrete projects, and informal interaction.

Leadership also plays a role by facilitating introductions among coalition members. For example, introductions during the first meetings could help members to:

- Identify common interests or potential disagreements.

- Share key information for strategy development.

- Set a tone of open communication.

The following are questions that could be answered during introductions:

- *Who are we?*

  – Who do we each represent?

- *Why are we each here?*

  – Why do we care about the issue?

  – Why do we need or want to join the coalition? What are our agendas?

- *What do we each bring?*

  – What is our perspective—individual and organizational?

  – What are our resources?

  – What can we do? What are our strengths?

- *What are our limits?*

  – Do any of us have resources that we cannot contribute to the coalition?

  – Can we each make decisions on behalf of our organizations?

  – Are there issues about which any of us are sensitive? For example, could a particular stand on an issue weaken our credibility with our constituents or threaten our sources of funding? How can we accommodate these sensitivities?

It may not be realistic to answer all of these questions when relationships are still new and trust is being developed. However, just thinking about the questions can help leaders to identify potential sources of misunderstanding or frustration among members and to find ways to address them in the full group.

Effective Communication and Conflict Management

Leadership needs to address conflicts and tensions as they emerge, helping coalition members to voice concerns or frustration, and to identify creative solutions drawn from multiple perspectives.

Creating space for open discussion is critical but can be difficult when members feel it's risky to speak up or when anger, distrust, or other emotions are involved. Leadership can create and strengthen an open environment in a number of ways:

- *Set the example that all voices should be heard.* Be aware of some members speaking more than others and what power dynamics among members may be involved. For example, members who are from groups with less traditional power—such as women, minorities, or representatives of smaller organizations—may find it difficult to speak up. Help the group develop and observe ground rules that prevent anyone from dominating discussions and encourage quieter members to participate.

- *Create "safe space."* That is, a comfortable environment where members feel listened to when they voice concerns. The avenues for voicing concerns can range from one-on-one conversations or anonymous feedback to caucuses or full-group discussion. For tensions that involve the full group, be sure to hear from everyone.

- *Discuss the "undiscussables."* That is, a tension or conflict that no one talks about openly, especially if one is afraid to offend someone or wants to avoid conflict. It's difficult to address a tension if you can't find its source. Set the example by talking about such unspoken taboos.

- *Take time for conflict management and problem solving.* It only takes one person to serve as a "bridge builder" and to help resolve conflict. Consult with members individually or carve out time during a coalition meeting. Focus on the key elements of mediating conflicts:

  - Identify common ground. Use this to focus the discussion as you address differences. Also, focus on the issue rather than the personalities involved in the conflict.

  - Ask questions to seek more information to manage the conflict. Make sure everyone has the chance to speak. Also, share all relevant information. Be specific. Use concrete examples.

  - Acknowledge the role of emotions. Do they help highlight critical issues? Or do they cloud judgment and the ability to problem solve? If necessary, allow emotions to cool down before problem solving. Give each person the chance to express their concerns without being challenged or corrected. Also, keep in mind that some strong emotions that are expressed may be unrelated to the conflict. Try not to take others' outbursts personally.

  - Maintain and demonstrate mutual respect for each other. Don't personalize criticism.

  - Don't question someone else's motives or place blame.

  - Don't act defensively if you disagree with someone. Ask questions to better understand others' perspectives, feelings, and ideas.

- *Listen well* to get to the heart of the matter and to draw out ideas for possible solutions. For example:

  - *Focus on the speaker and demonstrate that you are listening and understand.* Body language, eye contact, tone of voice, and the questions you ask all demonstrate that you are listening—rather than distracted, disinterested, or already decided on the matter.

  - *Avoid blocks to listening,* such as:

    - *Talking* without allowing someone else to speak.

    - *Deciding* on your opinion before someone finishes speaking or you've heard from more than one person.

    - *Rehearsing* a response in your head while the other person continues to speak.

- *Avoiding conflict* by agreeing with anything the speaker says.

- *Trying to "win" the argument* rather than focusing on common ground and possible solutions.

- *Being afraid to be wrong or assuming you're right.*

- *(In some contexts) Heated emotions.*

Summary of Key Points

"Collaboration" is working with individuals and groups who share a common focus or interest. The purpose may range from sharing information to taking joint action. While the distinctions are fluid and change over time, it can be helpful to consider informal "networks" at one end of the spectrum and more formal "coalitions" at the other. Whatever their name or structure, collaborative relationships are an essential ingredient in any advocacy effort.

If you are wary of working in a coalition without a compelling reason, then it probably isn't worth the investment of time, energy, and other resources. However, you do have alternatives, such as sharing information in an informal network or working together on a single event or short-term campaign.

Based on the experiences of the Advocacy Institute's facilitators and alumni, a number of ingredients are critical if you do choose to enter a coalition:

- Willingness to experiment and to learn from mistakes.

- Skilled and diverse leadership.

- Diverse membership and broad outreach.

- Basic coalition structures.

- Trusting relationships among members.

- Effective communication and conflict management.

Section 7
Information and Research

Information is needed throughout your advocacy effort, from understanding the problem and key audiences to developing alternative solutions and effective messages for each audience.

To help a group identify its information and research needs, this section is divided into four components:

- Frequently asked questions.

- Creating a research plan.

- Using creative analysis.

- Summary of key points.

Frequently Asked Questions

What Is "Information"?

Broadly defined, "information" means facts and findings, ranging from numbers to stories. Information is gathered from many sources through experience, observation, interviews, and other forms of research. Once gathered, information about an issue is analyzed to show relationships, patterns, trends, and contradictions.

How Is Information Used?

Throughout strategy development, action planning, and taking action, you need information to:

- Understand a problem—the causes, impact on people's lives, who benefits from the status quo, and so on.

- Identify key audiences and their positions on the issue.

- Identify possible entry points within the decision-making system.

- Develop objectives, a strategy, and an action plan based on what is possible.

- Identify or develop possible policy solutions.

- Develop effective messages for each key audience.

- Identify the best medium and messenger for each key audience.

Advocacy groups play one or more roles in using information:

- Research.

- Analysis.

- Dissemination.

The role your group plays at a given moment will depend on your capacity, expertise, and need. Keep in mind that you don't need to do the research yourself. Instead, many groups collaborate with, hire, or use information developed by their allies or other experts.

Creating a Research Plan

At its simplest, research is the process of identifying and gathering the various information you need. The information gathered can be in many forms, including:

- Data and analysis and interpretation of data, including statistics, studies, and reports.

- Laws, policies, budgets, and other public records.

- Newspaper articles.

- Opinion polls and surveys.

- Photos.

- Anecdotes, stories, and gossip.

To develop a research plan, ask yourself:

- *What information do we need?* What questions are we trying to answer?

- *Where can we look?* Who collects or has the type of information we need? Think about government offices, universities, private companies, other organizations, the library, the Internet, and so on.

- *How can we access the information?* Is the information readily available to the public? Is there a cost? Is the information available if we know the right "gatekeeper," such as a specific researcher or bureaucrat? If so, can we set up a meeting to build a new relationship?

- *Who will do the research?* Does our organization have the capacity to gather information? To understand or interpret it? To analyze it for patterns and trends?

  - If so, which people can be assigned to the task?

  - If not, who can we work with who does have the capacity? Do we need to hire a consultant?

- *What is our time frame?* When will we stop looking for information and begin to analyze it? As the National Campaign against Toxic Hazards in the United States advises, don't postpone action because of never-ending research. Once you begin analysis, if you discover you need more information, you can always do more research.

Creating a Research Plan

Developed by a group of India Advocacy Fellows who were asked to create a research plan for a hypothetical advocacy effort on children's right to life, to education, and to enjoy childhood.

- *Information needed on the issue.*

  - Background. All information should be broken down by sex, socioeconomics (class, caste, religion), and region (rural, urban).

    - *Health,* including immunization rates, and availability and cost of child health programs.

    - *Infant and child mortality,* including cause of death (malnutrition, female infanticide, etc.).

    - *Child marriage,* including average age of child brides and reasons for early marriage.

    - *Education,* including levels of education, quality of schooling and educational facilities, and dropout rates and causes.

    - *Employment,* including percentage of children employed, type of labor (formal and nonformal sectors), hours worked, and wages earned.

    - *Prostitution, trafficking, and other abuse.*

  - Government's plan of action.

    - Existing laws.

    - Existing policies.

    - Existing welfare programs.

  - Main decision makers and actors.

    - Government departments and bureaucrats.

    - Journalists.

    - NGOs, people's organizations, and other civil society organizations.

- *Sources of information.*
  - Census report and other government studies.
  - Government replies in Parliament.
  - Government committee reports.
  - Constitution and international conventions.
  - Independent surveys and research.
  - Reports of international organizations, like UNICEF.
  - Media.
  - Legal case histories.

In looking for information that is relevant to the issue, you may use one or more methods:

- Recycle what is already being used.
- Introduce existing information into public argument.
- Generate new information.

Recycle What Is Already Being Used

That is, use statistics and other information that are already part of public argument. By doing this, advocacy organizations can focus their energy and resources on analyzing information and reframing the debate or drawing attention to their position instead. (The concept "framing" is discussed in section 8, "Message Development.")

Introduce Existing Information into Public Argument

That is, find existing information and research that have been gathered by other organizations with the organizational capacity to conduct extensive fieldwork and to publish reports that are available to the public.

The following are possible sources of existing information and research:

- *Government departments, ministries, and agencies at the national, state, and local levels.* Government information ranges from the budget and census to research conducted to evaluate the government's policies and programs.

- *Universities, social science research institutions, and "think tanks."* Many disciplines—such as those related to public health, the environment, economics, and public policy—publish reports for the public, as well as journals written for other specialists in their field.

- *Advocacy groups,* including NGOs, CBOs, and other CSOs. Many organizations conduct their own studies to generate information and publish reports and guides to conducting research or finding specific types of information.

- *Investigative journalists.* Some may print in-depth, well-researched articles on your issue.

- *Corporations.* Some information (such as the names of its CEO, names of members of the board of directors, the company's holdings, and history of legal problems) may be public record.

- *Funding agencies.* Multilateral donors—like the World Bank and IMF—and private foundations often publish reports related to the projects they fund.

- *Other agencies,* such as the United Nations.

- *Internet.* E-mail and web pages are becoming rich sources of information that is both gleaned from the above sources and newly generated.

Generate New Information

Existing information about an issue may be incomplete and may not reflect your experiences. In this case, your organization can play a powerful role in generating information and introducing new perspectives into public argument.

Your group can work with its constituents, members, or members of the affected groups to generate information in many forms, including:

- *Anecdotes and stories.* Real stories that bring a human face to the problem can be a powerful illustration of the larger issue.

- *Surveys and participatory research.* These can be incredibly effective in generating quantitative data about the problem and organizing a community.

- *Model programs.* By testing a possible solution on a small scale, an organization can give valuable feedback about its strengths and weaknesses. Such information is particularly helpful when an issue is in its adolescence and alternative solutions are being considered.

- *Program evaluations.* Another way to give valuable feedback on a program is to monitor and document the impact of a specific policy solution once it is implemented. Such information can be helpful when an issue is in its renewal and decision makers are evaluating whether to continue or modify the program.

Regardless of how you do it, any information you generate and provide to others—decision makers, journalists, the public—must be accurate and well-supported. If it isn't, and your information is found to be wrong or misleading, your group's credibility will be damaged. Be ready to explain the methodology you used to generate information. A one-page explanation sheet can be particularly helpful.

Generating New Information

The following was contributed by Diana Autin, 1994 US Leadership Fellow and Executive Director of the Statewide Parent Advocacy Network (SPAN); adapted with permission from "Campaign for Resisting Dropouts from Primary Schools," by Rana Nishat Jahan, 1995 Bangladesh Advocacy Fellow; and adapted from the Advocacy Institute's Framing for Access: How to Get the Media's Attention, *number 5 in the* Blowing Away the Smoke *series of media advocacy advisories.*

In New Jersey, SPAN's Welfare and Human Rights Monitoring Project visits welfare offices and homeless shelters to collect information that no else has yet collected—stories and data from welfare recipients, those directly affected by welfare reform.

In Bangladesh, the Campaign for Popular Education (CAMPE) conducted a survey to count the number of school-age children in a selected area and to identify reasons why students drop out. The survey not only revealed the main causes of low attendance but was also a successful way to organize the community.

In Washington, D.C., the Junior League worked with sixth- and seventh-grade girls to count how many storefront ads and billboards for cigarettes they passed on their way to and from school. Not only did the survey demonstrate the dramatic effect of advertising on children, it gave the mass media an interesting angle for covering the story.

Using Creative Analysis

At its simplest, analysis is the process of reviewing information and looking for relationships, patterns, trends, and contradictions.

One tool that is particularly helpful is creative analysis or "social math": that is, placing large statistics—thousands of people, money in the millions and billions, and numbers of years—into a social context and using simple math to make the numbers easier for your audience to relate to.

Here are a few ways to use creative analysis or social math:

- *Scale down the numbers.* Divide annual figures into smaller units of time or divide the amount of money spent by the number of people. (See "Scaling Down the Numbers" for an example.)

- *Localize the numbers or bring the story home by identifying the impact on a specific community.*

- *Translate numbers* (the quantitative) *into comparisons* (the qualitative). Show that a number related to the issue is more or less, bigger or smaller in comparison to a more familiar number. (See "Scaling Down the Numbers" for an example.) This can be particularly effective in showing a great contrast or a surprising similarity.

In using social math, accuracy is absolutely vital. Your translation of the numbers must make sense and be free of error. Otherwise, neither your organization nor your message will be credible—and your audience won't listen.

To ensure your accuracy, here are a few tips:

- *Use information from a reliable source with a good reputation.*

- *Work carefully and methodically.* Attention to detail is a must. Always triple check your math. When possible, check with an expert (such as a researcher or the author of a study you cite). Journalists call this "double-sourcing" or using the "two-source rule." Your group is one source; the expert is the second.

- *Don't stretch the data too far.* Be sure the original information really supports your claim. If your claim sounds good but the numbers don't quite work, don't use them.

When using creative analysis or "social math," be prepared to be challenged by your opponents, skeptical journalists, and decision makers. Be ready to cite and provide copies of your information source and to explain how you used math to convert the numbers. A one-page explanation sheet can be particularly effective.

Scaling Down the Numbers

Suppose a study finds that, each year in your country, 1.3 million teenagers—people under the age of twenty—start smoking. This is a large number that may be difficult to relate to. However, if you have access to recent census data, you can scale down the numbers in at least three ways.

First, you can show what proportion of teenagers start smoking each year. If your country's teen population is 72 million, you can divide 72 million by 1.3 million. The result: one out of every fifty-five—or almost one in fifty—teenagers starts smoking each year.

Second, you can show how many teenagers start smoking *each day* in your country. Divide the annual number—1,300,000—by 365 days in a year. The result: almost 3,500 teenagers in your country start smoking *every day.*

Third, you can show how many teenagers start smoking *each day in your city.* Suppose your city's teen population is 2.4 million.

- First, divide 2.4 million by 72 million to show that your city's teen population is 3.3 percent of the country's teen population.

- Then multiply .033 (this is another way to write 3.3 percent) by 1.3 million to determine that 42,900 teenagers in your city start smoking each year.

- 42,900 is still a large number that may be difficult to relate to. Scale it down even more by dividing the annual number—42,900—by 365 days in a year.

The result: almost 120 teenagers in your city start smoking *every day.*

Making Comparisons

Adapted from "Brand Logo Recognition by Children Aged 3 to 6 Years," Journal of the American Medical Association *(1991), and the Advocacy Institute's* Framing for Access: How to Get the Media's Attention, *number 5 in the* Blowing Away the Smoke *series of media advocacy advisories.*

Six-year-old children in the United States are as familiar with the Joe Camel character used to sell cigarettes as they are with Walt Disney's Mickey Mouse.

After the US federal government found two Chilean grapes with cyanide on them, it halted all imports of Chilean fruit. Tobacco control advocates used this incident to make a comparison: the amount of cyanide in *one cigarette* is greater than the amount of cyanide in *several bushels* of tainted grapes. They then connected this surprising contrast to a policy question: Why would the government act so quickly and restrictively on one product while ignoring another common but more lethal product?

Summary of Key Points

Information is needed throughout an advocacy effort, from gathering intelligence on key audiences and what influences them to data on specific policies that help or worsen a problem.

Not all groups have the capacity to do original research. Instead, they can work with groups that do have the capacity or focus on using creative analysis to reframe the debate or draw attention to their position instead.

Regardless of how your group uses information, any information you use must be accurate and well-supported. If it isn't, and your information is found to be wrong or misleading, your group's credibility will be damaged.

Section 8
Message Development:
What Does Each Audience Need to Hear?

One goal of advocacy is to raise attention for an issue. However, before you have your audience's attention, do you know what message you want to convey?

To help a group answer this question, this section is divided into three components:

- Frequently asked questions.

- Basic principles of message development.

- Summary of key points.

Frequently Asked Questions

What Is a "Core Message"?

A core message is one or a few brief, straightforward statements that reflect:

- Your analysis of the problem.

- The problem's cause.

- Whom you hold responsible for solving the problem.

- Your proposed solution, if you have one.

- The actions you ask others to take in support of the solution.

The core message guides the tailored messages, slogans, sound bites, and stories that an advocacy effort uses at different times with different audiences.

What Is a "Tailored Message"?

A tailored message is a message created for a specific audience, based on an analysis of:

- What will be most persuasive for that audience.

- What information it needs to hear.

- What action you want that audience to take.

Such analysis will guide the message's:

- Content.

- Form (words, images, etc.).

- Length.

- Medium (mass media, one-on-one meeting, demonstration, street theater, etc.).

- Messenger or spokesperson (member of the affected group, an expert, etc.).

From Core Messages to Tailored Messages

Adapted from the Advocacy Institute's Getting the Message Right: Using Formative Research, Polling, and Focus Group Insights on the Cheap, *number 3 in the* Blowing Away the Smoke *series of media advocacy advisories.*

In 1995 the US Food and Drug Administration (FDA) proposed new tobacco regulations. Two audiences, the president and Congress, had the power to allow the FDA to act or to block it. President Clinton strongly supported the FDA rules, but Congress, with its fierce bias against government regulation and close ties to the tobacco industry, was likely to block the FDA. To neutralize congressional opposition, the Campaign for Tobacco-Free Kids developed a media campaign that focused on a set of core messages:

- Cigarette smoking is a "pediatric disease," in the words of FDA commissioner David Kessler. Kids are smoking at younger and younger ages—nine, ten, and eleven years old.

- Nicotine is addictive, and tobacco companies deliberately manipulate its content in cigarettes to hook kids and to keep them addicted.

- Tobacco companies have lied to the public about the hazards of smoking, the addictiveness of nicotine, and their targeted advertising to young people.

- To prevent public health authorities like the FDA from protecting kids, tobacco companies have spent millions of dollars on political campaign contributions, corrupting our democracy.

Using the tailored message "America's kids are not for sale," the campaign called upon all political candidates to "renounce and refuse" campaign contributions from tobacco companies. The campaign also seized every opportunity to highlight political ties between tobacco companies and Congress, stories calculated to enrage those voters who already distrusted both. The objective was to convince congressional leaders that any action to block the FDA was politically risky: the media and the voting public would assume such action was provoked by tobacco money they had accepted.

The extent of the message's impact can never be known, but the issue was never far from the news and Congress never moved to block the FDA.

Basic Principles of Message Development

Communications research shows that an effective message will use all or most of these basic principles of message development:

- Keep it simple.

- Put your frame around the issue.

- Know your audience.

- Invite the audience to "fill in the blank" and reach your conclusion on its own.

- Present a solution (if possible).

These principles are briefly discussed below.

Keep It Simple

That is, make the message easy to grasp, jargon-free, and relatively short or uncluttered.

Keep in mind that terms that your group uses frequently—such as "environmental racism" or "sustainable development"—may be jargon to the public. Such terms will need to be defined repeatedly when first introduced into public argument.

Also, remember that your message is *not* an elaborate argument of your position on the issue or an elaborate counterargument to your opponent's position.

The simpler the message, the more likely your audience is to understand it and to retain it. Also, people often need to hear a message again and again before they get it. Such saturation is *much more likely* if your audience continually hears the same message from you. It is *less* likely if you use multiple messages.

Put Your Frame around the Issue

Frames are boundaries that highlight specific parts of an issue, place others in the background, and leave out some entirely. They influence how the audience thinks about the issue, including who is responsible for the cause and its possible solutions.

Your frame guides the content of your messages, including the use of particular symbols, metaphors, and visual images. You need to frame the issue in a way that is as vivid and compelling as the opposition's frame and shifts the audience's attention to your perspective.

One Event, Three Frames, Three Solutions

Adapted from How to Tell and Sell Your Story, *edited by Timothy Saasta at the Center for Community Change in Washington, D.C.*

In her book *Prime Time Activism: Media Strategies for Grassroots Organizing,* Charlotte Ryan offers an example of how one event can be framed in many ways, with a profound impact on the event's meaning. Consider these three frames for the same event:

- "An infant left sleeping in his crib was bitten repeatedly by rats while his sixteen-year-old mother went to cash her welfare check."

- "An eight-month-old South End boy was treated yesterday after being bitten by rats while sleeping in his crib. Tenants said that repeated requests for extermination had been ignored by the landlord. He claimed that the tenants did not properly dispose of their garbage."

- "Rats bit eight-month-old Michael Burns five times yesterday as he napped in his crib. Burns is the latest victim of a rat epidemic plaguing inner-city neighborhoods. A Public Health Department spokesperson explained that federal and state cutbacks forced short-staffing at rat control and housing inspection programs."

"Each frame has a distinct definition of the issue, of who is responsible, and of how the issue might be resolved," explains Ryan.

The first version, by emphasizing the age and actions of the mother (leaving her baby to cash a welfare check), suggests that the problem is irresponsible teens having babies. The solution would be reforming welfare to discourage or punish such irresponsible behavior.

In version two, the issue is a landlord-tenant dispute about responsibility for garbage. The solution depends on the reader's perspective: either stronger enforcement of laws related to a landlord's responsibilities, or laws that would make it easier for a landlord to evict tenants.

Only the third version really gets into larger issues about how cuts in funding for basic services affect low-income communities.

Filling in the Blank

Adapted from "Unlocking the Power of Responsive Chord Communications," Trumpet Notes (July 1996), a publication of the Certain Trumpet Program, a partnership among the Advocacy Institute, the Benton Foundation, the Berkeley Media Studies Group, and others.

In 1994, Proposition 188 appeared on the California ballot. While framed as a clean-indoor-air law, it was actually designed to overturn strong local anti-tobacco laws. To build opposition to the proposition, the Wellness Foundation ran a series of newspaper ads that simply listed the main supporters of the proposition (including tobacco company Phillip Morris) and the main opponents (including the public health organization the American Cancer Society).

The ads forced the California public to choose between the integrity of two organizations. They worked because the audience was predisposed to believe that "anything Phillip Morris supports is bad" and "anything the American Cancer Society opposes is bad." The integrity of each organization was contrasted implicitly, not explicitly. The ads didn't supply these conclusions; the audience did and, thus, was much more likely to agree with them.

Know Your Audience

According to US media expert Tony Schwartz, the heart of communication is the interaction between the message that is sent and the minds of the audience that receives it. The more you know about a particular audience, the better you can create a message that strikes a "responsive chord" or resonates with the audience's knowledge, values, beliefs, feelings, needs, and priorities. By fitting what is already in the audience's mind, a responsive-chord message is more likely to be accepted and retained by the audience.

To determine an audience's responsive chords, think about their:

- *Knowledge.* Is there something the audience does not know that would change its position on the issue? Your message may focus on public education on the issue. Or a startling fact or comparison that causes the audience to re-think their position.

Putting It All Together: Evaluating Messages

Adapted from "The Minimum Wage Message" by Ericka Taylor in Trumpet Notes (April 1997), a publication of the Certain Trumpet Program, a partnership among the Advocacy Institute, the Benton Foundation, the Berkeley Media Studies Group, and others.

In 1996, the Association of Community Organizations for Reform Now (ACORN) spearheaded a campaign to raise the minimum wage in Denver, Colorado. The campaign lost badly, capturing only 22 percent of the vote. In the face of well-coordinated and well-resourced opposition, the campaign's only chance at victory may have been effective message development. They missed their chance.

One mistake was the campaign's message to undecided or "swing" voters. They tried to appeal to a sense of justice and basic human dignity. Unfortunately, a plea to do the right thing didn't touch the hearts of swing voters. Instead, the campaign should have stirred their quiet but righteous indignation, identifying their opponents as money-hungry, morally bereft tyrants unwilling to pay their employees a fair wage.

Another mistake was the campaign's use of multiple messages, ranging from "If you work, you should not be poor" to "Statistically, minimum wage increases do not increase unemployment." While their arguments were all valid points, none was a single, sharp message that reframed the debate or neutralized the opposition's message: "Don't destroy Denver jobs."

- *Values and beliefs.* What values does the audience hold most strongly?

- *Feelings.* What triggers the audience's compassion, outrage, or disgust?

- *Needs and priorities.* What does the audience care deeply about? What do they fear? Does your position on the issue help alleviate their fears?

Invite the Audience to "Fill in the Blank" and Reach Your Conclusion on Its Own

Schwartz takes his "responsive-chord" theory one step further: messages that convey more with less—that is, hold back from including every detail—implicitly invite the audience to participate in creating the message. By activating the audience's thought processes, such messages often lead the audience to reach the message's intended conclusion on its own. When this happens, the audience is even *more* likely to accept or agree with the message, and to retain it.

Present a Solution (If Possible)

According to research by US political scientist Shanto Iyengar on how people form political opinions, people are most responsive to messages that present solutions rather than those that focus on a problem's cause.

Summary of Key Points

Your use of a particular message should be based on an analysis of what you think will persuade a particular audience. Overall, the messages you use should be simple, to the point, and repeated frequently.

Section 9
Message Delivery

Developing the right message is half the art. The other half is choosing the right medium and messenger to make sure your audience hears the message.

To help a group understand the generic elements of message delivery, this section is divided into four components:

- Frequently asked questions.

- Choosing a medium.

- Choosing a messenger.

- Summary of key points.

Sections 10 to 11 focus on two specific forms of message delivery—working with the mass media and lobbying.

Frequently Asked Questions

What Are the Basic Principles of Message Delivery?

- Stay on message; repeat it again and again. Remember that people often need to hear the same message many times before they get it. Also, by repeating the same message, you reduce the chances that it will be distorted in the process.

- Choose a medium and messenger based on the audience you are trying to reach and what is possible given your context and organizational capacity.

What Is a "Medium"?

A "medium" is a means or channel of communication. "Media" is the plural of medium.

"Mass media" are those specific means used to communicate to large groups of people—for example, national newspapers, magazines, radio, and television. (Mass media are discussed further in section 10, "Message Delivery—Mass Media.")

The following are examples of the various media you may use to reach an audience at the local, national, and international levels:

- *People.*

  – One-on-one meetings.

  – Lobby visits. (These are discussed further in section 11, "Message Delivery—Lobbying.")

  – Group or community meetings.

  – Seminars.

  – Public hearings.

  – Protests, public demonstrations, and mass action.

  – Word of mouth and gossip.

- *Print.*

  – Newspapers and magazines.

  – Journals, bulletins, and other institutional publications.

  – Posters, leaflets, fliers, action alerts, press releases, reports, studies, and other organizational publications.

  – Billboards.

  – Letters to legislators, newspaper editors, and others.

- *Electronic.*

  – Radio.

  – Television.

  – Internet (e-mail, discussion lists, web pages).

– Videos.

– Slide shows.

• *Folk.*

 – Street theater and puppet shows.

 – Songs, music, and poems.

 – Dance.

Choosing a Medium

You will likely need multiple media to communicate your messages to your key audiences. For each audience, choose a medium based on your assessment of that audience, as well as your access to and capacity to work with that medium.

For each audience, think about:

• What are the audience's primary sources of information and influence? Who or what do they listen to? What do they read? What do they watch?

• What are the audience's characteristics? Where do they live or work? What language do they speak? Do they read? Can they afford to buy newspapers and other media? Do they have access to the Internet?

Once you have chosen a medium, assess whether it is possible to use it. Think about:

• How do we access the medium? Who owns it? Who are the gatekeepers?

• How do we get attention for that medium?

• Is it possible that the gatekeepers will distort our message? If so, is it worth it to use this medium? Why?

Next, assess whether you have the organizational capacity to work with that medium. Think about:

• What skills are needed?

• What resources are needed?

Choosing a Messenger

Choose a messenger based on the audience you are trying to reach. Think about:

• Who is most persuasive to the audience? Who has the most credibility?

The messengers you choose may include legislators, public leaders, community leaders, "experts" with technical knowledge, and "authentic voices," or those whose lives are immediately affected by the problem.

Once you choose a messenger, be sure they:

• Are knowledgeable about the issue.

• If public speaking is required, are poised, confident, and compelling.

• If writing is required, have strong writing and editing skills.

Remember, however, that knowledge and poise can be learned over time. They are not the key factors for choosing a messenger or spokesperson—credibility and influence with a key audience are.

Choosing the Right Medium

Adapted from a case story written by Paul Vleermuis, 1996 Namibia Advocacy Fellow, former Managing Director of the Rural Peoples' Institute for Social Empowerment (RISE), and current staff person at the Namibia National Farmers' Union.

The Rural Peoples' Institute for Social Empowerment (RISE) worked in rural southern Namibia to improve sanitation. To help communities air their views on preventative health, community hygiene, and the use of the bucket toilet system, RISE used three media:

• *Street dramas* were created based on information collected from house visits. Performances were done under trees, in front of shops and church halls, and so on. They highlighted problems that were associated with the bucket toilet systems and presented alternatives, such as ventilated-improved pit (VIP) latrines.

• *Community meetings* were held to follow up the street performances. People were given their chance to air their views and to make suggestions for community action.

• *A call-in radio show on the Nama-language radio station* allowed RISE officials and community members to discuss the alternative toilet systems and to respond to public queries. Members of the communities were urged to call and those without telephones were given access to phones.

Summary of Key Points

"Medium" can be defined as a means or channel of communication. "Media" is the plural of medium. Message delivery in an advocacy campaign can range from using people as a medium to using the "mass media," such as newspapers, radio, and television. Your use of a particular medium and messenger should be based on an analysis of what you think will persuade a particular audience.

Section 10
Message Delivery—Mass Media

Mass media are just one way to deliver messages. In some contexts where the mass media are owned, controlled, or heavily censored by the state, alternative media will be needed. However, in contexts that have a free press, the mass media can be an important way to deliver your message to multiple audiences, including the general public, decision makers, and others.

To help a group use the mass media for message delivery, this section is divided into seven components:

- Frequently asked questions.

- Assessing your mass media.

- Working with journalists.

- Creating "newsworthy" news.

- Preserving your message.

- Evaluating your efforts.

- Summary of key points.

Frequently Asked Questions

What Are "Mass Media"?

"Mass media" are those specific means used to communicate to large groups of people—for example, national newspapers, magazines, radio, and television.

If Your Context Allows It, Why Can It Be Important to Work with Mass Media?

- Mass media reach many critical audiences, including the general public and government decision makers.

- Mass media are influential. Most people don't have personal experience with most social problems. Instead, their knowledge and attitudes about an issue are often formed by the mass media—the issues covered, the parties held responsible for solving problems, and the alternative solutions presented.

- Mass media are free and, therefore, an especially helpful medium for groups with limited financial resources.

If Your Context Allows It, What Are Common Barriers to Working with Mass Media?

- Compared to the other media listed in section 9, "Message Delivery," advocates have much less control over whether the mass media cover their issue or deliver—or distort—their message.

- Mass media are businesses driven by profit, not public service. Stories that are "newsworthy"— focus on controversy, conflict, and so on—sell better and are more likely to be covered.

- According to communications research, media coverage of issues tends to be episodic, not thematic. That is, most stories are self-contained and focus on personal responsibility, rather than on the root causes of a problem and the need for institutional solutions.

- By their nature, most social justice advocacy issues are complex and long-standing—neither "new" and fresh every day nor easily captured in small, tidy stories. Advocates must find ways to fit their stories into newsworthy frames without compromising their values or distorting their message.

- Journalists write about what they know. However, advocacy groups often do not take time to educate and cultivate relationships with media gatekeepers—journalists, editors, producers, and so on—who decide whether and how to cover an issue.

- Mass media operate under tight deadlines that advocacy groups are not always able to meet.

Assessing Your Mass Media

The mass media are both a medium *and* a key audience. They may deliver your message, but, first, they are a key audience whose attention you will need to attract. Understanding your audience and what influences them is critical.

The first step is to assess the structure and nature of your mass media. The information you gather will

Figure 6.2. Understanding Audiences and Influences

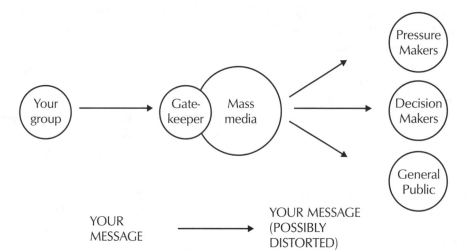

help you focus on the most helpful news organizations and journalists and determine how to frame your issue to attract their attention.

Begin by gathering basic information about your mass media. If necessary, call the news organization directly to find the answers.

- What are your key audiences' primary sources of information and influence? List specific mass media news organizations—newspapers, magazines, radio shows, TV news shows, professional journals, and so on—at the local, national, and international levels.

- How is each news organization structured? Is there a department or a specific journalist that covers your issue?

- What are the coverage options for each news organization? Articles, editorials, columns, political cartoons, letters to the editor, op-eds, radio talk shows, and so on?

- What is the timeline for each option? How much time does a journalist need or have to develop a story? Hours? Days? Weeks?

Next, observe your mass media for a month. Think about:

- Who are the gatekeepers, that is, those who decide whether to cover your issue, what frame is used,

what information is included, whose voices are represented? Does someone regularly cover your issue or related issues? Be as specific as you can in naming journalists, editors, producers, and others.

- How often is your issue covered? What frames are used most often? How is the issue described? Who is seen as responsible for solving the problem? Are alternative solutions discussed?

- What kinds of people are quoted in articles? What kinds of authors have their "letters to the editor" printed? Decision makers? Experts? NGO representatives? Members of the affected group? Others?

The answers to these questions will help you determine which news organizations are most likely to cover your issue and to deliver your message without distorting it.

Choosing the Right News Organizations

Adapted from the Advocacy Institute's Tobacco Control Media Advocacy in Communities of Color, *number 4 in the* Blowing Away the Smoke *series of media advocacy advisories.*

The Coalition against Uptown Cigarettes formed quickly when they heard a tobacco company planned to test market a new brand—Uptown cigarettes—that targeted African Americans. The coalition was extremely diverse—including health, religious, and community groups led by African Americans in the Philadelphia community—and was held together by a few basic principles:

- Focus on organizing in the African American community, including smokers.

- Focus attention on the tobacco company, RJR—*not* on other African Americans that might be on the wrong side of the issue.

- Keep the goal local—stop test marketing in Philadelphia.

These principles helped the coalition identify the media primarily as a tool to mobilize their community. Local media, then, was more important than national media, and local news organizations that "spoke to" African Americans were more important still.

After the first coalition meeting, the American Cancer Society (ACS)—one of the coalition members—received a call from the *New York Times* asking for a list of coalition members. Some thought the coalition should comply right away. After all, the *Times* is an important national news organization. For others, it was too soon to publish the list since, at the time, the coalition consisted mostly of the classic tobacco-control-movement groups—like ACS and the American Lung Association. Most African American groups still needed time to decide whether to support the coalition. Some were concerned that the story would say the coalition was the "same old players" and the issue had little attention in the African American community. The coalition decided to wait to release the list of members at an upcoming press conference after more groups had joined the effort.

The coalition faced a similar decision when a major television-network morning news show—*Good Morning America*—asked for a representative to come on the show to debate a marketing expert on the issue. The coalition turned down the opportunity because the marketing expert was African American, and they strictly opposed pitting African Americans against each other in public.

Eventually, the tobacco company withdrew the Uptown brand. Part of the coalition's success was due to their insistence on keeping the focus local and preventing the issue from dividing the African American community.

Working with Journalists

As with any other key audience, the quality of relationships you develop with the mass media can be very important. Once you know which gatekeepers control access to the various coverage options, you can focus on building relationships, educating them, and becoming a good source of information.

To help you work with journalists—the primary gatekeepers for the mass media—here are a few tips gathered from advocates and journalists alike:

- Provide information that the journalist needs, whether in person, by telephone, or in a press release. Key information may include:

  – Succinct, well-researched, substantiated information, supported by examples, if possible.

  – Background on the issue.

  – Your group's position on the issue, especially concrete, practical solutions.

  – Responses to counterarguments.

  If you don't know the answer to a question, say so. If possible, point the journalist to another source or offer to follow up later with the necessary information.

- Help identify spokespersons—members of the affected group, respected community leaders, experts—who can speak about the issue. If needed, help the spokespersons prepare so they will feel at ease speaking with the journalist.

- Respect the journalist's deadline. Be prepared to respond quickly. If you offer to follow up with more information, ask when they need it. If you can't answer the journalist's questions right away or if you need to consult your group first, ask what their deadline is and if you can call them back.

- Respect the journalist's objectivity and need to cover all sides of an issue. Don't expect coverage to focus only on your organization or position.

If your group doesn't have an existing relationship with a journalist, take time to introduce yourselves. Provide background information on:

- Your group, whom you represent, who supports you, the work you do.

- Your position on issues.

Educating Journalists

Drawn from case study research in Ecuador by Tamara L. Jezic and Gabrielle Watson for Part III, "Advocacy Case Studies."

In Ecuador, groups involved in a campaign against Texaco, a transnational oil corporation, told the "unofficial" story of oil contamination by organizing tours for journalists, legislators, and members of the military. In contrast to the "eco-tours" organized by the state oil company, these "toxi-tours" showed the very real pollution that Texaco and the state oil company had not cleaned up.

The tours were attractive to journalists for a number of reasons. First, they were able to speak directly to people affected by the pollution and the leaders of their popular organizations. Second, by accompanying the legislators and military personnel, the journalists were able to get quotes for their articles from these high-ranking decision makers and "experts."

The "toxi-tour" strategy had another benefit: it allowed the local people's organizations to build credibility in the media's eyes. Over time, journalists started going straight to these leaders for quotes and information.

This can lay the groundwork for raising their interest in your issue and for you becoming a source for them in the future.

Creating "Newsworthy" News

One challenge that advocates must meet is framing their issue in ways that are "newsworthy" but also stay true to their values and message.

The following are typical newsworthy frames:

- Controversy and conflict.

- Injustice, inequity, deception, and exploitation.

- Broad interest or meaningfulness to a large number of people.

- Things that are mysterious, inexplicable, or deeply unusual.

- Irony and dramatic contradictions that make us re-think something.

- Local impact of national stories.

"Newsworthy" News

Adapted from "Media-Advocacy Relationships: The View from the Other Side," written by Amanda C. Rawls in the Advocacy Institute's ChangeExchange *(October 1999).*

While discrimination in South Africa is "old news" and has been covered extensively, it still became a major headline in two examples from July 1999. In the first, a Black farm worker who trespassed by walking across a white farmer's land was caught by the farmer and sprayed from head to toe in silver paint. In the second, an AIDS activist who disclosed her HIV+ status at a meeting was later stoned to death. Both the human faces and the sense of injustice made them newsworthy stories.

During the US civil rights era, despite intensified media interest, there were several points when civil rights leaders thought the story was flagging and disappearing from the public's view. For example, after many consecutive days in which protesters were arrested without violence, the story was no longer "new" and, therefore, no longer "newsworthy."

The civil rights leaders overcame this by deliberately planning actions, such as the Freedom Rides, to attract the mass media's attention. The famous march on Birmingham, Alabama, by Martin Luther King Jr. and his followers was planned because leaders knew the police there were more likely to become violent with the protesters. They did, and the movement was back in the headlines again.

- Personal stories that give a human face and voice to a large issue and evoke the audience's compassion or outrage.

- Celebrities who are spokespersons for or personally affected by the issue.

- Breakthroughs or the first, best, or largest occurrence of something.

- Anniversary of an important milestone against which progress can be measured.

- Recurring stories, like annual holidays and the weather, which affect everyone.

- Visual images or pictures that tell the story as effectively as words would.

Think about your issue. How can you make it newsworthy?

Many advocates find that working in a group to brainstorm newsworthy frames for their issue unleashes creativity. Once a list is created, you can analyze and discuss each possibility until you find one that fits best—meaning it's "newsworthy" *and* fits your values and message.

Another helpful exercise is to observe your mass media. Make a note of any story that, from your perspective, covered the issue well. Then ask yourself what made the story "newsworthy" in the first place.

Preserving Your Message

Whenever you need to go through a gatekeeper to use a medium, you run the risk that your message will be distorted. The relationships you develop with individual gatekeepers will be tremendously important in helping them understand your message and issue.

There are also other options that allow you to maintain better control when working with the mass media:

- *Press releases and prepared statements* allow you to put into writing exactly what you want to say.

  Press releases are short, clearly written accounts of an event, accomplishment, or report. Ideally, the five *W*s and one *H*—who, what, when, where, why, and how—are covered in the first two paragraphs. This way, the most important information is at the beginning and is easier for a journalist, editor, or producer to glance at quickly. Your headline should also summarize the contents of the press release in one sentence. On the top of the first page, be sure to add your spokesperson's name and telephone number, along with your group name and other contact information.

  When writing press releases, be brief—use short words, short sentences, and short paragraphs. Write with active verbs to move the reader forward. Generally, press releases are no more than one and a half pages. If you use a second page, be sure to put "More" or "Continued" at the bottom of the first page. At the top of the second page, add an abbreviated headline and page number.

  Above all, make sure your press release is factual and accurate. Proofread it until it is perfect.

- *Letters to the editor and op-eds,* even though they will be edited for length, also allow you to put into writing exactly what you want to say.

  The letters-to-the-editor section of a newspaper is among the most highly read sections. It appears every day and is intended to—and often does—reflect the mood or a current debate within the community.

  You can use a letter to the editor to alert readers to the "other side" of an issue or to respond to a previous letter, article, or editorial. Generally, you would focus on important facts that were omitted, point out false or misleading information that was given, or clarify a key point that was made.

  Even a letter applauding another letter writer, journalist, or editorial position may be appropriate.

- *Spokespersons,* when well prepared, can help steer questions back to the two or three points that you are trying to convey.

  If possible, before an interview, have a colleague "interview" you so you can practice giving responses that are short and to the point.

  During the interview, stop to think through the answers carefully. Rephrase or clarify statements when necessary. It may be appropriate to provide background information that puts the comments into context, rather than assuming the journalist knows the context.

Evaluating Your Efforts

Regardless of the coverage option you choose, be sure to evaluate your efforts to work with mass media gatekeepers. Think about:

- Did your message appear in the news item?

- Was your message misunderstood, distorted, or lost entirely?

- Did the journalist use the information you provided?

- Was it worth it? Think about the organizational resources and capacities that were needed to work with the mass media.

- What would you do differently in the future?

Your answers will guide whether you should use the same news organizations or coverage options next time or if you need to develop better relationships with journalists or other capacities.

Summary of Key Points

The mass media are just one possible medium for delivering your message. Since they have control over whether and how your message is delivered, they should also be treated like a key audience and carefully analyzed and understood.

To work with the mass media, identify who the gatekeepers are at each news organization and which coverage option will best preserve your message. While you will have limited control over whether your message is delivered or distorted, a few things will help:

- Strong, professional relationships with journalists and other gatekeepers.

- Well-developed messages that are simple, to the point, and repeated frequently—whether delivered in conversation with a gatekeeper or in writing.

Section 11
Message Delivery—Lobbying

Lobby visits are one way to deliver messages in person to key decision makers or pressure makers. Even in contexts where access to formal decision makers is severely limited or impossible, lobbying skills can be used to great advantage with other key audiences, such as community leaders, journalists, funders, and so on.

To help a group prepare for a lobby visit, this section is divided into five components:

- Frequently asked questions.

- Before the lobby visit.

- During the lobby visit.

- After the lobby visit.

- Summary of key points.

Frequently Asked Questions

What Is "Lobbying"?

"Lobbying" is the art of educating and persuading your key audiences through direct, one-on-one contact.

Lobbying may be:

- *Formal,* such as visits with decision makers in their offices.

- *Informal,* such as waiting in the lobby of the capitol to discuss an issue with a legislator before it's voted on, networking at a reception, or talking with people at a community meeting.

When your lobbying target is a decision maker, think of lobbying as an "inside" tool, requiring you to work within the system and its corridors of power. Since you will rarely know exactly which advocacy tool will move your audience to act in the desired way, it is important to combine "inside" tools with "outside" tools—such as grassroots mobilization and working with the mass media—that involve pressure makers.

Why Is Lobbying an Important Advocacy Tool?

Lobby visits provide the opportunity to:

- Build relationships.

- Listen and collect information.

- Educate and provide information.

- Persuade.

These are all an integral part of advocacy.

Assuming You Have Access to Your Target Audience, What Are Common Barriers to Effective Lobbying?

- *Maintaining confidence.* During a lobby visit, advocates must find ways to stay focused on their main discussion points, despite any nervousness they may feel.

- *Unpredictability.* Will your audience be receptive to your views? Or argumentative? Will your audience ask questions to seek understanding? Share information? Or continually get sidetracked on irrelevant issues? During a lobby visit, advocates must find ways to adapt to unpredictable situations, keep lobby visits focused on the issue, and use their time effectively.

Before the Lobby Visit

Before a lobby visit, take time to prepare. The better you do so, the better you will be able to keep the discussion focused on your key points and to respond to any surprises or challenges. Preparation will also help build your confidence, especially if it is your first time lobbying.

- *Prepare the delegation.*

  - Who should participate in the lobby visit?

    - Who does your audience find most persuasive? Who knows the issue the best? Who is the most poised? Should the delegation include someone directly affected by the issue? An "expert" (for example, an academic or former government official)?

    - How many people should participate?

  - *Does everyone in the delegation share the same point of view* on the issue and what is wanted?

    Take time before the meeting to air differences and to reach consensus. This will help you convey a clear, consistent message during the actual visit.

  - *Does everyone know when to meet and where,* what to wear, and what to bring?

- *Prepare your presentation.*

  - *What is our issue?* Have we chosen one to focus on? Can we state this clearly and succinctly?

  - *What do we want from our audience?* Their vote? Leadership on the issue? Co-authorship of a bill? To persuade others to support the issue? Information? Be sure to ask something of your audience.

  - *What are the main points of our presentation?* What kinds of information will we use? Statistics? Testimony from someone affected by the issue? Tailor the message to your audience based on your assessment of what will persuade that person.

  - *What issues should* not *be discussed?* If they are raised, how will we steer the discussion back to our issue?

  - *What is negotiable?* What is non-negotiable? Determine this in advance so you can be prepared to compromise if needed.

  - *What do we have to offer our audience?* Information? Public support?

  - *How will we open the meeting?* If meeting with someone who has been supportive in the past, be sure to acknowledge your appreciation.

  - *Who will play which role during the meeting?* Who will say what? Who will open the conversation? Will someone facilitate? Who will "close the deal"? Will we have a notetaker?

  - *How will members of the delegation be introduced?* For example, "My name is...and I represent...." "My name is...and this is how I am directly affected by the issue."

- *Practice your presentation.* Role-plays can build confidence and help the delegation prepare for a range of possible responses from your audience. (See "Lobbying Role-Plays" for sample role-plays.)

- *Prepare your materials.* Be sure to leave your audience with something:

  - A summary of the issue and your main points.

  - Your contact information (for example, your business card).

Lobbying Role-Plays

The following two exercises have been used by the Advocacy Institute to simulate informal and formal lobbying situations, to help advocates build confidence, and to help them identify and prepare for a range of possible responses from their audiences.

Informal: The Reception

You are at a reception. A newly appointed public official turns to you and asks, "What does your organization do?" You have one minute. How do you respond?

Practice in pairs. Give each person the chance to play both roles. Afterward, everyone reports back to the full group.

Sample responses from Advocacy Institute workshop participants:

- Congratulate her on her new appointment.

- State your issue in one short sentence.

- Why should the issue be important to the minister?

- How can the minister give support? "We could use your vote."

- What can you offer the minister?

- Use simple language. Avoid technical jargon or complicated arguments.

- Leave room for listening.

- Give your business card. "Let's get together." Try to arrange a meeting.

Formal: The Lobby Visit

First, brainstorm possible scenarios for your visit. If you know anyone who has done a lobby visit before, ask them what types of things have gone wrong or surprised them.

Sample scenarios

- *Amount of time:* the full amount scheduled, or cut short or interrupted.

- *Target audience's position:* supporter, undecided, or hostile.

- *Target audience's behavior:* distracted, argumentative, talks too much, tries to divide the group, and so on.

- *Surprises:* the target audience isn't there; our group didn't agree on the main points; and so on.

Next, assign people to one of three roles:

- *Target audience.* Is your audience friendly, hostile, or a fence-sitter? Act out how this person might act during a real meeting. Draw from your own experiences in lobby visits, ask your colleagues for suggestions, or consider finding an ally—like a retired civil servant—who can help you prepare.

- *The delegation.* Act as if you are meeting with the actual decision maker.

- *Observers.* Watch the role-play as it is acted out. Then offer feedback to the full group.

Give everyone ten minutes to prepare for their roles. People assigned to observe can help either the target audience or delegation to brainstorm what they will do during the "meeting."

When everyone is ready, play out the scenario for approximately ten minutes. The facilitator or one of the observers should keep track of time or end the role-play when you think it is appropriate.

Give the "target audience" and "delegation members" a few minutes to shake off their roles and become themselves again.

Then evaluate the role-play as a group. Think about:

- How did you feel in your role?

- What did you do well?

- What was the most frustrating?

- Does the presentation fit the allotted time?

- Did you use simple language? Did you avoid using technical jargon?

- Were your points clear and succinct? Was your message lost in too much information?

- Can you adapt your arguments and still get your message across?

- Did you "close the deal"?

- What would you do differently next time?

During the Lobby Visit

Once you are actually meeting with your audience, keep in mind the four basic purposes for your visit:

- *Build relationships.*

  - Lobby visits can be used to develop new relationships or to strengthen existing ones.

  - Allow time in the beginning of the visit for small talk, but not too much. Remember, it's your meeting.

  - Maintain a tone of courtesy and respect.

  - Keep in mind the old advocacy adage, "No permanent friends, no permanent enemies." Even if you disagree on *this* issue, they may support you on a future one. Build the relationship so you can return at another time.

- *Listen and collect information.*

  - What issues are important to your audience?

  - What points do you agree on? Are there areas for common goals?

  - What are points of disagreement?

- If your audience is a "silent type," draw them out by asking questions.

- *Educate and provide information.*

  - Offer information that will strengthen or contradict your audience's opinion.

  - You don't have to be an expert on the issue. Your audience likely isn't one—many elected officials are generalists. However, if you think it is necessary, you may be able to be accompanied by someone who *is* an expert on the issue.

  - It's OK to say "I don't know" and offer to follow up with information after the meeting.

- *Persuade.*

  - Maintain a tone of courtesy and respect.

  - Be open to counterarguments but don't get stuck on them. Don't be argumentative or confrontational.

  - Stay on your point. If your audience talks a lot, look for openings to bring the discussion back to your point.

  - Use the right argument. Is your audience persuaded by logic? Statistics? Personal stories?

  - "Close the deal." After you make a request and have listened to your audience's reply, ask for a specific action. For example, if you want a decision maker's vote, confirm that their vote is secured. "So, we can tell our constituents that we can count on your vote on the bill?"

  - At minimum, make it difficult for your audience to say "no."

During the meeting, keep the following tips in mind:

- Be on time.

- Don't stay too long. Try to get closure on your issue. If you hear what you want, express your thanks and leave. If you reach an impasse, express your disappointment.

- Keep it simple. Too much information or technical jargon can distract from your message. Also, be sure to address no more than one or two issues.

- Take notes during the meeting. This can be an assigned role for one of the delegation members. The notes will be helpful when you report back to your constituents and allies.

- Don't become argumentative or push your point so much that your audience stops listening.

After the Lobby Visit

Lobby visits are not an end in themselves. Make sure you connect them with other activities:

- *Debrief with the delegation.* How did you do? What did you learn? What are next steps?

- *Bring it home.* Report back to your constituency and allies.

- *Follow up.*

  - Send a thank-you letter to your audience. Repeat your understanding of the commitments made during the meeting.

  - Send information if offered or requested.

  - Send a thank-you letter to staff members who were present or helped arrange the meeting.

- *Celebrate!* Remember that every meeting with a key audience is an opportunity to learn, build your confidence, and build your credibility in the audience's eyes. Feel proud of what you have accomplished.

Summary of Key Points

Lobbying is the art of educating and persuading your key audiences through direct, one-on-one contact. Lobbying is an "inside" persuasion tool that must be combined with "outside" pressure-making tools.

Lobby visits, whether informal or formal, provide the opportunity to:

- Build relationships.

- Listen and collect information.

- Educate and provide information.

- Persuade.

To be as effective as possible, practice and preparation are the keys.

Conclusion to Part II

Over the years the Advocacy Institute has learned there are many, many ways to engage in advocacy, pressure decision makers and power holders, mobilize ordinary people, amplify voices that are ignored, and, step by step, create long-term, sustainable, transformative change that truly affects people's daily lives.

Part II presents one set of models, theories, concepts, and examples drawn from the Advocacy Institute's work. Whether these are used and adapted or new ones are created, we hope they have stimulated the core qualities of any effective advocacy effort:

- Reflection.

- Observation.

- Analysis.

- Questioning.

- Listening.

- Creativity.

- Courage.

- Optimism.

We hope you—and your supporters—will find ways to recognize these qualities in your own work and to create ways to continue learning from your and others' work. Such learning and exchange are the life blood and spirit that fuel our efforts to create change.

Part III

Advocacy Case Studies

Gabrielle Watson

Chapter 7

Introduction to Part III[1]

Gabrielle Watson

The paradox of globalization is that people are more interconnected and interdependent, but inequity is endemic and increasing. At the same time, major decisions affecting the lives of the disenfranchised, especially poor people, are being made in ever more distant places. With globalization, social justice advocacy is more essential than ever. Poor people everywhere need to learn who makes the decisions affecting their lives and how to influence decision makers in still-unknown arenas. They need to learn different advocacy skills and approaches to advocacy. When issues span multiple decision-making arenas, they need to collaborate with other groups, working in alliances, coalitions, and networks.

This part of *Advocacy for Social Justice* presents six case studies of innovative and successful advocacy campaigns mounted by poor people across the globe. The cases describe what advocacy looks like; how it works; how grassroots and membership groups, national nongovernmental organizations (NGOs), and international NGOs do advocacy in different nations; and finally what they achieved. They ask: Which strategies worked and why? How did the advocacy allies learn to collaborate?

These stories tell how people organized to get oil companies to stop polluting the Ecuadorian Amazon, to defend human rights in Guatemala, to reform the land law in Cambodia, to fight racism in the United States, to combat violence against women in Senegal, and to fight for debt relief for the poorest developing countries, principally in Washington, D.C. The ad-

vocates are Oxfam America partner organizations or Oxfam staff and the allies they worked with. The advocacy strategies used range from mobilizing people for public protest to filing legal challenges in courts, drafting and lobbying for policy changes, and working from outside the system, when working within the system was impossible. The cases were developed in collaboration with the advocates and researchers from the case countries.

With the guidance of colleagues at Oxfam America, we chose a mix of cases, looking for common threads running through all the stories, providing some underlying "universal" insights for other social justice advocates. We chose cases where advocates engaged at the local and regional, the national and the global levels. We chose cases in countries where the advocates had varying degrees of political "space," from highly repressive governments to moderately open governments to full democracy. We sought diversity sufficient to show the range and breadth of advocacy approaches that grow out of very different social, political, cultural, economic, and historic contexts.

The cases give us some insight into how social justice advocacy works:

- Despite the narrow way some may define advocacy as lobbying and changing policies, all the cases show that social justice advocacy involves a range of interrelated activities from mobilizing protests to filing complex legal cases; from gaining access to decision-making processes to building capacity of grassroots groups and government officials alike.

- The cases demonstrate that more often than not advocacy is carried out beyond a particular arena (local, regional, or national) and draws on a range of actors and allies that have different perspectives and agendas. This has implications for building and

---

1. The Advocacy Learning Initiative case study project has involved a series of collaborations, first with the Advocacy Institute, then with colleagues in Oxfam America's regional programs and Washington, D.C., advocacy office, and finally with Oxfam America partner organizations and research collaborators from each case study country. I use the term "we" liberally in this text, to reflect this fact. However, the framing structure and conclusions, while an outgrowth of this collaborative process, are largely my own and do not necessarily reflect the views of the case study contributors.

maintaining coalitions, developing strategies, and determining what are acceptable outcomes.

- The cases also show that regardless of how open or closed the political system is, successful efforts employ a range of strategies, are flexible and responsive to changing circumstances, and are able to identify a range of leverage points, from the power of "rights" arguments to identifying sympathetic allies within otherwise hostile targets.

Starting Questions

There are many models and tools available to help groups develop and implement advocacy strategies, mostly building on US and European experiences. Parts I and II of *Advocacy for Social Justice* described advocacy concepts, tools, and models drawing on experiences from around the world. Part IV, "The Advocacy Resource Directory," lists capacity-building, funding, networking, and research organizations all over the world. We present these case studies from different parts of the globe in the belief that stories have power to teach that goes beyond models and words on a page.

We began the project with the following basic questions:

- What can we learn from organizations that have developed their own approaches to advocacy, based on their own experiences and their own contexts?

- What works and why?

- How did these groups learn to influence the outcome of decisions affecting their lives?

- To what extent did they learn from the experiences of others and their own trial and error?

- How can grassroots organizations, intermediary-support NGOs, and international advocacy groups collaborate to bring about change in a globalizing world?

Core Themes Running across the Cases

In developing the cases, the research collaborators, partner organizations, and I have sought to explore the starting questions by focusing on a number of core themes affecting how people think about and carry out advocacy. The themes are introduced here and explored throughout the cases and the conclusion.

Breadth of Advocacy Definitions

In each of the cases, we have asked the organizations being profiled what they understand advocacy to be and how they go about it. Much of the Western literature on advocacy sees it in relation to government and in terms of using tools such as lobbying, press releases, media work, report generation, drafting legislation for sympathetic politicians, and so on. This literature assumes that advocacy is happening in open political systems, where advocates have free access to information and decision makers. But the picture of advocacy that emerges from the cases includes a broader spectrum of political space and includes a whole spectrum of strategies for influencing change from protest to movement-building to policy influence to working outside the system. By engaging multiple voices in this dialogue, we hope to bring more perspectives to this conversation and contribute to the ongoing work to define advocacy within the social justice community.

Political Space and Advocacy Approaches

The majority of the world's poor live in societies that limit their access to decision making. Some live under repressive political regimes where speaking out can mean death. Some are part of an ethnic minority (or majority) blocked from formal access to power. Political and economic elites dominate decision-making processes, excluding the poor and disenfranchised. It is important, then, to understand how advocacy works in societies with varying degrees of political space, political freedoms, and rule of law.

Do some advocacy approaches work better under different degrees of political space? Looking at the cases as a whole, there is no simple answer to this question. They reveal a surprising mix of approaches across the different contexts. In some of the cases, approaches that seemed impossible, unlikely, or highly risky end up becoming key strategies because of chance occurrences no one could have predicted. The cases offer a hopeful and diverse picture of the kinds of advocacy strategies that work under different contexts.

Working at and Bridging the Local, National, and Global Levels

Intermediary-support NGOs—which help local and regionally based grassroots groups by getting involved with policy work at the national and global levels—often lose touch with the communities and issues that gave birth to their activism in the first place. In the process, just when the door seems to open, grassroots communities are excluded from the key decisions affecting them by the very groups they thought were there to help them. This is one of the classic advocacy dilemmas.

Most writing about social justice policy advocacy focuses at the national and international levels. But most of the world's poor have limited information about national-level policies, much less international-level dynamics, and they have limited access to decision making at either of these levels. This is one defining element of poverty. Yet decisions made in these distant arenas impact daily life at the local level. As Peter van Tuijl has argued, in globalization, "processes determining the 'public good' and social justice, or the lack of it, have become dislocated geographically and institutionally all over the world."[2] There is a growing crisis of representation, where those most affected do have less and less say in the decisions that affect them.

Being good at advocacy at one level does not guarantee effectiveness at another. The skills that make for successful projection of interests at the village, district, and regional levels are different from the skills needed to engage on issues like national budget allocations, constitutional reforms, or international debt. Making matters more difficult, national and global policy decisions are often made in small, exclusive circles, where events move quickly. There is rarely time for advocates to consult with their base, even in the best cases.

For these reasons, these are the key questions facing social justice advocates in today's globalizing context: How do advocates working at the national and global levels keep grounded in and accountable to the interests of the grassroots? How are the voices of excluded groups kept at the forefront in national- and global-

level advocacy work? The cases show how some groups have struggled to bring local, excluded voices to national and global arenas, seeking to work effectively at multiple levels simultaneously.

Building Effective Alliances and Collaborations

Because globalization now requires simultaneous and coordinated action in multiple arenas to effect change, working in alliances, networks, and coalitions becomes all the more important. But organizations do not always collaborate happily with each other. They fear losing control of the agenda strategy and tactics, not getting credit, losing clout with funders. Collaborations are also becoming more complex. They span national boundaries, cultures, languages, social classes, race, ethnicity, and varying degrees of access to communications technology. Collaboration takes a lot of time to do well—to build trust, understand each other's perspectives and strengths, identify what each can contribute, keep each other informed, make joint decisions, overcome conflict, resist attempts to divide coalition members, and so on.

The cases all underscore the importance of collaborations for making a difference. How they deal with coalition tensions varies greatly. In many cases, collaborating organizations crafted strategic alliances where the different aspects of the project are taken up by different organizations based on their special competencies. This helps avoid competition within the alliance, permits some variation in strategies and tactics, and builds on the comparative advantages of each alliance member. In some cases, legitimate differences have broken collaborations apart. In others, allies have agreed to disagree, each working semi-autonomously on the issue with some core shared goals. How groups collaborate in accountable and effective ways remains one of the greatest challenges to doing social justice advocacy in a globalizing world.

How to Evaluate Advocacy Impact

How do advocates know they have achieved something important? What if the outcome isn't what they initially set out to achieve? While the cases did not set out to answer these questions initially, it is a central question for social justice advocacy campaigns. The question asks us to return to the underlying search for a definition of advocacy. Is advocacy about policy change or does it also include the broader pro-

---

2. Peter van Tuijl, "Advocating Apart, Together: Southern NGOs and the Advocacy of Oxfam International" (photocopy), Discussion Paper for the Oxfam International Project Directors and Advocacy Coordinating Committee, January 1998.

cess of structural change in the balance of power and how representative institutions work? Is it about increasing the participation and engagement of affected constituencies? The answer to these questions affects how we think about and assess advocacy impact. The cases suggest some key elements for building an approach to advocacy evaluation, which is revisited in the conclusion.

Methodology of Case Selection and Field Work

The cases are drawn from Oxfam America partner-organization experiences plus one from Oxfam-coalition-policy-advocacy work. We chose cases we felt could present an especially innovative or successful advocacy experience from which to draw lessons. The selection process was designed to get a mix of regions around the world, a range of engagement at the local, national, and global arenas, and a range of political "space." Political space was understood to refer to the degree that civilian governance structures, rule of law, freedom of expression, and open access to information and decision-making channels exist in each country.

This sampling strategy uses the diversity of the cases to draw out underlying, generalizable lessons that are common to all the cases, representing fundamental processes at work. It also permits the identification of the unique factors that distinguish each of the cases. This sampling strategy also provides a global perspective, with diverse political, social, and cultural contexts for the cases. Because of the small number of cases, though, comparison across the cases for any one factor should be treated with caution.

Our selection criteria creates a built-in bias for advocacy campaigns that worked well and that focused on social justice issues, mainly from a rural and grassroots perspective. Oxfam America supports partners working for long-term structural solutions to poverty and inequity. Oxfam partners tend to work in rural areas, often work with indigenous communities, and typically are grassroots membership organizations or intermediary-support NGOs that work at the regional or national level to support grassroots groups. Conducting more case studies to examine less successful campaigns or campaigns with an urban focus would provide additional insight into some pitfalls of advocacy work (though some do emerge in the cases) and give a broader range of advocacy strategies for urban areas (though some of these appear here as well).

Range of Political Space and Level of Engagement

The "level of engagement" refers to the arena where the advocacy takes place. In almost all cases, there were multiple levels of engagement. Some cases, like Guatemala and Ecuador, could be categorized in all three levels for difference pieces of the advocacy work. Table 7.1 presents where the six cases fall along the range of political space and levels of engagement.

Research Methodology

The research methodology involved original fieldwork carried out in collaboration with researchers living in the countries involved. Research collaborators were chosen based on their familiarity or direct involvement with the issue of each case and their experience working with grassroots and social justice organizations. In two of the cases, Guatemala and the US Black-farmer cases, I collaborated directly with the Oxfam partner organization to carry out the field research. In all but one case, the research collaborators are nationals of the country the cases happen in. The research collaborators wrote three of the case studies and I wrote or co-wrote three of them—the Guatemala, US Black-farmer, and Cambodia case studies.

The fieldwork involved in-depth, unstructured interviews in which we asked key activists a set of standard questions based on the starting questions and core themes described above. We also carried out interviews with other participants in the initiative, external supporters (in country and out, including Oxfam and other funders), opponents, external observers (press, academics, etc.), and advocacy targets, if possible. Fieldwork involved between thirty and fifty interviews over a period ranging from two to five weeks. In addition, we reviewed organization records, press clippings, legal documents, past studies, survey data, and so on, to document the history of the initiative development. At the end of the fieldwork, we had consultative "ground-truthing" meetings with the partner organization to report on preliminary findings and make sure our understandings from the interviews and document review were accurate.

Table 7.1. Case Selection by Range of Political Space and Level of Engagement

	Closed	Moderately Open	Open
	Weak or nonexistent civilian governance structures. Systematic use of coercive force. Arbitrary and uneven application of rule of law. Civil society excluded from decision-making processes.	Moderately weak, uneven, civilian governance structures. Semi-professional police force coexists/competes with military. Periodic use of coercive force. Periodic violations of rule of law. Uneven access to decision-making processes.	Strong civilian governance structures at all levels. Professional police force. Sphere of military restricted to external matters. Rule of law prevails. Multiple channels of access to information and decision-making processes.
Local and Regional	Guatemala	Senegal Ecuador	United States: Black Farmers
National	Guatemala Cambodia	Ecuador Senegal	United States: Black Farmers United States: Debt Relief
International	Guatemala Cambodia	Ecuador	United States: Debt Relief

Conclusion

The social justice advocacy case studies set out to look at advocacy in action. What does advocacy look like in diverse social, political, and cultural contexts? By looking at these experiences, we hope to share how advocates around the world understand and engage in advocacy.

As you read through the cases, we invite you to read with the starting questions in mind:

- What can we learn from organizations that have developed their own approaches to advocacy, based on their own experiences and their own contexts?

- What works and why?

- How did these groups learn to influence the outcome of decisions affecting their lives? To what extent did they learn from the experiences of others and their own trial and error?

- How can grassroots organizations, intermediary-support NGOs, and international advocacy groups collaborate to bring about change in a globalizing world?

- How do the stories told here resonate with your own experiences? Are there lessons that emerge for you, from strategies that work to ways of collaborating with other advocates? What lessons could you add to these from your own experiences?

Chapter 8

Senegal: The APROFES Struggle to End Violence against Women

Codou Bop

Translated by Paul Takow, Nisrin Elamin, and Eric Tchatgen

Introduction

Incidents of domestic violence, rape, and incest are widespread in Senegal, but a "culture of silence" has kept families, doctors, police, politicians, and religious leaders from denouncing these crimes. The Association for the Advancement of Senegalese Women (APROFES) was founded in 1991, in Kaolack, the provincial capital in a region of five hundred thousand residents two hours from Dakar. APROFES has played a pioneering role in Senegal by raising the issue of gender violence and by having a strong and continuing impact on the status of gender rights in the Kaolack region. APROFES was started by a group of young local activists with limited educational and professional training. They developed an approach for using high-profile rape and murder lawsuits to mobilize public outrage and denounce violence against women in this predominantly Muslim nation. At the same time, they carefully cultivated allies within government and among religious leaders to support their cause.

In the process, APROFES mobilized both men and women in Kaolack and other parts of the country, including the capital city of Dakar. This mobilization sparked a national debate on gender and development among Dakar-based women's and human rights organizations. While APROFES's long-term work remains focused at the local level in and around Kaolack, the lawsuits served to focus national attention and energize the Dakar-based women's groups, who have gone on to play a leadership role in taking these issues forward. Ultimately, the mobilizations around the APROFES-initiated lawsuits led to the formation of a national coalition to work on gender violence. This coalition later secured the passage of a law that officially criminalizes violence against women throughout Senegal.

What made APROFES's strategies successful, and what can others learn from their experience? This case study explores the key elements of APROFES's work in building strong local-level alliances, reaching out to groups in other parts of the country, and using opinion shapers like religious leaders and the media to change not only laws and their implementation but also how people think about gender violence.

The story of APROFES also highlights how social justice advocacy can be highly interrelated and interdependent with economic development work. APROFES is made up of affiliated partner associations that promote the advancement of women in rural and urban areas in the Kaolack region. These are guided by peer leaders who come from the same background and communities and are well aware of the realities and difficulties that poor and working women face in these regions.

Along the way, APROFES has learned some important lessons about doing effective advocacy, which this case study examines in detail. The most important one deals with the necessity of having allies who come from diverse backgrounds; no one organization can have all the skills necessary to wage a full-scale advocacy campaign aimed at structural legal, policy, and attitudinal changes. Another is the importance of mobilizing people. Without broad popular mobilization, efforts by women's groups to influence government officials are much more difficult in Senegal. A key strategy has been to sensitize religious, economic, and political decision makers and opinion formers and those who exert a significant influence on them. APROFES has worked closely with these leaders in Kaolack to persuade them to denounce violence against women.

Specifically, a key lesson derived from APROFES bringing forward the lawsuit has been the importance of presenting strong and credible evidence and witnesses to convince the judge and jury during trials of those who perpetrate crimes or rapes. Perhaps one of the hardest lessons to replicate, because it requires long-term work to build trust in a community, is the importance of encouraging victims to report gender crimes to the police and to file complaints. Criminal charges can only be brought if women are willing to come forward. APROFES broke an unwritten rule perpetuated by families, medical professionals, police, religious leaders, state agencies, the courts, and the women themselves by enabling the first few women in Kaolack to come forward publicly to denounce their attackers.

The case study focuses on the role of APROFES in order to examine the role of local participants in national-level social justice causes.

The National and International Context for APROFES's Work

APROFES undertakes advocacy work in Senegal to end violence against women in a context in which democratization has been the trend at the national and region-wide level since the late 1980s. This context is characterized by political pluralism; the empowerment of civil society associations; the creation or multiplication of development-oriented NGOs, women's associations, and human rights associations; the consolidation of the women's movement; and the emergence of individual women's collectives.

The government of Senegal has been progressive in word, if not always in action, from a very early date. Beginning in 1978, the Senegalese government established a policy for advancing the status of women, thus concretizing commitments made during the 1975 International Conference on Women in Mexico. It created a ministry for women and elaborated action plans for women. The first of these was launched in 1982. In addition, Senegal is a signatory to the African Charter for Human Rights, the International Pact for Economic, Social, and Cultural Rights, the Convention for the Elimination of all Forms of Discrimination

against Women, as well as the Convention for Children's Rights. With regard to violence against women, however, the Senegalese penal code was still silent in the early 1990s. The government had passed no laws to protect women against gender violence.

It is important to note that Senegal, where 94 percent of the population are Muslim, is not immune to the resurgence of religious fundamentalism. Indeed, the Kaolack region, where APROFES makes its home, is the base for an important Muslim group called the Niassène brotherhood. Many fundamentalists individually, as well as in their organizations, have declared that the rights gained by women undermine family, religious, and traditional values of Senegalese society. This fact—combined with high levels of illiteracy; the general lack of understanding of Koranic texts, Islamic jurisprudence, and the Hadith (speeches and viewpoints of the Prophet Muhammad); as well as the proclamations of Senegalese fundamentalists that influence important groups in society—constitutes a serious challenge to those who defend women's rights and in a more specific manner defend their right to physical integrity.

An important external influence has been the emphasis on a "human rights" approach to development that has been particularly strong with regard to women's role in development. The Convention on the Elimination of All Forms of Discrimination against Women and the action plans of major international conferences such as the Conference on Human Rights (Vienna, 1993), the International Conference on Population and Development (Cairo, 1994), and the Beijing Conference on Women (1995) all were examples of this.

Other international trends affecting the Senegalese context were decentralization and structural adjustment policies promoted by international donors. These policies cut deeply into national funding for social programs and added responsibilities, but not necessarily financial resources, at the local level. As a consequence, local governments are relying more heavily on NGOs to carry out social programs at the local level.

A notable favorable development for APROFES's work has been the birth of a private, independent press. The media alert public opinion to human rights abuses, especially violence against women, and relate the measures taken by women's associations to mobilize and fight to eliminate such practices. With the extensive media network that has been established throughout Senegal, the private press has the ability to provide nationwide coverage of any form of violence perpetrated against women.

The advent of information and communication technologies, such as the Internet, has made it possible for human rights activists to inform like-minded international networks anywhere in the world and to solicit their support.

One can see that there are opportunities for advocacy in Senegal. But, while several institutions of government, the UN system, and civil society undertake advocacy work, the definitions they have and the methods they use to implement the concept of advocacy differ. Advocacy work can mean a single initiative aimed at raising awareness, or one for mobilization, or one for organizing alertness and solidarity campaigns. In an effort to describe the advocacy undertaken by her association, Mrs. Bineta Sarr, president of APROFES, explains, "The advocacy consists of an aggregate of concerted efforts aimed at changing given situations. In the long term it consists of a global strategy to consolidate several actions with the aim of winning a cause." We now turn to examine APROFES's vision and its work.

APROFES and Its Vision:
Economic Development and Women's Rights

APROFES was formed by young women from Kaolack and neighboring villages. Kaolack is the capital of the region with the same name, located about two hours' drive from Dakar in the central part of Senegal, with a population of about five hundred thousand inhabitants. APROFES's founding mothers had spent several fruitful years as activists in Sports and Cultural Associations (ASCs), which are social groups that developed from the popular movement for social change that attained prominence between 1970 and 1980. APROFES was founded in 1991 when a group of these women decided they wanted to do something concrete to respond to the economic and social justice issues of women in the region. Since then, APROFES has developed an innovative approach that strategically combines a focus on women's rights and the promotion of women's social, political, and economic

equality through financial and technical support to income-generation activities.

During their early years of activism, these young women realized that development strategies had been failing because women's interests and perspectives were not taken into account. To address this situation, they saw that it was necessary to set up a structure that could promote economic and social development for Senegalese women by reducing poverty and eliminating inequalities based on gender. This association would be a forum where women could meet together, share their experiences, analyze their problems, and seek solutions to them. It was this impetus that led to the creation of APROFES. The specific vision of the organization emerged through a collaborative process of analysis and critique of the prevailing development paradigm and key events that would lead its work to focus both on economic development and women's rights.

In Senegal during the 1980s and up until the Beijing Conference in 1995, the type of projects implemented for the advancement of women were limited to the approach of integrating women into development. The projects and programs aimed simply to improve women's living conditions by helping them acquire income or alleviate their domestic chores. The objective of these projects was not, however, to change power relations between men and women. This was important because gender relationships not only define the power relations between men and women but also deprive women of access to means and factors of production and decision-making spheres.

Mrs. Bineta Sarr, president and founding member of APROFES, says their vision developed after they had done an analysis of development programs, in particular those that were designed for women. They found that these programs were all framed in the same manner using standardized activities. They believed there was a need, however, for innovative approaches and implementation strategies that tackled the real challenges of gender inequality.

They also noted, after reflecting on the situation of the women's movement in Kaolack, that even though several NGOs were working in favor of women, their work was severely hampered by the lack of synergy among them. Moreover, the bulk of the work done, especially by the regional department in charge of women's affairs, did not address women's salient development needs. With the economic hardship prevailing in the region, particularly after the "shock" of the devalued West African currency, the CFA franc, and the imposition of the structural adjustment programs, local populations had few other options than to try to increase their access to trade opportunities and engage in political activism.

Determining the association's core area of activity was a central issue of debate, as members hesitated between the reduction of poverty and the promotion of women's rights. At that time, they were well aware that women were victims of violence, but even they could not grasp the full breadth of the problem. What sealed APROFES's decision was the series of murders and rapes of young girls and women in Kaolack and the expectations of the groups they work with that APROFES should do something about it. As Mrs. Bineta Sarr recalls, "From a strategic point of view, it was necessary to do both: improve women's living conditions *and* their rights." In practice, this meant that the association would promote and strengthen women's leadership with conviction, motivation, commitment, and a sense of innovation.

APROFES Programs

APROFES has five interdependent programs. First, it has a program aimed at improving the income and living conditions of women by consolidating their economic power. Second, it has a program to build women's leadership through activities aimed at sensitizing communities about the inequalities between men and women, issues of the rights of women and children, as well as those related to development in general. Third, it has a youth educational program for young girls between the ages of five and fifteen that emphasizes civic education, environmental education, conflict resolution, children's rights, girls education, the prevention of juvenile delinquency, family-life education, as well as the fight against AIDS. Fourth, it has a learning and research program, including exchange visits. And, finally, it has a program to fight the violence perpetrated against women, which is the focus of this case study. The first four programs are described in full in the Appendix.

APROFES Staff and Structure

APROFES has a staff of twelve, all of whom are women from Kaolack and neighboring villages. Culturally,

these women have similar backgrounds, as they were all activists in the Senegalese popular movement in the 1970s through the Sports and Cultural Association. Having shared the same experiences, difficulties, and accomplishments, they have a close relationship that makes it easier for them to adopt a democratic approach within the association. If one of them has an idea, she discusses it with all the others. And, if the idea is accepted, it is endorsed and put into practice by her colleagues in APROFES.

Unlike many local NGOs that depend on volunteers, APROFES has a professional staff. This is an advantage because workers are committed and ensure high-quality work and long-term commitment.

APROFES directs its rights work and income-generating activities toward local associations affiliated with APROFES that are committed to promoting women's development in rural and urban areas. These associations are guided by peer coordinators who have a good understanding of the cultural realities and social difficulties faced by the poor women in this region. The next section describes the APROFES campaigns to fight violence against women.

Campaigns to Stop Violence against Women

Special circumstances led APROFES to become involved in, and to ultimately lead, the fight to end violence against women in the Kaolack region. The death of a young woman from Kaolack and the rapes of young girls—all these acts perpetrated by people who believed themselves immune to punishment by law—pushed APROFES to take on a new kind of work. In the process, they pioneered an approach to fighting violence against women in Senegal using lawsuits, popular mobilization, and careful ally cultivation. Their struggle would also go on to have repercussions at the national level, sparking a movement to change the laws protecting women against gender violence. The next section of the case study tells the story of how this happened.

The Death of Doki Niasse

In 1992, twenty-two-year-old Doki Niasse was beaten to death. Her husband was accused of the crime, which was allegedly sparked by her refusal to prepare a meal for him during the holy month of Ramadan.

Outraged by this murder, women in her neighborhood mobilized to alert APROFES. Mrs. Bineta Sarr, president of APROFES, recalls that when this happened, APROFES "was the only NGO in Kaolack that worked systematically to promote women's development at the grassroots and that could monitor its initiatives to the very end." Without hesitation, APROFES organized a protest march that made history because it was the first time that a protest march was organized in the country to express concern about violence against women.

As the husband was a member of the large, renowned and influential family of a *marabouts,* or religious leader, there was every reason to fear it would be particularly difficult to bring a legal case against him. But APROFES and the women in the local community worked hard to mobilize public attention by organizing marches in Kaolack and then in Dakar. Their efforts probably changed the course of events, according to Dakar-based women's organization leaders. The husband was charged with the crime and brought to trial.

Although he was acquitted in the end "for lack of evidence," the mere fact that he had appeared before a court of law was a key first step toward ending a trend where husbands could beat their wives without being held accountable. Since then, the media and law enforcement officers have shown heightened interest in matters related to domestic violence. Even the manner in which incidents of violence against women are reported to the public has changed. As a result, the public now perceives violence against women as physical abuse and a violation of rights.

The Doki Niasse case has had major repercussions for the struggle of the Senegalese women's movement to defend the physical integrity of women. In fact, it was a galvanizing event for raising consciousness about violence against women throughout Senegal. In Dakar, as well as in certain regional capitals such as Saint Louis and Thies, marches were organized by women's and human rights associations on the day before the trial in an attempt to influence the verdict. The importance of this is stressed by Oulimata Gaye, coordinator of the legal program for CIJ/RADI in Dakar: "APROFES was the first organization to break the silence, to dare to speak out publicly. They got women to march. And remember, they were working from a remote area, just these women, and most of them with little or no education. These were not elite intellectuals. Yet they put the idea that conjugal violence is not acceptable on the national agenda. It opened up a whole new area for the women's movement."

The case also had a profound impact on how medical and police professionals deal with rape victims. "Before, nobody talked about violence against women," says Mrs. Ndaw Emilie Carva, a midwife at the Kaolack Maternity and Child Health Center. "As a worker at the health unit, I attended to young victims of rape. But I said nothing about their condition, because I felt bound by professional confidentiality. The parents of those victims also felt reluctant to say anything, as they did not want the public to learn about what their daughters had experienced. Besides, no rapist had ever been punished before. So, victims lacked a source of motivation and reference for legal action."

APROFES and the Senegalese women's movement learned crucial lessons through the Doki Niasse experience. Most important was the need to have solid evidence and reliable witnesses who are confident and determined to express themselves. For instance, during the trial, fifty witnesses lined up in front of the jury, and yet none agreed to reveal what they had seen or heard, which was obviously harmful to the plaintiff's case. Also, there was no autopsy report and no evidence presented at the trial. Reflecting on the case later, APROFES staff say this happened because the movement was spontaneous and, like most everyone else in the Senegalese women's movement, they lacked experience about legal issues and lawsuits. Also, they did not reach out to allies who might help with the evidentiary aspects of a criminal trial. They realized that if they were going to pursue a specific legal mechanism, they needed to learn how that system works and collaborate with others who could help them. These were hard lessons to learn, but APROFES and the women's movement were able to use the experience the next time they tried to bring justice for victims of violence against women.

Rape Cases

APROFES took the lead for the second time in a rape case to advocate for an end to violence against women. A nine-year-old girl had been raped. A sixty-year-old political and religious leader who had four wives and twenty-two children was accused of the rape.

APROFES again sprang into action, publicizing the case in a pamphlet with the words: "This evening, in the outskirts of Kaolack, a young girl sent on an errand by her mother was lured into a bedroom and raped savagely by a man. After the girl succeeded to escape from the clutches of her tormentor, she just had the time to denounce him before she fainted in a pool of her own blood."

APROFES had earned the trust and respect of Kaolack residents through its years of economic-development work and leadership development. As the mother of a young rape victim reports, "When the problem occurred, one of her aunts who is a member of a women's group supported by APROFES accompanied me to the association's office, where we were received and given advice. That is where I wrote my complaint. One member of APROFES and one from the African Network for Integrated Development (RADI) accompanied me to the police station, where the police commissioner received us. APROFES paid for all the charges—lawyers, medication, and medical bills."

Drawing on the lessons from the Doki Niasse case, this time APROFES worked closely with other women's organizations, legal aid groups, and human rights associations. Key allies in this effort included the Council of Senegalese Women (COSEF), the Legal Information Center of the African Network for Integrated Development (CIJ/RADI), the African Convention for the Defense of Human Rights (RADDHO), the Siggil Jigeen network (a network that brings together twenty women's associations nationwide), and the personal commitment of the late female lawyer Seyni Diagne. This collaborative work added strength to the initiative and also brought crucial technical and legal expertise to bear on the case.

While APROFES was mobilizing women and human rights NGOs, the political establishment in Kaolack, in particular the mayor, tried to protect the rapist. The mayor made threats and promises to the girl's family because the rapist was a member of the same political party as the mayor. In response, the coalition of organizations went to the state prosecutor's office and informed him of the strong resolve of civil society, in particular the NGOs working in the Kaolack region, to see the rapist brought to justice.

To add even more strength to their efforts, the group of associations circulated a petition, signed by twenty-two other local NGOs, calling attention to the fact that violence against women had never been punished and that no strategies existed to end it. They organized a forum on violence against women, which was attended by hundreds, including sympathetic government officials. The "Bamtaare" theater troupe opened the forum with a re-enactment of the rape scene, after which medical doctors and lawyers had a debate on violence against women. All these efforts had a powerful effect on public opinion in the judiciary. For the first time, a rapist was sentenced to a maximum term of ten years in prison. This victory opened new opportunities and gave the movement new strength and confidence.

APROFES got involved in a third case of violence in 1998, when a well-respected old man and family head threatened and raped a young girl, whom he had lured into his workshop one day at nightfall. As in the previous cases, APROFES acted quickly in conjunction with other NGOs to bring the culprit to justice. As a result, he was arrested, charged, and convicted, and given the maximum sentence of ten years.

APROFES showed the same commitment in bringing to justice a man who was accused of killing his very young wife in Gapakh village. The village has a women's group that APROFES had been working with on a regular basis for some time. They had created a community garden to produce market crops and other projects such as literacy training, consciousness-raising, and leadership development. APROFES's activities with this group was aimed at improving the living conditions of families through income generation and changing gender relations. When the killing happened, members of the women's group immediately went to APROFES to seek their help. Through all of APROFES's work in the community, there was a strong sense that this brutal act had been a rights violation and must be addressed. The man, in his shame, fled and sought refuge, but community members convinced him that he had to turn himself in to face the accusations.

In all these cases, the victims and their relatives suffered severe psychological trauma. The young girls who had been raped had to be hospitalized for several days. Upon their release, they continued to be under gynecological and psychological supervision, as these services were provided for free with help from APROFES. In all the cases, the victim's family received threats and warnings from the family of the rapist, as well as from the local political authorities who wanted the case withdrawn from court. Also, none of the rape victims received the compensation their violators were supposed to pay. The transition back into their communities after the rapes was so difficult for their families that they felt forced to move into other neighborhoods or send the child to another town, which created new problems of adaptation. For the survivors of murder, the horror of the violent deaths left lasting pain. Each time a psychological follow-up was necessary, and again APROFES helped out as best it could.

The overall successes in winning legal victory, bringing the cases to the attention of the media, and rallying numerous NGOs to support the causes contributed to opening up new opportunities and gave new impetus to building the movement. The most important results of this work were the creation of the National Committee to Fight Violence against Women in 1998 and its work to pass precedent-setting national legislation on gender violence, described below.

What was it about the way APROFES worked that allowed it to play this role in the Kaolack region and influence the course of the national campaign against gender violence? The next section analyzes the approach used by APROFES to build a broad base of support for its advocacy work, as well as some of the most important strategies and tactics used.

Behind the Scenes: APROFES Advocacy and Ally-Cultivation Strategies

Mrs. Bineta Sarr, president of APROFES, defines advocacy as "a set of concerted initiatives undertaken with a view to changing a situation. It is a global strategy involving several actions aimed at winning a cause." She sees a difference between lobbying and advocacy, in the sense that "advocacy is a long-term strategy, while lobbying aims to bring about policy changes through a well-defined course of action. In the context of military strategy, lobbying could be considered as one battle, while advocacy would be the war as a whole. But lobbying remains part of the general dynamic. Each victory won during lobbying exercises paves the way for the advocacy strategy. The struggle against rape deals with a precise case with well-defined

targets, while the promotion of women's rights is a long-term process."

Strengthening Women's Leadership

APROFES considers it essential for more women to become involved in leadership, especially as they have more difficulty gaining access to training and information. Giving managerial support, training, and information on women's rights to women's groups and encouraging women to participate in elections as voters or candidates have helped women enter into, and sometimes climb to the top of, political and economic structures. This, in turn, has helped to reduce the gender gap at the decision-making level and has promoted equity in access to resources.

On the issue of women's leadership, Mrs. Sarr comments, "Advocacy results from a certain vision of women's status and how they should relate to men and in society. A woman leader who is informed and can analyze situations critically has the potential for change. Most often she is more aware, more motivated, and places community interests above her own personal interests. For that reason, it is not just the act of lobbying per se that is most satisfying but rather the success achieved in raising awareness of women's rights in society. This is how social change in favor of women happens. Because if a women changes her mentality, then you get changes in the family and changes in the community."

The majority of women in urban and rural areas who receive support from APROFES are illiterate. In line with its objective to promote leadership among these poor women, APROFES has designed training modules suitable to their situation and committed its coordinators to lead trainings in national languages. Mrs. Sarr feels "it is also important for men to change their mentalities. In fact, if women change while men do not, women will always continue to depend on them. Moreover, if the change is limited to women only, there will always be conflict, especially for power."

Building Partnerships for Community Mobilization

The president of APROFES believes that "advocacy requires strong community mobilization, which makes it necessary to have allies." In choosing its allies, APROFES has been able to overcome one of the Senegalese women's movements prevailing weaknesses, a certain sectarianism. The association preferred to cast its net wide and to assemble a pool of allies who share its objective to end violence against women rather than try to work completely alone.

That is why APROFES established an informal united front in Kaolack with members from political parties (including the ruling party), human rights associations, regional government structures, women's groups, and traditional or religious leaders. With this coalition, APROFES has been able to build strategic alliances in the highest spheres, including the governor of the region and the ministerial departments concerned with violence against women. At the same time, it pools the resources that each member makes available, depending on their mandate and comparative advantage.

By involving multiple actors from government, religious organizations, and civil society, APROFES builds synergy in the town and region. At the same time, the association has sought to influence the actions and decisions of its allies from within this informal alliance. Rather than trying to persuade government and religious leaders through noisy protest from the outside—though protest marches were also part of its strategy on many occasions—APROFES uses a strategy of mutually beneficial collaboration to be able to gently influence them from within the framework of their alliance. Thus, many of APROFES's key advocacy targets in government and religious leaders have actually been their allies in the informal united front.

Allies and Targets among Kaolack Women and Men

To disseminate its ideas and solicit support for its actions in Kaolack, APROFES finds it most effective to organize forums and invite religious leaders and competent experts to participate in them. It circulates petitions, produces billboard posters, organizes protest marches, and uses the radio to rally as many women as possible to take part in its demonstrations. APROFES also utilizes its human resources to provide training, particularly in leadership, to its allies.

The men and women in Kaolack work with women's groups or individuals to provide broad-based support to activities aimed at informing the public about the need to put an end to violence against women. Mrs. Sarr observes that "men in Kaolack

are beginning to change. Today, they too come to APROFES for help when one of their sisters or relatives is a victim of violence. They have also started to condemn violence. In other cases, men have been at the forefront of the fight to end violence against women. There is a doctor, for example, who provides free medical follow-up and drugs when young girls are raped or women are physically assaulted."

Allies and Targets at the Ministerial Level

APROFES has key partners among sympathetic officials in government departments. These include the governor of Kaolack region, and local civil servants from the Ministry of Family, Social Affairs, and National Solidarity, from the Ministry of Health, and from the Ministry of Justice. APROFES was aided in its efforts to build partnerships with regional representatives of government ministries by the Senegalese decentralization process that encouraged collaboration between NGOs, ministries, and their regional divisions and also by the development of the media. The alliance with these key government authorities plays an important role in strengthening local leadership as well as in affirming the critique of resistant administrative authorities when they refuse to collaborate with civil society. It also serves to support the internal reformists within government, because they gain an ally who can strengthen their position vis-à-vis more conservative government officials.

Allies and Targets among Political Parties

Getting the issue of violence against women on the political agenda is crucial for advancing this cause. APROFES has worked with women parliamentarians from the ruling party and the opposition. Together with other women's activists, they have made these politicians aware of violence against women and mobilized them during court trials. These women parliamentarians further the cause by pushing to have the issue debated within their parties.

Allies and Targets among Religious and Traditional Leaders

In Senegal, religious leaders have considerable influence on public opinion. Hence, their support of a cause can attract even stronger public support. It was through the case of Doki Niasse, who belonged, along with her husband, to a powerful religious family in

Kaolack, that APROFES first began to create relationships in this religious circle. Given that there is no singular vision for social affairs among *marabouts* families and that Islam condemns serious violence perpetrated against women, APROFES formed links to sympathetic members of the *marabouts* families in order to lead them to condemn violent actions, particularly those committed in their circle. APROFES's strategy has been to approach and enter into dialogue with these religious leaders, advocating for patience and tolerance, citing social and religious values that condemn violence within the family and in society at large to their advantage. Thus, in the scandal when the nine-year-old girl was raped by a prominent religious figure in Kaolack, it was a woman, herself a religious leader from the powerful Niassène family, who issued a public statement to condemn the rape.

Allies and Targets among Civil Society Members in Kaolack and Dakar

APROFES sees itself as an active member of civil society—those individuals and organizations independent of the control of government and political parties. APROFES seeks to mobilize civil society as part of its struggle. APROFES works closely with many women's groups and human rights associations that have skills it does not possess, especially in the area of human rights and presenting legal cases. Thus, for example, APROFES collaborated with CIJ/RADI, a legal services NGO, and RADDHO, a human rights NGO, when it began working on the second major legal case in Kaolack.

Expanding initiatives through national and regional civil society structures has become a fundamental strategy by which APROFES pursues its work. The association is a member and regional representative of the Council of NGOs for Development (CONGAD), one of the most important national coalitions for NGOs and associations in Senegal. APROFES is a member of the National Council of Senegalese Women (COSEF), the Kaolack Development Committee (CODEKA), and the national Siggil Jigeen network. The members of APROFES are board members in all of these structures.

On the issue of violence against women specifically, mobilization among the international community has been gaining momentum since the early 1990s. In Senegal, women's rights activists set up the National Committee for the Prevention of Violence against Women in 1998 under the leadership of several Dakar-based women's rights groups. These groups worked to bring about legislation that would formally codify the demands of the women's movement in Senegal. On January 13, 1999, the government of Senegal took the important step of pressing the National Assembly to approve Law 06-99, which penalizes violence against women in a specific manner. The following are defined as violence under this law: rape, indecent assault, domestic violence, sexual harassment, female genital mutilation, and pedophilia.

Allies and Targets among the Media

APROFES has worked to cultivate relationships with key media professionals and build the credibility of the association in their eyes, so their work gets prominent attention in the press and on television. By relating information nationwide, media professionals have provided vital support to APROFES in its advocacy work. Mrs. Sarr remarks that media professionals today are very concerned about the question of violence. Whenever a case arises, they inform APROFES about it and ask what should be done. In her opinion, both the state-owned and private media have become key partners in the struggle to prevent violence against women.

How Partners See APROFES's Advocacy Work

This section presents the reflections of APROFES's partners on both their collaborative relationship and the impact of the association's work.

Within the NGO Community in Kaolack

One of the partners APROFES works most closely with in Kaolack is the regional branch office of the African Development Network's Legal Information Center (CIJ/RADI). Since it opened the Kaolack office in 1992, CIJ/RADI has been working to help local communities to understand how the law works and how they can use it to defend themselves. Although the center did not participate in the early stages of APROFES's work when the association launched the mobilization campaign to fight violence against women, it has been collaborating closely with APROFES since Oxfam America, their common funding partner, linked both of them after the Doki Niasse experience.

RADI/CIJ brings its legal expertise and deep understanding of court procedure to this collaborative work. The center works with APROFES's partner groups to broaden and deepen their understanding of the law in order to reduce the gap between mobilization and legal awareness activities. Mr. Babacar Ndiaye of CIJ/RADI's Kaolack branch office says, "The fact that APROFES is not made up of intellectuals, but of women who are often of similar backgrounds as those that they defend, lends credibility to their work. All staff members demonstrate the same level of commitment, such that whenever a victim goes to APROFES she is sure to obtain a prompt response from any staff member attending to her. There is a strong sense of solidarity in the association, because every member 'looks in the same direction.' One can say that APROFES has changed the way people in Kaolack perceive violence against women. In Senegal, Kaolack is not the area where violence against women is most pronounced, yet it is here that mobilization against this form of violence is strongest. This is a result of the work done by APROFES, which is capable of mobilizing the whole town."

Another partner that works very closely with APROFES is the Kaolack branch office of the African Human Rights Organization (RADDHO). Since it was set up in 1995, the RADDHO branch office has been working to enhance people's understanding of how the law works and to provide legal counsel to victims of violence. As Mr. Mbengue Mohamed Mamadou, manager of RADDHO's Kaolack branch office explains, "When there is a case of violence, APROFES informs us and we sensitize our target groups to the problem so that they can lend support to the victim and attend the court trial en masse."

The third partner with whom APROFES collaborates closely in Kaolack is the Council of Senegalese Women (COSEF). Mrs. Aminata Sarr, COSEF's representative, is a seasoned union activist and top opposition politician who serves as a resource person for APROFES. Mrs. Sarr says, "When a victim of gender-based violence comes to see me, I take her immediately to APROFES, where I am sure her problem will be addressed. I think APROFES has succeeded to generate a sense of unity and solidarity in that respect. So,

whenever there is a problem, all women and NGOs mobilize their efforts."

The partnership that has developed between APROFES, women's groups, human rights associations, and legal-service organizations has been instrumental in the establishment of the Regional Committee for the Prevention of Violence against Women. This partnership also facilitates collaborative work. Each of the members contributes resources to the regional committee. With RADI serving as its secretary, the regional committee helps families of victims bring legal actions and pay attendant charges. The committee is also poised to mobilize emergency responses when acts of violence occur.

Within Government Departments

APROFES has carefully cultivated relationships with numerous key government agencies, finding sympathetic and influential officials who can support its cause. In each case, these relationships have developed into collaborative alliances that are mutually beneficial to the association and the government officials. The viewpoints of a number of these allies are presented below.

APROFES collaborates closely with the regional services of the Ministry of Health. Mrs. Ndaw Emilie Carva, a midwife at the Kaolack Maternity and Child Health Center, mentioned that "we have received guidelines from the health ministry recommending that we should collaborate with NGOs. We see APROFES as a partner, especially in the prevention of violence against women. Before, victims lacked a source of motivation and reference for legal action. I can say that APROFES has worked to see to it that the authorities clamp down on the perpetrators of such forms of violence. The association is a source of hope for women, as they know that they can go there in times of trouble. APROFES has a lot of influence today because of its determination, force, and association with several other partners. Its approach is one that makes women feel at ease."

The Regional Directorate for Community Development, in charge of supervising NGO work, is another key partner that APROFES works with. This ministry, like all others doing social work, has experienced drastic cuts in its financial, material, and human resources since the government of Senegal instituted structural adjustment policies in 1991. These policies, promoted by the IMF and World Bank, have had a very negative impact on people's access to health services, education, and employment. The ministerial departments in charge of those sectors that are considered social were particularly affected by this policy, as their budgets and staffs were drastically reduced. Given the sexual division of labor, women in particular, who are among those who most utilize social services, suffered strongly from the negative impact of these policies. Acknowledging that there are many gaps in the way his department manages social affairs, Mr. Niang, the regional inspector of community development, praises the efforts made by NGOs to address the needs of local communities, seeing them as filling in for, if only partially, this agency's ability to respond to all the need.

With regard to efforts aimed at fostering women's development, Mr. Niang said, "APROFES is one of the most important NGOs in the Kaolack region. Our ministry encourages us to collaborate closely with APROFES, to participate in their activities, and to involve them in the activities we undertake. APROFES was actively involved in designing the Regional Action Plan for Women, which forms an important part of the national plan. I also served as chair in the Forum on Violence against Women that took place in Kaolack before the court trial of a young victim. There have been such drastic cuts in resources allocated to our ministry that we do not even have a counseling center. Therefore, we advise victims of violence to go to women's groups, which are most often better equipped. At our directorate, we consider APROFES a resource center for training facilitators."

From Civil Society Groups in Dakar

In Dakar, the capital of Senegal, APROFES is recognized as a leader in the prevention of violence against women. For Mrs. Martine Breault of the International Center for Studies and International Cooperation (CECI), "APROFES is a reference in the Kaolack region. When CECI wanted to set up a national committee in 1998 to promote the Women's March to the Year 2000, we could not have imagined doing so without involving APROFES. The association has built up a reputation for itself through its work to develop a methodology for the prevention of violence against women. When people go to APROFES, they

go to benefit from its experience in combating violence against women, and to learn how to tackle one problem or the other."

Mrs. Seynabou Gueye Tall, the program officer for UNIFEM (United Nations Development Fund for Women) in Senegal, has a similar point of view. She feels that "it is only recently that the international community started to give attention to violence against women. The focus used to be on how to improve the economic conditions of women. Human rights associations and NGOs have played a key role in bringing about this change. Here in Senegal, APROFES is a pioneer in that respect. As part of its program to fight violence against women, UNIFEM set out in November 1999 to travel across Senegal by bus and to project films and slides as a way of bringing the debate on violence against women to the public arena. APROFES was identified as a key ally in Kaolack for its work to fight violence against women. What determined the choice of this town was the courage with which APROFES had been working to end the culture of silence around violence against women. It was not because violence was more pronounced in this area than in any other. What's more, except for APROFES, few organizations work to promote women's rights in rural areas, where it is more difficult to work, and the local authorities and populations are more resistant to change."

APROFES's work to promote a vision of development based on gender equality and women's leadership has been recognized by ASHOKA–Innovators for the Public, an international foundation providing multi-faceted support to individuals and institutions that have innovative ideas for development but lack the resources to develop them. ASHOKA gave the president of APROFES a three-year grant to help her develop the association. Mrs. Kathy Diop, ASHOKA's representative in Senegal, sees the quality of the people involved, their innovative and replicable ideas, and their original strategies for implementation as the characteristics that influenced ASHOKA's decision to select APROFES's president as a grantee. The success APROFES has had working in rural areas shows that it is possible to bring about social change in these communities. Some of the strategies the association has designed for preventing violence against women are used today as the standard in Senegal, and peer NGOs use these strategies in their work.

APROFES: A Strong Advocacy Impact at the Local Level

Assessing the impact of APROFES's advocacy at the local and national levels is one of the key objectives of this case study. During the fieldwork interviews, all the respondents pointed to APROFES as a pioneer in raising the issue of violence against women at the national level and noted that it continues to play an influential role in preventing violence against women. But they stressed that the most visible and concrete impact of its work is confined to the Kaolack region. While APROFES's efforts in the Doki Niasse case first broke the "culture of silence" around violence against women, it has been Dakar-based women's groups that have taken the leadership role in keeping the issue alive and carrying it to the next level, in terms of securing national policy changes. Mrs. Oulimata Gaye, national coordinator of CIJ/RADI, says that "APROFES is an NGO working in a region where it has succeeded to make a name for itself. If they want to set up branch offices in other regions, it is certain that women will support them. But do they want to do that? I think they have committed themselves to the Kaolack region, where they can have the results they expect to have."

Mr. Mbengue, RADDHO's branch officer for the Kaolack region, adds: "In Kaolack, APROFES epitomizes the struggle to promote women's development. It has made an impact at several levels. On the one hand, it has raised the awareness about violence against women. On the other, it has made it possible for most women's groups or human rights associations to include violence against women in their strategies. Also, the number of associations working to prevent violence against women has increased."

There are many other people who, like Mrs. Gaye, believe that there is no need to question the level of impact APROFES has made through its work. Martine Breault of CECI feels "the association has the necessary skills to work at the grassroots level. But this is not the same as working at the national level, where the human, material, and financial resources required are more substantial than those that the association can presently afford."

However, other partners, like RADDHO, have criticized APROFES for limiting its work to the Kaolack region. "When women in Tambacounda, in the southern part of Senegal, suffer violence there is no response from APROFES even though it has the ability to intervene in these regions," says Aminata Dieye of RADDHO's Dakar office. "Instead of just confining its activities to Kaolack, APROFES should strengthen the skills of the National Committee for the Prevention of Violence against Women, which is headquartered in Dakar. It should send its theater troupe to other regions to work with other NGOs. APROFES shows a clear lack of willingness to share its experience at the national level."

This is perhaps due to the choices APROFES has made. Mrs. Bineta Sarr explains: "What we aim to do is to promote leadership at the regional level with women, associations, workers' unions, and political parties and to mobilize them around the objectives defined by APROFES." However, Mrs. Sarr argues that the association also undertakes activities at the national level, when invited, and at the international level as well. She believes that reinforcing partnerships with associations in other regions in Senegal is extremely important. It is within this capacity that APROFES has supported the Coordination of Women for the Development of Tambacounda (CFDT) since its formation in 1997, sharing its experience and knowledge of action and advocacy techniques with them. Mrs. Sarr also points to APROFES's involvement in another domestic violence case in 1998, the case of Fatou Dieng, a woman beaten by her husband, a high-ranking officer in the Senegalese army, who was ultimately condemned by the courts. In that case, APROFES ensured that the women of Diourbel, the Senegalese town in which the trial of the violent husband took place, were trained in organizing the forum as well as informed about court procedures.

According to Mrs. Sarr, APROFES also improved the international awareness of the violence Senegalese women endure through the campaign it led in 1997 during the Africa Viewpoint Festival in Canada. The question of human and material resources also has a bearing on APROFES's ability to be active in other parts of Senegal and at the international level. APROFES aims to contribute to the consolidation of and to the reinforcement of competency at the national level, but the means at its disposal are limited, and it must make strategic choices about just how much it can achieve.

Lessons from APROFES's Experience for National-Level Advocacy

The APROFES struggle to fight violence against women raises a number of lessons not only for APROFES itself but for the Senegalese national movement as well. Many of these lessons may spark new insights and realizations and may suggest new strategies for groups struggling to fight gender violence in their own countries.

1. Work with a wide cross-section of allies from different backgrounds capable, nonetheless, of presenting a determined and united front. Each ally brings different expertise and skills to bear on the work, such as legal expertise, knowledge of courtroom evidentiary rules, ability to rally large numbers of people for marches, contacts with media professionals, and so on.

2. Frame the problem in terms of rights, in particular those that protect women from physical abuse. Stating the problem this way mobilized a broad coalition of human rights organizations, women's groups, women parliamentarians, and pro-democracy forces and ultimately led to enactment legislation on violence against women in Senegal.

3. Design strategies for awareness-raising to conquer resistance from religious, traditional, or political leaders who can influence public opinion. APROFES used an innovative strategy to draw such leaders into their struggle as members of an informal coalition, allowing them to take partial credit for supporting what was clearly becoming a broad-based popular outcry to defend women's rights. In the process, APROFES and its allies gained strategic allies at the highest level of decision making and opinion making within Senegal.

4. Present evidence in court to convince the jury during trials of rapists or perpetrators of other forms of violence against women. During the Doki Niasse trial, for example, the husband was not convicted for lack of incriminating evidence like an autopsy report, medical certificate, or photographs of the injuries he was accused of inflicting on his wife. In subsequent cases, APROFES banded together with specialized legal-service and human rights groups that could help gather and present this kind of evidence.

5. Present reliable witnesses in court who are self-confident and determined to say what they have to say. During the Doki Niasse trial, over fifty witnesses appeared before the jury, but none of them was willing to tell the jury what they had seen or heard. Again, after learning this lesson, the next time APROFES knew to work closely with witnesses, preparing them carefully.

6. Prepare victims to go to the police and lodge their complaints: only when this happens can the state prosecutor institute legal proceedings for a breach of justice, using information from this hearing, other available proof, and a medical report attesting to the injuries sustained by the victim. Yet breaking the culture of silence and standing up to societal pressures coming from powerful people seeking to protect their impunity require a real act of courage. APROFES's strength in gaining the trust of victims and their families, built over years of work in the community, is likely a key ingredient and the least easy to replicate. It also may explain, in part, why APROFES has resisted expanding its reach beyond the area where it is known and trusted and can use this precious resource of trust to help women to come forward to denounce crimes against them.

Challenges and Implications for External Support

Although the Association for the Promotion of Senegalese Women (APROFES) has been able to make considerable gains, it still faces a number of challenges at this point in its history. These challenges were raised by partners and APROFES leadership alike.

Institutional Strengthening

Strengthening institutional capacity remains one of the biggest challenges for APROFES. First of all, the association needs to create an enabling environment that will make it possible for work to continue smoothly and effectively even after the "founding mothers" hand the organization over to a younger generation. The president, whose skills and charisma are recognized and admired by all, is particularly concerned about this. During the survey, respondents noted, for example, that there is a huge gap between the skills of the president and those of the support staff. For Martine Breault of CECI, "She has skills that put her too far ahead of the rest of the staff at APROFES. Even with the effective delegation of powers and division of labor, she is the one who has a global vision and can define objectives. The others merely seem to be there to carry out orders, as their experience is limited to the local level. Advocacy work is where the gap is widest because some staff members still do not fully master basic vocabulary and techniques. There is a need for them to undergo training to enable them to overcome some of those weaknesses."

APROFES's president is conscious that training staff members is a priority. She believes that it is absolutely necessary for staff members to have access to training, as this will make it possible for them to gain experience and for APROFES to develop. She believes exchange visits and training in other countries have an extremely positive impact. She explains, furthermore, that APROFES places strong emphasis on providing specialized training to its staff members because that is one way of strengthening institutional capacity.

There is indeed a lack of qualified staff who have specialized legal and communications skills. APROFES is also in need of a social assistant for its outreach efforts. Specifically with regard to leadership, APROFES would like its volunteers to receive formal professional training. Mrs. Sarr also believes that for institutional capacity-strengthening to be effective, programs should be diversified to include research and especially social theater for awareness-raising. Moreover, APROFES needs assistance in the production of teaching/learning aids and the instruction of trainers in advocacy so that it can further consolidate its advocacy work.

Financial Self-Reliance

Donor funding to African countries is dwindling, putting the programs undertaken by government ministerial departments and NGOs in jeopardy. To prepare for the challenge of generating its own funds, APROFES is building a house that will have a documentation center, a resource and training center for women, a restaurant, guest-rooms, and a store. It hopes the income-generating activities will make APROFES less reliant on external funding, as well as provide some employment opportunities for local residents.

Gender Bias in APROFES's Professional Staff

Mrs. Oulimata Gaye, of CIJ/RADI, pointed out that APROFES only employs women professionals. As APROFES promotes a holistic vision of society, she argues, it is necessary for the association to have men among its professional staff. Men should be more than just consultative committee members, volunteers, or consultants, she says. This, Gaye believes, would be more consistent with APROFES's commitment to changing gender relations in all areas of socioeconomic life, including the employment sector. While these may be fair comments, APROFES's officer in charge for cultural programs is a man, and APROFES has chosen to employ mainly women because of its commitment to building women leaders through its work.

Conclusion

Women's Rights Approach versus Poverty Reduction

As the number of women living in poverty continues to grow, especially in rural areas, one may question the relevance of APROFES's strategic focus on promoting women's rights while at the same time providing support for women's income-generation activities. Yet it is the commitment APROFES has to its mission, and the success it has achieved in its work, that gives the association the motivation to continue with this option.

This question is extremely important in thinking about the ways and means to change the extremely difficult living conditions women face while simultaneously transforming the gender relations with the objective of ensuring gender equity within the context of sustainable development. It is possible to improve women's living conditions (as in the case of countries in the North) without transforming their subordinate status, as long as the underlying sexual inequalities persist. APROFES aims both to improve women's living conditions as well as to transform their social status. In order to change the power relations between men and women, it seeks to improve women's power by giving them the ability to increase their income, to acquire knowledge or skills, and to make decisions for themselves, their family, or their community.

Relationship with the National Women's Movement against Gender Violence

Cases of domestic violence, rape, and incest are widespread in Senegal, but families, doctors, religious leaders, police, and politicians have been trying to shove these crimes into secret closets. APROFES and its partners succeeded in breaking this taboo. What was once hidden has now been brought out in the open. Police officers and law-makers now know that the ball is in their court and that they must bring justice to bear in these cases. APROFES achieved this because it showed it was indeed possible to bring culprits to trial, mobilize public opinion, and institute prompt legal action to ensure that the severest sentences are passed. But what have others learned from this experience?

The Senegalese feminist movement is extremely diverse. It consists of individuals and groups whose visions and actions are far from being homogenous. While a few consider themselves feminist, the majority are reformist and limit their actions to the reform level. In the long term, this does not improve women's living conditions. There are also individuals and groups within the Senegalese women's movement who are traditionalist or fundamentalist and whose actions aim to restore or retain traditional or religious values. It is within this general context that APROFES's advocacy must be analyzed.

Because it played a pioneering role in the prevention of violence against women, and has since initiated an innovative approach to work in this area, APROFES stands out today as a leader in advocacy work. Although some do not see APROFES as a leader, since other associations and individuals have also played an important role in advancing women's rights, especially at the national level, others feel it is a leader. They say APROFES should fully assume its leadership role by sharing its experience with less-experienced organizations throughout the country and involving them in more of the activities it undertakes. This question of leadership remains a sensitive issue for the women's movement in Senegal, because there is a diversity of approaches, experiences, successes, and failures, and also

a varied range of personalities among the individuals who make up the movement.

Within the more specific context of violence committed against women, APROFES was the first organization to mobilize itself, and then the women of Kaolack and eventually those of other regions including the capital city of Dakar. Given that Senegal is a patriarchal society where the illiteracy rate is relatively high, the result of this mobilization has been striking. On the one hand, it raised the national consciousness about the unacceptability of violence against women. On the other hand, it led to bringing the perpetrators in front of courts, where they have often been punished. Another outcome of this mobilization initiated by APROFES is the National Assembly's approval of a law that defines and criminalizes violence against women. The approval of this law means that Senegal is reconciling its legislation with its international commitments.

Notwithstanding its primarily local intervention, APROFES can certainly be considered a source of inspiration for women's associations and civil society throughout Senegal and beyond.

It is undeniable that APROFES, with its vision, approaches, and advocacy, occupies a special place at the heart of the Senegalese women's movement. By planning its advocacy as a long-term strategy to promote women's economic rights as well as the respect for their right to physical integrity, APROFES works to change unequal relationships between the sexes. Moreover, the struggle for the expansion and respect of women's rights was an integral part of the struggle to strengthen democracy in Senegal.

Appendix:
APROFES Programs

Improving Women's Income and Living Conditions

Consolidating women's economic power is a key area of APROFES's work. In rural and suburban areas, giving women access to funding that enables them to undertake income-generating activities constitutes a crucial factor in improving their living conditions. In 1992, APROFES established a microcredit scheme to support community-based projects and initiatives by women. These projects and initiatives include petty trading (the small-scale marketing of goods), market gardening, poultry farming, food processing and sales, and soap making. APROFES also sponsors a mutual credit and savings fund with CODEKA (Kaolack Development Committee). In addition, APROFES is a joint owner of a credit and savings union with other partners.

In rural areas where food is scarce before the harvest, APROFES supplies grain to the cereal banks that it has helped set up to ensure that families have food during the period that precedes the harvest. Similarly, APROFES provides village stores with primary foodstuffs so that local populations can access them easily without having to go to the larger commercial centers. In the urban and rural areas of Kaolack region, women have great difficulty in gaining access to clean water. The impact this has on their daily life is considerable. They spend a lot of time fetching water to clean their homes and immediate surroundings, and disposing of domestic waste. They also need water for their crops, especially women who engage in market gardening, which goes on even during the dry season. In light of this situation, APROFES has launched a program for hygiene, sanitation, and clean water in order to support women in these areas in their domestic and income-generating activities.

APROFES also works to increase women's access to technical skills and knowledge. The association arranges for a technician to train partner women's groups in market-gardening techniques. This has led to an increase in crop productivity. Appraising the impact this support from APROFES has had on their income-generating activities, the president of the women's collective in Gapakh, situated about fifty kilometers from Kaolack, says, "Building public taps in our village and wells on our farms has changed our lives. We have water for our homes and vegetable gardens. Today, we earn higher incomes. We can afford to cater better to our needs and those of our families. We have also won the esteem of our family members. We feel that we have more weight now than before."

Building Women's Leadership and Community Awareness

Building women's leadership and community awareness is one of the most important activities undertaken by APROFES. The program focuses on raising awareness of the inequalities between men and women and

sensitizing the community to women's and children's rights, as well as to development issues in general. Seeking to build women's leadership in social and economic development, the program addresses such issues as violence against women and reproductive health, while promoting income-generating activities, education, learning, and consciousness-raising among women. The ultimate goal of the program is to bring about a change in the relations between men and women and between people of different generations and social classes. The program's awareness-raising exercises take any of three forms: debates and conferences, role-playing or video shows, and popular theater.

APROFES has formed a popular education theater troupe called "Bamtaare," which means "development" in Pulaar—one of the seven national languages in Senegal. The role of the theater troupe is to raise public awareness in rural and urban areas. The troupe's twenty-five members are young men and women who, several years ago, participated actively in the cultural movement that was spearheaded by Sports and Cultural Associations (ASCs). During its performances, the troupe uses national languages (rather than French) to facilitate understanding among the mostly illiterate audiences and uses traditional dance forms, music, poetry, and role-playing to raise awareness and provoke discussion on such issues as violence against women, female genital mutilation, AIDS, polygamous marriages, and the impact of structural adjustment policies on the rural poor.

The idea of using this troupe to bring about social change is one that is quite original in the work of Senegal-based associations and rare even in the subregion, given that social theater is a genre that has developed mostly in Burkina Faso and Mali through the "Koteba"—which is also the name for popular theater in these two countries. The APROFES theater troupe has toured several African, European, and North American countries to raise awareness of the negative effects of macroeconomic policies, economic globalization, and debt in Africa. The troupe has performed in Belgium, Canada, and Burkina Faso, where it obtained a prestigious award for popular theater. APROFES has also produced two audiovisual aids for public awareness-raising. One of them deals with violence against women and forced marriages, and the other with the impact of structural adjustment policies and the devaluation of the West African currency, the CFA franc. Further, APROFES wants to establish collaborative ties with the national television service in Senegal to ensure that these videos are widely shown.

Youth Education

APROFES runs a community education center for girls between the ages five and fifteen who come from different Kaolack neighborhoods and social groups. The program's curriculum emphasizes civic education, environmental education, conflict resolution, children's rights, preventing juvenile delinquency, family life education, and AIDS prevention.

Learning and Research

APROFES carries out research work to support both its program and advocacy work. It has just completed a study on the socioeconomic situation of women in Kaolack region, an initiative that was conducted with funding from the International Center for Studies and International Cooperation (CECI) in Canada.

In addition, APROFES sponsors exchange visits to promote learning and growth among staff and its partner organizations. Exchange visits are organized between APROFES and other partner associations based in Kaolack, in other regions of the country like Podor and Tambacounda, and internationally. On a national level, APROFES participates in an exchange program with an organization called Coordination of Women for the Development of Tambacounda (CFDT), a region situated in eastern Senegal. APROFES had also organized a cultural exchange tour of the Bamtaare troupe in France, Belgium, Luxembourg, and Holland. At the village level, within the scope of its actions aimed at promoting the associations, APROFES also organizes exchange visits between village associations and international institutions. For instance, APROFES organized exchanges between the intervillage Federation of Mboss, which APROFES assists and guides; the Friends of Emmaus in France, a religious, charitable organization; and a group of farmers in Burkina Faso.

Chapter 9

United States: Black Farmers' Rights and the Struggle for Land[1]

John Zippert and Gabrielle Watson

Introduction/Overview

Black farmers have struggled to hold on to land since they first began farming it as free men and women, after the Civil War ended slavery in 1865. Like all small family farmers, they suffer from the challenges of unpredictable weather, unforgiving lenders, and the encroachment of industrial agriculture. But unlike white farmers, they also suffer from deep-seated racism from neighbors, bankers, and government bureaucrats. This case tells one piece of the story about the struggle of small Black and minority farmers to keep their land and challenge racial discrimination in the United States.

Country Context

The history of discrimination against Blacks in the United States has its roots in the legacy of slavery. The slave trade started in the 1600s. When the Civil War officially ended in 1865, there were four million Blacks who had experienced slavery in the United States. The Emancipation Proclamation abolished slavery and gave Black men (though not women) citizenship. Black men in the South were only able to vote in the short time from 1865 to 1876, when federal troops were withdrawn from the South and white southerners reasserted themselves and established racist and segregationist policies blocking Blacks from the vote.

Most Black Americans stayed in the South after the war and began farming independently. But living conditions and social structures were not too far from the days of slavery. Their presence as free Black men and women challenged the old ways of the plantation owners. White southerners created segregationist "Jim Crow" laws excluding Blacks from most public areas, denied Blacks the right to vote, and carried out a campaign of systematic violence. Many Blacks were trapped in a system of "debt peonage," working as sharecroppers and farm laborers on land where they had previously been slaves. White landowners furnished meager farming and living expenses for a portion, usually half of the crop, at harvest. In many cases under this system, Black farming people never were able to pay off their debts and lived in a perpetual system of economic and social subservience to whites.

Between 1865 and 1965 more than six thousand African Americans died in racial violence in the United States; over a third of them were lynched.[2] At its height at the turn of the century, two to three people were lynched every week. Railroads ran special excursion trains to lynching sites, and thousands gathered to watch the beating, hanging, and burning of human beings. Despite this, Black land ownership reached its peak in 1910, when there were 218,000 Black-owned farms, accounting for fifteen million acres of land. Over a million Blacks were involved in farming.[3] Since that time, Black land ownership has been in a free fall in the United States.

By 1973, Blacks had lost more than half their land, down to six million acres. This is two and a

---

1. This case study was prepared and written jointly by Gabrielle Watson and John Zippert. It reflects the opinions and assessments of the authors, based on interviews and personal recollections of the events. John Zippert is a long-term staff member of the Federation of Southern Cooperatives and was an active participant in many of the events described in this case study. The case study does not necessarily represent the Federation's view of the events described.

2. History of racial lynchings based on National Public Radio presentation, May 2000. "Lynching" is a North American term that refers to extra-judicial mob violence, usually murder by hanging and mutilation, usually against Blacks.

3. Federation of Southern Cooperatives/Land Assistance Fund (FSC/LAF), *25th Anniversary Annual Report* (1992).

half times the rate of white land loss for the period. Just five years later, in 1978, US Census of Agriculture figures showed the figure had dripped to 4.2 million acres, divided among fifty-seven thousand Black-owned farms. Between 1982 and 1987, Black farms declined by 30 percent while white farms declined by 6.6 percent. The 1992 US Census of Agriculture found that less than nineteen thousand Black-owned farms remained, accounting for approximately 2.3 million acres.[4]

By the time the devastation of Black family farms in the United States was coming to light in the 1970s and 1980s, the political landscape around this ongoing reality had changed. In the 1960s, the civil rights movement mobilized thousands of people to fight against racism in the South: the lack of voting rights, exclusion from basic public services, segregation of every conceivable public and private space, the torture and lynchings of Black men, and the impunity of the Ku Klux Klan.[5] After years of marches, demonstrations, boycotts, and legal court cases, the civil rights movement did bring some critical and necessary reforms: the Civil Rights Act of 1964 (banning discrimination because of color, race, national origin, religion, or sex) and the Voting Rights Act of 1965 (which asserted the rights of all citizens to vote). Other gains were made at the state and local levels.

The civil rights movement helped draw attention to the impact of systematic racism on Black family farmers. Numerous reports and blue ribbon panels were organized to look at, document, and denounce the decline of the Black family farm. In many of these cases, the reports and commissions were initiated because of pressure from Black farmers and their organizations. In 1973, the Black Economic Research Center published *Only Six Million Acres,* calling attention to the problems faced by Black farmers.

A decade later, in 1982, the US Commission on Civil Rights charged that discrimination by agencies of the US Department of Agriculture (USDA) was one of the main causes for Black farm losses. Not only were Blacks suffering from racism, the report found, but it was an official racism perpetrated by employees of government agencies. The report found that USDA officials did not give farm credit to Blacks on the same terms they gave it to whites or, worse, that Blacks were simply not told about credit programs at all. The County Committees, local bodies established to implement USDA loan, extension, forestry, and conservation service programs, were made up of white farmers. These whites favored their white farmer friends and excluded Black farmers from USDA benefits. This "good-old-boys" network, the report argued, shut Black farmers out from government supports their white counterparts enjoyed.

The 1982 report concluded with a grim prognosis, saying "unless government policies of neglect and discrimination are changed there may be no Black farmers by the year 2000." Another report in 1990 by the US Congress's House Committee on Government Operations found that little had changed since the 1982 report. In fact, the Farmers Home Administration had further contributed to the decline of minority family farmers.[6]

In 1998, the National Commission on Small Farms presented its finding to the secretary of agriculture, concluding that mergers, acquisitions, and government policy have contributed to the concentration of agricultural land into larger and larger farms. More to the point for government policy, it found that the USDA credit programs have not served small farmers, particularly minority farmers.[7] Despite these reports' stark findings and despite pleas by farmers, their representatives, and their organizations, USDA officials have—when not actively participating in the destruction of Black farms—stood by and watched as Black farmers continued to lose their land.

In the 1960s and early 1970s a number of Black-farmer organizations were formed to address these issues. Born out of the civil rights movement, these

---

4. Figures on ownership of farmland by Blacks are based on numerous sources: Black Economic Research Center, *Only Six Million Acres* (1973); Federation of Southern Cooperatives/Land Assistance Fund, *25th Anniversary Annual Report*; US Census of Agriculture, as cited by Jerry Pennick, *The Rural Agenda* (FSC/LAF journal) (February 1, 1997); John Zippert, "Minority Farmers Rights Bill Needed," photocopy of manuscript (1989); John Zippert, "Not One More Acre," *Christian Social Action* (October 1994). All figures are rounded and approximate because of the acknowledged lack of statistical accuracy of US Census of Agriculture figures.

5. The Ku Klux Klan is a secret order of American-born, primarily southern, whites that believes in white supremacy and advocates for white domination. Its members are responsible for numerous lynchings, cross-burnings, fire-bombings, threats, and acts of violence and intimidation against Blacks and other minority groups. Members dress in hooded white robes during their clandestine ceremonies to hide their identities, though some members openly acknowledge their affiliation with the "Klan."

6. FSC/LAF, *25th Anniversary Annual Report.*

7. US Department of Agriculture, National Commission on Small Farms, *A Time to Act* (January 1998).

groups sought to go beyond legal and social discrimination and to address the persistent and underlying economic discrimination that harms Blacks in America. The Federation of Southern Cooperatives is one of these organizations. Its mission is focused on retention and development of Black farmers and their landholdings.

The Federation of Southern Cooperatives

The Federation of Southern Cooperatives/Land Assistance Fund (the Federation) is a member-based organization involving over twenty thousand rural low-income families, organized in eighty-five active cooperatives and credit unions in twelve southern states. The Federation is both a service and an advocacy-oriented organization. The majority of staff time is spent providing technical assistance for cooperatives and credit unions and conducting training and education programs at the Rural Training and Research Center in Epes, Alabama. Other services provided include programs to help members gain access to housing and legal assistance. The Federation also carries out advocacy on public-policy issues related to family farms and rural economic development.

History

The Federation was started in the 1960s by Black family farmers who came together to create alternative community-economic-development models. Many founding organizers came out of the civil rights movement. They knew Blacks needed economic development to fight the exploitative and discriminatory practices they were subjected to on a daily basis. Work focused on supporting producer and consumer cooperatives and community credit unions, as two approaches to fuel economic development in rural communities. Setting out to "change the face of the South through cooperative development," the Federation of Southern Cooperatives was incorporated in 1967 with some twenty-five full- and part-time organizers and twenty-two cooperatives. It grew to one hundred member cooperatives by 1970, serving twenty-five thousand low-income families.[8] In 1985 the Federation merged with the

Emergency Land Fund, an organization focused on preventing Black land loss. The merger helped the Federation consolidate its mission to save Black- and minority-owned farms.

The Story: Minority Farmers' Rights and the Struggle for Land

This case study highlights two critical campaigns in the life of the Federation's work. The first campaign is on a policy initiative to include benefits to small Black farmers in the national farm bill, which is revised roughly every five years. The second campaign is on getting the federal government's farm-credit institutions to acknowledge and pay for systematic discrimination against small Black farmers. These campaigns are very different: one focused on influencing national policy to open new opportunities for Black and minority farmers and the other focused on using a class-action lawsuit to make a point and secure compensation for past harms. But they share the common overarching mission to assert Black farmers' rights to hold on to their land in the face of racist discrimination.

Working for a Just Agricultural Policy: Minority Farmers' Rights and the 1990 Farm Bill

The "Minority Farmers' Rights Bill" was the Federation's first major campaign that ended up in specific legislation. As a result of the Federation's efforts, the 1987 Agricultural Credit Act and the 1990 Farm Bill were the first farm legislation that contained programs specifically benefiting minority farmers. In the end, not all the provisions of the Federation-backed Minority Farmers' Rights Bill were incorporated. But there were some significant gains: new accountability provisions for the USDA and the Outreach and Education Program for Socially Disadvantaged Farmers (hereafter, "Outreach Program") and some targeting of credit programs to disadvantaged farmers. The Federation was one of only two community-based groups that would go on to earn contracts under the Outreach Program; all others were made to historically Black "land grant" colleges set up in 1890 with grants from the federal government. They serve, but do not always organize, Black farmers to advocate for their own interests. How was the Federation able to make this happen?

---

8. Ralph Paige, interview, "African American Farmers Organize against Republican 'Freedom to Farm' Bill," *In Motion* (1996); *http://www.inmotionmagazine.com/paige.html* (downloaded November 9, 1998).

The idea for working on a major piece of legislation started in 1985, when small-farmer advocacy groups in Washington, D.C., contacted the Federation. What was the Federation's opinion of the 1985 Food Security Act? they asked. That bill, and the 1987 Credit Act, both had pieces introduced by the D.C. groups to improve credit terms for small farmers. The problem was that most of the Federation's members had never had access to government-sponsored credit in the first place. If Black and minority farmers were going to benefit from federal and state legislation, the Federation was going to have to craft something different from what the other small-farmer advocacy groups had been working on before. It had to directly target assistance to Black and minority farmers and their specific issues. And the Federation staff knew they needed to start to prepare something ahead of time so that when Congress started to work on the next farm bill, they would be there with a specific draft proposal in hand.

Ben Burkett, of the Mississippi Association of Co-operatives, describes the process for defining the issues that went into the Federation's Farm Bill proposal: "We had state meetings, and each local co-op would kick the idea around. People would add things to the pot. Later, when we worked on the specific language, some things would get thrown out because the whole thing would get shot down if we left them in." Ezra Cunningham, a long-time Federation leader in rural Alabama, adds to the description: "We had state association meetings, our Vista volunteers[9] were out talking with members and bringing back their issues. Co-op members came together and discussed common problems. The Federation's role was to provide technical expertise on writing the proposals and come up with solutions."

John Zippert, director of programs for the Federation, is more modest: "We were basically learning as we went along, to a large extent, with the Minority Farmers' Rights Bill. We did some work on the Ag Credit Act of 1987 and learned that we would need a broad coalition of groups—including other farmers of color (this would include Indian tribal farmers), limited-resource farmers, labor union groups, religious organizations,

and other consumer organizations—to pass any meaningful national legislation."

For example, they learned from Alabama Democratic senator Howell Heflin that once a bill went into the conference committee for final drafting, it could be completely changed and didn't have to look anything like the original bill. They later experienced this firsthand when they lost some key pieces of their proposal when it went into a conference committee in the House of Representatives, the lower chamber of the US Congress. This was despite having what they thought was a solid ally and supporter in the conference committee. In retrospect, they realized that they should have worked as hard with their "ally" as they had with the "opposition," to convince him of their case.

Another lesson the Federation learned through the 1990 Farm Bill process was the importance of access to legislators' staffs. Most legislators employ policy analysts to work with them on specific issues. The interests of these staff people often determine a legislator's support for a particular issue. If a staff person is concerned with an issue, they can make the case to their boss, draft sympathetic proposals, influence the legislator to take up the issue, and help when the doors are closed and private sessions are held to complete details of legislative proposals.

In the 1990 Farm Bill work, the Federation identified an aide to Georgia Democratic senator Wyche Fowler, who became a champion of their proposal. In the House of Representatives, the proposal was sponsored by Democratic congressman Mike Espy, who later became the first Black secretary of agriculture in the Clinton administration. Fowler was initially interested because he saw the Federation's influence with Black voters, who made up a large part of his electoral constituency. Fowler assigned his aide, Rob Redding, to work with the Federation to refine their proposal. Redding's job was to put it into standard legislative language and make sure the bill didn't have any pieces that would trigger opposition from conservatives in Congress. Redding helped to coordinate and work with Espy's office and staff in the lower house to ensure similar language. In the process, the Federation had to make some compromises, but in the end the key issues were there.

Once the Federation had developed the draft language, they began to do the legwork in Congress to get the votes for it. Ben Burkett, who had been active

---

9. The Vista program provides federal funds to nonprofit organizations for hiring young people to work on community-based projects around the country. A number of Federation cooperatives use Vista volunteers, who are paid a very small stipend, for much of their outreach work with their members.

in political campaigns before joining the Federation, describes the process: "We used to go up to Washington three or four times a year to go around to senators' offices. We'd focus on getting the conservative ones at least not to oppose it, or even vote for it. Now they see it as a vote-getter, because for some, the Black vote is a huge part of their constituency."

A key resource the Federation brought to work on the Minority Farmers' Rights Bill was access to politicians built up over the years. Any small group like the Federation is competing with professional lobbyists paid by large businesses to influence legislation, and who collectively earned $1.4 billion in 1998 for work in the United States capital.[10] This precious resource of access, which the Federation has no budget to buy, had to be built bit by bit. A large part of this access comes from the legacy of the civil rights movement in the 1960s and the relationships forged during that time. Some people from the civil rights movement had moved on to new roles, becoming politicians and government administrators. Now those people could open doors for the Federation.

Some of the access also comes from campaign support by Federation members acting as individuals in their private activities, as well as participation in special "blue ribbon" panels and studies, where they are able to meet like-minded policy makers, academics, and politicians. For example, John Zippert and Ben Burkett participated in numerous panels and interfaith church programs relating to the 1990 Farm Bill effort where they made contact with people like David Harris, a lawyer with the North Carolina Land Loss Project. Harris recently served as USDA general counsel for civil rights. Ben Burkett worked with Senator Trent Lott, a conservative Republican congressman from Mississippi, in 1972, well before joining the Federation. Zippert and other Federation staff also participated in the USDA's Civil Rights Action Team (CRAT), which held listening sessions throughout the South to document racial discrimination. The CRAT report's 1997 findings were a key building block for the class-action lawsuit against the USDA.

In order to be effective in Washington, the Federation got crucial support from the "installed capacity" of other farmer advocacy organizations, like the Ru-

ral Coalition, the Land Loss Prevention Project, and church and civil rights groups. These groups had years of experience doing lobbying work in Congress. They helped to write position papers, hold press events, prepare farmers and other grassroots lobbyists for congressional visits, schedule visits with congresspeople, take notes in the meetings, and help with later follow-up to ensure results and success from the legislative visits. Their involvement was closely coordinated with the grassroots work of developing and refining proposals. It was key to building the coalition and to getting support for the bill.

These groups had been active in pushing the credit agenda for small farmers in 1985 and 1987, and they knew the players in Washington. "We needed all of them to get it passed," says Burkett. Zippert, who was one of the key Federation drafters of the bill, adds that having a diverse coalition allowed them to reach senators and representatives beyond the natural "Black belt" ties the Federation had cultivated. "We pulled together a large coalition in support of the bill, more than one hundred local and national organizations. The AFL-CIO, the NAACP (a national-level Black civil rights advocacy organization), church groups, environmental groups, Latinos, Native Americans. Each of these groups used their own ties to influence their state representatives; in this way we were able to expand legislative support to states beyond the South, which brought new votes and more bi-partisan support for the basic proposals," says Zippert.

The minority farmers' rights provisions were passed and added as an amendment to the 1990 Farm Bill in the US Senate on a floor vote without opposition. In the House of Representatives, only a portion of the proposal was adopted. The Senate-House conference committee, despite active efforts by Senator Fowler, accepted the weaker House language. "This meant we lost some significant parts of our hard-fought program through backroom political maneuvering," said Zippert. Even so, the final legislation signed by President George Bush was a breakthrough for Black and other people-of-color farmers[11] because it gave recognition to their plight and was the beginning of a formal government program to correct decades of neglect and discrimination.

---

10. Report by the Center for Responsive Politics, cited in the *New York Times*, July 29, 1999.

11. "People-of-color farmers" refers to non-white farmers in the United States.

The Federation learned that with a major allocation of staff time, grassroots lobbying, and calling on years of contacts and political good will, a small but significant legislative change could be achieved. The celebration was short-lived, however, because the Federation and its allies had to move on to secure funding—budgetary appropriations—for the new programs, which had only been authorized by the new Farm Bill legislation.

Each year the Congress needs to vote money into the programs, to make them real. It turned out that this didn't always happen, and the Federation and its coalition members embarked on an annual struggle to hold on to the gains promised in the 1990 Farm Bill. This meant that each year the Federation had to mobilize its allies and return to the corridors of Congress to lobby for putting real dollars into the program. One strategy the Federation used for this was to bring farmers, en masse, to Washington, D.C. In 1992, the Federation organized a caravan to Washington to call attention to minority farmers' plight. The caravan ended with a rally on the steps of the US Agriculture Department, with Black farmers demanding justice and equitable treatment from their government.

Another caravan was organized in 1995. Farmer John Boyd, an independent farmer from Virginia and president of the National Black Farmers Association, has become a familiar sight as "poster boy" of Black farmers' issues, arriving with his mule at the steps of the nation's Capitol. The Federation also joined small family farmers across the United States in a fund-raising and consciousness-raising initiative by musicians called Farm Aid, sponsored by country music legend Willie Nelson. Linking with Washington-based advocacy groups, the Federation worked to extend its voice, and the voice of its members, to the halls of power.

"The work to secure the 'Minority Farmers' Rights' provisions in the 1990 Farm Bill and our subsequent struggles to seek congressional budgetary appropriations and administrative changes in the USDA's civil rights enforcement policies have been worthwhile," concludes Ralph Paige, the Federation's executive director. "We focused national attention on this critical issue and moved an unshakable and racist federal bureaucracy to grudgingly make some positive changes which helped some of our members at the grassroots

to retain their land and continue to live and work in the rural South."

Saving Black- and Minority-Owned Land: Lawsuit against the USDA

This historic lawsuit will send a signal throughout the country that there is no room for racism within the government. Economic and social justice should be the goal of government policy makers and those who implement those policies. Black farmers and all others who are recipients of government services deserve nothing less than justice at the hands of government officials. Perhaps now some healing can begin and Black farmers can work toward becoming an integral part of American agriculture.—Ralph Paige, executive director of the Federation of Southern Cooperatives

"The main problem with the USDA is at the county committee level. But you have to solve it at the Glickman level," says farmer and activist Willie Head, referring to Department of Agriculture Secretary Dan Glickman. Head speaks from experience. Government agencies' denial of credit to him, and to thousands of small Black farmers, is at the root of the class-action lawsuit filed against the USDA in August of 1997.

How did the Federation decide to go after the USDA? After all, the Federation is a major beneficiary of USDA funding through the Outreach and Technical Assistance Program for Socially Disadvantaged Farmers and Ranchers, which funds half of the Federation's direct work with farmers. "We had to go after the power," says Wendell Paris. "All the USDA programs had the same issues," says Ezra Cunningham. "The money was short, the application process was skewed, loans were made too late in the season, and the only farmers who could get help were their favorite 'Uncle Tom' supporters.[12] Anyone else's application would have one thing or another wrong with it. In some counties, they wouldn't even entertain the application, if a Black came in for a loan."

The USDA discrimination suit was over ten years in the making, with multiple false starts and a lot of ground work, research, and writing to build the case

---

12. "Uncle Tom" refers to Harriet Beecher Stowe's 1852 book, *Uncle Tom's Cabin,* where the Black man held up as a model was subservient to whites.

against the USDA, waiting for the stars to line up. The first attempt to file a suit against the USDA was done in the early 1990s, jointly by the Land Loss Prevention Project (LLPP) of North Carolina and the Farmer's Legal Action Group (FLAG), based in Minnesota. This effort resulted in the USDA turning over thousands of pages of records on farmers' civil rights complaints under the Freedom of Information Act. LLPP and FLAG attempted to fashion a larger case from these records but did not have the time and resources to follow through. The LLPP and FLAG lawyers then began working with a small group of plaintiffs, including Welchell Long and Tim Pigford, who had received letters from the USDA indicating in writing that they had been discriminated against but were offered no compensation or redress for their grievances.

Meanwhile, the Federation began working in 1996 and early 1997 with Secretary Dan Glickman and his associate, Pearlie Reed, on the USDA Civil Rights Action Team (CRAT). With assistance from the Federation, the USDA held a series of "listening sessions" across the South and the nation, where farmers, employees, and other participants in USDA programs were able to present their experiences with the agency. These listening sessions, especially the ones in Albany, Georgia; Belzoni, Mississippi; and Memphis, Tennessee, attracted hundreds of Black farmers and developed a record of grievances and a pattern of discriminatory treatment over the years, especially by USDA credit agencies. The CRAT report, issued in March 1997, candidly documented the discriminatory history and record of the USDA and included ninety-seven recommendations for improvement. Many of the changes were recommended by farmers and co-op members connected with the Federation. The CRAT report also recognized that President Ronald Reagan had abolished the civil rights complaint mechanism within USDA at the start of his administration in 1981, blocking any way for Black farmers to address discrimination. The Federation continued to work with USDA officials after 1997 to implement the recommendations of the CRAT report.

One of the CRAT recommendations urged the secretary of agriculture to create a National Small Farms Commission to suggest ways the USDA could be more responsive to and effective in working with all family-farm producers. Secretary Glickman created this commission in mid-1997. Two Federation staff members, Ben Burkett and John Zippert, served on the commission. In January 1998, the commission's report, *A Time to Act,* was published. It included 146 practical recommendations for USDA to improve the conditions of and service to over 1.7 million American agricultural producers with gross receipts of $250,000 or less, including mostly all of the Black and people-of-color farmers in the nation. The Federation's contribution to both CRAT and the National Small Farm Commission was in the tradition of its work on improving farm legislation and developing grassroots solutions to national rural problems. These reports became a forum to illustrate the national impact and plight of almost a century of loss of Black farmland and upheaval in depressed rural counties of the "Black-belt" South.

On the legal front, James Myart, a Black attorney from San Antonio, Texas, took the cases over from LLPP and FLAG by convincing the plaintiff farmers that he could do a better job. Myart sought to finance his work with the farmers by establishing a "contingent fee" structure, where he would only get paid if the suit was successful. Under his proposal, a third or more of the farmers' settlement award would go to Myart, a typical amount in this kind of arrangement. This didn't seem fair to farmers, though, since they had so little to begin with. This led to distrust between farmers and Myart, and the farmers' organizations supporting the case decided to distance themselves from it. Myart's case was initially dismissed in federal court by an unfriendly judge. This, coupled with the disagreement over attorney's fees, led to the suit being withdrawn.

The suit finally got off the ground when Alexander J. Pires, an attorney experienced in defending white farmers with USDA credit problems, was approached by a group of Black farmers who had been trying to file suits against the USDA, including Tim Pigford of North Carolina, Lloyd Shaefer and Eddie Ross of Mississippi, and others. Pires suggested a different fee structure—attorneys' fees would be paid by the government under a civil rights statute and would not come out of farmers' settlements. He also brought experience with personal-injury and class-action litigation to the case. Ralph Paige and John Zippert, aware of the issues around lack of trust that came up in the previous attempt to bring a suit, encouraged civil rights attorney J. L. Chestnut of Selma, Alabama, to join the case. Chestnut was already representing several Black farmers in Alabama, including George Hall, at the time the sheriff of Greene County, Alabama, in a discrimination case against the government.

Chestnut is a long-time movement activist who represented Dr. Martin Luther King in the 1960s in Selma, Alabama, and leads the largest Black law firm in the state—Chestnut, Sanders, and Sanders. Chestnut is well known and well respected within Black communities throughout the South. For the Federation, it was also important to have someone who they trusted, like Chestnut and his firm, on the legal team. With this legal support and a fair fee system in place, the Federation was able to urge thousands of its members across the South to join as part of the lawsuit.

In order to strengthen support for the case, the Federation reached out to old allies from earlier battles over the various farm bills. They formed a broad coalition, the Coordinating Council of Black Farm Groups, to build unity among farmers, coordinate the efforts of Black farm groups, and serve as an advisory body to the legal team. The Federation served as the secretariat of this group throughout the case and has continued to lead efforts to monitor implementation of the settlement. Rev. Joseph Lowery, former president of the Southern Christian Leadership Conference, agreed to head the coordinating council. He brought a wealth of civil rights experience and leadership contacts to the task of helping to hold this coalition of groups together.

The Federation was also involved in creating the larger National Council of Community-Based Organizations (CBOs) in Agriculture, involving a larger number of organizations representing Black, Latino, and Native American farmers from across the United States, to support the case and press for implementation of the recommendations of the CRAT and National Small Farm Commission reports. Members of the National Council of CBOs included the Rural Coalition, Inter-Tribal Agriculture Council, Land Loss Prevention Project, Texas Landowners Association, Black Farmers and Agriculturalists Association, and others. The Federation played a key role in gathering these various organizations together in both the coordinating council and National Council of CBOs in Agriculture. "We don't have anything to lose, by working in coalitions," says Executive Director Ralph Paige. "Our agenda is too big. We can't do it alone.

We only have things to gain, if we're all clear on the agenda, and we stick with it."

The suit was filed on August 28, 1997, in Washington, D.C., on behalf of three Black farmers: Pigford, Shaefer, and Hall. Hundreds of other Black farmers joined the case as the pleadings were amended to show widespread support and lay a basis for making it a class action on behalf of all Black farmers who had tried to seek assistance from USDA agencies and programs. President Reagan's action to abolish the USDA civil rights compliance office in 1981 was used as the hallmark to measure the period of discrimination against the class of Black farmers.

US District Court Judge Paul Friedman declared the case a class-action suit on October 9, 1998. This opened the way for any Black farmer to join the suit if they could show USDA discrimination had harmed them during the fifteen-year period 1981 to 1996. Black farmers who stopped or were forced out of farming prior to 1981 were unfortunately not included in the suit. Nearly twenty thousand farmers ultimately joined the class. During the early phases of the case, the Federation used its structure of local cooperatives, state organizations, and annual membership meetings to get the word out to farmers. Farmers' concerns were brought to the lawyers working on the case in an effort to shape the structure of the settlement.

From the start, farmers had two key concerns. First, farmers wanted to be compensated for the losses they had suffered because they were wrongly denied access to loans and other USDA benefits, such as conservation assistance, emergency feed, crop allotments, forestry planning, and others. Second, they wanted to reform the structure that permitted discrimination by USDA county committees and loan agents of the Farmers Home Administration and Farm Services Agency in the first place. But part of the lawsuit story includes the breakdown between what the farmers wanted and what the lawyers leading the case were able to achieve.

At a point in the court proceedings, the judge asked the USDA and farmers' attorneys to enter into settlement negotiations. Once this settlement process began, it was difficult for the coalition of farmer groups supporting the case to play an active role and keep both their issues on the table. The shifting details of the negotiations and the pace of the process did not lend themselves to a consultative, consensus-based decision-making ideal many social justice advocacy groups strive to live up to. Just as in the case with the Minority Farmers' Rights Bill of the 1990 Farm Bill, pieces of the agenda were dropped in the course of developing the legal language of the settlement. But, unlike the drafting process for the Farm Bill, Federation staff and the coordinating council members were not fully involved in developing the legal strategy and had little control of the lawyers' negotiations with the USDA. Despite all the consultation they had done with their members, when the legal team drafted the final legal complaint, none of the coordinating council members were involved. As Paige notes, "The Federation didn't have a say, one way or another," in the drafting of the settlement.

Attorney J. L. Chestnut expressed concern that negotiations behind closed doors could take away the opportunity for farmers to have their day in court. More important, it could take away the chance for Black farmers to tell their story to the American public. "Americans need to hear from you. America needs to know what your own government has done to you over the years," said Chestnut to farmers during an open court session before the final decision came down.

In the end, the lawyers in the case calculated that structural reform of the USDA would not be winnable in the context of the lawsuit. The lawsuit provides primarily monetary compensation for farmers who could prove they were harmed by USDA discrimination and little in the way of systemic changes to USDA operations. Reforms of the USDA loan delivery system, including county committees, would have to wait for another day.

The lawyers' decision not to demand USDA reforms posed a challenge for the Federation and the coalition. Partly as a consequence, a number of coordinating committee member organizations presented countersuits to Judge Friedman during a fairness hearing on the settlement with class-action members. The key plaintiff named in the suit, Tim Pigford, was not satisfied and threatened to withdraw from the case. And Federation staff had to decide whether to support the suit at all.

The Federation did decide to stay with the suit, despite its partial victory. They still believed that, while not perfect, this was a landmark decision, and that they should support it. They owed it to their members and small Black farmers to give them a chance to get this benefit. For some, it would be enough money to help them keep farming, and for others it would let them pay off long-standing debts and obligations.

Attorney Chestnut advised the Federation that no legal settlement would be perfect or satisfy everyone. The settlement was a political compromise, in part negotiated under pressure from President Bill Clinton. Clinton wanted his own administration's Departments of Agriculture and Justice to resolve the long-standing problems of Black farmers. The basic monetary award of $50,000 per farmer, plus a tax payment to the Internal Revenue Service (IRS) of $12,500 and some debt relief, was the largest payment to date by the government in a class-action lawsuit. Chestnut said that without a negotiated settlement the case could go on for decades through appeals, and older farmers in the case might never see the benefits.

Another problem with the settlement was that the lawyers for the USDA tried to invoke a two-year "statute of limitations" period on claims, saying the case could not rightly cover discrimination that occurred fifteen years ago. This would have spelled the end of the lawsuit, if successful. Attorney Chestnut argued that the federal judge could make an exception to this statute in his ruling. Instead, a bipartisan group of senators, led by Democrat Charles Robb of Virginia and House members, supported by Speaker Newt Gingrich, passed a legislative exception to the statute of limitations for the farmer's class-action settlement, to cover the full period of 1981 to 1996. This was even better, since it didn't rely on the judge's decision. The Federation and other members of the Coordinating Council of Black Farm Groups worked to pass this legislation to make the legal settlement fully effective.

The Federation worked to get information out to farmers so they could decide for themselves whether to register as class members or not. Working in collaboration with local legal-service organizations, the Federation opened up their state and local offices for individual farmers to get one-on-one counseling from the legal-service staff. Federation staff members worked in a paralegal capacity helping hundreds of farmers to fill out their claim forms. Many of the farmers who benefited from this were not local co-op or even Federation members.

The claim settlement process has brought mixed

results, from the Federation's perspectives. As of August 15, 2000, according to the report of the court-appointed monitor in the case, there were a total of 20,675 claims filed by the initial October 12, 1999, deadline. Of these, 20,488 are eligible for the basic $50,000 settlement, and 187 are eligible for more than the basic settlement, if they can produce specific evidence of discrimination. Of the 20,488 eligible for the basic settlement, 18,062 (88 percent) had been reviewed, and of those 10,931 (61 percent) had been approved. The rest, 7,131, had been denied. As of August 2000, the government had paid out over $330 million in the settlement. An additional 20,000 late claims were filed by the September 15, 2000, final filing deadline, bringing the potential total class size to over 38,000. A determination on these late claims has yet to be made.

The Federation is continuing to work with the over 7,000 farmers whose initial claims were denied to prepare a petition for reconsideration to the monitor. The Federation feels the 39 percent denial rate is too high and reflects problems with the adjudicator's interpretation of the settlement and individual claims. Because so many claims were filed in a short period between April 14 and October 12, 1999, many farmers feel they did not file a complete or fully accurate claim because appropriate and sufficient technical and legal assistance was not available under the settlement. The Federation feels the case may continue for a long time once a determination is made on the late claims, which will start a new round of complaint filings. But despite the imperfect settlement process, the overall impact of the case is still a major success.

The victory of the Black farmers in this case sends a strong message to the USDA and to the American public: the government acknowledges it systematically excluded Black farmers from access to farm credit. Whether the monetary award of the lawsuit will eventually lead to systemic change within the USDA, such as ridding it of the "good-old-boy" networks that pervade the county committee structure, is an open question. For the plaintiffs in the suit, the money may never "make them whole," as lawyers say, meaning it will not undo or fully compensate for the harm they have suffered. Despite the huge loss of land by Black farmers and the comparatively small size of the settlement, the class-action suit does affirm that the farmers are right, that their government did them wrong, and

this carries tremendous importance. "This settlement does not make all farmers whole but it might provide many with resources for their continued participation in agricultural production. Our primary concern is the long-term impact and whether the settlement will have a positive effect within the USDA itself, especially as it relates to those farmers who are not a part of the settlement. We are hopeful that the spinoff of the settlement will open the doors for other minorities—including women—to increase their participation in America's agricultural system," stated Jerry Pennick, the Federation's director of land assistance.[13]

In the end, the victory—even if partial by some measures—is huge. The individual settlements are unprecedented. To put the case in perspective, ten years ago, the US Congress approved reparations of $20,000 to Japanese survivors of the World War II internment camps, where people of Japanese origin were placed after being stripped of their properties and taken from their communities. Said Jerry Pennick: "The settlement is a giant step in that direction. More importantly, it puts the USDA on notice that discrimination will not be tolerated any more." It will now be critical to continue the work of changing the USDA and actually getting the payments made to farmers, and it will be essential to keep pushing for structural changes to the USDA and its agencies.

Conclusion: The Federation's Impact

The Federation's advocacy efforts on behalf of Black farmers over the past fifteen years have been a success. The Federation has been able to make Black farmers' loss of their land and the elimination of Black farmers a visible issue and concern to the Black community and to a larger public audience in the United States. The scope of this public audience, which included the Congress and federal courts, led to some changes in the current conditions and potential outlook for Black farmers and the southern rural communities where they live.

As part of the Federation's mission to save Black farmers, to help them to retain their land, and through cooperatives to build a better way of life, it consciously decided and planned in the 1980s to make Federal agricultural policies recognize the plight of Black farm-

---

13. Federation of Southern Cooperatives, press release, April 2000.

ers and take some specific and compensatory steps to correct the historical reality, experience, and pattern of racial discrimination.

The Federation's planning was successful in helping to develop and secure passage of legislative provisions that recognize, target, and benefit Black and other people-of-color farmers as a response to past discriminatory treatment. The Federation also helped to do the groundwork, outreach, and support for a landmark class-action suit that provides monetary damages to individual Black farmers. Although it does not provide much in the way of systemic remedies or change the use of government resources to solve the problems of Black and people-of-color farmers, the suit put the issue in the public spotlight in a powerful way.

Through the Federation's coalition advocacy efforts, it helped secure authorization of the Outreach and Technical Assistance Program and the targeting of USDA farm ownership and operating loans to socially disadvantaged farmers and ranchers. Now, the USDA is mandated to provide special assistance to Black farmers and other farmers of color.

Yet, while the law is on the books, the Federation still needs to battle each year to get budgetary appropriations from Congress and the prevailing political administration, to implement these programs. The Outreach Program was authorized in 1990, for $10 million per year, a small program in USDA's total budget of over $60 billion per year. Since 1990, annual appropriations have never been above $3 million, and total annual spending on the program, which the secretary of agriculture supplemented with discretionary funds, has never exceeded $7.5 million. Total spending since 1990 on this worthwhile program to overcome years of discriminatory treatment is about $40 million, leaving a deficit between the actual and the potential spending of $60 million.

Similarly, in the case of the *Pigford v. Glickman,* the Black farmers' class-action lawsuit, the promise of justice and change was greater than the reality of the monetary benefits. The settlement of the lawsuit, which might have contained requirements for major systemic change of USDA agencies, operations, and employees, as well as requirements for full funding of the Outreach Program, institution of a minority farmers' registry, and establishment of a land-bank to begin restoration of the fifteen million acres once owned by Blacks, instead provides payments to individual farm-

ers without bringing systemic change at the USDA, which caused these serious problems of discrimination in the first place.

So in a democratic system, advocacy for legislative, administrative, and regulatory change is an incremental, not a revolutionary, process for change. The changes the Federation has achieved for Black farmers and rural communities are modest and require a continuing vigilance and fight to retain. The opposition is at work to reverse and contain these changes at every chance it can get. The Federation must work regularly to protect its legislative, regulatory, and policy gains, as well as battle to secure adequate funding to make them meaningful and effective.

Other lessons the Federation has learned in making its advocacy efforts effective include the need to develop coalitions to have as large and regionally dispersed and ethnically diverse support for its positions as possible. In both the legislative and the lawsuit work, the Federation embraced and led coalitions to work for broadening and deepening the support of these issues. The Federation's coalition work has also involved experts and organizations in Washington, D.C., like the Rural Coalition, National Family Farm Coalition, NAACP, labor unions, and others with more experience and contacts in Congress and other government agencies. Utilizing advice from experienced people helped to frame issues, locate allies, and analyze the political-power relationships necessary to make changes.

In addition to effective support from coalitions and experienced groups in Washington, D.C., the Federation also found that "grassroots lobbyists" have great power. Black farmers from its membership taking time to travel to Washington to meet with Congress people and other officials were the best and strongest spokespersons for their own cause. Rallies, demonstrations, and mobilizations like the 1992 Black Farmers' Caravan were critical to unifying the Federation's constituency, giving real voice to its concerns and helping to move forward the goals and agenda of its constituency. The impact of grassroots people in the context of a campaign was always strategic.

The Federation is a comprehensive organization. Advocacy is one strategic part of its overall mission to improve the lives of Black family farmers and other low-income rural people and make a difference for depressed rural communities. Its advocacy is coupled with service and technical assistance to Federation membership to build strong cooperatives and credit unions, as alternative economic structures to lift members and their communities out of poverty. The third element of the Federation's strategy is resource development to support the alternative economic development and legislative advocacy components of the Federation's work.

Chapter 10

Guatemala: Bringing Human Rights to Bear on the Culture of Impunity

Gabrielle Watson

Introduction

In February of 1999, the UN-sponsored Historical Clarification Commission released its report on the thirty-six-year civil war in Guatemala, using the word "genocide" to describe the atrocities committed by the Guatemalan security forces. This marked a crucial moment of official recognition for what Guatemalan social advocacy groups had been saying for years, despite consistent government denials. It also capped years of advocacy by countless organizations in Guatemala and the United States to hold the Guatemalan government and its US supporters in the CIA accountable for the systematic campaign against indigenous Mayan populations during the 1970s, 1980s, and 1990s. With the end of the civil war, Guatemalans are now struggling to rebuild the fractured society left in the wake of the brutal war. This case study tells the story and advocacy strategies of one of the organizations involved in this struggle, the Center for Human Rights Legal Action (CALDH—Centro para Acción Legal en Derechos Humanos).

CALDH is a Guatemalan human rights and grassroots support organization. It was founded in exile in the 1980s, working mainly to denounce government-perpetrated massacres in international forums like the Inter-American Court. In the early 1990s, when the political repression began to ease, CALDH opened an office in Guatemala. It then expanded its work beyond the legal cases against the Guatemalan government to bring a broad understanding of human rights to bear on the reconstruction of Guatemalan civil society. Much of the organization's work today involves building the leadership capacity of grassroots groups to articulate and promote their own interests in the area of human rights. It provides legal aid and strategic support to popular organizations and ex-cluded groups, including youth, women, indigenous communities, labor unions, and peasant organizations. "If you're really working for human rights, you have to work for democracy," says Frank La Rue, the president of CALDH.[1] He believes this means understanding human rights in its broadest sense, which includes both civil and political rights, social and economic rights, and the rights of excluded groups such as indigenous communities, women, and youth.

This case study highlights the multi-tiered advocacy approach used by CALDH that focuses on building the capacity of grassroots groups to advocate for their own interests, while simultaneously pushing a human rights agenda at the national and international levels. CALDH's work shows how one organization worked "backward" from the international to the national and to the local level, to work for its social justice advocacy goals from the grassroots up. Because CALDH works at multiple levels at the same time—the local, national, and international—this case study raises the question of accountability across these different arenas.

"Primary" and "Secondary" Spaces in Advocacy

CALDH's work with popular organizations sheds light on the distinction between advocacy "for" and advocacy "by" the group to benefit from the actions. It also speaks to issues of accountability in collaborative work across the local, national, and international levels. Charles Abugre, the Africa secretariat coordinator of the Third World Network, makes a distinction between "primary" and "secondary" spaces that is use-

---

1. Personal interview, Frank LaRue, director of CALDH, January 1999.

ful in exploring this question.[2] *Primary space* is an arena in which a given group is located (community, region, country) and where actions by that group will benefit its members. For example, when Guatemalan rural peasants, known as campesinos, engage at the municipal, departmental, or federal levels to promote their own interests, they are acting in their primary space. *Secondary space* is an arena outside of one's own primary space, where advocacy will benefit another group, but not the advocate directly. For example, when technical-support NGOs promote and do advocacy on campesino issues, they are working in their secondary space.

Looking at the CALDH experience in light of Charles Abugre's distinction between primary and secondary spaces suggests a number of questions for other NGO support organizations doing advocacy with counterpart grassroots organizations. Some specific questions to explore might include:

1. Are there "norms of conduct" for the various types of advocacy actors (membership organizations, intermediary-support NGOs, and professional advocates) working in their primary or secondary spaces? For example, can a group speak "on behalf of" the groups they work with when they are not working in their own primary space? Or are they bound to work with those groups in some way? What are the obligations?

2. Are intermediary-support NGOs by definition always working in a secondary space because they are not working in support of the interests of their own staff, but rather those of the groups they work with? Or are there some issues that are so universal that they are nobody's exclusive primary space?

3. Similarly, if a group is working to further its own interests, is there such a thing as secondary space? Put another way, can local grassroots groups still be working in their primary space when advocating their interests in international forums? Local and national boundaries are increasingly blurred in today's globalizing context, where decisions made at one level affect another. How do we deal with this?

---

2. Charles Abugre, Africa secretariat coordinator of the Third World Network, presentation to Oxfam International Advocacy Coordinating Committee, Washington, D.C., February 1999.

CALDH's work makes some interesting contributions to this discussion.

The Guatemalan Context

More than two hundred thousand people were killed or disappeared in Guatemala during the thirty-six-year civil war that officially ended when the government and the opposition coalition of guerrilla forces signed the UN-sponsored peace accords in December of 1996. The peace accords ushered in a process of demilitarization, resettlement and compensation for displaced civilians, police reforms, and UN monitoring and called for the creation of the independent Historical Clarification Commission to document human rights violations committed on both sides during the war.

The commission's report, released February 25, 1999, establishes that the government and allied paramilitary forces were responsible for 93 percent of the documented human rights violations, including torture, kidnapping, extra-judicial executions, and massacres. The report also found that "the structure and nature of the economic, cultural and social relationships in Guatemala, as well as racism, the closing of spaces for participation and the refusal by the state to promote substantive reform, were all factors that determined the origin and the outbreak of the armed confrontation."[3] Though the killing has now ended, the structural inequalities that sparked the civil war have not been changed in Guatemala and remain the central focus of social justice organizations there.

The worst of the violence occurred during the Romero Lucas García (1978–1982) and José Efraín Ríos Montt (1982–1983) regimes, when government forces systematically attacked Mayan communities suspected of sympathizing with the guerrilla forces. Entire villages were burned and their residents slaughtered, in an attempt to deny guerrillas possible supplies, intelligence, and shelter. At the same time, spaces for political participation were closed down throughout the country. Unions were shut down by the government. Teachers, university students, union members, progressive church members, and other civil society members were threatened, kidnapped, and killed. The press was censored, and as a result

---

3. *New York Times,* February 26, 1999.

Guatemalans living in the capital had little notion of the devastation going on in the rural villages and hamlets. The government created Civil Defense Patrol organizations (Patrullas de Autodefensa Civil, or PACs) composed of local residents armed and authorized to enforce security in their regions. The Civil Defense Patrols had little training, no legal accountability, and perpetrated many of the massacres that killed tens of thousands of Guatemalans. In many cases, government forces planned and gave the orders for the massacres and kept watch while the Civil Defense Patrols slaughtered defenseless peasants.

In the late 1970s and 1980s, many Guatemalans fled into exile in the United States, Canada, Europe, and other Latin American countries. Since it was impossible to fight against the atrocities being committed by the Guatemalan government from within the country, they began to work from the outside. The Organization of American States' Inter-American Court and the Inter-American Commission on Human Rights were the primary arenas for this work. "The Inter-American Commission reached its peak at the end of the 1980s. It was a really exciting time. The point then was to bring cases at a Latin American regional level. Since the national level was closed, we could only do it from the outside," says Frank La Rue of the early work CALDH and other organizations carried out to hold the Guatemalan government accountable.[4]

Then, in 1993, the so-called self-coup of then-president Serrano opened up new space for Guatemalan civil society organizations. Serrano's attempt to stage a coup to consolidate his own power backfired, and there was internal purging within the government that brought more democratically oriented people into the government. Activists who had fled into exile began to return and slowly expand the space for doing social justice advocacy and bring legal cases within the national context. The Roman Catholic Church launched a three-year investigation in 1995 to document human rights abuses on both sides during the war. That report was published in 1998, the year before the UN-sponsored report came out, and identified specific military officers and guerrilla groups responsible for crimes. But as a signal that not so much has changed in Guatemala, days after the report came out, Roman Catholic bishop Juan José Gerardi was beaten

to death with a concrete block. The military was widely suspected to be behind the murder.

In 1996, after years of negotiations, the UN-brokered peace accords were signed. The peace accords not only involved a halt to armed combat but set time frames for significant structural reforms such as the resettlement of returning refugees, legal reforms, and constitutional revisions, as well as the Truth Commission's work. The peace accords have provided a legal framework and organizing vehicle for progressive civil society groups to carry out broad-based, civic educational work to expand the scope and substance of democratic participation in the national reconstruction process.

By the time the Historical Clarification Commission's report came out in February 1999, much of the peace accord's elements were well under way, but still of a tentative nature. Significant resettlement had happened, a new constitution had been drafted, there was a new penal code, and so on. With the end of the military government, the Inter-American Court began to play a decreasing role in leveraging accountability at the national level. Yet the national legal system was not yet robust enough to respond to the human rights cases that needed to be brought. As people finally began to dig up their loved ones' bodies buried in mass graves, and tentatively talk about the massacres, some wanted to seek justice and bring legal cases against the perpetrators. But while the reformed legal system allows bringing human rights cases, the government prosecutors remained reluctant to delve into these old stories. The message sent by Bishop Gerardi's brutal death was not lost on them.

CALDH's work follows the story of Guatemala's transition through the dark period of the late 1970s and early 1980s up to the more recent period of tentative transition to democracy. It tells about the advocacy strategies used by CALDH and its allies to use the ideals of human rights to rebuild the fabric of civil society and culture of democracy.

CALDH—Origins and the Struggle for Human Rights in the Face of Impunity

The Center for Human Rights Legal Action, CALDH, is a "full-service" human rights organization based in Guatemala City, with over fifty staff. CALDH's work spans the international, national, and local levels and

---

4. LaRue, interview.

includes work on gender rights, indigenous rights, youth, disabled people, rural workers, and fledgling labor union movements. CALDH monitors and accompanies the Guatemalan peace accords process, using the accords and other legal and policy breakthroughs as vehicles for building citizen involvement in the democratic transition process.

In the 1970s, Frank La Rue and other founding CALDH members had been running a legal services agency serving Guatemalan labor unions. By the early 1980s, when the unions were forced to shut down because of death threats and fire bombings, they left Guatemala, leaving behind their union activism, friends, and families. "I went to Washington; another union activist went to Canada. We had to look for a way to continue our work. But we realized we had to shift our focus from labor to human rights issues," says La Rue.[5] The national context had polarized. Internal social justice work was no longer possible. Friends were disappearing; teachers, labor union activists, and church lay workers were being targeted by the death squads. And the military was carrying out massacres against Mayan villages in the highlands.

When they moved into exile, La Rue and others began to link up with exiled activists from the Guatemalan indigenous movement. La Rue had begun to work with indigenous activist and 1982 Nobel Peace Prize winner Rigoberta Menchú in 1982. They were lobbying the United Nations to bring a resolution to condemn the Guatemalan government. "The strategy at the time was to bring legal cases as a way to highlight victims within the country. We wanted to bring international pressure, but we wanted to focus on what was going on within the country, too. But we had to do it from outside Guatemala because the internal space didn't exist."[6] From that work, La Rue saw a way to use his legal background to continue his work from outside of Guatemala. This was the start of CALDH as an organization.

Xavier Mena, a UN human rights official who worked as an Organization of American States (OAS) intern at the time, says CALDH was the NGO that brought the most petitions to that body. "They were there all the time. They did very serious, profes-

sional work. And they were extremely brave, given the personal risks they were taking," he recalls.[7]

Frank La Rue pulled together a group of lawyers in the US who worked with groups that continued to work in Guatemala, such as GAM (Grupo de Apoyo Mutuo—Mutual Support Group) and CONAVIGUA (Coordinadora Nacional de Viudas de Guatemala—National Council of Guatemalan Widows), a group of Guatemalan widows, to get key information out of the country. CALDH would then use this information to build legal cases and present petitions to the Inter-American Human Rights Commission of the OAS. Until the end of the Ríos Montt regime, however, they could not do much more than bring generic petitions. Evidence gathering was nearly impossible. "The country was a graveyard," remembers La Rue. "No one could talk."[8]

After Ríos Montt left the government in 1983, things opened up enough so that by 1989, Frank La Rue and others were able to send a delegation of US lawyers to Guatemala to investigate a massacre that had occurred in the town of Aguacate. When they came back, they wrote a report on their findings and presented it to the OAS. "This was a turning point for us. It was our first big case," says La Rue.[9] By that time, they were able to get more information out of the country. Though La Rue was stopped and denied entry at the airport three times between 1988 and 1990, others were able to get in and bring crucial evidence out.

Seeing that some limited work was again possible within Guatemala, CALDH staff decided to take a calculated risk and open an office in Guatemala City in 1991. A North American lawyer went down and quietly began working alone, gradually building relationships with other groups. Then, in 1993, a group of British women wanted to do accompaniment work with returning refugees. They approached CALDH and proposed collaborating. "This is when we really began to grow as an organization," says La Rue.[10] Further, 1993 was the year of a failed coup attempt, the so-called self-coup, that created new political space as more conservative forces within the government were

---

5. LaRue, interview.
6. LaRue, interview.

7. Xavier Mena, human rights official, UN mission to Guatemala, personal opinion expressed during interview, January 1999.
8. LaRue, interview.
9. LaRue, interview.
10. LaRue, interview.

purged. Groups throughout Guatemala began to take advantage of this new space by taking a more aggressive posture toward organizing—holding marches and protests and publicizing their views. More CALDH staff began moving back to Guatemala. When La Rue returned, his friends advised him against staying. A close friend had tried to stay the year before and was disappeared and killed. La Rue decided to face his fears and his enemies head on. "I called a journalist and did a full-page interview with photos and everything," he recounts. "If they wanted to find me now, they'd know exactly where to go."[11] But there would also be the repercussion of national and international public attention. At least this was La Rue's gamble. And so CALDH's national foothold was firmly established, and the organization began to grow.

The move back shifted the focus of CALDH's work from international forums to Guatemalan forums. More of the legal cases were targeted at Guatemalan courts, and the international cases served more as an additional leverage point, a mechanism for increasing national-level legal accountability.

The next sections describe CALDH's campaign to bring a genocide case against the Guatemalan government and its work to support campesino and indigenous communities' advocacy on land issues.

Building Justice through Genocide Cases

In 1993, CALDH began the slow process of constructing the pieces of a genocide case against the Lucas García (1978–1982) and Ríos Montt (1982–1983) regimes for the systematic massacre and cultural destruction of indigenous communities. In the end, according to La Rue, the genocide case is a struggle to end the culture of impunity in Guatemala and to rebuild the fabric of civil society. As Miguel Nort of CALDH's legal team says, "International decisions are important. But much more important is the change that happens at the national level. If there's no national action, there's no point in doing international-level work. The point is to re-create democratic space within the country, to call them to account for what they did."[12]

CALDH was one of the few organizations in Guatemala in 1999 that could represent human rights

cases at the international level and one of only a few equipped to carry out exhumations of massacre sites. CALDH's international legal staff, made up of Guatemalans and foreigners, bring their prior experience in international courts. They know the laws and how the international process works. (Today there are other groups capable of bringing international cases, which is a positive step.) CALDH's national legal and local forensics teams work closely with communities to gain the trust and confidence of victims' relatives and perform the exhumations in a way that allows for healing within the community. But the exhumations must also be done under careful scientific guidelines, in order for the evidence to hold up in court. So the forensic teams must walk a very careful line, respecting both needs and helping family members understand the need for reliable forensic evidence. In some cases, the communities do not want to bring cases against the perpetrators, but forensics staff work with them to bury their relatives with respect, bringing some sense of closure.

CALDH's strategy for bringing a genocide case against the Guatemalan government is to build a large enough set of massacre cases to demonstrate a pattern and practice of genocide. Miguel Nort of the legal department estimates that it will take some twenty cases from the Lucas García and Ríos Montt periods to do this. They will then combine the massacre cases with documentation proving the Guatemalan government was using its scorched-earth, model-villages, and civilian-patrol policies to carry out an intentional program of cultural destruction against indigenous Mayan peoples. The *tierra arrasada,* or scorched-earth, policy was aimed at removing areas of possible refuge for armed anti-government forces by destroying villages, primarily indigenous, that were suspected of aiding guerrilla forces. Model villages were refugee settlements that were under the control of the military and that were considered free of guerrillas.

Each massacre case has to be investigated, developed, presented, and adjudicated individually before it can be combined in the genocide case, and this could take many years. "The Truth Commission and the church's work have already established that this happened at a moral and social level. But it still needs to be established legally, that there was a concerted plan to commit genocide," says Nort. "Now we have to show that behind the PACs (Patrullas de Autodefensa

---

11. LaRue, interview.
12. Personal interview, Miguel Nort, lawyer with CALDH international legal team, January 1999.

Civil—Civilian Defense Patrols), the 'model villages,' behind all the people fleeing for their lives, there was a strategic intent of cultural genocide."[13]

The Rio Negro Massacre Case

The Rio Negro massacre occurred on March 13, 1982. Approximately 270 men, women, and children were killed by the Civilian Defense Patrol of Xococ, as part of the government's scorched-earth policy.[14] The Rio Negro massacre occurred in two parts. First, the PAC killed nearly all the men. The one who survived fled into the surrounding hills. Then, a month later, the PAC returned and killed the women and children. One man and eighteen children survived the massacre. Some of the children were taken as work slaves by Xococ PAC members.[15]

Eleven years after the massacre, in 1993, a group of survivors formed a group to search for closure. They sought out CALDH and other human rights organizations, initiating one of the first massacre exhumations in Guatemala. "The exhumations are important," says CALDH's Miguel Nort. "There's a dual purpose of healing the hurt, but also of gathering evidence. Sometimes these two goals can be at odds."[16] Survivors need to find a way to lay their relatives' remains to rest in a way that respects their beliefs and traditions. This normally means relatives want to remove and re-bury the remains as quickly as possible. But careful forensic work is needed to present strong evidence in court, if a case is brought. So the forensic teams must work with survivors to find a way to both allow survivors to grieve and say good-bye to their relatives and document the crime. "We try to find ways to increase the confidence of the people, develop their sense of self-esteem," says Edgar Pérez of CALDH's national legal team. "We have to work for a long time to develop their trust, so they can decide whether they want to go forward with a case."[17] Sometimes, survivors do not want to bring a case, and the forensic teams focus on the healing process only.

"There are real risks" with bringing a criminal case against the perpetrators of a massacre, observes Miguel Nort. "It's impossible to fully protect witnesses, for one." Villagers know that former PAC members and their military supporters still live in the area. Everyone knows who they are, and everyone knows they have no interest in the full truth coming out. "And it's hard to do the technical work. We work with the Forensics Foundation and the Office of the Archbishop on Human Rights (ODHA), but it's hard. You need to have solid evidence to bring a case and be able to follow through," says Nort.[18] Part of CALDH's work has involved the behind-the-scenes tasks of witness preparation and witness protection, to the extent possible. Edgar Pérez, of CALDH's national legal team, believes the witness-preparation work for the Rio Negro case was crucial. They held workshops for witnesses with mock trials and role-playing to get them used to court proceedings and so they would know what to expect at trial. CALDH staff have also worked to make the legal process work the way it is supposed to, denouncing intimidation and threats against witnesses in court to push the Public Ministry to take action to protect them, calling for evidence checks, and doing some cautious media work to raise public support for the case while trying to shield witnesses from any more danger than they already face.

On November 30, 1998, the Guatemalan courts convicted three PAC members of a brutal massacre in the Rio Negro village in Rabinal, in the department of Baja Verapaz. This was the first legal decision in Guatemala against any of the perpetrators of massacres. The Rio Negro conviction was also the first massacre case to gain national public attention, re-opening the old wounds and old memories of the dark days of the armed conflict. It had taken five years to investigate and prosecute the case, including efforts by CALDH and many other national advocacy groups such as the Forensics Foundation and the ODHA. The Rio Negro case was also the first building block of CALDH's genocide case.

The three members of the Xococ PAC were condemned to death by lethal injection for their involvement in the massacre. The Rio Negro decision got front-page coverage within Guatemala, bringing the first break in the silence surrounding the bloody history of the war. This was the first test, too, of the limits to the peace accord's amnesty program. The

---

13. Nort, interview.

14. *Siglo 21,* December 1, 1998; *El Periódico,* December 7, 1998; *Prensa Libre,* November 6, 1998; *El Gráfico,* December 1, 1998.

15. *El Periódico,* February 12, 1998.

16. Nort, interview.

17. Personal interview, Edgar Pérez, lawyer with CALDH national legal team, January 1999.

---

18. Nort, interview.

amnesty covers armed forces on both sides of the conflict but does not shield either from accusations of "crimes against humanity." Much of the press coverage focused on the death sentences. "The judgement was very good, but the death sentence was very bad," comments Miguel Nort.[19] Walter Valencia, of CALDH's local powers project, was quoted in the press as saying that as a human rights organization, CALDH must defend all rights, and that it is categorically opposed to the death penalty.[20]

Miguel Nort also stressed that the Rio Negro conviction was only a start. "The PAC in Xococ did all the killing, but the army circled the town and kept everyone there. They also gave the orders."[21] So the Rio Negro case set a precedent, but the work to end the impunity for the crimes still remains to be done. "CALDH's task is to push to find the intellectual authors of the crime, not just the material authors," adds Edgar Pérez. "For this, we need to do more detailed investigation. The government prosecutors won't do this. They know who's really responsible, and they're afraid."[22] In the judge's sentence of the three PAC members, he determined that the rest of the PAC was also responsible, and the army as well. This lays the legal groundwork for a second case against those responsible higher up in the command structure.

The Rio Negro case was the first piece of CALDH's genocide case against the Guatemalan government. CALDH had another twelve cases underway in early 1999, with all but two in the forensics-investigation stage, according to Nort.

Rebuilding the Fabric of Civil Society: Peasant and Indigenous Organizations

The lawsuits are trying to bring justice to heal Guatemala's wounds. But CALDH also wants to look to the future and create new ways of working that bring excluded voices forward. When CALDH began to build its Guatemala office in the early 1990s, it expanded its focus to bring a human rights perspective to its work on local-governance issues and excluded groups, to begin to rebuild Guatemalan democratic practices from the ground up.

Two key groups in the work to reconstruct Guatemalan democracy have been peasants and indigenous communities displaced by the war. Working with these groups presented a challenge to CALDH staff, whose prior professional training and advocacy experience had centered on using high-level national and international legal structures to carry out their work. Now they were working with grassroots constituencies that were just barely emerging from years of repression and fragmentation. "This was really different from the old 'central-planning' model. Now the big challenge was to build from the grassroots up. This is much more difficult than the old vision of top-down change guided by ideological dogma," says La Rue. "We started a Local Powers Project, once we moved back," says La Rue. "For us, if you're really working for human rights, you have to work for democracy. In the end, the challenge of reconstructing the relationship between civil society and the state happens at the local level."[23]

How did CALDH learn to work in this qualitatively different way? And how did the organization structure itself in order to do this? This section explores these questions by looking at one program area, the Technical Unit for Analysis, Relations, and Support, UTARA (Unidad Técnica de Análisis, Relaciones y Asesoría), which focuses on local governance issues within the context of land conflicts.

The Technical Unit's role within CALDH is to provide support to groups at the local level that are trying to reconstruct and reinvent themselves after the war. Most of these groups are dealing with land-conflict issues, so much of the Technical Unit's work centers on land, land reform, resettlement, and land conflict resolution, a majority of which is linked to the peace accords. "The popular sectors were destroyed during the war," says Enrique Torres of the CALDH Technical Unit. "Now, what few leaders there are lack a national, systemic vision. The war also destroyed connections among popular sectors. They're all very locally focused now." Torres and the others in the Technical Unit focus primarily on excluded groups in the rural areas—indigenous, peasant, and fledgling union and popular organizations. At the same time, they're keenly aware of the need to link these organizations to national-level policy debates on the issues that affect them. "There's a national-political-party process,

---

19. Nort, interview.
20. *Siglo 21,* December 1, 1998.
21. Nort, interview.
22. Pérez, interview.

23. LaRue, interview.

but it isn't grounded in local issues," observes Torres. "CALDH is trying to build a national network and the capacity of local groups to participate in that network."[24]

The Technical Unit uses a three-pronged approach to its work, according to the unit's Walter Valencia. First, they provide legal advice and support on land-conflict issues, as they arise, though they don't function as legal counsel or legal representatives. Second, they help popular organizations carry out strategic planing, also on land-conflict and land-policy issues. Their role involves providing contextual analysis of national policies on land issues and helping organizations develop strategies for taking advantage of openings provided by the peace accords and emerging legal or political opportunities. And, third, they carry out leadership-development work focused on political, electoral, and representative structures, but always maintaining a staunch nonpartisan position. While the Technical Unit works directly with membership organizations such as peasant groups, indigenous communities, and displaced people's organizations, they also support local technical teams that do most of the day-to-day work, as described in more detail below.

"A Counterpart for Everything We Do"

The Technical Unit works in a number of regions of Guatemala: San Marcos, Quetzaltenango, Quiché, Ixcan, Alta Verapaz, Isabal, Livingston, and the Petén. In order to have such a broad area of operations, given that the Technical Unit is composed of less than five staff people, they always work with local counterpart organizations. More important, CALDH's work with counterparts also stems from a commitment to play a support role, as opposed to a representational role. "We have clarity on playing a support role," says Valencia. "It's framed within the analysis that indigenous and popular sectors need to take a leadership role in decision making."[25] CALDH staff seek to pass this philosophy on to the local support organizations they work with.

"We always have a counterpart for everything we do," says CALDH president Frank La Rue. "If there

isn't one, we help organize it."[26] They work with, and help train and organize, small technical teams to provide legal services to rural workers. Most of the teams work for the local Catholic diocese, as part of the church's pastoral work on land issues. Others teams are made up of members of peasant and indigenous groups who have had some higher education or committed professionals from local municipal governments, teachers unions, or state and federal technical-assistance agencies. Some are local staff of national and international development organizations. The church and other organizations welcome CALDH's support in training their local staff because CALDH staff bring specialized knowledge about the legal and policy environment.

The CALDH Technical Unit staff help these teams develop work plans for providing legal services and doing organizing work in the communities. They also provide consulting-type services, accompanying the teams as they navigate through government institutions and the decision-making process. Through this interaction, the technical teams develop a knowledge and skill base that they can use on their own, without Technical Unit staff assistance. "After just two years we are already seeing a big change in the capacity of local leaders to take key facts, pull them together, relate them to the local context, and make proposals," says Valencia.[27] In this way, Technical Unit staff are cultivating a network of regionally based resources for the emerging rural indigenous, peasant, and labor movements. Not only does the Technical Unit expand its reach and impact, but it is building a network of skilled support organizations that will ultimately support the autonomy of local organizations.

In Quetzaltenango, for example, the Technical Unit works with the local church-based Pastoral de Tierra (Land Pastoral Team). "It's a very young, but very energetic team," says Valencia.[28] There, the communities' concern isn't access to land, as it is in much of the rest of the country, but labor issues. Most of the region's poor are landless, and there is a high unemployment rate. The CALDH role in Quetzaltenango has been to support the local Pastoral de Tierra team, providing legal advice and training to their lawyers and holding ongoing contextual-analysis workshops that

---

24. Personal interview, Enrique Torres, CALDH Technical Unit staff person, January 1999.
25. Personal interview, Walter Valencia, CALDH Technical Unit staff person, January 1999.

26. LaRue, interview.
27. Valencia, interview.
28. Valencia, interview.

analyze the changing agrarian, labor, and constitutional frameworks. They also help to carry out regional investigations into labor issues so the local unions can have an analytical and factual basis for developing proposals to resolve the unemployment problem.

In another region, the northern part of Isabal, CALDH has been supporting local indigenous organizations facing an increase in land conflicts. This area suffered numerous massacres during the war, and CALDH has been involved in bringing two human rights cases to the Inter-American Court. It had organized into formally registered organizations with the help of a national indigenous federation. But when the national federation became involved in the peace accords, they weren't able to continue their work in the region, and the groups had faltered. A local priest working with the communities wanted to help them develop autonomous organizations to deal with their land problems and contacted CALDH for support, knowing that they worked with peasant and indigenous groups in other parts of the country.

The Technical Unit helped the communities do a mapping project to see what the key issues were. Based on this work, they proposed that the community form a municipal-level organization around the land issue. At a second meeting they got a much broader attendance, including members of the Protestant church and people with the municipal government. This larger group appointed a small team to carry the work forward, composed of a lawyer who speaks the local Kekchi language, a social worker from the town, a local teacher, and an agronomist. Once this rather heterogeneous group formed, CALDH worked to advise and support it. The team helped residents formally create an association for local development—the issue that united this diverse group. They developed a two-pronged strategy of negotiations with the government for land assistance and pursuing legal cases, giving continuity to the unfinished business of dealing with the massacres. CALDH's role at this point is helping the association and the local technical team, supporting them to access and navigate national-level agencies that can help resolve the land-conflict issues.

Successful Counterpart Relationships: What It Takes

The Technical Unit's collaboration with church-based and non-affiliated technical teams has a number of key features that make it a successful model. First, it builds on the long-standing relationship between the church and other local support organizations and the communities they work with. For many years, the church was the only place where rural people could safely come together to talk about their concerns and the repression that they were facing. The church was not immune from violence by the state, but it was able to continue providing a relatively safe place for the rural population. This gives CALDH the ability to reach into arenas that, as a national-level organization based in Guatemala City, it would be unable to do on its own.

Second, it builds and strengthens the capacity of these groups to do increasingly sophisticated work, as the opportunities for organized collective engagement with the state increase. Once that capacity has been developed, CALDH's role in promoting the interests of these groups will become less central and will take place on an as-needed, advisory basis only. In essence, this serves to rebuild the social fabric of civil society, increasing the capacity of groups to articulate their own needs in the newly opening political spaces.

Third, the local technical teams' geographic distribution permits an intensive interaction with rural organizations that the Technical Unit is not able to have itself. CALDH would need to dramatically increase its staff and create regional offices if it were to do this work itself. The relationship with counterpart organizations builds on the comparative advantages of each: CALDH provides the analytical, institutional, organizing, and policy "know how," and the counterpart groups provide the day-to-day interaction with the grassroots groups.

And, fourth, each of the local teams is multidisciplinary, including some generalists with specialized legal training or paralegals who have roots in the region they are working in. These paraprofessionals play the key role of listening to the multiple issues faced by rural workers and tailoring ways of working that will respond to these multiple needs. Their work is labor-intensive, detailed, and requires strong commitment and interpersonal skills. Combining these attributes with the more specialized skills of the team lawyer makes for an effective team that can gain the trust and confidence of popular organizations in a way that outsiders could never do.

CALDH Advocacy: Working Definition and Changes with Shifting Political Space

CALDH staff people see themselves as advocates, but what does advocacy mean to them? "Advocacy is the promotion of the interests of excluded popular organizations," says Enrique Torres of the Technical Unit.[29] This definition is different from some definitions of advocacy because it does not identify a subject and an object of advocacy. Advocacy is not necessarily done by one group "for" another group. But it is also not necessarily done by the group directly interested in the outcomes of the advocacy. The definition is agnostic; it could be either of the interpretations.

In fact, as the CALDH work described here shows, the way the staff understand advocacy includes both interpretations—advocacy "for" and advocacy "by" excluded groups. At one end of the spectrum, advocating on behalf of others, is CALDH's legal work in international courts. Bringing legal cases and representing clients is one of the most traditional forms of advocacy: the lawyer representing the interests of the client, using highly technical skills in a complex, inaccessible arena—at least for most clients. In the case of the early international human rights work in the US, this representation was far removed from the "clients," not only by physical distance but by language, by time, and by virtue of working one step removed through the "third-party" organizations that did the direct work with witnesses, relatives, and physical evidence.

At the other end of the spectrum is CALDH's popular-mobilization work in Guatemala, where CALDH staff plays a support role, and the advocacy is done directly by the groups themselves. CALDH Technical Unit staff provide advice and strategic analysis of the policy environment, but the ultimate goal is for grassroots groups to advocate and negotiate on their own behalf. CALDH builds their capacity to investigate and articulate their collective needs, analyze the policy and development context, navigate the key public and private institutions, and develop concrete proposals to address their issues. This kind of support varies from helping groups officially register as legal entities, to providing workshops on contextual analysis of the peace accords and ongoing legal reforms. CALDH staff do not have a representational

---

29. Torres, interview.

relationship in this work. In one case, where popular organizations have difficult access to federal-level government bodies due to physical distances and lack of knowledge, CALDH has signed formal contractual agreements to be the official conduit for the organizations' business. Yet even in this instance, the use of legal agreements codifying this relationship only highlights the clear boundaries between CALDH, in its support role, and the membership-based popular organization.

Shifting Advocacy Strategies and Advocacy Targets Based on Political Space

From the early 1980s to the present, CALDH has been reinventing its advocacy work to suit the context, the opportunities, and the constraints it works in. The starting point has been the basic skills of the majority of the members—lawyers and union, indigenous, and peasant-movement activists—and the core commitment of promoting the interests of marginalized sectors. When the political context closed down the possibility to work on labor rights, CALDH used the same skills to "reinvent" itself. When the political context opened up, CALDH again redefined its role and brought in new skills and staff representing a broader set of interests, to occupy more of the expanding democratic space. The thread running through all of the work is the struggle to democratize Guatemala and open up society to excluded groups.

CALDH started bringing human rights cases to the Organization of American States' (OAS) Inter-American Commission on Human Rights. But why bring cases, and why human rights cases? Human rights advocacy was actually a "second generation" of work for La Rue. Like many of CALDH's current staff, La Rue started out working as a lawyer for labor unions until they were forced to shut down, and the members fled into exile in the late 1970s and early 1980s. The focus on international human rights cases, then, was not just a change in venue and tactics. It represented an entirely new arena (from national to international courts) and a change in substantive focus (from labor law to human rights).

CALDH made this radical shift in advocacy focus because of the contraction in the political space in Guatemala. By 1979, Guatemala was characterized by the persecution of all forms of organized civil society, the absence of the rule of law, and the dominance of a military that was using coordinated coercive force to eliminate voices of dissent. Shifting to human rights issues enabled CALDH to directly address the atrocities being committed by the government. The context had changed, and so the advocacy strategy needed to change with it. The new area of work also represented a shift from using formal, national channels to engage government decision-making structures (a strategy appropriate to open political systems), to going completely outside of government (international courts) to bring defensive collective grievances against government (a hybrid strategy suited to closed systems [working externally to the system] and to relatively open systems [the international court system]).

Now that the national context is opening up, CALDH has shifted its focus back to the national level. The focus now is on building the capacity of local groups to formulate and articulate their own interests and to form and strengthen networks. In a sense, CALDH has gone through the opposite trajectory from what one usually sees, where groups get increasingly out of touch with their grassroots base as time passes, and they get more engaged with national- and international-level advocacy work. How has CALDH managed to break this mold?

"Dual-Track" Approach to Policy Work and Grassroots Organizing

Part of the reason CALDH has managed to keep its links with popular sectors has been a purposeful "dual-track" strategy of grassroots mobilization work, on the one hand, and policy engagement, on the other. One key example of this has been CALDH's work around the Guatemalan peace accords. CALDH staff have had sharp criticisms for the failings of the peace accords and have worked both during and after the accords to make them work better for the poor. "We worked in the background during the peace process, but at the same time criticized them for their lack of popular engagement," says Frank La Rue.[30] CALDH staff worked to pressure the UN mission to Guatemala (MINUGUA), established to monitor the peace accords, to push their agenda for popular participation. For example, CALDH has tried to get MINUGUA to address the issue of the death penalty, a very unpopular opinion in Guatemala today. When MINUGUA

finally decided to hold a conference on the death penalty, CALDH took advantage of the opening and worked to get trade unions and other key organizations to attend. In this way CALDH was able to use MINUGUA's "outsider" role as a vehicle for getting a difficult issue into public debate.

At the same time, CALDH has used the peace accords as an organizing vehicle and as a capacity-building opportunity in its organizing work with popular organizations. The peace accords opened significant opportunities for excluded groups to gain access to resources and political processes. In order for this to happen, though, people needed to know what the accords actually meant. Much of the Technical Unit's work with indigenous and peasant communities has involved providing orientation on the peace accords so they can take advantage of the new opportunities, framing their issues in the context of the rights established by the accords.

Challenges

CALDH's biggest challenge has been its success. Rapid growth and broadly dispersed geographic programmatic work, combined with the expansion into new functional areas, have created an organization that is high-strung and fast-paced, but not necessarily tightly focused. CALDH started with a limited focus on human rights cases brought in international courts and grew to include accompaniment of returning refugees, exhumation and legal cases brought within Guatemala, and now finally a wide range of activities from civil society support work, to many kinds of anti-discrimination work (gender, youth, disabled, sexual preference, etc.), to environmental monitoring of oil-industry violations.

Expansion into multiple program areas is not unique to CALDH and points to the need for organizational-development services for the nonprofit sector in general. Most organizations would benefit from organizational-development support to build links among programs, improve administrative and reporting systems, develop strategic-planning skills, and so on. CALDH has been carrying out annual strategic-planning sessions, is aware that its diverse programs don't interact as they might, and has been working to find ways to link them better. CALDH leadership has not wanted to reduce the number of

---

30. LaRue, interview.

programs, however, deciding that the breadth of the work is essential to address the multi-faceted nature of human rights issues in Guatemala.

Conclusion

The CALDH case offers some significant lessons on how advocacy works in political systems that drastically reduce advocates' maneuvering space. Moving from a highly repressive, authoritarian regime to a gradually opening society, CALDH staff first fled into exile and used international courts to try to reform the government from the outside and then cautiously returned and began to work through national courts and at the grassroots to slowly rebuild the fabric of a democratic society. The key lessons that emerge are:

- Respecting the right of grassroots groups to set their own agendas and do their own advocacy, while providing key analytical, legal, and technical support.

- Shifting "backward" from international advocacy to local-level advocacy.

- Focusing simultaneously on legal victories, opening political space for civil society, and building social movements at the grassroots level.

Setting Agendas in Collaboration with Grassroots Groups

When groups team up to do collaborative advocacy, the issue of how agendas get set—who participates in agenda setting, how alliance members influence changes in the agenda, and so on—comes to the forefront. CALDH's contribution to the question of how agendas get set in structurally unequal alliances comes from the work that the Technical Team and the indigenous program are doing. In both cases, the relationship between CALDH, as grassroots support organization, and the counterpart organization is one of support, and not representation, as discussed in the section of definitions of advocacy.

But there is a fine line that CALDH staff must walk. The organizations they are working with are just beginning the process of mapping and analyzing their context, of defining their agenda, and of crafting strategies for achieving their goals. "Yes, we need to keep winning and opening up space," says Walter Va-

lencia of CALDH's Technical Unit. "And CALDH's role is specific to our expertise—including legal and strategic analysis and proposing alternatives. But the groups themselves need to decide the direction they want to go."[31] Yet, in supporting this process, it is almost impossible not to influence it in some way. CALDH staff try to compensate for this by presenting options and pushing their counterpart organizations to make the final selection.

By virtue of the national spread of their programmatic work, CALDH staff are able to see common patterns that individual groups aren't aware of, and they are able to monitor national-level political opportunities in a way that remote groups cannot. In this sense, there is a natural "comparative advantage" to playing an advisory role, steering popular organizations away from some options, and toward others. But there must remain a distinction between CALDH's agenda—which is to support and strengthen excluded groups of civil society—and the agenda of the groups it works with.

How do support NGOs that engage in advocacy work balance power relationships across inherently unequal partnerships, and how are effective alliances and collaborations established? CALDH's work with counterpart organizations offers a useful model for other organizations. The Technical Unit's work with church-based and local technical teams is one example of strategic advocacy alliances. The Technical Unit could have chosen to build its own network of regional technical teams. Instead, it works with local groups that have organic ties in the region and are institutionally supported by separate organizations—in some cases the church and in others, outside funders, development organizations, and local and state agencies. The advantages for CALDH is it gets access to teams that have in-depth knowledge and experience in each region and that have independent sources of support, providing a secure source of sustenance for the work. CALDH, for its part, brings the national perspective and negotiations and legal skills developed through years of labor union and human rights work.

By working with the comparative advantages of counterpart organizations, each organization has a strong position within the alliance. The other advantage is that this tends to reinforce the autonomy of

---

31. Valencia, interview.

each alliance or collaboration participant, since they are valued precisely because of their distinct set of skills or organizational capacities.

Shifting from International- to National- to Local-Level Advocacy

Unlike many advocacy organizations that lose connection to their social bases over time, CALDH has gone in the opposite direction. It made the transition from essentially "elite" advocacy work—highly technical, specialized human rights advocacy at the international level—to increasingly grassroots-based advocacy work, focusing more on rebuilding the social fabric that was destroyed during the war in Guatemala. In this transition, it has continued its work at all levels—local, national, and international. How has this been possible?

CALDH has had a purposeful focus on promoting the interests of popular sectors, as part of the core mission of the organization. This has defined its work and ensured that it has indeed maintained its grassroots ties. The staff have not worked on human rights in the abstract, or judicial reform, or indigenous rights, or monitored the peace accords, and so on, for their own sake. The focus has always been to use a particular issue as a vehicle to promote the interests of the excluded group and simultaneously build its capacity to engage effectively in the national and international policy-making processes.

Advocating at Multiple Levels Simultaneously

CALDH's work focuses on three primary arenas: the legal system, to gain formal "paradigmatic" victories that set precedents favoring popular organizations; the political system, to open up space for popular organizations; and social movements, to help reconstruct the social fabric of Guatemalan civil society.

Three structural characteristics of the organization contributed to CALDH's ability to work well at multiple levels simultaneously. The first characteristic entails having a large enough operation to have a mix of skills on hand. CALDH includes lawyers, paraprofessionals, staff with international and labor union experience, and people from the women's and indigenous movements. The diversity of the staff, and the organic ties staff bring to CALDH from their previous organizing work, enables the organization to keep grounded in grassroots interests and at the same time

extend its action to national and international policy levels.

The second organizational characteristic involves having staff that move comfortably across multiple boundaries, from very local grassroots organizations to high-level national organizations. This attribute also derives from the previous organizing experiences staff bring to their work with CALDH. The ability to move across multiple levels makes it possible to implement multiple, simultaneous advocacy strategies. In much of CALDH's work, staff have employed a "dual-track" approach, combining consultation and agenda setting with grassroots groups and high-level policy engagement.

The third characteristic involves the working relationship with counterpart organizations at the local level that either are themselves part of membership organizations or are organically tied to grassroots organizations. This gives CALDH a kind of long-term relationship by proxy with these organizations. CALDH benefits from the counterparts' knowledge of the nuances that can only be known from working with groups for an extended period of time. It also eliminates the need for CALDH staff themselves to work at the local level, which would be impossible for the size of the organization. Thus, CALDH can remain relatively agile, build the strength of local organizations, and foster their independence, at the same time.

Primary and Secondary Space, Revisited

What does the CALDH experience tell us about Charles Abugre's formulation of primary and secondary space? How would his distinction help us analyze CALDH's work, and what might this suggest about the roles of membership organizations and intermediary-support NGOs working at the local, national, and international levels, in this case?

CALDH's work with campesino groups is an example of working in a *secondary space* because staff are neither campesinos nor have concerns having to do with land. CALDH's work on the genocide case is a bit more complex. On the one hand, they are supporting the decisions of local communities, whether or not they decide to prosecute the perpetrators of massacres. In this sense, they are working in their secondary space. On the other hand, CALDH is also building a case of genocide against two past administrations that will set a national precedent. They are working to assert the human rights of all Guatemalans, themselves included. So CALDH's work on the long-term genocide case is in the staff's own primary space.

CALDH's work offers some possible answers to the question whether there are "norms of conduct" for working outside one's own primary space. In the Technical Unit's work with campesinos, program staff have made a specific decision not to advocate on behalf of these groups. There is a strong support and advising relationship, but not a representational relationship. They see their role as helping to build their counter-part organizations' capacity to advocate on their own behalf. In the case of individual massacre cases, the legal and forensics units are also playing an advisory and support role. The ultimate decision about what to do rests with the community. In CALDH's work on the genocide case, it has taken a lead role in setting the agenda, defining strategies, and speaking in its own voice on the issue. Here it is not seeking to put others' voices forward, or restricting itself to a supporting role only. Perhaps human rights are a global primary space, the domain of all people, independent of nationality.

Chapter 11

Cambodia: Revising the Land Law[1]

Srey Chanthy and Gabrielle Watson

Introduction

Cambodia is only now emerging from a devastating history of genocide, foreign occupation, and the halting reconstruction of a democratic state. The Khmer Rouge rule from 1975 to 1979 left Cambodia and civil society[2] decimated. The subsequent Vietnamese-installed government (1979–1991) and UN transitional government (1991–1993) reintroduced some semblance of order, and the elected Cambodian governments since 1993 have begun to reconstruct a new national order. Cambodia is living with the legacy of an extraordinarily brutal past, a closed political system, and a weak civil society, which is struggling to define its role as the country re-creates itself.

One of the central issues facing this primarily agrarian country is natural-resource decision making. How are lands allocated, forests managed, and in the midst of all of this, how are poor people's needs met? Landlessness is a growing crisis in Cambodia. A combination of land grabbing and land speculation, the return of refugees, an outmoded and cumbersome land-titling process, and corruption of government officials are pushing poor rural Cambodians off their land.

This case study describes the early steps in an advocacy initiative to revise the land law in favor of poor and landless farmers and highland indigenous communities. It focuses on the significant role international nongovernmental organizations (NGOs) have played in the initiative and shows how national and local or-

ganizations have engaged in the processes initiated by the international NGOs. International NGOs worked in collaboration with national NGOs and the UN mission to propose a land law that would address the issues of growing landlessness and land-tenure conflicts in Cambodia. Multiple advocacy approaches were used by various initiative participants. Because the advocacy initiative described in this case study was still in progress as the case was written, the final outcomes are not presented. Assessment of the different advocacy approaches are based on interviews.

Country Context[3]

Cambodia emerged in 1991 from the devastation of the Khmer Rouge and the control of a Vietnamese-installed government with a decimated civil society, low levels of literacy and formal education, and a still-smoldering conflict between the remaining Khmer Rouge fighters and the Cambodian military. The Khmer Rouge (1975–1979) wanted to create a utopian agrarian society and sought to destroy all foreign influences. The Khmer Rouge brought Cambodia back almost a century in human, technological, economic, and political terms. Of a starting population of seven million in 1975, an estimated 1.5 to 2 million Cambodians were killed, starved, or worked to death during the Khmer Rouge period. The Khmer Rouge's Pol Pot carried out a policy of mass internal migrations that emptied the cities, separated families, and created a society of forced manual labor in subsistence activities. All the social, economic, and physical infrastructure of the country was destroyed. Intellectuals were targeted for especially severe treatment, and often worked to death.

---

1. This case study was written by Srey Chanthy, an independent Cambodian consultant with expertise in natural-resource management and agricultural development. The final case study was developed by Gabrielle Watson from Srey Chanthy's drafts and supplemented by her field notes. The two researchers conducted interviews in Cambodia in April 1999. All affiliations refer to those at the time of fieldwork, April 1999, and are not necessarily current.

2. The term "civil society" is used in this case study to refer to nongovernmental organizations and popular organizations independent of direct government control.

3. This section draws, in part, from Curtis Grant, *Cambodia Reborn? The Transition to Democracy and Development* (Washington, D.C., and Geneva: Brookings Institution Press and The United Nations Research Institute for Social Development, 1998).

Having experienced these atrocities, Cambodians are extremely cautious of organized groups and feel unsafe engaging in overtly political activities. During the Khmer Rouge period there was a saying that people should "plant the kapok tree" (the *doeum ko* tree, in Khmer). *Ko* means dumb, and the phrase meant that people were to pretend they knew nothing of their leader's acts. To save their lives, they had to plant the culture of silence and pretend to be blind, deaf, and dumb about the atrocities of the Khmer Rouge.

In 1979, the Vietnamese invaded Cambodia, ended control of the Khmer Rouge, and installed a government managed from Vietnam. During the eleven years of Vietnamese control over Cambodia, the country suffered under a US–led embargo while Khmer Rouge forces continued to fight from the countryside. Despite aid from Vietnam and the Soviet Union, Cambodia endured a decade of economic privation and isolation as the superpowers struggled to win the Cold War.

Peace accords signed in 1991 ushered in a transitional period overseen by the United Nations. Once the internationally recognized government was established, UN agencies such as the World Food Program, United Nations Development Program (UNDP), and UNICEF came in with the mission to support the Royal Government of Cambodia. The UN Transitional Authority of Cambodia (UNTAC) (1991–1993) initiated a slow process of national reconstruction, in the face of ongoing fighting and fragile peace accords. With UNTAC came huge amounts of foreign aid and a wave of international NGOs. These organizations took on the role of civil society within Cambodia, providing development services, helping local communities rebuild themselves, and carrying out various campaigns, such as the campaign to remove land mines left from the fighting. In 1993, UN-organized elections were held. Democratic space slowly began to open up. Some UN agencies like the UN High Commission for Refugees, the UN Center for Human Rights, and CARERE (Cambodia Area Rehabilitation and Regeneration) continued their work beyond 1993, with the goal of building government capacity and consolidating the emerging democratic state.

The whole structure of society and the legal system from before the Khmer Rouge period had been completely destroyed, and what remained were out-of-date French models, no longer accepted in the new Southeast Asian reality. Following the elections, new laws were passed and others began to be drafted. While a new legal framework is welcomed, the process for drafting new laws is less than transparent for Cambodian civil society, and it has been a struggle to participate in the process.

In addition to the lack of laws, law-enforcement mechanisms are also still weak. Lawlessness and impunity prevail. Neutrality of the judiciary system has not yet been established. There is limited training available for police, lawyers, and judges. Low pay prevents the emergence of a fair and just legal system. Poor victims rarely receive justice from court judgments. Trials are highly politicized and bribes are common. These problems extend from the local to the national levels.

The combination of the absence of a modern, legal governance framework and the lack of respect for what laws do exist makes life difficult for everyone. There is a high level of violence in the country. Military officers exercise arbitrary and informal power over all aspects of Cambodian society and are linked with powerful economic interests. For example, logging firms use military guards to protect their activities and have known connections to politicians as well. The majority of cases of illegal logging and land grabbing involve soldiers and police.

Some regions of the country continued to see fighting with the remaining Khmer Rouge troops until the last Khmer Rouge left from their forest hide-outs in 1999. Factional street fighting in Phnom Penh between competing political parties in 1997 and a high level of petty crime left Cambodians with a deep feeling of insecurity.

Over the past decade, Cambodia has begun a process of market-oriented development, with an emphasis on foreign direct investment and private ownership of productive assets such as land. The signs of economic development are beginning to show, at least in Phnom Penh: buildings are going up all over, more and more people own motor scooters, and some even own cars. At the same time, rapid economic development has occurred without adequate protections for poor Cambodians unable to compete with foreign capital and in a context of widespread government corruption. This has resulted in a concentration of land ownership and increased poverty and landlessness in Cambodia.

Although Cambodia is a small country, about the size of Senegal or Uruguay, poor infrastructure and communications leave parts of the country isolated. As a result, most rural communities are beyond the reach of media, basic public services such as health care, and the government offices. Many rural areas are only visited by the NGOs working in their region.

Reemergence of Civil Society

There was no civil society activity in Cambodia during the Khmer Rouge regime, which completely monopolized all associational activities through its organization, known as Ankar. During the Vietnamese-installed government, the country was opened up and some international NGOs came in. During the 1980s a few international NGOs began to work on ending the US-led embargo against Cambodia: the American Friends Service Committee, the Mennonites, and Oxfam America. When UNTAC came in the early 1990s, there was a rapid influx of larger international development NGOs, which focused on service delivery. International NGO staff became a prominent part of the Phnom Penh landscape, driving around in large, white off-road vehicles while the rest of the population walked, biked, or got around on motor scooters. But there was still little space for Cambodians to organize independent associations. There was almost no history of national NGO activity before the war. There had been strict royal government control during the French colonial period and absolute restriction of autonomous organizing under the Khmer Rouge. In fact, some argue that except for the Buddhist support structures, Cambodian civil society is a brand new, totally imported phenomenon.[4]

International NGOs work on issues ranging from land mines to literacy, environment to women's workloads. Over the course of the 1990s, as the UN presence diminished and the national government became established, the international NGOs began to transfer the reins of their Cambodian operations to Cambodian nationals, at least in name. This process, referred to as "indigenization" of international NGOs, has been slow, and questioned by some. Critics say

that, in fact, it is little more than Cambodian window-dressing on what continue to be Western-funded organizations following Western-driven agendas and programs. Yet, at the same time, a few new and entirely Cambodian NGOs, especially in the human rights field, have begun to fill the space being granted by the government and the UNTAC period.

"We're basically in year seven in civil society development in Cambodia," said Joel Charny, former Oxfam America policy director and deputy program manager of the UNDP CARERE program in Cambodia.[5] Talking about the influx of international NGOs, and the gradual transition to Cambodian-led NGOs, he says: "First, NGOs focused on survival. Then, it was figuring out what to work on. Now, maybe on to policy work." There are currently close to three hundred NGOs in Cambodia, of which about half are run by Cambodians.

Reformers within Government

Some government agencies, such as the Ministry of Rural Development (MRD) and the Ministry of Environment (MoE), share civil society concerns about poverty. They also want to reform Cambodian laws to be more transparent and benefit all Cambodians. These ministries, newly established in the 1990s, have been struggling to defend themselves from competition and administrative jealousies from other government agencies, but have provided a source of allies inside government for many of the NGO initiatives in Cambodia.

For example, MRD has advocated for participatory processes focusing on the decentralization process. Under its programs, about twenty-four hundred people's organizations, known as Village Development Committees (VDCs), have been created. The VDCs are democratically elected by community members with NGO and MRD support, and work to forward the interests of village members in local development initiatives. The MoE has been raising environmental concerns such as pollution, toxic wastes, wildlife poaching, and the need for environmental impact assessments of major projects. Both of these initiatives have been supported by various donor agencies such as the World Bank and the Asia Development Bank.

4. Personal interview, Joel Charny, former deputy Program manager, UNDP CARERE project, November 2000.

5. Charny, interview, April 1999.

But these receptive ministries and officials at all levels of government who support more transparent and participatory government also face risks for taking the positions they do, particularly if they become involved in controversial issues like logging and land ownership. In both these areas, powerful interests stand to lose a great deal if the status quo is changed. Cambodians pursuing human rights and illegal logging investigations have disappeared in the past.

Despite these exceptions, most Cambodian government ministries, and the military especially, are not accessible or accountable to civil society. Unchecked, corruption is widespread, and arbitrary acts of violence are common and go unpunished. One area where this has profound impact on the poor in Cambodia is land ownership. The next section discusses efforts by international and national NGOs to address issues of land conflicts and landlessness that are emerging, in part, as a result of government corruption, predatory private-sector development practices, and the unchecked abuse of official power.

Land Tenure and Land Conflicts in Cambodia

More than 85 percent of Cambodians are farmers, living in rural areas and relying entirely on agriculture. The poorest 70 percent of Cambodians hold only 4 percent of all land. Landlessness is growing rapidly in Cambodia. At present, the number of landless poor amounts to 10 percent in some regions. It is still an emerging phenomenon, but will prove disastrous if nothing is done to reverse the trend. Multiple factors are leading to the growing crisis. There is increased population resulting from returning refugees and natural population growth. There has been a loss of common-property resources under the present land law. With the shift to market-based development, private development is encroaching on wetlands, forests, and fisheries. Land disputes are on the rise, and there is less land available for cultivation. Land grabbing by powerful figures and land speculations by local and foreign investors are widespread, much of it by or with the complicity of military personnel. By one estimate, one rural family in five is affected by land disputes.[6]

Based on this new reality, development and human rights NGOs realized that the situation of landlessness would only worsen if nothing were done. Further, increasing landlessness threatened to put the government's poverty-eradication policy in question. Because of this, the landlessness issue began to draw the attention of external donor agencies.

The current land-tenure structure was established in 1989, at the end of the Vietnamese occupation of Cambodia. Unlike China and Vietnam, which have taken cautious steps toward revamping their economies, then-fledgling socialist Cambodia undertook its reform process quickly and with limited knowledge of legal frameworks. As a consequence, the laws created were problematic. The Vietnamese-installed Phnom Penh government dissolved collective production groups (*krom samaki*) and distributed all lands to their individual members. Since then, each household in Cambodia has theoretically had private holding or ownership of land. But they rarely possess land-title documentary evidence.

A new land law was enacted by the State of Cambodia in 1992. But the 1992 land law does not provide enough protection for vulnerable groups, since only about 10 percent of the total population have land-title documents, which require long and complex administrative procedures to obtain. Officials in charge of land titling are sometimes corrupt. Those who have title reside mainly in urban areas, leaving most people in rural areas unprotected by the law.

The Cambodian government, with pressure and support from NGOs, local communities, and donors, particularly the Asia Development Bank (ADB), is now revising the existing land law. The stakes are high, not only for Cambodian farmers but for the NGOs that work with them. Both NGOs and affected communities have struggled to raise their concerns with the government.

Oxfam Great Britain and UNDP Work on the Land Law

NGOs and UN programs working in Cambodia became involved in the land-law revision process because of three major concerns: (1) rights abuses, (2) the failure of poverty-alleviation efforts, and (3) success and sustainability of their projects.

---

6. R. Biddulph, *Making the Poor More Visible—Where Has All the Land Gone?* vol. 4 (Phnom Penh: Oxfam Great Britain, 2000).

The majority of NGOs in Cambodia work with the rural poor. Their many micro-projects—rice banks, animal banks, saving and credit schemes, improvement and rehabilitation of irrigation facilities, provision of technical training and extension, and so on—were aimed at improving agricultural productivity in order to increase food security and reduce poverty. But the landless poor could hardly benefit from their projects. Realizing the growing landlessness issue threatened the success and sustainability of their poverty-alleviation efforts, international and local NGOs began to turn their attention to the land law, seeking a more structural solution to the problem.

To tackle the problem they have combined different approaches to influence land law: (1) gathering facts and information from affected communities, (2) collecting petitions from affected groups, (3) networking with each other to share information and raise awareness through various workshops and other activities, and (4) using pressure from donor agencies and governments to convince the Cambodian government to open the process to civil society input.

Oxfam Great Britain (Oxfam GB) and the United Nations Development Program (UNDP) collaborated with a group of Cambodian NGOs to play a lead role in the land-law revision process. The next sections describe how they collaborated with national and local NGOs and the Cambodian government to influence the land law.

Oxfam Great Britain and the Land Law Working Group: Alliance Advocacy Using Traditional Western Advocacy Approaches

Oxfam Great Britain had been aware of landlessness and land-tenure issues through its program work over the years in Cambodia and decided to start a program to address the policy issues directly. Oxfam GB hired a project coordinator, Shaun Williams, to start working on it. Based in Phnom Penh, Williams worked with the NGO Forum on Cambodia, a Phnom Penh–based networking NGO that provides space for NGO community discussions and carries out advocacy training for NGO leaders. Together, they identified and contacted national NGOs with community-development programs throughout the country. Together they formed the Land Law Working Group.

The Land Law Working Group was made up of the Cambodian Human Rights and Development Association (ADHOC), the Bar Association of the Kingdom of Cambodia, and Legal Aid of Cambodia, among others. Its goal was to curb the trend in landlessness and institute land-ownership protections for the rural poor by influencing the new land law using common Western policy-influence strategies.

A major opening for the Land Law Working Group happened when the government of Cambodia agreed to open the land-law review process to civil society input. Getting this opening was remarkable, given the Hun Sen government's historic resistance to this kind of input, and the extremely hierarchical nature of Cambodian society, in general. How did this happen?

The Land Law Working Group knew that the government was not going to allow nongovernmental involvement, based on its history. The members also knew that Cambodia is highly dependent on donor funding, representing 167 percent of the country's annual revenues.[7] Cambodia's accumulated foreign debt amounts to 80 percent of current gross domestic product (GDP).[8] They decided to take a roundabout way and try to get funders to put open consultation with civil society as a condition of ongoing funding. Williams attended a Consultative Group[9] meeting in Tokyo to lobby donors. There, he made contact with staff from the Japanese International Volunteer Committee (JVC), whom he had worked with before. They were also interested in the land-law reform issue. Through this connection, Williams began to feed land-law information to JVC. They translated the documents into Japanese and shared with other NGOs in Japan. The Japanese NGOs got very interested in the issue and began to mobilize to put pressure on the Japanese government. The Japanese government became uncomfortable with all the pressure from NGOs and put pressure on the ADB to push the Royal Government of Cambodia to change the land law. Under mounting pressure, the ADB put revision of the land law—with civil society input—as a condi-

---

7. M. Godfrey et al., *Technical Assistance in an Aid-Dependent Economy: The Experience of Cambodia,* CDRI Working Paper 15 (Phnom Penh: CDRI, 2000).

8. World Bank, *Cambodia Country Assistance Strategy* (Washington, D.C.: World Bank, 2000).

9. Consultative Group meetings are annual meetings of donor governments and multilateral donor agencies like the World Bank and the Asia Development Bank, when donors agree to a set of common priorities and coordinate lending programs.

tionality[10] for continued aid. "We turned a threat into an opportunity by using international NGO networking to good effect," says Williams, adding that "now comes that hard part," of developing specific proposals with the rest of the NGO community, doing stakeholder consultations, building alliances, negotiating, and making compromises.[11]

Once the process was opened for civil society input into the land-law revision process, Oxfam GB's Williams and the Land Law Working Group began to mount a campaign to develop a unified and informed NGO position on the land law. They commissioned two case studies on land expropriations and the lack of legal recourse in Cambodia. They developed a land-dispute database to catalog and quantify the extent of the land-dispute issue. They developed a report arguing for specific changes to the land-titling process and hired a media person to mount a public opinion campaign on the land law. "This is a new model for Cambodia, participating in policy development," says Shaun Williams. "Obviously, it can't be built overnight."[12]

During the period of proposal development, Oxfam GB, ADHOC, the Cambodian Bar Association, and Legal Aid of Cambodia met biweekly on an informal basis to plan and coordinate their activities. They began drafting an "NGO" proposal for the land law and shared the proposal with the larger NGO community. Translations were an important part of their outreach and consultation process. They were key to fostering participation from NGOs and their constituencies that don't speak English.

At the same time, Oxfam GB's Shaun Williams focused on building the advocacy capacity of initiative partners. He wanted the process to increase their knowledge of the substantive issues but also develop their advocacy skills. He used collaborative research and case studies on specific issues as a vehicle for this. Together they looked at policy and its implications in the specific cases and developed hypothetical advocacy campaigns. For example, in one case study, they looked at a village where Oxfam GB had been working. Landlessness had increased from 0 to 35 percent, but no one

knew why. When they did the fieldwork, they discovered that the Oxfam-supported irrigation project had created land speculation. This was causing the consolidation of land ownership and pushing the poorest people off their lands. They concluded that part of the problem was that the project designers had not talked with the local people and only worked through the district development council. By looking at this level, it was also easy to see that there was a growing issue of land speculation, and a need to address it at the policy level.

UNDP Land-Law Advocacy: Collaboration with Local-Level Government in the Interest of Communities

At the same time that Oxfam GB was working with national NGOs in the Land Law Working Group, the UNDP was also working on the land law. But its approach was much more collaborative with the Cambodian government. As part of its mission to build the capacity of the new government, the UNDP worked hand-in-hand with government institutions, particularly at the local level. One example of UNDP local-level engagement with the government on land-law issues comes from Ratanakkiri Province in northeast Cambodia, along the Laos and Vietnamese boarders.

The UNDP CARERE project hired a natural-resources-management consultant, contracted with ADHOC to do land-ownership research, and helped establish the local Land Study Group in Ratanakkiri Province. There, highland indigenous groups are struggling to protect their rights to ancestral forests in the face of logging concessions granted at the central government level. Also, because of land speculation and land concentration, prime lowland agricultural lands are coming under control of private companies based outside the region. The local Land Study Group is made up of local staff from the NGOs, the Non-Timber Forest Products group (NTFP), the Comité International pour le Développment et la Solidarité Européen (CIDSE), the UNDP/CARERE Seila Program, ADHOC, and provincial officials from the Land Title Department and the Forestry Department, among others. Their role is to work with local communities to analyze local land-conflict issues and present alternatives.

The Land Study Group helped local communities prepare natural-resource-management plans and

---

10. "Conditionality" is the term used by donors to refer to specific policy or program-implementation requirements attached to loans.
11. Personal interview, Shaun Williams, Oxfam Great Britain, April 2000.
12. Williams, interview.

community-based forestry-management plans. These plans helped show that communities were willing and able to propose development strategies, and wanted to contribute to a new land-tenure structure. The plans were developed in consultation with local government, and got approval and buy-in at the local-government level. Although the plans alone are not enough to change the land law, they serve as concrete evidence of the need for the new law to encompass collective-ownership structures and community management over common resources, such as forests and fisheries.

Ratanakkiri Province Land Conflicts, Local Advocacy, and the Land Law

Highlander communities in Ratanakkiri Province are worried about degradation of the forest that they rely on for non-timber forest products. Their forests are threatened by lumber-extraction activities by foreign companies granted concessions by the national government. The highlander communities want to protect their community forests, which they self-manage based on traditional practices of hunting and harvesting nuts, rattan, bamboo, and other forest products. One of the aims of the NGO proposal for the land law is to enable highlander groups to continue managing their forests in a sustainable manner. Under the proposed land law, community forest areas would be legally recognized and protected.

Highlander communities have witnessed the negative impacts of forest degradation due to logging. They stress the importance of sustainable management of their forest that they have followed since the beginning of time. Their goal is to hold on to their community forests and to participate in timber-extraction concession planning and monitoring in order to ensure that timber companies are not intruding on their ancestral lands. NTFP and CIDSE have been working with highlander communities to develop community forestry plans that demonstrate their ongoing management of non-timber forest products and delineate the areas traditionally used by villagers. Despite work on these plans, without participation in the concession process, the national technical agencies have often granted concessions to private timber-extraction companies in villagers' ancestral spirit forests and villages. In many cases, concessions have been granted on top of designated protected areas and national parks.

The Taiwanese Hero timber company had been granted a concession by the central Cambodian government in one of the areas traditionally used by the highlander ethnic Kreung peoples. The villagers consider the area near their village their "spirit forest" because it holds their ancestors' spirits. Hero had cut a road right past their villages to access their concession area. The members of one village decided they did not want the loggers coming in because they did not trust them to respect their spirit forest. So they detained some Hero company staff and demanded a "fine." After the fine was paid, they were allowed to go. But the message was clear: the loggers were no longer welcome in the Kreung area. One villager commented:

> Before, we were like animals in the forest. We were illiterate and uneducated. We did not know anything, and lived in an isolated world. We had very limited access to information and knowledge. When we saw strangers, good or bad, we would run away. But we did know about our traditional rights, which we inherited from our ancestors, to the forest and land on which we live. But now we have learned a lot from these organizations working with us about human rights, legal rights to resources, about illegal logging, and how to manage our community forests sustainably. With this knowledge we now stand firm against those illegal logging operators and outside pressures.[13]

They now had the full attention of the provincial officials. Ministry of Environment officials went out with Hero company officials to negotiate with the villagers, but had no luck changing their minds. Hero company staff tried to appease village leaders with gifts of rice, but the village stood firm. Realizing that the villagers were steadfast in their position, local Ministry of Forestry officials from Ratanakkiri Province called a meeting with Hero company officials and the two NGOs working in the Kreung villages, NTFP and CIDSE. The forestry officials realized that they had no control over the villages and sought the support of NGO staff to bring them in line. The NGOs argued that Kreung villagers should be at the meeting, but the forestry official held the meeting before they could come.

---

13. Personal interview, Tumpoun villager, highland area in Ratanakkiri Province, April 1999.

NTFP's position at the meeting was that it could not speak for the villagers and that the forestry officials should negotiate directly with them. During the meeting, Hero company and the forestry officials were pushing to grant the Kreung access only to degraded forestry areas in exchange for their letting the Hero company log the prime areas of the concession. They wanted NTFP staff to "agree" to this on behalf of the villagers. "What can NTFP do? We can do research with the community to see what they want. But the role of negotiations with the community and Hero is the forestry ministry's. We are happy to coordinate, if that is helpful," said Gordon Paterson, the American director of NTPF. "No, we want you to be the representative," responded the official from the forestry ministry, adding that "what we agree today, you will explain to the communities." But NTFP staff stood firm, and by the end of the meeting, they had hammered out an agreement to form a research team of Hero officials, NTFP and CIDSE staff, and forestry and land-title representatives. The team would work with the villagers to delineate areas to be preserved for community forestry, according to the villages' plans.[14]

The highlander villagers were not only concerned with the specific timber concession near their villages. Through CIDSE and NTFP, they were participating in the land-law consultation process. "We heard recently that the land law is being re-drafted. We want to have our concerns considered and incorporated into the new land law," said one ethnic highlander Kreung villager.[15] But in order for them to participate in the concession process and secure their rights to community forests under the new land law, they need the help of outsiders. They lack access to government officials and many do not even speak Khmer. They also face real risks in making their concerns public, because it could be seen as a challenge to government officials who may be benefiting from the concessions. "To make our voice stronger, we need to join with people in other villages. But above all else, we need legal and official recognition from the national government that we have rights to the resources here so that we can have a ground to defend ourselves against abuses. To make this happen, we need outside organizations to help us deal with the government, because we rarely see government officials here in our village."[16]

As the Ratanakkiri example shows, through the UNDP's support, local communities and NGOs have an opportunity to have face-to-face dialogue about the issue with central-government officials. The Land Study Group has arranged for central-government officials to visit Ratanakkiri Province to observe the local situation. At the same time, the UNDP has undertaken research and information collection (such as a case study on the Prek Thnaot Multi-purpose Water Project, the Land Study in Ratanakkiri, and others). Their contribution to the process is crucial because they present the local situations to decision makers, lawmakers, legal experts, various stakeholders, and others for appropriate consideration and action through formal channels.

The UNDP approach to the land law is different from the Land Law Working Group supported by Oxfam Great Britain. It stems from the UNDP mission to work in collaboration with government agencies and their staff, crafting proposals together with them. "Effective collaboration with government is very important. Groups doing advocacy can't define themselves as being 'in opposition' to things" in Cambodia, says Rosemary McCreery, director of the UN Center for Human Rights.[17] The Oxfam Great Britain–supported Land Law Working Group's work also sought to make constructive proposals, but working as an external actor that was able to challenge government somewhat more than UNDP.

The Land Law Working Group and the UNDP used multiple advocacy approaches to influence the land-law revision process: case studies, natural-resource and community-forestry plans, a database of land disputes, and the draft NGO-proposed land-law text. Through these, they were able to play a critical role in advising the central government on the land-law revision. They had gathered technical experts, conducted case studies, collected evidence from their land-disputes database and the case studies, and used the demonstration effect of community natural-resource-management plans. And they presented concrete proposals for the land law. Although this case study was prepared before the final outcome

---

14. This section is based on personal observations during the meeting, April 1999.

15. Personal interview, ethnic highlander Kreung villager in Ratanakkiri Province, April 1999.

16. Kreung villager, interview.

17. Personal interview, Rosemary McCreery, director of the UN Center for Human Rights, April 1999.

of the land-law revision campaign, it is clear that the process had captured the imagination of community groups and national NGOs alike. And it was clear that government officials were beginning to take notice of the campaign.

The next section draws on the reflections of national and international NGOs and on the land-law revision experience to describe an evolving understanding of advocacy in Cambodia.

Advocacy in Cambodia: Emerging Definitions[18]

Advocacy was just emerging in Cambodia in the 1990s. The idea of collective action and participating in (never mind challenging) the government's activities was so strongly suppressed during the Khmer Rouge period that it is difficult to discuss. Advocacy is often seen by government, and some in civil society, as being against government. NGOs are *anti*-governmental organizations, and therefore political, and should be stopped. Many consider it dangerous to do advocacy in Cambodia. Civil society organizations in Cambodia are struggling to construct a new Cambodian understanding of advocacy and a new way of doing advocacy. Some tentative ideas are emerging from this effort.

"Struggling for an Idea"

No single word in Khmer can fully express the meaning of the English word "advocacy." Most English-Khmer dictionaries translate it as *Kamtror,*[19] which means "support." Long discussions in the NGO community in Cambodia were sponsored by the NGO Forum on Cambodia to identify a Khmer phrase that can represent advocacy as Cambodian civil society understands it. The participants decided that the phrase *karts Umti*, meaning "struggling for an idea," should be used. It is already entering the lexicon in Cambodia. But there is a feeling among some that it is too strong, since the notion of *struggling* may connote more of an adversarial relationship, and po-

lite diplomacy better describes how most advocacy actually works in Cambodia.

"Lobbying for an Idea"

This phrase reflects a definition of advocacy, expressed by many groups, similar to "struggling for an idea." But it is a bit softer, referring to a more polite, humble mode of working, especially when dealing with high-ranking government officials. It suggests an effort to persuade government to accept a view, which is of importance and value to all of society. Advocacy in this sense would be to offer solutions that help government address a concern that is shared by many people. It is the opposite of accusing or demanding action, which would be considered very clumsy and offensive, and would generate animosity among government officials.

Doing Political Work

Some groups believe that advocacy is and should be political work. They believe that development work alone is not enough to help poor and marginalized people. Civil society organizations should speak out against unfair decisions, views, and policies of the government. While they feel this approach to advocacy enables them to be more active in government decision making, they acknowledge that it is dependent on democratic space. Although there is more space in Cambodia now, it is still tentative. When advocacy is viewed as political work, it raises the fear that it would be seen as something against the government. And political activists have real reason to fear for their lives in Cambodia. "Advocacy is risky, yes, but if we don't do it, who will? No one wants to go back to the dictatorship. So we have to move forward," said a Cambodian environmental activist.[20] Yet many still shy from taking approaches that could be seen as political or challenging government.

Amplification of the Voice of Others

Many NGOs work directly with communities on development work and focus on the interests of these communities. They often come to see their role as making the voice of these people heard, at least by the national government, and as influencing policy

---

18. This section draws heavily on the work of the NGO Forum on Cambodia, which had held numerous workshops to discuss advocacy in Cambodia and the Khmer language. It also draws on our interviews, in which we asked members of civil society to reflect on their understandings of advocacy in Cambodia today.

19. This Khmer word can also be transliterated into English as *KaMRT.*

---

20. Personal interview, Cambodian activist, April 1999.

and decision making at that level. A number of international NGOs have carried out advocacy projects in Cambodia based on this view. They see advocacy as the amplification of the voice of the communities they work with. They feel that having that voice heard is important to the success of their projects and the long-term benefit of the communities and justifies taking a direct advocacy role on behalf of the communities.

One example of this is the work of Global Witness, a small NGO based out of the United Kingdom that has done pioneering work to expose the practice of illegal logging by the Khmer Rouge and the Cambodian government. "Global Witness has put the mining and logging issues on the map," says Joel Charny.[21] "They're basically like environmental cowboys, going in under cover, taking pictures, getting documents, and sneaking back out again," says Ngan Nguyen, program coordinator for Oxfam America's Southeast Asia Program.[22] "I would attribute 100 percent of the success on logging to Global Witness," says Doug Henderson, Phnom Penh–based independent consultant on community forestry and resource management, referring to the significant decrease in illegal logging between 1997 and 1999.[23] Global Witness reports documenting logging practices—including classified government documents demonstrating complicity with the illegal trade—made a tremendous impact on World Bank lending policies to Cambodia. As in the land-law revision experience, it was this outside pressure that proved the key to turning the situation around. At the same time, the NGO Forum on Cambodia translated their reports and distributed them widely throughout Cambodia. Government officials frequently had stray Global Witness reports lying on their tables during interviews and referred to them frequently to report on their efforts to curb the logging.

"It would have been unconceivable that anyone would do anything about illegal logging locally," says Kathy Knight, former Oxfam America advocacy officer who helped Global Witness make preliminary contacts with World Bank staff in Washington, D.C.[24] In the mid 1990s, the rate of deforestation in Cam-

bodia was seven to eleven times the sustainable yield. According to the World Bank, if logging continued at its current rate, there would be no forests left by the year 2000. Under these circumstances, something had to be done. "You cannot be ideological, take an a priori position that advocacy has to be done by Cambodians. No Cambodians would have been able to do what Global Witness has done, and probably won't for another five years," says Joel Charny.[25]

As the political space opens, however, it becomes more and more possible for international and national NGOs to collaborate on advocacy efforts and for national NGOs to lead advocacy. One important initiative to support the transition to Cambodian-led advocacy is the NGO Forum on Cambodia's work to demystify advocacy and build the advocacy capacity of national NGO staff and members of grassroots organizations.

Conclusion

Civil society is just recently emerging in Cambodia, and the practice of advocacy is completely new. This study is a first attempt to explore Cambodian civil society concepts of and ways of doing advocacy. It documents some of the advocacy experiences by local community groups, national NGOs, and international NGOs working within and outside of Cambodia, focusing on decision making in natural-resource management specifically in relation to the land-law revision process. We hope it can form the foundation for future discussions within and outside of Cambodia.

The definitions of advocacy that emerge from our interviews with civil society organizations in Cambodia are numerous. But the weight seems to be put on polite engagement rather than combative criticism or denunciation. Nevertheless, advocacy has a political element, because it seeks to change the power relations between poor and excluded groups—mainly rural farmers, hillspeople, and landless peasants—and governing forces, including the military. Therefore, it has been seen as a dangerous activity, because it is seen as acting against the government, and democratic space is still limited in Cambodia.

21. Charny, interview.

22. Personal interview, Ngan Nguyen, Oxfam America Southeast Asia program coordinator, March 1999.

23. Personal interview, Doug Henderson, independent consultant, April 1999.

24. Personal interview, Kathy Knight, former Oxfam America Policy Department staff, March 1999.

25. Charny, interview.

There are many difficulties and challenges in doing advocacy in Cambodia today. The influence of civil society in decision making around natural-resource management and the environment, as well as in other spheres, would not be possible without pressure from international actors such as donors and development organizations. The opportunities for advocacy also depend on democratic space. There is still a long distance to go.

At present, to best support advocacy or civil society in Cambodia, numerous kinds of support are needed. Capacity building, ongoing funding support, and continued international presence in the country are needed. In addition, the national government should be encouraged to enact adequate laws and enforcement mechanisms and to gradually widen the democratic space for civil society to participate in decision making. At the same time, civil society organizations in Cambodia must begin to forge their own path and become self-sufficient.

Chapter 12

Ecuador: The Campaign against Texaco Oil

Tamara L. Jezic

We must let the world know how the Cofan People have suffered because of Texaco. There has been continuous disease in our communities since the arrival of the company. Our waters are completely contaminated. Pregnant women have spontaneous abortions and children are born with illnesses we have never seen before. Many people are dying of cancer. Because of the roads and colonization of the forest, we are losing our customs as a people. I can tell you how much a piece of wood costs, but not the value of a young Cofan who has lost his culture. That has no price.[1]

In this statement, José Quenamá, a leader of the Cofan indigenous nationality of Ecuador's Amazon rain forest, describes how his people have struggled for physical and cultural survival since Texaco Petroleum Company began oil operations in traditional Cofan lands. Quenamá is one of the thirty thousand indigenous and settler residents of the Ecuadorian Amazon affected by Texaco's exploration and exploitation activities from 1967 to 1992. According to Ecuadorian government estimates, Texaco spilled 16.8 million gallons of crude oil into the Amazon River system and dumped 19 billion gallons of toxic waste waters directly into the environment during its operations.[2] The company built a network of roads that opened up 2.5 million acres of tropical rain forest to deforestation and colonization, resulting in the displacement of Cofan, Secoya, and Siona peoples from their traditional lands.[3] As this case study is being written, no action has been taken to undo the harm done by past oil development. Today, the Ecuadorian national oil company

continues to use the same equipment left behind by Texaco, and the contamination continues.

The Cofan, Secoya, Siona, and settler populations of the Ecuadorian Amazon are among the key actors in a precedent-setting, ten-year campaign to hold Texaco Petroleum Company accountable for its harms to the Amazonian people and environment. One of the most successful aspects of the Texaco campaign has been its ability to bring together participants at the grassroots, national, and international levels. The strategies implemented by the various actors have included organization and popular education among Amazonian communities, protests in Quito, engagement with Ecuadorian government officials, and a class-action lawsuit against Texaco in US federal court. The longevity of the campaign can be attributed to these strategies all interacting, depending upon, and sustaining one another. The Texaco campaign seeks to change the course of decades of corporate impunity for devastation caused in Southern countries, expand international law, and hold a US transnational corporation accountable for its damages abroad—for the first time—under US and international human rights law.

This case study examines the context of oil development in Ecuador and describes Texaco's operations and impacts on the Amazonian people and their environment. It explores the Texaco campaign through its various stages, focusing on local organizing and national mobilizations and later when the US federal lawsuit became the focal point for ongoing campaign activities. The case notes, but does not explore in detail, international solidarity actions around the Texaco campaign. The study concludes with an analysis of the most important successes, particularly forming and strengthening settler and indigenous organizations, increasing the capacities of local communities to articulate and press for their rights, and raising

---

1. Personal interview, José Quenamá, Organización Indígena de la Nacionalidad Cofan del Ecuador (ONICE), September 1999.
2. Judith Kimerling, *Amazon Crude* (New York: Natural Resources Defense Council, 1991), 65–69.
3. Kimerling, *Amazon Crude,* 75–77.

the consciousness of Ecuadorian citizens about the importance of the Amazon and its people.

The Ecuadorian Context

The Ecuadorian Amazon, known as the "Oriente," encompasses an area of over thirteen million hectares (thirty-two million acres) of tropical rain forest and is one of the most biologically diverse ecosystems in the world.[4] The Oriente is home to approximately two hundred thousand indigenous people of nine nationalities—Shuar, Achuar, Quichua, Huaorani, Secoya, Siona, Cofan, Shiwiar, and Zapara—who have lived in the rain forest for centuries. Most indigenous communities rely on hunting, fishing, and cultivation of crops for nourishment, use hundreds of plant species for medicinal, religious, and domestic purposes, and bathe, cook, fish, and wash clothes in rivers, streams, and lakes.[5]

The Ecuadorian Amazon is also home to 250,000 to 300,000 settlers, also called *colonos* or campesinos, who followed the oil roads into the rain forest. Settlers were encouraged by Ecuadorian laws of the 1960s and 1970s that proclaimed colonization of the Oriente an urgent national priority, declared the Oriente "uninhabited," and offered title to settlers who cleared the land and put it to "productive" use.[6] Conflicts have existed between settler and indigenous groups for years, as settlers' arrival placed greater pressure on indigenous peoples' land, natural resources, and culture.

Oil-producing zones of the Oriente are home to some of the poorest communities in Ecuador, which lack potable water and basic health and sanitation services.[7] While oil revenues account for approximately 45 percent of the national budget, less than 3 percent of the budget is invested in oil-producing areas.[8] Furthermore, while its economy experienced rapid growth during the oil boom years, Ecuador emerged from this period with a crippling foreign debt, growing from $500 million in 1975 to $14.7 billion in 1996.[9] Today 70 percent of Ecuadorians live in poverty.[10]

Additionally, the structure and policies of the Ecuadorian government favor the interests of foreign corporations at the expense of its citizens and environment. The executive branch dominates the government, which reestablished democracy in 1979 after seven years of military rule.[11] The judiciary is characterized by corruption, lack of resources, and vulnerability to political and economic pressures.[12] The state retains ownership rights to all subsurface minerals and provides incentives to foreign firms through favorable foreign investment laws and minimal environmental protection. Although the Ecuadorian Constitution has recognized the "right to live in an environment free from contamination" since 1984, environmental protection laws remain weak, nonexistent, or unenforced.[13]

Ecuadorian society and government discriminate against indigenous people, Afro-Ecuadorians, and the poor. Indigenous peoples, who make up 45 percent of the country's population, have been organizing since the 1960s and have emerged as a powerful sector in Ecuadorian society and politics. CONAIE, the Confederación de Nacionalidades Indígenas del Ecuador (Confederation of Indigenous Nationalities of Ecuador), was founded in 1986 to unite highland and Amazonian indigenous peoples in claiming their rights to land, bilingual education, and respect for their identity.[14] In 1990, thousands of indigenous people awakened Ecuadorian society to the importance of indigenous peoples in a week-long *levantamiento* (uprising), which shut Ecuador down with roadblocks, land seizures, and occupations of local government offices.[15] Since then, the indigenous movement has held several nationwide mobilizations,

4. Kimerling, *Amazon Crude*, 31–33.

5. Kimerling, *Amazon Crude*, 37.

6. Kimerling, *Amazon Crude*, 39–40.

7. Centro de Derechos Económicos y Sociales (CDES), *De Necesidades a Derechos: Reconociendo el Derecho a la Salud en el Ecuador* (Quito: CDES, 1998), 9.

8. Diana Jean Schemo, "Ecuadoreans Want Texaco to Clear Toxic Residue," *New York Times*, February 1, 1998.

9. *El Comercio*, September 29, 1997; cited in CDES, *De Necesidades a Derechos*, 8.

10. UNICEF, "Características de la Proforma Presupuestaria y del Gasto Social para el 2001" (November 2000).

11. Judith Kimerling, "The Environmental Audit of Texaco's Amazon Oil Fields: Environmental Justice or Business as Usual?" *Harvard Human Rights Journal* 7 (1994): 202.

12. Organization of American States, Inter-American Commission on Human Rights, *Report on the Situation of Human Rights in Ecuador* (Washington, D.C., 1997), 29.

13. Kimerling, "Environmental Audit," 207–8.

14. Personal interview, Ampam Karakas, Confederación de Nacionalidades Indígenas del Ecuador (CONAIE), September 1999.

15. Suzana Sawyer, "The 1992 Indian Mobilization in Lowland Ecuador," *Latin American Perspectives* 24 (1997): 69–70.

demanding legal recognition of ancestral territories, constitutional reform, participation in national policy formulation, and recognition of Ecuador as a plurinational state. Each indigenous *levantamiento* has forced the government to open dialogue with indigenous and other sectors of civil society to address their demands.

After years of protests, proposals, and dialogue with the government, the indigenous movement achieved two historic successes in 1998: Ecuador's ratification of International Labor Organization (ILO) Convention 169 concerning Indigenous and Tribal Peoples in Independent Countries and constitutional recognition of collective rights for indigenous peoples. The new Ecuadorian Constitution, adopted in 1998, declares Ecuador to be a "democratic, pluricultural, and multiethnic state"[16] and declares indigenous peoples to be subjects of collective rights, including the right to be consulted about exploration and exploitation of non-renewable resources in their lands, the right to participate in the benefits of these projects, and the right to receive compensation for the harms that these projects cause.[17] Rights of indigenous peoples remain largely declaratory, however, as the Ecuadorian government has never "consulted" indigenous peoples about plans concerning exploitation of natural resources in indigenous territories, and indigenous peoples have never enjoyed "participation" in the benefits of oil exploitation.

The voices of the people impacted by oil development are rarely heard in governmental and industry decisions affecting their lives, health, land, and culture. The Texaco campaign seeks to alter that reality.

Texaco's Operations and Impacts on Oriente Residents

The environmental, social, cultural, and economic effects of Texaco's activities were devastating. Texaco dumped over 4.3 million gallons of highly toxic production waters per day into unlined pits throughout the Oriente,[18] instead of re-injecting those toxic wastes deep into the earth as the company does in the United States.[19] Texaco was also responsible for thirty major spills in the 498 kilometer Trans-Ecuadorian Pipeline that runs from the Oriente to the west coast of Ecuador, spilling 16.8 million gallons of oil directly into the environment, more than 1.5 times the 10.8 million gallons spilled by the *Exxon Valdez* into Alaska's Prince William Sound.[20]

In 1992, Texaco's contract with the Ecuadorian government ended and the company handed over its operations to Petroecuador, the Ecuadorian national oil company. Petroecuador continues to operate approximately 235 oil wells designed and constructed by Texaco and continues to dump untreated production waters into hundreds of waste pits throughout the northern Oriente.[21]

Texaco's operations in the Oriente, a 1994 study by the Center for Economic and Social Rights (CESR) revealed, resulted in the release of waste waters containing toxic products linked to cancer. Oriente residents now face increased risk of cancer and neurological and reproductive problems as a result. The drinking, bathing, and fishing waters contain levels of toxic products ten to one hundred times the amount permitted by the US Environmental Protection Agency.[22]

Oil roads opened close to 2.5 million acres of indigenous territory to colonization, land speculation, deforestation, and other extractive industries.[23] This led to the appropriation of indigenous lands, introduction of new diseases to indigenous communities, undermining of traditional indigenous economies, and degradation of the natural resources on which the people depend.[24] In areas previously inhabited by thousands of indigenous peoples, today only hundreds remain.

---

16. Constitución Política de la República del Ecuador, Art. 1.

17. Constitución Política de la República del Ecuador, Art. 84.

18. Ministry of Energy and Mines, "I. Producciones de Petróleo, Agua de Formación y Gas Natural, Dic/89" (Quito, 1989), cited in Kimerling, *Amazon Crude*, 65.

19. During oil production, petroleum, natural gas, and highly toxic wastes known as "production waters" are extracted and pumped to a separation facility, where oil is separated from production waters and gas and sent through the pipeline. Production waters come from thousands of feet below the earth's surface and contain heavy metals, oil, and toxic levels of salt, as well as chemicals that have been used in the extraction process, drilling muds, and industrial cleaning solvents.

20. Kimerling, *Amazon Crude*, 69.

21. Kimerling, "Environmental Audit," 205.

22. Center for Economic and Social Rights, *Rights Violations in the Ecuadorian Amazon: The Human Consequences of Oil Development* (New York: CESR, 1994).

23. Kimerling, "Environmental Audit," 206.

24. Kimerling, *Amazon Crude*, 75–81.

Early Organization and Popular Education among Oriente Communities

During the initial years of oil development in the 1970s, people did not talk about problems of oil contamination or make the connection between health problems and contamination, even when they lived next to toxic waste pits. Arnulfo Angüisaca, a Shushufindi community leader, remembered: "The majority of campesinos thought that Texaco was good; they controlled the dust on the roads by pouring oil on the roads and people asked the oil truck to give them some crude. They didn't know that the company was poisoning their home and their animals."[25] When people began to get sick and saw that their cows and fish were dying, they didn't understand why. They thought it was destiny, bad luck, or the will of God.[26] Siona leader William Criollo related: "The Siona People didn't understand that oil could cause grave harm. The government and the indigenous leaders didn't know anything about oil. When the company came, they gave little gifts, food, tools, and clothes to the Siona People. The Siona culture began to transform. We thought, 'This is good. This is development.' The leaders trusted Texaco."[27]

The process of community organization and popular education slowly began to change the lack of understanding about effects of oil contamination. People began to question their beliefs that illness and contamination were inevitable. Settler communities began to organize in the late 1970s to reflect and act upon the problems they faced, especially conflicts over land with the Ecuadorian government.[28] When a 1987 earthquake destroyed the roads leading to the northern Oriente and left the region isolated, women's, farming, and Catholic organizations united to confront urgent necessities.[29] Local human rights committees were established in coordination with the Catholic Church in response to rights violations by the Ecuadorian military. Later, human rights committees expanded to include other social organizations and began to re-

spond to violations such as domestic violence and conflicts between oil workers and companies.[30]

Indigenous communities in the area affected by Texaco began to organize in the 1970s in response to the forces that were encroaching upon their lands and threatening their survival. The Cofan, Secoya, Siona, and Quichua peoples formed OINCE, OISE, ONISE, and FCUNAE, respectively, to press for legalization of their ancestral territories and respect for their language, cultures, and identities.

The Capuchin and Carmelite Catholic missions worked with settler and indigenous communities to raise awareness of the impacts of oil activities and to introduce the idea that Texaco's contamination was a violation of human rights.[31] They also helped local people write letters of complaints. Angüisaca remembered, "When the company damaged our land, we thought the state and the company had all the rights. As we carried out critical analysis in popular education with the missions, we saw that we were equal as persons and that we had the same rights and the same obligations. And we began to realize that they didn't have to keep contaminating us."[32] Catholic missions began to frame the problem of oil contamination in terms of human rights violations in the 1980s, planting the seed for organizing and advocacy work in the 1990s.

The Campaign to Hold Texaco Accountable

Texaco's environmental and cultural impacts were first brought to international attention in 1991 by Judith Kimerling's seminal book, *Amazon Crude*. Also in the early 1990s, international activist organizations and committed legal professionals began to work with fledgling indigenous and settler organizations. Rain Forest Action Network (RAN), the Center for Economic and Social Rights,[33] Oxfam America, and the Coalition for Amazonian Peoples

---

25. Personal interview, Arnulfo Angüisaca, leader from Shushufindi community, September 1999.

26. Personal interviews, Arnulfo Angüisaca; Manuel Pallares, biologist; Isauro Puente, medical doctor, September 1999.

27. Personal interview, William Criollo, Organización de la Nacionalidad Indígena Siona del Ecuador (ONISE), September 1999.

28. Personal interview, Angüisaca.

29. Personal interview, Luis Yanza, president, Frente de Defensa de la Amazonía, September 1999.

30. Personal interview, Carmen Allauca, president, Comité de Derechos Humanos del Nororiente, September 1999.

31. Personal interview, Paulina Garzón, executive director, Centro de Derechos Económicos y Sociales, March 2000.

32. Personal interview, Angüisaca.

33. The Center for Economic and Social Rights (CESR) established a Latin American office, Centro de Derechos Económicos y Sociales (CESR), in Quito in 1997. In this case study, "Center for Economic and Social Rights" refers to the US-based international NGO, while "Centro de Derechos Económicos y Sociales" refers to the Quito-based, Ecuadorian NGO.

and their Environment, as well as some key individuals, put out publications, coordinated international solidarity actions, and began to bring the plight of Oriente residents to the attention of the international community.[34]

RAN, together with CONFENIAE, the Confederación de Nacionalidades Indígenas de la Amazonía Ecuatoriana (Confederation of Indigenous Nationalities of the Ecuadorian Amazon, created in the early 1980s), and Ecuadorian environmental NGOs visited the Ecuadorian Amazon several times, speaking with indigenous organizations and disseminating information about oil contamination in Ecuador internationally. The combination of nascent community organizing, an emerging debate on human rights violations of oil activity, and involvement of international activists all provided a favorable environment for a campaign to challenge Texaco's irresponsible oil development in the Oriente.[35]

The Quito-based NGO Acción Ecológica (Ecological Action) assumed the role of leading and coordinating the campaign to challenge petroleum exploitation in the Amazon. In March 1990, a coalition of environmental NGOs came together to launch the Amazonía por la Vida (Amazon for Life) campaign, which focused on protecting indigenous territories and ecologically fragile areas of the Amazon from oil activity. The campaign centered on preventing Conoco Oil Company from exploring for oil in Yasuní National Park and on pressing for a moratorium of all oil activity in sensitive areas.[36]

It soon became clear to Acción Ecológica that the Texaco case was going to be a huge part of the struggle to hold oil companies accountable for their actions in Ecuador. Acción officially launched its campaign against Texaco with a nonviolent occupation of Texaco's office in Quito on June 28, 1991. Acción focused on two main strategies in the early years: pressuring the Ecuadorian government to carry out an environmental audit to determine Texaco's impacts and costs of environmental remediation and promoting a national and international letter-writing campaign and a Texaco boycott.[37]

Texaco's concession for oil development reached its end in 1992, and Texaco pulled out of Ecuador. In response to pressure from environmental and indigenous groups, Petroecuador announced that HBT Agra Limited, a Canadian consulting firm, would conduct an "independent and impartial" environmental audit of Texaco's activities.[38] The audit was viewed, however, as neither impartial nor independent. Texaco and Petroecuador not only selected the firm to carry out the audit but designed the audit's terms of reference as well.[39] When the report came out, its conclusions were denounced as absurd by local environmental groups, congresspeople, and industry experts alike.[40] The report mentioned animals that do not exist in the Amazon, grossly understated oil damages, and called for a woefully inadequate program to clean up the mess.[41]

Acción Ecológica began to work with María Eugenia Lima, a sympathetic congressperson and president of the Congressional Oversight Commission. Acción, the Congressional Oversight Commission, and popular organizations of the Oriente coordinated visits to contaminated areas of the rain forest. They brought government and Petroecuador officials, national and international journalists, and international support organizations to the Oriente in order to raise awareness of the impacts of Texaco's activities and to call for the audit's cancellation.[42]

Involving Congress in the campaign "brought legitimacy and recognition to the campaign."[43] The Congressional Oversight Commission had the power to require the Ministry of Energy and Mines to hand over confidential information, which sympathetic commission members passed along to NGOs and popular organizations. The organizations then used these to formulate more informed and precise challenges and criticisms.[44] At the same time, congressional involvement in the campaign opened Congress to the necessity of working on environmental issues and

---

34. Personal interview, Garzón, March 2000.
35. Personal interview, Garzón, March 2000.
36. Personal interview, Garzón, March 2000.
37. Acción Ecológica, "La Campaña contra la Texaco" (unpublished document, Acción Ecológica, 1993).

38. Kimerling, "Environmental Audit," 200.
39. Acción Ecológica, "La Campaña contra la Texaco."
40. Personal interviews, Esperanza Martinez, Acción Ecológica; Giovanni Rosanía, Petroleum Industry Engineer; María Eugenia Lima, former congressperson, September 1999.
41. Personal interviews, Lima and Pallares, September 1999.
42. Personal interview, Lima.
43. Personal interview, Martinez.
44. Personal interview, Lima.

establishing contact with popular organizations and NGOs.[45]

Acción Ecológica, CONFENAIE, and CONAIE also worked with allies in Europe and the United States to support and join the campaign against Texaco. These organizations were invited to participate in "Texaco Week" in July 1993. International delegates visited Texaco's contamination sites, met with affected indigenous and settler communities, participated in seminars in Quito, and publicized their observations. International organizations then joined Ecuadorian groups in calling for a truly independent and comprehensive investigation, open to public participation and scrutiny, of Texaco's activities.[46] The Ministry of Energy and Mines eventually declared the first audit invalid and agreed to carry out a second one.

Other strategies in the early years of the campaign included nonviolent occupations of gas stations, oil company offices, and the Ministry of Energy and Mines in Quito; publication and dissemination of educational materials; and holding concerts and other public events to bring attention to the problem. Campaign coalition members attended Texaco shareholder meetings in the United States and presented information on Texaco's activities in the Amazon developed by the Ecuadorian networks. They lobbied multilateral lending institutions to stop funding destructive projects in the Oriente.[47]

Turning Points

Coordination among the Ecuadorian environmental NGOs that made up the Amazonía por la Vida campaign faltered within the first few years of its creation because of political differences and competition for a leadership role. European environmental groups ceased to play a significant supporting role after 1993, but US groups such as Rain Forest Action Network, the Center for Economic and Social Rights, Oxfam America, and the Coalition for Amazonian Peoples and Their Environment continued to support the Ecuadorian campaign.[48]

Two international legal actions presented in the early 1990s brought even more international attention to the problem of oil contamination in the Oriente. In 1990, the Sierra Club Legal Defense Fund presented a complaint before the Inter-American Human Rights Commission of the Organization of American States on behalf of the Huaorani people affected by Conoco Oil Corporation's plans to explore for oil in Huaorani lands. The petition led the commission to visit the Oriente five years later and to dedicate a section of its 1997 country report on Ecuador to human rights violations of oil development in the Oriente.[49] In 1992, an Ecuadorian NGO specializing in environmental law, CORDAVI (Corporación para la Defensa de la Vida—Corporation for the Defense of Life), presented a case before the International Water Tribunal in the Netherlands against Texaco, Petroecuador, and City Investing Company. The water tribunal's jury agreed that the companies caused grave environmental destruction and adversely affected settler and indigenous peoples of the area.[50] Although the two legal actions brought international attention and provided more credibility and motivation to the Ecuadorian campaign, neither was the subject of organizing or follow-up of Ecuadorian civil society and neither Texaco nor the Ecuadorian government had to carry out the international organizations' recommendations.[51]

In 1993, another legal challenge changed the focus of the international and national campaign against Texaco when an Ecuadorian-born US lawyer filed a class-action lawsuit against Texaco in a US federal court.

The US Lawsuit against Texaco

Cristobal Bonifaz, a Massachusetts attorney born in Ecuador, learned of Texaco's damage to the Ecuadorian Amazon after reading Judith Kimerling's *Amazon Crude* and literature published by Northern campaign participants RAN and Oxfam America. During trips to the Oriente, Bonifaz collected evidence of Texaco's damage with the help of legal and scientific experts from the Center for Economic and Social Rights and

45. Personal interview, Garzón, September 1999.

46. Acción Ecológica, "La Campaña contra la Texaco."

47. Acción Ecológica, "La Campaña contra la Texaco," and personal interview, Garzón, March 2000.

48. Personal interview, Garzón, March 2000.

49. Organization of American States, *Human Rights in Ecuador.*

50. Second International Water Tribunal, "Petroleum in the Ecuadorian Amazon: Water Pollution due to Petroleum Exploitation," *In Pollution* (the Netherlands: International Books, 1994), 69–174.

51. Chris Jochnick, "The Right to a Healthy Environment: Advocacy Obstacles and Strategies," paper presented at New Strategies for Human Rights Advocacy conference, Peru, July 1999.

gathered plaintiffs for a class-action lawsuit. Upon his return to the United States, together with the law offices of Kohn, Nast, and Graf, a firm that specializes in class-action suits, Bonifaz prepared a complaint against Texaco on behalf of thirty thousand settler and indigenous Oriente residents.

At the same time the lawyers were preparing the suit, a group of fifteen Oriente residents were studying community leadership on a scholarship in Amherst, Massachusetts, in the same building as the office of Cristobal Bonifaz. Bonifaz convinced the leaders to join the suit. On November 3, 1993, the lawyers and the Oriente residents presented *María Aguinda et al. v. Texaco* in the US District Court for the Southern District of New York.

In a bold legal strategy, the Texaco suit stands to expand the scope of international law by holding a US corporation accountable under the Alien Tort Claims Act (ATCA) for violations of international human rights law. The ATCA allows an alien victim of a tort committed in violation of customary international law to sue its aggressor in a US court and is generally used by foreigners suing their human rights abusers for human rights violations such as torture and genocide. The lawsuit claims that Texaco violated three international human rights of the Oriente residents: the right to a healthy environment, protection from cultural genocide, and protection from racial and ethnic discrimination.[52]

The case calls for Texaco to clean up its old oilfields in the Ecuadorian Amazon; modernize the obsolete technologies the company designed, constructed, and left behind in Ecuador; and compensate Oriente residents harmed by the company's actions. Lawyers for the plaintiffs estimate damages at over a billion dollars.[53]

Texaco denies the charges and insists it acted within all Ecuadorian laws and accepted international petroleum industry standards of the time.[54] Texaco argues the case should be tried in Ecuador, since the company's challenged actions happened there.[55] Texaco also argues that the Ecuadorian government,

the majority shareholder in the Texaco-Petroecuador consortium after 1977, was responsible for decisions about the operations.[56]

But plaintiffs argue that Texaco made key operational decisions at its corporate headquarters in White Plains, New York. Most of the evidence about Texaco's decisions is in the United States, they argue, and only a US court can make those documents available for trial. Plus, they say, they could not possibly find justice in Ecuador. Even high-level officials admit the Ecuadorian judicial system is weak, inefficient, and corrupt.[57] As the former minister of energy and mines Manuel Navarro said, "While the Constitution declares the equality of all Ecuadorians before the law, it is public knowledge that the poor, indigenous peoples and marginalized sectors in general have no real possibilities of obtaining just treatment from persons socially influential and economically powerful."[58] In addition, Ecuador's Congress recently passed a law, "Law 55," that declares that if Ecuadorian citizens bring a case in a foreign court, Ecuador's courts will not accept the case if it is dismissed abroad. Because of the law, plaintiffs would be denied a hearing in Ecuador if the New York court were to dismiss the case on the grounds it should be tried in Ecuador.[59]

With this lawsuit, the plaintiffs and their lawyers hope to change the course of legal history by holding a US transnational corporation accountable for its actions in a foreign country (for the first time) in a US court. The suit also has the potential to bring about a significant increase in the power wielded by affected communities by bringing their demands to national and international attention and giving them legitimacy in both public debates and policy decisions. Especially in the early years, the case received wide coverage in Ecuadorian national newspapers and brought much attention to the environmental disaster and problems borne by indigenous and settler communities of the Ecuadorian Amazon. It also served as a rallying point around which affected communities organized and built their strength.

52. *http://www.texacorainforest.com,* the website of the plaintiffs against Texaco and their lawyers.

53. Plaintiffs' website.

54. Texaco Public Relations, "Texaco Statement concerning February 1, 1999 Court Hearing: Aguinda v. Texaco and Jota v. Texaco."

55. Defendant's Motion to Dismiss Based on Forum Non Conveniens, *Aguinda v. Texaco, Inc.* (No. 93 Civ. 7527).

56. Schemo, "Toxic Residue."

57. Plaintiffs' website.

58. Affidavit of Manuel E. Navarro, minister of energy and mines during Ecuador's military regime, March 3, 1994.

59. Plaintiffs' website.

Local Organizing in the Amazon around the Lawsuit: The Frente de Defensa de la Amazonía

Residents of the Oriente viewed the case as a major opportunity to organize and fight against contamination. The fifteen people who presented the lawsuit in the District Court of New York returned to the Amazon in 1993 and formed the Comité de Demandantes contra la Texaco (Plaintiffs against Texaco Committee). Luis Yanza, then-president of the Coordinadora de Organizaciones Populares del Nororiente (Coordinator of Popular Organizations of the Northern Oriente), heard an interview on the local radio station about the case and called a meeting of the plaintiffs' committee and other interested Oriente residents. The group of settlers then resolved to create a coordinating body among campesino organizations of the three Oriente provinces affected by Texaco to support and sustain the lawsuit. On May 15, 1994, the Frente de Defensa de la Amazonía (Amazon Defense Front) was founded.[60]

Many local, national, and international organizations supported the Frente's work. Catholic missions and human rights committees helped Oriente residents present complaints about oil contamination to human rights organizations and governmental bodies in Quito. The local radio station Radio Sucumbíos aired a program called "Café y Petróleo" (Coffee and Oil), on the problems of oil contamination and the struggle to hold companies responsible. Acción Ecológica helped the Frente establish links with governmental bodies and mass media in Quito and collaborated with local groups to establish an extensive popular education and monitoring network around oil impacts, as described below. The US-based organizations Rain Forest Action Network, the Coalition for Amazonian People and Their Environment, Oxfam America, and the Center for Economic and Social Rights provided educational, technical, and financial support and exercised international pressure on Texaco.[61]

Today, the Frente consists of over twenty-five campesino organizations of the northern Oriente. Its goals include organizing Amazonian people to protect their rights and environment; proposing sustainable alternatives for natural-resource management in the Oriente; and denouncing environmentally harmful

activities.[62] Its activities include visiting congressional representatives and attorneys general to obtain their support of the plaintiffs' case in US federal court, keeping the issue alive in the Ecuadorian press, and continually meeting with community leaders to inform them of the status of the case. Frente president Luis Yanza acts as an intermediary between the affected communities and their lawyers in the United States, informing the lawyers of communities' questions and expectations as well as situations that may present problems to the case. In addition to carrying out activities concerning the Texaco case, the Frente provides information and training about impacts of oil development among indigenous and settler communities of the Oriente, organizes community monitoring of a number of oil companies in the northern Amazon, and coordinates visits from international NGOs and journalists to the Oriente.

Indigenous organizations in the northern Oriente have chosen not to be members of the Frente. Only indigenous organizations can speak for indigenous peoples, they say, and the Frente is a coordinating body of settler organizations. Indigenous peoples' central demands—including legalization of ancestral territories and respect for their language, culture, and identity—are formulated, in part, in response to the pressures generated by the settlers' arrival. Still, indigenous organizations coordinate a variety of activities with the Frente, such as mobilizations in Quito, visits to the United States to publicize the Texaco issue, and workshops on rights affected by oil development. Indigenous and settler leaders state that in spite of the historical differences between indigenous peoples and settlers, indigenous and settler communities are united in their struggle against Texaco.

Popular Education and Community Organizing around Human Rights Violations by Oil Companies

One of the most important local initiatives of the Texaco campaign has been the creation of a citizens' monitoring network in the Oriente, including extensive popular education on impacts of oil development and strategies to hold oil companies accountable. Organizing and popular education work have highlighted the issue in terms of human rights. Chris

---

60. Personal interview, Yanza.
61. Personal interview, Garzón, September 1999.

62. Frente de Defensa de la Amazonía, educational pamphlet.

Jochnick of the Centro de Derechos Económicos y Sociales (CDES) observes:

> Framing the problem of oil contamination in terms of rights has provided legitimacy to the complaints of affected communities and has encouraged a long-overdue sense of injustice that has helped in organizing and mobilizing these communities. Community members are more likely to risk/dare raising their complaints in front of government and industry officials and the general public if they can be supported by legally recognized rights. Calling a long-accepted problem a "rights violation" suggests that things could be different and that somebody is responsible.[63]

In order to assert and defend their rights, residents needed to first recognize and name the problem, then document just what was going on and bring their plight to public attention. Various supporting organizations, including Acción Ecológica, Catholic Church missions, independent researchers, and legal activists, had started holding consciousness-raising sessions with local residents in the early 1990s. Attorney Judith Kimerling brought photographs and discussed the harmful effects of oil on people, animals, and the Amazonian ecosystem. Later, the Center for Economic and Social Rights held workshops on oil development in the context of human rights and provided training and legal support to residents.[64] Numerous workshops focused on the technical aspects of oil development so residents could discuss complex industry activities and the impacts on their lives. This was essential if residents were going to engage with industry representatives and policy makers. This work led to a recognition that Ecuadorian oil operations had to be seen in the broader context of national and international development policies.

Through these meetings, workshops, and discussions, it became clear early on that no one—government, residents, or supporting organizations—was monitoring the ongoing devastation caused by oil activities. So the affected communities of the Oriente and their supporting organizations resolved to create a permanent community-based environmental monitoring and popular education network.

The Red de Monitoreo Ambiental (Environmental Monitoring Network) was officially launched on September 24, 1996. It was supported by Acción Ecológica staff based in the region, the Center for Economic and Social Rights, local human rights groups, the Frente, local radio stations, and various Catholic missions. It encompassed fifteen communities, each of which had an environmental "promoter" who led local popular education and monitoring activities.

While the Red de Monitoreo Ambiental still exists, its most active period lasted for the first two or three years. The network carried out a series of workshops during the first two years to train the promoters in impacts of the petroleum industry, environmental-monitoring skills, and national and international rights and laws. The monitoring network helped Oriente residents publicly denounce problems with oil companies. The network promoters helped people write reports about oil spills, fires, confrontations with company officials, and other problems. The reports used testimonies from local residents, photos, videos, and water samples to show damages and also contained legal arguments and recommendations.[65]

With the help of local human rights groups, environmental promoters sent the reports to local authorities, the Congressional Environment Commission, the Ministry of Energy and Mines, and oil company officials to demand environmental remediation and compensation. They sent complaints and monitoring reports to local and national media, generating weekly articles in the press. This, in turn, encouraged people from other communities to come forward and file complaints about their experiences with oil contamination, creating a period of heightened national press attention on oil impacts around the country.[66]

The work of the Red de Monitoreo Ambiental has had a significant impact on public opinion, local and national authorities, and oil companies operating in the northern Oriente. National newspapers reported stories of environmental contamination almost weekly during the first year of the network's activities. The Ministry of Energy and Mines started to make an effort to take public responsibility for impacts of the

---

63. Jochnick, "The Right to a Healthy Environment."
64. Personal interview, Martinez.

65. Personal interviews, Garzón and Yanza, September 1999, and documents of the Red de Monitoreo Ambiental, on file with the Frente de Defensa de la Amazonía, Lago Agrio, Ecuador.
66. Personal interviews, Garzón and Yanza, September 1999, and documents of the Red de Monitoreo Ambiental.

oil industry. Local authorities and politicians began to outline plans to confront environmental contamination.[67] "Companies now respond to the pressure to clean up their damage or provide compensation to the people, although the results are never completely just. But the companies know they are being watched. They are showing the communities more respect," commented Yanza.[68]

The creation of the Frente, the formation of the Red de Monitoreo Ambiental, and popular education among Oriente communities have had transformative effects on Oriente residents' understanding of oil development and human rights. Carmen Allauca, president of the Comité de Derechos Humanos del Nororiente (Human Rights Committee of the Northern Oriente), explained:

> When the companies began, the people didn't know anything about rights; they didn't know they could denounce oil companies. We told the people, "Don't be afraid; we must denounce the contamination." When we first started, we faced a kind of disbelief among the people. The state owned the subsurface rights and the company was the big God; what they said was what you had to do. There was no understanding that you could oppose the company and claim your rights. Now people have begun to realize that they can and they should denounce the contamination and that they don't have to be afraid. Now people feel supported and they come forward.[69]

Secoya leader Colón Piaguaje stated, "We didn't have an organized way to confront the attacks on our people and culture. We didn't know anything about laws to defend ourselves. We know we have rights and we must be respected."[70]

Lawsuits, Negotiations, and the Impact on Community Organizing

At the time of this writing, the Texaco lawsuit has gone on for more than seven years. During this time,

it has survived six attempts by Texaco to have it dismissed, and it has seen five changes in the Ecuadorian administration and eight different Ecuadorian attorneys general. It has been the focus of numerous mass mobilizations to demand and sustain government support of the plaintiffs' right to sue Texaco in the United States. It also has stimulated continuous education and consciousness-raising on human rights and the environment among impacted communities and in the larger national and international communities.

Along the way, the challenges have required local organizers to rally to defend the core principles of the case: the right to sue Texaco in the United States and Texaco's need to clean up its damage and compensate the people harmed. At each of the stumbling blocks along the way, local groups and the Quito-based support organizations have managed to overcome the threats. In the end, the campaign has been strengthened, but the struggles continue.

One of the ongoing struggles of the case has been over whether to negotiate with Texaco or to push for a court decision that could bring all or nothing and could set a key precedent, or not, depending on the jury's final say. Members of the suit and supporters are divided over this point. "Class-action lawsuits are always difficult. Even in the United States, when the plaintiffs are all in the same place, it's hard," says Cristobal Bonifaz, lead lawyer for the Texaco suit. "Imagine this case. We're arguing complex points of law. We're up here; the plaintiffs are down there. There's all kinds of opportunities for things to get confused. And sure, people are poor. You put a thousand dollars on the table and they'll take it. That's the tragedy of this case."[71]

Affected communities first faced the negotiation dilemma in May 1995. Texaco proposed negotiated agreements via the Ecuadorian government with two Quichua federations and four local governments. Texaco agreed to pay five million dollars to the two Quichua groups and the four municipalities. In exchange, they all agreed to drop any future claims against Texaco and effectively dropped out of the suit. Texaco then attempted to use the agreements to get the New York judge to dismiss the case. The Frente and the Cofan, Secoya, and Siona organizations de-

---

67. Personal interview, Garzón, September 1999.
68. Personal interview, Yanza.
69. Personal interview, Allauca.
70. Personal interview, Colón Piaguaje, Organización Indígena Secoya del Ecuador (OISE), September 1999.

---

71. Personal interview, Cristobal Bonifaz, lead Texaco lawsuit attorney, September 2000.

nounced the agreement in the press and in a letter to the US court and resolved to continue their support of the lawsuit.[72] Frente president Luis Yanza explained, "Texaco's intentions were to continue conquering people. They tried to use [Ecuadorian] authorities to negotiate with individuals and communities. We had to fight hard to prevent this. Ultimately we became more united."[73] The Frente and its supporters vigorously denounced the clean-up operation in the press as symbolic and ineffectual. In June 1995, the court rejected Texaco's motion to dismiss the case.[74]

Surviving Legal Delays

Other challenges to the suit have come in a series of legal maneuvers by Texaco that have been met with coordinated legal, political, and public-opinion strategies involving everything from street protests, to carefully targeted lobbying of key decision makers, to media and information campaigns and international solidarity.

From 1993 to 1996, the Ecuadorian government was adamantly opposed to the lawsuit in New York. This presented a huge obstacle to the Ecuadorian plaintiffs, but also presented opportunities for mobilizations that eventually brought about and sustained an about-face in the Ecuadorian government's position and kept the lawsuit alive. When the suit was filed in 1993, the government of Sixto Durán Ballén (1992–1996) opposed the lawsuit, declaring that it was an affront to national sovereignty, threatened the Ecuadorian economy, and was a disincentive to US companies considering investing in Ecuador.[75] Texaco sought to dismiss the suit based to a large extent on the Ecuadorian government's opposition to the suit. In a landmark decision, the late judge Vincent Broderick allowed the case to continue for the purpose of discovery to determine if decisions made by Texaco in New York resulted in damages to the Ecuadorian

plaintiffs.[76] In March 1995, Judge Broderick died of cancer and the case was eventually reassigned to Judge Jed Rakoff in 1996.

The re-assignment to Judge Rakoff presented the next and ongoing challenge to the suit. Judge Rakoff dismissed the case in November 1996 based to a large extent on the Durán Ballén administration's opposition to the suit.[77] Plaintiffs had ten days to petition for reconsideration of the decision. Abdalá Bucaram had been elected president of Ecuador in August 1996 and the plaintiffs' lawyers needed a letter from the new Ecuadorian government expressing its support of the case. The Frente and Acción Ecológica organized a mobilization of campesinos, indigenous people, congressional representatives, and environmental and human rights NGOs and held a peaceful takeover of Attorney General Leonidas Plaza Verduga's offices. They demanded that the new Abdalá Bucaram government support the lawsuit in New York. Their efforts succeeded in getting a letter from the Ecuadorian administration declaring that the lawsuit was not an affront to national sovereignty but rather protected the interests of Ecuadorian citizens.[78]

But in February 1997, President Abdalá Bucaram was impeached by the Ecuadorian Congress on the grounds of mental incapacity, and the next month, Judge Rakoff requested that the interim government of President Fabián Alarcón clarify its position. Once again, the Frente, indigenous organizations, and NGOs in Quito mobilized and took over the offices of the new attorney general, Milton Alava Ormaza, until they left with a letter expressing the Alarcón government's support of the plaintiffs' right to sue Texaco in New York.[79]

Although two successive governments had expressed their support of the plaintiffs' case in New York, on August 12, 1997, Judge Rakoff denied the plaintiffs' motion for reconsideration and dismissed the case.[80] The plaintiffs' attorneys filed an appeal of Rakoff's decision before the US Court of Appeals for the Second Circuit in New York in September 1997.

72. Frente de Defensa de la Amazonía, Centro de Derechos Económicos y Sociales, Comité de Demandantes contra la Texaco, "La Texacontaminación en el Ecuador" (1999).

73. Personal interview, Yanza.

74. Jack Epstein, "Ecuadorans Wage Legal Battle against US Oil Company," *Christian Science Monitor,* September 12, 1995.

75. Amicus Brief of the Government of Ecuador, cited in Victoria C. Arthaud, "Environmental Destruction in the Amazon: Can U.S. Courts Provide a Forum for the Claims of Indigenous Peoples?" *Georgetown International Environmental Law Review* 7 (1994): 230.

76. Judge Broderick, memorandum, *Aguinda v. Texaco, Inc.* (S.D.N.Y.) (No. 93-7527) (issued April 11, 1994).

77. *Aguinda v. Texaco, Inc.,* 945 F.Supp. 625 (S.D.N.Y. 1996).

78. Frente de Defensa de la Amazonía et al., "La Texacontaminación en el Ecuador."

79. Frente de Defensa de la Amazonía et al., "La Texacontaminación en el Ecuador."

80. *Aguinda v. Texaco, Inc.,* 175 F.R.D. 50 (S.D.N.Y. 1997).

The court of appeals reversed Rakoff's decision in October 1998 and sent it back, telling him to require Texaco's consent to Ecuadorian jurisdiction, to reconsider the arguments of both parties, and to reconsider the position of the Ecuadorian government in regards to the suit.[81] Essentially, the court of appeals had told Judge Rakoff he'd made a bad ruling.

Jamil Mahuad had been elected president of Ecuador in August 1998. Frente president Luis Yanza and NGO representatives made several attempts to meet with governmental officials in order to obtain the government's continued support of the suit. But they were denied appointments or told the government would not take a position on the matter.[82]

So on December 2, 1998, the Frente and Quito-based NGOs again took over the offices of the new attorney general, Ramón Jiménez Carbo. They demanded the attorney general support the litigation in New York. After an intense seven-hour meeting with eight delegates from the Frente, NGOs, and indigenous organizations, the attorney general agreed to support the plaintiffs' right to sue Texaco in New York. He also agreed to cooperate with the court, provide necessary information, and implement any environmental remediation the court ordered.[83]

By late 1999, Judge Jed Rakoff had yet to announce his decision. The presidents of the Frente and the Cofan people traveled to the United States, sponsored by their lawyers, to launch a newspaper, TV, and radio ad campaign in the United States publicizing Texaco's damages to the people and environment of the Oriente and charging the company with racism.[84] The ad campaign came three years after Texaco paid a $176.1 million settlement to African American employees who sued the company for racial discrimination. Texaco responds that the charges of racism are "inflammatory" and "baseless." Texaco CEO Peter I. Bijur sent a letter to Frente president Luis Yanza stating that he was "deeply saddened" by the charges and indicated interest "in working together toward a fair, reasonable and comprehensive resolution."[85]

In January 2000, in protest of the government's inability to control the spiraling economic crisis and the broken promises the government had made to CONAIE, eight thousand indigenous people marched on Quito demanding the renunciation of the three branches of the Ecuadorian government. On January 21, CONAIE united with leaders of a military faction and the former president of the Ecuadorian Supreme Court and ousted President Jamil Mahuad.

In light of the coup, Judge Rakoff expressed his concerns regarding "the ability of the Ecuadorian courts to dispense independent, impartial justice" and ordered lawyers for the plaintiffs and for Texaco to submit additional evidence on corruption in the Ecuadorian judiciary before he decided on whether the case would proceed in the United States.[86]

Approaching Negotiated Settlements

With the September 1999 letter from Texaco implying possible intentions to settle the case and in view of Rakoff's order, the Frente and the Cofan, Secoya, and Siona groups organized a series of events with indigenous and settler communities in early 2000. The goal was to discuss and reflect upon the past six years of the struggle, consider possible scenarios, and develop strategies for responding to them. What if Texaco offered a settlement proposal? What if Judge Rakoff accepted jurisdiction for the case in New York and it went into the next phase of litigation? What if he dismissed the case and there had to be yet another appeal or possibly a lawsuit in the courts of Ecuador?

Some Oriente residents and NGO members don't trust settlement negotiations, given the history of oil companies' negotiations with settler and indigenous communities in Ecuador. Oil companies are notorious for signing contracts with indigenous communities in which communities agree to allow companies access to their lands in exchange for "trinkets" such as outboard motors, medicine chests, solar panels, or the construction of schools, health centers, or soccer fields. After what happened in 1995 when Texaco negotiated with the Ecuadorian government, Quichua organizations, and Oriente municipalities, many residents have good reason to see negotiations with Texaco as divisive and ultimately a recipe for defeat. They want to see the case litigated to the end in order to set a global precedent

81. *Jota v. Texaco, Inc.*, 157 F.3d 153 (2d Cir. 1998).

82. Personal interview, Garzón, March 2000.

83. Frente de Defensa de la Amazonía et al., "La Texacontaminación en el Ecuador."

84. Plaintiffs' website.

85. Letter from Peter I. Bijur to Luis Yanza, September 28, 1999.

86. Jed Rakoff, memorandum, *Aguinda v. Texaco, Inc.* (S.D.N.Y.) (No. 93-7527) (issued January 31, 2000).

of holding a transnational corporation accountable to indigenous peoples and campesinos in a US federal courtroom. "The suit is a good process. No one was an expert on oil. The Siona leaders, the government, no one knew what it meant. Now we are changing all that. We are confronting the oil company," said one Siona leader. "Negotiation is weakness. If we go to final judgment, we will win their respect."[87]

At the same time, many Oriente residents and members of the NGO community would welcome a settlement to avoid costly, risky litigation that could last for years. The Frente has maintained that it will only consider a settlement proposal that assures the three basic demands of the lawsuit: that Texaco clean up old contamination, bring in modern technology, and compensate for residents' losses.[88] Leaders of the Frente and the Cofan, Secoya, and Siona organizations have insisted that should Texaco propose a settlement offer, the leaders would not have the power to accept the settlement in the name of the communities, but rather that "the ultimate decision would be in the hands of the affected people and the plaintiffs."[89] The leaders agree that there must be a broad consultative, participatory process among the base communities before presenting or accepting any settlement proposal.

This position was put to the test in July of 2000, when Texaco presented a settlement offer of twenty million dollars, plus all attorneys fees for Bonifaz and the Philadelphia firm of Kohn, Nast, and Graf. The lawyers presented the proposal to the Frente and other groups representing plaintiffs, and they rejected it.[90] With damages, remediation, and new technology valued at well over a billion dollars, what is twenty million dollars going to do? they asked. But Texaco gambled that the chance to earn attorney fees after so many years of work would be enough to get the lawyers to convince their clients to accept the offer. For Bonifaz, it wasn't. "The case can be settled, sure, but that's not the point. The point is to get a decision saying this kind

of case can be tried in the United States," he says.[91] In the meantime, settlers and indigenous communities have yet again stood firm for their beliefs, tested by the sweet offer of quick money.

In the latest twist as this case study is being written, the *New York Times* broke a story about judges accepting "junkets"—expense-paid trips for conferences in resort areas—sponsored by a business-friendly organization and paid for by numerous corporations. It turns out that Judge Rakoff was one of the judges, Texaco was one of the funders, and former Texaco chairman and chief executive officer Alfred DeCrane was one of the lecturers. At the conference in question, which took place in September 1998 just before the court of appeals overturned Judge Rakoff's decision in favor of Texaco, attendees spent six days listening to presentations, dining, riding horses, and socializing together. Attorney Bonifaz filed a petition asking Judge Rakoff to voluntarily step down from the case, given the clear perception of influence from Texaco. Rakoff refused and the court of appeals upheld his ruling. Meanwhile, major US newspapers have printed editorials pointing to this case and calling for sweeping reform of judicial education and compensation systems so that judges will be less likely to be exposed to this kind of potentially corrupting influence.[92]

Campaign Tensions: Divergent Goals and Competing Strategies

The Texaco campaign has required a broad network of environmental groups, settler and indigenous organizations, legal activists, and sympathetic government officials and politicians, as well as international supporters. But divisions and tensions among the different groups have arisen and at times threatened the campaign.

When Acción Ecológica launched the Texaco campaign, its main goals were to pressure Texaco to clean up the damage it had left in the Ecuadorian Amazon and to set a precedent of accountability to all companies acting in Ecuador.[93] While these were the explicit goals of the NGO leading the campaign, other par-

---

87. Personal group interview, Siona leaders, September 1999.
88. Frente de Defensa de la Amazonía et al., "La Texacontaminación en el Ecuador."
89. "Acuerdo Oficial entre OINCE, ONISE, OISE, Comité de Demandantes y Frente de Defensa de la Amazonía" (December 6, 1999).
90. Agencia Informativa Púlsar, "Petrolera Texaco Intenta Dividir a Comunidades Indígenas," Latin America and Caribbean Internet News Agency, July 4, 2000.

91. Personal interview, Bonifaz.
92. See "A Threat to Judicial Ethics," *New York Times,* September 15, 2000, and "Judicial Junketeering," *Boston Globe,* September 24, 2000. Personal interview, Bonifaz.
93. Acción Ecológica, "La Campaña contra Texaco."

ticipants had different goals. Oriente residents, for example, prioritized economic compensation for their harms suffered. Since affected people did not have the resources or abilities to structure and promote a campaign, environmental reparation was prioritized over social and economic compensation in the public campaign activities.[94]

Because the Quito-based NGOs have easier access to national politicians, journalists, international NGOs, and the lawyers in the United States, they often end up playing a default role of spokesperson for the affected communities. Once the Frente began to establish its own credentials with the national press and politicians, this uneven balance of power within the coalition shifted somewhat. But the physical distance between the Oriente and Quito, never mind the United States, lack of Spanish fluency of many indigenous residents, and the self-imposed requirements for careful member consultation in moments of major decision making have presented structural challenges for full and equal participation of affected communities in campaign agenda-setting. Events often move more quickly in political and legal worlds than precarious communication systems, unreliable public transport, and community deliberations can accommodate.

Yet the affected communities hold the most important card of all in the campaign. In the end, they are the ones who have suffered and who embody the interests being defended by the campaign and the lawsuit. The Frente and indigenous organizations have used this fact to counterbalance the other relative disadvantages they have in the campaign coalition. For example, the Frente and indigenous leaders have chosen to withdraw when they have disagreed with certain campaign strategies, effectively withholding the source of legitimacy the Quito-based NGOs need. Frente and indigenous leaders have also recognized the need to be in direct communication with the US legal team and other outside supporters. This has also diminished one source of coalition imbalance caused by the fact of their remote location. It takes money for phone lines and international calls and in the case of indigenous communities, battery-powered radios.

Important differences in agendas, strategies, and tactics also simmered among Quito-based NGOs and their international supporters. One key difference has been whether the NGOs' role is to support local groups in whatever they chose to fight for or rather to push an agenda in the campaign and in the lawsuit that is independent of local community decisions. "The first group of environmental lawyers was different [from those that came later]," says Byron Real about the early legal cases brought in the late 1980s and early 1990s by CORDAVI. "We were not trying to change the system, but to be a legal support to people affected by pollution. We had a militant perspective on our role."[95] Following this explicitly support-oriented and advisor-oriented role, CORDAVI focused on providing a legal framework for the settler communities' issues and carried out legal and environmental research to bring legal cases.

Meanwhile, Acción Ecológica focused on denouncing oil development as a manifestation of a corrupt and exploitative development model that destroys Ecuador's natural and cultural heritage and allows international corporations to be accountable to no one. Oil development had to be resisted at all costs, they argued—and still argue. "If one person in the community wants to resist oil development, we will help that community resist," says Alexandra Almeida of Acción. Reflecting on Acción's position, she adds, "If you affirm resistance of the development model, you affirm the identity of the campesino and indigenous realities."[96] So while CORDAVI and the more mainstream environmental groups in Quito focused on formal legal and legislative strategies to fight oil pollution, Acción Ecológica took to the streets in the name of resisting all oil development. They occupied Texaco's corporate offices, stopped traffic with marches, staged sit-ins at government offices, and helped organize an international boycott against Texaco.

When the Center for Economic and Social Rights (CESR) became active in the campaign from the United States in 1994, their approach also focused on providing a legal framework for the issue, like CORDAVI. But they also placed an explicit emphasis on rights—environmental, social, and economic. Further, they focused on the rights of the communities to have an active, informed voice in decisions affect-

---

94. Personal interview, Garzón, March 2000.

95. Personal interview, Byron Real, environmental lawyer, September 1999.
96. Personal interview, Alexandra Almeida, Acción Ecológica, September 1999.

ing them, not only about oil development but also within the lawsuit and the campaign. When CESR staff established the Centro de Derechos Económicos y Sociales in Quito in 1997, they continued to pursue this rights-based approach.

Framing the problem of oil contamination in terms of human rights violations has had a major impact on the campaign, Chris Jochnick says. First, rights serve as a powerful mobilizing tool among communities affected by oil development. Second, calling a problem a "rights violation" increases public pressure on the government and oil industry. Third, the language of rights engages international and governmental institutions such as the US State Department, the United Nations, and the OAS. Fourth, rights violations play a role in attracting media and public attention. Finally, rights violations have provided "a common rallying point" among social sectors and NGOs pressing for new legislation, regulations, or improved industry conduct.[97]

Paulina Garzón of the Centro de Derechos Económicos y Sociales believes that while NGOs and affected people may have held different priorities in the campaign, the diverse goals can be united in terms of human rights. The main goals of the campaign were always to stop human rights violations and to restore those rights—the rights to health, a healthy environment, and compensation for damages, and the rights to a say in the matter. While campaign activists initially did not frame the campaign goals in terms of restitution of rights, the language of rights today centers the campaign, she argues. Garzón says the language of human rights provides the "axis" to unite different priorities and strategies of such a complex and multi-faceted campaign.[98]

Multiple and Interdependent Campaign Actions

While often uncoordinated, the multiple strategies and tactics used by campaign participants have proven to be mutually dependent, with each one feeding off of and supporting the others. Former minister of the environment Yolanda Kakabadse commented that "the campaign's different strategies—activist, intellectual, critical, and propositive—have complemented each

other."[99] A major lesson of the campaign has been the necessity to work on many strategies simultaneously, maintaining flexibility to prioritize and change.[100]

Street protests brought national press attention and forced governmental officials to dialogue with social sectors rather than make decisions behind closed doors.[101] Protests have also served to educate urban Ecuadorians about the problems faced by indigenous and settler communities of the Amazon and to question a model of development based on petroleum exploitation.[102]

At the same time, meetings with government officials helped campaign activists keep informed about shifting governmental positions, identify allies within the public sector, and come up with new campaign strategies. Meetings with government officials also served to remind the Ministry of Energy and Mines that its actions are continually monitored by a vigilant NGO community.[103] Working with allies in the Ecuadorian Congress provided a very public forum for making the case against Texaco and brought legitimacy to the campaign. It also pushed Congress to begin working on environmental and indigenous issues. Congress started working on an environmental protection law and finally approved it in May 1999.

Use of the media—from Radio Sucumbíos in Lago Agrio, to major newspapers in Quito, to CNN, CBS, and the *New York Times*—has been a continual strategy in the campaign. Opposition to neoliberal policies of Sixto Durán Ballén in the early 1990s in both Ecuadorian media and society made the media sympathetic to the Oriente plaintiffs' plight, using the case as another critique against the government. The press uncovered links between oil companies and the government. The fact that indigenous peoples presented their case in an international forum, holding press conferences in traditional dress on the doorstep of the New York courthouse, made a strong impact in the national and international press.[104] The Frente continually hosted visits by journalists to the Oriente and provided information from the Monitoring Network's

97. Jochnick, "The Right to a Healthy Environment."

98. Personal interview, Garzón, March 2000.

99. Personal interview, Yolanda Kakabadse, former Ecuadorian minister of the environment, September 1999.

100. Personal interview, Garzón, September 1999.

101. Personal interview, Ivonne Ramos, Acción Ecológica, September 1999.

102. Personal interview, Garzón, September 1999.

103. Personal interview, Garzón, September 1999.

104. Personal interview, Martin Pallares, journalist, September 1999.

research. "The visits hosted by the local people were important, because the legal representative of Texaco in Ecuador was always hosting press conferences and taking journalists to nice places where Texaco had reforested or built schools," commented journalist Martin Pallares.[105]

Dr. Francisco Huerta, former minister of government, former editor of the Guayaquil-based newspaper *El Expreso,* and long-time supporter of the campaign, says street protests often have been the only thing that got press attention to the problem of oil contamination in the Oriente. "Scandal is one of the most important factors. Protest puts the issue on the front page." Huerta noted that the consciousness among Ecuadorian journalists of the links between health, the environment, and human rights is still incipient and that campaign activists should take a more active role in training journalists in these themes.[106]

There have been multiple legal initiatives throughout the Texaco campaign, some directly and some indirectly related to Texaco. But the relationship between each legal action and the larger campaign has been different in some important ways that have affected their long-term impact. The two early international legal actions—the petition before the Organization of American States in 1990 and the International Water Tribunal Case in 1992—did not involve much national or international media work or campaign organizing by local groups or NGOs. While they attracted some international attention and validated claims of human rights violations, they were not able to influence either the oil companies involved or Ecuadorian government policy. But these cases showed the way for others to follow. They helped form the relationships between local residents and NGOs; they taught affected communities that they could have their voice heard; and they provided a first exposure to how legal and government structures work.

Following in these footsteps and applying important lessons from their shortcomings, the lawsuit presented in US federal court in Texaco's home state of New York has been the most successful. The suit has generated tremendous media attention in Ecuador and internationally, generated intense local organizing and education, raised awareness about rights, and

generated much activity on the part of civil society and the government. Lawsuits of this dimension are highly risky, time- and resource-consuming, and therefore difficult to duplicate. But domestic cases or cases before international tribunals, if they are part of larger campaigns, can also serve powerful organizational and educational goals.[107] Lawsuits can also press the boundaries of accepted legal doctrine on social and economic rights; for example, they serve to press the idea that poverty and environmental destruction are not inevitable results of development, but the results of deliberate actions and omissions, and those responsible must be held accountable.[108]

Challenges Going Forward

While the campaign has contributed to a growing consciousness in the Ecuadorian government of the need to protect the environment, many of the changes in governmental policy have been "cosmetic."[109] The Undersecretary of Environmental Protection was created in 1990, but as a bureau within the Ministry of Energy and Mines, where protecting the environment has been subordinated to protecting the interests of industry. The Ministry of Energy and Mines promulgated environmental regulations for the petroleum industry in 1992, but advocates maintain that these regulations are woefully inadequate.

And while the government has demonstrated growing sensitivity to the environmental matters, sensitivity to social and cultural impacts of oil development is still largely lacking. The 1998 Constitution declares that people potentially affected by environmental decision making shall have the right to information and participation in those decisions.[110] To this day, however, there are few real opportunities for affected people to participate in environmental decisions that affect them.

Conclusion: Analyzing Campaign Impacts

The campaign against Texaco has brought some important changes to the landscape of the Ecuadorian

---

105. Personal interview, Martin Pallares.
106. Personal interview, Francisco Huerta, September 1999.

107. Jochnick, "The Right to a Healthy Environment."
108. See Centro de Derechos Económicos y Sociales, *De Necesidades a Derechos.*
109. Personal interview, Huerta.
110. Constitución Política de la República del Ecuador, Art. 88.

Amazon. Some of the lessons about advocacy strategies that come from this experience are:

- The importance of organizing the affected population around oil impacts, emphasizing those people's rights, and creating the network for monitoring oil impacts.

- The power of the human rights framework to give voice to campesino and indigenous communities' demands for justice.

- The mutually reinforcing strategies of protest and lobbying when directed at specific targets with a specific aim.

- The role of the lawsuit to legitimize the arguments of affected communities and raise awareness for their plight both nationally and internationally.

The Texaco campaign has yet to meet its most tangible goals of getting Texaco to clean up its environmental destruction, modernize the obsolete technology it left behind in Ecuador, and pay for damages. But the campaign has brought about other kinds of successes.

Perhaps the greatest success has been the formation and strengthening of local organizations, especially the creation of the Frente de Defensa de la Amazonía. The Frente has been successful in unifying diverse settler communities from three provinces affected by Texaco's operations and in working in coordination with indigenous organizations of the area. Through workshops, meetings, popular educational work, and use of the local radio, the Frente has raised the consciousness of Oriente residents about environmental contamination. People now dare to denounce contamination and violations of their rights and protest the government's oil policies in Quito. Speaking out about oil development is no longer only for "technical experts"; now people see they can and have the *right* to express their opposition to oil activities and policies. Oriente residents have learned there are ways to be heard: in the press, in the Congress, before ministries, before the attorney general, before Petroecuador officials, and before a foreign court.[111]

Another major impact of the campaign against Texaco has been to raise the consciousness of Ecuadorian citizens about the importance of the Amazon and its people, the problems caused by oil development in the Oriente, and the conflicts with a development model based on uncontrolled exploitation of natural resources. The nature of public discourse on the campaign issues has been fundamentally changed. Environmental issues are no longer seen in a vacuum, but as intertwined with human health, social, and cultural issues. The campaign has also brought international attention to the problems caused by Texaco and to the reality lived by the people affected by Texaco's destruction. Both of these factors have been crucial in rallying support for the Oriente residents' cause.

In another victory, the New York lawsuit against Texaco sparked a national dialogue about the inability of Ecuadorians to find justice in their own court system. Protests and public debate about the Ecuadorian government's position in relation to the lawsuit spurred a national discussion about national sovereignty. Citizens questioned and debated, "What does national sovereignty mean? What is the role of the government? Should the government protect the interests of the transnational corporations or of its citizens?"[112] Citizens' outrage over Amazonian devastation pushed the Ecuadorian government to support—or at least not oppose—the legal case against Texaco. This impact has also shifted, if only slightly, the nature of debate on actions by foreign corporations in Ecuador.

One of the campaign's greatest policy impacts to date has been changing and sustaining the government's position in regards to the suit. The government went from staunch opposition to the US federal lawsuit to sustained support for the plaintiffs' rights to bring the case and choose the forum in which their complaint is heard. Thanks to protests, mass mobilizations, hours of negotiations, and public pressure, the governments of Bucaram, Alarcón, and Mahuad supported the plaintiffs' right to search for relief in a foreign forum and agreed to cooperate with any decisions of the New York court. The success in winning the support of Ecuadorian public opinion was one critical factor in achieving and holding on to this important victory that is crucial for keeping the lawsuit alive.

Finally, the campaign has had a notable, though still incomplete, effect on the behavior of oil companies currently operating in Ecuador. "The campaign has served as a warning to other companies," noted

---

111. Personal interview, Manuel Pallares.

112. Personal interview, Bolívar Beltrán, indigenous rights lawyer, September 1999.

Claudino Blanco, a Carmelite priest working in the northern Oriente. The first thing companies say in their public discourse is, "We're not Texaco. We re-inject production waters."[113] Companies are using more advanced, less-contaminating technology today, commented former undersecretary of the environment Jorge Albán, adding, "There is no way that the Texaco experience can happen again."[114] This is a success of degree, because while oil companies are improving their environmental performance somewhat, they are still guilty of committing gross social and cultural harm among indigenous communities. Although changing oil companies' behavior in other areas isn't an explicit goal of the lawsuit, it is one of the goals of the larger campaign. Any movement toward holding oil companies accountable must be seen as a positive impact, even if it is incomplete.

While the lawsuit is still pending and Oriente residents affected by Texaco are still confronting environmental and cultural impacts of oil development, the Texaco campaign charts one way for dealing with oil development. Settler and indigenous organizing, education, and monitoring work on the ground have combined with work by environmental and social justice organizations in Quito to raise national and international awareness of the issue. The New York lawsuit has proved a powerful campaign vehicle that has raised the profile and legitimacy of the Oriente residents' claims. Not without its own risks, the lawsuit has helped consolidate local organizations' strength, demanded the attention of the national government, and, if successful, could set a precedent with implications for US corporate accountability all over the world.

---

113. Personal interview, Claudino Blanco, Carmelite priest, September 1999.

114. Personal interview, Jorge Albán, former Ecuadorian undersecretary of the environment, September 1999.

Chapter 13

International Financial Institutions:
The Campaign for Debt Relief[1]

Andrew Bauck

Introduction

When the Cold War ended, so too did much of the foreign aid that developing countries depended on. This was especially true of aid from the United States, which had long used foreign aid as a tool to secure political influence. As aid to developing countries declined dramatically, they were left with less money available to repay old debts, loans that in some cases had been given to corrupt regimes in exchange for ideological allegiance. In the early 1990s, just a handful of organizations in Washington, D.C., were working to bring attention to the growing debts of poor countries and their effect on human development. By the end of the 1990s, a broad coalition of churches, unions, and civil society organizations had come together under Jubilee 2000/USA, which had become a powerful voice for debt relief. These groups had united around the simple moral argument that it was unacceptable for impoverished countries to devote large portions of their budgets to foreign debt service while their own people's needs went unmet. Furthermore, this coalition was part of a worldwide movement that had grown tremendously in just a few years, primarily due to the strong support of religious groups. By the summer of 2000, newspaper editorials echoed charges originally made by activists, linking large debt burdens to an inability to improve human development, especially in sub-Saharan Africa.

Even the World Bank and International Monetary Fund (IMF), long seen by activists as part of the problem, now recognized that many poor countries could not possibly repay their debts and that continued high levels of debt service inhibited economic growth and human development. As a result of these economic realities, combined with international pressure, in 1996 the World Bank and IMF implemented the Heavily Indebted Poor Country (HIPC) Initiative, a new program with the explicit goal of reducing poor-country debt burdens to sustainable levels. As evidence grew that the program was failing to achieve its aims, it was expanded in 1999 to provide greater levels of debt relief to more countries.

Many challenges remained, however. Most immediately, reluctance to pay for debt relief created a risk that promises made internationally would not be kept due to insufficient financing from developed countries. Furthermore, countries with severe debt problems such as Haiti, Nigeria, and Jamaica were not included in the program. Other countries that could potentially benefit, including Ethiopia and Sudan, had seen their entry into the program postponed indefinitely by conflict. Even for countries that had been promised debt relief, the process was proceeding at a glacial pace and required many difficult conditions, and there was concern that in the end they would not receive enough debt relief to sufficiently address poverty reduction. Finally, despite the tangible gains that had been made, there was still a long way to go toward the much larger goal of reforming the IMF and World Bank so that effective poverty reduction was their primary mission.

This case study tells the story of how activists and advocates brought international attention to the economic and social problems caused by the huge foreign debts of many of the world's poorest countries. The case focuses specifically on the roles of Oxfam America

1. Research for this case study was undertaken by Andrew Bauck with support from Oxfam America and the Daniel J. Evans School of Public Affairs at the University of Washington. It also appears, in its original form, as part of the Electronic Hallway series of public-policy case studies for graduate students (*http://www.hallway.org*). Except where otherwise noted, all quotes are based on personal communication between July and August 2000.

(OA), Oxfam International (OI),[2] and Jubilee 2000 in key parts of the struggle for debt relief. This focus is intended to highlight both the coalition work and how one organization participated as part of the larger coalition. It is not in any way meant to diminish the critical roles played by countless other individuals and organizations, nor to claim disproportionate credit for Oxfam in the campaign for debt relief of the late 1990s.

Oxfam Policy Advocacy

All Oxfams engage in advocacy to affect policy decisions of their home governments, but Oxfam America is in a unique position to affect policy on a more global level. First, because the United States is the wealthiest and most powerful nation in the world, decisions relevant to poverty reduction in the developing world made in the United States are likely to have broad reverberations. Second, Washington, D.C., is home to powerful international financial institutions (IFIs) such as the World Bank and the IMF whose policies affect vast numbers of people in developing countries. To take advantage of the opportunities to affect policy globally, Oxfam America and Oxfam International share an advocacy office in Washington, D.C. Although their work is complementary, Oxfam America's focus is mainly on influencing US government policy while Oxfam International works to make the IFIs more attentive to the needs of the world's poor.

The Oxfam America Policy Department uses an advocacy approach based on direct lobbying of policy makers and spreading their message through the media. The alignment of advocacy goals and strategy through Oxfam International amplifies the message and reach of each individual Oxfam. For example, Oxfam advocates in the United States, the United Kingdom, and Canada lobbied their home finance ministries simultaneously with a unified message, helping to push forward the debt-relief debate in the Group of Seven (G7).[3] Because Oxfam's positions are backed by

---

2. Oxfam International is a federation of the eleven national Oxfam organizations formed in 1995 to better coordinate advocacy, relief, and marketing efforts of the member organizations. The primary focus of all the Oxfams is making grants to partner organizations for sustainable development and poverty alleviation.

3. The Group of Seven (G7) refers to the leading industrial nations (the United States, Britain, Canada, Germany, France, Japan, and Italy), which meet in summits annually to discuss issues of mutual concern. Although this group has been formally expanded to the G8 with the addition of Russia, it is the original G7 that determine finance policy.

credible, field-based research, Oxfam advocates have been able to cultivate relationships with senior staff in Congress, the Clinton administration, and institutions such as the World Bank and the US Treasury. At the same time, Oxfam uses an aggressive media strategy based on gaining the trust of key journalists, which results in sympathetic op-ed pieces and editorials in influential newspapers and coverage of issues raised by Oxfam at press conferences.

Early Debt Advocacy

Large foreign-debt burdens in developing countries were first acknowledged to be a problem in 1982 when Mexico stopped servicing debt owed primarily to international commercial banks. Other middle-income countries in Latin America followed suit. In 1989, many of these countries were able to reduce their debt stock to more sustainable levels through the Brady Plan, which swapped debt for bonds backed by guarantees from developed countries.

Meanwhile, the debt burden of heavily indebted poor countries (HIPCs) grew quietly throughout the 1980s and 1990s. In contrast to the countries benefiting from the Brady Plan, these countries' debts were primarily bilateral (owed to the governments of developed countries) and, increasingly, multilateral (owed to IFIs such as the World Bank and IMF). The proportion of multilateral debt rose steadily as new IFI loans allowed other creditors to be paid off and aid flows declined following the fall of the Berlin Wall in 1989. By 1994, multilateral debt accounted for over 30 percent of the HIPCs' long-term external debt stocks. Furthermore, because the IFIs are preferred creditors and serve as gatekeepers for loans from other sources, meaning they must be paid back first, poor-country remittances to multilaterals grew even more, to about half of their total foreign-debt-service paid.

Because of the priority given to repayment of multilateral debt, poor countries increasingly failed to service debt to bilateral creditors. In recognition of the fact that much of this debt was unlikely to ever be repaid, the Paris Club group of bilateral creditors agreed on a series of measures to reduce debt owed to them, starting in the late 1980s. Positions of the creditor countries on poor-country debt were varied, and the UK, under the leadership of Chancellor of the Exchequer Kenneth Clarke, took the lead in pushing forward bilateral debt forgiveness. In 1994, the Paris Club announced the Naples Terms, which granted countries that had successfully completed three years of an IMF structural adjustment program (SAP)[4] a 67 percent reduction of "pre-cutoff" debt—debt accrued before the country had first appealed to the Paris Club for debt rescheduling. Despite these measures, the debt burdens of poor countries continued to grow due to declining aid flows, falling prices for the commodity goods that made up the majority of most HIPCs' exports, and the fact that Paris Club debt relief never had the explicit goal of reducing debt stocks to levels that would be sustainable in the long term.

In the 1980s and early 1990s, the Debt Crisis Network, a US coalition made up primarily of religious groups but also including environmental, family-farm, and labor organizations, led advocacy on debt in Washington. Despite some successes in pushing forward relief for bilateral and commercial debts, discussion of debt receded from the spotlight once the immediate crisis in Latin American passed.

Calls to reduce multilateral debt stocks, more of an issue than commercial debt for the poorest countries, many of which are in sub-Saharan Africa, were resisted fiercely by the IFIs. Although in practice new IFI lending was frequently used to pay old IFI loans, masking the fact that many countries were essentially in default on commitments to IFIs, the World Bank's AAA credit ratings rested in part on the supposition that it was not legally possible to default on its loans. Granting debt relief threatened this belief, and officials of the World Bank feared that doing so would hurt its credit rating and make it more expensive for it to borrow in the markets, which would in turn raise the costs of borrowing for the countries that are the bank's clients. The IMF and others warned of the risk of "moral hazard": the fear that debtors would agree to future loans that they couldn't pay because of the expectation that a third party would bail them out if they were unable to keep their commitments. The credit-rating and moral-hazard fears remained the principal arguments of opponents to IFI debt relief.

---

4. A structural adjustment program (SAP) is a series of economic policy measures typically demanded by the World Bank and IMF in exchange for low-interest loans. Generally, they have the short-term goal of reducing balance of payments imbalances by increasing foreign exchange earnings and decreasing domestic demand. Many activists and NGOs are critical of SAPs because of the risk that reducing demand in low-consumption economies will further exacerbate poverty.

Finding Inside Allies

As the World Bank and IMF geared up to celebrate their fiftieth anniversary in 1994, a diverse group of activists came together in a new coalition to challenge the legacy of the Bretton-Woods institutions. Oxfam America joined over one hundred other development, environmental, religious, and human rights organizations as a founding member of 50 Years Is Enough.[5] Activist and confrontational in style, 50 Years Is Enough used rallies and street demonstrations to call for multilateral debt reduction in addition to increasing transparency in World Bank and IMF decision making, eliminating SAPs, reforming World Bank programs to be focused on poverty reduction, ending World Bank projects resulting in environmental destruction and forced resettlement, and reducing the power of the IMF and World Bank in the global financial system.

The activists' persistence paid off as more people began to openly question the role of the IFIs and the World Bank became increasingly concerned about its image. Although uncomfortable with the militancy of 50 Years Is Enough, Anthony Gaeta of the World Bank's HIPC Implementation Unit gives the group some of the credit for the bank's move toward more openness and dialogue with civil society in recent years, stating that "in the beginning, 50 Years Is Enough was needed in order to get the bank to listen."

In January 1995, Oxfam International (OI) opened its Washington office and began advocacy work on debt reduction. Advocacy Director Justin Forsyth and Senior Advocacy Officer Veena Siddharth worked together to build relationships with policy makers within the World Bank and IMF and with journalists who could bring the problems of unsustainable debt to a wider audience. They were backed by rigorous, field-based Oxfam International research reports prepared by Oxfam Great Britain's policy department that highlighted the threat multilateral debt posed to long-term development prospects in poor countries.

According to Siddharth, "Multilateral debt relief was not acknowledged to be necessary at that time. The IMF and World Bank both claimed that the Paris Club's Naples Terms were enough." Earlier ad-

---

5. Oxfam America stopped being a member of the 50 Years Is Enough coalition in 1997, though informal discussions and coordination continued to take place on key issues after that point.

vocacy had been unable to persuade the IFIs to take calls for multilateral debt relief seriously. In addition to the moral-hazard and credit-rating arguments outlined above, the standard response was that developing countries that followed the economic policies prescribed by the World Bank and IMF would achieve high growth rates and grow themselves out of their debt problems. As late as February 1995, a joint World Bank/IMF report submitted to executive directors concluded that "for most of the heavily indebted poor countries, multilateral debt service burdens are manageable."[6]

In the spring of 1995, Siddharth and Forsyth made contact with Nawal Kamel, director of the World Bank group that produces the annual World Debt Tables (now called Global Development Finance), who had found that a significant portion of funds from the International Development Association (the World Bank's concessional lending arm) were being used to pay back debt. According to Siddharth, Kamel took a personal interest in debt, and shared her findings with Oxfam International, but encountered strong resistance from the key Vice Presidency of Financing and Resource Mobilization within the World Bank. Oxfam International's cooperation with Kamel is representative of Oxfam's "inside-outside" advocacy strategy: finding allies within the IFIs and working with them to push the issue forward from the inside, while at the same time generating outside pressure through the media and in collaboration with other organizations and activists.

In the summer of 1995, James Wolfensohn had just been selected as the new president of the World Bank. Because of his Wall Street background, 50 Years Is Enough was skeptical of the new leader and warned that his actions would be closely scrutinized. But on a trip to Great Britain even before taking office, Wolfensohn displayed a willingness to reach out to civil society by meeting with nongovernmental organizations (NGOs) including Oxfam. The World Bank had already begun to promote NGO participation in its activities, but so far this was limited to assisting with projects. Oxfam told him that the participation of NGOs in policy making as well was essential for the World Bank to succeed in its mission of reduc-

ing poverty and urged him to raise the profile of the debt issue. Wolfensohn also went to Africa early on, and in Uganda, Tony Burdon of Oxfam Great Britain helped facilitate meetings with local NGOs, including the Uganda Debt Network.

From the start, Wolfensohn vowed to make poverty alleviation one of the bank's top priorities and showed a willingness to address multilateral debt. With Wolfensohn as its head, the World Bank joined the British government as the leading institution working to overcome resistance to debt relief from the IMF and some members of the G7, notably Germany and Japan.

Shortly after assuming his position, Wolfensohn convened a Multilateral Debt Task Force headed by Nawal Kamel. The task force's confidential report concluded that growing debt burdens were an intractable problem for many poor countries and proposed that their debts be addressed comprehensively for the first time through the creation of a Multilateral Debt Facility, which would act as a trust fund to pay the multilateral debt service of qualifying countries for a specified period of time. When a copy of this report was leaked to the press in September 1995, the IMF and some governments of developed countries were furious that the World Bank was considering new debt-relief measures without consulting them. An anonymous IMF official quoted in the *Financial Times* said, "By raising the issue of multilateral debt relief, the World Bank has scored an own goal."[7] Although Wolfensohn was upset by the leak, it did serve to bring renewed attention to multilateral debt and push forward a debate that had become stalled.

Managing Success

At the IMF–World Bank annual meetings later in the fall of 1995, governments directed the institutions to continue searching for a solution to the crisis, and a joint task force was commissioned to study ways to address debt comprehensively. Oxfam International, other Washington-based NGOs including Bread for the World and Center of Concern, and the Religious Working Group on the World Bank and IMF continued their strategy of moving entrenched opposition, especially at the IMF, by lobbying and

---

6. As quoted by George Graham, "Multilateral Debt Dogma Questioned," *Financial Times*, April 26, 1995.

7. As quoted by Michael Holman, "IMF Cool to World Bank Debt Document," *Financial Times*, September 15, 1995.

generating media coverage of the debt issue. Meanwhile, in Europe, the European Network on Debt and Development (EURODAD), the Catholic Fund for Overseas Development (CAFOD), and Christian Aid, Oxfam International, and Oxfam Great Britain took the lead in debt advocacy, producing persuasive policy papers for decision makers linking the growing multilateral debt burdens of poor countries to poverty and low human development and using moral and economic arguments to persuade officials of the need for debt reduction.

During 1996, Oxfam America began its own advocacy work on debt. Senior Policy Advisor Lydia Williams worked out of the Washington office and co-ordinated lobbying efforts with Oxfam International. While Forsyth and Siddharth worked to influence the Washington-based IFIs, Williams targeted US institutions such as the administration, the US Treasury, and Congress. The US Treasury plays an important role in implementing debt relief because it negotiates the terms for forgiveness of US bilateral debt and because Treasury has US jurisdiction over the World Bank, the IMF, and the regional development banks. Furthermore, the United States controls the largest share of votes at the IMF and World Bank, making Treasury's role even more critical.[8] As Siddharth had found in lobbying efforts at the IFIs, the reception to debt relief at Treasury was varied. One person who did take an interest was Deputy Secretary Lawrence Summers, who became secretary in 1999.

When the proposal submitted by the new IMF–World Bank committee was approved at the IMF–World Bank annual meetings in September 1996, Wolfensohn said, "It is very good news for the poor of the world."[9] In any analysis, the Heavily Indebted Poor Countries (HIPC) Initiative was indeed a significant departure from previous efforts at debt reduction. For the first time, all creditors, including the multilateral institutions, were being asked to work in concert to reduce debt, with the explicit goal of making poor countries' debt burdens fiscally sustainable so that they could exit from their debt problems. "Sustainable debt" was defined as having a net present value of debt stock to exports of 200–250 percent or debt service to

exports of 20 to 25 percent. The target ratios were given a range in recognition that some countries are especially economically vulnerable, for example due to reliance on a single major commodity export. An alternative fiscal target of net present value of debt to fiscal revenue of 280 percent was added later. To receive debt reduction under the fiscal criteria, countries needed to meet thresholds of revenue collection of at least 20 percent of gross domestic product (GDP) and exports of at least 40 percent of GDP. Based on eligibility criteria, a list of forty-one countries was drawn up, although it was only expected that about half of these would ultimately qualify for debt relief under the terms of the plan.

To qualify for the program, a country first needed to establish a three-year period of compliance with an IMF structural adjustment program. After that, the country reached the "decision point," when two-thirds of eligible Paris Club debt was canceled under the Naples Terms. A debt-sustainability analysis was then carried out, and if it was determined that the country would still be above the thresholds in three years, it became eligible for further debt reduction following another three years of compliance with an IMF program. After the second three-year period, the country reached the "completion point" and received debt-stock reduction of 80 percent from Paris Club and other bilateral creditors. Finally, the debt stock was reduced to previously defined sustainable levels by reductions in multilateral debt stocks. Multilateral institutions covered the cost of debt reduction from their own resources and through the HIPC Trust Fund, which was financed by donations from developed-country governments. Securing sufficient funding for the trust fund was crucial to the success of the program.

Oxfam International greeted the announcement of the HIPC Initiative with a press release acknowledging it as a bold step forward. At the same time, OI highlighted the deficiencies of the new program:

- The debt-to-export ratio was too high to provide real debt sustainability.

- The six-year time frame was too long given the countries' urgent needs.

- There was no explicit link between debt relief and poverty reduction.

---

8. Currently, the US shares of votes at the IMF and World Bank are 17.67 and 16.5 percent, respectively.

9. As quoted on the World Bank's HIPC website: *http://www.worldbank.org/hipc/about/hipcbr/hipcbr.htm*.

- Civil society in eligible countries would not be involved in the process.

Despite the fact that the press release identified problems with the initiative, some activists criticized Oxfam for appearing to cooperate with the World Bank and accepting a debt-reduction plan that included structural adjustment and preserved the roles of the IMF and World Bank.

More outspoken HIPC Initiative critics such as 50 Years Is Enough and Witness for Peace argue that structural adjustment programs harm the poor through their reductions in government spending, promotion of export agriculture and trade liberalization, and emphasis on controlling inflation by reducing demand. According to Witness for Peace Executive Director Steve Bennett, "We need to be true to what our partners in the South ask for. They're saying there should be no conditions." Bennett adds that although the civil society organizations in developing countries that Witness for Peace works with oppose structural adjustment and are generally disappointed with the HIPC Initiative, they are willing to accept any debt relief available, and thus his organization does not work to undermine the HIPC process.

Although critical of the inattention to poverty reduction in traditional structural adjustment programs, Oxfam America and the other Oxfams do not discount the need for economic reform in many developing countries. First, they recognize that prior to structural adjustment, most of the poor countries in question did not have fiscal policies geared toward poverty reduction and were indeed faced with economic crises. The question then becomes how to construct policies that facilitate both economic stability and poverty reduction. As Siddharth points out, "Some kind of reform was necessary, but the adjustment that took place in the '80s and '90s was not poverty-focused." With respect to the HIPC Initiative specifically, Oxfam observed that under traditional Paris Club debt relief, three years of compliance with an IMF program were seen as sufficient to avert moral hazard, but now the bar had been raised to six years for no obvious reason. In addition, Oxfam pointed out that two-thirds of structural adjustment programs in HIPCs break down before their completion point due to design problems and a "lack of ownership," that is, a low level of commitment to a reform program conceived largely by outsiders. The poor track record of structural adjustment implementation means that this condition was likely to prohibit many poor countries from receiving HIPC Initiative benefits.

The divergence in responses to the HIPC Initiative illustrates a divide that would remain present within the diverse and growing constellation of NGOs doing debt advocacy. While Oxfam is willing to engage policy makers in order to achieve whatever is politically possible in the medium term, some allies assume a prophetic stance, refusing to budge from their vision of the way things should be. As Oxfam's Media Spokesperson Seth Amgott put it, "My law of Washington is that people who are making more compromises than you are sellouts who don't know why they're in this business. And people who are making less compromises than you are wild-eyed idealists who have no idea how to accomplish something and would rather be right than make any change in the real world. Virtually everyone sees themselves as the midpoint in that spectrum."

Regardless of where groups lie on the spectrum, they almost universally claim to base their position on feedback from partner organizations in developing countries. Although the extent to which Northern NGOs have developed relationships with Southern partners varies widely, the fact that they may reach different conclusions does not necessarily mean that consultations never took place—there are naturally a diversity of opinions and approaches among civil society within the indebted countries themselves.

Involvement of Southern partners takes a wide variety of forms. Northern advocates sometimes host their partners in Washington so that they can meet with policy makers directly, which can be especially effective when they are briefed by their hosts on what to expect from a given official. Another strategy is to include partner organizations directly when developing positions. This strategy works well for organizations such as Oxfam, which have a presence in developing countries and well-developed networks of partner NGOs. Central American NGOs were especially influential in helping Oxfam International develop positions on post-Hurricane Mitch reconstruction in Honduras and Nicaragua. Partner organizations that have helped Oxfam build positions in Africa include the Mozambique Debt Group and the Uganda Debt Network. In recent years, the worldwide spread of information technology has greatly facilitated communication, and groups with well-established connections are now able to easily consult and share information with partners by e-mail before making policy decisions. Finally, although most groups would be reluctant to admit it, positions that must be taken quickly may be formed based on past experience without direct input from the developing countries themselves.

After the implementation of the HIPC Initiative, Oxfam America and the other members of Oxfam International focused their advocacy energy toward working to make the framework deliver deeper, broader, and faster debt relief—yielding greater debt reduction for more countries in a shorter time frame. Strategies included lobbying to have countries considered, pushing for shorter completion points, and analyzing debt sustainability by the World Bank and IMF. Advocates suspected the IMF of attempting to limit the amount of debt relief for poor countries by inflating the economic projections upon which HIPC relief was based. For example, Siddharth examined projections for Rwanda and found that they assumed an unrealistically high export-revenue growth rate in 1995—just one year after the country had been torn apart by genocidal violence. The figure was revised after Oxfam International, Oxfam Canada, and others lobbied the IMF's executive directors.

Again, allies within the World Bank such as Nawal Kamel and her successor as head of the HIPC Implementation Unit, Axel van Trotsenberg, proved invaluable in negotiating with the other parties to the process to secure the best possible terms for qualifying countries. As Anthony Gaeta of the World Bank's HIPC Implementation Unit points out, "Veena [Siddharth] and Kevin [Watkins, with Oxfam International in the United Kingdom] know as much about debt as people in the HIPC Unit, so of course we're going to listen to them." At the same time, Oxfam continued cultivating relationships with Washington journalists, and sympathetic discussion of debt issues began appearing in newspapers influential to policy makers, such as the *Financial Times* and *Washington Post*, with increasing frequency.

Maintaining a Coalition

According to Siddharth, since 1996 groups from developing countries have come to the forefront of the debate on debt reduction. This can be attributed in part to a growing awareness on the part of NGOs in the global South that despite its deficiencies, the HIPC Initiative does represent a significant opening. No less important is the impact of Jubilee 2000, a worldwide movement for debt cancellation that gathered momentum in the late 1990s.

Jubilee 2000 was started in Great Britain in April 1996 and has since spread to sixty-five countries around the world. Its platform calls for "a one-off cancellation of the unpayable debts of the world's poorest countries by the end of the year 2000, under a fair and transparent process."[10] Basing its case on moral arguments, the movement takes its name and inspiration from biblical reference to a "Jubilee Year" every fifty years when debts were forgiven and slaves set free. The symbolism of the year 2000 and the notion that poor countries should be allowed a fresh start in the new millennium provided a catalyst. Jubilee 2000 has attracted strong support from the Catholic Church and major Protestant denominations, but its endorsers also include unions, environmental, human rights, and development organizations. It boasts a cast of celebrity supporters including Ewan McGregor, Muhammad Ali, Madonna, and Bono, among many others.

Jubilee 2000/USA was formed in 1997 from the informal Religious Working Group on the World Bank and the IMF, itself composed of the more progressive Catholic orders and Protestant denominations. Today it is a coalition with a steering committee of forty-nine organizational members, including Oxfam America as well as numerous religious, solidarity, and development organizations. Jubilee 2000 coalitions throughout the world are organized similarly and together create a broad global network of debt-relief activists.

Although the moral arguments of Jubilee 2000 are not dissimilar from those used in the many Oxfam policy papers that highlight the human cost of debt, Jubilee was extremely successful in using the simple message that human needs should come before debt repayment to spur a broad popular campaign in a way that organizations focused on lobbying could not. Religious leaders including Pope John Paul II, Archbishop Desmond Tutu, Pat Robertson, Billy Graham,

---

10. See the Jubilee 2000 website: *www.jubilee2000uk.org/main.html.*

and the Dalai Lama have endorsed the Jubilee 2000 vision and issued emotional moral appeals for debt relief. At the same time, Jubilee 2000's roots in churches provide a ready way to disseminate information and inspire action. Technology unavailable to earlier debt activists has also aided the dispersed movement, as information can be spread quickly and easily via the Internet.

Although the primary motivating factor for most Jubilee 2000/USA members is faith-based belief in the moral responsibility to assist the world's poorest and the injustice of worldwide inequality, other organizations see debt reduction as part of their mission for different reasons. In explaining why an environmental organization has taken on debt relief, Friends of the Earth's Carol Welch says, "We see a connection between high levels of debt and exploitation of natural resources. We go after the root causes of environmental destruction, and we see debt as one of those root causes."

The movement first came to international attention in May 1998, when Jubilee 2000 mobilized over fifty thousand supporters to form a human chain around the site of the G7 meeting in Birmingham, UK, forcing a meeting with Prime Minister Tony Blair. But calls for debt relief beyond the existing program were rebuffed at the meeting, especially by resistance from Germany.

The chain, which represents the chains of debt, is the symbol of the Jubilee 2000 movement. Jubilee 2000 actions since Birmingham have been equally creative. An ongoing petition drive boasts over seventeen million signatories and aims to become the largest petition in history. Jubilee 2000 organizers were able to make their voices heard at the G7 summit in remote Okinawa, Japan, in July 2000 through a "Net the Debt" campaign in which supporters checked a website for the e-mail and fax numbers of G7 embassies and sent messages calling for debt cancellation.

Tragedy also brought debt relief to public attention in 1998 when Hurricane Mitch tore through Central America, setting back development by a generation in already vulnerable countries like Nicaragua and Honduras. In keeping with its emphasis on addressing poverty by focusing on the root causes rather than short-term humanitarian aid, Oxfam joined a broad network of organizations in Nicaragua and Honduras in calling for immediate cancellation of those countries' debts. In response, creditors said they

would consider postponing debt service due while the countries recovered.

As a broad coalition including both moderate groups such as Oxfam America and more radical ones like 50 Years Is Enough, there was tension on the Jubilee 2000/USA steering committee from the start. This tension turned into a crisis in early 1999 when some members of the Public Policy Subcommittee, including Oxfam America's Lydia Williams and Seth Amgott, formed the Legislative Group and began searching for a way to push debt relief forward in the US Congress.

Until this point, US debt-relief policy had remained inside Treasury, which was now reluctant to push expansion of the HIPC program due to fear that the Republican-dominated Congress would not fund it. Therefore, the Legislative Group sought to move the debate out of Treasury and into the political arena by actively seeking out sympathetic Republicans. The result was an agreement from Representative Jim Leach of Iowa to introduce legislation based on recommendations of the Legislative Group. H.R. 1095, the Debt Relief for Poverty Reduction Act of 1999, was introduced to the House of Representatives in March 1999 and currently boasts 140 cosponsors, although it has never come to the floor for a vote. Among the bipartisan supporters of the Leach Bill, one of the most passionate was Republican representative Spencer Bachus of Alabama, a devout Southern Baptist who, according to Amgott, was strongly influenced by moral arguments for debt relief. Bachus has since become one of the most forceful voices for debt relief in the House, saying, "This decision will define us as either a loving people, a people filled with grace and compassion, or it will define us as a people focused on the monetary, the temporal."[11]

In addition to providing US funding for the HIPC Trust Fund and authorizing the sale of some of the IMF's gold reserves to finance its portion of the relief package, the Leach Bill would have gone beyond existing US commitments under the HIPC framework by canceling all bilateral debt to eligible countries (not just pre-cutoff debt) and urging the president to seek modification to the HIPC Initiative so that the waiting period would be reduced to a maximum of

---

11. As quoted by Mike McManus, "Jubilee 2000 Is Debt Relief for the Poor," *The News Herald*, October 16, 1999; available online at: *www.newsherald.com/archive/religion/ra101699.htm.*

three years and countries would be required to show a commitment to poverty reduction. Still, some Jubilee 2000/USA Steering Committee members felt unable to support a bill that would retain the IMF and World Bank as the gatekeepers for debt reduction and ultimately fall short of the goal of canceling all unpayable debt through a transparent process. Njoki Njehu, Director of 50 Years Is Enough, argues that "the Leach Bill will not work in the long run, because it maintains structural adjustment programs and it keeps the World Bank and IMF in charge of debt relief." Others maintained that pursuing such a legislative strategy would dilute Jubilee 2000's prophetic vision and allow politicians to co-opt the movement. According to Carole Collins, former national coordinator for Jubilee 2000/USA, "Jubilee South fears that the position of Jubilee 2000/USA becomes a ceiling, not a floor."

According to Williams, however, "Pressure on the administration through the Leach Bill yielded direct results by strengthening Clinton's hand going into the Cologne G7 meeting." By this time, Seth Amgott, who served as media spokesperson for both Oxfam America and Oxfam International, had joined Williams in Oxfam's Washington office. He too claimed success for the legislative strategy of pushing debt relief forward politically by bringing Republicans on board, saying that "Secretary Summers told Bachus shortly after becoming secretary that the administration can no longer afford to have Spencer Bachus to its left on this issue. Which said that Lydia and my strategy worked."

Jubilee 2000 did not lend its name to the legislation, due not only to the internal conflict but also to the realization that once introduced into Congress the bill was beyond their control and could be amended to the point where it was unrecognizable. Still, the issue revealed a rift that nearly tore the coalition apart. In the end, Steering Committee members realized they had more to gain than lose by continuing to work together privately, while maintaining different public profiles and positions.

Keeping the Momentum

As the Jubilee 2000 movement gathered support internationally, discussion of debt relief broadened and became more visible in 1999. Meanwhile, the World Bank and IMF began a review of the HIPC pro-

gram. In an effort to mute criticism that the institutions were closed and unwilling to engage in dialogue with outsiders, comments from civil society were actively sought. The fact that this would have been unthinkable even a few years before illustrates the movement toward greater openness that had occurred during Wolfensohn's tenure. In response, Oxfam International repeated the arguments it had been making in policy papers for years:

Debt relief is being delivered too slowly. By April 1999, two years after the program had been implemented, just two countries, Uganda and Bolivia, had actually reached the completion point and begun to receive debt reduction. Uganda had been undergoing economic reforms for over a decade, and OI charged that it should have been given relief a year earlier and had lost $190 million in benefits because of the delay.

Sustainability thresholds are too high. OI pointed out that in Uganda, debt servicing in 1998–1999 fell from $165 million to $128 million, but still accounted for 18 percent of government revenue, leaving insufficient resources to implement the ambitious national poverty-eradication plan. Furthermore, due to a fall in the price of coffee, Uganda's debt burden would not meet the sustainability target set by the World Bank and IMF. Meanwhile, the bank and the fund judged Senegal's debt to be sustainable, despite the fact that debt service absorbs 25 percent of government revenue, in a country where adult literacy is 33 percent.

HIPC relief is unconnected to human development. Due to the extreme human-development needs in the poorest indebted countries, OI argued that there should be a more explicit link between debt relief and poverty reduction and that further resources were needed.

To address these concerns, OI proposed a Human Development Window, which would offer countries incentives to turn debt reduction into human-development investments. Instead of compliance with structural adjustment programs, conditionality would be based on a willingness to allocate 70 to 100 percent of budgetary savings to poverty reduction, development of a Poverty Action Framework with input from civil society, and the transfer of debt savings into a national poverty fund. Countries agreeing to these guidelines would be rewarded with debt relief within one to two years under lowered sustainability thresholds.

Uganda, which was widely viewed as the biggest HIPC success story, provided a model of what could be done. All of Uganda's budget savings from debt were allocated to the Poverty Action Fund, which spent money in a transparent fashion according to priorities identified in the national Poverty Eradication Action Plan that had been developed in consultation with civil society. As a result, primary-school enrollment more than doubled between 1997 and 1999, setting Uganda on a course to achieve its ambitious goal of universal primary education.

On the other side of the issue, critics such as Karl Ziegler of the Centre for Accountability and Debt Relief argued that debt reduction will likely benefit only the elites in poor countries, due to corruption, and should therefore be dependent on repatriation of wealth stolen by leaders and strictly audited commitments to invest the savings in social programs. Ziegler singles out Uganda as a truly deserving country that has been able to turn savings achieved from debt relief into poverty reduction due to a strong record of economic and political reform. According to Ziegler, "Many [of the world's poor] are now effectively disenfranchised and will most likely continue to be ruled largely by kleptocrats, selfish ruling elites and unaccountable, inefficient governments. Such governments are hardly likely to convert the proceeds of debt relief into social programs in which they don't get a piece of the action. Unless a new, more realistic policy is proposed and implemented, the poor will remain frustrated."[12] Debt-relief advocates counter that the poor should not be required to suffer for their leaders' past sins, that safeguards can be put in place to link debt relief to increased social spending, and that attempting to track down stolen money would create an unacceptable delay in countries with desperate human-development needs.

Also in 1999, Oxfam launched Education Now, its first international campaign. Coordinated by Oxfam International and with varying levels of participation from the other Oxfams, the campaign combined in-depth research and reports with a simple, media-friendly message that all the world's children deserved a basic primary education. Campaign literature highlighted the ambitious human-development goals set by the world community of halving the incidence of poverty, reducing child deaths by two-thirds, and achieving universal primary education by 2015. As the campaign progressed, Oxfam made explicit connections between unsustainable debt, inadequate spending on education in the HIPCs, and insufficient progress toward meeting the agreed human-development goals. Just as debt relief was seen as a wedge issue to force broader reform geared toward poverty reduction within the IFIs, Oxfam used education as a wedge to push debt relief forward.

In promoting the message that development should be specifically oriented toward human needs, Oxfam challenged head-on the dominant discourse that economic growth is synonymous with development and would be sufficient to bring people out of poverty. With the Education Now campaign, Oxfam showed that economic growth by itself did not guarantee that benefits were spread equitably and that education outcomes were dependent on policy choices and investment in education. According to Williams, this strategy was particularly effective in getting Treasury Secretary Summers to recognize the human needs that lay beyond the numbers and economic data.

At the G7 summit meeting in Cologne, Germany, in June 1999, Jubilee 2000 again organized a human chain to bring attention to the debt crisis in developing countries. This time, the assembled dignitaries were more openly receptive, as there was a growing recognition that the HIPC Initiative had failed to end the debt crisis and a political consensus that more needed to be done. Japan, the world's largest creditor nation, had been previously skeptical of debt relief, but had slowly changed its position, and Germany's new government had abandoned the reluctance of its predecessor. The summit ended with G7 leaders announcing that total HIPC debt relief would be increased from approximately $52.5 billion to $100 billion, including an approximate doubling of multilateral debt reduction to $50 billion.[13]

---

12. Karl Ziegler, "Bankrolling Despots: Count Me Out," May 15, 1998; available online at *www.painsley.org.uk/justice/debt/19980515-12.html.*

---

13. Although the $100 billion headline figure sounds impressive, $20 billion of that represents the cancellation of concessional bilateral loans (Official Development Assistance), almost none of which was being serviced anyway.

The enhanced HIPC framework, ratified at the annual meetings of the IMF and World Bank in September 1999, essentially amounted to the deeper, broader, and faster debt relief that Oxfam and others had been advocating for. The Enhanced HIPC Initiative increased Naples Terms bilateral debt relief from 80 to 90 percent, lowered debt-sustainability ratios, and provided for lower debt service in the period between the decision and completion points. In an attempt to link debt relief to poverty reduction, the IMF's Enhanced Structural Adjustment Facility (ESAF) was renamed the Poverty Reduction and Growth Facility (PRGF), and qualifying HIPCs would now be required to produce a Poverty Reduction Strategy Paper (PRSP), which would be developed in conjunction with civil society. Although the PRSP does include traditional macroeconomic adjustment measures, it also incorporates some aspects of the proposed Human Development Window by seeking to link debt relief to poverty reduction through a transparent process. Finally, debt relief would be based on actual economic indicators available at the decision point, not on projections of what the debt ratios will be at the completion point. In the past, a country that had already reached the completion point could not receive additional relief if exports were less than expected, resulting in a debt-to-export ratio above what was targeted.

Oxfam welcomed the improvements, citing the global debt movement as a critical factor in getting this far, but called for further action, saying that the enhancements to HIPC had brought the world halfway toward solving the poor-country debt crisis. There was skepticism within the NGO community about the commitment of the World Bank and IMF to poverty reduction, and many charged that the PRGF was just structural adjustment by a different name. Some rejected the Enhanced HIPC process outright because the World Bank and IMF led it and conditionality was still based on SAPs. According to Njehu, "We are very clear that we share the views of Jubilee South and other voices in the South that the Cologne initiative polishes rather than breaks the chains of debt."

Nonetheless, at least at the rhetorical level, the Enhanced HIPC Initiative represented a significant shift away from the IFIs' association of development solely with growth and toward an understanding of poverty reduction and the addressing of human needs as part of the development process. Both institutions loudly proclaimed that poverty reduction was now their primary mission. Whether this change goes beyond rhetoric and becomes incorporated into a new model of development remains to be seen, and likely depends on the vigilance of Oxfam and other World Bank and IMF critics.

Shortly after it was agreed, the Enhanced HIPC Initiative was in danger of dying an early death due to a lack of contributions to the HIPC Trust Fund. Furthermore, the World Gold Council was vociferously opposed to a proposed sale of some of the IMF's gold, which was to finance the IMF's share of the program. In order to sell its gold, the IMF had to have a vote of 85 percent of the executive directors. With 17 percent of the votes, the United States had a de facto veto, and congressional leaders of both parties made it clear that they sided with the gold industry in opposing an open-market sale. The IMF could also gain the necessary resources by revaluing its gold, which was kept on the books at far below its current market value, but the IMF's governing articles required a vote in the national legislature of every member country in order to do this, a nearly insurmountable obstacle.

After doing some research, Williams and Amgott came up with a creative, back-door way to refinance the gold via an off-market sale. A country owing money to the IMF would buy the gold and then use it to repay its debt to the fund. The gold would never leave the building and could be revalued through the transaction by an 85 percent vote of the executive directors without the approval of every national legislature. Williams and Amgott presented the plan to Representative Bachus, who supported it publicly and gained the support of Secretary of the Treasury Summers. Because the plan did not require an open-market sale, the gold industry was not opposed, and in the end Congress approved the revaluation of nine-fourteenths of the IMF's gold stock. The rest of the G7 agreed and the plan was implemented, freeing up the necessary resources for the IMF's share of the plan.

Also in the 1999 session, Congress approved funds to meet US bilateral commitments under Enhanced HIPC, but failed to appropriate the US contribution to the HIPC Trust Fund, despite strong support from the Clinton administration. As a result, the Inter-

American Development Bank could not finance debt relief for countries expected to qualify, and other creditor nations were balking at donating to the Trust Fund until the US funds were released.

By early 2000, the US Congress remained the biggest obstacle to achieving even the limited debt relief promised through the Enhanced HIPC Initiative. In the spring, a number of organizations pushing debt relief through Capitol Hill lobbying, including Oxfam America, Bread for the World, the Catholic Conference, and the Episcopal Church, began meeting informally to coordinate their efforts through the Debt Roundtable. Despite stated support for debt relief from a majority of Congress, by summer, prospects for securing sufficient US support for the HIPC Trust Fund didn't look good. In the House, the Republican leadership was trying to prevent a floor vote so that debt-relief funds could be used as a bargaining chip with the president in the budget fight expected in the fall. Meanwhile, Senator Phil Gramm was insisting on linking appropriations for the HIPC Trust Fund to reform of the IMF.

Finally, after a relentless lobbying campaign by Oxfam and many of the other groups that make up Jubilee 2000, Congress approved legislation to fully fund the US contribution to the HIPC Trust Fund, which was signed by President Clinton on November 6, 2000. In addition, the legislation authorized additional IMF gold sales to fund the program. With the resources needed to meet existing HIPC commitments secured, campaigners continue to monitor the process and ensure that the debt relief granted benefited the world's poor to the greatest degree possible.

Conclusion: Advocacy Lessons

From a policy perspective, debt-relief advocacy achieved fantastic gains in the second half of the 1990s. In the space of just five years, the World Bank and IMF moved from a position of resolute opposition to any discussion of multilateral debt relief to implementing a program granting just that, and then expanded it when it became obvious that it would not meet its goals. Of course, it would be presumptuous to say that advocacy by Oxfam, Jubilee 2000, and other organizations was solely responsible for this progress; other factors were also at play including World Bank president Wolfensohn's commitment to openness and

poverty reduction and the leadership shown by Britain within the G7.

Nonetheless, it is clear that the advocacy campaign described here was successful in pushing the debate forward at key junctures. Several factors were instrumental to this success. First, by identifying and cultivating relationships with sympathetic insiders in key institutions such as the World Bank, US Congress, and the US Treasury, campaigners found influential allies who would listen to their arguments and advance them from the inside. In addition, these insider allies shared information with advocates and thus helped them craft their strategy. At the same time, campaigners kept the pressure on from the outside through the media by gaining the trust of journalists who helped spread their message through sympathetic coverage and editorials. This dual strategy proved extremely successful and may be useful as a model for future advocacy campaigns.

But perhaps the single greatest factor contributing to the success of debt-relief advocacy was the construction of a broad coalition that was able to conduct a grassroots campaign to complement the lobbying efforts of advocates. Jubilee 2000 member organizations ranged in their tactics from those who refused to budge from their position that all poor-country debt should be canceled immediately with no conditions, to those willing to work within the system to achieve pragmatic short-term gains far short of complete cancellation. Despite these differences, Jubilee 2000 avoided collapsing at a critical moment and was able to maintain its moral argument for debt relief to sway hundreds of thousands of people, both citizens and policy makers. If Jubilee 2000 offers a lesson to be learned about how to build and maintain a coalition of disparate organizations, it is by showing the value of unifying around a simple fundamental principle that makes sense to large numbers of people—in this case the immorality of poor-country debt.

Partially as a byproduct of the debt-relief campaign, governance at the IFIs has become much more open in the past several years. This is illustrated most tangibly by the active solicitation of input from civil society when revisions to the HIPC Initiative were being considered. In addition, the Poverty Reduction Strategy Papers, as envisioned, are a way to involve civil society in poor countries in setting priorities for spending the savings from debt reduction. In the past, civil society was invited to help at the implementation stage of World Bank projects, but was never asked for input in actual policy making. It remains to be seen whether advocacy groups will be able to build on these steps and achieve more fundamental reform in the governance of the IFIs. But certainly, the success of the campaign for debt relief provides reason for hope to advocates seeking broader changes within the global financial architecture.

Chapter 14

Comparative Lessons
from Social Justice Advocacy Case Studies[1]

Gabrielle Watson

In writing case studies on advocacy, the case study authors and I wanted to explore the basic question of how advocacy is conceived of and carried out in different contexts from a practitioner's perspective. In each of the case studies, we asked organizations what they understand advocacy to be and how they go about it. We also looked at what they are actually doing to answer this question. By engaging in this dialogue, we hope to bring more voices to this conversation.

The case selection process purposefully sought out "success stories" where advocates pioneered innovative and effective advocacy strategies. All the campaigns described had significant impact in some aspects of their struggles, even if the final outcome was less than they sought or is still unknown. Many of these cases represent years of struggle with both advances and setbacks. Although limited in number and focused on "successes," they offer some essential insights into how to navigate through the challenges that inevitably come up in the course of advocacy campaigns. Reviewing the core lessons from the cases, one notices a number of broad patterns that run through them. Some may not apply in all countries and contexts, but they were evident in enough of the cases that they can serve as a tentative guide—both cautionary and hopeful—for social justice work around the globe.

The cases also suggest some basic insights about social justice advocacy:

- Social justice advocacy seeks to change the balance of power to favor excluded groups by acting simultaneously in multiple arenas, including influencing policies and laws, opening channels of participa- tion in decision-making forums, and building civil society.

- More often than not, advocacy in a globalized world is carried out beyond a particular arena (local, regional, national or "global") and draws on a range of actors and allies that have different perspectives, agendas, and access to resources. This has implications for mutual responsibilities in building and maintaining coalitions, sharing information, protecting those most at risk, developing strategies, and determining what are acceptable outcomes.

- Regardless of how open or closed the political system is, successful efforts employ a range of strategies, are flexible and responsive to changing circumstances, and identify a range of leverage points from the power of "rights" arguments, to filing complex legal cases, to identifying sympathetic allies within otherwise hostile targets.

This conclusion returns to the "starting questions" of the case study project: how groups define advocacy and how they learn to be effective advocates in different social, political, and cultural contexts. It begins with a discussion of definitions of advocacy and then examines the correlation between advocacy approaches and political space. In "Strategies That Work," it analyses the major advocacy strategies that run across multiple cases. Then it looks at how groups struggled to bridge local, regional, national, and global political arenas to be effective in their advocacy campaigns. Some key challenges common to multiple cases, and how groups sought to rise above them, are discussed in "Challenges to Overcome." Key advocacy skills and "assets" that helped groups be effective advocates are presented next. Finally, the conclusion ends

---

1. The analysis and the framing issues raised here are based on my own interpretation of the six case studies. They are not necessarily shared by the case study research collaborators, though many of the ideas emerged during our joint fieldwork and appear in their case studies.

with a preliminary framework for evaluating advocacy impact.

Definitions of Advocacy

The cases present a diverse landscape of advocacy issues, arenas, campaign participants, and approaches. They suggest a multi-dimensional understanding of advocacy, held together by the core principles of social justice, human rights, equity, and equal power for all members of society. Social justice advocacy is about shifting the balance of power in favor of excluded groups. It involves advocacy to win specific policies, laws, and programs that shift power, affirm human rights, and make a difference in people's lives. It involves winning the right to *be* at the table, creating governance structures and mechanisms that give civil society groups standing in decision-making processes. It also involves civil society groups struggling to be clear and unified in their positions, when they get to the table, and transforming power relations and cultures within civil society.[2] That is, advocacy seeks impact at three levels:

- Specific policy, law, and program gains benefiting excluded groups.

- Governance gains, changing the rules of the game to open up channels for excluded groups to participate in decision-making processes.

- Civil society gains, building the capacity of excluded groups to influence powerful actors and

create democratic and accountable internal structures. It involves building networks of civil society so excluded groups can articulate their interests and it involves building knowledge of substantive issues and processes for engaging and influencing decision makers.

This multi-dimensional definition of advocacy is broader than the traditional understanding that includes only the first dimension—policy influence. The cases argue, through their lived experiences, that social justice advocacy is deeper and touches on the basic power structures within societies. At the end of the conclusion, I return to this definition to explore how groups can think about evaluating advocacy impact using a multi-dimensional framework.

Political Space and Advocacy Approaches

When we began this project, one of the key questions had to do with the relationship between political space and advocacy. How does the degree of political space—the presence or absence of responsive governance structures, rule of law, freedom of expression, and open access to information and decision-making channels—affect how social justice groups engage in advocacy? Is it even possible to engage in advocacy work when political space is closed? This is important because most advocacy guides focus on lobbying and media strategies that presume responsive governments, a free press, and open and transparent decision-making structures. They assume citizens can seek to influence policies without fearing reprisals. But this is not the reality in many places.

Degrees of political space affect advocates' access to decision-making processes. The more open and transparent the process, the more access advocates have to information and decision makers. This understanding of political space suggested some working hypotheses that we used as a starting point when we began our fieldwork. We expected that advocacy would look very different in closed and open political systems. We also expected that as political space opened, advocacy efforts would transition from protest as a major advocacy approach to one of constructive engagement. Protest would be aimed at opposing harmful policies and programs and demanding access to decision-making structures. Engagement would involve a more

---

2. This understanding of advocacy echoes and builds on work by Valerie Miller and others. See especially Valerie Miller, "NGO and Grassroots Policy Influence: What Is Success?" *IDR Reports* 11, no. 5 (1994); Valerie Miller and Jane Covey, *Advocacy Sourcebook: Frameworks for Planning, Action, and Reflection* (Boston: Institute for Development Research, 1997); Leslie M. Fox and Priya Helweg, "Advocacy Strategies for Civil Society: A Conceptual Framework and Practitioner's Guide," unpublished, prepared for the Center for Democracy and Governance, USAID, 1997; and Chris Roche, *Impact Assessment for Development Agencies: Learning to Value Change* (Oxford: Oxfam GB, 1999). One definition of advocacy that gives a clear statement of this multi-dimensional perspective comes from Lisa Jordan and Peter van Tuijl: "Using information as a key tool, it entails the ambition to change the course of human development by promoting equal power relationships in national and international arenas. NGO advocacy is to organize the strategic articulation of information to democratize unequal power relations. . . . NGO advocacy also entails a fight against cynicism and despair to which powerless communities tend to fall victim, in the face of massive political and practical obstacles impairing them to improve their lot. . . . NGO advocacy includes lobby[ing], development education and campaigning, all aimed at strategically articulating information to democratize unequal power relations" (Lisa Jordan and Peter van Tuijl, "Political Responsibility in Transnational NGO Advocacy," *World Development* 28, no. 12 [2000]).

dialogue-based approach where groups discuss policies with government and other decision makers to raise concerns and put forward proposals.[3]

In countries transitioning toward democracy in Latin America, for example, social movements moved from protest to more nuanced and politically sophisticated advocacy as the opportunities to actually engage with government in constructive debate increased. The more government and political space opened, the more advocates were able to put forward proposals and negotiate solutions. This created a dialectic of "virtuous circles" where political openings allowed civil society organizations to engage more with government, which led to increased openness, more substantive engagement, and so on. That said, it is important to recognize that degrees of political space can often be uneven, making generalizations difficult. Democratic openness can seem robust at times, and then suffer retreats. Some aspects of government may be more open than others and vary widely at the local, regional, and national levels and across geographic regions within the same country. Pockets of open political processes may coexist with "old" forms of exclusion and the use of coercive force.

We intentionally chose cases from countries with a range of political spaces. Two cases, Guatemala during the 1980s and 1990s and Cambodia over a similar time period, are examples of closed political systems. Of course, these two cases cannot represent all societies with closed political systems. We hoped they would help us expand our understandings and perhaps develop some preliminary ideas about what might be possible, even in the worst contexts.

So we started with a "protest-to-proposal" model for thinking about advocacy under different political regimes (see Figure 14.1 on the following page). According to this model, advocacy approaches suited to the degree of political space might be laid out along the trajectory described by the arrow, with lobbying, media work, legislative work, and lawsuits all clus-

tered at the top right end, and protest marches, sit-ins, and everyday acts of resistance clustered down at the bottom left end.

But as we look at this starting model in light of the cases, right away something is missing. Not only don't the cases follow the expected "trajectory"—that is, the cases with closed political systems clustered around protest and the cases with open political systems clustered around proposal strategies—but they suggest a much broader range of advocacy approaches and strategies.

To start with, in Guatemala and Cambodia, the two cases with the least amount of political space, protest was not an option. People who engaged in active protest faced almost certain death in both cases. Instead, advocates used "exit"—leaving the country altogether—to protect themselves. But, especially in the Guatemalan case, they didn't stop trying to influence the course of events within their country. Their "exit" strategies included working from the outside, leveraging external influence on the government through the United Nations and the Organization of American States, since the avenue for direct influence was closed to them. This strategy has also been one of the key approaches used in Cambodia. There, groups used the World Bank to push the government to put policies into effect that would protect forests from predatory illegal logging companies. The World Bank was not necessarily interested in furthering the interests of excluded indigenous peoples—they were concerned with the level of corruption and economically unsustainable extractive forestry policies. But they were a natural ally in this work and had the power to make the Cambodian government crack down on illegal loggers, at least to some extent.

The model also does not fit in countries with medium and high political space, where we might expect it to. In open or moderately open contexts like the United States, Senegal, and Ecuador, protest was a frequent strategy, used in tandem with more propositional strategies like drafting legislation, working with political and religious leaders, and filing lawsuits. Then there are examples of very collaborative engagement in countries with low and moderate political space, like Senegal and during recent years in Cambodia, where groups have worked with government agencies to provide human rights training and legal services.

---

3. The idea behind this framework draws, in part, from my previous work on urban social movements in Brazil and the political science literature on democratic transitions (Gabrielle Watson, "Water and Sanitation in São Paulo, Brazil: Successful Strategies for Service Provision in Low-Income Communities" (master's thesis, Massachusetts Institute of Technology, 1992). See also Alfred Stepan, ed., *Democratizing Brazil: Problems in Transition and Consolidation* (New York: Oxford University Press, 1989); and Maria Helena Moreira Alves, *State and Opposition in Military Brazil* (Austin: University of Texas Press, 1988).

Figure 14.1. Starting Mental Model: Relationship between Political Space and Advocacy Approaches

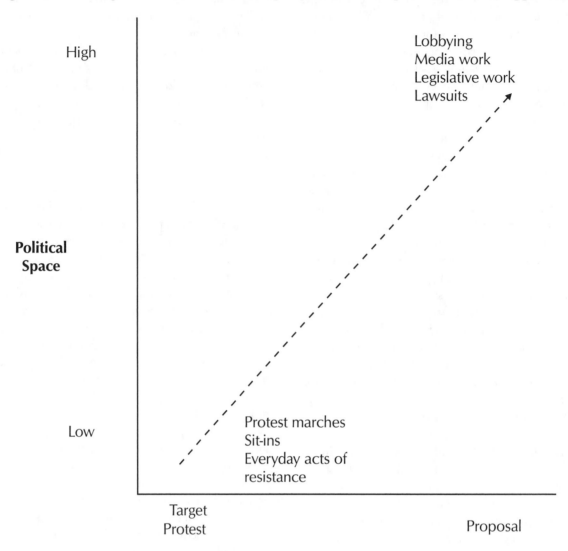

Advocacy Approach

Other counter-examples to the model come from the United States and Guatemala, where we see examples of group members "becoming government." The Federation of Southern Cooperatives encouraged its members to get elected to local, state, and national offices. And in Guatemala, where the political space has increased in recent years, but is still low to moderate, we also see this approach, with indigenous leaders getting elected to municipal governments. In this way, groups seek to place, *within* government, receptive reformers who can work from the inside to further their change objectives. This is not to say that people cannot

be corrupted or co-opted after they enter office; this often does happen. People cannot be naïve about it; it can go terribly wrong. But the cases show that working with government, and sometimes purposefully placing reformists within it, can be one long-term strategy for social justice advocacy.

A final counter-example to what the model would predict comes again from the US farmer case, where we see local groups side-stepping government and creating parallel technical-assistance services where government has failed to meet the groups' needs. This could be seen as another form of

Figure 14.2. Revised Mental Model:
Relationship between Political Space and Advocacy Approaches from the Case Studies

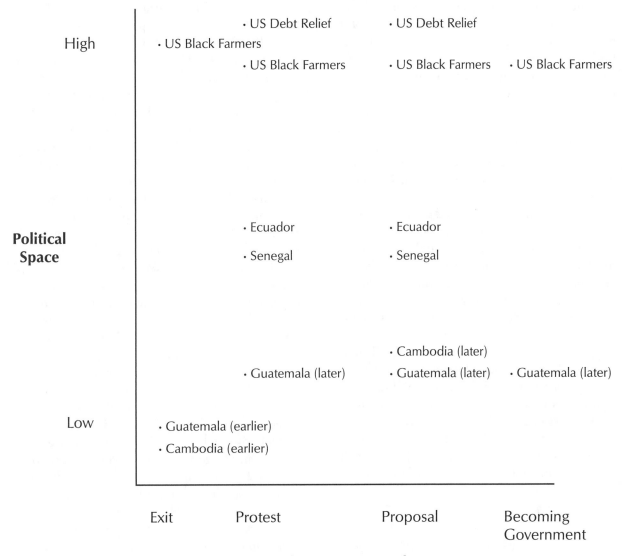

"exit" without physically leaving the local or national context.

If we plot out all these "points" of different kinds of advocacy strategies from the cases, a couple of things become obvious (see Figure 14.2). First, there is no linear association between political space and advocacy approach. The cases demonstrate there are opportunities for advocacy in most systems and that effective social change agents draw on a repertoire of strategies. The approaches that work are varied and overlapping. Second, the case studies are much more hopeful than

the original model. Instead of having fewer options available in closed systems, they show it *is* possible to engage governments of closed political systems. It may require going outside the sphere of influence of that government to bring external pressure to bear, such as in Guatemala and Cambodia. But there are alternative approaches that work, besides protest or going "underground." It may require "polite" engagement with the government by carefully assuring it that groups just want to help. This strategy worked in Cambodia, when human rights groups offered training services to military personnel to "help them" comply with UN requirements.

Third, the cases show there is no "natural" progression *from* protest *to* proposals. In fact, one of the most effective strategies in nearly all the cases involved the combination of protest and proposal in a "good cop–bad cop" strategy. In this approach, one group is more protest-oriented, and another group pushes a specific legislative, legal, or policy agenda with decision makers. In Senegal, for example, protest marches were organized, but they were part of a larger campaign to push for the inclusion of gender rights in the Senegalese legal system and society. Because the groups on the "outside" are making the advocacy target uncomfortable through their loud and hard-to-ignore protests, the "polite" policy-oriented group is able to present their proposals to the "inside" players as a reasonable solution to an uncomfortable situation. We see other examples in Ecuador, with the combined street protests and lobbying work. In work in the United States to reduce debt, we see 50 Years Is Enough in the streets while Oxfam America staff work the halls of the US Congress and at World Bank/IMF annual meetings. It is such a successful strategy that you could get the impression that it is intentional. But in most of the cases we looked at here, the ultimate success of the strategy was accidental, wasn't necessarily based on shared goals—though sometimes it was—and, in fact, was a source of tension in some of the cases, as discussed later on in the "Good Cop–Bad Cop" section.

Strategies That Work

Some of the strategies that worked in the case studies have already been mentioned: the "good cop–bad cop" strategy of combining protest and targeted lobbying; the "triangulation" strategy of bringing external forces like the UN or World Bank or the Asia Development Bank to bear on governments that do not respond to internal pressures. This section analyzes these and other strategies in detail. Drawing on the case studies, the section looks at successful strategies common to multiple cases and analyzes what made them effective.

Dual Strategy of Policy Influence and Grassroots Organizing

In many of the cases, advocates pursued a multi-pronged strategy that included two very different kinds of advocacy work: grassroots organizing and policy influence. In Ecuador, the latter part of the campaign against Texaco centered around the lawsuit in New York. But a major part of the work on the ground in Ecuador involved community education, environmental monitoring, and mobilization work to ensure people affected by Texaco's pollution were actively involved in the case. In Guatemala, the effort to bring indigenous concerns into the new constitution focused on the specifics of the constitutional reform process. But this would not have been possible if there hadn't been a network of membership-based organizations consulting with each of their constituencies and bringing their ideas back to develop a unified platform. In the United States, the discrimination lawsuit against the US Department of Agriculture brought national attention to the plight of small Black farmers. But the lawsuit grew out of decades of work by dozens of organizations working on the day-to-day problems of poor Black farmers. These often service-oriented organizations brought Black farmers' issues back to their leadership, who crafted a national strategy to go after the root cause of the problem.

Codou Bop argues in her case study on Senegal's APROFES that their success was due to the simultaneous focus on women's rights and economic development. APROFES "seeks to improve women's power by giving them the ability to gather income, to acquire knowledge or skills, and to make decisions for themselves, their family, or community." In this way, the two kinds of work are indivisible, Bop argues. "It is the commitment APROFES has to its mission, and the success it has achieved in its work, that give the association the motivation to continue its work."[4]

This dual policy-influence–grassroots-organizing approach runs across nearly all of the cases. It provides a strong argument that successful social justice advocacy goes beyond lobbying decision makers and getting key policies and legislation passed to also include grassroots organizing and mobilization work. The cases offer three arguments for this dual approach. The first argument is about accountability and legitimacy: in order to formulate policy positions that represent the needs of the poor and excluded, you need to involve the poor and excluded in the formulation

---

4. Personal interview, Bineta Sarr, president of APROFES, March 1999.

process. We see this in the Guatemala constitutional reform work, in the US Black-farmer lawsuit, and in the Ecuadorian campaign against Texaco.

The second argument is that people who make policy won't change unless pressure is placed on them to abandon the old policy and practices. The third argument for a broader approach to advocacy is about what constitutes change: in order to change the balance of power in development decision making, you have to address the economic and social structures that underlie inequities. In at least two of the cases, economic empowerment helped give the basis for political empowerment. This was particularly true in the Senegalese and the US Black-farmer cases, where organizations carried out economic-development activities with their constituents using both direct-service and technical-assistance models. Both organizations view this part of their work as a form of advocacy, by providing alternative development models and giving their bases ways to get around structural barriers that exclude their access to resources.

The Power of the Human Rights Framework

Most of the advocacy groups profiled here centered their campaigns on human rights arguments, specifically on social and economic rights. The Ecuador case, for example, shows how indigenous and settler communities have come to frame their demands against Texaco in the context of rights. In Senegal, gender rights provided the foundation for APROFES's work against domestic violence. In Guatemala, every aspect of CALDH's work comes from a human rights perspective. The Cambodian case showed how local groups brought human rights to bear on the issue of land access. In the United States, the lawsuit against the US Department of Agriculture (USDA) was grounded on the basic civil right to protection against discrimination. The debt-relief coalition in the United States and Europe founded its work on a belief that debt represented a denial of the social and economic rights of poor people. When poor countries spend more on debt payments than they do on basic education, health care, and other fundamental needs, this condemns their citizens to perpetual poverty.

Human rights have had both the power of moral argument, as in the US debt work, and provided a tactical vehicle for making public arguments, as in the Guatemala work on genocide. The work to incorporate the

rights of indigenous people into the Guatemalan constitution and the Ecuadorian work to show how oil development practices and policies violated the social and economic rights of settler and indigenous communities are other examples. The fact that human rights was an organizing and framing concept in all these cases suggests the power of human rights for social justice work.

Triangulation Using External Forces to Leverage Change

Many of the campaigns described in the cases used a strategy that relied heavily on outsiders to press from "above" or "outside" to influence policy change. Usually this was accompanied by simultaneous policy-influence and mobilization strategies at the local or national level to press from "below" (see Figure 14.3).[5]

Figure 14.3. Triangulation Advocacy Approach

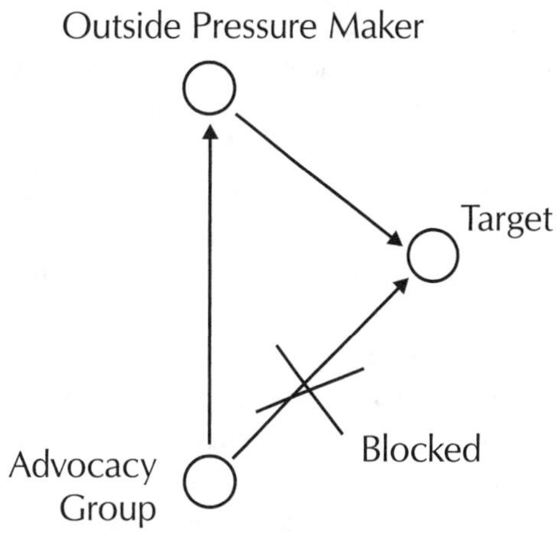

One of the best examples of the triangulation strategy comes from Cambodia. There, work on the land law began with an initiative from a network of human rights, community-forestry, environmental, and legal-rights civil society organizations together with international development organizations like Oxfam Great

---

5. This concept is presented in useful detail by Margaret Keck and Kathryn Sikkink in what they call the "boomerang pattern of influence" (Margaret E. Keck and Kathryn Sikkink, *Activists beyond Borders* [Ithaca, N.Y.: Cornell University Press, 1998]). See also Jonathan A. Fox's "sandwich strategy" (Jonathan A. Fox, *The Politics of Food in Mexico: State Power and Social Mobilization* [Ithaca, N.Y.: Cornell University Press, 1992]) and Jonathan A. Fox, "The Difficult Transition from Clientelism to Citizenship: Lessons from Mexico," in *The New Politics of Inequality in Latin America: Rethinking Participation and Representation,* ed. Douglas A. Chalmers et al. (Oxford: Oxford University Press, 1997).

Britain and the UNDP. But the Cambodian government only put land-law reform on the table when it was pressed from the outside by the Asia Development Bank (ADB). How did that happen? The ADB had been pressed by the Japanese government, which in turn had been lobbied by Japanese NGOs, with the help and urging of Oxfam Great Britain and the Cambodian network. Their agenda was to get the Cambodian government to carry out a participatory reform process. But they needed to rely on their national and international NGO networks to make it happen. Cambodia is dependent on donor money, so officials there had to listen to the ADB. Meanwhile, the NGO network working on the land law had done research, prepared case studies, and organized a consultation process in the regions. Once the ADB made consultation a requirement for further loans to Cambodia, they were ready to "solve the government's problems" by offering that service.[6]

The triangulation strategy was also used in Guatemala, where the Organization of American States was used as a vehicle for Guatemalan government reform during a time when the legal and political systems inside the country were closed down. These two cases suggest that the triangulation strategy, using outsider influence to get at non-responsive or unaccountable advocacy targets, is one useful way to deal with closed political systems.

The Ecuador case has an interesting variation of the triangulation strategy. There, Quito-based NGOs got many Ecuadorian attorneys general to take a position favorable to the plaintiff's case against Texaco in New York, as a way to influence the progress in that suit. Any effort to lobby the judge directly is considered illegal influence and would jeopardize the case.

"Paradigmatic" Legal Cases

A number of the cases involved "paradigmatic" legal cases to illustrate and challenge a pervasive and systemic injustice. They were paradigmatic because they focused on an example that resonated deeply with the larger social justice aspirations of society and challenged dominant paradigms of exclusion, repression, racism, sexism, and exploitation. These cases were both symbolic and pragmatic, in that they sought to

make a fundamental point about justice and equity and also sought real gains for the people involved.

In the United States, the USDA class-action lawsuit aimed to win compensation for Black farmers wronged by widespread discrimination and, at the same time, show there was a "pattern and practice" of discrimination that required systemic changes to the way the USDA works. In Senegal, domestic violence and rape cases broke the culture of silence in that country and also sought justice for the victims and their families. In Ecuador, the class-action lawsuit against Texaco seeks compensation and remediation of the pollution Texaco caused, but also seeks to make a statement about accountability. It is not acceptable for foreign companies to come to the Ecuadorian Amazon and run roughshod over the environment, livelihoods, and culture of the indigenous and settler communities living there. In Guatemala, legal cases against the military for massacres seek to bring a sense of healing and closure for the survivors. They also seek to bring this dark part of the war's history out in the open by naming it genocide, after years and years of official denials and public ignorance.

All these paradigmatic legal cases served as powerful advocacy vehicles for the social justice organizations involved. The cases put the social justice issue in the public realm. They got widespread media attention. They told the story of the injustice in human terms. They brought the issue forward in a concrete and authoritative way, giving it a legitimacy and enabling the message to reach an audience often far beyond the mobilizing capacity of the groups involved. They also provided a center around which organizations could focus their members on shared goals and build their strength.

But while lawsuits can be a vehicle for achieving significant changes in the balance of power between excluded groups and powerful institutions, they can also be a difficult way to win a victory. First, they usually take years to complete. The Texaco lawsuit has been going on since 1993. The Black farmers' lawsuit was over a decade in the making before it was filed in 1997, and then took three years to conclude.

Second, legal cases cost a lot of money in lawyers' fees, require large amounts of staff time, and can take a toll on organizations. It is hard to keep people organized and focused on the larger social justice issue over years and years of legal maneuvering. Perhaps more

---

6. Personal interview, Shaun Williams, Oxfam Great Britain, April 1999.

important, the staff time and investment required to support large legal cases can draw all an organization's attention and leave little for other parts of the advocacy campaign. Many participants in the campaign against Texaco, for example, say this has been one of their frustrations with the focus on the New York lawsuit.

A third difficulty with legal strategies is they can raise expectations that may or may not be met in the end. Lawyers are under tremendous pressure to reach closure to the case quickly because this is usually when they are paid. In the process, it is difficult, especially in class-action lawsuits, for the interests of all the plaintiffs to be heard.

And finally, lawsuits can bring compensation to the plaintiffs but leave the underlying injustice intact. The lawsuit against the USDA, for example, brought monetary awards for farmers but didn't require the USDA to institute any reforms. As this is being written, there are some preliminary signs that the financial pain and public embarrassment are pushing the USDA to undertake serious internal reform. Hearings are being held to review the structure of the white-farmer-dominated county committees, and Federation of Southern Cooperative members are giving testimony at these hearings. But whether the farmers' suit will end discrimination within the agency is something only time will tell.

Perhaps the lesson to draw from all these cautionary notes is that lawsuits should be seen more as one component in a larger strategy, understanding that there are many risks that come with the benefits.

There are some situations where bringing legal cases is not a viable advocacy option. In Cambodia, for example, there was a potentially powerful paradigmatic case evolving where highland villages were being overtaken by private-sector loggers with questionable rights to develop the area. The villagers, in a rare act of resistance, had blocked a logging road and temporarily held logging company staff in their village. But no advocacy group in Cambodia was planning to file a lawsuit. "The legal approach doesn't work where the legal system doesn't work," observed Shaun Williams of Oxfam Great Britain.[7] Instead, local-development advocacy groups collaborated with the regional UN office to hold meetings with logging-company officials and the provincial government sponsoring their activities. "Our role [as advocates] is to help the community and government understand the issues and find a fair solution benefiting both sides, both government and the people," said one local NGO field-worker.[8] This is a much more gentle, polite form of advocacy. Meanwhile, national and international NGOs in Cambodia focused on reforming the land law, a much slower, lower-profile process. Activists believed this approach was not as likely to be seen by government as a frontal challenge and provoke a reaction, such as deporting foreign-born NGO staff or killing people.

Working with Reformers

In nearly all the cases, we see community-based organizations and support NGOs seeking out and collaborating with receptive government, industry, or religious leader reformers. This challenges the idea that social justice advocacy must use only "oppositional" strategies, fighting from outside government or other targets to challenge the status quo. In Senegal, for example, case writer Codou Pop uses the terms "target" and "allies" almost interchangeably. There, APROFES enlisted high-level government officials and Muslim leaders in the Kaolack region to help raise awareness of gender violence. Were they targets? Yes, because APROFES sought to influence them and gain their high-profile support for their cause. Were they allies? Also yes, because these leaders worked with APROFES in a coordinated and decisive way, once they were on board.

In the US debt-relief work, case writer Andrew Bauck describes what he calls the Oxfam "inside-outside" advocacy strategy. The Oxfam strategy involved "finding allies within the IFIs [international financial institutions] and working with them to push the issue forward from the inside, while at the same time generating outside pressure through the media and in collaboration with other NGO activists."[9] In this case, they challenged the use of concessionary International Development Association (IDA) funds to pay back debt instead of funding poverty-alleviation projects through the actions of a reform-minded insider. By supporting the insider, who was facing resistance within the World Bank, with information and

---

7. Williams, interview.

8. Personal interview, Non Forest Timber Products (NTFP) staff person in Ratanakkiri Province, Cambodia, April 1999.

9. See Andrew Bauck, this volume.

arguments, the debt-relief coalition effectively gained an internal "spokesperson" for their point of view.

In Ecuador, the Texaco campaign organizers also sought out receptive government and elected officials to further their agenda. For example, they worked with legislators to initiate a congressional investigation of the government- and Texaco-sponsored environmental-impact report that allegedly described all of Texaco's environmental impacts before that company could end its obligations to the state of Ecuador. The report was of questionable reliability, listing animals that didn't even live in the Ecuadorian Amazon. Having a congressional investigation on the report meant that classified government documents could be subpoenaed, government officials required to testify under oath, and new information revealed. The campaign organizers worked with the legislators to provide key background information, develop the investigation's focus, and formulate lines of questioning for government officials. This gave them power and access and brought a level of legitimacy to the campaign they would not have had without the support of the sympathetic legislators.

In the Black-farmer work in United States, one of the Federation of Southern Cooperatives' key accomplishments is the generation of "progeny," former Federation members who have gone on to elected office and high-level policy positions. These former Federation members were nurtured and came of age, so to speak, through their work with the Federation, but are now in positions to push for Black-farmer interests from *within* the system. Also, the Federation and its allies have worked hard to identify and collaborate with sympathetic politicians from across the country to get small-farmer issues on the table. In fact, the legislative advocacy strategy would be impossible without the help of reform-minded politicians and government bureaucrats.

In Cambodia, international NGOs and UN organizations helped get a consultative land-law review process by collaborating with reformers in the Japanese government and the ADB, who convinced the Cambodian government to open up the process.

Each of these cases makes a compelling argument to seek out and work with receptive insider reformers in the target organization or in organizations that can influence it. Of course, there is always a danger of insider "reformers" not being able to leverage any

real change from within, and this argues for continued vigilance and pressure from the outside even while working with the reformer. It also means that high-quality research on who the key decision makers are is crucial for this strategy to work. When it does work, there is often a symbiotic relationship between social justice organizations and these reformers. On the one hand, the reformers need the broad-based support and legitimacy brought by the grassroots organizations and their NGO supporters. On the other hand, the grassroots groups need the legal, legislative, and political knowledge and savvy the reformist insiders bring to the equation.[10]

Strategic Alliances to Bring in Technical or Advocacy Expertise

Many of the organizations and campaigns profiled in the case studies involved collaborations among quite different kinds of social justice organizations. The collaborations allowed them to combine their diverse strengths to carry out multiple kinds of advocacy strategies and bring different skills to bear on their efforts. The range includes grassroots membership groups, grassroots service-oriented organizations, technical-support organizations, and capital-city-based policy organizations and international NGOs. When they were able to do it successfully, the collaborations proved advantageous for all of the groups.

For grassroots groups just beginning to engage in advocacy around an issue they have identified, their success hinged on teaming with groups with technical expertise and advocacy experience. These groups helped them "learn the ropes" on building evidence to support their case, such as how to prepare witnesses for trial in Senegal or taking photos and water samples in contaminated areas in Ecuador. They also brought staff with skills the grassroots groups might not have, such as lobbyists familiar with the insider scene in capital cities, or lawyers knowledgeable about international human rights laws and courts.

For the technically oriented support NGOs and policy organizations, linking with grassroots groups brought legitimacy to their work, because they could

---

10. For more on "reformist bureaucrats," see Marilee S. Grindle, "The Sexenio and Public Careers in Mexico," in *Bureaucrats, Politicians, and Peasants in Mexico: A Case Study in Public Policy* (Berkeley: University of California Press, 1977); Judith Tender, *New Lessons from Old Projects: The Dynamics of Development in Northeast Brazil* (Washington, D.C.: World Bank, 1991); Fox, *Politics of Food*; and Fox, "Difficult Transition."

point to the constituency of their allies as evidence of the broad-based need for change. It also enabled them to combine their efforts with grassroots mobilizations, marches, and protests. Mass mobilizations were important elements, if not turning points, in a number of the cases, such as the march on Dakar in the Senegalese struggle against gender violence, the mass Black-farmer caravan to Washington, and the Jubilee 2000 demonstrations around the world. Without the alliance with mass-based grassroots groups, the policy and technical organizations would be restricted to lobbying, preparing research papers, holding conferences, testifying during hearings, and so on. Even in these "technical" areas, lobbying and research are strengthened by grassroots collaboration. The information is more accurate, its impact on affected groups is clearer, and the identified solutions are more likely to have a real impact.[11] The collaboration across different types of organizations allowed campaigns to use the "dual strategy" of policy influence and grassroots organizing and the "good cop–bad cop" strategy described next.

Good Cop–Bad Cop Strategy

The "good cop–bad cop" strategy involves putting both "gentle" and "hard-ball" pressure on the target simultaneously from two different fronts so that the "gentle" group seems to present an attractive alternative to the more extreme demands of the "hard-ball" group. The idea suggests a coordinated team of police officers (in this case advocates) where one pushes hard on the suspect (the advocacy target) while the other appears sympathetic and helpful, and manages to extract the key information or cooperation the two are looking for. This strategy appears most clearly in two case studies, Ecuador and the US work on debt relief. Interestingly, it was not necessarily an intentional strategy in either case, and in fact was often the source of considerable tension among campaign participants. In Ecuador, Acción Ecológica frequently played a more protest-oriented role, denouncing government policies, staging sit-ins of government offices, and organizing marches and rallies. At the same time, the Center for Social and Economic Rights and other NGOs in Quito engaged in collaborative work with government agencies, trying to expand environmen-

tal legislation via the legislative and legal processes. In interviews, most government policy makers recall the role of Acción Ecológica, likely because their public actions drew the most attention. But the detailed formulation of new policies and reversals of bad policies also involved more painstaking, collaborative advocacy efforts.

In the US debt-relief work, the 50 Years Is Enough coalition and Witness for Peace presented a staunch opposition to Highly Indebted Poor Country (HIPC) and Structural Adjustment Program (SAP) initiatives of the World Bank/International Monetary Fund. Meanwhile, Oxfam and other debt-relief allies had a more nuanced critique that acknowledged the validity of some of the World Bank concerns for moral hazard and the need for fiscal reforms in receiving countries, while still pushing a poverty-focused agenda. Much of the Oxfam and Jubilee 2000 advocacy agenda has now made it into standard World Bank parlance. But this would have been very difficult if groups like 50 Years Is Enough and Global Witness weren't pushing for much more radical reforms of the institutions. "In the beginning, 50 Years Is Enough was needed in order to get the bank to listen," reported one World Bank official, confirming the crucial importance of militant groups in getting large institutions to pay attention to previously ignored issues.[12]

As mentioned, the different advocacy approaches and stances taken by campaign participants often led to internal tensions and divisions. This is not to say that groups should seek to work happily together when their legitimate disagreements simply do not permit this. In the US debt-relief work, for example, each group claimed to be representing the interests of their Southern counterparts. In Ecuador, the campaign participants had real differences. This strategy can be so effective, though, that it is worth pursuing it intentionally. Basic agreement on key fundamental, long-term goals of the campaign is likely essential if groups are to withstand the frictions that inevitably come up when different strategies and tactics are used. The "good cop–bad cop" strategy works best with shared objectives and strategies among campaign participants, with only the tactics being different. If strategies are different as well, at minimum participants need to see them as complementary.

---

11. I am grateful to Diana MTK Autin for reminding me of this point.

12. As cited by Andrew Bauck, this volume.

Agreeing to disagree may be easier in theory than in practice. But the alternative, silencing a voice that is also working for social justice, is worse. Lisa Jordan and Peter van Tuijl argue that social justice advocacy should "open up space to strategically articulate a plurality of development aspirations, at peoples' own conditions and risks, using their own time-frames, speaking their own language and applying their own design of political expression or association."[13] The challenge for social justice campaigns is as much about winning as it is about respecting the interests of the most vulnerable, they argue. The next section talks about accountability, political responsibility, and mutual influence within social justice coalitions.

Bridging Local, National, and Global Arenas with Accountability

Many of the case studies involve collaborative work across the local, national, and international arenas. This kind of work raises the question of what kind of accountability groups have to each other as they work across national, political, social, and cultural boundaries and must bridge differences in language, culture, geography, and access to information, financial resources, technology, and decision makers. There are also historic reasons for deep distrust in North-South work: slavery, colonialism, neo-colonialism, imperialism, and so on. As Jonathan A. Fox points out, "overcoming the vast chasms of culture and power differences within [transnational campaign coalitions] will be a permanent challenge."[14] Are there some guidelines to help NGOs working in social justice campaigns bridge political arenas in a respectful and accountable way? Various researchers and activists offer some ways for thinking about this question, and the cases offer some tentative lessons, summarized at the end of this section.

Primary and Secondary Space

Charles Abugre, the Africa secretariat coordinator of the Third World Network, makes a distinction between "primary" and "secondary" advocacy spaces,

explored in the Guatemala case study. He defines *primary space* as an arena in which a given group is located (community, region, country) and where actions by that group will benefit its members. *Secondary space* is an arena outside of one's own primary space, where advocacy will benefit another group, but not the advocate directly. By making the distinction, Abugre suggests these two spaces are different and that groups need to take special care when they're acting in someone else's political space.

Jonathan Fox and David Brown argue in their book on accountability and transnational coalitions that one of the pivotal moments in coalition building is when the main problem is defined. What is the issue we are working on, and how do we define the problem? The problem's definition will shape the strategies and tactics needed to solve the problem.[15] This, for its part, will dictate which groups in the coalition are most important for carrying out the strategies and tactics. As a consequence, these groups will generally have more say over the day-to-day decisions of the campaign and have first access to and control over information flows and, ultimately, more power. Campaigns focused on local issues will tend to give local groups more power in campaign coalitions; campaigns focused on national issues will give power to national groups; and campaigns on international issues will favor international NGOs.

Lisa Jordan and Peter van Tuijl make a similar point in their article on NGO advocacy and globalization, but go a step further. They argue that a key element of accountability within advocacy campaigns is the political responsibility all actors have for the risks faced by the most vulnerable.[16] They list seven areas of coalition work where groups have to pay attention to their political responsibility to other coalition members: dividing political arenas (who has expertise and knowledge in which political arenas, and respecting that), setting agenda and strategies, raising and sharing financial resources, making information available to other members, making it available in a timely way and in an appropriate format, and formalizing coalition relationships. They argue that NGOs should strive to achieve campaigns that "at

---

13. Jordan and van Tuijl, "Political Responsibility."

14. Jonathan A. Fox, "Thinking Locally, Acting Globally: Bringing the Grassroots into Transnational Advocacy," presentation given at "Regional Worlds–Latin America: Cultural Environments and Development Debates," Center for Latin American Studies and the Globalization Project, University of Chicago, May 21–23, 1998.

15. Jonathan A. Fox and L. David Brown, eds., *The Struggle for Accountability: The World Bank, NGOs, and Grassroots Movements* (Cambridge, Mass.: MIT Press, 1998).

16. Jordan and van Tuijl, "Political Responsibility."

minimum . . . leave room for a variety of objectives in different political arenas . . . [and] respect the interests or aspirations of the most vulnerable groups involved in the campaign."[17]

Are there "norms of conduct" for the various types of advocacy actors (grassroots and membership organizations, intermediary-support NGOs, and national and international policy NGOs) working in their primary or secondary spaces? For example, can a group advocate "on behalf of" the groups it works with when it is not working in its own primary space? The cases reveal some different answers to this question.

Respecting Primary Space

In Guatemala, the country had gone through a devastating period of repression. Civil society had not been completely destroyed, but it was atomized. The role of the staff of CALDH (Centro para Acción Legal en Derechos Humanos), an intermediary-support NGO, was to provide technical and analytical support to strengthen grassroots indigenous and campesino groups and begin to rebuild the connections linking civil society. They would not make decisions or act in the place of these groups, though. Instead, their role was to help them take up issues and advocate on their own behalf. At the same time, CALDH had its own agenda of building a genocide case against the former government and had the skills to bring human rights cases at the national and international levels. Communities that had suffered massacres during the period of military rule had to decide if they wanted to bring a legal case. If they decided to bring a case, then CALDH provided legal and political support for the case, coordinating with the local communities.

CALDH was respecting the primary space of the indigenous and campesino communities to define their strategy. If the groups chose to bring a massacre case, only then would CALDH take an active role in bringing the case forward. The communities and CALDH had different agendas, but they were mutually reinforcing, and CALDH respected the communities' decisions in each case. If CALDH had chosen to take cases forward without the consent of the affected communities, they would have been violating the primary space of the community members and potentially putting them at real risk without their con-

---

17. Jordan and van Tuijl, "Political Responsibility."

sent. CALDH's actions demonstrate its respect for the decisions of their more vulnerable partners, while still pursuing their own advocacy agenda.

The Comparative-Advantage Approach

In a number of the cases where groups collaborated across multiple political and geographic arenas, they worked to define parallel strategies building on each group's comparative advantage, knowledge base, skills, and abilities. The "comparative-advantage" strategy was often an attempt to avoid competition among campaign participants in any one political space and acknowledge the specific contribution of each group. Where this worked, it was based on fundamental shared goals and involved ongoing negotiations to get clarity and agreement about each group's respective roles at key points in the campaign.

In the case of the US Black-farmer work aimed at holding the US Department of Agriculture (USDA) accountable, all groups wanted to set a precedent and gain leverage to change the culture and policies within the USDA to benefit Black and minority farmers. Some groups, like the Federation of Southern Cooperatives, brought organic ties to affected farmers and were able to mobilize large numbers to participate in the lawsuit. Other groups, like the Rural Coalition, brought a broad range of grassroots groups together and had strategic knowledge and experience working within the political structures in Washington, D.C. There was room for divergence in focus of particular strategies, but everyone shared the central goal concerning the USDA. Making this work, however, required repeated discussions to clarify roles and reaffirm commitment to the central goals.

In the Senegal case, the locally grounded APROFES worked with local human rights groups and religious organizations as well as Dakar-based human rights and women's groups to support changes in public opinion and in the legal system. Working alone, APROFES would not have been able to marshal the legal expertise in the cases or bring broad-based support to bear on the issue of gender violence in Senegal. In that case, the groups came together around high-profile cases of gender violence that both demanded and greatly benefited from collaboration among the multiple groups. With the clarity and unity of purpose the lawsuits demanded, it was relatively easy to define each group's roles and leadership for separate parts of the multi-strategy campaign.

The Role of Outsiders in Closed Political Space

In the Cambodian case, the experience is quite different. There, civil society was completely decimated and is just now rebuilding itself. In the meantime, many international NGOs, including Oxfam Great Britain, have taken an active role advocating within and outside Cambodia on Cambodian issues. They and others argue that the issues they are dealing with, like illegal logging, cannot wait until national NGOs develop the capacity to mount their own advocacy campaigns. If they waited, all the forests would be gone in a matter of years. Oxfam Great Britain staff worked in collaboration with national NGOs on the land law, providing advocacy training and setting agendas together with national NGOs. They relied on national NGOs to work with local communities to define their interests around community forestry and other issues.

Yet the international NGOs were still doing advocacy in Cambodia on Cambodian issues. They were acting outside their primary space and acting "on behalf of" Cambodians. Some might say they were acting "in place of" Cambodians. But they worked to share information, include local NGOs and community organizations in strategy development, and engage with the local actors to the extent possible. Because of the weakness of civil society and the restrictions placed on civil society participation by the Cambodian government, there were real restrictions on local actors taking a lead role in the land-law campaign. So Oxfam Great Britain used the land-law campaign as an opportunity to build local-NGO advocacy capacity while simultaneously trying to use the process to open more political space for future local-NGO participation.

Outsiders as Coalition Partners

Sometimes, no matter how good the intentions of support NGOs and representative grassroots groups working on a campaign, certain strategies can make accountability difficult because the strategies place outside actors in defining positions within the campaign. In Ecuador, we saw a grassroots and international campaign evolve into one focused primarily on a class-action lawsuit in the United States. In the course of this evolution, the lawyers bringing the case became some of the primary actors in the campaign. In the US

Black-farmer struggle against the US Department of Agriculture, we also saw a major part of the preexisting campaign shift its focus to a lawsuit. Again, the lawyers played a central role in defining the terms of the case and shaping the outcomes. These cases add a layer of complexity and raise a dilemma for achieving accountability in NGO advocacy campaigns. The campaign participants may share some specific goals, but this does not guarantee that the lawyers working on a lawsuit will.

At best, these two cases involved a generally symbiotic relationship between the attorneys and the affected communities. The lawyers needed the communities (and to a much lesser extent their representative organizations and collaborating NGOs) to take the lawsuits forward. The communities saw the cases as a powerful vehicle for the campaigns to hold Texaco and the USDA accountable for what they had done. They also saw the cases as a vehicle for achieving immediate, tangible benefits in the form of cash settlements. The communities were dependent on the lawyers to bring the cases forward.

The representative grassroots organizations and NGOs involved in these two cases have worked hard to keep communities informed about the cases so they can make informed choices. But it has proved difficult to influence the lawyers or the course of the cases. These two lawsuit-oriented campaigns point up the promise and the pitfalls of using legal strategies, especially when money is involved. While suits can change public opinion and set powerful precedents, the temptation of cash settlements is so great it can override the goals that started the campaign in the first place. The risks of a legal strategy should be weighed carefully against potential gains. Advocates need to be prepared to be aggressive in ensuring that the interests of the most vulnerable are kept front and center during the whole process.

Tentative Lessons on Coalition Accountability

The "rules of engagement" for working outside one's own primary space seem to vary by national, political, and cultural context, but a few tentative lessons do emerge from the cases.

First, many NGOs agree there is a "political responsibility," as Jordan and van Tuijl say, to strive for more accountability and mutual influence within campaign coalitions. Much of this centers around information sharing and co-development of agendas and advocacy strategies. A large part of this involves keeping the interests and potential risks of the most vulnerable at the center of the advocacy work.

Second, where civil society is weak and the political opportunities for influencing decision making are limited or nonexistent, international and intermediary NGOs at the regional and national levels can play a disproportionately dominant role. They can help overcome problems of weak civil society and recalcitrant and hostile actors at the local level. In the cases of Guatemala and Cambodia, groups shared information, provided advocacy training, and used campaign work as an opportunity to build local capacity as a way to compensate for the power imbalance within the coalition. With exit and triangulation as the key advocacy strategies in closed systems, international and intermediary NGOs helped grassroots groups access external actors and learn to influence them and opened more space for national civil society participation. By working in coalition and investing significant resources in increasing the capacity of national NGOs and grassroots organizations, international NGOs and national NGOs working from outside the country used their position of relative power responsibly and with an eye to the long-term sustainability of joint advocacy work.

Third, when campaigns center on strategies that place outside actors in decisive positions, the other campaign members have a responsibility to offset the imbalance of power by active information sharing. They also may need to advocate, within the campaign coalition, for the interests of the most vulnerable. This is especially true when legal strategies involving the possibility of cash settlements take a central place in advocacy campaigns.

A Cautionary Note on Accountability and Universal Space

Are there some issues that are so universal that they are nobody's exclusive primary space? What are the "rules of engagement" in that case? This question came up in a number of cases, where intermediary and international NGOs were working on issues like human rights (Guatemala, Senegal, and Ecuador), environmental devastation (Cambodia and Ecuador), and global financial structures (US debt-relief work). These issues have broad development implications for

civil society everywhere. The lead campaigners in each of these cases felt the issues were so universal that they had to work on them, whether or not they were able to do so in tandem with grassroots organizations.

For example, in Cambodia, there was fear that the forests would be destroyed if international NGOs waited for Cambodian civil society to develop and the political opportunities for Cambodians to safely participate to emerge. In Ecuador, some of the campaign participants felt that oil companies should be blocked at all costs, because of the environmental and cultural devastation they cause, even if local communities were not in full agreement with this perspective.

The lessons from the cases do not provide a clear or satisfying answer to the question of what norms of conduct or rules of engagement might apply for groups working outside their primary space on "universal" issues such as the environment, human rights—including economic, cultural, and social rights—or global rule-making, which are the concern of all yet the exclusive domain of no one. Perhaps all the lessons above do apply, but there is a need for a certain caution. Advocates must not succumb to the real temptation to act independently, with no contact with or accountability to those whose daily lives could be affected by the advocacy efforts.

Challenges to Overcome

The campaigns described in the cases point to many challenges that had to be overcome in order to be effective. In some cases, the challenges were external, dictated by the nature of political space. In others, the challenges had more to do with the nature of the organizations and their own experiences. Some of the most common challenges that ran across the cases are presented here, with some of the strategies used by groups to overcome them.

Lack of Political Space

In closed political systems, where personal and political freedoms are restricted, it is obviously difficult, if not impossible, to organize effectively. Guatemala and Cambodia are the two cases that best illustrate this challenge, though both countries are now emerging from their dark periods of repression. In the Guatemala case, one of the key strategies used was "exit." Activists literally left the country and worked from outside the national context from a place of relative safety, using "triangulation" to get external actors to influence events within the country. The United Nations and Organization of American States were two key levers used, as well as US and European public opinion. The other key strategy was to develop a campaign centering around a human rights framework. Appealing to the universal rights articulated in human rights, Guatemalan activists sought to draw attention and bring external pressure to bear on the Guatemalan government. It was not until the country began to open up again that they were finally able to return and work from within the country, though even then not without risk.

The Cambodian experience was more severe, in many ways. While the fabric of civil society was torn apart in Guatemala, the entirety of civil society was decimated in Cambodia. Anyone with education, who spoke a foreign language, or who had any dealings with anything non-Cambodian was lucky to survive the Khmer Rouge regime. All associative action outside of the Khmer Rouge itself was prohibited and punishable by death, leaving a deeply rooted distrust of any organizing efforts that lasts to this day. The Vietnamese tightly controlled all organizations during their decade-long occupation, and this was followed by another massive "invasion" of international NGOs that came with the United Nations in the early 1990s. Until quite recently, there was no organized Cambodian civil society to speak of, and what existed was often "supply driven," focusing their work on issues defined by foreign funders' agendas. At the same time, the newly emerging Cambodian government was not receptive to internal criticisms, and the general level of political instability led all groups to fear invoking the wrath of anyone, lest conflicts erupt into violence. As Joel Charny, former deputy director of the UNDP CARERE project based in Phnom Penh and former Oxfam America policy director, says, there is a great tension between harmony and impunity that colors all advocacy work in Cambodia. "All anyone wants is for there to be no more violence. But how do you take into account the need for social harmony when people are still engaging in arbitrary, unchecked, and unpunished violence?"

One of the answers from Cambodia, like in Guatemala, was exit. But in the Cambodian case, this was much more difficult to do because of how quickly the Khmer Rouge regime took control of and laid waste to the country. Another answer, also used in the Guatemalan case, is to focus on a discourse and framework of human rights. First political and civil rights, then social and economic rights. The strongest Cambodian advocacy groups are human rights groups headed by Cambodians who spent most of the past twenty-five years in exile and who bring experience gained during that time. The other Cambodian strategy for dealing with limited and unpredictable political space is to take a highly collaborative, polite approach to advocacy work. With few exceptions, Cambodians doing advocacy use a respectful and solicitous approach with government officials. This demonstrates their good intentions to bring benefit to all Cambodians and help the officials in their work. This does not mean this is what's driving them, but in order to keep dialogue open with officials, they must be seen as contributing to problem solving, and not being "NATO—No Action, Talk Only," as one Cambodian Environment Ministry official complained about many NGOs.

Not Knowing the "Texts" (Laws, Policies, Norms, Etc.)

One of the greatest challenges facing groups is a basic unfamiliarity with the laws, policies, players, and decision-making processes. Linked to this, advocates often have limited access to current and readily useable information on their issue. Government officials frequently criticize NGOs, and especially grassroots organizations, for advocating positions that don't correspond with current debates or are so out of step as to be unworkable. NGOs that are able to draft laws, present timely research on current legislative debates, provide expert testimony, and so on, are more likely to achieve concrete policy changes. Changing actual behaviors and power relations may be a whole separate challenge, but policies and laws remain one of the key dimensions of advocacy work. If they're going to have policy influence, groups need to learn the official "texts" and access key information on their issues in order to develop strategies tailored to the right forums and decision makers.

There were three paths groups took to learn the "texts." The first was a gradual process of learning-by-doing, slowly feeling their way through the maze of decision making, both formal and informal, until they were able to find the pressure points, arguments, and strategies that could affect the outcome. The second involved partnering with other groups that already knew the "texts"—the players, laws, policies, procedures, and so on. These two paths were almost always intertwined. The third strategy or path involved getting more or less formal orientation from support NGOs about laws, policies, and decision-making processes. In that case, the intermediary-support NGO that provides technical and capacity-building support but does not "represent" the constituency it works with may or may not itself be involved in the advocacy efforts related to the education and orientation process.

The case of APROFES in Senegal is an example of a combination of the first two strategies. There, APROFES teamed up with local and Dakar-based human rights groups to help them bring their legal cases, but they also went through their own internal learning process where they developed experience they could apply the next time they brought a gender-violence case.

In the US Black-farmer experience, the Federation of Southern Cooperatives also went through an internal learning process during its first major experience lobbying to insert specific provisions in the US Farm Bill. At the same time, it worked in tandem with Washington, D.C.–based organizations that brought a significant amount of experience to the effort. By the end of the process, the Federation had learned a lot about developing legislative language, working with legislative aids, the US legislative committee process, and building bipartisan support for its proposals.

The Guatemala experience provides an example of support NGOs providing orientation and training on the "texts." In that case, CALDH brought experience with and understanding of new constitutional provisions benefiting indigenous and peasant communities and held orientation sessions for them on the new laws. Indigenous and peasant groups could then use their new knowledge of the laws in their own work. Except in the genocide cases, CALDH's role was to provide support and orientation, rather than partnering with the indigenous and peasant organizations. This is an example of intermediary NGOs playing an advocacy support role. Popular education and orientation about rights and legal frameworks can provide one of the crucial elements for developing advocacy strategy. This

educational work on the official "texts" is essential for effective advocacy by grassroots groups.

"Leaderitis"

Concentration of control, strategic decision making, vision, and organizational capacity in one charismatic leader happens everywhere. This is because outside organizations gravitate to the leader, work with and share information with the leader, and the leader has the relationships with funders. Over time, the leaders' power and control and indispensable role grow and grow, whether intended or not. These leaders often provide powerful direction for the organization, but there is always the danger that when they leave, the organization will fall apart.

In the cases presented here, there were a number of examples of this, though the case studies themselves don't always raise it as an issue. In Ecuador, the Frente de Defensa de la Amazonía has a quietly charismatic leader who has almost single-handedly shepherded the organization along during the last seven years in the Texaco lawsuit. But who would take over if he left? In Guatemala, CALDH's leader, Frank LaRue, is internationally recognized as a pioneer for his work against impunity and genocide. And there are strong leaders within the organization, each working on their own program areas. But what would happen without LaRue's connections and vast experience both within and outside of Guatemala? Would CALDH continue to have the same level of impact? In Senegal, Bineta Sarr is a powerful and inspirational leader, surrounded by a highly dedicated and cohesive staff. But a transition from her leadership could be difficult. Many of the APROFES staff are not comfortable speaking French and are not well connected with Dakar-based organizations. Ms. Sarr is currently working to build the leadership skills of a "second tier" of leaders within the organization, dedicating significant organizational resources to this. It may be that the organizational focus shifts somewhat when and if she leaves, but she is determined to lay the groundwork for her eventual succession.

Two organizations, the Federation of Southern Cooperatives and Oxfam America, largely avoided the *leaderitis* problems. At the Federation of Southern Cooperatives, there is more sharing of leadership responsibilities, and they do not seem to suffer so much from "leaderitis." Various Federation staff take the lead on different initiatives. Executive Director Ralph Paige is not the only one who appears in press releases, who gives interviews, and who presents testimony during hearings on Black-farmer issues. The Federation can spread leadership responsibilities because it is more decentralized, with multiple state offices, and a regional training center. Of necessity, each regional entity has developed its own leadership structure and relatively autonomous programs, and the various state office leaders have a say in overall Federation decision making. Another possible reason is the origins of the Federation, which brought together many civil rights leaders into one organization. It was not created around the vision or impetus of one charismatic leader, but began as a collaborative effort of committed and experienced activists.

For more "professionalized" advocacy organizations, like Oxfam America and Oxfam International, staff playing leadership roles are hired employees with a high degree of autonomy for specific campaign initiatives. When they leave, another is hired to take over the initiative. This can be an issue for continuity on specific campaigns, because the outgoing staff member often takes with them their particular skills, contacts, and commitments. But consistency in the agency's overall mission and direction is supported by a larger structure of the executive director and board of directors.

Christmas Tree Effect

A number of organizations faced the challenge of trying to do many things at once without linking activities in terms of advocacy agendas, key constituency groups, or strategies used. Some people call this the "Christmas tree" effect. Like decorations hung on evergreen trees at Christmas time, they look great, but each one is isolated. Both internal self-critiques and external coalition allies pointed to this as a potential block to effectiveness on any one issue.

The clearest example of this is CALDH, which has programs ranging from gender rights, youth, massacre exhumations, indigenous-movement organizing, and labor rights. While linked by an overarching agenda to rebuild the fabric of civil society based on a human rights framework, each program had a high degree of autonomy and isolation from the others. Organizational consultants were invited to advise CALDH on their structure after the case study was written.

They recommended that CALDH restructure itself as an umbrella organization, with each group having explicit autonomy, and share the administrative resources of the parent organization. CALDH rejected this, but after that decision, staff of the Technical Unit for Analysis, Relations, and Support left to form their own organization. CALDH still has a Technical Unit, but it has had to re-staff the group and has lost the strong staff it had. But the vision of a united organization outweighed that risk for CALDH.

APROFES also has multiple programs that work with different constituencies on different kinds of activities that range from income generation for women to women's leadership development, youth education, and socioeconomic learning and research. But for APROFES, each of the activities is linked to the others by a clearly articulated, specific, and tangible goal of increasing the power of women to control their own lives. The importance of each group's work is clear to all the other groups, because their activities have an interlocking and mutually reinforcing effect. The success of one program feeds the success of all the others.

Groups need to balance the potential promise against the difficulties of managing a multi-faceted organization. Natural competition among programs can make staff feel their work is either more important than the others', and therefore merits more attention and resources, or less important, and therefore is undervalued by the organization. Either way, program leaders may withhold information from each other as a way to protect themselves. As a result, people in the same organization can end up unaware of what their colleagues are doing, including major advocacy victories that may be common knowledge among those in only certain circles of the organization. The lesson these cases suggest is that the promise of bridging issues related by overarching goals is potentially very powerful, but not always easy. To do this, groups need to articulate clearly how each program links, supports, and is supported by the work of all the other programs in reaching this goal. APROFES's example suggests having one common constituency makes these linkages more natural.

Tensions between Service and Advocacy

One challenge that came up in many of the cases is a tension between service-related work and advocacy work. Service work involves more technical projects, such as helping women learn how to plant, irrigate, harvest, and market vegetables to generate income in Senegal, or helping Black farmers organize credit co-operatives. The case studies have focused more on the advocacy work, but each organization does some amount of service-related work as well. The tension arises because activists fear that their service-related work can distract from advocacy work and set up a dependent relationship with their "customers," who then expect the organization to "deliver" goods and services. These expectations can lead, they fear, to a passive attitude that carries over into the advocacy work as well. There are also tensions of competing priorities, with service work taking away from advocacy work since the need always outstrips the resources. And staffing an organization that does both can be difficult, either in finding staff who can work in both areas or in ensuring that staff talk with each other and share ideas, if they are separated.

Another fear is that service-related work will make organizations dependent on service-contract funding and end up not having the time or the autonomy to carry out advocacy work. For example, Oxfam America made a choice in the 1970s not to accept US government funds to carry out emergency-relief activities. The argument at the time was that Oxfam was advocating against the US government's role in Central America. If it took US government money, it would lose the autonomy to be critical of the US government. Also, staff feared Oxfam America could become too focused on emergencies and lose the core focus on long-term structural solutions to poverty.

On the positive side, having some service-related activities keeps organizations engaged with the day-to-day realities of their base constituency. That way, they can identify issues long before they build to a crisis or identify "orphan" issues that other groups have missed.

According to the case studies, these fears and tensions are real but have been largely overcome. It should be noted that the case-selection process purposefully sought out innovative success stories, and we may have selected groups less likely to fall prey to the down-side of the service-advocacy dilemma. What the cases do offer are some structures that may help inoculate organizations against the pitfalls of combining service and advocacy.

The Federation of Southern Cooperatives is the strongest example of successfully combining advocacy and service activities. The Federation is one of the only nongovernmental recipients of major funding from the US Department of Agriculture for the Black-farmer outreach program, and this program constitutes a major part of the Federation's annual operating budget. Yet the Federation not only led advocacy efforts to create the program but has driven the lawsuit against the USDA. Why hasn't the USDA just cut off their funding? Could this only happen in America? The cases show a number of organizations managed to combine their advocacy and service-related work successfully, and maintain their autonomy despite being in service contracts.

In Cambodia, for example, one of the key human rights organizations, ADHOC, has pushed to expand the land-law reform process and make it more transparent, but it also provides training services to national police on human rights issues, under contract with the government of Cambodia. This work is service provision, but it is also a form of advocacy, because it is changing the attitudes and behaviors of government personnel. And in Senegal, APROFES staff organically link their economic-development and advocacy work to support their larger goal of increasing the power of women. They see the two as integrally interrelated.

The Kind *of Services and* Ways *They Are Provided Matter*

In these cases, the services relate directly to the groups' larger missions. For the Federation of Southern Cooperatives, the service expands Black-farmer access to key USDA services. For ADHOC, training Cambodian police officers helps build a culture free of violence, impunity, and human rights violations. Their "customers" were also their targets, and they used the service relationship as a vehicle for getting their message across. For APROFES, economic development and income generation are key pieces of the struggle to increase women's control over their lives. So part of the answer is to be strategic about what *kinds* of service-oriented work to take on. Providing services is not necessarily incompatible with advocacy work, but groups have to be careful what kinds of services they take on. Does it support the overall mission? Does it feed the long-term advocacy-oriented work the organization does? Is it building the strength of the constituency or just making them dependent? Is there an actual or implied agreement with the funder not to criticize or seek to change it?

The question of creating dependent and passive "customers" by engaging in service-oriented work is difficult to analyze from the cases, because we did not focus on the details of the service work, and the evidence is more anecdotal than comparative. For the Federation of Southern Cooperatives, one of the challenges has been to avoid participating in the delivery of material goods as part of their service contracts with government. Seed deliveries, especially, left long memories. When asked what was the most important thing the Federation has done, some farmers only remembered the seed distributions and not the policy-advocacy work for Black farmers. So the Federation tries to stay away from this, if possible.

APROFES's service work involves intensive community empowerment because local leaders are responsible for organizing the activities, not APROFES staff. This way they avoid being placed in the "deliverer" role. So the *way* services are provided is as important as the kind of services chosen. APROFES set up autonomous organizations that are able to find the resources they need to keep going from other places—the market, government agencies, and other organizations. APROFES staff are available to advise and encourage the organization, but their role is not to lead or provide subsidies, only to support and encourage. Helping constituents access resources is OK, but actually handing out goods is more problematic.

Key Advocacy Assets and Advocacy Capacity Building

Looking across the cases, there are a number of "assets" that the especially effective groups shared. By "assets" I mean specific skills, knowledge, and experiences used to inform advocacy work and craft advocacy strategies. Some of these came from formal advocacy capacity building, but most came from life experiences and technical and professional training the advocates brought to their work. Together, they give something of a road map for the kind of skills that groups might try to bring together to make themselves effective advocacy organizations.

Radical Roots

Nearly all of the case studies involve organizations that evolved or grew out of earlier "radical" organizing activities. CALDH staff came out of the labor union movement in Guatemala, and their time in exile. APROFES grew out of a youth sports and culture organization with links to a left-wing political party. Cambodian human rights organizations were formed by people who survived the Khmer Rouge and Vietnamese periods in exile. The Federation of Southern Cooperatives is made up of former civil rights activists. Ecuadorian NGOs and community-based organizations come from radical environmental backgrounds, student activism, and indigenous-rights movements. The radical roots of these organizations brought them a clarity of purpose and a long-term commitment to social justice. Radical roots also brought the wisdom and patience that come with long-seasoned experience and reflection. Most of the time their roots in social justice struggles also brought a deep commitment to helping excluded communities gain power and act on their own behalf.

This coincidence is more descriptive than prescriptive. That is, it would not be possible to introduce radical roots if the group didn't have them already. But groups that don't come from radical-activist backgrounds can link with other groups that do and bring a grounded and committed strength to their advocacy work.

Ability to Act Fluidly at Multiple Levels Simultaneously

Most of these cases involve advocacy that crosses local, regional, and sometimes national boundaries. In nearly all the cases, they involve developing campaigns with local communities where educational levels and access to information are extremely low, and people may not speak the dominant language used by decision makers. They also involve efforts to influence public policy, public opinion, media coverage, corporate behavior, legal precedents, and international tribunals, which usually require specialized technical knowledge and skills. Yet for groups that are committed to fully include local communities as equal partners in advocacy work, they must be able to move fluidly across these cultural, geographic, linguistic, and technology divides.

Based on the case studies, below is a list of the skills, assets, and organizational structures that have made for effective advocacy work at different levels:

Local Level

- Speaking the local language(s).

- Organic ties between popular-movement leadership and support organizations.

- Long track record of work in the regional and/or local area.

- Using paraprofessionals for outreach—either local folks with some technical knowledge or extension workers with local ties.

- Ability to identify and provide support for local grassroots organizational structures.

- Knowledge of and ability to clearly explain the regional, national, or international decision-making processes, to help local groups navigate through them.

- Ability to frame issues in the larger socioeconomic-political and human rights context, stimulate reflection, and help form analytical capacity.

- Listening closely to people's issues, fears, hopes, and desires.

Regional/National Level

- Knowledge of the bureaucracy and the decision-making processes in order to know where the key points of intervention are.

- Personal contacts and social and political networks to open up access to power arenas.

- Ability to use highly technical skills as an entry-point into issues (i.e., legal skills, technical and environmental expertise, legislative experience, etc.).

- Playing a broker role in opening doors, getting organization members a seat at the table at higher levels of power.

- Ability to identify and cultivate receptive subgroups within bureaucracies.

- Finding "campaign vehicles" that resonate deeply, but also get at the core issues (i.e., paradigmatic human rights cases, outrage over domestic violence,

boycotts against notorious corporations, the notion of a Jubilee Year when all debts are forgiven).

International Level

- Physical presence, personal ties, or other connections in this arena.

- Knowledge of the system, doctrines, laws, procedures, and so on (UN, OAS, etc.).

- Special competency (policy knowledge, technical skills, legal skills, etc.).

- Friends and allies who can open doors and provide guidance on skills needed to act at this level.

Evaluating Impact

At the beginning of this conclusion, I argued that social justice advocacy involves having an impact on three levels:

- Policy impacts, which bring changes in specific policies, laws, programs, or practices to benefit excluded groups.

- Governance impacts, which open and consolidate channels of participation, voice, and power for civil society to engage in decision-making processes affecting their lives.

- Civil society impacts, which increase the ability of civil society organizations to fight for their interests with powerful actors and to create internal cultures, practices, and structures consistent with their social justice ideals.

Going back to look at the cases to see how these three dimensions can help us evaluate advocacy impact, it's clear that the distinctions among the three categories are often blurred. We see links among the three dimensions of impact, with gains in one category often feeding advances in another. And the causal relationships flow in all directions, with civil society gains advancing governance and policy gains, and visa versa. Yet each of the dimensions has its own importance and merits attention as a distinct entity. To help navigate this interconnectedness among the dimensions, I suggest making a distinction between impacts that are instrumental in achieving gains in another dimension

Table 14.1. Impact Analysis for Social Justice Advocacy

Dimension of Advocacy Impact		Policy	Governance Structures	Civil Society
Definition				
	Instrumental	Policies, laws, programs, or practices that lead to other policy, governance, or civil society gains	Access to decision-making processes that facilitates policy gains or civil society gains	Increasing the ability of civil society organizations to articulate and fight for their interests with powerful actors and hold government and the private sector accountable
	Structural	Specific policies, laws, programs, and practices that have direct benefit for excluded groups, when implemented	Opening and consolidating channels of participation, voice, and power for civil society to engage in decision-making processes affecting their lives	Creating internal cultures, practices, and structures consistent with their social justice ideals and holding representative structures accountable
Strategies		• Lobbying to promote a position • Proposing alternatives • Media campaigns to influence decision makers • Research, monitoring, and investigations • Investigations by proxy (media, watchdog agencies) • Policy alliances with decision makers to increase leverage	• Changing public discourse • Creating, opening, and consolidating channels for civil society participation • Strategic alliances for articulating common interests to increase power • Strengthening vehicles for expressing civil society interests (media, governance structures, courts, etc.)	• Grassroots organizing • Popular education on social justice and human rights issues • Strengthening of representative organizations • Creating bridging organizations to link civil society organizations • Building sense of dignity, courage, and self-respect to fight cynicism and despair
Indicators of Success		Policy, law, program, precedent, etc. instituted and implemented	• Democratic space expanded • New channels for participation • Freedom of action, engagement • Position, credibility, and power of campaign participants strengthened	• Strong grassroots organizations and NGOs with representative and accountable structures • Ability to articulate rights (political, civil, social, and economic) and formulate proposals to assert these rights • Increased awareness of members and other sectors of civil society and public about issues at stake

of impact and impacts that are structural, representing a gain unto themselves.[18]

To illustrate, in Ecuador the emergence of the Frente de Defensa de la Amazonía and organized indigenous communities was a civil society gain that strengthened the power of Oriente residents to defend and assert their rights. This was also instrumental in the campaign against Texaco because it created a unified block of Oriente residents that government officials in Quito had to acknowledge and negotiate with. By creating more access to decision makers, the existence of Oriente residents' organizations led to a governance impact, opening new channels of participation, however tenuous. That impact, in turn, was

instrumental in achieving one of the major policy victories of the campaign: securing the support of the Ecuadorian government for the lawsuit against Texaco. But the arrows of causality point in the other direction too. The Ecuadorian government's support for the New York court case helped stop the judge from throwing it out during the early stages. If the Oriente residents win the case in New York, they will achieve a major governance victory, opening the global arena to the possibility of international corporate accountability. Coming full circle, the lawsuit has fed and animated the Frente and indigenous organizations, which represent long-term structural civil society gains because they are forums for articulating interests, building shared understandings, and developing processes for engaging and influencing decision

---

18. I am grateful to Valerie Miller for helping me clarify and draw out this point.

Table 14.2. Case Study Impact Analysis

Dimension of Advocacy Impact	Policy	Governance Structures	Civil Society
Ecuador	• Changed Ecuadorian government position to support or not oppose lawsuit in New York • Changed other oil company environmental practices (but not culturally destructive practices)	• Awareness raising and opinion formation of public—Ecuador, US, Europe • Change in public discourse on oil development to include justice, human rights, corporate accountability, and sovereignty • Small but significant gains in access to government decision makers	• Frente and indigenous organizations strengthened; provide channel for Oriente residents to articulate interests • Residents willing to denounce rights violations of private and public oil companies
Guatemala	• Win in Rio Negro massacre case • Bringing other cases to trial (ongoing) • Bringing genocide case (future)	• Asserting right to bring human rights cases in Guatemala • Building competency, accountability of Guatemalan courts (incipient) • Growing public awareness of massacres	• Massacre victims gaining courage to bring legal cases • Massacre victims healing through reburial of relatives • Reconstruction of indigenous and peasant organizations
US Black Farmers	• Minority Outreach and Education Program inserted into 1990 Farm Bill • Annual appropriations funding outreach program • Lawsuit victory against US Department of Agriculture	• Putting official discrimination in public light • Linking with other small-farmer groups to defend interests of small farmers against corporate agriculture	• Multi-state network of Black-farmer associations
Senegal	• Man brought to trial for killing wife for first time • Rapists sentenced to maximum prison term in two cases	• Putting gender violence in public discourse for first time in Senegal • Building awareness and sensitivity to gender violence of police, religious leaders, and doctors • Feeding national movement that led to national legislation penalizing violence against women	• Long-term gender awareness, leadership development, and economic development for women in Kaolack • Shifting culture at the regional level • Regional network of civil society organizations focused on violence against women
US Debt Relief	• Enhanced debt-relief framework of 1999 • Debt relief conditioned on requirement for civil society input in creation of poverty-reduction strategies, nationally • Revaluation of gold to fund debt relief • US congressional funding secured	• Opening door for civil society input to poverty-reduction strategy development in indebted countries • Helped consolidate access of NGOs to international financial institutions	• Creation of Jubilee 2000 campaign network around the world • Empowering advocates from developing countries to speak for themselves • Raised awareness of public in Northern country of debt issues
Cambodia	• Secured revision of Cambodian land law with requirement for civil society input	• Including Cambodian civil society in land-law revision through triangulation strategy	• Incipient civil society re-emergence and engagement in policy debates

makers. It also helped forge structures for internal decision making among settlers and indigenous communities and, importantly, between these two groups as well.

Building on this discussion, Table 14.1 presents the framework for analyzing social justice advocacy. Table 14.2 uses the framework to analyze the key victories and successes of the case studies.

From Table 14.2, analyzing the key victories and successes of the case studies, it is clear that activities and impacts in each of these categories are often fused with impacts in other categories. If APROFES hadn't built a strong regional network around gender rights, its activities would not have sparked a national debate on violence against women. Likewise, if international NGOs hadn't managed to force the Cambodian government to open up the land-law revision to national civil society, those groups would not have won a seat at the table. This mutual reinforcement and mutual dependence show that looking at advocacy as simply involving laws, policies, and programs misses the much larger dynamics of power, change, and social justice.

The framework suggests some areas for further social justice advocacy research not directly addressed by the case studies. We looked primarily at the interaction between political space and advocacy approaches that work. But we didn't look at the interaction between the strength of civil society and advocacy approaches. The cases and the framework suggest that the strength or weakness of civil society may be an even greater defining factor in advocacy work. How can social justice work go forward when civil society is fractured or nonexistent? What is possible, who can do it, and how to do it? What can outside groups do? Are there "right" and "wrong" ways to go about it? The cases presented here only begin to answer these questions, which merit further attention.

Another area for further research is the allocation of financial resources in collaborative advocacy work. Especially in transnational advocacy alliances, the question of which organizations have access to financing, how much, and how it is shared can have a strong impact on campaign success, the ability to continue a struggle over a long period, and the stability of the organizations involved. As organizations such as Oxfam America become increasingly involved in collaborative advocacy work with counterparts in the South, this question will demand honest and direct attention.

Conclusion

The case studies offer many lessons, both hopeful and cautionary. Some of the cases had advocacy impacts that have transformed the day-to-day lives of many people far beyond what any "brick-and-mortar" or emergency-response project ever could. In other cases, the impacts have been partial, tentative, or it's still too early to know the final tally. Yet in all the cases, the groups involved have shown the way for some incredibly innovative and creative approaches to advocacy. Purposefully combining grassroots organizing with high level policy influence, using the power of the social- and economic-rights framework, using paradigmatic cases that resonate deeply and bring justice for large numbers of people, and playing strategies off each other to influence decision makers are some of the ones highlighted in this conclusion.

The groups profiled in the cases have struggled with and in some cases pioneered ways to bridge local, regional, national, and global arenas with mutual respect and with impact. Social justice organizations of all shapes and sizes will need to continue constructing "norms of conduct" for working across arenas. And there are other ongoing challenges facing social justice advocates: opening more political space, strengthening civil society, learning the rules and "texts" for effective policy influence, creating learning organizations not dependent on a single charismatic leader, building a unifying vision that informs all the organization's activities. The cases show the promise of overcoming these difficulties and at the same time remind us that the ideal is just an ideal, and reality is much messier and complex.

The multi-dimensional understanding of advocacy that emerges from the experiences in the cases resonates with how social justice advocates are beginning to understand their work around the world. It reflects an integrated understanding of how social justice change happens, an understanding that includes changing laws and policies, opening up governance structures, and building civil society and social movements. The framework presented here systematizes this understanding and may help organizations think more intentionally about the multiple aspects of their social justice advocacy work, pushing to broaden their impact at all levels.

Part IV

Advocacy Resource Directory

Gabrielle Watson

with Angela Orlando, Jennifer Shea, and Karin Lockwood

Introduction

The Advocacy Resource Directory was created for development practitioners and social justice activists around the world who wish to increase their advocacy impact. It provides concise, high-quality information about advocacy support organizations around the world in an easy-access format. It will also be of interest to organizations that support nongovernmental organizations working to strengthen civil society and democratic practices and build social capital.

The directory includes descriptions and contact information for 272 advocacy support organizations from Africa, Asia, Europe, Latin America, the Middle East, and North America. The directory lists organizations that support advocacy through:

- Advocacy capacity building

- Nongovernmental organization (NGO) networking

- Development policy analysis and research

- Advocacy funding

The Advocacy Resource Directory is also available on the Advocacy Institute/Oxfam America *Advocacy for Social Justice* web page in a significantly expanded and searchable format. The web page features organizational profiles with concise, self-reported descriptions of the mission and advocacy-related work of each organization as well as contact information for each regional office. In addition, the website contains a listing of over 350 key Internet and printed advocacy resources, including books, catalogs, manuals, guides, and websites with contact information for locating them. The *Advocacy for Social Justice* web page can be reached from the Advocacy Institute and Oxfam America websites, at *www.advocacy.org* and *www.oxfamamerica.org,* respectively.

Method for Gathering Information

The directory is the result of one and a half years of research, outreach, double- and triple-checking of information by a team of dedicated consultants and volunteers coordinated by Gabrielle Watson, and a peer-review process by a Directory Advisory Committee. An underlying goal of the directory is to foster grassroots-to-grassroots networking and learning and to disseminate the large and growing pool of available resources around the world. The criterion for inclusion in the directory was that the organization works to build advocacy capacity of a relatively large potential constituency through training, research, financial support, networking, or dissemination of capacity-building materials. Organizations that only work with very specific groups, or that provide non-advocacy-oriented capacity building, were not included. The directory also does not include organizations whose primary work is *doing* advocacy. While their work is extremely important, it isn't necessarily aimed at helping other organizations increase their advocacy impact.

The vast majority of organizations profiled here provided the information directly to us. The directory production team asked organizations to complete a profile questionnaire or sent them draft profiles based on available information, which they then modified and sent back. Some profiles are based on web page information. In these cases, the directory production team took the liberty of assuming implicit agreement for publication of their activities, based on their own publication on the Internet.

The directory production team contacted organizations through the networks of Oxfam America, the Advocacy Institute, and Oxfam International. Many suggestions were provided by other advocacy-capacity-building organizations, most notably World Learning's School for International Training, the Institute for Development Research, and The Asia Foundation. This initial "casting of the net" identified many organizations from all over the world to include in the directory.

Nevertheless, the Advocacy Resource Directory cannot claim to be comprehensive or complete. There are many organizations that the directory team was not able to learn about, contact, or obtain sufficient information from to confidently include in this directory. Some organizations chose not to be included for a variety of reasons that must be respected. The *Advocacy for Social Justice* web page will ultimately serve as a mechanism for updating and expanding the directory, leading to a more comprehensive printed edition in the future.

The directory production team made a difficult

decision not to include *individuals* who provide advocacy-capacity-building services. There is a small but growing community of advocacy consultants that provides crucial support to grassroots groups and support NGOs working with them. However, it would be unfair to the many not identified or contacted to include only the few the team learned about.

The directory includes some advocacy support organizations working exclusively with North American or central/eastern European NGOs but does not attempt to provide a comprehensive listing for either of these regions. This choice was made in part because more complete directories and resources are already available for Northern-based organizations, and it would not be to this directory's comparative advantage to try to duplicate them. These resources are listed in the "Resources" section of the *Advocacy for Social Justice* web page.

Directory Organization

The directory has four principal parts: capacity-building organizations, NGO networking organizations, development-research and policy-analysis organizations, and funding organizations. In addition, there is an index of organizations by the countries in which they work. Organizational profiles provide contact information, the organization's main issue areas, regions and languages they work in, and the types of advocacy resources and services they provide. Each organization is listed by its "primary" advocacy resource category though it may also work in other areas as well. Most organizations have self-identified their primary resource category. In some cases, the directory team made the determination based on published materials.[1]

Index of Organizations by Country of Operation

To help identify organizations, an index of organizations by the countries in which they work is presented first. If you are looking for organizations active in a particular country, this index will tell you the sections of the directory where you will find their profiles.

Capacity-Building Organizations

This resource category includes organizations that provide advocacy training, degree programs, technical assistance, workshop facilitation, and advice and mentoring to help organizations improve specific advocacy skills and competencies.

NGO Networking Organizations

This resource category includes organizations that create the opportunity for networking among people's organizations, NGOs, and other civil society organizations. They may provide meeting space, coordinate organized advocacy working groups, organize conferences, connect organizations with common advocacy agendas, and engage in other activities to strengthen advocacy initiatives and civil society more broadly.

Development-Policy and Research Organizations

This resource category includes organizations that do research and/or analysis of development and policy issues, make research studies and publications available to the public, or help community groups and NGOs engage in monitoring, research, and policy-analysis activities.

Funding Organizations

This resource category includes organizations that directly fund advocacy, democracy, and civil-society-strengthening work.

---

1. These four "resource categories" were chosen based on the primary types of resources either sought or offered by activists and advocacy support organizations. During the process of compiling this directory, it became clear that many organizations do not fit neatly into one category or another, and the directory team frequently had to make an assessment of how best to classify them. The team received a number of requests to categorize organizations by the substantive areas of their work, such as gender, environment, human rights, economic development, and so on. Due to the time and resource limitations of this project, and the difficulty of choosing categories that are understood the same way by all organizations around the world, this level of classification was not possible.

Index of Organizations by Program Country

Organization Name	Directory Section

Afghanistan

| Christian Aid (CAID) | Policy/Research |
| International NGO Training and Research Centre (INTRAC) | Capacity Building |

Albania

| Microfinance Centre for Central and Eastern Europe and the NIS (MFC) | Capacity Building |
| Open Society/Soros Foundation | Funding |

Angola

| American Friends Service Committee (AFSC) | Capacity Building |
| Kulima | Capacity Building |

Antigua and Barbuda

| Instituto Interamericano de Cooperación para la Agricultura (IICA) | NGO Networking |

Argentina

Abya Yala Fund (AYF)	Funding
Asociación Latinoamericana de Organizaciones de Promoción (ALOP)	NGO Networking
Centro de Estudios de Estado y Sociedad (CEDES)	Policy/Research
Centro de Estudios Legales y Sociales (CELS)	Policy/Research
Centro Latinoamericano de Economía Humana (CLAEH)	Policy/Research
Citizen Power Foundation (Fundación Poder Ciudadano)	Capacity Building
Esquel Group Foundation	Policy/Research
Instituto Interamericano de Cooperación para la Agricultura (IICA)	NGO Networking
Master of Arts Program in Public Policy and Administration—Universidad de San Andrés	Capacity Building
Posgrado en Organizaciones sin Fines de Lucro	Capacity Building
Servicio Habitacional y de Acción Social (SEHAS)	Capacity Building
Women's Eyes on the World Bank—Latin America Chapter	NGO Networking

Armenia

| Microfinance Centre for Central and Eastern Europe and the NIS (MFC) | Capacity Building |
| Open Society/Soros Foundation | Funding |

Australia

Human Rights and Peoples Diplomacy Training	Capacity Building
Oxfam Australia/Community Aid Abroad (CAA)	Funding
Tambuyog Development Center, Inc. (TDC)	Capacity Building

Austria

IFEX Clearing House	NGO Networking
Microfinance Centre for Central and Eastern Europe and the NIS (MFC)	Capacity Building

Azerbaijan

IFEX Clearing House	NGO Networking
Open Society/Soros Foundation	Funding
Sisterhood Is Global Institute (SIGI)	Capacity Building

Bahamas

Instituto Interamericano de Cooperación para la Agricultura (IICA)	NGO Networking

Bangladesh

ActionAid (AA)	Capacity Building
Bangladesh Centre for Advanced Studies (BCAS)	Policy/Research
Bangladesh Rural Advancement Committee (BRAC)	Capacity Building
CUSO	Capacity Building
Focus on the Global South	Policy/Research
Forum of Environmental Journalists of Bangladesh (FEJB)	Capacity Building
Initiatives for Research, Education and Development in Asia (INASIA)	NGO Networking
Institute for Development Policy Analysis and Advocacy at Proshika (IDPAA)	Policy/Research
International NGO Training and Research Centre (INTRAC)	Capacity Building
Oxfam Australia/Community Aid Abroad (CAA)	Funding
PRIP Trust	Capacity Building
Sisterhood Is Global Institute (SIGI)	Capacity Building
South Asian Coalition on Child Servitude (SACCS)	NGO Networking
South Asia Partnership Canada—SAP Canada	Capacity Building
Tambuyog Development Center, Inc. (TDC)	Capacity Building
Unnayan Shahojogy Team (UST)	Policy/Research

Barbados

Caribbean Association for Feminist Research and Action (CAFRA)	Capacity Building
Instituto Interamericano de Cooperación para la Agricultura (IICA)	NGO Networking

Belarus

International NGO Training and Research Centre (INTRAC)	Capacity Building
Microfinance Centre for Central and Eastern Europe and the NIS (MFC)	Capacity Building
Open Society/Soros Foundation	Funding

Belgium

IFEX Clearing House	NGO Networking
Via Campesina (VC)	NGO Networking

Belize

Asociación Latinoamericana de Organizaciones de Promoción (ALOP)	NGO Networking
Caribbean Association for Feminist Research and Action (CAFRA)	Capacity Building
CUSO	Capacity Building

Fundación Arias para la Paz y el Progreso Humano—Centro para la Participación Organizada (ARIAS)	Policy/Research
Instituto Interamericano de Cooperación para la Agricultura (IICA)	NGO Networking
Society for the Promotion of Education and Research (SPEAR)	Policy/Research
Washington Office on Latin America (WOLA)	Policy/Research

Benin

Environment and Development Action in the Third World (ENDA TM)	Policy/Research
Helvetas—Swiss Association for International Cooperation	Capacity Building

Bhutan

Helvetas—Swiss Association for International Cooperation	Capacity Building

Bolivia

Abya Yala Fund (AYF)	Funding
Apoyo para el Campesino-Indígena del Oriente Boliviano (APCOB)	Capacity Building
Asociación Latinoamericana de Organizaciones de Promoción (ALOP)	NGO Networking
Centro de Educación Popular Qhana (QHANA)	Capacity Building
Centro de Estudios de la Realidad Económica y Social (CERES)	Policy/Research
Centro de Estudios Jurídicos e Investigación Social (CEJIS)	Policy/Research
Centro de Estudios para el Desarrollo Laboral y Agrario (CEDLA)	Policy/Research
Coordinadora de la Mujer	NGO Networking
CUSO	Capacity Building
Environment and Development Action in the Third World (ENDA TM)	Policy/Research
Esquel Group Foundation	Policy/Research
Instituto Interamericano de Cooperación para la Agricultura (IICA)	NGO Networking
Investigación Social y Asesoramiento Legal Potosí (ISALP)	Capacity Building
Japan International Volunteer Center (JVC)	Funding
Oxfam America	Funding
Women's Eyes on the World Bank—Latin America Chapter	NGO Networking

Bosnia-Herzegovina

Microfinance Centre for Central and Eastern Europe and the NIS (MFC)	Capacity Building

Botswana

African Science & Technology Exchange (ASTEX)	Policy/Research
Association of African Women for Research & Development (AAWORD)	Policy/Research
Collaborative Centre for Gender and Development (CCGD)	Capacity Building
Development Innovations and Networks (IRED)	Policy/Research
Emang Basadi Women's Association (EB)	Capacity Building
Forum for Women in Democracy (FOWODE)	Capacity Building
ZERO Environment Regional Organization (ZERO)	Policy/Research

Brazil

ActionAid (AA)	Capacity Building
American Friends Service Committee (AFSC)	Capacity Building
Asociación Latinoamericana de Organizaciones de Promoción (ALOP)	NGO Networking
Center of Concern (COC)	Policy/Research

Esquel Group Foundation	Policy/Research
Federação de Orgãos para Assistencia Social e Educacional/Association of Organizations for Social and Educational Assistance (FASE)	Capacity Building
Ford Foundation	Funding
Global Exchange	Policy/Research
Grassroots International	Funding
Instituto Interamericano de Cooperación para la Agricultura (IICA)	NGO Networking
John D. and Catherine T. MacArthur Foundation	Funding
Polis Instituto de Estudos, Formação e Assessoria em Politicas Sociais	Policy/Research
Via Campesina (VC)	NGO Networking
W. Alton Jones Foundation	Funding

Bulgaria

Microfinance Centre for Central and Eastern Europe and the NIS (MFC)	Capacity Building
Open Society/Soros Foundation	Funding

Burkina Faso

Association Nationale pour la Promotion Active (ANPA)	Capacity Building
Association of African Women for Research & Development (AAWORD)	Policy/Research
CUSO	Capacity Building
Oxfam America	Funding

Burma (Myanmar)

International Centre for Human Rights and Democratic Development (ICHRDD)	NGO Networking

Burundi

ActionAid (AA)	Capacity Building
Association of African Women for Research & Development (AAWORD)	Policy/Research
Christian Aid (CAID)	Policy/Research

Cambodia

American Friends Service Committee (AFSC)	Capacity Building
Cambodian Human Rights Association (ADHOC)	Policy/Research
International NGO Training and Research Centre (INTRAC)	Capacity Building
Japan International Volunteer Center (JVC)	Funding
NGO Forum on Cambodia	NGO Networking
NGO Forum on the Asian Development Bank	NGO Networking
Oxfam America	Funding
Oxfam Australia/Community Aid Abroad (CAA)	Funding
Tambuyog Development Center, Inc. (TDC)	Capacity Building
W. Alton Jones Foundation	Funding

Cameroon

Association of African Women for Research & Development (AAWORD)	Policy/Research
Helvetas—Swiss Association for International Cooperation	Capacity Building

Canada

Canadian Human Rights Foundation—International Human Rights Training Program (IHRTP)	Capacity Building
IFEX Clearing House	NGO Networking
Institute for Agriculture and Trade Policy (IATP)	Policy/Research
Instituto Interamericano de Cooperación para la Agricultura (IICA)	NGO Networking
International Centre for Human Rights and Democratic Development (ICHRDD)	NGO Networking
NGO Forum on the Asian Development Bank	NGO Networking
Public Law Center (TPLC)	Capacity Building
South Asia Partnership Canada—SAP Canada	Capacity Building
Tambuyog Development Center, Inc. (TDC)	Capacity Building
Via Campesina (VC)	NGO Networking

Cape Verde

Association of African Women for Research & Development (AAWORD)	Policy/Research

Chile

Abya Yala Fund (AYF)	Funding
Asociación Latinoamericana de Organizaciones de Promoción (ALOP)	NGO Networking
Centro de Estudios Nacionales de Desarrollo Alternativo (CENDA)	Policy/Research
CUSO	Capacity Building
Esquel Group Foundation	Policy/Research
Ford Foundation	Funding
Instituto Interamericano de Cooperación para la Agricultura (IICA)	NGO Networking
Oxfam Canada	Policy/Research
Women's Eyes on the World Bank—Latin America Chapter	NGO Networking

China

Center of Concern (COC)	Policy/Research
Ford Foundation	Funding
NGO Forum on the Asian Development Bank	NGO Networking
Oxfam America	Funding
Oxfam Australia/Community Aid Abroad (CAA)	Funding
Oxfam Hong Kong	Funding
W. Alton Jones Foundation	Funding

Colombia

Abya Yala Fund (AYF)	Funding
American Friends Service Committee (AFSC)	Capacity Building
Asociación Latinoamericana de Organizaciones de Promoción (ALOP)	NGO Networking
Christian Aid (CAID)	Policy/Research
Colombia Human Rights Network	NGO Networking
Confederacion de ONGs (CCONG)	NGO Networking
Corporación para el Desarrollo de la Educación Básica (CORPOEDUCACION)	Capacity Building
Corporación Viva la Ciudadanía	Policy/Research
CUSO	Capacity Building
Environment and Development Action in the Third World (ENDA TM)	Policy/Research
Fundación Antonio Restrepo Barco (FRB)	Policy/Research

Denmark

Center of Concern (COC)	Policy/Research
IFEX Clearing House	NGO Networking

Djibouti

Oxfam Canada	Policy/Research

Dominica

Caribbean Association for Feminist Research and Action (CAFRA)	Capacity Building
Instituto Interamericano de Cooperación para la Agricultura (IICA)	NGO Networking

Dominican Republic

ActionAid (AA)	Capacity Building
Asociación Latinoamericana de Organizaciones de Promoción (ALOP)	NGO Networking
Caribbean Association for Feminist Research and Action (CAFRA)	Capacity Building
Colectivo de Investigación, Desarrollo y Educación entre Mujeres (CIDEM)	Capacity Building
Environment and Development Action in the Third World (ENDA TM)	Policy/Research
Helvetas—Swiss Association for International Cooperation	Capacity Building
Instituto Interamericano de Cooperación para la Agricultura (IICA)	NGO Networking
Public Law Center (TPLC)	Capacity Building
Women's Eyes on the World Bank—Latin America Chapter	NGO Networking

East Timor

Oxfam Australia/Community Aid Abroad (CAA)	Funding

Ecuador

Abya Yala Fund (AYF)	Funding
Asociación Latinoamericana de Organizaciones de Promoción (ALOP)	NGO Networking
Centro de Derechos Económicos y Sociales (CDES)	Policy/Research
Esquel Group Foundation	Policy/Research
Fondo Ecuatoriano Populorum Progressio (FEPP)	Capacity Building
Instituto Interamericano de Cooperación para la Agricultura (IICA)	NGO Networking
Oxfam America	Funding

Egypt

Arab Center for the Independence of the Judiciary and the Legal Profession (ACIJLP)	Capacity Building
Association of African Women for Research & Development (AAWORD)	Policy/Research
Center for Development Services (CDS)	Capacity Building
Ford Foundation	Funding
Institute of Cultural Affairs—Middle East and North Africa (ICA-MENA)	Capacity Building
Legal Research and Resource Center for Human Rights (LRRC)	Policy/Research
Sisterhood Is Global Institute (SIGI)	Capacity Building

El Salvador

Asociación Latinoamericana de Organizaciones de Promoción (ALOP)	NGO Networking
Centro Latinoamericano de Economía Humana (CLAEH)	Policy/Research
CUSO	Capacity Building
Development Innovations and Networks (IRED)	Policy/Research

Fundación Arias para la Paz y el Progreso Humano—Centro para la Participación
    Organizada (ARIAS)   Policy/Research
Fundación Nacional para el Desarrollo (FUNDE)   Policy/Research
Fundación Salvadoreña para la Promoción Social y el Desarrollo Económico
    (FUNSALPRODESE)   Capacity Building
Funding Exchange   Funding
Instituto Interamericano de Cooperación para la Agricultura (IICA)   NGO Networking
Oxfam America   Funding
Oxfam Canada   Policy/Research
Washington Office on Latin America (WOLA)   Policy/Research
Women's Eyes on the World Bank—Latin America Chapter   NGO Networking

Eritrea

Grassroots International   Funding

Estonia

Open Society/Soros Foundation   Funding

Ethiopia

ActionAid (AA)   Capacity Building
African Women's Development and Communications Network (FEMNET)   NGO Networking
Christian Aid (CAID)   Policy/Research
Collaborative Centre for Gender and Development (CCGD)   Capacity Building
Environment and Development Action in the Third World (ENDA TM)   Policy/Research
Ethiopian Women Lawyers Association (EWLA)   Policy/Research
International NGO Training and Research Centre (INTRAC)   Capacity Building
Japan International Volunteer Center (JVC)   Funding
Legal Research and Resource Center for Human Rights (LRRC)   Policy/Research
Oxfam America   Funding
Oxfam Australia/Community Aid Abroad (CAA)   Funding
Oxfam Canada   Policy/Research

Fiji

CUSO   Capacity Building
IFEX Clearing House   NGO Networking

Former Yugoslavia

American Friends Service Committee (AFSC)   Capacity Building
IFEX Clearing House   NGO Networking

France

IFEX Clearing House   NGO Networking
Microfinance Centre for Central and Eastern Europe and the NIS (MFC)   Capacity Building
NGO Forum on the Asian Development Bank   NGO Networking

Gambia, The

ActionAid (AA)   Capacity Building
Association of Non-governmental Organizations (TANGO)   NGO Networking

| International NGO Training and Research Centre (INTRAC) | Capacity Building |
| Oxfam America | Funding |

Georgia

| Microfinance Centre for Central and Eastern Europe and the NIS (MFC) | Capacity Building |
| Open Society/Soros Foundation | Funding |

Germany

| African Women's Development and Communications Network (FEMNET) | NGO Networking |
| Association of African Women for Research & Development (AAWORD) | Policy/Research |

Ghana

ActionAid (AA)	Capacity Building
African Women's Development and Communications Network (FEMNET)	NGO Networking
Association of African Women for Research & Development (AAWORD)	Policy/Research
CUSO	Capacity Building
Integrated Social Development Centre (ISODEC)	Capacity Building
International NGO Training and Research Centre (INTRAC)	Capacity Building

Greece

| IFEX Clearing House | NGO Networking |

Grenada

| Instituto Interamericano de Cooperación para la Agricultura (IICA) | NGO Networking |

Guatemala

Abya Yala Fund (AYF)	Funding
Acción Ciudadana	NGO Networking
ActionAid (AA)	Capacity Building
Asociación Latinoamericana de Organizaciones de Promoción (ALOP)	NGO Networking
Christian Aid (CAID)	Policy/Research
Coordination of NGOs and Cooperatives (CONGCOOP)	Policy/Research
CUSO	Capacity Building
Fundación Arias para la Paz y el Progreso Humano—Centro para la Participación Organizada (ARIAS)	Policy/Research
Fundación Nacional para el Desarrollo (FUNDE)	Policy/Research
Funding Exchange	Funding
Global Exchange	Policy/Research
Helvetas—Swiss Association for International Cooperation	Capacity Building
Instituto Interamericano de Cooperación para la Agricultura (IICA)	NGO Networking
International Centre for Human Rights and Democratic Development (ICHRDD)	NGO Networking
Open Society/Soros Foundation	Funding
Oxfam America	Funding
Oxfam Australia/Community Aid Abroad (CAA)	Funding
Oxfam Canada	Policy/Research
Washington Office on Latin America (WOLA)	Policy/Research

Guinea

| African Science & Technology Exchange (ASTEX) | Policy/Research |

Guinea-Bissau

Environment and Development Action in the Third World (ENDA TM)   Policy/Research
Oxfam America   Funding

Guyana

Caribbean Association for Feminist Research and Action (CAFRA)   Capacity Building
Instituto Interamericano de Cooperación para la Agricultura (IICA)   NGO Networking
Oxfam Canada   Policy/Research

Haiti

ActionAid (AA)   Capacity Building
American Friends Service Committee (AFSC)   Capacity Building
Christian Aid (CAID)   Policy/Research
Funding Exchange   Funding
Grassroots International   Funding
Helvetas—Swiss Association for International Cooperation   Capacity Building
Instituto Interamericano de Cooperación para la Agricultura (IICA)   NGO Networking
International Centre for Human Rights and Democratic Development (ICHRDD) NGO Networking
Open Society/Soros Foundation   Funding
Oxfam America   Funding

Honduras

Abya Yala Fund (AYF)   Funding
Asociación Latinoamericana de Organizaciones de Promoción (ALOP)   NGO Networking
Fundación Arias para la Paz y el Progreso Humano—Centro para la Participación
    Organizada (ARIAS)   Policy/Research
Fundación Nacional para el Desarrollo (FUNDE)   Policy/Research
Instituto Interamericano de Cooperación para la Agricultura (IICA)   NGO Networking
Oxfam America   Funding
Oxfam Australia/Community Aid Abroad (CAA)   Funding
Via Campesina (VC)   NGO Networking
Washington Office on Latin America (WOLA)   Policy/Research

Hong Kong

Center of Concern (COC)   Policy/Research
Institute for Popular Democracy (IPD)   Policy/Research
NGO Forum on the Asian Development Bank   NGO Networking

Hungary

American Friends Service Committee (AFSC)   Capacity Building
Public Law Center (TPLC)   Capacity Building
Rockefeller Brothers Fund   Funding

India

ActionAid (AA)   Capacity Building
Centre for Youth and Social Development (CYSD)   Policy/Research
Christian Aid (CAID)   Policy/Research
Developing Initiatives for Social and Human Action (DISHA)   Capacity Building

Environment and Development Action in the Third World (ENDA TM)	Policy/Research
Focus on the Global South	Policy/Research
Ford Foundation	Funding
Indian Social Institute	Policy/Research
Initiatives for Research, Education and Development in Asia (INASIA)	NGO Networking
International NGO Training and Research Centre (INTRAC)	Capacity Building
John D. and Catherine T. MacArthur Foundation	Funding
Lutheran World Relief (LWR)	Capacity Building
National Centre for Advocacy Studies (NCAS)	Policy/Research
NGO Forum on the Asian Development Bank	NGO Networking
Oxfam America	Funding
Oxfam Australia/Community Aid Abroad (CAA)	Funding
PAIRVI	Capacity Building
PREPARE—India Rural Reconstruction and Disaster Response Service	Capacity Building
Ryan Foundation International	Funding
Sisterhood Is Global Institute (SIGI)	Capacity Building
South Asian Coalition on Child Servitude (SACCS)	NGO Networking
South Asia Partnership Canada—SAP Canada	Capacity Building
Via Campesina (VC)	NGO Networking
W. Alton Jones Foundation	Funding

Indonesia

Ford Foundation	Funding
IFEX Clearing House	NGO Networking
Institute for Popular Democracy (IPD)	Policy/Research
Institute for Social Transformation (INSIST)	Policy/Research
International Centre for Human Rights and Democratic Development (ICHRDD)	NGO Networking
Lembaga Studi dan Advokasi Masyarakat (ELSAM)	Policy/Research
Oxfam Australia/Community Aid Abroad (CAA)	Funding
Southeast Asia Regional Institute for Community Education (SEARICE)	Policy/Research
Tambuyog Development Center, Inc. (TDC)	Capacity Building

Iran

Center for Development Services (CDS)	Capacity Building
Sisterhood Is Global Institute (SIGI)	Capacity Building
W. Alton Jones Foundation	Funding

Iraq

American Friends Service Committee (AFSC)	Capacity Building

Israel

American Friends Service Committee (AFSC)	Capacity Building
Funding Exchange	Funding

Jamaica

Caribbean Association for Feminist Research and Action (CAFRA)	Capacity Building
CUSO	Capacity Building

Instituto Interamericano de Cooperación para la Agricultura (IICA)	NGO Networking
Red Latinoamericana y del Caribe sobre la Banca Multilateral de Desarrollo (RedBancos)	NGO Networking

Japan

NGO Forum on the Asian Development Bank	NGO Networking
W. Alton Jones Foundation	Funding

Jordan

Center for Development Services (CDS)	Capacity Building
Sisterhood Is Global Institute (SIGI)	Capacity Building

Kazakhstan

International NGO Training and Research Centre (INTRAC)	Capacity Building
Open Society/Soros Foundation	Funding

Kenya

ActionAid (AA)	Capacity Building
African Science & Technology Exchange (ASTEX)	Policy/Research
African Women's Development and Communications Network (FEMNET)	NGO Networking
Anglican Church of Kenya (ACK)	Policy/Research
Associates for Change	Policy/Research
Association of African Women for Research & Development (AAWORD)	Policy/Research
Center of Concern (COC)	Policy/Research
Christian Aid (CAID)	Policy/Research
CUSO	Capacity Building
Ford Foundation	Funding
Forum for Women in Democracy (FOWODE)	Capacity Building
Horn of Africa Relief	Capacity Building
IFEX Clearing House	NGO Networking
Institute for Education Democracy (IED)	Policy/Research
Integrated Social Development Centre (ISODEC)	Capacity Building
International Centre for Human Rights and Democratic Development (ICHRDD)	NGO Networking
International NGO Training and Research Centre (INTRAC)	Capacity Building
Media Institute, The (MI)	Policy/Research
People against Torture—Kenya (PAT)	NGO Networking
PREPARE—India Rural Reconstruction and Disaster Response Service	Capacity Building

Korea

American Friends Service Committee (AFSC)	Capacity Building
W. Alton Jones Foundation	Funding

Kyrgyzstan

Helvetas—Swiss Association for International Cooperation	Capacity Building
International NGO Training and Research Centre (INTRAC)	Capacity Building
Open Society/Soros Foundation	Funding

Lao PDR

American Friends Service Committee (AFSC)	Capacity Building
CUSO	Capacity Building
Focus on the Global South	Policy/Research
International NGO Training and Research Centre (INTRAC)	Capacity Building
Japan International Volunteer Center (JVC)	Funding
Oxfam Australia/Community Aid Abroad (CAA)	Funding
Oxfam Hong Kong	Funding
Southeast Asia Regional Institute for Community Education (SEARICE)	Policy/Research

Latvia

Open Society/Soros Foundation	Funding

Lebanon

American Friends Service Committee (AFSC)	Capacity Building
Center for Development Services (CDS)	Capacity Building
Sisterhood Is Global Institute (SIGI)	Capacity Building

Lesotho

Collaborative Centre for Gender and Development (CCGD)	Capacity Building
Helvetas—Swiss Association for International Cooperation	Capacity Building

Liberia

ActionAid (AA)	Capacity Building

Lithuania

Open Society/Soros Foundation	Funding

Macedonia

Microfinance Centre for Central and Eastern Europe and the NIS (MFC)	Capacity Building

Madagascar

Environment and Development Action in the Third World (ENDA TM)	Policy/Research

Malawi

ActionAid (AA)	Capacity Building
African Women's Development and Communications Network (FEMNET)	NGO Networking
Collaborative Centre for Gender and Development (CCGD)	Capacity Building
Development Innovations and Networks (IRED)	Policy/Research
Emang Basadi Women's Association (EB)	Capacity Building
Forum for Women in Democracy (FOWODE)	Capacity Building
International NGO Training and Research Centre (INTRAC)	Capacity Building
Zimbabwe Women's Resource Center and Network (ZWRCN)	Capacity Building

Malaysia

Helvetas—Swiss Association for International Cooperation	Capacity Building
Sisterhood Is Global Institute (SIGI)	Capacity Building
Southeast Asia Regional Institute for Community Education (SEARICE)	Policy/Research

Mali

Associates for Change	Policy/Research
Association of African Women for Research & Development (AAWORD)	Policy/Research
Christian Aid (CAID)	Policy/Research
Comité de Coordination des Actions des ONG au Mali (CCA/ONG)	NGO Networking
Forum Malien d'Appui a la Democratie et aux Droits Humains (FOMADDH)	Capacity Building
Helvetas—Swiss Association for International Cooperation	Capacity Building
Oxfam America	Funding

Mauritius

Associates for Change	Policy/Research

Mexico

Abya Yala Fund (AYF)	Funding
Alianza Cívica	Capacity Building
American Friends Service Committee (AFSC)	Capacity Building
Asociación Latinoamericana de Organizaciones de Promoción (ALOP)	NGO Networking
Casa Alianza/Covenant House Latin America	NGO Networking
Centro de Estudios y Publicaciones Alforja (CEP)	Capacity Building
Centro Mujeres, AC	Capacity Building
Chiapas Media Project (CMP)	Capacity Building
Colectivo de Investigación, Desarrollo y Educación entre Mujeres (CIDEM)	Capacity Building
CUSO	Capacity Building
Democracy Center	Capacity Building
Equidad de Género: Ciudadanía, Familia y Trabajo	Policy/Research
Ford Foundation	Funding
Fundación Nacional para el Desarrollo (FUNDE)	Policy/Research
Funding Exchange	Funding
Global Exchange	Policy/Research
Grassroots International	Funding
IFEX Clearing House	NGO Networking
Institute for Agriculture and Trade Policy (IATP)	Policy/Research
Instituto Interamericano de Cooperación para la Agricultura (IICA)	NGO Networking
International Centre for Human Rights and Democratic Development (ICHRDD)	NGO Networking
John D. and Catherine T. MacArthur Foundation	Funding
Oxfam Australia/Community Aid Abroad (CAA)	Funding
Oxfam Canada	Policy/Research
Red Latinoamericana y del Caribe sobre la Banca Multilateral de Desarrollo (RedBancos)	NGO Networking
Red Mexicana de Acción Frente al Libre Comercio (REMALC)	NGO Networking
Red Nacional de Organismos Civiles de Derechos Humanos	NGO Networking
W. Alton Jones Foundation	Funding
Washington Office on Latin America (WOLA)	Policy/Research
Women's Eyes on the World Bank—Latin America Chapter	NGO Networking

Moldova

Open Society/Soros Foundation	Funding
Microfinance Centre for Central and Eastern Europe and the NIS (MFC)	Capacity Building
Public Law Center (TPLC)	Capacity Building

Mongolia

National CEDAW-Watch Network Center (CEDAW Watch)	NGO Networking
Open Society/Soros Foundation	Funding

Morocco

Association of African Women for Research & Development (AAWORD)	Policy/Research
Environment and Development Action in the Third World (ENDA TM)	Policy/Research
International NGO Training and Research Centre (INTRAC)	Capacity Building

Mozambique

ActionAid (AA)	Capacity Building
African Science & Technology Exchange (ASTEX)	Policy/Research
American Friends Service Committee (AFSC)	Capacity Building
Associates for Change	Policy/Research
Association of African Women for Research & Development (AAWORD)	Policy/Research
Centre for Conflict Resolution (CCR)	Capacity Building
CUSO	Capacity Building
Development Innovations and Networks (IRED)	Policy/Research
Helvetas—Swiss Association for International Cooperation	Capacity Building
Kulima	Capacity Building
LINK—Forum de ONGs	NGO Networking
Oxfam America	Funding
Oxfam Australia/Community Aid Abroad (CAA)	Funding
Oxfam Canada	Policy/Research
Southern African Research and Documentation Centre (SARDC)	Policy/Research
ZERO Environment Regional Organization (ZERO)	Policy/Research

Namibia

Centre for Conflict Resolution (CCR)	Capacity Building
Collaborative Centre for Gender and Development (CCGD)	Capacity Building
Emang Basadi Women's Association (EB)	Capacity Building
Forum for Women in Democracy (FOWODE)	Capacity Building
IFEX Clearing House	NGO Networking
Namibia Non-governmental Organisations' Forum (NANGOF)	Capacity Building
Oxfam Canada	Policy/Research
ZERO Environment Regional Organization (ZERO)	Policy/Research

Nepal

ActionAid (AA)	Capacity Building
Helvetas—Swiss Association for International Cooperation	Capacity Building
Initiatives for Research, Education and Development in Asia (INASIA)	NGO Networking
International NGO Training and Research Centre (INTRAC)	Capacity Building
National Centre for Advocacy Studies (NCAS)	Policy/Research
South Asian Coalition on Child Servitude (SACCS)	NGO Networking
South Asia Partnership Canada—SAP Canada	Capacity Building

Netherlands

African Women's Development and Communications Network (FEMNET)	NGO Networking
IFEX Clearing House	NGO Networking
Institute for Popular Democracy (IPD)	Policy/Research

Netherlands Antilles

Caribbean Association for Feminist Research and Action (CAFRA)	Capacity Building

New Zealand

NGO Forum on the Asian Development Bank	NGO Networking

Nicaragua

Abya Yala Fund (AYF)	Funding
Asociación Latinoamericana de Organizaciones de Promoción (ALOP)	NGO Networking
Centro de Estudios y Acción para el Desarrollo (CESADE)	Capacity Building
Centro para la Participacion Democratica y el Desarrollo Cenzontle (CENZONTLE)	Capacity Building
Colectivo de Investigación, Desarrollo y Educación entre Mujeres (CIDEM)	Capacity Building
Comité Nacional Feminista (CNF)	Capacity Building
CUSO	Capacity Building
Environment and Development Action in the Third World (ENDA TM)	Policy/Research
Fundación Arias para la Paz y el Progreso Humano—Centro para la Participación Organizada (ARIAS)	Policy/Research
Fundación Nacional para el Desarrollo (FUNDE)	Policy/Research
Funding Exchange	Funding
Instituto de Investigación y Desarrollo—Universidad Centroamericana (NITLAPAN)	Policy Research
Instituto Interamericano de Cooperación para la Agricultura (IICA)	NGO Networking
International NGO Training and Research Centre (INTRAC)	Capacity Building
Oxfam America	Funding
Oxfam Canada	Policy/Research
Red Latinoamericana y del Caribe sobre la Banca Multilateral de Desarrollo (RedBancos)	NGO Networking
Washington Office on Latin America (WOLA)	Policy/Research

Niger

Association of African Women for Research & Development (AAWORD)	Policy/Research

Nigeria

ActionAid (AA)	Capacity Building
African Science & Technology Exchange (ASTEX)	Policy/Research
Association of African Women for Research & Development (AAWORD)	Policy/Research
CUSO	Capacity Building
Development Innovations and Networks (IRED)	Policy/Research
Ford Foundation	Funding
IFEX Clearing House	NGO Networking
International Centre for Human Rights and Democratic Development (ICHRDD)	NGO Networking
International NGO Training and Research Centre (INTRAC)	Capacity Building
John D. and Catherine T. MacArthur Foundation	Funding

Pakistan

ActionAid (AA)	Capacity Building
Development Foundation (DevFound)	Capacity Building
IFEX Clearing House	NGO Networking
International Centre for Human Rights and Democratic Development (ICHRDD)	NGO Networking
International NGO Training and Research Centre (INTRAC)	Capacity Building
NGO Resource Centre (A Project of Aga Khan Foundation) (NGORC)	Capacity Building
Sisterhood Is Global Institute (SIGI)	Capacity Building
South Asian Coalition on Child Servitude (SACCS)	NGO Networking
South Asia Partnership Canada—SAP Canada	Capacity Building
SUNGI Development Foundation (SDF)	Capacity Building
Sustainable Development Policy Institute (SDPI)	Policy/Research
W. Alton Jones Foundation	Funding

Palau

Tambuyog Development Center, Inc. (TDC)	Capacity Building

Palestine

American Friends Service Committee (AFSC)	Capacity Building
Center for Development Services (CDS)	Capacity Building
General Union of Disabled Palestinians (GUDP)	Policy/Research
Grassroots International	Funding
Japan International Volunteer Center (JVC)	Funding

Panama

Asociación Latinoamericana de Organizaciones de Promoción (ALOP)	NGO Networking
Fundación Arias para la Paz y el Progreso Humano—Centro para la Participación Organizada (ARIAS)	Policy/Research
Instituto Interamericano de Cooperación para la Agricultura (IICA)	NGO Networking
Washington Office on Latin America (WOLA)	Policy/Research
Women's Eyes on the World Bank—Latin America Chapter	NGO Networking

Papua New Guinea

CUSO	Capacity Building
NGO Forum on the Asian Development Bank	NGO Networking
Oxfam Australia/Community Aid Abroad (CAA)	Funding
Ryan Foundation International	Funding

Paraguay

Asociación Latinoamericana de Organizaciones de Promoción (ALOP)	NGO Networking
Centro Latinoamericano de Economía Humana (CLAEH)	Policy/Research
Helvetas—Swiss Association for International Cooperation	Capacity Building
IFEX Clearing House	NGO Networking
Instituto Interamericano de Cooperación para la Agricultura (IICA)	NGO Networking
W. Alton Jones Foundation	Funding

Peru

Abya Yala Fund (AYF)	Funding
Asociación Latinoamericana de Organizaciones de Promoción (ALOP)	NGO Networking
Centro de Asesoría Laboral del Peru (CEDAL)	Capacity Building
Centro Peruano de Estudios Sociales (CEPES)	Policy/Research
Coordinadora Nacional de Derechos Humanos (CNDDHH)	NGO Networking
CUSO	Capacity Building
Esquel Group Foundation	Policy/Research
Grupo Mujer y Ajuste Estructural	Policy/Research
IFEX Clearing House	NGO Networking
Instituto de Defensa Legal (IDL)	Policy/Research
Instituto Interamericano de Cooperación para la Agricultura (IICA)	NGO Networking
International Centre for Human Rights and Democratic Development (ICHRDD)	NGO Networking
International NGO Training and Research Centre (INTRAC)	Capacity Building
Oxfam America	Funding
Oxfam Canada	Policy/Research
PROTERRA	Capacity Building
Red Latinoamericana y del Caribe sobre la Banca Multilateral de Desarrollo (RedBancos)	NGO Networking
Women's Eyes on the World Bank—Latin America Chapter	NGO Networking

Philippines

Action for Economic Reform (AER)	Policy/Research
Ateneo Center for Social Policy and Public Affairs (ACSPPA)	Policy/Research
Caucus of Development NGO Networks (CODE-NGO)	NGO Networking
Focus on the Global South	Policy/Research
Ford Foundation	Funding
Helvetas—Swiss Association for International Cooperation	Capacity Building
IFEX Clearing House	NGO Networking
Institute for Popular Democracy (IPD)	Policy/Research
Institute of Politics and Governance (IPG)	Policy/Research
Lutheran World Relief (LWR)	Capacity Building
MineWatch Philippines—Bantay Mina (MWP—BM)	Capacity Building
NGO Forum on the Asian Development Bank	NGO Networking
Philippine International Forum (PIF)	Policy/Research
Philippine Legislators Committee on Population and Development Foundation, Inc. (PLCPD)	Policy/Research
Oxfam America	Funding
Philippine Peasant Institute (PPI)	Policy/Research
Southeast Asia Regional Institute for Community Education (SEARICE)	Policy/Research
Tambuyog Development Center, Inc. (TDC)	Capacity Building
Upland NGO Assistance Committee (UNAC)	Policy/Research

Poland

Microfinance Centre for Central and Eastern Europe and the NIS (MFC)	Capacity Building
Open Society/Soros Foundation	Funding
Rockefeller Brothers Fund	Funding
Via Campesina (VC)	NGO Networking

Puerto Rico

Caribbean Association for Feminist Research and Action (CAFRA)   Capacity Building

Romania

Open Society/Soros Foundation   Funding

Russia

Barbara Delano Foundation (BDF)   Funding
Charles Stewart Mott Foundation   Funding
Ford Foundation   Funding
IFEX Clearing House   NGO Networking
Land Tenure Center (LTC)   Policy/Research
Open Society/Soros Foundation   Funding
Public Interest Law Initiative in Transitional Societies (PILI)   Capacity Building
Rockefeller Brothers Fund   Funding
W. Alton Jones Foundation   Funding

Rwanda

ActionAid (AA)   Capacity Building
Christian Aid (CAID)   Policy/Research
Collaborative Centre for Gender and Development (CCGD)   Capacity Building
International Centre for Human Rights and Democratic Development (ICHRDD)   NGO Networking
Oxfam America   Funding

Saint Kitts and Nevis

Instituto Interamericano de Cooperación para la Agricultura (IICA)   NGO Networking

Saint Lucia

CUSO   Capacity Building
Instituto Interamericano de Cooperación para la Agricultura (IICA)   NGO Networking

Saint Vincent and the Grenadines

Caribbean Association for Feminist Research and Action (CAFRA)   Capacity Building
Instituto Interamericano de Cooperación para la Agricultura (IICA)   NGO Networking
Oxfam Canada   Policy/Research

Senegal

Action Group for Community Development (GADEC)   Policy/Research
Association of African Women for Research & Development (AAWORD)   Policy/Research
Environment and Development Action in the Third World (ENDA TM)   Policy/Research
Gorée Institute   Capacity Building
Oxfam America   Funding

Sierra Leone

ActionAid (AA)   Capacity Building

Slovak Republic

Rockefeller Brothers Fund   Funding

Slovenia

Open Society/Soros Foundation	Funding

Solomon Islands

CUSO	Capacity Building
Oxfam Australia/Community Aid Abroad (CAA)	Funding

Somalia

American Friends Service Committee (AFSC)	Capacity Building
Horn of Africa Relief	Capacity Building
Oxfam Canada	Policy/Research
Ryan Foundation International	Funding

Somaliland

ActionAid (AA)	Capacity Building
International NGO Training and Research Centre (INTRAC)	Capacity Building
Oxfam Australia/Community Aid Abroad (CAA)	Funding

South Africa

African Women's Development and Communications Network (FEMNET)	NGO Networking
Association of African Women for Research & Development (AAWORD)	Policy/Research
Centre for Applied Legal Studies (CALS)	Capacity Building
Centre for Conflict Resolution (CCR)	Capacity Building
Charles Stewart Mott Foundation	Funding
Collaborative Centre for Gender and Development (CCGD)	Capacity Building
Co-operative for Research and Education (CORE)	Policy/Research
CUSO	Capacity Building
Democracy Center	Capacity Building
Development Innovations and Networks (IRED)	Policy/Research
Emang Basadi Women's Association (EB)	Capacity Building
Ford Foundation	Funding
Forum for Women in Democracy (FOWODE)	Capacity Building
Funding Exchange	Funding
IFEX Clearing House	NGO Networking
Institute for Democracy in South Africa (Idasa)	Policy/Research
Institute for Popular Democracy (IPD)	Policy/Research
International NGO Training and Research Centre (INTRAC)	Capacity Building
Japan International Volunteer Center (JVC)	Funding
Legal Research and Resource Center for Human Rights (LRRC)	Policy/Research
National AIDS Convention of South Africa (NACOSA-KZN)	NGO Networking
National Land Committee (NLC)	Policy/Research
Open Society/Soros Foundation	Funding
Oxfam Australia/Community Aid Abroad (CAA)	Funding
Oxfam Canada	Policy/Research
Public Law Center (TPLC)	Capacity Building
Rockefeller Brothers Fund	Funding
South African National NGO Coalition (SANGOCO)	Capacity Building

ZERO Environment Regional Organization (ZERO)	Policy/Research
Zimbabwe Women's Resource Center and Network (ZWRCN)	Capacity Building

Sri Lanka

Centre for Women's Research (CENWOR)	Policy/Research
Helvetas—Swiss Association for International Cooperation	Capacity Building
IFEX Clearing House	NGO Networking
Initiatives for Research, Education and Development in Asia (INASIA)	NGO Networking
International NGO Training and Research Centre (INTRAC)	Capacity Building
NGO Forum on the Asian Development Bank	NGO Networking
Oxfam Australia/Community Aid Abroad (CAA)	Funding
South Asian Coalition on Child Servitude (SACCS)	NGO Networking
South Asia Partnership Canada—SAP Canada	Capacity Building

Sudan

African Women's Development and Communications Network (FEMNET)	NGO Networking
Center for Development Services (CDS)	Capacity Building
Christian Aid (CAID)	Policy/Research
International NGO Training and Research Centre (INTRAC)	Capacity Building
Oxfam America	Funding
Oxfam Australia/Community Aid Abroad (CAA)	Funding
Oxfam Canada	Policy/Research

Suriname

Caribbean Association for Feminist Research and Action (CAFRA)	Capacity Building
Instituto Interamericano de Cooperación para la Agricultura (IICA)	NGO Networking

Swaziland

African Women's Development and Communications Network (FEMNET)	NGO Networking
Association of African Women for Research & Development (AAWORD)	Policy/Research
Collaborative Centre for Gender and Development (CCGD)	Capacity Building
Emang Basadi Women's Association (EB)	Capacity Building
ZERO Environment Regional Organization (ZERO)	Policy/Research

Switzerland

African Women's Development and Communications Network (FEMNET)	NGO Networking
Associates for Change	Policy/Research
Helvetas—Swiss Association for International Cooperation	Capacity Building

Syria

Sisterhood Is Global Institute (SIGI)	Capacity Building

Tajikistan

International NGO Training and Research Centre (INTRAC)	Capacity Building
Open Society/Soros Foundation	Funding

Tanzania

ActionAid (AA)	Capacity Building
African Science & Technology Exchange (ASTEX)	Policy/Research
African Women's Development and Communications Network (FEMNET)	NGO Networking
Associates for Change	Policy/Research
Association of African Women for Research & Development (AAWORD)	Policy/Research
Collaborative Centre for Gender and Development (CCGD)	Capacity Building
CUSO	Capacity Building
Helvetas—Swiss Association for International Cooperation	Capacity Building
International NGO Training and Research Centre (INTRAC)	Capacity Building
PREPARE—India Rural Reconstruction and Disaster Response Service	Capacity Building
ZERO Environment Regional Organization (ZERO)	Policy/Research

Thailand

Assembly of the Poor (AOP)	Policy/Research
CUSO	Capacity Building
Focus on the Global South	Policy/Research
IFEX Clearing House	NGO Networking
Initiatives for Research, Education and Development in Asia (INASIA)	NGO Networking
Institute for Popular Democracy (IPD)	Policy/Research
International Centre for Human Rights and Democratic Development (ICHRDD)	NGO Networking
Japan International Volunteer Center (JVC)	Funding
Southeast Asia Regional Institute for Community Education (SEARICE)	Policy/Research
Tambuyog Development Center, Inc. (TDC)	Capacity Building
Via Campesina (VC)	NGO Networking

Togo

Collaborative Centre for Gender and Development (CCGD)	Capacity Building
CUSO	Capacity Building
Helvetas—Swiss Association for International Cooperation	Capacity Building
International Centre for Human Rights and Democratic Development (ICHRDD)	NGO Networking

Trinidad and Tobago

Caribbean Association for Feminist Research and Action (CAFRA)	Capacity Building
Instituto Interamericano de Cooperación para la Agricultura (IICA)	NGO Networking

Tunisia

Association of African Women for Research & Development (AAWORD)	Policy/Research
Environment and Development Action in the Third World (ENDA TM)	Policy/Research

Uganda

ActionAid (AA)	Capacity Building
African Science & Technology Exchange (ASTEX)	Policy/Research
African Women's Development and Communications Network (FEMNET)	NGO Networking
Associates for Change	Policy/Research
Association of African Women for Research & Development (AAWORD)	Policy/Research
Collaborative Centre for Gender and Development (CCGD)	Capacity Building
Development Innovations and Networks (IRED)	Policy/Research

Development Network of Indigenous Voluntary Associations (DENIVA)	NGO Networking
Emang Basadi Women's Association (EB)	Capacity Building
Forum for Women in Democracy (FOWODE)	Capacity Building
International NGO Training and Research Centre (INTRAC)	Capacity Building
Uganda Debt Network (UDN)	Capacity Building
Uganda Women's Network (UWONET)	NGO Networking

Ukraine

Open Society/Soros Foundation	Funding

United Kingdom

IFEX Clearing House	NGO Networking

United States

African Women's Development and Communications Network (FEMNET)	NGO Networking
Alliance for Justice	NGO Networking
American Friends Service Committee (AFSC)	Capacity Building
Associates for Change	Policy/Research
Association of African Women for Research & Development (AAWORD)	Policy/Research
Bread for the World	Policy/Research
Center for Economic and Social Rights—US (CESR)	Policy/Research
Center for Popular Economics (CPE)	Capacity Building
Center of Concern (COC)	Policy/Research
Charles Stewart Mott Foundation	Funding
Colombia Human Rights Network	NGO Networking
Columbia Program on Teaching Human Rights Law	Capacity Building
Democracy Center	Capacity Building
Funding Exchange	Funding
Hauser Center for Nonprofit Organizations	Capacity Building
Highlander Research and Education Center	Capacity Building
IFEX Clearing House	NGO Networking
Institute for Agriculture and Trade Policy (IATP)	Policy/Research
Institute for Not-for-Profit Management (INM)	Capacity Building
Instituto Interamericano de Cooperación para la Agricultura (IICA)	NGO Networking
Land Tenure Center (LTC)	Policy/Research
Open Society/Soros Foundation	Funding
Oxfam America	Funding
Project South	Capacity Building
Public Law Center (TPLC)	Capacity Building
Rockefeller Brothers Fund	Funding
Ruckus Society	Capacity Building
Social Action and Leadership School for Activists (SALSA)	Capacity Building
Tambuyog Development Center, Inc. (TDC)	Capacity Building
United for a Fair Economy (UFE)	Capacity Building
Washington College of Law—Summer Session on Human Rights and Humanitarian Law	Capacity Building
Washington Office on Africa (WOA)	NGO Networking
Women's Eyes on the World Bank—Latin America Chapter	NGO Networking
Women's Peacepower Foundation, Inc. (WPPF)	Funding

Uruguay

Asociación Latinoamericana de Organizaciones de Promoción (ALOP)	NGO Networking
Centro Latinoamericano de Economía Humana (CLAEH)	Policy/Research
Esquel Group Foundation	Policy/Research
Instituto Interamericano de Cooperación para la Agricultura (IICA)	NGO Networking
Red Latinoamericana y del Caribe sobre la Banca Multilateral de Desarrollo (RedBancos)	NGO Networking

Uzbekistan

International NGO Training and Research Centre (INTRAC)	Capacity Building
Open Society/Soros Foundation	Funding
Sisterhood Is Global Institute (SIGI)	Capacity Building

Vanuatu

CUSO	Capacity Building
Oxfam Australia/Community Aid Abroad (CAA)	Funding

Venezuela

Abya Yala Fund (AYF)	Funding
Asociación Latinoamericana de Organizaciones de Promoción (ALOP)	NGO Networking
Centro al Servicio de la Acción Popular (CESAP)	NGO Networking
Instituto Interamericano de Cooperación para la Agricultura (IICA)	NGO Networking
Women's Eyes on the World Bank—Latin America Chapter	NGO Networking

Vietnam

ActionAid (AA)	Capacity Building
American Friends Service Committee (AFSC)	Capacity Building
CUSO	Capacity Building
Environment and Development Action in the Third World (ENDA TM)	Policy/Research
Ford Foundation	Funding
Helvetas—Swiss Association for International Cooperation	Capacity Building
Japan International Volunteer Center (JVC)	Funding
Oxfam America	Funding
Oxfam Australia/Community Aid Abroad (CAA)	Funding
Oxfam Hong Kong	Funding
Southeast Asia Regional Institute for Community Education (SEARICE)	Policy/Research
Tambuyog Development Center, Inc. (TDC)	Capacity Building

West Bank

Funding Exchange	Funding

Yemen

Center for Development Services (CDS)	Capacity Building

Zambia

African Women's Development and Communications Network (FEMNET)	NGO Networking
Association of African Women for Research & Development (AAWORD)	Policy/Research
Catholic Commission for Justice and Peace (CCJP)	NGO Networking
Forum for Women in Democracy (FOWODE)	Capacity Building

ZERO Environment Regional Organization (ZERO)	Policy/Research
Zimbabwe Women's Resource Center and Network (ZWRCN)	Capacity Building

Zanzibar

Collaborative Centre for Gender and Development (CCGD)	Capacity Building

Zimbabwe

Associates for Change	Policy/Research
Centre for Conflict Resolution (CCR)	Capacity Building
Christian Aid (CAID)	Policy/Research
Collaborative Centre for Gender and Development (CCGD)	Capacity Building
CUSO	Capacity Building
Development Innovations and Networks (IRED)	Policy/Research
Environment and Development Action in the Third World (ENDA TM)	Policy/Research
Housing People of Zimbabwe (HPZ)	Capacity Building
International NGO Training and Research Centre (INTRAC)	Capacity Building
Legal Resources Foundation (LRF)	Policy/Research
Organization of Rural Associations for Progress (ORAP)	Capacity Building
Oxfam America	Funding
Oxfam Australia/Community Aid Abroad (CAA)	Funding
Oxfam Canada	Policy/Research
Poverty Reduction Forum	Policy/Research
Sisterhood Is Global Institute (SIGI)	Capacity Building
Southern African Research and Documentation Centre (SARDC)	Policy/Research
ZERO Environment Regional Organization (ZERO)	Policy/Research

Capacity-Building Organizations

ABANTU for Development

Wanjiru Kihoro, Director
1 Winchester House
11 Crammer Road
London SW9 6EJ, United Kingdom
Tel: (44-20) 7229-8022
Fax: (44-20) 7820-0088
E-mail: *people@abantu.org*
Website: Not available

Main Issue Areas
Conflict; Gender; Governance; Information and communications technology; Poverty and economic empowerment; Training and capacity building

Areas Where Organization Works
Africa, Europe

Working Languages
English

Types of Resources Available
NGO networking; Policy/research; Training

Regional Offices
Ghana, Kenya, United Kingdom

ActionAid (AA)

Hilary Coulby, Head of Corporate Advocacy; David Norman, Advocacy Training Coordinator
Hamlyn House
Macdonald Road, Archway
London N19 5PG, United Kingdom
Tel: (44-20) 7561-7561
Fax: (44-20) 7263-7599
E-mail: *mail@actionaid.org.uk*
Website: *http://www.actionaid.org*

Main Issue Areas
Basic rights; Civil society building; Conflict resolution; Disability; Education; Emergencies; Gender equity; Health; HIV/AIDS; Income generation

Areas Where Organization Works
Africa: Burundi, Ethiopia, The Gambia, Ghana, Kenya, Liberia, Malawi, Mozambique, Nigeria, Rwanda, Sierra Leone, Somaliland, Tanzania, Uganda; *Asia:* Bangladesh, India, Nepal, Pakistan, Vietnam; *Latin America:* Brazil, Dominican Republic, Guatemala, Haiti

Working Languages
English, French, Local languages, Portuguese, Spanish

Types of Resources Available
Funding/Funding information; NGO networking; Policy/research; Technical assistance; Training

Regional Offices
Bangladesh, Brazil, Guatemala, India, Kenya, Nepal, Zimbabwe

Advocacy Institute (AI)

Maureen Burke, Senior Director of Programs; Colin Moffett, Program Associate
1629 K Street NW
Suite 200
Washington, DC 20006, USA
Tel: 1 (202) 777-7575
Fax: 1 (202) 777-7577
E-mail: *info@advocacy.org*
Website: *http://www.advocacy.org*

Main Issue Areas
Corporate accountability; Environmental preservation; Gender equity; Public health; Social, economic, and political justice; Sustainable development; Universal human rights

Areas Where Organization Works
Worldwide

Working Languages
English

Types of Resources Available
NGO networking; Technical assistance; Training

Alianza Cívica

Yosemite 45
Col. Napoles
Mexico, D.F. 03810, Mexico
Tel: (52-5) 682-3811; 536-2073; 543-3799
Fax: (52-5) 543-3037
E-mail: *alianza@laneta.apc.org*

271

Website: *http://www.laneta.apc.org/alianza/marcos.htm*

Main Issue Areas

Monitoring of elections; Transparency

Areas Where Organization Works

Latin America: Mexico

Working Languages

Spanish

Types of Resources Available

NGO networking; Training

American Friends Service Committee (AFSC)

Susan Gunn, Director, International Division; David Bronkema

1501 Cherry Street

Philadelphia, PA 19102-1479, USA

Tel: 1 (215) 241-7000

Fax: 1 (215) 241-7275

E-mail: *afscinfo@afsc.org*

Website: *http://www.afsc.org*

Main Issue Areas

Agriculture; Community development; Democratization; Education; Emergency response; Environment; Global economy and economic development; Human rights; Labor; Minority issues; Nonviolence; Poverty; Sustainable development; Women

Areas Where Organization Works

Africa: Angola, Mozambique, Somalia, Southern Africa; *Asia:* Cambodia, Korea, Lao PDR, Vietnam; *Europe:* former Yugoslavia, Hungary; *Latin America/Caribbean:* Andean region, Brazil, Central America, Colombia, Cuba, Haiti, Mexico; *Middle East:* Israel, Iraq, Lebanon, Palestine; *North America:* United States

Working Languages

English

Types of Resources Available

Funding/funding information; Technical assistance; Training

Apoyo para el Campesino-Indígena del Oriente Boliviano (APCOB)

Graciela Zolezzi, Area de Sistematizacion, Deputy Director

Calle Cuatro Ojos #80

Casilla de Correo 4213

Santa Cruz de la Sierra, Bolivia

Tel: (59-13) 542-119; 539-954

Fax: (59-13) 542-120

E-mail: *apcob@bibosi.scz.entelnet.bo*

Website: *http://www.latinwide.com/apcob/*

Main Issue Areas

Cultural development; Democracy promotion; Gender; Natural-resource protection

Areas Where Organization Works

Bolivia

Working Languages

Spanish

Types of Resources Available

Technical assistance; Training

Arab Center for the Independence of the Judiciary and the Legal Profession (ACIJLP)

Nasser Amin, General Director

8/10 Mathaf Al-Manyal

Floor 11

Cairo, Egypt

Tel: (20-2) 362-0732; 531-0027

Fax: (20-2) 362-0732; 531-0027

E-mail: *acijlp@thewayout.net*

Website: *http://www.arabrights.org/acijlp.html/*

Main Issue Areas

Human rights

Areas Where Organization Works

Arab countries, Egypt

Working Languages

Arabic, English

Types of Resources Available

NGO networking; Policy/research; Technical assistance; Training

Asia Foundation, The (TAF)

Dick Fuller, Senior Director Country Programs
465 California Street
San Francisco, CA 94104, USA
Tel: 1 (415) 982-4640
Fax: 1 (415) 392-8863
E-mail: *info@asiafound.org*
Website: *http://www.asiafoundation.org*

Main Issue Areas

Access to justice; Democracy and governance; Economic reform; Human rights; Rule of law; US–Asia Pacific relations; Women's political participation

Areas Where Organization Works

Asia-Pacific

Working Languages

English

Types of Resources Available

Funding/funding information; NGO networking; Technical assistance; Training

Regional Offices

Bangladesh, Cambodia, China, Indonesia, Japan, Korea, Mongolia, Nepal, Pakistan, the Philippines, Sri Lanka, Thailand, Vietnam, Washington, DC

Asia Monitor Resource Centre Ltd. (AMRC)

Leung Po Lam, Executive Director
444 Nathan Road, 8-B
Yaumatei, Kowloon, Hong Kong
Tel: (852) 2332-1346
Fax: (852) 2358-5319
E-mail: *amrc@pacific.net.hk*
Website: *http://www.amrc.org.hk/*

Main Issue Areas

Labor

Areas Where Organization Works

Asia/Pacific

Working Languages

Bahasa, Chinese, English, Tagalog

Types of Resources Available

Policy/research; Technical assistance; Training

Association Nationale pour la Promotion Active (ANPA)

André-Eugène Ilboudo, Director
05 BP 6274 Ouagadougou 05
Ouagadougou, Burkina Faso
Tel: (226) 311-636
Fax: (226) 385-280
E-mail: *aeugene@fasonet.bf*
Website: Not available

Main Issue Areas

Human rights (especially women's rights, children's rights, and freedom of the press)

Areas Where Organization Works

Burkina Faso

Working Languages

French

Types of Resources Available

Training

Bangladesh Rural Advancement Committee (BRAC)

Golam Samdani Fakir, Director, Training Division; Kamrul Aman, Senior Trainer, Training Division
BRAC Centre
75 Mohakhali
Dhaka 1212, Bangladesh
Tel: (880-2) 884-180; 884-051; 988-1265
Fax: (880-2) 883-542; 883-614
E-mail: *brac@bdmail.net*
Website: *http://www.brac.net*

Main Issue Areas

Essential health care; Gender and quality action learning; Human rights and legal education; NGO development; Non-formal primary education program; Nutrition-facilitation program; Reproductive health and disease control; Rural development; Social-development program; Rural-health-delivery partnership

Areas Where Organization Works

Bangladesh

Working Languages

Bangla, English

Types of Resources Available

NGO networking; Technical assistance; Training

Canadian Human Rights Foundation— International Human Rights Training Program (IHRTP)

Lawrence Lefcort, IHRTP Coordinator
Canadian Human Rights Foundation
1425 René-Lévesque Blvd. West, Suite 307
Montreal, Quebec H3G 1T7, Canada
Tel: (514) 954-0382
Fax: (514) 954-0659
E-mail: *lawrence@chrf.ca*
Website: *http://www.chrf.ca/english/programmes_eng/files/ihrt.htm*

Main Issue Areas
Current human rights issues; Human rights education; Human rights law

Areas Where Organization Works
Canada

Working Languages
English, French

Types of Resources Available
NGO networking; Training

Caribbean Association for Feminist Research and Action (CAFRA)

Nelcia Robinson, Coordinator; Margarette May Macaulay, Chairperson; Jeanne Henriquez, Deputy Chairperson
PO Bag 442
Tunapuna Post Office
Tunapuna, Trinidad & Tobago
Tel: (868) 662-1231; 663-8670
Fax: (868) 663-6482
E-mail: *cafrainfo@wow.net*
Website: Not available

Main Issue Areas
Education and training; Human rights; Institutional development; Politics; Reproductive rights; Sex tourism; Sustainable development; Trade policy; Women and agriculture

Areas Where Organization Works
Barbados, Belize, Cuba, Dominica, Dominican Republic, Guyana, Jamaica, Netherlands Antilles, Puerto Rico, St. Vincent, Suriname, Trinidad & Tobago

Working Languages
English, Spanish

Types of Resources Available
Policy/research; Technical assistance; Training

Caribbean Initiative on Equality and Non-Discrimination

Mike McCormack, Convenor
Guyana Human Rights Centre
56'B" Hadfield St. & Austin Place 3; PO Box 10653
Georgetown, Guyana
Tel: (592-2) 61-789; 74-911
Fax: (592-2) 74-948
E-mail: *ghra.guy@solutions2000.net*
Website: Not available

Main Issue Areas
Children' rights (CRC); HIV-positive people; Indigenous peoples (ILO 169); People with disabilities; Women's rights (CEDAW)

Areas Where Organization Works
Caribbean

Working Languages
Amharic, Dutch, English, Eritrean, Haitian Creole, Somali

Types of Resources Available
Training

Center for Development Services (CDS)

Alaa Saber, Director; Ali Mokhtar, Program Manager
4 Ahmed Pasha Street, 6th Floor
Citibank Building, Garden City
Cairo 11451, Egypt
Tel: (20-2) 355-7558
Fax: (20-2) 354-7278
E-mail: *cds@neareast.org*
Website: *http://www.neareast.org*

Main Issue Areas
Children's rights; Community participation; Disadvantaged groups; Economic development; Education; Environment; Health

Areas Where Organization Works
Egypt, Iran, Jordan, Lebanon, Palestine, Sudan, Yemen

Working Languages
Arabic, English, French, Spanish
Types of Resources Available
NGO networking; Policy/research; Technical assistance; Training
Regional Offices
Israel, Jordan, Sudan

Center for Legislative Development (CLD)

Socorro L. Reyes, President; Sheila E. Villaluz, Executive Director
P.O. Box 13929 G/F OCAI Bldg. MB 35
Pasig City 1600, Philippines
Tel: (63-2) 687-2083
Fax: (63-2) 687-2082
E-mail: *cld@info.com.ph; rcld@info.com.ph*
Website: *http://www.cld.org*
Main Issue Areas
Citizen participation in the legislative process; Women's political participation; Women's rights
Areas Where Organization Works
Central Asia, Pacific Islands, Southeast Asia
Working Languages
English, Filipino
Types of Resources Available
NGO networking; Training

Center for Popular Economics (CPE)

PO Box 785
Amherst, MA 01004-0785, USA
Tel: 1 (413) 545-0743
Fax: Not available
E-mail: *info@ctrpopec.org*
Website: *http://www.ctrpopec.org*
Main Issue Areas
Economic justice; Popular economics
Areas Where Organization Works
North America
Working Languages
English
Types of Resources Available
Policy/research; Technical assistance; Training

Center for Sustainable Human Rights Action: Strengthening Human Rights Communities (CeSHRA)

Mona Chun, Director
122 West 27th Street
10th Floor
New York, NY 10001, USA
Tel: 1 (212) 691-8020
Fax: 1 (253) 390-0781
E-mail: *ceshra@ceshra.org*
Website: *http://www.ceshra.org*
Main Issue Areas
Grassroots development; Human rights; Women's and indigenous people's groups
Areas Where Organization Works
Worldwide
Working Languages
English, French, Spanish
Types of Resources Available
Technical assistance; Training

Center for Women's Global Leadership

Charlotte Bunch, Executive Director
Douglass College—Rutgers, The State University of New Jersey
160 Ryders Lane
New Brunswick, NJ 08901-8555, USA
Tel: 1 (732) 932-8782
Fax: 1 (732) 932-1180
E-mail: *cwgl@igc.org*
Website: *http://www.cwgl.rutgers.edu*
Main Issue Areas
Human and women's rights; Sexual and reproductive health; Socioeconomic well-being; Violence against women
Areas Where Organization Works
Worldwide
Working Languages
English
Types of Resources Available
Policy/research; Training

Centre for Applied Legal Studies (CALS)

David Unterhalter, Director
University of the Witwatersrand
Private Bag 3
Wits Gauteng 2050, South Africa
Tel: (27-11) 403-6918
Fax: (27-11) 403-1990
E-mail: *125ta2ti@solon.law.wits.ac.za*
Website: Not available

Main Issue Areas
AIDS issues; Competition and trade law; Gender; Human rights; Labor; Land; Legal and constitutional issues; Legislative formulation and drafting; Migration policy

Areas Where Organization Works
South Africa

Working Languages
English

Types of Resources Available
NGO networking; Policy/research; Training

Centre for Conflict Resolution (CCR)

L. N. Nathan, Executive Director
UCT
Private Bag
Rondebosch 7701, South Africa
Tel: (27-21) 422-2512
Fax: (27-21) 422-2622
E-mail: *mailbox@ccr.uct.ac.za*
Website: *http://ccrweb.ccr.uct.ac.za/*

Main Issue Areas
Constructive conflict management and resolution; Defense and security issues; Peace education and peacemaking

Areas Where Organization Works
Mozambique, Namibia, South Africa, Zimbabwe

Working Languages
English

Types of Resources Available
Policy/research; Technical assistance; Training

Centre for Development and Population Activities (CEDPA)

Peggy Curlin, President
1400 16th Street, NW
Suite 100
Washington, DC 20036, USA
Tel: 1 (202) 667-1142
Fax: 1 (202) 332-4496
E-mail: *cmail@cedpa.org*
Website: *http://www.cedpa.org*

Main Issue Areas
Advocacy; Capacity-building for NGOs; Human rights; Nonformal education/literacy; Reproductive health services/education; Women's leadership training; Women's political participation; Youth development

Areas Where Organization Works
Africa, Asia, Eastern Europe/NIS, Latin America, Middle East

Working Languages
Arabic, English, French, Portuguese, Romanian, Russian, Spanish

Types of Resources Available
NGO networking; Technical assistance; Training

Centro de Asesoría Laboral del Peru (CEDAL)

Luis Miguel Sirumbal, Director Ejecutivo
Jr. Talara No. 769, Jesús María
Lima, Peru
Tel: (51-1) 433-3207; 433-3472
Fax: (51-1) 433-9593
E-mail: *postmaster@cedal.org.pe;*
emoura@cedal.org.pe
Website: Not available

Main Issue Areas
Defense of human rights, especially labor, economic, social, and cultural rights

Areas Where Organization Works
Peru

Working Languages
Spanish

Types of Resources Available
Policy/research; Technical assistance; Training

Centro de Educación Popular Qhana (QHANA)

Mario Molina Guzman
Calle Landaeta No. 522
La Paz, Bolivia
Tel: (591-2) 353-855; 373-960
Fax: (591-2) 391-892
E-mail: *qhana@qhana.rds.org.bo*
Website: Not available

Main Issue Areas
Sustainable development; Local governance; Environmental protection; Human rights

Areas Where Organization Works
Bolivia

Working Languages
Aymara, Spanish

Types of Resources Available
NGO networking; Technical assistance; Training

Centro de Estudios y Acción para el Desarrollo (CESADE)

Allan Fajardo Reina, Director Ejecutivo
Montoya 2 c. al Este 1/2 c. al Sur #7
Colonia Pereira, Barrio El Carmen
Managua, Nicaragua
Tel: (505-2) 669-186; 687-264
Fax: (505-2) 669-270
E-mail: *cesade@nicaro.org.ni*
Website: Not available

Main Issue Areas
Central American integration; Citizen advocacy; Empowerment of rural women; Environment, especially in dry-tropic areas; Globalization; Participatory rural development in the dry tropics; Post–Hurricane Mitch redevelopment; Strengthening civil society organizations to develop advocacy capabilities

Areas Where Organization Works
Central America, Nicaragua

Working Languages
English, Spanish

Types of Resources Available
NGO networking; Policy/research; Technical assistance; Training

Centro de Estudios y Publicaciones Alforja (CEP)

Oscar Jara, President; Cecilia Diaz, Director
De la Iglesia de San Pedro
100 Mt. Sur, 175 M. Este
San Jose 369-1000, Costa Rica
Tel: (506) 280-6540
Fax: (506) 253-7023
E-mail: *cep@alforja.or.cr*
Website: *http://www.alforja.or.cr/quees/centros/ceppa .shtml*

Main Issue Areas
Engage in popular education processes with grassroots organizations in urban and rural areas; Municipalities; Women's organizations

Areas Where Organization Works
Central America, Costa Rica, Mexico

Working Languages
Spanish

Types of Resources Available
Training

Centro Mujeres, AC

Monica Jasis, Co-director
Avenida Marquez de Leon 480 B
Colonia Centro
La Paz, Baja California Sur, CP 23000, Mexico
Tel: (52-11) 223-570; 223-342
Fax: (52-11) 223-570
E-mail: *cmujeres@balandra.uabcs.mx*
Website: *http://www.bajatravel.com/centromujeres*

Main Issue Areas
Reproductive health and rights; Sexual health and rights

Areas Where Organization Works
Latin America, Mexico

Working Languages
English, Spanish

Types of Resources Available
NGO networking; Policy/research; Training

Centro para la Participacion Democratica y el Desarrollo Cenzontle (CENZONTLE)

Malena de Montis, Directora Ejecutiva
De la Cruz Roja Nicaraguense 50 vrs. Al lago Cas No. 5
Reparto Belmonte
Managua 5334, Nicaragua
Tel: (505-2) 652-983; 651-425
Fax: Not available
E-mail: *Cenzontl@ibw.com.ni*
Website: Not available

Main Issue Areas
Advocacy at the local, national, and international levels; Credit; Political participation of women; Women's business and community leadership training and technical assistance

Areas Where Organization Works
Nicaragua

Working Languages
English, Spanish

Types of Resources Available
Policy/research; Technical assistance; Training

Chiapas Media Project (CMP)

Alexandra Halkin, Co-Director
4834 N. Springfield Ave.
Chicago, IL 60625, USA
Tel: 1 (773) 583-7728
Fax: 1 (773) 583-7738
E-mail: *msn@mexicosolidarity.org*
Website: *http://www.chiapasmediaproject.com*

Main Issue Areas
Democracy; Human rights, especially rights for women and indigenous peoples; Land reform

Areas Where Organization Works
Mexico

Working Languages
English, Spanish

Types of Resources Available
NGO networking; Technical assistance; Training

Citizen Power Foundation (Fundación Poder Ciudadano)

Miguel Perellano
Rodriguez Pena 681 2 Of 4
Capital Federal, Buenos Aires 1020, Argentina
Tel: (54-11) 4375-4925; 4375-4926
Fax: (54-11) 4375-0398
E-mail: *mpellera@podciu.org.ar*
Website: *http://www.podciu.org.ar*

Main Issue Areas
Citizen participation; Controlling corruption; Democracy network; Education for participation; Justice; Political representation

Areas Where Organization Works
Argentina, Latin America

Working Languages
English, Spanish

Types of Resources Available
Training

Colectivo de Investigación, Desarrollo y Educación entre Mujeres (CIDEM)

Mayela García Ramirez, General Coordinator
2a Privada de Rebsamen No. 50
Col. Martires de Chicago
Xalapa, Veracruz 91090, Mexico
Tel: (52-28) 181-732; 190-055
Fax: (52-28) 181-732; 190-055
E-mail: *cidem@edg.net.mx*
Website: Not available

Main Issue Areas
Advocacy on gender policy; Citizenship; Communication; Development and the environment; Health and sexual and reproductive rights; Women's leadership development

Areas Where Organization Works
Costa Rica, Dominican Republic, Mexico, Nicaragua

Working Languages
Spanish

Types of Resources Available
NGO networking; Policy/research; Technical assistance; Training

Collaborative Centre for Gender and Development (CCGD)

Wanjiku Mukabi Kabira, Consultant Coordinator
Golden Gate, House number 34B, Sadi Road Gate
"A" off Kapiti Road, South
PO Box 4869
Nairobi 254-02, Kenya
Tel: (254-2) 537-100; 537-101
Fax: (254-2) 537-100
E-mail: *ccgd@nbnet.co.ke*
Website: Not available
Main Issue Areas
Economic empowerment; Education; Gender-based human rights; Political empowerment
Areas Where Organization Works
Botswana, Ethiopia, Lesotho, Malawi, Namibia, Rwanda, South Africa, Swaziland, Tanzania, Togo, Uganda, Zanzibar, Zimbabwe
Working Languages
English, French, Swahili
Types of Resources Available
Technical assistance; Training

Columbia Program on Teaching Human Rights Law

Professor Catherine Powell, Executive Director
Columbia Law School, Human Rights Institute
435 West 116th Street, D-19
New York, NY 10027, USA
Tel: 1 (212) 854-5705
Fax: 1 (212) 854-2640
E-mail: *cpowell@law.columbia.edu*
Website: *http://www.law.columbia.edu/hri/index .html*
Main Issue Areas
Human rights
Areas Where Organization Works
North America; Worldwide
Working Languages
English
Types of Resources Available
Degree program

Comité Nacional Feminista (CNF)

Maria Teresa Blandon; Sofía Montenegro; Dorotea Wilson
Apdo. postal 18-33
Managua, Nicaragua
Tel: (505-2) 225-355
Fax: Not available
E-mail: *corrient@ibw.com.ni*
Website: Not available
Main Issue Areas
Women's leadership and development; Women's movement
Areas Where Organization Works
Nicaragua
Working Languages
Spanish
Types of Resources Available
Policy/research; Technical assistance; Training

Conflict Transformation Program of Eastern Mennonite University

Vernon E. Jantzi, Director of Conflict Tranformation Program
Eastern Mennonite University
1200 Park Road
Harrisonburg, VA 22802-2462, USA
Tel: 1 (540) 432-4490
Fax: 1 (540) 432-4444
E-mail: *info@emu.edu; ctprogram@emu.edu*
Website: *http://www.emu.edu/ctp/ctp.html*
Main Issue Areas
Conflict transformation; Peace-building
Areas Where Organization Works
Worldwide
Working Languages
English
Types of Resources Available
Degree program; Training

Cooperative for American Relief Everywhere, Inc. (CARE)

Andrew Pugh, Advocacy Coordinator
151 Ellis Street, NE
Atlanta, GA 30303-2439, USA
Tel: 1 (404) 681-2552; 1 (800) 521-CARE
Fax: 1 (404) 577-1205
E-mail: *info@care.org*
Website: *http://www.care.org*

Main Issue Areas
Economic development; Education; Emergency relief and rehabilitation; Environmental protection; Food security; Health and population

Areas Where Organization Works
Africa, Asia, Caribbean, Caucasus, central Asia, Latin America, Pacific

Working Languages
English

Types of Resources Available
Technical assistance; Training

Regional Offices
Australia, Canada, Denmark, Germany, Japan, Norway, Austria, France, United Kingdom

Corporación para el Desarrollo de la Educación Básica (CORPOEDUCACION)

Margarita Pena, Executive Director
Carrera 20 No. 84
Oficina 402
Bogotá, DC, Colombia
Tel: (57-1) 530-5128; 530-5129; 530-5130
Fax: (57-1) 691-6070
E-mail: *corpoedu@colnodo.apc.org*
Website: *http://www.corpoeducacion.org.co*

Main Issue Areas
Basic education

Areas Where Organization Works
Colombia

Working Languages
Spanish

Types of Resources Available
Policy/research; Training

CUSO

Susan Learoyd, Advocacy Coordinator
2255 Carling Avenue
Suite 400
Ottawa, Ontario K2B 1A6, Canada
Tel: (613) 829-7445, ext. 210
Fax: (613) 289-7996
E-mail: *susan.learoyd@cuso.ca*
Website: *http://www.cuso.org*

Main Issue Areas
Community health; Economic alternatives; Environment; Food security; Human rights; Micro-enterprise; Natural-resource management; Women's issues

Areas Where Organization Works
Africa: Burkina Faso, Ghana, Kenya, Mozambique, Nigeria, South Africa, Tanzania, Togo, Zimbabwe; *Asia:* Bangladesh, Fiji, Lao PDR, Papua New Guinea, Solomon Islands, Thailand, Vanuatu, Vietnam; *Latin America:* Belize, Bolivia, Chile, Colombia, Costa Rica, El Salvador, Guatemala, Jamaica, Mexico, Nicaragua, Peru, St. Lucia

Working Languages
English, French, Local languages

Types of Resources Available
Funding/funding information; NGO networking; Policy/research; Technical assistance; Training

Regional Offices
Costa Rica, Ghana, Indonesia

Democracy Center

Jim Shultz, Executive Director
Casilla 5283
Cochabamba, Bolivia
Tel: (978) 383-1269
Fax: (978) 383-1269
E-mail: *Jshultz@democracyctr.org*
Website: *http://www.democracyctr.org*

Main Issue Areas
The center has worked with a wide variety of issue areas, including: Education and children's issues; Health care; Human and immigrant rights; Political reform; and Tax and budget issues

Areas Where Organization Works
Central/South America, Mexico, South Africa, United States

Working Languages
English, Spanish
Types of Resources Available
Policy/research; Technical assistance; Training
Regional Offices
United States

Developing Initiatives for Social and Human Action (DISHA)

Madhusudan Mistry, Managing Trustee
9, Mangaldeep Flats, Near Parikshit Bridge
Gandhi Ashram PO
Ahmedabad, Gujurat 380 027, India
Tel: (91-79) 755-9842
Fax: (91-79) 755-6782
E-mail: *disha@ad1.vsnl.net.in*
Website: Not available
Main Issue Areas
Budget analysis; Human rights; Labor; Tribals
Areas Where Organization Works
India
Working Languages
English, Gujarati, Hindi
Types of Resources Available
NGO networking; Policy/research; Technical assistance; Training

Development Foundation (DevFound)

Abdul Majid, Chief Executive; Rana Riaz Saeed, Project Officer
97 Street 96, I-8/4
PO Box 2640
Islamabad, Pakistan
Tel: (92-51) 447-076; 443-054
Fax: (92-51) 449-621
E-mail: *majid@devfound.sdnpk.undp.org*
Website: Not available
Main Issue Areas
Capacity building; Political development; Research; Socioeconomic development
Areas Where Organization Works
Pakistan
Working Languages
English, Urdu
Types of Resources Available
Funding/funding information; Policy/research; Technical assistance; Training

Emang Basadi Women's Association (EB)

Keboitse Machangana, Executive Director
Plot 551, South Ring Road, Extension 4
Private Bag 00470
Gaborone, Botswana
Tel: (267) 309-335
Fax: (267) 309-335
E-mail: *ebasadi@global.bw*
Website: Not available
Main Issue Areas
Gender; Resource and documentation center; Women's human rights
Areas Where Organization Works
Botswana, Malawi, Namibia, South Africa, Swaziland, Uganda
Working Languages
English, Setswana
Types of Resources Available
Policy/research; Training

Federação de Orgãos para Assistencia Social e Educacional/Association of Organizations for Social and Educational Assistance (FASE)

Jorge Eduardo Saavedra Durao, National Executive Director
Rua das Palmeiras 90
Botafogo
Rio de Janeiro, RJ 22270-070, Brazil
Tel: (55 21) 286-1441
Fax: (55-21) 286-1209
E-mail: *jdurao@fase.org.br*
Website: *http://www.fase.org.br*
Main Issue Areas
Citizenship; Environment and development; Public policy; Urban issues; Work and income
Areas Where Organization Works
Brazil
Working Languages
Portuguese
Types of Resources Available
Funding/funding information; NGO networking; Policy/research; Technical assistance; Training

Fondo Ecuatoriano Populorum Progressio (FEPP)

Jose Tonello Foscarini, Executive Director
Mallorca 427 y Coruna
Quito, Pichincha 17-110-5202, Ecuador
Tel: (593-2) 520-408; 592-372
Fax: (593-2) 520-408; 504-978
E-mail: *fepp@uio.satnet.net*
Website: Not available

Main Issue Areas

Applied research; Capacity building; Community organizing; Conservation and environmental management; Cooperative marketing; Creation of rural financial systems; Gender equity; Infrastructure development (housing, domestic and agricultural water supplies); Microenterprises; Production; Support for legalization of ancestral land title; Sustainable development

Areas Where Organization Works

Ecuador

Working Languages

Local languages, Spanish

Types of Resources Available

Funding/funding information; NGO networking; Technical assistance; Training

Forum for Women in Democracy (FOWODE)

Winnie Byanyima, Chairperson; Patricia Munabi, Acting Director
Plot 5, Dewinton Road
Kampala, PO Box 7176, Uganda
Tel: (256-41) 342-130
Fax: (256-41) 342-123
E-mail: *fowode@starcom.co.ug*
Website: Not available

Main Issue Areas

Economics; Human rights; Land; Research; Skills development

Areas Where Organization Works

Botswana, Kenya, Malawi, Namibia, South Africa, Uganda, Zambia

Working Languages

English, Local languages

Types of Resources Available

Policy/research; Technical assistance; Training

Forum Malien d'Appui a la Democratie et aux Droits Humains (FOMADDH)

Abdoulaye Lansar, Coordinateur
PO Box 1481
Bamako, Mali
Tel: (223) 218-091
Fax: (223) 218-091
E-mail: *abdoulansar@yahoo.fr*
Website: Not available

Main Issue Areas

Broadcasting international conventions; Democratic governance; Human rights

Areas Where Organization Works

Mali

Working Languages

French

Types of Resources Available

Technical assistance

Forum of Environmental Journalists of Bangladesh (FEJB)

Quamrul Islam Chowdhury
42/1 Kha 9, 2nd Floor
Segun Bagicha
Dhaka 1000, Bangladesh
Tel: (880-2) 956-3383; (880-19) 343-500
Fax: Not available
E-mail: Not available
Website: Not available

Main Issue Areas

Environment; Health; Water

Areas Where Organization Works

Bangladesh, South Asia

Working Languages

Bangla, English

Types of Resources Available

Training

Fundación Salvadoreña para la Promoción Social y el Desarrollo Económico (FUNSALPRODESE)

Rolanda Mata Fuentes
27 C. Pte Y 17 Av. Nte. No. 1434, Col. Layco
San Salvadore 1953, El Salvador
Tel: (503) 225-0414; 225-0416
Fax: (503) 225-5261
E-mail: *funsal@es.com.sv*
Website: Not available
Main Issue Areas
Agriculture; Education; Environment; Health
Areas Where Organization Works
El Salvador
Working Languages
Spanish
Types of Resources Available
Funding/funding information; Technical assistance

Global Partnership Postgraduate Diploma Course (GP)

Roberto Mugnani, Coordinator of Program Development, Center for Social Policy and Institutional Development
School for International Training
Kipling Road, PO Box 676
Brattleboro, VT 05302-676, USA
Tel: 1 (802) 258-3339
Fax: 1 (802) 258-3248
E-mail: *info@worldlearning.org*
Website: *http://www.sit.edu/gp/#degree*
Main Issue Areas
NGO leadership and management
Areas Where Organization Works
Asia, North America, Africa
Working Languages
English
Types of Resources Available
Degree program

Gorée Institute

Social Advocacy Program Coordinator
BP 05
Goree, Senegal
Tel: (221) 823-5339; 821-0562
Fax: (221) 822-5476
E-mail: *gorin@telecomplus.sn; Goree@enda.sn*
Website: *http://www.gorin.org*
Main Issue Areas
Advocacy against exclusion; Advocacy capacity building; Education; Environment; Health; Gender issues; Leadership and empowerment; Policy
Areas Where Organization Works
Africa
Working Languages
English, French, Wolof
Types of Resources Available
NGO networking; Policy/research; Technical assistance; Training

Hauser Center for Nonprofit Organizations

Neida M. Jiménez, Program Coordinator
Harvard University
79 John F. Kennedy Street
Cambridge, MA 02138, USA
Tel: 1 (617) 496-5675
Fax: 1 (617) 495-0996
E-mail: *neida_z@harvard.edu; hauser_center@harvard.edu*
Website: *http://www.ksghauser.harvard.edu*
Main Issue Areas
Education; Nonprofit practitioner engagement; Research
Areas Where Organization Works
United States
Working Languages
English
Types of Resources Available
Policy/research; Training

Helvetas—Swiss Association for International Cooperation

E. Werner Kulling, Secretary General
St. Moritzstrasse 15
PO Box 181
Zurich 8042, Switzerland
Tel: (41-1) 368-6500
Fax: (41-1) 368-6580
E-mail: *helvetas@helvetas.ch*
Website: *http://www.helvetas.ch*

Main Issue Areas
Culture; Education; Rural infrastructure; Sustainable natural-resource management

Areas Where Organization Works
Benin, Bhutan, Cameroon, Colombia, Dominican Republic, Guatemala, Haiti, Kyrgyzstan, Lesotho, Malaysia, Mali, Mozambique, Nepal, Paraguay, Philippines, Sri Lanka, Switzerland, Tanzania, Togo, Vietnam

Working Languages
English, French, German, Spanish

Types of Resources Available
Funding/funding information; Technical assistance

Highlander Research and Education Center

1959 Highlander Way
New Market, TN 37820, USA
Tel: 1 (865) 933-3443
Fax: 1 (865) 933-3424
E-mail: *HREC@highlandercenter.org*
Website: *http://www.highlandercenter.org*

Main Issue Areas
Social justice

Areas Where Organization Works
United States

Working Languages
English

Types of Resources Available
NGO networking; Policy/research; Technical assistance; Training

Horn of Africa Relief

Fatma Jama Jibrell, Managing Director
PO Box 70331
Nairobi, Kenya
Tel: (254-2) 724-193
Fax: (254-2) 724-193
E-mail: *horn-rel@nbnet.co.ke*
Website: Not available

Main Issue Areas
Advocacy against female genital mutilation; Agriculture; Education/adult literacy and skill training; Empowering the youth; Environmental awareness and rehabilitation; Marine resource management; Natural-resource management; Public health/human health; Women's advocacy for human rights; Women in political participation; Women's peace advocacy initiatives and peace process

Areas Where Organization Works
Kenya, Somalia

Working Languages
English, Somali

Types of Resources Available
NGO networking; Training

Housing People of Zimbabwe (HPZ)

Regis Mtutu, Training Officer
PO Box CY
2686 Causeway
Harare, Zimbabwe
Tel: (263-4) 739-610; 737-044
Fax: (263-4) 252-977
E-mail: *hpz@samara.co.zw*
Website: *http://www.icon.co.zw/housingpeople*

Main Issue Areas
Urban housing development

Areas Where Organization Works
Zimbabwe

Working Languages
English, Ndebele, Shona

Types of Resources Available
NGO networking; Technical assistance; Training

Human Rights Advocates Training Program

Center for the Study of Human Rights
Columbia University
New York, NY 10027, USA
Tel: 1 (212) 854-2479
Fax: 1 (212) 316-4578
E-mail: Not available
Website: *http://www.columbia.edu/cu/humanrights/adv*

Main Issue Areas
Human rights, including rights for minorities, women, children, and gays

Areas Where Organization Works
Worldwide

Working Languages
English

Types of Resources Available
Degree program

Human Rights and Peoples Diplomacy Training

Diplomacy Training Program
Faculty of Law, University of New South Wales
Sydney 2052, Australia
Tel: (61-2) 9385-2277; 9385-2807
Fax: (61-2) 9358-1778
E-mail: *dtp@unsw.edu.au*
Website: *http://www.law.unsw.edu.au/centres/dtp/index.html*

Main Issue Areas
Conflict; Governance; Human rights

Areas Where Organization Works
Asia-Pacific, Australia

Working Languages
English

Types of Resources Available
Degree program; Training

Human Rights Program, Visiting Fellowships

Peter Rosenblum, Project Director
Harvard University
Pound Hall 401
Cambridge, MA 02138, USA
Tel: 1 (617) 495-9362
Fax: 1 (617) 495-1110
E-mail: *prosenbl@law.harvard.edu*
Website: *http://www.law.harvard.edu/programs/HRP/Fellows.html*

Main Issue Areas
Human rights

Areas Where Organization Works
North America, Worldwide

Working Languages
English

Types of Resources Available
Training

Institute for Conflict Analysis and Resolution at George Mason University

Kevin P. Clements, Director
Institute for Conflict Analysis and Resolution
George Mason University
Fairfax, VA 22030-4444, USA
Tel: 1 (703) 993-1300
Fax: 1 (703) 993-1302
E-mail: *icarinfo@osf1.gmu.edu*
Website: *http://www.gmu.edu/departments/icar*

Main Issue Areas
Major research interests include the analysis of deep-rooted conflicts and their resolution; the exploration of conditions attracting parties to the negotiation table; the role of third parties in dispute resolution; and the testing of a variety of conflict-intervention methods in community, national, and international settings

Areas Where Organization Works
North America, Worldwide

Working Languages
English

Types of Resources Available
Degree program

Institute for Development Research (IDR)

Jane Covey, President; Valerie Miller, Senior Associate
44 Farnsworth Street
Boston, MA 02210-1211, USA
Tel: 1 (617) 422-0422
Fax: 1 (617) 482-0617
E-mail: *idr@jsi.com*
Website: *http://www.jsi.com/idr*

Main Issue Areas
Civil society groups; Cooperatives; Education; Indigenous movements; NGOs that work on environmental issues

Areas Where Organization Works
Eastern, southern, and western Africa; South Asia, Southeast Asia

Working Languages
English, French, Spanish

Types of Resources Available
Policy/research; Technical assistance; Training

Institute for Not-for-Profit Management (INM)

Columbia Executive Education
Armstrong Hall, 4th Floor
2880 Broadway, MC 5926
New York, NY 10025, USA
Tel: 1 (212) 854-4226
Fax: 1 (212) 316-1473
E-mail: *inm@columbia.edu*
Website: *http://www.gsb.columbia.edu/execed/INM/index.html*

Main Issue Areas
Leadership capacity building; Not-for-profit management

Areas Where Organization Works
United States

Working Languages
English

Types of Resources Available
Degree program

Institute of Cultural Affairs—Middle East and North Africa (ICA-MENA)

Hala El Kholy, Executive Director
10 Road # 23, Maadi El Sarayat
PO Box 23, Maadi
Cairo 11431, Egypt
Tel: (20-2) 375-1320; 375-0088
Fax: (20-2) 375-1756
E-mail: *ica@link.com.eg; ica@idsc.gov.eg*
Website: *http://www.icaworld.org/mena/index.html*

Main Issue Areas
Agriculture and environment; Capacity building; Credit and microenterprise; Health and education; Media and publications; Training and consultancies; Women's enhancement

Areas Where Organization Works
Egypt

Working Languages
Arabic, English

Types of Resources Available
NGO networking; Policy/research; Technical assistance; Training

Regional Offices
Autonomous, national member institutes (ICAs) are located in: Australia, Belgium, Benin, Bosnia and Herzegovina, Brazil, Canada, Chile, Egypt, Cote d'Ivoire, Egypt, Germany, Ghana, Guatemala, Hong Kong, India, Japan, Kenya, Korea, Malaysia, Mexico, Nepal, Netherlands, Nigeria, Peru, Philippines, Spain, Sri Lanka, Taiwan, Tanzania, Uganda, United Kingdom, United States, Venezuela, Zambia

Institute of Development Studies (IDS)

Keith Bezanson, Director
University of Sussex
Brighton BN1 9RE, United Kingdom
Tel: (44) 1273-606261
Fax: (44) 1273-621202
E-mail: *ids@ids.ac.uk*
Website: *http://www.ids.ac.uk*

Main Issue Areas
Democracy and governance; Education; Environment; Employment; Finance; Food issues; Gender; Globalization; Health; Poverty reduction; Social policy; Trade and industry

Areas Where Organization Works
Throughout most of the Third World, with a focus on Africa and South and East Asia. It is also increasingly involved in eastern Europe and the countries of the former Soviet Union.
Working Languages
English
Types of Resources Available
Degree program; Policy/research; Technical assistance; Training

Integrated Social Development Centre (ISODEC)

Charles Abugre, Executive Director
PO Box 19452, Accra-North
4th Sakumono Link, Lartebiokoshie
Accra, Greater Accra, Ghana
Tel: (233-21) 306-069; 301-064
Fax: (233-21) 311-687
E-mail: *isodec@ncs.com.gh*
Website: Not available
Main Issue Areas
Education; Environment; Micro-finance; Newspaper publishing; Public interest law; Rights-based approach to health; Water
Areas Where Organization Works
Ghana, Kenya
Working Languages
English
Types of Resources Available
NGO networking; Policy/research; Technical assistance; Training

International Budget Project of the Center on Budget and Policy Priorities (CBPP)

Isaac Shapiro (CBPP) and Waren Krafchick (Idasa, South Africa)
820 First Street, NE
Suite 510
Washington, DC 20002, USA
Tel: 1 (202) 408-1080
Fax: 1 (202) 408-1056
E-mail: *shapiro@cbpp.org; warren@idasaact.org.za*
Website: *http://www.internationalbudget.org*

Main Issue Areas
Applied budget work; Budget analysis; Budget decision making; Budget process
Areas Where Organization Works
Worldwide
Working Languages
English
Types of Resources Available
NGO networking; Policy/research; Technical assistance; Training

International NGO Training and Research Centre (INTRAC)

Brian Pratt
PO Box 563
Oxford, Oxfordshire OX1 2BE, United Kingdom
Tel: (44-1865) 201-851
Fax: (44-1865) 201-852
E-mail: *intrac@gn.apc.org*
Website: *http://www.intrac.org*
Main Issue Areas
Advocacy-related research; Education; Emergency relief; International development; Organizational assistance
Areas Where Organization Works
Africa: Ethiopia, The Gambia, Ghana, Kenya, Malawi, Morocco, Nigeria, Somaliland, South Africa, Sudan, Tanzania, Uganda, Zimbabwe; *Asia:* Afghanistan, Bangladesh, Cambodia, India, Lao PDR, Nepal, Pakistan, Sri Lanka; *Central Asia:* Belarus, Kazakhstan, Kyrgyzstan, Tajikistan, Uzbekistan; *Latin America:* Colombia, Nicaragua, Peru
Working Languages
English, Russian, Spanish
Types of Resources Available
Policy/research; Technical assistance; Training
Regional Offices
Kyrgyzstan, Malawi

Investigación Social y Asesoramiento Legal Potosí (ISALP)

Marco Antonio Castro Gamarra
Calle Sucre #69
Potosí Frias Casilla 326, Bolivia
Tel: (591) 622-4192
Fax: (591) 622-6228
E-mail: *isalp@cedro.pts.entelnet.bo*
Website: Not available

Main Issue Areas
Environmental defense; Indigenous organizations; Judicial defense of women, farmers, indigenous peoples

Areas Where Organization Works
Bolivia

Working Languages
Spanish

Types of Resources Available
Technical assistance; Training

Johns Hopkins Institute for Policy Studies—Third Sector Project

Carol Wessner, Program Manager, Third Sector Project
Center for Civil Society Studies
3400 N. Charles Street, Wyman Building, 5th Floor
Baltimore, MD 21218, USA
Tel: 1 (410) 516-5389
Fax: 1 (410) 516-8233
E-mail: *cwessner@jhu.edu*
Website: *http://www.jhu.edu/ips/Programs/ThirdSectorProject/*

Main Issue Areas
Advocacy; Nonprofit management training

Areas Where Organization Works
Central Asia, central and eastern Europe

Working Languages
English

Types of Resources Available
Funding/funding information; NGO networking; Policy/research; Technical assistance; Training

Kulima

Domenico Liuzzi, General Coordinator
Avenue Karl Marx 1452
Maputo, Maputo 4404, Mozambique
Tel: (258-1) 430-665; 421-622
Fax: (258-1) 421-510
E-mail: *Kulima@mail.tropical.co.mz*
Website: Not available

Main Issue Areas
Decentralization of political structures; Democracy and governance; Participatory planning; Strengthening participation of civil society

Areas Where Organization Works
Angola, Mozambique

Working Languages
English, Local languages, Portuguese

Types of Resources Available
Funding/funding information; NGO networking; Training

Lutheran World Relief (LWR)

Jim Bowman, Director of Public Policy
122 C Street, NW
Suite 125
Washington, DC 20001, USA
Tel: 1 (202) 783-6887
Fax: 1 (202) 783-5328
E-mail: *Jbowman@lwr.org; lwr@lwr.org*
Website: *http://www.lwr.org*

Main Issue Areas
Debt; Democracy; Gender; Human-centered development; Land; Natural resources; Peace with Justice; Relief

Areas Where Organization Works
Andean region, Central America, East Africa, India, Philippines, West Africa

Working Languages
English, Spanish

Types of Resources Available
NGO networking; Technical assistance; Training

Master of Arts Program in Public Policy and Administration—Universidad de San Andrés

Carlos Acuna, Director
Graduate Program in Administration and Public Policy
Vito Dumas 284
Victoria, Provincia de Buenos Aires 1644, Argentina
Tel: (54-11) 4725-7000; 4725-7017
Fax: (54-11) 4725-7010
E-mail: *chacu@udesa.edu.ar*
Website: *http://www.udesa.edu*

Main Issue Areas
Public policy and administration

Areas Where Organization Works
Argentina

Working Languages
Spanish

Types of Resources Available
Degree program; Policy/research; Training

Microfinance Centre for Central and Eastern Europe and the NIS (MFC)

Maria Nowak, Chairperson
ul. Koszykowa 60/62 m. 52
00-673 Warszawa, Poland
Tel: (48-22) 622-3465
Fax: (48-22) 622-3485
E-mail: *microfinance@mfc.org.pl*
Website: *http://www.mfc.org.pl*

Main Issue Areas
Micro-finance

Areas Where Organization Works
Eastern Europe/FSU: Albania, Armenia, Belarus, Bosnia-Herzegovina, Bulgaria, Croatia, Georgia, Macedonia, Moldova, Poland; *Western Europe:* Austria, France

Working Languages
English, Polish

Types of Resources Available
Training

MineWatch Philippines—Bantay Mina (MWP-BM)

Virgilio Reoma, National Coordinator
No. 14 Mabait Street, Teachers Village, Diliman
Quezon City, Philippines
Tel: (63-2) 925-7777
Fax: (63-2) 925-3729
E-mail: *bantay-mina@phil.gn.apc.org*
Website: Not available

Main Issue Areas
Information-education campaigns at the local level; Mass mobilization and rallies; Policy-engagement dialogues with key government officials; Research work, documentation, and publications; Strategic support-group formation among indigenous peoples

Areas Where Organization Works
Philippines, Asia-Pacific

Working Languages
Bisaya, English, Filipino, Ilocano, Tagalog

Types of Resources Available
Policy/research; Training

Namibia Non-Governmental Organisations' Forum (NANGOF)

Uhuru Dempers, Executive Directory
Caesar Str. 196, Wanaheda, Katutura
PO Box 70433
Windhoek-West, Khomasdal 9000, Namibia
Tel: (264-61) 239-469
Fax: (264-61) 239-471
E-mail: *nangof@iafrica.com.na*
Website: Not available

Main Issue Areas
Community natural-resource management; Human-resource development; Land reform; Legislative reform; NGO capacity building; Policy advocacy and networking

Areas Where Organization Works
Namibia

Working Languages
English

Types of Resources Available
NGO networking; Policy/research; Training

NGO Resource Centre (A Project of Aga Khan Foundation) (NGORC)

Asad Azfar, Director
D-114, Block 5
Clifton
Karachi SINDH 75600, Pakistan
Tel: (92-21) 586-5501; 586-5502
Fax: (92-21) 586-5503
E-mail: *info@ngorc.khi.sdnpk.undp.org*
Website: Not available

Main Issue Areas
Democracy and civil society; Institutional development; Organizational development

Areas Where Organization Works
Pakistan

Working Languages
English, Sindhi, Urdu

Types of Resources Available
NGO networking; Policy/research; Training

Organization of Rural Associations for Progress (ORAP)

Tomson Dube
15 Founders Road, Richmond
PO Box 4139
Bulawayo, Zimbabwe
Tel: (263-9) 74-209; 68-588; 68-538
Fax: (263-9) 72-127; 31-088
E-mail: *oraphq@acacia.samara.co.zw*
Website: *http://www.people2people.org/voices/orap1.html*

Main Issue Areas
Food security and environment; Gender empowerment; Microcredit; Self-employment and sufficiency; Sustainable agriculture; Traditional medicine; Training and education

Areas Where Organization Works
Eight hundred village groups in Zimbabwe

Working Languages
English

Types of Resources Available
Technical assistance; Training

Pact

Traer Sunley, Vice President of Communications
1901 Pennsylvania Avenue, NW
5th Floor
Washington, DC 20006, USA
Tel: 1 (202) 466-5666
Fax: 1 (202) 466-5669
E-mail: *pact@pacthq.org*
Website: *http://www.pactworld.org*

Main Issue Areas
Civil society; Communication and information technology; Ecology (sustainable natural-resource management); Education; Financial sustainability (private-sector initiative); Legal NGO frameworks; Health

Areas Where Organization Works
Worldwide

Working Languages
English, French, Portuguese, Spanish

Types of Resources Available
Funding/funding information; NGO networking; Technical assistance; Training

PAIRVI

P. M. Paul, Promoter
JG-2/ 33, Khirki Extension
New Delhi, Malviya Nagar 110 017, India
Tel: (91-141) 591-950; 592-022
Fax: (91-141) 591-950
E-mail: Not available
Website: Not available

Main Issue Areas
Caste; Class; Development; Environment; Gender; Human rights

Areas Where Organization Works
India

Working Languages
English, Hindi

Types of Resources Available
Technical assistance; Training

Partners of the Americas (POA)

Martha Cecilia Villada, Director Citizen Participation Program; Polly Donaldson, Director of Public Outreach
1424 K Street, NW
Suite 700
Washington, DC 20005, USA
Tel: 1 (202) 628-3300
Fax: 1 (202) 628-3306
E-mail: *mcv@partners.poa.com;*
Pd@partners.poa.com; info@partners.poa.com
Website: *http://www.partners.net*

Main Issue Areas

Agriculture; Capacity building; Citizen participation; Environment; Health; Human rights; Organizational development; Women's legal rights

Areas Where Organization Works

Caribbean, Latin America, United States

Working Languages

English, Portuguese, Spanish

Types of Resources Available

NGO networking; Technical assistance; Training

Population Concern

Wendy Thomas, Chief Executive
Studio 325, Highgate Studios
53-79 Highgate Road
London NW5 1TL, United Kingdom
Tel: (44-20) 7241-8500
Fax: (44-20) 7267-6788
E-mail: *info@populationconcern.org.uk*
Website: *http://www.populationconcern.org.uk*

Main Issue Areas

Sexual and reproductive health and rights, with a special focus on young people

Areas Where Organization Works

Africa, Asia, Latin America/Caribbean

Working Languages

English

Types of Resources Available

NGO networking; Technical assistance

Posgrado en Organizaciones Sin Fines de Lucro

Gabriel Berger
Minones 2177, PB
Buenos Aires 1428, Argentina
Tel: (54-11) 4783-3410
Fax: (54-11) 4783-3220
E-mail: *pdssc@utdt.edu*
Website: *http://www.utdt.edu/departamentos/ politica/*

Main Issue Areas

Nonprofit organizations management

Areas Where Organization Works

Argentina

Working Languages

English, Spanish

Types of Resources Available

Degree program; Policy/research; Training

PREPARE—India Rural Reconstruction and Disaster Response Service

Jacob D. Raj, Executive Secretary; Daisy Dharmaraj
4 Sathalvar Street
Mogappair West
Chennai 600 058, India
Tel: (91-44) 635-7854; 625-3254; 624-4211
Fax: (91-44) 625-0315
E-mail: *prepare@md2.vsnl.net.in*
Website: *http://www.pcsadvt.com/prepare*

Main Issue Areas

Democratic governance; Domestic governance; Food security; Gender equity; Human rights; Nature conservation; Poverty alleviation; Securing livelihoods

Areas Where Organization Works

India, Kenya, Tanzania

Working Languages

English, Local languages

Types of Resources Available

Policy/research; Technical assistance

PRIP Trust

Aroma Goon, Executive Director
59/A, Satmasjid Road
Dhanmondi R
Dhanmondi R/A
Dhaka 1209, Bangladesh
Tel: (880-2) 819-111
Fax: (880-2) 816-429
E-mail: *prip@prip.org*
Website: Not available

Main Issue Areas
Capacity building; Networking and support services; Organizational development; Women's development

Areas Where Organization Works
Bangladesh

Working Languages
Bengali, English

Types of Resources Available
NGO networking, Technical assistance

Project South

9 Gammon Avenue
Atlanta, GA 30315 USA
Tel: 1 (404) 622-0602
Fax: 1 (404) 622-7992
E-mail: *projectsouth@igc.org*
Website: *http://www.peacenet.org/projectsouth/*

Main Issue Areas
Social and economic justice

Areas Where Organization Works
United States

Working Languages
English

Types of Resources Available
NGO networking; Policy/research; Training

PROTERRA

Walter Valdez
Madrid #166—Miraflores
Lima 18, Peru
Tel: (51-1) 242-0239
Fax: (51-1) 446-6363
E-mail: *wvaldez@mail.cosapidata.com.pe*
Website: Not available

Main Issue Areas
Citizens' rights; Environmental law; Environmental policies; Legal defense (especially in community-based organizations); Promotion of environmental policies; Public education; Social capacity building

Areas Where Organization Works
Peru

Working Languages
English, Spanish

Types of Resources Available
Funding/funding information; Policy/research; Technical assistance; Training

Public Interest Law Initiative in Transitional Societies (PILI)

Edwin Rekosh, Director
Columbia Law School
435 West 116th Street, Mail Code 3525
New York, NY 10027, USA
Tel: 1 (212) 851-1060
Fax: 1 (212) 851-1064
E-mail: *erekosh@law.columbia.edu;*
pili@law.columbia.edu
Website: *http://www.pili.org*

Main Issue Areas
Access to justice; Clinical legal education; Human rights; Public interest law

Areas Where Organization Works
Central and eastern Europe, central Asia, Russia

Working Languages
English, Russian

Types of Resources Available
Degree program; NGO networking; Policy/research; Training

Public Law Center (TPLC)

David A. Marcello, Executive Director
6329 Freret Street
Suite 351
New Orleans, LA 70118, USA
Tel: 1 (504) 862-8850
Fax: 1 (504) 862-8851
E-mail: *dmarcello@law.tulane.edu*
Website: *http://www.law.tulane.edu/ildi/public.htm*

Main Issue Areas
Citizen participation; Judicial reform; Legislative drafting; Rule of law

Areas Where Organization Works
Canada, Dominican Republic, Hungary, Moldova, South Africa, United States
Working Languages
English
Types of Resources Available
Degree program; Policy/research; Technical assistance; Training

Ruckus Society
2054 University Avenue
Berkeley, CA 94704, USA
Tel: 1 (510) 848-9565
Fax: 1 (510) 848-9541
E-mail: *ruckus@ruckus.org*
Website: *http://www.ruckus.org*
Main Issue Areas
Environment; Human rights; Nonviolent civil disobedience
Areas Where Organization Works
United States
Working Languages
English
Types of Resources Available
Technical assistance; Training

Servicio Habitacional y de Acción Social (SEHAS)
Carlos Buthet, Director
Bvrd. del Carmen No. 680, Villa Siburu
Estafeta 14
Córdoba 5003, Argentina
Tel: (54-351) 480-5031; 488-0292
Fax: (54-351) 489-7541
E-mail: *sehasmb@nt.com.ar; sehas@nt.com.ar*
Website: Not available
Main Issue Areas
Banking; Civil society; Housing; Organizational development; Poor urban youth; Social development
Areas Where Organization Works
Argentina
Working Languages
Spanish
Types of Resources Available
NGO networking; Policy/research; Technical assistance; Training

Sisterhood Is Global Institute (SIGI)
Greta Hofmann Nemiroff
1200 Atwater Avenue
Suite 2
Montreal, Quebec H3Z 1X4, Canada
Tel: (514) 846-9366
Fax: (514) 846-9066
E-mail: *sigi@qc.aibn.com*
Website: *http://www.sigi.org*
Main Issue Areas
Human rights; Human rights education; Violence against women; Women and civil society; Women and development; Women and leadership; Women's rights
Areas Where Organization Works
Azerbaijan, Bangladesh, Egypt, India, Iran, Jordan, Lebanon, Malaysia, Pakistan, Syria, Uzbekistan, Zimbabwe
Working Languages
English, Local languages
Types of Resources Available
NGO networking; Policy/research; Technical assistance; Training

Social Action and Leadership School for Activists (SALSA)
733 15th Street NW
Suite 1020
Washington, DC 20005, USA
Tel: 1 (202) 234-9382, ext. 229
Fax: 1 (202) 387-7915
E-mail: *salsa@reply.net*
Website: *http://www.hotsalsa.org*
Main Issue Areas
Activist skill building
Areas Where Organization Works
United States
Working Languages
English
Types of Resources Available
Training

South African National NGO Coalition (SANGOCO)

Safoora Sadek, Executive Director
PO Box 31471
Braamfontein, Gauteng 2017, South Africa
Tel: (27-11) 403-7746
Fax: (27-11) 403-8703
E-mail: *ngocoal@wn.apc.org*
Website: *http://www.sangoco.org.za*

Main Issue Areas
Adult education; Children; Disabled people; Electoral education; Environment; Health; Human rights; Land; Media; Research; Rural and urban development; Women

Areas Where Organization Works
South Africa

Working Languages
English, Local languages

Types of Resources Available
Policy/research, Training

South Asia Partnership Canada—SAP Canada

Richard Harmston, Executive Director
1 Nicholas Street
Suite 200
Ottawa, Ontario K1N 7B7, Canada
Tel: (613) 241-1333
Fax: (613) 241-1129
E-mail: *sap@web.ca*
Website: *http://www.sapcanada.org*

Main Issue Areas
Civil society; Community development; Capacity building; Human development; Human rights; Local governance; NGO networking; Peace

Areas Where Organization Works
Bangladesh, Canada, India, Nepal, Pakistan, Sri Lanka

Working Languages
English

Types of Resources Available
NGO networking; Technical assistance

SUNGI Development Foundation (SDF)

Advocacy Support Unit Programme Manager; Mushtaq Gadi, Principal Program Coordinator
Number 17, Street 67 G-6/4 (Liaison Office)
Islamabad, Pakistan
Tel: (92-51) 273-272; 276-589; 276-579
Fax: (92-51) 823-559
E-mail: *mail@sungi.sdnpk.undp.org;*
naeemasu@hotmail.com
Website: Not available

Main Issue Areas
Agriculture; Civic rights; Credit; Development; Forestry; Health and sanitation; Livestock; Non-formal education; Rural crafts; Small enterprise development; Social mobilization; Sustainable livelihoods

Areas Where Organization Works
Pakistan

Working Languages
English, Hindko, Pushto, Urdu

Types of Resources Available
NGO networking; Policy/research; Technical assistance; Training

Tambuyog Development Center, Inc. (TDC)

Rebecca R. Guieb, Executive Director; Dinna Umengan, Advocacy Officer
Room 108A, Phil. Social Science Center
Commonwealth Avenue, Diliman
Quezon City, Dillman 1102, Philippines
Tel: (63-2) 456-1908; 456-1907; 922-9621 (local 346)
Fax: (63-2) 926-4415
E-mail: *tambuyog@netgazer.com.ph*
Website: *http://www.skyinet.net/~tambuyog/*
tambuyog.htm

Main Issue Areas
Agriculture; Environment; Fisheries

Areas Where Organization Works
Australia, Bangladesh, Cambodia, Canada, Indonesia, Palau, Philippines, Thailand, United States, Vietnam

Working Languages
English, Filipino
Types of Resources Available
NGO networking; Policy/research; Technical
assistance; Training

Uganda Debt Network (UDN)

Zie Gariyo, Coordinator
PO Box 21509
Kampala, Uganda
Tel: (256-41) 543-974
Fax: (256-41) 534-856
E-mail: *udn@infocom.co.ug*
Website: *http://www.uganda.co.ug/debt*
Main Issue Areas
Accountability and transparency; Budgetary poli-
cies; Economic and social justice; External debt
Areas Where Organization Works
Uganda
Working Languages
English
Types of Resources Available
NGO networking; Policy/research; Training

United for a Fair Economy (UFE)

Chuck Collins, Co-Director
37 Temple Place
Boston, MA 02111, USA
Tel: 1 (617) 423-2148
Fax: 1 (617) 423-0191
E-mail: *info@ufenet.org*
Website: *http://www.ufenet.org*
Main Issue Areas
Fair taxation; Fair trade; Global trade; Government
spending; Income inequality
Areas Where Organization Works
North America
Working Languages
English
Types of Resources Available
Policy/research; Training

Washington College of Law—Summer Session on Human Rights and Humanitarian Law

4801 Massachusetts Avenue, NW
Washington, DC 20016-8084, USA
Tel: 1 (202) 274-4000
Fax: Not available
E-mail: *humlaw@wcl.american.edu*
Website: *http://www.wcl.american.edu/pub/humright*
Main Issue Areas
Humanitarian law; Human rights
Areas Where Organization Works
United States
Working Languages
English
Types of Resources Available
Training

Women's Political Participation, The Asia Foundation (WPP)

Carol Yost, Director; Lisa VeneKlasen, Assistant
Director
1779 Massachusetts Avenue, NW
Suite 815
Washington, DC 20036, USA
Tel: 1 (202) 588-9420
Fax: 1 (202) 588-9409
E-mail: *gwip@dc.asiafound.org*
Website: *http://www.asiafoundation.org*
Main Issue Areas
Advocacy and leadership training; Citizen participa-
tion; Capacity building of civil society organizations;
Gender and governance; Women's economic and
legal rights; Women's political participation
Areas Where Organization Works
Asia-Pacific and other regions, working with re-
gional and local partners
Working Languages
English
Types of Resources Available
NGO networking; Technical assistance; Training
Regional Offices
Bangladesh, Cambodia, China, Indonesia, Japan,
Korea, Mongolia, Nepal, Pakistan, Philippines, Sri
Lanka, Taiwan, Thailand

Women, Law and Development International (WLDI)

Molly Reilly, Director of Programs
1350 Connecticut Avenue, NW
Suite 407
Washington, DC 20036, USA
Tel: 1 (202) 463-7477
Fax: 1 (202) 463-7480
E-mail: *wld@wld.org*
Website: *http://www.wld.org*

Main Issue Areas
Women's human rights

Areas Where Organization Works
Africa, central and eastern Europe, central Asia, Latin America

Working Languages
English, Russian, Spanish

Types of Resources Available
Policy/research; Technical assistance; Training

Regional Offices
Russia

World Learning and the School for International Training (SIT)

Roberto Mugnani, Coordinator of Program Development, Center for Social Policy and Institutional Development
PO Box 676, Kipling Road
Brattleboro, VT 05302-0676, USA
Tel: 1 (802) 258-3339
Fax: 1 (802) 258-3248
E-mail: *policy.advocacy@sit.edu; cspid@sit.edu*
Website: *http://www.worldlearning.org*

Main Issue Areas
Basic education; Democracy and governance; Grassroots development; Institutional capacity building; NGO leadership and management; Organizational leadership and development; Policy advocacy; Project design and planning; Societies in transition; Strategic and financial management; Training of trainers

Areas Where Organization Works
Africa, Asia, Caribbean, central and eastern Europe, new independent states

Working Languages
English, French, Spanish

Types of Resources Available
Degree program; NGO networking; Training

Zimbabwe Women's Resource Center and Network (ZWRCN)

Thoko Matshe, Director
Box 2192
Harare, Zimbabwe
Tel: (263-4) 702-198
Fax: (263-4) 720-331
E-mail: *thoko@zwrcn.org.zw*
Website: Not available

Main Issue Areas
Information sharing; Women's rights

Areas Where Organization Works
Malawi, South Africa, Zambia

Working Languages
English, Ndebele, Shona

Types of Resources Available
Policy/research; Technical assistance; Training

Networking Organizations

Acción Ciudadana

Rudy López Reyes, Analista
5a. Avenida 15-45, Zona 10 Centro Empresarial
Torre
Oficina 1004
01010 Guatemala
Tel: (502) 363-2719; 363-2729
Fax: (502) 363-2739
E-mail: *acciongt@quik.guate.com*
Website: *http://www.quik.guate.com/acciongt/index*
.html
Main Issue Areas
Civic participation; Democratization
Areas Where Organization Works
Guatemala
Working Languages
Spanish
Types of Resources Available
NGO networking

Advocates International

Samuel E. Ericsson, President; John E. Langolis,
Board Chairman
9691 D Main Street
Fairfax, VA 22031-3754, USA
Tel: 1 (703) 764-0011
Fax: 1 (703) 764-0077
E-mail: *info@advocatesinternational.org*
Website: *http://www.advocatesinternational.org*
Main Issue Areas
Conflict resolution; Human rights; Professional
ethics; Reconciliation; Religious freedom
Areas Where Organization Works
Advocates in over one hundred nations
Working Languages
English
Types of Resources Available
NGO networking

African Women's Development and Communications Network (FEMNET)

Sarah Macharia, Program Officer
PO Box 54562
Nairobi, Kenya
Tel: (254-2) 741-320; 741-301
Fax: (254-2) 742-927
E-mail: *femnet@africaonline.co.ke*
Website: *http://www.africaonline.co.ke/femnet/index*
.html
Main Issue Areas
Gender equity
Areas Where Organization Works
Africa: Ethiopia, Ghana, Kenya, Malawi, South
Africa, Sudan, Swaziland, Tanzania, Uganda,
Zambia; *Western Europe:* Germany, the Netherlands,
Switzerland; United States
Working Languages
English, French
Types of Resources Available
NGO networking; Training

Alliance for Justice

John Pomeranz and Kay Guinane, Nonprofit
Advocacy Council
2000 P Street, NW
Suite 712
Washington, DC 20036, USA
Tel: 1 (202) 822-6070
Fax: 1 (202) 822-6068
E-mail: *pomeranz@afj.org; kay@afj.org*
Website: *http://www.afj.org*
Main Issue Areas
Children's issues; Civil rights; Consumer rights;
Environment; Health; Women's issues
Areas Where Organization Works
United States
Working Languages
English
Types of Resources Available
NGO networking; Technical assistance; Training

Asian Forum for Human Rights and Development (FORUM-ASIA)

Somchai Homlaor, Secretary General
c/o Union for Civil Liberty
111 Suthisarnwinitchai Road
Hueykwang, Bangkok 10320, Thailand
Tel: (66-2) 275-4231; 275-4233; 276-9846
Fax: (66-2) 693-4939
E-mail: *Chalida@Mozart.inet.co.th*
Website: Not available
Main Issue Areas
Human rights
Areas Where Organization Works
South Asia
Working Languages
English
Types of Resources Available
NGO networking; Training

Asociación Latinoamericana de Organizaciones de Promoción (ALOP)

Manuel Chiriboga, Executive Secretary
Apartado 265-1350, Barrio Escalante
Casa 3144, de la Iglesia Santa Tersita, 300m. norte,
275m. este
San Jose, Costa Rica
Tel: (506) 283-2122
Fax: (506) 283-5898
E-mail: *info@alop.or.cr*
Website: *http://www.alop.or.cr*
Main Issue Areas
Aid and development; Habitat; Human rights;
Rural development; Social exclusion; Trade and
trade agreements
Areas Where Organization Works
Latin America: Argentina, Belize, Bolivia, Brazil,
Chile, Colombia, Costa Rica, Cuba, Dominican
Republic, Ecuador, El Salvador, Guatemala, Honduras, Mexico, Nicaragua, Panama, Paraguay, Peru,
Uruguay, Venezuela
Working Languages
Spanish
Types of Resources Available
Policy/research; Technical assistance; Training
Regional Offices
Belgium

Association of Non-governmental Organizations (TANGO)

Fatma Baldeh-Njie, Director
PMB 392
Serrekunda
Kanifing KSMD, The Gambia
Tel: (220) 497-771
Fax: (220) 497-772
E-mail: *tango@qanet.gm*
Website: Not available
Main Issue Areas
Advocacy; Information and resource center for
NGOs; Training and capacity building
Areas Where Organization Works
The Gambia
Working Languages
English, Local languages
Types of Resources Available
NGO networking; Training

Casa Alianza/Covenant House Latin America

Bruce Harris, Executive Director of Latin America
Programs
SJO 1039
PO Box 025216
Miami, FL 33102-5216, USA
Tel: (506) 253-5439 [Costa Rica]
Fax: (506) 224-5689 [Costa Rica]
E-mail: *bruce@casa-alianza.org*
Website: *http://www.casa-alianza.org*
Main Issue Areas
Advocacy; Education; Health; Human rights; Legal
defense; Social service; Training
Areas Where Organization Works
Central America, Mexico
Working Languages
English, Spanish
Types of Resources Available
NGO networking; Policy/research; Training
Regional Offices
Guatemala, Honduras, Mexico, Nicaragua

Catholic Commission for Justice and Peace (CCJP)

Joe Komakoma, Executive Secretary; Sam Mulafu-lafu, Assistant Executive Secretary
PO Box 31965
Lusaka 10101, Zambia
Tel: 1 (260-1) 227-854; 227-855
Fax: 1 (260-1) 220-996; 225-289
E-mail: *zecccjp@zamnet.zm*
Website: *http://www.ccjp.org.zm*

Main Issue Areas
Civic education; Human rights; Social teaching of the churches

Areas Where Organization Works
Southern and eastern Africa, Zambia

Working Languages
English, Local languages

Types of Resources Available
NGO networking; Training

Caucus of Development NGO Networks (CODE-NGO)

Danielo A. Songco, National Coordinator
Social Development Complex
Ateneo de Manila University, Loyola Heights
Quezon City 1108, Philippines
Tel: (63-2) 426-5938
Fax: (63-2) 426-5938
E-mail: *caucus@codewan.com.ph*
Website: *http://www.codewan.com.ph/*

Main Issue Areas
Policy development and advocacy (including development finance, local governance, and democracy); Strengthening organizations; Raising the standards of development work (developing a successor generation of NGO leaders and workers); Strengthening regional (local) member networks; Promoting an NGO certification mechanism; Internal reform initiative

Areas Where Organization Works
Philippines

Working Languages
English, Filipino

Types of Resources Available
NGO networking; Policy/research

Centro al Servicio de la Acción Popular (CESAP)

Armando Janssens, Presidente; Santiago Martínez, Enlace CESAP-ALOP
San Jose del Avila a San Isidro (al lado de la Abadia)
Edif. Grupo Social CESAP
Caracas, Venezuela
Tel: (58-2) 862-3605; 862-8997; 862-7423; 861-6257; 861-6438
Fax: (58-2) 862-7182
E-mail: *cesap@eldish.net*
Website: *http://www.cesap.org*

Main Issue Areas
Civic participation; Economic and social equity

Areas Where Organization Works
Venezuela

Working Languages
Spanish

Types of Resources Available
NGO networking; Policy/research; Technical assistance; Training

CIVICUS: World Alliance for Citizen Participation

Kumi Naidoo, Secretary General and CEO
919 18th Street, NW
3rd Floor
Washington, DC 20006, USA
Tel: 1 (202) 331-8518
Fax: 1 (202) 331-8774
E-mail: *info@civicus.org*
Website: *http://www.civicus.org*

Main Issue Areas
Civil society support

Areas Where Organization Works
Africa, Arab region, Asia/Pacific, Europe, Latin America and the Caribbean, Newly independent states, North America

Working Languages
English

Types of Resources Available
NGO networking; Technical assistance

Regional Offices
Budapest, Colombia, Egypt, Kenya

Colombia Human Rights Network

Not Available—this operates as an electronic network
in Colombia
Tel: Not available
Fax: Not available
E-mail: *mediac@erols.com*
Website: *http://www.igc.org/colhrnet/index.htm*
Main Issue Areas
Human rights
Areas Where Organization Works
Colombia, United States
Working Languages
English, Spanish
Types of Resources Available
NGO networking

Comité de Coordination des Actions des ONG au Mali (CCA/ONG)

Yerefolo Malle, Executive Director
Hippodrome, Rue 339, Porte 119
Bamako BPE 3216, Mali
Tel: (223) 212-112; 218-083
Fax: (223) 212-359; 295-359
E-mail: *cca@malinet.ml*
Website: Not available
Main Issue Areas
Capacity building; Decentralization; Environment; Gender; Information/communication; National development policy making; Population; Sensitizing decision makers and partners
Areas Where Organization Works
Mali
Working Languages
French
Types of Resources Available
NGO networking; Policy/research; Technical assistance; Training

Confederacion de ONGs (CCONG)

Ines Useche de Brill, Director
Avenida Caracas No. 46–47
Bogotá, Colombia
Tel: Not available
Fax: (57-1) 288-5872
E-mail: *confe@colnodo.apc.org*
Website: *http://www.ccong.org.co/ccong.html*

Main Issue Areas
Civil society; Participation; Role of NGOs in decision making
Areas Where Organization Works
Colombia
Working Languages
Spanish
Types of Resources Available
NGO networking; Policy/research; Technical assistance; Training

Coordinadora de la Mujer

Diana Urioste, Executive Secretary
Calle Aspiazu 382, 3rd Floor
(address between 08/6 and 10/20)
La Paz 9136, Bolivia
Tel: (591-2) 335-471; 356-291
Fax: (591-2) 335-471
E-mail: *coordinadora@kolla.net*
Website: Not available
Main Issue Areas
Civic rights; Development; Gender
Areas Where Organization Works
Bolivia
Working Languages
Spanish
Types of Resources Available
NGO networking; Policy/research; Technical assistance; Training

Coordinadora Nacional de Derechos Humanos (CNDDHH)

Sofía Macher, Executive Secretary
Av. Tupac Amaru 2467, Lince
Lima 14, Peru
Tel: (51-1) 441-1533
Fax: (51-1) 442-4827
E-mail: *postmast@cnddhh.org.pe*
Website: *http://www.cnddhh.org.pe*
Main Issue Areas
Human rights (civil, political, economic, social, and cultural)
Areas Where Organization Works
Peru
Working Languages
English, French, Local languages, Spanish
Types of Resources Available
NGO networking; Policy/research; Training

Development Network of Indigenous Voluntary Associations (DENIVA)

Jassy B. Kwesiga, Executive Secretary
490 Makerere Road, Kagugube Zone
Block 9 (near Law Development Centre), PO Box 11224
Kampala, Uganda
Tel: (256-41) 530-575; 531-150
Fax: (256-41) 531-236
E-mail: *denivaug@infocom.co.ug*
Website: Not available

Main Issue Areas
Capacity building; Human rights; Policy research/development

Areas Where Organization Works
Uganda

Working Languages
English

Types of Resources Available
NGO networking; Policy/research; Training

Global Coalition for Africa (GCA)

1750 Pennsylvania Avenue, NW
Suite 1204
Washington, DC 20006, USA
Tel: 1 (202) 458-4338
Fax: 1 (202) 522-3259
E-mail: Not available
Website: *http://www.gca-cma.org/emenu.htm*

Main Issue Areas
Development

Areas Where Organization Works
Africa

Working Languages
English, French

Types of Resources Available
NGO networking

IFEX Clearing House

490 Adelaide Street West
Suite 205
Toronto, Ontario M5V 1T2, Canada
Tel: (416) 703-1638
Fax: (416) 703-7034
E-mail: *ifex@web.net*
Website: *http://www.ifex.org*

Main Issue Areas
Freedom of expression

Areas Where Organization Works
Africa: Congo, Kenya, Namibia, Nigeria, South Africa; *Asia/Pacific:* Fiji, Indonesia, Pakistan, Philippines, Sri Lanka, Thailand; *Eastern Europe/FSU:* Azerbaijan, former Yugoslavia, Russia; *Latin/South America:* Mexico, Paraguay, Peru; *Middle East; North America:* Canada, United States; *Western Europe:* Austria, Belgium, Denmark, France, Greece, the Netherlands, United Kingdom

Working Languages
Arabic, English, French, Spanish

Types of Resources Available
NGO networking

Initiatives for Research, Education and Development in Asia (INASIA)

Sunimal Fernando, General Convenor; John Samuel, Hon. General Co-ordinator
5, Sadicha Apts., Near Sadal Baba
Deccan College Road, Yerawada
Pune, Maharashtra 411 006, India
Tel: (91-20) 669-2659
Fax: (91-20) 669-2659
E-mail: *bodhi@vsnl.com*
Website: Not available

Main Issue Areas
Environment; Human rights; People-centered economic initiatives; People's rights over livelihood resources; Social justice

Areas Where Organization Works
Bangladesh, India, Nepal, Sri Lanka, Thailand

Working Languages
English

Types of Resources Available
NGO networking; Policy/research

Instituto del Tercer Mundo (ITeM)

Roberto Bissio, Executive Director
Jackson 1136
Montevideo 11200, Uruguay
Tel: (598-2) 409-6192
Fax: (598-2) 401-9222
E-mail: *item@chasque.apc.org*
Website: *http://www.item.org.uy*

Main Issue Areas
Communication; Development; Education; Environment; Human rights; Information

Areas Where Organization Works
Caribbean, Latin America

Working Languages
English, Spanish

Types of Resources Available
NGO networking; Policy/research; Training

Instituto Interamericano de Cooperación para la Agricultura (IICA)

Centro Regional Central
1a. Avenida 8-00, Zona 9
Ciudad de Guatemala, C.A. 01009, Guatemala
Tel: (502) 361-0905; 361-0915;
361-0925; 361-0935
Fax: (502) 332-6795
E-mail: *crc@iica.org.gt*
Website: *http://www.iicanet.org/info/iica.asp*

Main Issue Areas
Agricultural health; Natural resources; Politics and trade; Sustainable rural development; Technology

Areas Where Organization Works
Caribbean: Antigua and Barbuda, Bahamas, Barbados, Dominica, Dominican Republic, Grenada, Guyana, Haiti, Jamaica, Saint Kitts and Nevis, Saint Lucia, Saint Vincent and the Grenadines, Suriname, Trinidad and Tobago; *Latin America:* Argentina, Belize, Bolivia, Brazil, Chile, Colombia, Costa Rica, Ecuador, El Salvador, Guatemala, Honduras, Nicaragua, Panama, Paraguay, Peru, Uruguay, Venezuela; *North America:* Canada, Mexico, United States

Working Languages
English, French, Portuguese, Spanish

Types of Resources Available
NGO networking

Inter-African Network for Human Rights and Development (AFRONET)

Muleya Mwananyanda
Church House, 1st Floor, Cairo Road
PO Box 31145
Lusaka, Zambia
Tel: 1 (260-1) 251-813
Fax: 1 (260-1) 251-776
E-mail: *afronet@zamnet.zm*
Website: *http://www.afronet.org.za/afronet.htm*

Main Issue Areas
Democracy; Ethics in government; Human rights; NGO management and governance

Areas Where Organization Works
Africa

Working Languages
English

Types of Resources Available
NGO networking

International Centre for Human Rights and Democratic Development (ICHRDD)

Warren Allmand, President; Iris Almeida, Director of Programmes
63 de Bresoles
Suite 100
Montreal, Quebec H2Y 1V7, Canada
Tel: (514) 283-6073
Fax: (514) 283-3792
E-mail: *ichrdd@ichrdd.ca; ialmeida@ichrdd.ca*
Website: *http://www.ichrdd.ca*

Main Issue Areas
Democratic development; Globalization and human rights; Human rights; Impunity and the rule of law; Rights of indigenous peoples; Women's human rights

Areas Where Organization Works
Africa: Democratic Republic of Congo, Kenya, Nigeria, Rwanda, Togo; *Latin America:* Guatemala, Haiti, Mexico, Peru; *Asia:* Burma (Myanmar), Indonesia, Pakistan, Thailand; *North America:* Canada

Working Languages

English, French, Spanish

Types of Resources Available

Funding/funding information; NGO networking; Policy/research; Technical assistance; Training

International Institute of Rural Reconstruction (IIRR)

Pratima Kale, President

Y. C. James Yen Center

Silang, Cavite 4118, Philippines

Tel: (63-46) 414-2417; 414-2418; 414-2419

Fax: (63-46) 414-2420

E-mail: *execoff@cav.pworld.net.ph*

Website: *http://www.interaction.pair.com/members/ iirr.html*

Main Issue Areas

Agriculture; Community health and nutrition; Environment; Institutional capacity building

Areas Where Organization Works

Africa, Asia, Latin America

Working Languages

English

Types of Resources Available

NGO networking; Policy/research; Technical assistance; Training

Regional Offices

Ecuador, Ethiopia, Kenya, Nepal

Latin American Working Group (LAWG)

110 Maryland Avenue, NE

Box 15, Suite 203

Washington, DC 20002, USA

Tel: 1 (202) 546-7010

Fax: 1 (202) 543-7647

E-mail: *lawg@lawg.org*

Website: *http://www.lawg.org*

Main Issue Areas

Human rights; Peace; Sustainable development

Areas Where Organization Works

Caribbean, Latin America

Working Languages

English, Spanish

Types of Resources Available

NGO networking; Policy/research

LINK—Forum de ONGs

Flavia Gemo, Manager F & A; José Piquitai, Assistant F & A Rua Dr. António José de Almeida 191

Maputo 2187, Mozambique

Tel: (258-1) 496-279; 496-280

Fax: (258-1) 496-304; 496-306; 423-377

E-mail: *forum@link.uem.mz*

Website: Not available

Main Issue Areas

Humanitarian assistance; Development work

Areas Where Organization Works

Mozambique

Working Languages

English; Portuguese

Types of Resources Available

NGO networking; Technical assistance; Training

National AIDS Convention of South Africa (NACOSA-KZN)

Nomaswazi Mlaba, Advocacy Programme Coordinator

Room 61, 20 Saint Andrews Street, NACOSA-KZN

Durban, Kwazulu, Natal 4001, South Africa

Tel: (27-31) 307-1712

Fax: (27-31) 307-1694

E-mail: *nackzn@wn.apc.org*

Website: Not available

Main Issue Areas

Education; Environment; HIV/AIDS treatment and care; Human rights

Areas Where Organization Works

South Africa

Working Languages

English, Zulu

Types of Resources Available

NGO networking; Policy/research; Technical assistance; Training

National CEDAW-Watch Network Center (CEDAW Watch)

Zanaa Jurmed, Director
Post Office 99
Ulaanbatar 13, Mongolia
Tel: (976-1) 328-798
Fax: (976-1) 328-798
E-mail: *mmsa@magicnet.mn*
Website: Not available

Main Issue Areas
Advocacy based on CEDAW Alternative Report; Coordination of CEDAW Alternative Report; Gender and CEDAW training; Monitor government's performance on the National Plan for Action on the Advancement of Women

Areas Where Organization Works
Mongolia

Working Languages
English, Mongolian, Russian

Types of Resources Available
Funding/funding information; NGO networking; Policy/research; Technical assistance; Training

Network of East-West Women (NEWW)

Kristen Hansen and Erin Barclay, Executive Directors; Tatiana Andronova, Director Assistant
1601 Connecticut Ave., NW
Suite 603
Washington, DC 20009, USA
Tel: 1 (202) 265-3585
Fax: 1 (202) 265-3508
E-mail: *eastwest@neww.org*
Website: *http://www.neww.org*

Main Issue Areas
Women's rights

Areas Where Organization Works
More than forty countries in the newly independent states (NIS) and central and eastern Europe (CEE) and countries of the former Soviet Union

Working Languages
English, Russian

Types of Resources Available
NGO networking; Policy/research

Regional Offices
Poland, Russia

NGO Forum on Cambodia

Russell Peterson, Representative
#35, St.178 (CCC Building)
PO Box 2295
Phnom Penh-3, Cambodia
Tel: (855-23) 360-119; 723-242
Fax: (825-23) 723-242
E-mail: *admin@ngo.forum.org.kh*
Website: *http://www.camnet.com.kh/ngoforum/*

Main Issue Areas
Cambodia Information Project; Civil society; Development banks; Development values; Environment; Landmines; Women

Areas Where Organization Works
Cambodia

Working Languages
English, Khmer

Types of Resources Available
NGO networking; Policy/research; Training

NGO Forum on the Asian Development Bank

Takahiro Nanri, International Convenor; Melinda Mae B. Ocampo, Information/Liaison Officer; Norly Grace G. Mercado, Project Officer
Secretariat, c/o LRC-KsK/FoE Phils
2nd Floor Puno Building, #47 Kalayaan Avenue
Diliman, Quezon City 1101, Philippines
Tel: (63-2) 927-9670; 927-9644
Fax: (63-2) 920-7172
E-mail: *ocampom@philonline.com*
Website: Not available

Main Issue Areas
Environmental concerns: agriculture, energy, fisheries, forestry, water; *Policy dialogues:* corruption, development paradigm, governance/accountability, information disclosure, inspection function, poverty reduction, private-sector operations, structural adjustment; *Social concerns:* displacement, education, health, indigenous peoples, labor, population, women

Areas Where Organization Works
Cambodia, Canada, China, France, Hong Kong, India, Japan, New Zealand, Papua New Guinea, Philippines, Sri Lanka

Working Languages
English, Local languages
Types of Resources Available
NGO networking; Policy/research; Technical assistance; Training

Pacific Peoples Partnership (PPP)

Stuart Wulff, Executive Director
1921 Fernwood Road
Victoria, British Columbia V8T 2T6, Canada
Tel: (250) 381-4131
Fax: (250) 388-5258
E-mail: *sppf@sppf.org*
Website: *http://www.sppf.org*
Main Issue Areas
Community development; Environment; Indigenous science/knowledge; Nuclear testing and militarization; Sovereignty and decolonization; Sustainable development
Areas Where Organization Works
South Pacific
Working Languages
English
Types of Resources Available
Funding/funding information; NGO networking; Policy/research; Training

People against Torture—Kenya (PAT)

Beatrice Gathoni Kamau, Chairperson; Wilfred Omariba, Coordinator
52780
Nairobi 02, Kenya
Tel: (254-2) 569-960
Fax: (254-2) 569-960
E-mail: *atn@africaonline.co.ke*
Website: Not available
Main Issue Areas
Civic and paralegal education; Health; Human rights advocacy
Areas Where Organization Works
Kenya
Working Languages
English, Kiswahili, Local languages
Types of Resources Available
NGO networking; Policy/research; Technical assistance; Training

Red Latinoamericana "Mujeres Transformando la Economía"

Maria Adela Rivera, Santander Mieses
Av. Almirante Guisse 1137
Jesus Maria
Lima 11, Peru
Tel: (51-1) 265-8540
Fax: (51-1) 472-0625
E-mail: *postmast@mujecon.org.pe*
Website: Not available
Main Issue Areas
Gender and the economy; Women and debt
Areas Where Organization Works
Latin America
Working Languages
Spanish
Types of Resources Available
NGO networking; Policy/research

Red Latinoamericana y del Caribe sobre la Banca Multilateral de Desarrollo (RedBancos)

Not available
Tel: Not available
Fax: Not available
E-mail: *redbanco@chasque.apc.org*
Website: *http://fp.chasque.net:8081/redbancos/*
Main Issue Areas
Energy; Environment; Multilateral development bank reform
Areas Where Organization Works
Latin America/Caribbean: Jamaica, Mexico, Nicaragua, Peru, Uruguay
Working Languages
English, Spanish
Types of Resources Available
NGO networking; Policy/research

Red Mexicana de Acción Frente al Libre Comercio (REMALC)

Godard #20
Col. Guadalupe Victoria, DF 04120, Mexico
Tel: (52-5) 355-1177
Fax: (52-5) 355-1177
E-mail: *rmalc@laneta.apc.org*
Website: *http://www.rmalc.org.mx*

Main Issue Areas
Debt; Economic alternatives; Environmental protection; Fair trade; Labor rights; Sustainable development
Areas Where Organization Works
Mexico
Working Languages
Spanish
Types of Resources Available
NGO networking

Red Nacional de Organismos Civiles de Derechos Humanos

Secretaria Tecnica
Puebla No. 45, 1er piso
Col. Roma.
DF CP 06700, Mexico
Tel: (52-5) 207-1824
Fax: (52-5) 207-9316
E-mail: *redtdt@redtdt.org.mx*
Website: *http://www.redtdt.org.mx*
Main Issue Areas
Environment; Human rights; Justice; Public and national security
Areas Where Organization Works
Mexico
Working Languages
Spanish
Types of Resources Available
NGO networking

South Asian Coalition on Child Servitude (SACCS)

Kailash Satyarthi, Chairperson
L-6 Kalkaji
Delhi 110019, India
Tel: (91-11) 622-4899; 647-5481
Fax: (91-11) 623-6818; 621-8210
E-mail: *saccs@ndf.vsnl.net.in*
Website: *http://www.globalmarch.org*
Main Issue Areas
Bonded child labor; Child labor; Primary education for all
Areas Where Organization Works
South Asia: Bangladesh, India, Nepal, Pakistan, Sri Lanka

Working Languages
English, Hindi
Types of Resources Available
NGO networking

Uganda Women's Network (UWONET)

Sheila Kawamara, Coordinator
Plot 144, Kiira Road, Kamokya
PO Box 27991
Kampala, Uganda
Tel: (256-41) 543-968
Fax: (256-41) 543968
E-mail: *uwonet@starcom.co.ug*
Website: Not available
Main Issue Areas
Advocacy skills training; Combating gender violence; Economic issues; Increasing women's participation and power; Policy dialogues
Areas Where Organization Works
Uganda
Working Languages
English
Types of Resources Available
NGO networking; Training

Via Campesina (VC)

Nettie Wiebe, North American Coordinator
Secretaria Operativa Internacional
Apartado Postal 3628
Tegucigalpa M.D.C., Honduras, C.A.
Tel: (504) 232-2198
Fax: (504) 235-9915
E-mail: *viacam@gbm.hn*
Website: *http://www.sdnhon.org.hn/via*
Main Issue Areas
Agrarian reform; Alternative agriculture; Biodiversity and genetic resources; Credit and external debt; Food sovereignty; Gender; Human rights; Rural development; Trade and investment
Areas Where Organization Works
Belgium, Brazil, Canada, Cuba, Honduras, India, Poland, Thailand
Working Languages
English, French, Spanish
Types of Resources Available
NGO networking, Policy/research

Washington Office on Africa (WOA)

Leon P. Spencer, Executive Director
212 East Capitol Street
Washington, DC 20003, USA
Tel: 1 (202) 547-7503
Fax: 1 (202) 547-7505
E-mail: *woa@igc.apc.org*
Website: *http://www.woaafrica.org*

Main Issue Areas
Development aid; Economic justice toward and in Africa; International debt; Trade

Areas Where Organization Works
Africa, United States

Working Languages
English

Types of Resources Available
NGO networking; Policy/research; Technical assistance; Training

Women's Eyes on the World Bank— Latin America Chapter

Laura Frade Rubio, Campaign Coordinator
Alternativas de Capacitación y Desarrollo Comunitarión A.C., Calle Chapultepec No. 257 B
Apdo. Postal No. 46
Creel, Chihuahua 33200, Mexico
Tel: (52-1) 456-0078; 456-0134
Fax: (52-1) 456-0078
E-mail: *alcadeco@infosel.net.mx*
Website: Not available

Main Issue Areas
Education; Environment; Health; Macroeconomic issues

Areas Where Organization Works
Argentina, Bolivia, Caribbean, Chile, Colombia, Dominican Republic, El Salvador, Mexico, Panama, Peru, United States, Venezuela

Working Languages
English, Spanish

Types of Resources Available
NGO networking; Policy/research

World Rainforest Movement (WRM)

Ricardo Carrere
Maldonado 1858
Montevideo 11200, Uruguay
Tel: (598-2) 409-6192 ext. 119
Fax: (598-2) 408-0762
E-mail: *wrm@chasque.apc.org*
Website: *http://www.wrm.org.uy*

Main Issue Areas
Biodiversity; Deforestation; Forest people; Rain forest; Sustainable development

Areas Where Organization Works
Africa, Asia, Europe, Latin America, North America, Oceania/Pacific

Working Languages
English, French, Portuguese, Spanish

Types of Resources Available
NGO networking; Policy/research

Regional Offices
United Kingdom

Development-Policy and Research Organizations

Academy for Educational Development (AED)

Support for Analysis and Research in Africa Project
1825 Connecticut Avenue, NW
Washington, DC 20009, USA
Tel: 1 (202) 884-8700
Fax: 1 (202) 884-8447
E-mail: sara@aed.org
Website: http://www.aed.org/sara
Main Issue Areas
Basic education; Health; Population
Areas Where Organization Works
Africa
Working Languages
English
Types of Resources Available
NGO networking; Policy/research

Action for Economic Reform (AER)

Filomeno Sta. Ana, Coordinator
PO Box 242
University of the Philippines Campus
Quezon City, Diliman 1101, Philippines
Tel: (63-2) 927-9686 loc. 270
Fax: (63-2) 927-9686 loc. 270
E-mail: *action@codewan.com.ph*
Website: Not available
Main Issue Areas
Education; Exchange-rate policy; Health; Monetary policy; Poverty reduction; Public expenditures and investments; Social development; Taxation
Areas Where Organization Works
Philippines
Working Languages
English, Filipino
Types of Resources Available
NGO networking; Policy/research

Action Group for Community Development (GADEC)

Aissatou Ndiaye, President
BP 123
Tambacounda, Senegal
Tel: (221) 981-1220
Fax: (221) 981-1720
E-mail: *bachastu@sonatel.senet.net;*
gadectba@telecomplus.sn
Website: Not available
Main Issue Areas
Community-based economic development; Environmental development; Environmental protection; Political development; Poverty alleviation
Areas Where Organization Works
Senegal
Working Languages
French, Wolof
Types of Resources Available
Policy/research; Technical assistance

African Gender Institute (AGI)

Amina Mama, Director; Jennifer Radloff, Communications
University of Cape Town
Private Bag Rondebosch 7701
Cape Town 7701, South Africa
Tel: (27-21) 650-2970
Fax: (27-21) 685-2124
E-mail: *Agi@humanities.uct.ac.za*
Website: *http://www.uct.ac.za/org/agi*
Main Issue Areas
Gender-based violence in education; Gender and women's studies; Information and communications technologies; Institutional transformation
Areas Where Organization Works
Africa

Working Languages

English

Types of Resources Available

NGO networking; Policy/research; Technical assistance; Training

African Science & Technology Exchange (ASTEX)

Alex Tindimubona, BSc, PhD
Plot 6, 2nd Street (The Creations)
PO Box 10382
Kampala, Uganda
Tel: (256-41) 347-563
Fax: (256-41) 34-5597
E-mail: *astex@imul.com; atindi@yahoo.com*
Website: Not available

Main Issue Areas

Environment; Information and communication technology; Natural resource management; Sustainability

Areas Where Organization Works

Africa: Botswana, Guinea, Kenya, Mozambique, Nigeria, Tanzania, Uganda

Working Languages

English, French, Rukiga, Swahili

Types of Resources Available

NGO networking; Policy/research; Technical assistance; Training

Anglican Church of Kenya (ACK)

Harold Mwang'ombe
PO Box 40502
Nairobi, Kenya
Tel: (254-2) 718-801
Fax: (254-2) 711-782
E-mail: *ackjpc@insightkenya.com*
Website: Not available

Main Issue Areas

Human rights protection; Peace; Youth

Areas Where Organization Works

Kenya

Working Languages

English, Kiswahili

Types of Resources Available

Policy/research; Training

Assembly of the Poor (AOP)

Prasittiporn Kan-onsri, Noi, Advisor
99, 3rd Floor
Nakorn Sawan Road
Pom Prab, Bangkok 10100, Thailand
Tel: (66-2) 281-2595; 281-1916
Fax: (66-2) 281-1916
E-mail: *fopthai@asiaaccess.net.th; fopthai@hotmail.com*
Website: Not available

Main Issue Areas

Development policy; Environment; Human rights

Areas Where Organization Works

Thailand

Working Languages

English, Thai

Types of Resources Available

NGO networking; Policy/research

Associates for Change

Florence Butegwa
Suite 11, Plot 29/29 A, Nkrumah Road
PO Box 9627
Kampala, Uganda
Tel: (256-41) 342-230
Fax: (256-41) 250-993
E-mail: *butegwa@starcom.co.ug*
Website: Not available

Main Issue Areas

Gender and development; Participation in governance; Women's rights

Areas Where Organization Works

Kenya, Mali, Mauritius, Mozambique, Switzerland, Tanzania, Uganda, USA, Zimbabwe

Working Languages

English, Kiswahili, Luganda, Runyoro

Types of Resources Available

Policy/research; Technical assistance; Training

Association of African Women for Research & Development (AAWORD)

Yassine Fall, Executive Secretary
SICAP Sacre Coeur I, & 8798
BP 15367 Dakar Fann
Dakar, Senegal
Tel: (221) 824-2053
Fax: (221) 824-2056

E-mail: *aaword@telecomplus.sn*
Website: Not available
Main Issue Areas
Equity; Gender issues and analysis; Governance, democratization, and women's political empowerment; Information technology; Natural-resource management and reproductive health for sustainable human development; Struggle for women's rights and prevention of violence against women; Transformation of economic and social-policy reforms in Africa
Areas Where Organization Works
Botswana, Burkina Faso, Burundi, Cameroon, Cape Verde, Cote d'Ivoire, Egypt, Germany, Ghana, Kenya, Mali, Morocco, Mozambique, Niger, Nigeria, Senegal, South Africa, Swaziland, Tanzania, Tunisia, Uganda, United States, Zambia
Working Languages
English, French
Types of Resources Available
NGO networking; Policy/research

Ateneo Center for Social Policy and Public Affairs (ACSPPA)

Fernando T. Aldaba, Executive Director
Social Development Complex, Ateneo De Manila University, Katipunan Road
Loyola Heights
Quezon City 11008, Philippines
Tel: (63-2) 426-6061; 426-6062
Fax: (63-2) 426-5999
E-mail: *ftaldaba@pusit.admu.edu.ph*
Website: *http://www.ateneo.net/auxiliary/csppa/default.htm*
Main Issue Areas
Economics; Politics and governance; Policy research
Areas Where Organization Works
Philippines
Working Languages
English
Types of Resources Available
Policy/research; Training

Bangladesh Centre for Advanced Studies (BCAS)

Saleemul Huq
House 620, Road 10A
Dhanmondi
Dhaka, Bangladesh
Tel: (880-2) 815-829
Fax: (880-2) 811-344
E-mail: *saleemul@citechco.net*
Website: *http://www.bcas.net*
Main Issue Areas
Environment; Sustainable development
Areas Where Organization Works
Bangladesh, South Asia
Working Languages
Bangla, English
Types of Resources Available
NGO networking; Policy/research; Technical assistance; Training

Bank Information Center (BIC)

Kay Treakle, Executive Director
733 15th Street NW
Suite 1126
Washington, DC 20005, USA
Tel: 1 (202) 737-7752
Fax: 1 (202) 737-1155
E-mail: *info@bicusa.org*
Website: *http://www.bicusa.org*
Main Issue Areas
Multilateral Development Bank reform and accountability; NGO networking in global South and North with social movements, grassroots groups, indigenous peoples, and women's organizations
Areas Where Organization Works
Worldwide
Working Languages
English, Spanish
Types of Resources Available
NGO networking; Policy/research; Technical assistance; Training

Brazilian Institute of Social and Economic Analyses (IBASE)

Candido Grzybowski, Director
Rua Visconde de Ouro Preto, 5-7 andar
Botafogo
Rio de Janeiro, RJ 22250-180, Brazil
Tel: (55-21) 553-0676
Fax: (55-21) 552-8796
E-mail: *ibase@ibase.br*
Website: *http://www.Ibase.br*

Main Issue Areas
Environment; Family forum agriculture; Food security; Globalization and economic policies of multilateral organizations; Human rights; Job creation; Labor policy; Land reform; Local sustainable development; Public budgeting and social accounting

Areas Where Organization Works
Africa, Europe, Latin America, North America

Working Languages
Portuguese

Types of Resources Available
Policy/research

Bread for the World

David Beckmann, President
50 F Street
Suite 500
Washington, DC 20001, USA
Tel: 1 (800) 82-BREAD; 1 (202) 639-9400
Fax: 1 (202) 639-9401
E-mail: *bread@bread.org*
Website: *http://www.bread.org*

Main Issue Areas
Debt relief; Hunger; Poverty

Areas Where Organization Works
Africa, United States

Working Languages
English

Types of Resources Available
Policy/research

Cambodian Human Rights Association (ADHOC)

Thun Saray, President; Chun Sath, Acting Secretary General
Number 1, Street 158 Oukghna Troeung Kang
Beng Raing Daun Penh
Phnom Penh, Cambodia
Tel: (855-23) 218-653
Fax: (855-23) 217-229
E-mail: *adhoc@forum.org.kh*
Website: *http://www.cambodia-hr.org/adhoc/Default.htm*

Main Issue Areas
Human rights education; Human-rights-violation monitoring; Lobbying and advocacy; Women's issues

Areas Where Organization Works
Cambodia

Working Languages
English, Khmer

Types of Resources Available
Policy/research; Technical assistance; Training

Center for Economic and Social Rights – US (CESR)

Roger Normand, Policy Director; Sarah Zaidi, Research Director
25 Ann Street
6th Floor
New York, NY 10038, USA
Tel: 1 (212) 634-3424
Fax: 1 (212) 634-3425
E-mail: *rights@cesr.org*
Website: *http://www.cesr.org*

Main Issue Areas
Economic and social rights, including the right to work, the right to food, the right to health and a healthy environment, the right to housing, and the right to education

Areas Where Organization Works
Latin America, Middle East, United States

Working Languages
Arabic, English, Spanish

Types of Resources Available
NGO networking; Policy/research; Training

Regional Offices
Ecuador, Palestine, United Kingdom

Center of Concern (COC)

James E. Hug, SJ, President
1225 Otis Street, NE
Washington, DC 20017, USA
Tel: 1 (202) 635-2767
Fax: 1 (202) 832-9494
E-mail: *coc@coc.org*
Website: *http://www.coc.org/coc*

Main Issue Areas
Agriculture/food security; Civil society participation; Debt; Global financial architecture; Globalization; Human rights; Labor/workers' rights; Women's issues/rights

Areas Where Organization Works
Worldwide

Working Languages
English

Types of Resources Available
NGO networking; Policy/research; Training

Centre for Southern African Studies (CSAS)

Lisa Thompson
University of Western Cape
Private Bag X17
Bellville, Western Cape 7535, South Africa
Tel: (27-21) 959-3040
Fax: (27-21) 959-3041
E-mail: Not available
Website: Not available

Main Issue Areas
Development; Environment; Gender; Human rights; Migration; Security

Areas Where Organization Works
Southern Africa

Working Languages
English

Types of Resources Available
Policy/research; Training

Centre for Women's Research (CENWOR)

Kamalini Wijayatilake
225/4, Kirula Road
Colombo 05, Sri Lanka
Tel: (94-1) 502-828; 502-153
Fax: (94-1) 502-153; 502-828
E-mail: *cenwor@slt.lk; cenwor@panlanka.net*
Website: *http://www.cenwor.lk*

Main Issue Areas
Decision making; Economic participation; Education and training; Environment; Health; Human rights; Media; Situation of women in armed conflict; Social change; Violence against women

Areas Where Organization Works
South Asia, Southeast Asia, Sri Lanka

Working Languages
English, Sinhala, Tamil

Types of Resources Available
NGO networking; Policy/research; Technical assistance; Training

Centre for Youth and Social Development (CYSD)

Jagadananda, Member-Secretary
E-1, Institutional Area
PO RRL
Bhubaneswar, Orissa 751013, India
Tel: (91-674) 582-377; 583-725; 583-739
Fax: (91-674) 583-726
E-mail: *cysdbbsr@dte.vsnl.net.in*
Website: Not available

Main Issue Areas
Basic services; Development; Food security; Right to resources and livelihood (special focus on women's rights); Sustainable agriculture and entrepreneurship

Areas Where Organization Works
India

Working Languages
English, Oriya

Types of Resources Available
NGO networking; Policy/research; Technical assistance; Training

Centro de Derechos Económicos y Sociales (CDES)

Paulina Garzon, Latin America Program Coordinator; Chris Jochnick, Legal Director
Lizardo García 512 y Diego Almagro
Quito 17-07-8808, Ecuador
Tel: (593-2) 563-517; 529-125
Fax: (593-2) 560-449
E-mail: *cesr@accessinter.net*
Website: Not available

Main Issue Areas
Debt alleviation; Economic, social, and cultural rights; Inequality; Participation; Poverty issues; Right to development; Right to health and a healthy environment

Areas Where Organization Works
Ecuador, Latin America

Working Languages
English, Spanish

Types of Resources Available
NGO networking; Policy/research; Technical assistance; Training

Centro de Estudios de Estado y Sociedad (CEDES)

Ines Gonzalez Bombal, Co-Director of Civil Society and Social Development Areas
Bustamante 27
Buenos Aires 1173, Argentina
Tel: (54-11) 4486-1144; 4486-5204
Fax: (54-11) 4486-5080
E-mail: *socivcedes@arnet.com.ar*
Website: *http://www.clacso.edu.ar/~cedes*

Main Issue Areas
Citizenship; Health; Rights; Social development

Areas Where Organization Works
Argentina, Latin America

Working Languages
English, Spanish

Types of Resources Available
NGO networking; Policy/research; Technical assistance; Training

Centro de Estudios de la Realidad Económica y Social (CERES)

Roberto Laserna, Director
Pasaje Warisata No 1
Av. Circunvalación y Potosí
Cochabamba, Bolivia
Tel: (591-4) 293-149
Fax: (591-4) 293-145
E-mail: *ceres@albatros.cnb.net*
Website: *http://www.cnb.net/~ceres*

Main Issue Areas
Drug policy; Environment; Local development and decentralization; Social action and democratic participation

Areas Where Organization Works
Bolivia

Working Languages
English, Quechua, Spanish

Types of Resources Available
Policy/research; Training

Centro de Estudios Jurídicos e Investigación Social (CEJIS)

Alejandro Almaraz Ossio
Alfredo Jordan #79
Santa Cruz, Bolivia
Tel: (591-3) 532-714; 533-809
Fax: (591-3) 535-169
E-mail: *cejis@scbbs-bo.com*
Website: Not available

Main Issue Areas
Human rights; Indigenous and peasant rights

Areas Where Organization Works
Bolivia

Working Languages
Spanish

Types of Resources Available
NGO networking; Policy/research; Technical assistance; Training

Centro de Estudios Legales y Sociales (CELS)

Martin Abregu, Executive Director
Rodriguez Pena 286
Piso 1
Buenos Aires 1020, Argentina
Tel: (54-11) 4371-9968; 4371-3790
Fax: (54-11) 4375-2075
E-mail: *cels@cels.org.ar*
Website: Not available
Main Issue Areas
Human rights
Areas Where Organization Works
Argentina
Working Languages
Spanish
Types of Resources Available
NGO networking; Policy/research; Technical assistance; Training

Centro de Estudios Nacionales de Desarrollo Alternativo (CENDA)

Hugo Fazio, Executive Director; Jacobo Schatan, Director Economics/Environmental Department
Vergara 578
Santiago, Chile
Tel: (562) 688-3760; 688-6763
Fax: (562) 688-3761
E-mail: *cenda@cep.cl*
Website: Not available
Main Issue Areas
Environmental problems and their relationships to economic policies; Elaboration of a database with information on major economic and financial issues (since 1992); Income distribution and poverty; Labor and social security policies; Macroeconomic developments
Areas Where Organization Works
Chile
Working Languages
Spanish
Types of Resources Available
NGO networking; Policy/research; Technical assistance; Training

Centro de Estudios para el Desarrollo Laboral y Agrario (CEDLA)

Javier Gomez Aguilar, Executive Director
Avenue Jaimes Freire Number 2940, Esquina Munoz Cornejo
La Paz, Bolivia
Tel: (591-2) 412-429; 413-175; 413-223
Fax: (591-2) 414-625
E-mail: *cedla@caoba.entelnet.bo*
Website: *http://www.cedla.com*
Main Issue Areas
Labor; Productive development; Social development
Areas Where Organization Works
Bolivia
Working Languages
Spanish
Types of Resources Available
NGO networking; Policy/research; Technical assistance; Training

Centro de Investigación Económica para el Caribe (CIECA)

Jefrey Lizardo, Executive Director; Miosotis Rivas Pena, Vice Executive Director
Calle Osvaldo Baez 5 Gazcue
Santo Domingo 3117, Dominican Republic
Tel: (809) 686-8696; 685-1266
Fax: (809) 686-8687
E-mail: *cieca@codetel.net.do; cieca@aacr.net*
Website: *http://www.serex.gov.do/cieca*
Main Issue Areas
Integration; Public expenditure; Social expenditure (health, education); Sustainable development; Trade and civil society issues
Areas Where Organization Works
Caribbean, Central America
Working Languages
English, Spanish
Types of Resources Available
NGO networking; Policy/research; Training

Centro Latinoamericano de Economía Humana (CLAEH)

Pablo Cayota, Director
Zelmar Michelini 1220
Montevideo 11100, Uruguay
Tel: (598-2) 900-7194
Fax: (598-2) 902-1127
E-mail: *info@claeh.org.uy*
Website: *http://www.claeh.org.uy*

Main Issue Areas

Economic, health, and social policy; Environment; Local development; Small-enterprise development

Areas Where Organization Works

Argentina, El Salvador, Paraguay, Uruguay

Working Languages

Spanish

Types of Resources Available

Policy/research; Technical assistance; Training

Centro Peruano de Estudios Sociales (CEPES)

Fernando Eguren, Presidente; Juan Rheineck, Director Ejecutiva
Ave. Salaverry No. 818
Lima 11, Peru
Tel: (51-1) 433-6610
Fax: (51-1) 433-1744
E-mail: *cepes@cepes.org.pe; jrheinec@cepes.org.pe*
Website: *http://www.cepes.org.pe*

Main Issue Areas

Agrarian issues

Areas Where Organization Works

Peru

Working Languages

Quechua, Spanish

Types of Resources Available

Policy/research; Technical assistance

Christian Aid (CAID)

Sebele Abera, Team Administrator Policy Teams; Clare Moberly, Capacity Building Officer
PO Box 100
London SE1 7RT, United Kingdom
Tel: (44-20) 7620-4444
Fax: (44-20) 7620-0719
E-mail: *sabera@christian-aid.org; cmoberly@christian-aid.org*
Website: *http://www.christian-aid.org.uk*

Main Issue Areas

Disaster mitigation and preparedness; Environmental sustainability; Food security and sustainable agriculture; Health and education; Human rights; Improved position of women; Microenterprise and credit; Southern advocacy; Trade

Areas Where Organization Works

Sixty countries worldwide

Working Languages

English, French, Portuguese, Spanish

Types of Resources Available

Funding/funding information; NGO networking; Policy/research; Technical assistance

Regional Offices

Burundi, Colombia, Ethiopia, Guatemala, Haiti, Horn of Africa, Mali, Kenya, Pakistan, Rwanda, Zimbabwe

Co-operative for Research and Education (CORE)

Phiroshaw Camay
62 Marshall Street
PO Box 42440
Fordsburg 2033, South Africa
Tel: (27-11) 836-9942
Fax: (27-11) 836-9944
E-mail: Not available
Website: Not available

Main Issue Areas

Capacity building; Information dissemination; Training

Areas Where Organization Works

South Africa, southern Africa

Working Languages

English

Types of Resources Available

Policy/research; Training

Coordination of NGOs and Cooperatives (CONGCOOP)

Helmer Velasquez, Coordinator Generale
2a Calle 16-60, Zona 4 Mixco
Edificio Atanasio Tsul, 2do. Nivel
Residencias Valle del Sol, Guatemala
Tel: (502) 592-0966; 591-4638
Fax: (502) 593-4779
E-mail: *congcoop@guate.net*
Website: *http://www.rds.org.gt/congcoop*

Main Issue Areas
Agrarian and campesino issues; International aid;
Land tenancy; Reinsertion and migration; Uprooted
peoples

Areas Where Organization Works
Guatemala

Working Languages
Spanish

Types of Resources Available
NGO networking; Policy/research

Corporación Viva la Ciudadanía

Jorge Arturo Bernal, Director
Calle 54 No. 10-81
7th Floor
Santafe de Bogotá, Cundinamarca, Colombia
Tel: (57-1) 348-0781; 348-0782; 249-6303
Fax: (57-1) 212-0467
E-mail: *vciudada@colnodo.apc.org*
Website: *http://colnodo.apc.org/home/viva*

Main Issue Areas
Citizenship; Democracy; Education; Employment;
Health

Areas Where Organization Works
Colombia

Working Languages
Spanish

Types of Resources Available
NGO networking; Policy/research; Technical
assistance; Training

Development Innovations and Networks (IRED)

Rudo Chitiga
3 Rue de Varembe Case 116
Geneva 20 GE 1211, Switzerland
Tel: (41-22) 734-1716
Fax: (41-22) 740-0011
E-mail: Not available
Website: *http://www.ired.org*

Main Issue Areas
Democratization; Economic empowerment; Food
security; Local participatory governance

Areas Where Organization Works
Africa: Botswana, Congo, Malawi, Mozambique,
Nigeria, South Africa, Uganda, Zimbabwe; *Europe;*
Latin America: El Salvador

Working Languages
English, French

Types of Resources Available
NGO networking; Policy/research; Training

Regional Offices
Bangladesh, Democratic Republic of Congo, El
Salvador, Italy, Nigeria, South Africa, West Africa,
Zimbabwe

Environment and Development Action in the Third World (ENDA TM)

Muthoni M. Muriu, Programme Officer
7 Rue Kleber
BP 3370, Dakar, Senegal
Tel: (221) 821-7037; 823-5754
Fax: (221) 822-2695
E-mail: *syspro2@enda.sn*
Website: *http://www.enda.sn/*

Main Issue Areas
Alternative consumption patterns; Alternative
energy technologies; Communication for development; Environment; Gender; Health; Human
rights; Innovative agricultural systems; International
policy advocacy; Microcredit; Participatory training; Urban management; Youth

Areas Where Organization Works
Africa: Benin, Ethiopia, Guinea Bissau, Madagas-
car, Morocco, Senegal, Tunisia, Zimbabwe; *Asia:*
India, Vietnam; *Latin America:* Bolivia, Colombia,
Dominican Republic, Nicaragua

Working Languages
English, French, Spanish
Types of Resources Available
Funding/funding information; NGO networking; Policy/research; Technical assistance; Training

Equidad de Género: Ciudadanía, Familia y Trabajo

Patricia Mercado, Executive Director; Elena Tapia, Chairperson
Isabela Católica 921, Colonia Postal
Mexico City, DF 03410, Mexico
Tel: (52-5) 696-9024
Fax: (52-5) 696-9025
E-mail: *equidad@laneta.apc.org*
Website: Not available
Main Issue Areas
Family; Human rights; Labor
Areas Where Organization Works
Latin America, Mexico
Working Languages
English, Spanish
Types of Resources Available
NGO networking; Policy/research; Training

Esquel Group Foundation

Kenneth H. Cole, President
1003 K St. NW
Suite 800
Washington, DC 20001-4425, USA
Tel: 1 (202) 347-1796
Fax: 1 (202) 347-1797
E-mail: *info@esquel.org*
Website: *http://www.esquel.org*
Main Issue Areas
Civil society
Areas Where Organization Works
Latin America
Working Languages
English, Portuguese, Spanish
Types of Resources Available
NGO networking; Policy/research
Regional Offices
Esquel Group Foundation is a network with branches in Argentina, Bolivia, Brazil, Chile, Ecuador, Peru, and Uruguay

Ethiopian Women Lawyers Association (EWLA)

Meaza Ashenafi, Executive Director
Woreda 21 Kebele 04, House Number 538/19
PO Box 13760
Addis Ababa, Addis Ababa, Ethiopia
Tel: (251-1) 531-867; 531-701; 519-148
Fax: (251-1) 531-818
E-mail: *ewla@telecom.net.et*
Website: Not available
Main Issue Areas
Women's rights
Areas Where Organization Works
Ethiopia
Working Languages
Amharic, English
Types of Resources Available
Policy/research; Technical assistance; Training

Focus on the Global South

c/o Cusri
Wisit Prachuabmoh Bldg., Chulalongkorn University
Phythai Road
Bangkok 10330, Thailand
Tel: (66-2) 218-7363; 218-7364; 218-7365
Fax: (66-2) 255-9976
E-mail: *admin@focusweb.org*
Website: *http://www.focusweb.org*
Main Issue Areas
Civil society; Democracy; Human security; Market economy; Natural resources; Social inequality and economic development; Trade and investment liberalization
Areas Where Organization Works
Bangladesh, India, Lao PDR, Philippines, Thailand
Working Languages
English
Types of Resources Available
NGO networking; Policy/research; Technical assistance; Training

Food First/Institute for Food and Development Policy

Anuradha Mittal, Policy Director
398 60th Street
Oakland, CA 94618, USA
Tel: 1 (510) 654-4400
Fax: 1 (510) 654-4551
E-mail: *foodfirst@foodfirst.org*
Website: *http://www.foodfirst.org*

Main Issue Areas
Economic and social justice; Environment; Human rights (with focus on economic and social human rights); Hunger; Poverty; Sustainable agriculture

Areas Where Organization Works
Worldwide

Working Languages
English, Hindi, Spanish

Types of Resources Available
Policy/research; Training

Fundación Antonio Núñez Jiménez de la Naturaleza y el Hombre

Lic. Lilliana Núñez Velis, Vicepresidente
Calle 5ta B & 6614 e/66 y 70 Miramar
La Habana, Ciudad de la Habana 11600, Cuba
Tel: (537) 242-985
Fax: (537) 240-438
E-mail: *funat@artsoft.cult.cu*
Website: Not available

Main Issue Areas
Cultural services; Environmental programs; Publication of works of Antonio Núñez Jiménez

Areas Where Organization Works
Cuba

Working Languages
Spanish

Types of Resources Available
Policy/research; Technical assistance; Training

Fundación Antonio Restrepo Barco (FRB)

Angela Maria Robledog, Director of Social Division;
Marco Antonio Cruz, Executive Director
Carrera 7 U 73-55
Piso 12
Santa Fe de Bogotá, Colombia
Tel: (91) 312-1511
Fax: (91) 312-1182
E-mail: *frbarco@latino.net.co*
Website: Not available

Main Issue Areas
Children's rights; Education; Health; Welfare; Youth

Areas Where Organization Works
Colombia

Working Languages
Spanish

Types of Resources Available
Policy/research; Training

Fundación Arias para la Paz y el Progreso Humano – Centro para la Participación Organizada (ARIAS)

Fernando Duran-Ayanegui, Executive Director;
Paula Antezana, Director of Center for Organized Participation
Apartado 8-6410-1000
San Jose, Costa Rica
Tel: (506) 255-2955
Fax: (506) 255-2244
E-mail: *cpo@arias.or.cr*
Website: *http://www.arias.or.cr/fundarias/cpo/*

Main Issue Areas
Civil society; Democratic consolidation

Areas Where Organization Works
Belize, Costa Rica, El Salvador, Guatemala, Honduras, Nicaragua, Panama

Working Languages
Spanish

Types of Resources Available
NGO networking; Policy/research; Technical assistance; Training

Fundación Nacional para el Desarrollo (FUNDE)

Alberto Enriquez, Director of Local/Regional Development
15 Calle Pte 4362, Colonia Escalón
San Salvador, Apartado Postal 1774, Centro de Gobierno El Salvador
Tel: (503) 264-4938; 264-4939; 264-4940; 264-4941
Fax: (503) 263-4537
E-mail: *funde@es.com.sv*
Website: Not available

Main Issue Areas

Agrarian policies; Central American integration; Community economic development; Decentralization; Local and regional development; Structural adjustment; Sustainable development

Areas Where Organization Works

Cuba, El Salvador, Guatemala, Honduras, Mexico, Nicaragua

Working Languages

Spanish

Types of Resources Available

NGO networking, Policy/research, Technical assistance, Training

General Union of Disabled Palestinians (GUDP)

Nizar Basalat, Chairman; Ziad Amro, Executive Manager
PO Box 31
Ramallah, West Bank
Tel: (972-2) 295-9097; 298-6815
Fax: (972-2) 295-9097
E-mail: *Gudpal@palnet.com*
Website: Not available

Main Issue Areas

Advocacy; Empowerment; Legislation; Public awareness; Rights for people with disabilities

Areas Where Organization Works

Palestine

Working Languages

Arabic, English

Types of Resources Available

NGO networking; Policy/research; Technical assistance; Training

Global Exchange

Medea Benjamin, Executive Director
2017 Mission Street
Suite 303
San Francisco, CA 94110, USA
Tel: 1 (415) 255-7296
Fax: 1 (415) 255-7498
E-mail: *info@globalexchange.org*
Website: *http://www.globalexchange.org*

Main Issue Areas

Community organizing and self-help; Corporate accountability; Fair trade; Macroeconomic issues

Areas Where Organization Works

Latin America/Caribbean: Brazil, Colombia, Cuba, Guatemala, Mexico

Working Languages

English

Types of Resources Available

Funding/funding information; NGO networking; Policy/research; Technical assistance; Training

Grupo Mujer y Ajuste Estructural

Maria Adela Rivera-Santander Mieses
Av. Almirante Guisse 1137
Jesus Maria
Lima 11, Peru
Tel: (51-1) 265-8540; 470-0625
Fax: (51-1) 472-0625
E-mail: *postmast@mujecon.org.pe*
Website: *http://micasa.yupi.com/churru*

Main Issue Areas

Economic, social, and cultural rights; Gender and the economy; Structural adjustment; Women and the economy

Areas Where Organization Works

Peru, Latin America

Working Languages

Spanish

Types of Resources Available

NGO networking; Policy/research; Technical assistance; Training

Indian Social Institute

Ambrose Pinto, SJ, Director
10 Institutional Area
Lodi Road
New Delhi 110 003, India
Tel: (91-11) 462-2379; 461-1745; 462-5015
Fax: (91-11) 469-0660
E-mail: *p_ambrose@hotmail.com*
Website: Not available

Main Issue Areas
Globalization; Human rights; Marginalized groups;
Women's issues

Areas Where Organization Works
India

Working Languages
English, Hindi

Types of Resources Available
NGO networking; Policy/research; Training

Institute for Agriculture and Trade Policy (IATP)

Mark Ritchie, President; Dale Wiefoff, Communications; Kristin Dawkins, Program Director for Trade and Ag.; Bill Vorley, Program Director for Food and Ag.; Phil Guillery, Program Director for Forestry
2105 First Avenue South
Minneapolis, MN 55404, USA
Tel: 1 (612) 870-0453
Fax: 1 (612) 870-4846
E-mail: *iatp@iatp.org*
Website: *http://www.iatp.org*

Main Issue Areas
Biotechnology; Digital-organizing group; Environment and agriculture; Food and agriculture; Forestry; Healthcare without harm; Human rights; Trade and agriculture

Areas Where Organization Works
Europe, Latin America, North America, Southeast Asia

Working Languages
English, French, Spanish

Types of Resources Available
NGO networking; Policy/research; Technical assistance; Training

Institute for Democracy in South Africa (Idasa)

Warren Krafchik
6 Spin Street, Church Square
PO Box 1739
Cape Town 8001, South Africa
Tel: (27-21) 461-2559
Fax: (27-21) 461-2589
E-mail: *info@idasa.org.za*
Website: *http://www.idasa.org.za*

Main Issue Areas
Development of Democracy and civil society

Areas Where Organization Works
South Africa

Working Languages
English

Types of Resources Available
NGO networking; Policy/research; Training

Institute for Development Policy Analysis and Advocacy at Proshika (IDPAA)

Mahbubul Karim, Shah Newaz
I/1 Ga, Section-2
Mirpur Dhaka 1216, Bangladesh
Tel: (880-2) 805-945; 805-946
Fax: (880-2) 805-811
E-mail: *idpaa@proshika.bdonline.com*
Website: *http://www.proshika.org*

Main Issue Areas
Democratization and governance; Employment and income generation; Gender relations; Human-resource development; Poverty eradication; Sustainable management

Areas Where Organization Works
Bangladesh; Asia

Working Languages
Bangla, English

Types of Resources Available
Policy/research; Technical assistance; Training

Institute for Education Democracy (IED)

Marren Akasta-Bukachi
Adams Arcade, Off Elgeyo Marakwet Road
PO Box 43874
Nairobi, Kenya
Tel: (254-2) 566-871; 576-566
Fax: (254-2) 576-567
E-mail: *ied@nbnet.co.ke*
Website: Not available

Main Issue Areas
Civic education; Elections observation; Human rights; Voters' rights

Areas Where Organization Works
Kenya

Working Languages
English, Kiswahili

Types of Resources Available
NGO networking; Policy/research; Training

Institute for Popular Democracy (IPD)

Joel Rocamora
45 Matimtiman Street
Teachers Village
Quezon City, Diliman 1101, Philippines
Tel: (63-2) 921-8409; 434-8859
Fax: (63-2) 926-2893
E-mail: *joelroc@popdem.org*
Website: *http://www.popdem.org*

Main Issue Areas
Agrarian reform; Constitutional reform; Democratization; Electoral mapping; Local financing; Local governance

Areas Where Organization Works
Hong Kong, Indonesia, Netherlands, Philippines, South Africa, Thailand

Working Languages
English, Filipino, Indonesian, Malay

Types of Resources Available
NGO networking; Policy/research; Technical assistance; Training

Institute for Social Transformation (INSIST)

Mansour Fakih
Sekip Blok T-7/ 38
Yogyakarta 55281, Indonesia
Tel: (62-274) 561-847
Fax: (62-274) 561-847
E-mail: *insist@yogya.wasantara.net.id*
Website: Not available

Main Issue Areas
Democratization; Environment; Gender; Human rights

Areas Where Organization Works
Indonesia

Working Languages
English, Indonesian

Types of Resources Available
Policy/research; Training

Institute of Politics and Governance (IPG)

Adrian Cristobal Jr., Chairperson
70 Matahimik Street
Teacher's Village, Diliman
Quezon City, Philippines
Tel: (63-2) 436-2041
Fax: (63-2) 436-1942
E-mail: Not available
Website: *http://handel.pacific/net/ph/~ipg/*

Main Issue Areas
Electoral participation and reform; Governance; Political analysis and studies

Areas Where Organization Works
Philippines

Working Languages
English

Types of Resources Available
Policy/research; Technical assistance

Instituto de Defensa Legal (IDL)

Ernesto de la Jara Basombrio, Director; Carlos
Basombrio Iglesias, Sub-director
Jiron Toribio Polo 248
Lima 18, Peru
Tel: (51-1) 441-0192; 441-6128; 442-4037;
221-1237
Fax: (51-1) 441-0192; 441-6128; 442-4037;
221-1237
E-mail: *ernesto@idl.org.pe; carlosb@idl.org.pe*
Website: Not available
Main Issue Areas
Civil and political rights; Civilian-military rela-
tionships; Democracy; Discrimination; Freedom of
speech; Human rights; Impunity; Justice
Areas Where Organization Works
Peru
Working Languages
Spanish
Types of Resources Available
NGO networking; Policy/research; Technical
assistance; Training

Instituto de Investigación y Desarrollo – Universidad Centroamericana (NITLAPAN)

Arturo Grigsby, Director; Eva Margarita Sánchez,
Project Director
Campus Universitario, UCA
Universidad Centroamericana
Managua, Nicaragua
Tel: (505-2) 781-343; 781-344
Fax: (505-2) 670-436
E-mail: *grigsby@ns.uca.edu.ni*
Website: Not available
Main Issue Areas
Economic development; Policy research and devel-
opment
Areas Where Organization Works
Nicaragua
Working Languages
Spanish
Types of Resources Available
Policy/research; Technical assistance

Instituto Venezolano de Estudios Sociales y Políticos (INVESP)

Francine Jacome, Director
Qta. Marielvi, Avenida Gil Fortoul con Calle Simon
Planas
Santa Monica
Caracas, DF 1080, Venezuela
Tel: (58-2) 661-2933
Fax: (58-2) 662-1655; 661-5196
E-mail: *Invesp@cantv.net*
Website: Not available
Main Issue Areas
Civil society; Democracy and governance; Global-
ization; Integration; Regionalization
Areas Where Organization Works
Caribbean, Latin America
Working Languages
English, Spanish
Types of Resources Available
Policy/research; Training

International Center for Research on Women (ICRW)

Cheryl Morden
1717 Massachusetts Avenue, NW
Suite 302
Washington, DC 20036, USA
Tel: 1 (202) 797-0007
Fax: 1 (202) 797-0020
E-mail: *cmorden@icrw.org*
Website: *http://www.icrw.org*
Main Issue Areas
Women's issues in developing and transition
countries
Areas Where Organization Works
Africa, Asia, Europe, Latin America/Caribbean,
Middle East
Working Languages
English
Types of Resources Available
Funding/funding information; Policy/research;
Technical assistance

International Development Research Centre (IDRC)

PO Box 8500
Ottawa, Ontario K1G 3H9, Canada
Tel: (613) 236-6163
Fax: (613) 238-7230
E-mail: *info@idrc.ca*
Website: *http://www.idrc.org*

Main Issue Areas

Environment; Gender; Information and communication technology; Knowledge systems; Social and economic equity

Areas Where Organization Works

Africa, Asia, eastern Europe, Latin America

Working Languages

English, French

Types of Resources Available

Funding/funding information; Policy/research; Technical assistance; Training

Regional Offices

Egypt, India, Kenya, Singapore, Senegal, South Africa, Ukraine, Uruguay

International Water and Sanitation Centre (IRC)

Dick de Jong, Advocacy Manager
PO Box 2869
Delft 2601, CW, Netherlands
Tel: (31-015) 219-2961
Fax: (31-015) 219-0955
E-mail: *jong@irc.nl*
Website: *http://www.irc.nl*

Main Issue Areas

Community-based technologies; Community water-resource management; Gender awareness; Hygiene promotion; Information management; Monitoring and evaluation; Operation and maintenance; Participation and community management; Resource-center development; Water and environmental sanitation

Areas Where Organization Works

Africa, Asia, Latin America

Working Languages

English, French, Portuguese, Spanish

Types of Resources Available

NGO networking; Policy/research; Technical assistance; Training

Land Tenure Center (LTC)

Harvey M. Jacobs, Director
University of Wisconsin—Madison
1357 University Avenue
Madison, WI 53715, USA
Tel: 1 (608) 262-3657
Fax: 1 (608) 262-2141
E-mail: *hmjacobs@facstaff.wisc.edu*
Website: *http://www.wisc.edu/ltc*

Main Issue Areas

Agrarian reform; Credit; Labor; Land reform; Land registration and titling; Land tenure; Property rights; Resource sustainability; Social and cultural conflicts; Water; Women's rights

Areas Where Organization Works

Africa, Central America, central Asia, eastern Europe, Russia, South America, United States

Working Languages

English, French, Portuguese, Russian, Spanish

Types of Resources Available

Policy/research; Technical assistance; Training

Legal Research and Resource Center for Human Rights (LRRC)

Amir Salem
7 Al-Higaz Street
Heliopolis
Cairo, Roxi, Egypt
Tel: (20-2) 2452-0977
Fax: (20-2) 259-6622
E-mail: *lrrc@brainy1.ie-eg.com; lrrc.geo@yahoo.com*
Website: *http://www.geocities.com/~lrrc*

Main Issue Areas

Censorship and freedom of expression; Informal human rights education; Law-reform campaigns; Women's and gender issues

Areas Where Organization Works

Egypt, Ethiopia, South Africa

Working Languages

Arabic, English

Types of Resources Available

NGO networking; Policy/research; Training

Legal Resources Foundation (LRF)

Eileen Sawyer, National Director; Miss DE Barron, National Administrator
PO Box 918
Harare, Zimbabwe
Tel: (263-4) 728-212; 728-211
Fax: (263-4) 728-213
E-mail: *lrfhre@mail.pci.co.zw*
Website: *http://www.icon.co.zw/lrf*
Main Issue Areas
Human rights; Legal education
Areas Where Organization Works
Zimbabwe
Working Languages
English, Ndebele, Shona
Types of Resources Available
NGO networking; Policy/research; Technical assistance; Training

Lembaga Studi dan Advokasi Masyarakat (ELSAM)

Abdul Hakim G Nusantara, Board Director; Ifdhal Kasim, Executive Director
Jl Siaga II No 31 Pejaten Barat
Pasar Minggu
Jakarta 12510, Indonesia
Tel: (62-21) 797-2662, 7919-2564
Fax: (62-21) 7919-2519
E-mail: *elsam@nusa.or.id; advokasi@rad.net.id*
Website: Not available
Main Issue Areas
Democracy; Human rights; Indigenous people; Urban poor; Women's issues
Areas Where Organization Works
Indonesia
Working Languages
English, Indonesian
Types of Resources Available
NGO networking; Policy/research; Technical assistance; Training

Media Institute, The (MI)

David Makali, Director
Cargen House, 2nd Floor, Harambee Avenue
PO Box 46356
Nairobi, Kenya
Tel: (254-2) 217-082; 217-209
Fax: (254-2) 219-768
E-mail: *mediainst@iconnect.co.ke*
Website: *http://www.kenyanews.com/about-mi.html*
Main Issue Areas
Democracy; Freedom of the press; Human rights
Areas Where Organization Works
Kenya
Working Languages
English
Types of Resources Available
Policy/research

National Centre for Advocacy Studies (NCAS)

John Samuel, Executive Director
Flat 2, Santosh Apartment
Sheelavihar Colony, Paud Road
Pune, Maharashtra 411 038, India
Tel: (91-20) 346-460; 235-543; 235-694
Fax: (91-20) 346-460
E-mail: *ncas@pn2.vsnl.net.in*
Website: *http://education.vsnl.com/ncas*
Main Issue Areas
Environment; Gender rights; Governance and policies; Human rights; Laborers; Rights of tribals and dalits; Social action and advocacy
Areas Where Organization Works
India, Nepal
Working Languages
English, Hindi, Marathi
Types of Resources Available
NGO networking; Policy/research; Training

National Land Committee (NLC)

Zakes Hlatshwayo
PO Box 30944
185 Smit Street, Auckland House Building, 9th
Floor, West Wing
Braamfountein, Gauteng 2017, South Africa
Tel: (27-11) 403-3803
Fax: (27-11) 339 6315
E-mail: *nlc@wn.apc.org*
Website: *http://wn.apc.org./nlc/*
Main Issue Areas
Environment; Human rights; Land reform; Rural
development
Areas Where Organization Works
South Africa, southern Africa (working in all
fourteen SADC countries)
Working Languages
Afrikaans, English, Pedi, Setho, Xloja, Zulu
Types of Resources Available
NGO networking; Policy/research; Training

Oxfam Canada

Rieky Stuart, Executive Director
294 Albert Street
Suite 300
Ottawa, Ontario K1P 6E6, Canada
Tel: (613) 237-5236
Fax: (613) 237-0524
E-mail: *enquire@oxfam.ca*
Website: *http://www.oxfam.ca*
Main Issue Areas
Democracy; Development finance; Food security;
Gender; Health; Youth
Areas Where Organization Works
Africa: Djibouti, Ethiopia, Mozambique, Namibia,
Somalia, South Africa, Sudan, Zimbabwe; *Latin
America and Caribbean:* Chile, Cuba, El Salvador,
Guatemala, Guyana, Mexico, Nicaragua, Peru,
Saint Vincent and the Grenadines
Working Languages
English, Spanish

Types of Resources Available
Funding/funding information; NGO networking;
Policy/research; Technical assistance; Training
Regional Offices
Offices in Canada: Halifax, Saskatoon, St. John's,
Toronto, Vancouver; *Overseas offices:* Addis Ababa,
Durban, Havana, Managua, Maputo, Windhoek

Oxfam International

Phil Twyford, Director of Advocacy
733 15th Street, NW
Washington, DC 20005, USA
Tel: 1 (202) 783-3331
Fax: 1 (202) 783-5547
E-mail: *advocacy@oxfaminternational.org*
Website: *http://www.oxfaminternational.org*
Main Issue Areas
Capacity building; Debt relief; Education; Equity;
Literacy; Networking; Peace; Reconstruction
Areas Where Organization Works
Worldwide
Working Languages
English
Types of Resources Available
NGO networking; Policy/research

Philippine International Forum (PIF)

Judith Guinto-Agnoletto, Coordinator
146, Matimtiman Street, Sikatuna Village
PO Box AC502, 1135 Cubao
Sikatuna Village, Quezon City, Philippines
Tel: (63-2) 434-4415
Fax: (63-2) 426-1580
E-mail: *pif@wtouch.net*
Website: Not available
Main Issue Areas
Development issues; Politics
Areas Where Organization Works
Philippines
Working Languages
Cebuano, Dutch, English, Filipino, German
Types of Resources Available
NGO networking; Policy/research

Philippine Legislators Committee on Population and Development Foundation, Inc. (PLCPD)

Teresa Aquino-Oreta, Co-Chair; Luwathati R. Antonino, Co-Chair; Roberto M. Ador, Executive Director
611 Northwing
House of Representatives
Quezon City 1126, Philippines
Tel: (63-2) 931-5354; 931-5001 (local 7430)
Fax: (63-2) 931-5354; 931-5001 (local 7430)
E-mail: *plcpd@skyinet.net*
Website: *http://www.infoteam.com/nonprofit/plcpd*

Main Issue Areas
Human and social development; Population; Sustainable development

Areas Where Organization Works
Philippines

Working Languages
English, Filipino

Types of Resources Available
Policy/research; Training

Philippine Peasant Institute (PPI)

Romeo Royandoyan, Executive Director
Room 339, PSSC Building, Commonwealth Avenue, Diliman
PO Box PACS 19
Quezon City, MM, Philippines
Tel: (63-2) 922-9621; 929-6211 loc. 314/339
Fax: (63-2) 924-3767
E-mail: *ppi@qinet.net*
Website: *http://www.ppi.org.ph*

Main Issue Areas
Agrarian reform and rural development; Peasant sector

Areas Where Organization Works
Philippines

Working Languages
English, Filipino

Types of Resources Available
NGO networking; Policy/research; Technical assistance; Training

Polis Instituto de Estudos, Formação e Assessoria em Politicas Sociais

Nelson Saule Junior
Rua Conego Eugenio Leite Number 433 Pinheiros
São Paulo, São Paulo, CEP 05414010, Brazil
Tel: (55-11) 853-6877
Fax: (55-11) 852-5050
E-mail: *polis@ax.apc.org*
Website: Not available

Main Issue Areas
Citizenship; Cultural policies; Cultural sustainability; Democratic management of the cities; Democratization of local power; Environment; Food security; Good governance; Human rights; Local economic development; Popular participation; Quality of life; Urban planning; Urban reform

Areas Where Organization Works
Brazil

Working Languages
Portuguese

Types of Resources Available
NGO networking; Policy/research; Technical assistance; Training

Poverty Reduction Forum

Muriel Mafico
Institute of Development Studies, University of Zimbabwe
MP 167 Mt. Pleasant; Box 880
Harare, Zimbabwe
Tel: (263-4) 333-341; 333-342
Fax: (263-4) 333-345
E-mail: *ids@ids1.uz.zw*
Website: Not available

Main Issue Areas
Poverty reduction

Areas Where Organization Works
Zimbabwe

Working Languages
English, local languages

Types of Resources Available
Funding/funding information; NGO networking; Policy/research; Technical assistance; Training

Programme for Development Research (PRODDER)

Yzette Terreblanche, Development Information Officer; David Barnard, Coordinator
Private Bag X41
Pretoria, Gauteng 0001, South Africa
Tel: (27-12) 302-2999
Fax: (27-12) 302-2497
E-mail: *YzetteT@.hsrc.ac.za*
Website: *http://www.hsrc.ac.za/prodder.html*
Main Issue Areas
Development research
Areas Where Organization Works
Southern Africa
Working Languages
English
Types of Resources Available
NGO networking; Policy/research

Society for the Promotion of Education and Research (SPEAR)

Diane Haylock, Executive Director
38 Freetown Road
PO Box 1766
Belize City, Belize
Tel: (501-2) 31-668
Fax: (501-2) 32-367
E-mail: *spear@btl.net*
Website: *http://www.spear.org.bz*
Main Issue Areas
Advocacy; Community empowerment; Political education; Public information
Areas Where Organization Works
Belize
Working Languages
English, Spanish
Types of Resources Available
NGO networking; Policy/research; Technical assistance; Training

Southeast Asia Regional Institute for Community Education (SEARICE)

Elenita C. Dano, Executive Director
Unit 331 Eagle Court Condominium
26 Matalino Street, Central District, Diliman
Quezon City 1100, Philippines
Tel: (63-2) 433-7182; 924-7544
Fax: (63-2) 922-6710
E-mail: *searice@philonlinecom.ph*
Website: Not available
Main Issue Areas
Biodiversity conservation; Environment; Plant genetic-resources conservation
Areas Where Organization Works
Indonesia, Lao PDR, Malaysia, Philippines, Thailand, Vietnam
Working Languages
English, Filipino
Types of Resources Available
NGO networking; Policy/research; Technical assistance; Training

Southern African Research and Documentation Centre (SARDC)

Phyllis Johnson, Executive Director
13 Bath Road
Belgravia
Harare, Zimbabwe
Tel: (263-4) 738-694; 738-695; 738-696
Fax: (263-4) 738-693
E-mail: *sardc@sardc.net*
Main Issue Areas
Conflict; Democracy and governance; Emergency response; Environment; Gender; Regional economic development
Areas Where Organization Works
Mozambique, Zimbabwe, southern Africa
Working Languages
English, Portuguese
Types of Resources Available
NGO networking; Policy/research; Training

Sustainable Development Policy Institute (SDPI)

Shahrukh Rafi Khan, Executive Director; Saba Gul Khattak, Deputy Director
PO Box 2342
3 UN Boulevard Diplomatic Enclave-1, G-5
Islamabad, Pakistan
Tel: (92-51) 278-134
Fax: (92-51) 278-135
E-mail: *main@sdpi.org*
Website: *http://www.sdpi.org*

Main Issue Areas
Economy; Environment; Governance; Human development; Policy advising; Sustainable development

Areas Where Organization Works
Pakistan

Working Languages
English

Types of Resources Available
NGO networking; Policy/research; Training

Third World Network (TWN)

228 Macalister Road
Penang 10400, Malaysia
Tel: (60-4) 226-6728; 226-6159
Fax: (60-4) 226-4505
E-mail: *twn@igc.apc.org; twnet@po.jaring.my*
Website: *http://www.twnside.org.sg*

Main Issue Areas
Agriculture; Economic and social development issues; Environment; Health; Humanitarianism; Trade

Areas Where Organization Works
Africa, Asia-Pacific, Latin America, western Europe

Working Languages
English

Types of Resources Available
NGO networking; Policy/research

Regional Offices
Delhi, India; Montevideo, Uruguay; Geneva; London; and Accra, Ghana

Unitarian Universalist Service Committee (UUSC)

Valora Washington, Executive Director
130 Prospect Street
Cambridge, MA 02139, USA
Tel: 1 (617) 868-6600, ext. 226
Fax: 1 (617) 492-9824
E-mail: *bgleason@uusc.org*
Website: *http://www.uusc.org*

Main Issue Areas
Community development; Emergency relief; Indigenous peoples; Human rights; Reproductive health; Women's rights

Areas Where Organization Works
Africa, Asia, Caribbean, Latin America

Working Languages
English

Types of Resources Available
Funding/funding information; Policy/research; Technical assistance; Training

United States Institute of Peace (USIP)

Patrick Cronin
1200 17th Street, NW
Suite 200
Washington, DC 20036-3011, USA
Tel: 1 (202) 429-3891
Fax: 1 (202) 429-6063
E-mail: Not available
Website: *http://www.usip.org*

Main Issue Areas
Conflict resolution

Areas Where Organization Works
Worldwide

Working Languages
English

Types of Resources Available
Policy/research; Training

Unnayan Shahojogy Team (UST)

Khorshed Alam, Network, Advocacy & Policy Lobbying Department
House No. 739, Road No. 9, Baitul Aman Housing Society
Adabor, Shamoli
Dhaka 1207, Bangladesh
Tel: (880-2) 324-431; 329-503; 912-8347

Fax: (880-2) 816-758
E-mail: *ust@citechco.net*
Website: Not available
Main Issue Areas
Advocacy for people-centered development; Children's rights; Community health; Development training and education; Grassroots organization; Income generation and employment; Local organization building, training, and education; Productive income generation and employment; Social and legal awareness; Sustainable environmental development
Areas Where Organization Works
Bangladesh
Working Languages
Bangla, English
Types of Resources Available
NGO networking; Policy/research; Technical assistance; Training

Upland NGO Assistance Committee (UNAC)

Ramon Derige, Executive Officer
59 C. Salvador Street
Loyola Heights
Quezon City 1108, Philippines
Tel: (63-2) 436-0706
Fax: (63-2) 436-0706
E-mail: *unac@skyinet.net*
Website: Not available
Main Issue Areas
Environment; Indigenous peoples' rights; Natural-resource-management planning; Upland marketing and agroforestry
Areas Where Organization Works
Philippines
Working Languages
English, Filipino
Types of Resources Available
Policy/research; Technical assistance

Washington Office on Latin America (WOLA)

Susan Peacock, Associate for the Advocacy Training Project
1630 Connecticut Avenue, NW
Suite 2
Washington, DC 20009, USA
Tel: 1 (202) 797-2171
Fax: 1 (202) 797-2172
E-mail: *speacock@wola.org*
Website: *http://www.wola.org*
Main Issue Areas
Economic and trade policies; Human rights; Police reform; US anti-narcotics policy; Women's rights
Areas Where Organization Works
Belize, Costa Rica, El Salvador, Guatemala, Honduras, Mexico, Nicaragua, Panama
Working Languages
English, Spanish
Types of Resources Available
Policy/research; Technical assistance; Training
Regional Offices
El Salvador, Guatemala

Women in Law and Development in Africa (WiLDAF)

Lynette Matimba, Communications Manager
2nd Floor Zambia House, Union Avenue
PO Box 4622
Harare, Zimbabwe
Tel: (263-4) 752-105; 751-189
Fax: (263-4) 781-886
E-mail: *wildaf@wildaf.org.zw*
Website: *http://www.wildaf.org.zw*
Main Issue Areas
Women's rights
Areas Where Organization Works
East Africa, southern Africa, West Africa
Working Languages
English, French
Types of Resources Available
NGO networking; Policy/research; Technical assistance; Training

ZERO Environment Regional Organization (ZERO)

Dorothy Manuel, Acting Director
158 Fife Avenue, Greenwood Park
PO Box 5338
Harare, Zimbabwe
Tel: (263-4) 791-333; 732-858;
700-030; 720-405
Fax: (263-4) 732-858
E-mail: *zero@internet.co.zw*
Website: Not available

Main Issue Areas
Capacity building; Enhancing land-reform strategies; Land reform; Networking and advocacy on land reform in South Africa

Areas Where Organization Works
Botswana, Mozambique, Namibia, South Africa, Swaziland, Tanzania, Zambia, Zimbabwe

Working Languages
English, Shona

Types of Resources Available
NGO networking; Policy/research; Training

Funding Organizations

Abya Yala Fund (AYF)

Nilo Cayuqueo, Co-Director
PO Box 28386
Oakland, California 94604, USA
Tel: (510) 763-6553
Fax: (510) 763-6588
E-mail: *abyayala@earthlink.net*
Website: *http://www.nativeweb.org/abyayala/ayf*

Priority Areas for Funding
Education; Environment; Gender; Health; Indigenous culture recuperation; Indigenous human rights

Regions in Which Projects Are Funded
Central America, South America

Working Languages
English, Spanish

Types of Resources Available
Funding/funding information; NGO networking; Technical assistance; Training

Ashoka—Innovators for the Public

1700 North Moore Street
Suite 1920
Arlington, VA 22209, USA
Tel: 1 (703) 527-8300
Fax: 1 (703) 527-8383
E-mail: *info@ashoka.org*
Website: *http://www.ashoka.org*

Priority Areas for Funding
Education; Environment

Regions in Which Projects Are Funded
Thirty-three developing countries in Africa, Asia, central Europe, and Latin America

Working Languages
English, Portuguese, Spanish

Types of Resources Available
Funding/funding information; Technical assistance

Regional Offices
Argentina, Brazil, Bolivia, Mexico

Aspen Institute Nonprofit Sector Research Fund

David Williams, Program Coordinator
One Dupont Circle, NW
Suite 700
Washington, DC 20036, USA
Tel: 1 (202) 736-5800
Fax: 1 (202) 293-0525
E-mail: *nsrf@aspeninst.org*
Website: *http://www.aspeninst.org/nppf/nppf-nsrf.asp*

Priority Areas for Funding
International study of peace and conflict-resolution activities

Regions in Which Projects Are Funded
Worldwide

Working Languages
English

Types of Resources Available
Funding/funding information; NGO networking; Policy/research; Training

Barbara Delano Foundation (BDF)

Peter Knights, Program Director
450 Pacific Avenue
2nd Floor
San Francisco, CA 94133, USA
Tel: 1 (415) 834-1758
Fax: 1 (415) 834-1759
E-mail: *bdf@igc.org*
Website: *http://www.bdfoundation.org*

Priority Areas for Funding
Protection of endangered species and protected areas

Regions in Which Projects Are Funded
Africa, Asia, Latin America, Russia

Working Languages
English

Types of Resources Available
Funding/funding information; Technical assistance

Charles Stewart Mott Foundation

Office of Proposal Entry
1200 Mott Foundation Building
Flint, Michigan 48502-1851, USA
Tel: 1 (810) 238-5651
Fax: 1 (810) 766-1753
E-mail: *infocenter@mott.org*
Website: *http://www.mott.org*

Priority Areas for Funding
Civil society; Environment; International finance
and trade

Regions in Which Projects Are Funded
Central/eastern Europe, Latin America, Russia,
South Africa, United States

Working Languages
English

Types of Resources Available
Funding/funding information

Cottonwood Foundation

Paul Moss, Executive Director
PO Box 10803
White Bear Lake, MN 55110, USA
Tel: 1 (651) 426-8797
Fax: 1 (651) 426-0320
E-mail: *cottonwood@igc.org*
Website: *http://www.pressenter.com/~cottonwd*

Priority Areas for Funding
Cultural diversity; Empowerment; Environment;
Volunteers

Regions in Which Projects Are Funded
Worldwide

Working Languages
English

Types of Resources Available
Funding/funding information

Development and Peace

10 St. Mary Street
Suite 420
Toronto, Ontario M4Y 1P9, Canada
Tel: (416) 922-1592; (800) 494-1401
Fax: (416) 922-0957
E-mail: *ccodp@devp.org*
Website: *http://www.devp.org*

Priority Areas for Funding
Agrarian reform; Cooperative movements; Educa-
tion and job opportunities; Environment; Housing;
Women's rights

Regions in Which Projects Are Funded
Africa, Asia, Middle East, Latin America/Caribbean

Working Languages
English, French, Spanish

Types of Resources Available
Funding/funding information

Dorothea Haus Ross Foundation

Wayne Cook, Executive Director
1036 Monroe Avenue
Rochester, NY 14620, USA
Tel: (716) 473-6006
Fax: (716) 473-6007
E-mail: *dhrossfnd@excelonline.com*
Website: Not available

Priority Areas for Funding
Relieving suffering among children who are sick,
handicapped, injured, disfigured, orphaned, or
otherwise vulnerable, through programs of direct
service or medical research; we do not fund day-to-
day operations, individuals, conferences, day care,
or public education; we encourage organizations
applying to us from foreign countries to call our
office for further instructions.

Regions in Which Projects Are Funded
Worldwide

Working Languages
English

Types of Resources Available
Funding/funding information; Policy/research;
Technical assistance

Ford Foundation

Secretary
320 East 43rd Street
New York, NY 10017, USA
Tel: (212) 573-5000
Fax: (212) 351-3677
E-mail: *office-secretary@fordfound.org*
Website: *http://www.fordfound.org*
Priority Areas for Funding
There are three main priority areas (1) Asset Building
and Community Development, (2) Peace and Social
Justice, and (3) Education, Media, Arts, and Culture.
(Grant-seekers are encouraged to look carefully at
Ford's Annual Report and Grant Guidelines at
www.fordfound.org)
Regions in Which Projects Are Funded
Africa, Asia, Latin America, Middle East, Russia
Working Languages
English
Types of Resources Available
Funding/funding information
Regional Offices
Egypt, Brazil, Chile, China, India, Indonesia,
Mexico, Namibia, Nigeria, Philippines, Kenya,
Russia, South Africa, Vietnam

Funding Exchange

Angela Moreano
666 Broadway
Suite 500
New York, New York 10012, USA
Tel: 1 (212) 529-5300
Fax: 1 (212) 982-9272
E-mail: *fexexc@aol.com*
Website: *http://www.fex.org*
Priority Areas for Funding
Civil and human rights; Cultural and media
activism; Environmental and economic justice;
International solidarity with progressive movements
Regions in Which Projects Are Funded
El Salvador, Guatemala, Haiti, Israel, Mexico,
Nicaragua, South Africa, USA, West Bank
Working Languages
English, Spanish
Types of Resources Available
Funding/funding information; Technical assistance

Fundación Corona

Guillermo Carvajalino, Director
Calle 100 No.8 A55 Torre C Piso 9
Santafe de Bogotá, Colombia
Tel: (57-1) 610-5555
Fax: (57-1) 610-7620
E-mail: *fundacion@corona.com.co*
Website: *http://www.fundacioncorona.org.co*
Priority Areas for Funding
Farmers' and indigenous organizations working in
defense of the environment; Indigenous organiza-
tions (Ayllus); Judicial defense
Regions in Which Projects Are Funded
Colombia
Working Languages
English, Spanish
Types of Resources Available
Policy/research; Technical assistance; Training

Global Fund for Women (GFW)

Laila Machuria
425 Sherman Avenue
Suite 300
Palo Alto, CA 94306-1823, USA
Tel: (650) 853-8305
Fax: (650) 328-0384
E-mail: *gfw@globalfundforwomen.org*
Website: *http://www.globalfundforwomen.org*
Priority Areas for Funding
Women's health; social, economic, and political
rights; grants range from $500 to $15,000
Regions in Which Projects Are Funded
Global South, only outside the United States
Working Languages
English
Types of Resources Available
Funding/funding information; NGO networking

Grassroots International

Kevin Murray, Executive Director
179 Boylston Street
4th Floor
Jamaica Plain, MA 02130, USA
Tel: 1 (617) 524-1400
Fax: 1 (617) 524-5525
E-mail: *kmurray@igc.org*
Website: *http://www.grassrootsonline.org*
Priority Areas for Funding
Democratic development; Human rights
Regions in Which Projects Are Funded
Brazil, Eritrea, Haiti, Mexico, Palestine
Working Languages
Arabic, English, Haitian Creole, Portuguese, Spanish
Types of Resources Available
Funding/funding information; NGO networking;
Policy/research

Humanist Institute for Cooperation with Developing Countries (HIVOS)

HIVOS Head Office
Raamweg 16
The Hague, 2596 HL, Netherlands
Tel: (31-70) 376-6500
Fax: (31-70) 362-4600
E-mail: *hivos@hivos.nl*
Website: *http://www.dds.nl/~hivos/*
Priority Areas for Funding
Human rights; Pluralism; Democratization
Regions in Which Projects Are Funded
Support is concentrated in a limited number of regions and countries; in 1998, financial support went to over 750 organizations in more than thirty countries in Central and South America, the Caribbean, southern and east Africa, and South, Southeast, and central Asia
Working Languages
Dutch, English
Types of Resources Available
Funding/funding information; Technical assistance
Regional Offices
Costa Rica, India, Zimbabwe

Institute of International Education—International Human Rights Internship Program (IHRIP)

Ann Blyberg, Executive Director
1400 K Street, NW, Suite 650
Washington, DC 20005, USA
Tel: 1 (202) 326-7725
Fax: 1 (202) 326-7763
E-mail: *ihrip@iie.org*
Website: *http://www.iie.org*
Priority Areas for Funding
Human rights
Regions in Which Projects Are Funded
Africa, Asia, east central Europe, Latin America/Caribbean, Middle East, the former Soviet Republics
Working Languages
English
Types of Resources Available
Funding/funding information; Training

Intermon (Oxfam in Spain)

Ignasi Carreras, Executive Director
Roger De Illuria, 15
Barcelona 08010, Spain
Tel: (34-93) 482-0700
Fax: (34-93) 482-0707
E-mail: *Intermon@intermon.org*
Website: *http://www.intermon.org*
Priority Areas for Funding
Development cooperation (strengthening of civil society, improving access to basic services, production initiatives, both rural and urban); Development education; Empowering women; Fair trade; Policy analysis and lobbying
Regions in Which Projects Are Funded
Africa, India, Latin America
Working Languages
Catalan, English, French, Portuguese, Spanish
Types of Resources Available
Funding/funding information; NGO networking;
Policy/research

Japan International Volunteer Center (JVC)

Michiya Kumaoka
6 F Maruko Building
1-20-6 Higashiueno, Taito-ku
Tokyo 110, Japan
Tel: (81-3) 3834-2388
Fax: (81-3) 3835-0519
E-mail: *jvc@jca.ax.apc.org*
Website: *http://www.jca.ax.apc.org/jvc/english/index-e.html*

Priority Areas for Funding

Agriculture; Education; Emergency-relief assistance; Environment; Health; Human rights advocacy; Rural development; Small-scale industrial development; Urban development; Vocational training; Women's issues

Regions in Which Projects Are Funded

Africa: Ethiopia, South Africa; *Asia:* Cambodia, Lao PDR, Thailand, Vietnam; *Middle East:* Palestine; *Latin America:* Bolivia

Working Languages

English, Japanese

Types of Resources Available

Funding/funding information; NGO networking; Training

John D. and Catherine T. MacArthur Foundation

Ray Boyer, Program Officer
140 Dearborn Street
Suite 1100
Chicago, IL 60603, USA
Tel: 1 (312) 726-8000
Fax: 1 (312) 917-0334
E-mail: *4answers@macfdn.org*
Website: *http://www.macfdn.org*

Priority Areas for Funding

Arms reduction and security; Ecosystem conservation; New partnerships; Population; US interests

Regions in Which Projects Are Funded

Worldwide, with some emphasis on Brazil, India, Mexico, Nigeria, and the former Soviet Union

Working Languages

English

Types of Resources Available

Funding/funding information

NOVIB

Greetje Lubbi, Director Advocacy & Press
PO Box 30919
Den Haag, 2500 GX, Netherlands
Tel: (31-70) 342-1777
Fax: (31-70) 361-4461
E-mail: *Greetje.Lubbi@novib.nl*
Website: *http://www.novib.nl/*

Priority Areas for Funding

Advocacy with specific attention to human rights; Basic social services; Environment and gender issues; Strengthening civil society

Regions in Which Projects Are Funded

Africa, Asia, eastern Europe, Latin America

Working Languages

Dutch, English, French, Portuguese, Spanish

Types of Resources Available

Funding/funding information; Policy/research

Open Society/Soros Foundation

400 West 59th Street
New York, NY 10019, USA
Tel: (212) 548-0600
Fax: (212) 548-4679
E-mail: *osnews@sorosny.org*
Website: *http://www.soros.org*

Priority Areas for Funding

Art and culture; Education; Health—medicine; Human rights

Regions in Which Projects Are Funded

Central and eastern Europe and the former Soviet Union, but also in other parts of the world going through a transition to democracy

Working Languages

English

Regional Offices

Hungary

Oxfam America

Raymond Offenheiser, President
26 West Street
Boston, MA 02111, USA
Tel: 1 (800) 77-OXFAM
Fax: 1 (617) 728-2594
E-mail: *info@oxfamamerica.org*
Website: *http://www.oxfamamerica.org*

Priority Areas for Funding
Community-based resource management; Access
to financial resources; Promoting democratic
participation in civil society; Cultural integrity;
Gender equity; Human rights; in 1999, Oxfam
America made more than two hundred grants to
partner organizations in more than thirty countries;
the average annual grant size is $28,000.

Regions in Which Projects Are Funded
Africa, Asia, Caribbean, Latin America, United
States

Working Languages
English, French, local languages, Portuguese,
Spanish

Types of Resources Available
Funding/funding information; NGO networking;
Policy/research; Technical assistance

Regional Offices
Cambodia, El Salvador, Peru, Senegal, Zimbabwe

Oxfam Australia/Community Aid Abroad (CAA)

Jeremy Hobbs, Executive Director; Andrew Hewett,
Director Public Education and Policy
156 George Street
Fitzroy, Victoria 3065, Australia
Tel: (61-3) 9289-9444
Fax: (61-3) 9419-5318
E-mail: *Enquire@caa.org.au*
Website: *http://www.caa.org.au*

Priority Areas for Funding
Advocacy; Environment; Gender; Human rights;
Indigenous peoples; Natural resources; grant size
ranges from AU$2,000 to AU$250,000

Regions in Which Projects Are Funded
Africa: Ethiopia, Mozambique, Somaliland, South
Africa, Sudan, Zimbabwe; *Asia/Pacific:* Australia,
Bangladesh, Cambodia, China, East Timor, India,
Indonesia, Lao PDR, Papua New Guinea, Sri Lanka,
Solomon Islands, Vanuatu, Vietnam; *Latin America:*
Guatemala, Honduras, Mexico

Working Languages
Chinese, English, Indonesian, Portuguese, Spanish

Types of Resources Available
Funding/funding information; NGO networking;
Policy/research

Oxfam Belgium (Oxfam-Solidarité/Oxfam-Solidariteit)

Stefan Declerq, Executive Director
39 Rue du Conseil
Bruxelles 1050, Belgium
Tel: (32-2) 501-6700
Fax: (32-2) 514-2813
E-mail: *oxfamsol@oxfamsol.be*
Website: *http://www.oxfamsol.be*

Priority Areas for Funding
Food security; Basic services; Socioeconomic and
people's rights

Regions in Which Projects Are Funded
South and Central America and Caribbean; Africa
(southern, central, western, Horn, and Sahara);
Southeast Asia; Palestine and Lebanon

Working Languages
Dutch, French

Types of Resources Available
Funding/funding information; NGO networking;
Policy/research; Technical assistance

Regional Offices
Burkina Faso, Caribbean, El Salvador, Mozambique,
Nicaragua, Vietnam

Oxfam Great Britain

David Bryer, Executive Director
274 Banbury Road
Oxford OX27DZ, United Kingdom
Tel: (44-1865) 311-311
Fax: (44-1865) 312-600
E-mail: *oxfam@oxfam.org.uk*
Website: *http://www.oxfam.org.uk*

Priority Areas for Funding
Education; Gender equity; Health; Humanitarian
and emergency relief work; Livelihoods; Strengthening civil society and good governance

Regions in Which Projects Are Funded
Africa, Asia, eastern Europe, Latin America

Working Languages
English, French, Spanish

Types of Resources Available
Funding/funding information

Regional Offices
Oxfam GB has a number of regional offices in
Africa, Asia, eastern Europe, and Latin America;
contact the main office for further information.

Oxfam Hong Kong

Chong Chanyau, Director
9/F Breakgrough Centre
91 Woosung Street, Jordan, Kwoloon
Hong Kong, China
Tel: (852) 2520-2525
Fax: (852) 2527-6307
E-mail: *info@oxfam.org.hk*
Website: *http://www.oxfam.org.hk*

Priority Areas for Funding
Advocacy/research; Agriculture; Education; Emergency relief, rehabilitation, and disaster prevention; Health and clean water; Income generation; Multisector programs; Partner support/capacity building; Training and counseling

Regions in Which Projects Are Funded
China, Indochina: Vietnam, Lao PDR

Working Languages
Chinese, English

Types of Resources Available
Funding/funding information; Technical assistance; Training

Oxfam Ireland

Brian Scott, Executive Director
9 Burgh Quay
Dublin 2, Ireland
Tel: (353-1) 672-7662
Fax: (353-1) 672-7680
E-mail: *Oxireland@oxfam.ie*
Website: *http://www.oxfamireland.org*

Priority Areas for Funding
Capacity building to local civil society groups; Conflict resolution; Environmental health; Food security; Housing; Human rights with a particular focus on children, youth, women, and refugee and indigenous communities; Income generation; Water supply. Criteria for funding include: existing Oxfam Ireland programming involvement in country or district; high level of need in the country or district; link between programming and Oxfam Ireland advocacy work; potential to develop strong links between donor groups and projects

Regions in Which Projects Are Funded
Africa, Asia, Central America, Middle East, Pacific

Working Languages
English

Types of Resources Available
Funding/funding information; NGO networking; Policy/research

Oxfam New Zealand

Terri-Ann Scorer, Executive Director
PO Box 68357
Auckland 1032, New Zealand
Tel: (0-800) 400-666; (64-9) 355-6500
Fax: (64-9) 355-6505
E-mail: *Oxfam@oxfam.org.nz*
Website: *http://www.oxfam.org.nz*

Priority Areas for Funding
Agriculture; Education; Environment; Health; Human rights; Hunger and poverty relief; Women's rights

Regions in Which Projects Are Funded
Africa, Asia, Latin America, Pacific

Working Languages
English

Types of Resources Available
Funding/funding information

Oxfam Quebec

Pierre Veronneau, Executive Director; Mohammed Chikhaoui, Advocacy Manager
2330 Rue Notre-Dame Ouest
Bureau 200
Montreal, Quebec H3J 2Y2, Canada
Tel: (514) 937-1614
Fax: (514) 937-9452
E-mail: *info@oxfam.qc.ca*
Website: *http://www.oxfam.qc.ca*

Priority Areas for Funding
Capacity development; Education; Environment; Fair trade; Food security; Health; Human rights; Labor rights; Training; Women in development

Regions in Which Projects Are Funded
Africa, Asia, Caribbean, Latin America, Middle East

Working Languages
English, French

Types of Resources Available
Funding/funding information; NGO networking; Policy/research

Presbyterian Committee on the Self-Development of People

Sherri Hunter
100 Witherspoon Street
Louisville, Kentucky 40202-1396, USA
Tel: 1 (502) 569-5782; 569-5783
Fax: 1 (502) 569-8963
E-mail: Not available
Website: *http://www.pcusa.org/wmd/sdop*

Priority Areas for Funding
Empowerment and self-reliance of poor people

Regions in Which Projects Are Funded
Worldwide

Working Languages
English

Types of Resources Available
Funding/funding information

Public Welfare Foundation

Larry Kressley, Executive Director
2600 Virginia Avenue, NW
Washington, DC 20037, USA
Tel: 1 (202) 965-1800
Fax: 1 (202) 625-1348
E-mail: *general@publicwelfare.org*
Website: *http://www.publicwelfare.org*

Priority Areas for Funding
Community economic development; Criminal justice; Participation; The elderly; Environment; Global security; Health; Human rights; Reproductive health; Youth. Grant size range: $500–$250,000, average size $25,000–$50,000

Regions in Which Projects Are Funded
Africa, Caribbean, Central America

Working Languages
English

Types of Resources Available
Funding/funding information

Rockefeller Brothers Fund

Benjamin R. Shutes Jr., Secretary
437 Madison Avenue
New York, NY 1022-7001, USA
Tel: (212) 812-4200
Fax: (212) 812-4299
E-mail: *rock@rbf.org*
Website: *http://www.rbf.org*

Priority Areas for Funding
Arts; Culture; Education; Global security; Health; Nonprofit sector; Sustainable resource use. Grant size range: $1,000 to $250,000; average size: $25,000 to $200,000.

Regions in Which Projects Are Funded
Central and eastern Europe, North America, South Africa

Working Languages
English

Types of Resources Available
Funding/funding information

Ryan Foundation International

Felix Ryan
8 W. Mada Street, Srinagar Colony, Saidapet
Madras 600 015, India
Tel: (91-44) 235-1993
Fax: (91-44) 491-0746
E-mail: Not available
Website: Not available

Priority Areas for Funding
Environment; Health; Rural Energy; Water

Regions in Which Projects Are Funded
Worldwide, especially Africa and Asia

Working Languages
English

Types of Resources Available
Funding/funding information; NGO networking; Policy/research; Technical assistance; Training

Tides Foundation

Adam Davis, Communications Associate
PO Box 29903
San Francisco, CA 94129-0903, USA
Tel: 1 (415) 561-6400
Fax: 1 (415) 561-6401
E-mail: Not available
Website: *http://www.tides.org*

Priority Areas for Funding

Civic participation; Economic development; Economic justice; Environment; Environmental justice; Gay, lesbian, bisexual, and transgender issues; HIV/AIDS; Media and arts; Native American communities; Spirituality; Women's issues/reproductive health; Youth programs. The Central American Relief Fund: the Tides Foundation facilitated this fund to support organizations working on reconstruction and relief in the wake of Hurricane Mitch. Tides donors contributed over $275,000.

Regions in Which Projects Are Funded

Africa, Asia, Latin America, North America

Working Languages

English, Spanish

Types of Resources Available

Funding/funding information; NGO networking; Policy/research; Technical assistance; Training

W. Alton Jones Foundation

JP Myers, Director
232 East High Street
Charlottesville, VA 22902, USA
Tel: (804) 295-2134
Fax: (804) 295-1648
E-mail: *earth@wajones.org*
Website: *http://www.wajones.org*

Priority Areas for Funding

Maintaining ecological biodiversity; Nuclear non-proliferation; Renewable energy. Grants size range: $1,000 to $200,000; average size: $5,000 to $100,000

Regions in Which Projects Are Funded

Worldwide

Working Languages

English

Types of Resources Available

Funding/funding information; Policy/research; Technical assistance; Training

Women's Peacepower Foundation, Inc. (WPPF)

Candice Warmke, President and CEO; Diane McCabe, Director of Development
PO Box 2056
Dade City, FL 33526, USA
Tel: 1 (352) 567-9116
Fax: 1 (352) 567-0809
E-mail: *peace@peacepower.org*
Website: *http://www.peacepower.org*

Priority Areas for Funding

Domestic violence; Peace; Women's human rights; Women's issues

Regions in Which Projects Are Funded

United States; Countries where organizations must have a 501(c)(3) fiscal sponsor

Working Languages

English

Types of Resources Available

Funding/funding information; Technical assistance

World Bank Small Grants Program

Michael MacHarg, Coordinator
Social Development Department, MC 5-172
The World Bank, 1818 H Street, NW
Washington, DC 20433, USA
Tel: (202) 473-8637
Fax: (202) 522-3247
E-mail: *smallgrantsprgm@worldbank.org*
Website: *http://www.worldbank.org*

Priority Areas for Funding

International development; enhancing local and national dialogue on development

Regions in Which Projects Are Funded

Worldwide

Working Languages

English

Types of Resources Available

Funding/funding information; NGO networking; Technical assistance

Selected References and Further Reading

Part I: Reflections on Advocacy

Popular Education

Freire, Paulo. *Education for Critical Consciousness.* Trans. Myra B. Ramos. New York: Continuum, 1973.

Freire, Paulo. *Pedagogy of the Oppressed: 20th Anniversary Edition.* Trans. Myra B. Ramos. New York: Continuum, 1992.

Nadeau, Denise. *Counting Our Victories: Popular Education and Organizing.* 1996. Contact Repeal the Deal, c/o Canadian Auto Workers, 326 12th Street, 2nd Floor, New Westminster, BC, V3M 4H6, Canada; tel. (604) 522-7911; fax (604) 522-8975.

Public Argument, Public Judgment, and Free Spaces

Briand, Michael K. *Practical Politics: Five Principles for a Community That Works.* Champaign: University of Illinois Press, 1999.

Cohen, David. "Effective and Lasting Ways to Defeat Poverty." *Research in Social Policy* 5 (Stamford, Conn.: JAI Press) (1997).

Cohen, David. "Elements of Advocacy." Washington, D.C.: Advocacy Institute, 1995. Unpublished.

Evans, Sara M., and Harry C. Boyte. *Free Spaces: The Sources of Democratic Change in America.* Chicago: University of Chicago Press, 1992.

Fellman, Gordon. *Rambo and the Dalai Lama: The Compulsion to Win and Its Threat to Human Survival.* Albany: State University of New York Press, 1998.

Friedman, Lawrence M. *The Horizontal Society.* New Haven, Conn.: Yale University Press, 1999.

Huq, Saleemul. "Political Protest: Search for Alternatives." *ChangeExchange* 1, no. 5 (Washington, D.C.: Advocacy Institute) (1999).

James, Maureen, and Liz Rykert. *From Workplace to Workspace: Using E-mail Lists to Work Together.* Ottawa, Canada: International Development Research Centre, 1998. See *http://www.idrc.ca/books/848/index_.html.*

Rustin, Bayard. "From Protest to Politics." In *Down the Line.* Quadrangle Books, 1971. See *http://www.socialdemocrats .org/protopol.html.*

Yankelovich, Daniel. *Coming to Public Judgment: Making Democracy Work in a Complex World.* Syracuse, N.Y.: Syracuse University Press, 1991.

Civil Society

Cohen, David. "Moving towards Civil Society." Washington, D.C.: Advocacy Institute, 1995. Unpublished.

Cohen, David. "A Vibrant Civil Society." *Discourse* 1, no. 1 (Dhaka, Bangladesh: Institute for Development Policy Analysis and Advocacy at Proshika) (1996).

de Oliveira, Miguel Darcy, and Rajesh Tandon, coordinators. *Citizens: Strengthening Global Civil Society.* Washington, D.C.: CIVICUS, 1994.

Gordimer, Nadine. *Living in Hope and History: Notes from Our Century.* New York: Farrar, Straus, and Giroux, 1999.

Korten, David C. *Globalizing Civil Society: Reclaiming Our Right to Power.* New York: Seven Stories Press, 1998.

Margalit, Avishai. *The Decent Society.* Cambridge, Mass.: Harvard University Press, 1996.

Saul, John Ralston. *The Unconscious Civilization.* Toronto: Anansi, 1995.

Storytelling

Coles, Robert. *The Call of Stories.* Boston: Houghton Mifflin, 1989.

Leadership

Fox, Jonathan A.. "Democratic Rural Development: Leadership Accountability in Regional Peasant Organizations." *Development and Change* 23, no. 2 (Thousand Oaks, London, and New Delhi: Sage) (1992).

Gardner, John W. *On Leadership.* New York: The Free Press, 1993.

Pertschuk, Michael. *Lead Us Not.* Forthcoming.

NGOs and Organizational Development

Carroll, Thomas F. *Intermediary NGOs: The Supporting Link in Grassroots Development.* West Hartford, Conn.: Kumarian Press, 1992.

Fisher, Julie. *Nongovernments: NGOs and the Political Development of the Third World.* West Hartford, Conn.: Kumarian Press, 1998.

Fowler, Alan. *Striking a Balance: A Guide to Making Nongovernmental Organizations Effective.* London: Earthscan Publications, 1997.

Knowles, Malcolm S., Elwood R. Holton, and Richard A. Swanson. *The Adult Learner: The Definitive Classic in Adult Education and Human Resources Development.* Houston: Gulf Publishing, 1998.

Senge, Peter M., et al. *The Fifth Discipline Fieldbook: Strategies and Tools for Building a Learning Organization.* New York: Currency Doubleday, 1994.

Movement-Building

Advocacy Institute. *A Movement Rising: A Strategic Analysis of U.S. Tobacco Control Advocacy.* Washington, D.C.: Advocacy Institute, 1999.

Kennard, Byron. "Ten Ways to Kill a Citizen Movement." *Not Man Apart* (1983).

Korten, David C. *Getting to the 21st Century: Voluntary Action and the Global Agenda.* West Hartford, Conn.: Kumarian Press, 1990.

Piven, Frances F., and Richard A. Cloward. *Poor People's Movements: Why They Succeed, How They Fail.* New York: Vintage Books, 1979.

Political Liberalization, Democracy, and Governance

Diamond, Larry J. *Developing Democracy: Toward Consolidation.* Baltimore: Johns Hopkins University Press, 1999.

O'Donnell, Guillermo, and Philippe C. Schmitter, eds. *Transitions from Authoritarian Rule: Tentative Conclusions about Uncertain Democracies.* Baltimore: Johns Hopkins University Press, 1986.

Tismaneanu, Vladimir, ed. *The Revolutions of 1989.* New York: Routledge, 1999.

Touraine, Alain. *What Is Democracy?* Trans. David Macey. Boulder, Colo.: Westview, 1997.

Economic Liberalization and Globalization

Brecher, Jeremy, and Tim Costello. *Global Village or Global Pillage: Economic Reconstruction from the Bottom Up.* Boston: South End Press, 1998.

Cohen, David. "Stripping Away the Gloss of Global Capitalism: William Greider's *One World Ready or Not.*" *Discourse* 1, no. 2 (Dhaka, Bangladesh: Institute for Development Policy Analysis and Advocacy at Proshika) (1997).

Fox, Jonathan A., and L. David Brown, eds. *The Struggle for Accountability: The World Bank, NGOs, and Grassroots Movements.* Cambridge, Mass., and London: MIT Press, 1998.

Held, David, et al. *Global Transformations: Politics, Economics, and Culture.* Stanford, Calif.: Stanford University Press, 1999.

Jameson, Fredric, and Masao Miyoshi, eds. *The Cultures of Globalization.* Durham, N.C.: Duke University Press, 1998.

Karliner, Joshua. *The Corporate Planet: Ecology and Politics in the Age of Globalization.* San Francisco: Sierra Club Books, 1997.

Korten, David C. *When Corporations Rule the World.* West Hartford, Conn.: Kumarian Press, 1995.

Krugman, Paul. *The Return of Depression Economics.* New York: W. W. Norton & Company, 1999.

O'Malley, Padraig, ed. *Southern Africa: The People's Voices.* Bellville, South Africa: National Democratic Institute for International Affairs and the University of the Western Cape School of Government, 1999.

Sassen, Saskia. *Globalization and Its Discontents: Essays on the New Mobility of People and Money.* New York: The New Press, 1998.

Sassen, Saskia. *Losing Control: Sovereignty in an Age of Globalization.* New York: Columbia University Press, 1996.

Scott, James C. *Seeing Like a State: How Certain Schemes to Improve the Human Condition Have Failed.* New Haven, Conn., and London: Yale University Press, 1998.

Sennet, Richard. *The Corrosion of Character: The Personal Consequences of Work in the New Capitalism.* New York: W. W. Norton & Company, 1998.

Elections

Dambula, George. "Malawi: Elections and the Role of Civil Society." *ChangeExchange* 1, no. 6 (Washington, D.C.: Advocacy Institute) (1999).

Domi, Tanya L. "The Role of Media in the Conduct of Fair and Free Elections." *ChangeExchange* 1, no. 6 (Washington, D.C.: Advocacy Institute) (1999).

Harsono, Andreas. "The Future for Media Freedom in Post-Suharto Indonesia." *ChangeExchange* 1, no. 5 (Washington, D.C.: Advocacy Institute) (1999).

Corruption and Transparency

Morgan, Amanda L. *Corruption: Causes, Consequences, and Policy Implications, a Literature Review.* Washington, D.C.: The Asia Foundation, 1998.

Pope, Jeremy, ed. *National Integrity Systems: The TI Source Book.* Berlin: Transparency International, 1997.

Budget Analysis

Budlender, Debbie. *The Third Women's Budget.* Cape Town, South Africa: Idasa, 1998.

Falk, Stefan, and Isaac Shapiro. *A Guide to Budget Work: A Systematic Overview of the Different Aspects of Effective Budget Analysis.* Cape Town, South Africa, and Washington, D.C.: International Budget Project, 1999. See *http://www.internationalbudget.org/resources/guide/index.htm.*

Samuel, John, ed. *Understanding the Budget: As If People Mattered.* Pune, India: National Centre for Advocacy Studies, 1998.

UN Conferences, Human Rights, and International Law

Nazarali-Stranieri, Farah. "Using International Law to Advocate for Human Rights." *ChangeExchange* 1, no. 6 (Washington, D.C.: Advocacy Institute) (1999).

Pandit, Vivek. *A Handbook on Prevention of Atrocities (Scheduled Castes and Scheduled Tribes).* Usgaon, Maharashtra, India: Vidhayak Sansad, 1995.

Tsekos, Mary Ellen. "International Law as a Tool for Advocacy." *ChangeExchange* 1, no. 3 (Washington, D.C.: Advocacy Institute) (1998).

United Nations. See the University of Minnesota's Human Rights Library at *http://www.umn.edu/humanrts.*
"Convention on the Elimination of All Forms of Discrimination against Women (CEDAW)." 1981.
"International Covenant on Civil and Political Rights." 1966.
"International Covenant on Economic, Social, and Cultural Rights." 1966.
"Universal Declaration of Human Rights." 1948.

van Tuijl, Peter. "NGOs and Human Rights: Sources of Justice and Democracy." *Journal of International Affairs* 52, no. 2 (New York: Columbia University School of International and Public Affairs) (1999).

Women's Environment and Development Organization. *Mapping Progress: Assessing Implementation of the Beijing Platform.* New York: WEDO, 1998.

Other

Levinson, David. *Family Violence in Cross-Cultural Perspectives.* Frontiers of Anthropology Series, number 1. Thousand Oaks, London, and New Delhi: Sage, 1989.

Touraine, Alain. *Critique of Modernity.* Trans. David Macey. Oxford: Blackwell, 1995.

Part II: Advocacy Skills

General Strategy Development and Advocacy Skill Building

Bobo, Kim, Jackie Kendall, and Steve Max. *Organizing for Social Change: A Manual for Activists in the 1990s.* Santa Ana, Calif.: Seven Locks Press, 1991.

Centre for Development and Population Activities. *Cairo, Beijing, and Beyond: A Handbook on Advocacy for Women Leaders.* Washington, D.C.: CEDPA, 1995.

Fox, Leslie M., and Priya Helweg. "Advocacy Strategies for Civil Society: A Conceptual Framework and Practitioner's Guide." 1997. Unpublished. Prepared for the Center for Democracy and Governance, USAID.

Miller, Valerie. "NGOs and Grassroots Policy Influence: What Is Success?" *IDR Reports* 11, no. 5 (Boston: Institute for Development Research) (1994).

Miller, Valerie, and Jane Covey. *Advocacy Sourcebook, Frameworks for Planning, Action, and Reflection.* Boston: Institute for Development Research, 1997.

Public Interest Law Initiative. *Public Interest Law Handbook.* 2000. See *http://www.pili.org.*

Ruthrauff, John, Tania Palencia, and Rob Everts. *Advocacy and Negotiation: A Process for Changing Institutional and Governmental Policies.* Silver Spring, Md.: Center for Democratic Education, 1997.

Shultz, Jim. *The Initiative Cookbook: Recipes and Stories from California's Ballot Wars.* San Francisco: Democracy Center/Advocacy Institute West, 1996.

South African NGO Coalition. *Advocacy Training Manual.* Johannesburg: SANGOCO, 1998.

STAR Project of Delphi International. *Public Policy Advocacy: Women for Social Change in the Yugoslav Successor States.* Zagreb: STAR Project, 1998.

VeneKlasen, Lisa. *The Action Guide for Advocacy and Citizen Participation.* Forthcoming.

Washington Office on Latin America. *La Planificación Participativa para la Incidencia Política: Una Guía Práctica.* Washington, D.C.: WOLA, 1998.

Collaboration and Coalitions

Advocacy Institute. "Stone Soup: Recipe for Successful Coalition Building." Washington, D.C.: Advocacy Institute, 1994. Unpublished.

Fisher, Roger, and William Ury. *Getting to Yes: Negotiating Agreement without Giving In.* New York: Viking Penguin, 1991.

Fox, Jonathan A., and L. David Brown, eds. "Transnational Civil Society Coalitions and the World Bank: Lessons from Project and Policy Influence Campaigns." 1999. Unpublished. Prepared for the Conference on NGOs in a Global Future.

Keck, Margaret E., and Kathryn Sikkink. *Activists beyond Borders: Advocacy Networks in International Politics.* Ithaca, N.Y.: Cornell University Press, 1998.

Ury, William. *Getting Past No: Negotiating Your Way from Confrontation to Cooperation.* New York: Bantam Books, 1993.

Information and Research

"By the Numbers: A Guide to the Tactical Use of Statistics and Positive Policy Change." *Blowing Away the Smoke* 2 (Washington, D.C.: Advocacy Institute) (1998).

Children's Defense Fund. *An Advocate's Guide to Using Data.* Washington, D.C.: CDF, 1990.

Gaventa, John. "Citizen Knowledge, Citizen Competence, and Democracy Building." *The Good Society* 5, no. 3 (College Park, Md.: PEGS, Department of Government and Politics, University of Maryland) (1995).

National Campaign against Toxic Hazards. *The Citizens' Toxic Protection Manual.* Boston: National Campaign, 1988.

Message Development and Delivery

"Framing for Content: Shaping the Debate on Tobacco." *Blowing Away the Smoke* 6 (Washington, D.C.: Advocacy Institute) (1998).

"Getting the Message Right: Using Formative Research, Polling, and Focus Group Insights on the Cheap." *Blowing Away the Smoke* 3 (Washington, D.C.: Advocacy Institute) (1998).

Saasta, Timothy, ed. "A Guide to Developing Effective Messages and Good Stories about Your Work." In *How to Tell and Sell Your Story.* Part 2. Washington, D.C.: Center for Community Change, 1998.

Schwartz, Tony. *The Responsive Chord.* Garden City, N.Y.: Anchor Press/Doubleday, 1973.

Taylor, Ericka. "The Minimum Wage Message." *Trumpet Notes* 1, no. 3 (Washington, D.C.: Certain Trumpet [Advocacy Institute]) (1997).

"Tobacco Control Media Advocacy in Communities of Color." *Blowing away the Smoke* 4 (Washington, D.C.: Advocacy Institute) (1998).

"Unlocking the Power of Responsive Chord Communications." *Trumpet Notes* 1, no. 3 (Washington, D.C.: Certain Trumpet [Advocacy Institute]) (1996).

Mass Media

Bales, Susan. "Doing Communications Strategically: Toward a Working Definition." 1998. Unpublished. Prepared for a Council on Foundations meeting.

Center for Democracy and Governance. *The Role of Media in Democracy: A Strategic Approach.* Washington, D.C.: USAID Center for Democracy and Governance, 1999.

"Framing for Access: How to Get the Media's Attention." *Blowing Away the Smoke* 5 (Washington, D.C.: Advocacy Institute) (1998).

"Introduction to the Series." *Blowing Away the Smoke* 1 (Washington, D.C.: Advocacy Institute) (1998).

Iyengar, Shanto. *Is Anyone Responsible? How Television Frames Political Issues.* Chicago: University of Chicago Press, 1994.

McCaulay, Moco. "Breaking through a Culture of Silence: An Interview with Kenneth Best." *ChangeExchange* 1, no. 4 (Washington, D.C.: Advocacy Institute) (1999).

Rawls, Amanda C. "Media-Advocacy Relationships: The View from the Other Side." *ChangeExchange* 1, no. 6 (Washington, D.C.: Advocacy Institute) (1999).

Ryan, Charlotte. *Prime Time Activism: Media Strategies for Grassroots Organizing.* Boston: South End Press, 1991.

Saasta, Timothy, ed. "A Guide to Media for Community Groups and Other Nonprofits." In *How to Tell and Sell Your Story.* Part 1. Washington, D.C.: Center for Community Change, 1997.

Schwartz, Tony. *Media: The Second God.* New York: Random House, 1982.

Wallack, Lawrence, et al. *Media Advocacy and Public Health: Power for Prevention.* Thousand Oaks, London, and New Delhi: Sage, 1993.

Wallack, Lawrence, et al. *News for a Change: An Advocate's Guide to Working with the Media.* Thousand Oaks, London, and New Delhi: Sage, 1999.

Lobbying

Sheekey, Kathleen D. "Six Practical Tips on How to Lobby Your Legislator or Elected Official." Washington, D.C.: Common Cause, 1989.

Smucker, Bob. *The Nonprofit Lobbying Guide.* Washington, D.C.: Independent Sector, 1999.

Case Studies

Pertschuk, Michael. *Giant Killers.* New York: W. W. Norton & Company, 1986.

Pertschuk, Michael, and Wendy Schaetzel. *The People Rising: The Campaign against the Bork Nomination.* New York: Thunder's Mouth Press, 1989.

Themba, Makani N. *Making Policy, Making Change: How Communities Are Taking Law into Their Own Hands.* Oakland, Calif.: Chardon, 1999.

Part III: Advocacy Case Studies

Alves, Maria Helena Moreira. *State and Opposition in Military Brazil.* Austin: University of Texas Press, 1988.

Fox, Jonathan A. "The Difficult Transition from Clientelism to Citizenship: Lessons from Mexico." In *The New Politics of Inequality in Latin America: Rethinking Participation and Representation,* ed. Douglas A. Chalmers et al. Oxford: Oxford University Press, 1997.

Fox, Jonathan A. *The Politics of Food in Mexico: State Power and Social Mobilization.* Ithaca, N.Y.: Cornell University Press, 1992.

Fox, Jonathan A. "Thinking Locally, Acting Globally: Bringing the Grassroots into Transnational Advocacy." Presentation given at "Regional Worlds–Latin America: Cultural Environments and Development Debates." Center for Latin American Studies and the Globalization Project, University of Chicago, May 21–23, 1998.

Fox, Jonathan A., and L. David Brown, eds. *The Struggle for Accountability: The World Bank, NGOs, and Grassroots Movements.* Cambridge, Mass.: MIT Press, 1998.

Fox, Leslie M., and Priya Helweg. "Advocacy Strategies for Civil Society: A Conceptual Framework and Practitioner's Guide." 1997. Unpublished. Prepared for the Center for Democracy and Governance, USAID.

Grindle, Marilee S. "The Sexenio and Public Careers in Mexico." in *Bureaucrats, Politicians, and Peasants in Mexico: A Case Study in Public Policy.* Berkeley: University of California Press, 1977.

Jordan, Lisa, and Peter van Tuijl. "Political Responsibility in Transnational NGO Advocacy." *World Development* 28, no. 12 (2000).

Keck, Margaret E., and Kathryn Sikkink. *Activists beyond Borders.* Ithaca, N.Y.: Cornell University Press, 1998.

Kimerling, Judith. *Amazon Crude.* Natural Resources Defense Council, 1991.

Miller, Valerie. "NGOs and Grassroots Policy Influence: What Is Success?" *IDR Reports* 11, no. 5 (Boston: Institute for Development Research) (1994).

Miller, Valerie, and Jane Covey. *Advocacy Sourcebook: Frameworks for Planning, Action, and Reflection.* Boston: Institute for Development Research, 1997.

O'Donnell, Guillermo, and Philippe C. Schmitter, eds. *Transitions from Authoritarian Rule: Tentative Conclusions about Uncertain Democracies.* Baltimore: Johns Hopkins University Press, 1986.

Stepan, Alfred, ed. *Democratizing Brazil: Problems in Transition and Consolidation.* New York: Oxford University Press, 1989.

Tender, Judith. *New Lessons from Old Projects: The Dynamics of Development in Northeast Brazil.* Washington, D.C.: World Bank, 1991.

van Tuijl, Peter. "Advocating Apart, Together: Southern NGOs and the Advocacy of Oxfam International." Photocopy. Discussion paper for the Oxfam International Project Directors and Advocacy Coordinating Committee, January 1998.

Watson, Gabrielle. "Water and Sanitation in São Paulo, Brazil: Successful Strategies for Service Provision in Low-Income Communities." Master's Thesis, Massachusetts Institute of Technology, 1992.

About the Institutions

Advocacy Institute

The Advocacy Institute is a US-based global organization dedicated to strengthening the capacity of political, social, and economic justice advocates to influence and change public policy.

The Advocacy Institute makes a difference around the world by strengthening leadership and movements for political, social, and economic justice. Working with our partners to help make democratic institutions accountable, our work links us with a global community of grassroots activists and non-governmental organization (NGO) leaders tackling critical human rights issues—such as public health, gender equity, peace, ending poverty, sustainable development, and preserving the environment.

The institute's work includes advocacy leadership development, movement-building, strategy development and analysis, advocacy-skills-building, facilitating alliance building, strategic counseling, and networking of advocates from all over the world.

Advocacy Institute
1629 K Street, NW,
Suite 200
Washington, DC
20006-1629
(202) 777-7575
fax (202) 777-7577
www.advocacy.org

Oxfam America

Oxfam America seeks lasting solutions to poverty, hunger, and social inequities around the world. We know that poverty and hunger are preventable problems, and we work to eliminate the root causes of social and economic inequities. By directing expertise and resources to local organizations in poor communities, Oxfam builds on community strengths and promotes lasting change that will allow families and individuals to break the cycle of poverty. Oxfam America is also widely known and respected for its effective humanitarian responses to natural disasters and political crises. Since 1970, Oxfam America has disbursed more than $100 million in program funding and technical support to hundreds of partner organizations in Africa, Asia, the Caribbean, and the Americas, including the United States. Through collaboration with the ten other autonomous members of Oxfam International, we extend our reach and our effectiveness around the world.

Through national and international policy research and advocacy, Oxfam America pursues systemic solutions to inequities rooted in social, political, and economic systems. Because poverty thrives on ignorance, Oxfam America aggressively promotes universal education for children around the world. Through our educational programs we offer the public opportunities to become informed and involved in world affairs and development issues.

Oxfam America
26 West Street
Boston, MA 02111-1206
(800) 77-OXFAM—(800) 776-9326
fax (617) 728-2562
www.oxfamamerica.org
info@oxfamamerica.org